The Secrets of Fat-Free Cooking Collection

Also by Sandra Woodruff, M.S., R.D.

Light and Easy Holiday Cooking
The Good Carb Cookbook
The Best-Kept Secrets of Healthy Cooking
Secrets of Cooking for Long Life
Secrets of Fat-Free Italian Cooking
Secrets of Living Fat-Free

The Secrets of Fat-Free Cooking Collection

Sandra Woodruff, M.S., R.D.

Includes recipes from *Secrets of Fat-Free Cooking,*
Secrets of Fat-Free Baking, and *Secrets of Fat-Free Desserts*

AVERY
A MEMBER OF PENGUIN PUTNAM INC.
NEW YORK

The recipes contained in this book are to be followed exactly as written. Neither the publisher nor the author is responsible for your specific health or allergy needs that may require medical supervision or for any adverse reactions to the recipes contained in this book.

AVERY

a member of
Penguin Putnam Inc.
375 Hudson Street
New York, NY 10014
www.penguinputnam.com

ISBN 1-58333-134-4

Printed in the United States of America

10 9 8 7 6 5 4 3 2 1

Contents

Preface

As a nutritionist, I have long been aware of the need to help people eliminate fat from their diet. I also know the importance of creating nutrient-rich dishes made with whole grains, fresh vegetables, and other ingredients that are as close as possible to their natural state. And because of my work as a teacher, I know that foods must be more than just healthy. They must be visually appealing and absolutely delicious, and they must be quick and easy to prepare. If they are not the former, people simply will not eat them. If they are not the latter, people simply will not make them.

The Secrets of Fat-Free Cooking Collection is the perfect book for people who want to reduce the fat in their diet, maximize their nutrition, and treat family and friends to delicious meals. From Golden French Toast, to Pot Roast With Sour Cream Gravy, to Hearty Oven Fries, to Refreshing Fruit Pie, every recipe has been designed to reduce fat and boost nutrition. Just as important, every recipe has been kitchen-tested to make sure that you enjoy success each and every time

you make it, and people-tested to make sure that every dish you create is a hit.

The Secrets of Fat-Free Cooking Collection is a compilation of three of my previously published books: *Secrets of Fat-Free Cooking, Secrets of Fat-Free Baking,* and *Secrets of Fat-Free Desserts.* It begins by explaining just why dietary fat should be reduced, and just how much fat is allowable in a healthy diet. You will also learn about the many nonfat and low-fat ingredients that will help you reduce fat without reducing taste, and you will learn about the nutritional analysis that accompanies each and every recipe in this book.

Following this important information, each chapter focuses on a specific meal of the day or a specific type of dish. Looking for breakfast foods that are not only tempting enough to lure family members out of bed, but also nutritious enough to give them the energy they'll need until lunch time? Chapter 2, "Breakfasts for Champions," presents a wide selection of breakfast dishes, from Applesauce Pancakes to Zucchini Frittata. Or perhaps you want to serve fresh-baked breads, rolls, muffins, and biscuits that will add that special touch to family meals without wreaking havoc on your healthy lifestyle. "Bountiful Breads" will lead the way with a sumptuous selection of low- and no-fat homemade goodies that are as easy to prepare as they are delicious and nutritious. Still other chapters will show you how to make festive hot and cold hors d'oeuvres, like Chicken Fingers with Honey Mustard Sauce; warming soups, like Fresh Corn Chowder; refreshing salads, like Dillicious Potato Salad; wholesome vegetable side dishes, like Cranapple Acorn Squash; savory past dishes, like Bow Ties with Spicy Artichoke Sauce; hearty home-style entrées, like

Simply Delicious Chicken and Dumplings; and meatless main dishes, like Eggplant Parmesan. And because for some of us, the meal just isn't complete until we've enjoyed dessert, there's a mouthwatering selection of cakes, cobblers, crisps, puddings, pies, cookies, and other treats designed to provide a sweet but nutritious conclusion to your fat-free meal.

It is my hope that *The Secrets of Fat-Free Cooking Collection* will provide to you, your family, and your friends, that any meal can be delicious and satisfying without being rich and fattening. So eat well and enjoy! As you will see, it is possible to do both—at every meal, and on every day of the year.

Introduction

Making and eating great food is one of life's simplest yet greatest pleasures. And there is nothing wrong with enjoying good food—except that for too long, *good* often meant *greasy*. Butter, margarine, oil, mayonnaise, cheese, and other fatty ingredients were long considered essential for good cooking. We now know that all this fat—along with excess sugar and salt—has a tremendous impact on health. In fact, after smoking, diet is the number-one killer of Americans. Moreover, diet-related diseases like obesity, heart disease, cancer, and diabetes greatly affect the quality of life for millions of Americans.

The good news is that this awareness has led people to explore new ways of cooking and eating. As a result, many low-fat cookbooks are now available. But while these cookbooks do provide low-fat recipes, they often reduce fat and calories by using artificial fat substitutes and sweeteners, and they often rely on many highly refined, processed foods, as well. Because of these ingredients, nutrition is often compromised. *The Secrets of Fat-Free Cooking Collection* is a very different kind of cookbook. It was designed to help you create delicious low- and no-fat foods that are also high in nutrition.

As a nutritionist and teacher, I began looking for ways to reduce or totally eliminate the fat in foods long before anyone heard the term "fat-free." Through years of experimentation and kitchen testing, I developed simple ways to do just this. But the recipes in this book are more than just low-fat. I have further improved the nutritional value of these recipes by using natural sweeteners like fruits and juices whenever possible to reduce the need for added sugar. Whole grains and whole grain flours have also been incorporated into these recipes for fiber and extra nutritional value. As an added bonus, the use of herbs, spices, and other seasonings, as well as minimal reliance on processed foods, has helped keep sodium under control.

Perhaps the best part of these recipes, though, is their simplicity. Every effort has been made to keep the number of ingredients, pots, pans, and utensils to a minimum. This will save you time and make cleanup a breeze—important considerations for most people today.

As you will see, watching your fat intake does not have to mean dieting and deprivation. This book is filled with easy-to-follow recipes for delicious dishes that your whole family will enjoy, as well as plenty of ideas for getting the fat out of your own favorite recipes. I wish you the best of luck and health with all your fat-free cooking!

1

Mastering Fat-Free Cooking

Who says you can't have your cake and eat it, too? If you know the secrets of fat-free cooking, you can have just about anything you want—deceptively rich cheesecake, creamy fettucine Alfredo, crispy Cajun chicken, cheese-filled lasagna, hearty Western omelettes, luscious quiches, and much more.

For too many years, eating healthfully has meant limited choices, deprivation, and extra hours spent shopping and cooking. "If it's good for you, it probably tastes awful," was the attitude that emerged. Fortunately, this is far from true. *The Secrets of Fat-Free Cooking Collection* introduces you to new fat-free cooking techniques, and shows you how to use the latest nonfat and low-fat products in all your meals. The result? Foods that are never bland or boring, that are simple to prepare, and that your whole family will love.

In these pages, you will find recipes for a wide variety of delicious low-fat and fat-free dishes. You will be delighted by "defatted" versions of old favorites, as well as tempting new creations that will let you eat the foods you love without guilt. Perhaps just as impor-

tant, this book will show you that contrary to popular belief, changing over to a low-fat lifestyle does not have to be an ordeal. As you will see, the recipes in this book will save you not just fat and calories, but time and effort, too. Most of these recipes are very simple to prepare, even for beginners, and are designed to create as little mess as possible, saving you cleanup time.

This chapter will explain why dietary fat should be reduced, and will guide you in budgeting your daily fat intake. In addition, you will learn about the various healthful ingredients used throughout this book—ingredients that will enable you to prune fat from every meal of the day.

BIG FAT PROBLEMS

Excess fat may well be the number-one dietary problem in America. With more than twice the calories of carbohydrates or protein, fat is a concentrated source of calories. Compare a cup of butter or margarine (almost pure fat) with a cup of flour (almost pure carbohydrates). The butter has 1,600 calories, and the flour has 400 calories. It's easy to see where most of our calories come from.

Besides being high in calories, fat is also readily converted into body fat when eaten in excess. Carbohydrate-rich foods eaten in excess are also stored as fat, but they must first be converted into fat—a process that burns up some of the carbohydrates. The bottom line is that a high-fat diet will cause 20 percent more weight gain than will a high-carbohydrate diet, even when the two diets contain the same number of calories. So a high-fat diet is a double-edged sword for the weight-conscious person. It is high in calories, and it is high in the kind of nutrient that is most readily stored as body fat.

But high-fat diets pose a threat to much more than our weight. When fatty diets lead to obesity, diseases like diabetes and high blood pressure can result. And specific types of fats present their own unique problems. For example, eating too much saturated fat— found in meat, butter, and other solid fats— raises blood cholesterol levels, setting the stage for heart disease. Polyunsaturated fat, once thought to be the solution to heart disease, can also be harmful when eaten in excess. A diet overly rich in vegetable oils like corn, sunflower, and safflower oil, as well as products made from these oils, can alter body chemistry to favor the development of blood clots, high blood pressure, and inflammatory diseases. Too much polyunsaturated fat can also promote free-radical damage to cells, contributing to heart disease and cancer.

Where do monounsaturated fats fit in? Monounsaturated fats—found in olive oil, canola oil, avocados, and nuts—have no known harmful effects other than being a concentrated source of calories, like all fats.

Considering the problems caused by excess fat, you may think it would be best to completely eliminate fat from your diet. But the fact is, we do need some dietary fat. For instance, linoleic acid, a polyunsaturated fat

naturally abundant in nuts and seeds, is essential for life. The average adult needs a minimum of 3 to 6 grams of linoleic acid per day—the amount present in one to two teaspoons of polyunsaturated vegetable oil, or one to two tablespoons of nuts or seeds. Linolenic acid, a fat present mainly in fish and green plants, is also essential for good health. And some dietary fat is needed so that we may absorb fat-soluble nutrients like vitamin E.

Unfortunately, many people are getting too much of a good thing. The liberal use of foods like mayonnaise, oil-based salad dressings, margarine, and cooking oils has created an unhealthy overdose of linoleic acid in the American diet. And, of course, most people also eat far too much saturated fat. How can we correct this? We can minimize the use of refined vegetable oils and table fats, and eat a diet rich in whole grains, vegetables, and fruits, with moderate amounts of nuts and seeds, fish, and lean meats, if desired. This is what *The Secrets of Fat-Free Cooking Collection* is all about. In the remainder of this chapter, you will learn how to budget your daily fat intake, and you will become acquainted with the healthful foods that will help you prune the fat from your diet and maximize the nutrients. Throughout the rest of the book, you will learn how to use these foods to create delicious, healthful fare that you will be proud to serve, and your family will love to eat.

BUDGETING YOUR FAT

For most people, close to 40 percent of the calories in their diet come from fat. However, currently it is recommended that fat calories constitute no more than 30 percent of the diet, and, in fact, 20 to 25 percent would be even better in most cases. So the amount of fat you should eat every day is based on the number of calories you need. Because people's calorie needs depend on their weight, age, gender, activity level, and metabolic rate, these needs vary greatly among people. Most adults, though, must consume 13 to 15 calories per pound to maintain their weight. Of course, some people need even fewer calories, while very physically active people need more.

Once you have determined your calorie requirements, you can estimate a fat budget for yourself. Suppose you are a moderately active person who weighs 150 pounds. You will probably need about 15 calories per pound to maintain your weight, or about 2,250 per day. To limit your fat intake to 20 percent of your calorie intake, you can eat no more than 450 calories derived from fat per day (2,250 x .20 = 450). To convert this into grams of fat, divide by 9, as one gram of fat has 9 calories. Therefore, you should limit yourself to 50 grams of fat per day (450 ÷ 9 = 50).

The table at the bottom of this page shows two maximum daily fat gram budgets—one based on 20 percent of calorie intake, and one based on 25 percent of calorie intake. If you are overweight or underweight, go by the weight you would like to be. And keep in mind that although you have budgeted *X* amount of fax grams per day, you don't *have* to eat that amount of fat—you just have to avoid going over budget.

HOW LOW SHOULD YOU GO?

If you are like most people, you have discovered that for maximum health, you must reduce your daily fat intake. How low should you go? As discussed earlier, some fat is *necessary* for good health. Therefore, you should not try to consume less than 20 grams of fat per day. Of course, if you eat a balanced diet rich in whole, natural foods, it would be almost impossible to eat less than this anyway. On the other hand, if you eat a diet rich in fat-free refined and processed foods, you could be at risk for a deficiency of essential fats, as well as deficiencies of other essential nutrients. This is why the recipes in this book so often use whole grains and other natural foods, and minimize the use of refined and processed foods.

Realize, too, that a very low-fat diet is not for everyone. If you have a specific medical problem, be sure to check with your physician or nutritionist before making any dramatic dietary changes.

Maximum Daily Fat Intakes

Weight	Recommended Daily Calorie Intake (13–15 calories per pound)	Fat Grams Allowed (20% of Calorie Intake)	Fat Grams Allowed (25% of Calorie Intake)
100	1,300–1,500	29–33	36–42
110	1,430–1,650	32–37	40–46
120	1,560–1,800	34–40	43–50
130	1,690–1,950	38–43	47–54
140	1,820–2,100	40–46	51–58
150	1,950–2,250	43–50	54–62
160	2,080–2,400	46–53	58–67
170	2,210–2,550	49–57	61–71
180	2,340–2,700	52–60	65–75
190	2,470–2,850	55–63	69–79
200	2,600–3,000	58–66	72–83

ABOUT THE INGREDIENTS

Never before has it been so easy to eat healthfully. Nonfat and low-fat alternatives are available for just about any ingredient you can think of. This makes it possible to create a dazzling array of healthful and delicious foods, including low-fat versions of many of your favorite dishes. In the pages that follow, we will take a look at low-fat and nonfat cheeses, fat-free spreads and dressings, fat-free egg substitutes, ultra-lean meats, and many other ingredients that will insure success in all your fat-free cooking adventures.

Low-Fat and Nonfat Cheeses

Americans have long had a love affair with cheese. For many years, though, people who wanted to reduce the fat in their diet had to also reduce the cheese, or even eliminate cheese entirely. Fortunately, a wide range of nonfat and low-fat products is now available, making it possible to have your cheese and eat it, too. Let's learn about some of the cheeses that you will be using in your fat-free recipes.

Cottage Cheese. Although often thought of as a diet food, full-fat cottage cheese has 5 grams of fat per 4-ounce serving, making it far from diet fare. Instead, choose nonfat or low-fat cottage cheese. Puréed until smooth, these healthful products make a great base for dips and spreads, and add richness and body to casseroles, quiches, cheesecakes, and many other recipes. Select brands with 1 percent or less milk fat. Most brands of cottage cheese are quite high in sodium, with about 400 milligrams per half cup, so it is best to avoid adding salt whenever this cheese is a recipe ingredient. As an alternative, use unsalted cottage cheese, which is available in some stores.

Another option when buying cottage cheese is dry curd cottage cheese. This nonfat version is made without the "dressing" or creaming mixture. Minus the dressing, cottage cheese has a drier consistency; hence its name, "dry curd." Unlike most cottage cheese, dry curd is very low in sodium. Use dry curd cottage cheese as you would nonfat cottage cheese in casseroles, quiches, dips, spreads, salad dressings, and cheesecakes.

Cream Cheese. Regular full-fat cream cheese contains about 10 grams of fat per ounce, making this popular spread a real menace if you are trying to reduce dietary fat. A tasty alternative is light cream cheese, which has only 5 grams of fat per ounce. Another reduced-fat alternative is Neufchâtel cheese, which contains 6 grams of fat per ounce. And, of course, nonfat cream cheese contains no fat at all. Like light cream cheese and Neufchâtel, nonfat cream cheese may be used in dips, spreads, and sauces. Look for brands like Philly Free and Healthy Choice, and use the block-style cheese for best results.

When substituting nonfat cream cheese for full-fat cheese in cheesecakes, you may find that the texture of the cake is softer—more puddinglike—than that of traditional cheesecake. If this happens, try adding a tablespoon of flour to the batter for each cup of nonfat cream cheese used. This should produce a firm, nicely textured cake that is remarkably low in calories and fat.

Firm and Hard Cheeses. Both low-fat and nonfat cheeses of many types—including Swiss, Cheddar, Monterey jack, and mozzarella—are available in most grocery stores. Reduced-fat cheeses generally have 3 to 5 grams of fat per ounce, while nonfat cheeses contain no fat at all. Compare this with whole-milk varieties, which contain 9 to 10 grams of fat per ounce, and you will clearly see your savings in fat and calories.

Nonfat and reduced-fat firm and hard cheeses can be used in casseroles, in sauces—in any way that you might use their full-fat counterparts. Look for brands like Alpine Lace, Cracker Barrel Lite, Healthy Choice,

Kraft ⅓ Less Fat, Kraft Free, Lifetime, Sargento Light, Jarlsberg Lite Swiss, and Weight Watchers.

Parmesan Cheese. Parmesan typically contains 8 grams of fat and 400 milligrams of sodium per ounce. Fortunately, reduced-fat and nonfat versions are available. A little bit of this flavorful cheese goes a long way, so even if you use regular Parmesan in any of the recipes in this book, the amount of fat per serving will be quite low.

Pasteurized Processed Cheese. Sold in blocks, in slices, and preshredded, this cheese is designed to melt smoothly, and so is intended as a cooking cheese for use in hot cheese dips, sauces, and similar dishes. When buying nonfat processed cheeses, look for brands like Healthy Choice, Lifetime, and Alpine Lace.

Ricotta Cheese. Ricotta is a mild, slightly sweet creamy cheese that may be used in dips, spreads, and traditional Italian dishes like lasagna. As the name implies, nonfat ricotta contains no fat at all. Low-fat and light ricotta, on the other hand, have 1 to 3 grams of fat per ounce, while whole-milk ricotta has 4 grams of fat per ounce.

Soft Curd Farmer Cheese. This soft, spreadable white cheese makes a good low-fat substitute for cream cheese. Brands made with skim milk have about 3 grams of fat per ounce, compared with cream cheese's 10 grams. Soft curd farmer cheese may be used in dips, spreads, and cheesecakes, and as a filling for blintzes. Some brands are made with whole milk, so read the label before you buy. Look for a brand like Friendship Farmer Cheese.

Yogurt Cheese. A good substitute for cream cheese in dips, spreads, and cheesecakes, yogurt cheese can be made at home with any brand of yogurt that does not contain gelatin. Simply place the yogurt in a funnel lined with cheesecloth or a coffee filter, and let it drain into a jar in the refrigerator for eight hours or overnight. When the yogurt is reduced by half, it is ready to use. The whey that collects in the jar may be used in place of the liquid in bread and muffin recipes.

Nondairy Cheese Alternatives. If you choose to avoid dairy products because of a lactose intolerance or for another reason, you'll be glad to know that low-fat cheeses made from soymilk, almond milk, and Brazil nut milk are now available in a variety of flavors. Look for brands like Almondrella, Veganrella, and Tofurella.

Measuring Cheese

Throughout the recipes in this book, I have usually expressed the amount of cheese needed in cups. For instance, a recipe may call for one cup of cottage cheese or one-fourth cup of grated Parmesan. Since you will sometimes buy cheese in chunks and grate it in your own kitchen, or buy packages marked in ounces when the recipe calls for cups, it is useful to understand that the conversion of cheese from ounces (weight) to cups (volume) varies, depending on the texture of the cheese. When using the recipes in *The Secrets of Fat-Free Cooking Collection,* the following table should help take the guesswork out of these conversions.

Cheese Equivalency Amounts

Cheese	Weight	Equivalent Volume
Cheddar	8 ounces	2 cups shredded or crumbled
Cottage Cheese	8 ounces	1 cup
Cream Cheese	8 ounces	1 cup
Farmer Cheese	8 ounces	1 cup
Mozzarella	8 ounces	2 cups shredded or crumbled
Parmesan	8 ounces	2¼ cups grated
Ricotta	8 ounces	1 cup

Other Low-Fat and Nonfat Dairy Products

Of course, cheese isn't the only dairy product we use in our everyday cooking. How about the sour cream in dips, casseroles, and sauces, and the buttermilk in your favorite biscuits? Fortunately, there are low-fat and nonfat versions of these and other dairy products as well.

Buttermilk. Buttermilk adds a rich flavor and texture to baked goods like biscuits, muffins, and cakes, and lends a "cheesy" taste to sauces, cheesecakes, and casseroles. Originally a by-product of butter making, this product should perhaps be called "butterless" milk. Most brands of buttermilk contain from 0.5 to 2 percent fat by weight, but some brands contain as much as 3.5 percent fat. Choose brands that contain no more than 1 percent milk fat.

If you do not have buttermilk on hand, a good substitute can be made by mixing equal parts of nonfat yogurt and skim milk. Alternatively, place a tablespoon of vinegar or lemon juice in a one-cup measure, and fill the measure to the one-cup mark with skim milk. Let the mixture sit for five minutes, and use as you would nonfat buttermilk.

Evaporated Skim Milk. This ingredient can be substituted for cream in a variety of dishes. Use it to add creamy richness—but no fat—to quiches, sauces, cream soups, custards, and puddings.

Milk. Whole milk, the highest-fat milk available, is 3.5 percent fat by weight and has 8 grams of fat per cup. Instead, choose skim (nonfat) milk, which—with all but a trace of fat removed—has only about 0.5 gram of fat per cup. Another good choice is 1-percent milk, which, as the name implies, is 1 percent fat by weight and contains 2 grams of fat per cup.

Nonfat Dry Milk. Like evaporated skim milk, this product adds creamy richness, as well as important nutrients, to quiches, cream soups, sauces, custards, and puddings. One cup of skim milk mixed with one-third cup of nonfat dry milk powder can replace cream in most recipes. Or add this ingredient to fat-free cookies and brownies to enhance flavor and promote browning. For best results, always use *instant* dry milk powder, as this product will not clump.

Sour Cream. As calorie- and fat-conscious people know, full-fat sour cream can contain almost 500 calories and about 48 grams of fat per cup! Use nonfat sour cream, though, and you'll save 320 calories and 48 grams of fat. Made from cultured nonfat milk thickened with vegetable gums, this product beautifully replaces its fatty counterpart in dips, spreads, and sauces.

All brands of nonfat sour cream can substitute for the full-fat version in dips, dressings, and other cold dishes. However, some brands will separate when added to hot dishes like sauces and gravies. For these recipes, use a brand like Land O Lakes, which holds up well during cooking.

Yogurt. Yogurt adds creamy richness and flavor to sauces, baked goods, and casseroles. And, of course, it is a perfect base for many dips and dressings. Like some brands of nonfat sour cream, however, yogurt will curdle if added to hot sauces or gravies. To prevent this, first let the yogurt warm to room temperature. Then stir one tablespoon of cornstarch or two tablespoons of unbleached flour into the yogurt for every cup of yogurt being used. You will then be able to add this tasty ingredient to your dish without fear of separation.

In your low-fat cooking, select brands of yogurt with 1 percent or less milk fat. If you must avoid dairy products, look for soy yogurt, which is available in health food stores and many grocery stores.

Fat-Free Spreads and Dressings

Like cheeses, spreads and dressings were long a major source of fat and calories. Happily, many low-fat and nonfat alternatives to our high-fat favorites are now available. Let's learn a little more about these fat-saving products.

Margarine. If you are used to spreading foods with margarine, you can easily reduce your dietary fat by switching to a nonfat or reduced-fat margarine and using it sparingly. Every tablespoon of nonfat margarine that you substitute for regular margarine will save you 11 grams of fat. You may be surprised to learn that you can also *bake* with reduced-fat margarine—and with light butter, too. Crisp cookies, light and tender cakes, biscuits, pie crusts, and other goodies can easily be prepared with half the fat by substituting reduced-fat margarine or butter for the full-fat products, and by making simple adjustments in the recipe. (For details on using these products in your baked goods, see the Low-Fat Cooking Tip on page 288.)

Mayonnaise. Nonfat mayonnaise is highly recommended over regular mayonnaise, which is almost pure fat. How can mayonnaise be made without all that oil? Manufacturers use more water and vegetable thickeners. Some commonly available nonfat brands are Kraft Free, Miracle Whip Free, and Smart Beat. Reduced-fat mayonnaise is also available, with half to two-thirds less fat and calories than regular mayonnaise. Look for brands like Hellman's Reduced-Fat, Kraft Light, Miracle Whip Light, Blue Plate Light, and Weight Watchers.

Salad Dressings. Now made in a number of flavors, fat-free dressings contain either no oil or so little oil that they have less than 0.5 gram of fat per tablespoon. Use these dressings instead of oil-based versions to dress your favorite salads or as a delicious basting sauce for grilled foods.

Fat Substitutes for Baking

Almost any moist ingredient can replace the fat in cakes, muffins, quick breads, and other baked goods. The recipes in this book use a variety of fat substitutes. Most of these substitutes, including applesauce, fruit purée, fruit juice, nonfat buttermilk, yogurt, and mashed pumpkin, are readily available in grocery stores. Two additional substitutes—Prune Butter and Prune Purée—can be easily made at home using the recipes found in Chapter 6.

Egg Whites and Egg Substitutes

Everyone who cooks knows the value of eggs. Eggs are star ingredients in quiches, add lightness to casseroles, and are indispensable in a wide range of baked goods. Of course, eggs are also loaded with cholesterol. For this reason, the recipes in this book call for egg whites or fat-free egg substitute. Just how great are your savings in cholesterol and fat when whole eggs are replaced with one of these ingredients? One large egg contains 80 calories, 5 grams of fat, and 210 milligrams of cholesterol. The equivalent amount of egg white or fat-free egg substitute contains 20 to 30 calories, no fat, and no cholesterol. The benefits of these substitute ingredients are clear.

You may wonder why some of the recipes in this book call for egg whites while others call for egg substitute. In some cases, one ingredient does, in fact, work better than the other. For instance, egg substitute is the best choice when making quiches and puddings. In addition, because they have been pasteurized (heat treated), egg substitutes are safe to use uncooked in eggnogs and salad dressings. On the other hand, when recipes require whipped egg whites, egg substitutes do not work.

In most recipes, egg whites and egg substitutes can be used interchangeably. Yet, even in these recipes, one may sometimes be listed instead of the other due to ease of measuring.

For example, while a cake made with three tablespoons of fat-free egg substitute would turn out just as well if made with three tablespoons of egg whites, this would require you to use *one and a half* large egg whites, making measuring something of a nuisance.

Whenever a recipe calls for egg whites, use large egg whites. When selecting an egg substitute, look for a fat-free brand like Egg Beaters. (Some egg substitutes contain vegetable oil.) When replacing egg whites with egg substitute, or whole eggs with egg whites or egg substitute, use the following guidelines:

---

1 large egg = 1½ large egg whites

---

l large egg = 3 tablespoons egg substitute

---

1 large egg white = 2 tablespoons egg substitute

Ultra-Lean Poultry, Meat, and Vegetarian Alternatives

Because of the high fat and cholesterol contents of meats, many people have sharply reduced their consumption of meat, have limited themselves to white meat chicken or turkey, or have totally eliminated meat and poultry from their diets. The good news is that whether you are a sworn meat eater, someone who only occasionally eats meat dishes, or a confirmed vegetarian, plenty of lean meats, lean poultry, and excellent meat substitutes are now available.

The most important point to remember when including meat in meals is to keep portions to a modest 6 ounces or less per day. For perspective, a 3-ounce portion of meat is about the size of a deck of cards. Here are

Using Purées as Fat Substitutes

Looking for a healthful and delicious way to get the fat out of your favorite baked goods? Think fruit. By now, nearly everyone has heard about using applesauce as a fat substitute, but a variety of other fruit products—including puréed pears, peaches, and apricots, as well as mashed bananas and Prune Purée (page 223)—can also replace part or all of the fat in quick breads, cakes, and other baked goods, lending versatility and extra flavor to your recipes.

How do fruit purées work? Fat performs many vital functions in baking, some of which can be duplicated by fruit purées. For instance, fat adds moistness and flavor, imparts tenderness, and promotes browning. Fruit purées reduce the need for fat because their fiber and naturally occurring sugars hold moisture into baked goods. The fiber, sugar, and mild acids in fruit purées also help tenderize baked goods, while fruit sugars help promote browning.

When substituting fruit purées for fat, be sure to choose a purée that complements your recipe. In some cases this is easy, as many recipes already contain a fat substitute. For instance, when making banana bread, simply replace the fat with extra bananas. When you want a fat substitute that will not alter the color or flavor of your recipe, use applesauce. Puréed canned pears also have a very mild flavor that will not interfere with the taste of the finished product. When you want to add a fruity flavor to a recipe, try puréed pears, mashed bananas, or Prune Purée.

How do you go about substituting fruit purées and other ingredients for the fat in your recipes? Throughout this book, you'll find helpful insets that will guide you in using these great fat-saving ingredients in a variety of baked goods.

some suggestions for choosing the leanest possible poultry and meat.

Turkey

Although both chicken and turkey have less total fat and saturated fat than beef and pork, your very best bet when buying poultry is turkey. What's the difference between the fat and calorie contents of chicken and turkey? While 3 ounces of chicken breast without skin contain 139 calories and 3 grams of fat, the same amount of turkey breast without skin contains only 119 calories and 1 gram of fat.

Your best defense when preparing and eating poultry is removing the skin and any underlying visible fat. Doing just this eliminates over half the fat. Is there any advantage to removing the skin *before* cooking? A slight one. Poultry cooked without the skin has about 20 percent less fat than poultry that has the skin removed after cooking. And, of course, when the skin is removed after cooking, so is the seasoning. For this reason, the recipes in this book all begin with skinless pieces.

All of the leanest cuts of turkey come from the breast, so that all have the same amount of fat and calories per serving. Here is what you are likely to find at your local supermarket:

Turkey Cutlets. Turkey cutlets, which are slices of turkey breast, are usually about ¼-inch thick and weigh about 2 to 3 ounces each. These cutlets may be used as a delicious and ultra-lean alternative to boneless chicken breast, pork tenderloin slices, or veal.

Turkey Medallions. Sliced from turkey tenderloins, medallions are about 1 inch thick and weigh about 2 to 3 ounces each. Turkey medallions can be substituted for pork or veal medallions in any recipe.

Turkey Steaks. Cut from the turkey breast, these steaks are about ½ to 1 inch in thickness. Turkey steaks may be baked, broiled, grilled, cut into stir-fry pieces or kabobs, or ground for burgers.

Turkey Tenderloins. Large sections of fresh turkey breast, tenderloins usually weigh about 8 ounces each. Tenderloin may be sliced into cutlets, cut into stir-fry or kabob pieces, ground for burgers, or grilled or roasted as is.

Whole Turkey Breast. Perfect for people who love roast turkey but want only the breast meat, turkey breasts weigh 4 to 8 pounds each. These breasts may be roasted with or without stuffing.

Ground Turkey. Ground turkey is an excellent ingredient for use in meatballs, chili, burgers—in any dish that uses ground meat. When shopping for ground turkey, you'll find that different products have different percentages of fat. Ground turkey breast, which is only 1 percent fat by weight, is the leanest ground meat you can buy. Ground dark meat turkey made without the skin is 8 to 10 percent fat by weight. Brands with added skin and fat usually contain 15 percent fat. The moral is clear. Always check labels before making a purchase!

Chicken

Although not as low in fat as turkey, chicken is still lower in fat than most cuts of beef and pork and therefore is a valuable ingredient in low-fat cooking. Beware, though: Many cuts of chicken, if eaten with the skin on, contain more fat than some cuts of beef and pork. For the least amount of fat, choose the chicken breast and always remove the skin—preferably, before cooking.

Does ground chicken have a place in low-fat cooking? Like ground turkey, ground chicken often contains skin and fat. Most brands contain at least 15 percent fat, in fact, so read the labels carefully before you buy.

Beef and Pork

Although not as lean as turkey, beef and pork are both considerably leaner today than in decades past. Spurred by competition from the poultry industry, beef and pork producers have changed breeding and feeding practices to reduce the fat content of these products. In addition, butchers are now trimming away more of the fat from retail cuts of meat. The result? On average, grocery store cuts of beef are 27 percent leaner today than in the early 1980s, and retail cuts of pork are 43 percent leaner.

Choosing the Best Cuts and Grades. Of course, some cuts of beef and pork are leaner than others. Which are the smartest choices? The following table will guide you in selecting those cuts that are lowest in fat.

The Leanest Beef and Pork Cuts

Cut (3 ounces, cooked and trimmed)	Calories	Fat
Beef		
Eye of Round	143	4.2 grams
Top Round	153	4.2 grams
Round Tip	157	5.9 grams
Top Sirloin	165	6.1 grams
Pork		
Tenderloin	139	4.1 grams
Ham (95% lean)	112	4.3 grams
Boneless Sirloin Chops	164	5.7 grams
Boneless Loin Roast	165	6.1 grams
Boneless Loin Chops	173	6.6 grams

While identifying the lowest-fat cuts of meat is an important first step in healthy cooking, be aware that even lean cuts have varying amounts of fat because of differences in *grades*. In general, the higher and more ex-pensive grades of meat, like USDA Prime and Choice, have more fat due to a higher degree of *marbling*—internal fat that cannot be trimmed away. USDA Select meats have the least amount of marbling, and therefore the lowest amount of fat. How important are these differences? A USDA Choice piece of meat may have 15 to 20 percent more fat than a USDA Select cut, and USDA Prime may have even more fat. Clearly, the difference is significant. So when choosing beef and pork for your table, by all means check the package for grade. Then look for the least amount of marbling in the cut you have chosen, and let appearance be your final guide.

Ground Beef. While ground turkey breast is the leanest ground meat you can find, low-fat ground beef is also available, giving you another option. The leanest ground beef commonly available is 95-percent lean. Can't find this meat in your store? Select a lean piece of top round and ask the butcher to trim off the fat and grind the remaining meat. Made this way, ground beef is about 95-percent lean. Your next best choice is 93-percent lean ground beef. Available in many grocery stores, this beef, as the label implies, is only 7-percent fat by weight.

How significant are the differences in ground beef with varying percentages of fat? Beef that is 95-percent lean contains 4.9 grams of fat and 132 calories per 3-ounce serving. Compare this with regular ground beef (73-percent lean) with 17.9 grams of fat and 248 calories for the same-size serving, and your savings are clear.

Lean Processed Meat

Because of our new fat-consciousness, low-fat sausage, ham, bacon, and lunch meats are now available, with just a fraction of the fat of regular processed meats. Many of these low-fat products are used in the recipes in this book. Here are some examples:

Sausage. Low-fat sausages are made either from turkey or from a combination of turkey, beef, and pork. These products contain a mere 30 to 40 calories and 0.75 to 3 grams of fat per ounce. Compare this with an ounce of full-fat pork sausage, which contains over 100 calories and almost 9 grams of fat, and your savings are clear.

When a recipe calls for smoked turkey sausage, try a brand like Healthy Choice, which has less than 1 gram of fat per ounce. When a recipe calls for ground turkey breakfast sausage, try a brand like Louis Rich. Many stores also make their own fresh turkey sausage, including turkey Italian sausage. When buying these fresh sausages, always check the package labels and choose the leanest mixture available.

Bacon. Turkey bacon, made with strips of light and dark turkey meat, looks and tastes much like pork bacon. But with 30 calories and 2 grams of fat per strip, turkey bacon has 50 percent less fat than crisp-cooked pork bacon, and shrinks much less during cooking. Besides being a healthier alternative to regular breakfast bacon, turkey bacon may be substituted for pork bacon in Southern-style vegetables, casseroles, and other dishes.

Lunch Meats. Many varieties of ultra-lean lunch meats are now available, including pastrami, corned beef, ham, and roast beef. These meats are ideal substitutes for fatty cold cuts in sandwiches and party platters. Keep in mind, though, that just like their full-fat counterparts, these meats are high in sodium, and so should be used in moderation.

Some processed meats are now labelled "fat-free." Since all meats naturally contain *some* fat, how can this be? The manufacturer first starts with a lean meat such as turkey breast, and then adds enough water—and usually extra salt and artificial flavors, as well—to dilute the fat to a point where the product contains less than 0.5 gram per serving. This

means that part of your dollar actually pays for water, rather than meat. Fortunately, it is not necessary to go to this extreme when purchasing lean meats. Meats that are labelled 96- to 99-percent lean—and therefore contain from 0.3 to 1 gram of fat per ounce—are lean enough to be included in a low-fat diet.

Vegetarian Alternatives

Nonmeat alternatives to ground meat can be substituted for ground beef or ground poultry in any of the recipes in this book. Two good options found in the freezer case of your grocery store are Green Giant Harvest Burger for Recipes and Morningstar Farms Burger Style Crumbles. Made from vegetable proteins, these products are fat-free and rich in protein. Both substitutes look like cooked crumbled ground beef, and can be used in casseroles, spaghetti sauces, and similar dishes.

Two other products can also replace cooked crumbled ground meat in dishes like tacos and chili. The first—texturized vegetable protein (TVP)—is made from defatted soy flour. TVP comes packaged as dry nuggets that you rehydrate with water. The other ground meat alternative is Tofu Crumbles. These precooked, mild seasoned bits of tofu come ready to use. For more information on using these products in cooking, see the inset on page 182.

Fish and Other Seafood

Of the many kinds of fish that are available, some types are almost fat-free, while others are moderately fatty. However, the oil that fish provide contains an essential substance known as omega-3 fatty acids—a substance that most people do not eat in sufficient quantities. Omega-3 fatty acids are valuable because they can help reduce blood cholesterol, lower blood pressure and prevent deadly blood clots from forming. This means that all kinds of fish, including the higher-fat varieties, are considered healthful.

Many fish are now raised on "farms." Do these fish offer the same health benefits as do fish caught in natural habitats? No. Farm-raised fish are fed grains, instead of a fish's natural diet of plankton and smaller fish. As a result, farm-raised fish contain as much or more fat than wild fish do, but are much lower in the beneficial omega-3 fatty acids.

What about the cholesterol content of shellfish? It may not be as high as you think it is. With the exception of shrimp, a 3-ounce serving of most shellfish contains about 60 milligrams of cholesterol, placing it well under the upper limit of 300 milligrams per day. An equivalent serving of shrimp has about 160 milligrams of cholesterol—just over half the recommended daily limit. Keep in mind, though, that all seafood, including shellfish, is very low in saturated fat, which has a greater cholesterol-raising effect than does cholesterol.

Fish is highly perishable, so it is important to know how to select a high-quality product. First, make sure that the fish is firm and springy to the touch. Second, buy fish only if it has a clean seaweed odor, rather than a "fishy" smell. Third, when purchasing whole fish, choose those fish whose gills are bright red in color, and whose eyes are clear and bulging, not sunken or cloudy. Finally, refrigerate fish as soon as you get it home, and be sure to cook it within forty-eight hours of purchase.

Grains and Flours

Just because a food is fat-free does not mean it is good for you. Fat-free products made from refined white flour and refined grains provide few nutrients, and can actually deplete nutrient stores if eaten in excess. Whole grains and whole grain flours, on the other hand, contain a multitude of nutrients such as vitamin E, zinc, magnesium, chromium, potassium, and many other nutrients that are lacking in refined grains. Whole grain products also add fiber to our diets, making our meals more satisfying. You see, fiber—like fat—provides a feeling of fullness. Fiber also helps maintain blood sugar levels, which helps keep hunger at bay. Adequate fiber is, in fact, an important part of a successful low-fat eating plan, as a diet of fat-free and low-fat refined foods is sure to leave you hungry.

Fortunately, once accustomed to the heartier taste and texture of whole grains, most people prefer them over tasteless refined grains. Following is a description of some whole grain products used in the recipes in this book. Many of these products are readily available in grocery stores, while others may be found in health foods stores and gourmet shops. If you are unable to locate a particular grain or flour in your area, it is probably available by mail order. (See the Resource List on pages 491–492.)

Barley. This grain has a nutty light flavor, making it a great substitute for rice in pilafs, soups, casseroles, and other dishes. Hulled barley, like brown rice, cooks in about 50 minutes. Quick-cooking barley, which retains most of the fiber and nutrients of the long-cooking variety, can be prepared in only 10 to 12 minutes.

Barley Flour. Made from ground barley kernels, this flour is rich in cholesterol-lowering soluble fiber. Slightly sweet-tasting, barley flour adds a cake-like texture to baked goods, and can be used interchangeably with oat flour in any recipe.

Bread Flour. Made from high-gluten wheat flour, this product is made especially for use in yeast breads. Bread flour also contains dough conditioners, such as ascorbic acid (vitamin C), that make doughs rise better.

Brown Rice. Brown rice is whole-kernel rice, meaning that all nutrients are intact. With a slightly chewy texture and a pleasant nutty flavor, brown rice makes excellent pilafs and stuffings.

Brown Rice Flour. Brown rice flour is simply finely ground brown rice. It has a texture similar to cornmeal, and adds a mildly sweet flavor to baked goods. Use it in cookies and waffles for a crisp and crunchy texture.

Buckwheat. Buckwheat is technically not a grain, but the edible fruit seed of a plant that is closely related to rhubarb. Roasted buckwheat kernels, commonly known as kasha, are available in most grocery stores, and make delicious pilafs and hot breakfast cereal.

Buckwheat Flour. Made from finely ground whole buckwheat kernels, buckwheat flour is delicious in pancakes, waffles, breads, and muffins.

Cornmeal. This grain adds a sweet flavor, a lovely golden color, and a crunchy texture to baked goods. Select whole grain (unbolted) cornmeal for the most nutrition. By contrast, bolted cornmeal is nearly whole grain, and degermed cornmeal is refined.

Millet. A staple in Oriental and African diets, this tiny round grain cooks in 15 to 20 minutes. Millet absorbs more water than most grains, and so is lower in calories. With the bland taste, millet is a good substitute for rice in almost any dish, and also makes an excellent hot cereal.

Oat Bran. Made of the outer part of the oat kernel, oat bran has a sweet, mild flavor, and is a concentrated source of cholesterol-lowering soluble fiber. Oat bran helps retain moisture in baked goods, making it a natural for fat-free baking. Look for it in the hot cereal section of your grocery store, and choose the softer, more finely ground products, like Quaker Oat Bran. Coarsely ground oat bran makes excellent hot cereal, but is not the best choice for baking.

Measuring Ingredients

Because different measuring techniques can result in varying amounts of an ingredient being added to a recipe—and, in some cases, in dramatically different results—proper measuring is critical to the success of your fat-free cooking and baking endeavors. The recipes in this book were developed using the following measuring methods. By using the same techniques carefully and consistently in your own kitchen, you will enjoy greater success when using the recipes in this book.

Measuring Dry Ingredients. When measuring flour, sugar, and other dry ingredients, use a dry measuring cup that has the exact capacity you wish to measure. Scoop the ingredient directly from the canister, bin, or bag; then level the top off with the back of a knife. Do not pack any dry ingredient except for brown sugar.

Measuring Liquid Ingredients. Use a clear glass or plastic measuring cup to measure liquids. Place the cup on a level surface, and bend down so that the mark you wish to read is at eye level. Then fill the cup to that mark. If your recipe calls for more than one liquid ingredient to be added at the same time, you can place them all in the same cup. For instance, if your recipe calls for ¾ cup of milk and ¼ cup of egg substitute, first fill the cup to the ¾-cup mark with the milk. Then add enough egg substitute to reach the 1-cup mark.

Measuring Semisolid Ingredients. When measuring ingredients like fruit purées, applesauce, and yogurt, use a dry measuring cup that has the exact capacity you wish to measure. Spoon the ingredient into the cup; then level the top off with the back of a knife.

Oat Flour. This mildly sweet flour is perfect for cakes, muffins, and other baked goods. Like oat bran, oat flour retains moisture in baked goods, reducing the need for fat. To add extra fiber and nutrients to your own recipes, replace up to one-third of the refined flour with an equal amount of oat flour. If you can't find oat flour in your local stores, you can easily make it at home by grinding quick-cooking rolled oats in a blender.

Oats. Loaded with cholesterol-lowering soluble fiber, oats add a chewy texture and sweet flavor to muffins, quick breads, pancakes, cookies, and crumb toppings. They are also delicious in breakfast cereals and other dishes. Most of the recipes in this book use quick-cooking rolled oats. (Look for oats that cook in one minute.) Old-fashioned oats, which are cut slightly thicker, cook in 5 minutes.

Unbleached Flour. This is refined white flour that has not been subjected to a bleaching process. Unbleached white flour lacks significant amounts of nutrients compared with whole wheat flour, but does contain more vitamin E than bleached flour.

Wheat Bran. Unprocessed wheat bran— sometimes called miller's bran—is made from the outer portions of the whole wheat kernel. This grain product adds fiber and texture to breads, muffins, and other foods.

Whole Grain Wheat. Available in many forms, this grain is perhaps the easiest to use in the form of bulgur wheat. Cracked wheat that is precooked and dried, bulgur wheat can be prepared in a matter of minutes and can be used to replace rice in any recipe.

Whole Wheat Flour. Made of ground whole grain wheat kernels, whole wheat flour includes the grain's nutrient-rich bran and germ. Nutritionally speaking, whole wheat flour is far superior to refined flour. Sadly, many people

grew up eating refined baked goods, and find whole grain products too heavy for their taste. A good way to learn to enjoy whole grain flours is to use part whole wheat and part unbleached flour in recipes, and gradually increase the amount of whole wheat used over time.

When muffin, quick bread, cake, and cookie recipes call for whole wheat flour, **whole wheat pastry flour,** also called whole grain pastry flour, works best, and is recommended for the recipes in this book. Whole wheat pastry flour produces lighter, softer-textured baked goods than regular whole wheat flour because it is made from a softer (lower-protein) wheat and is more finely ground.

White whole wheat flour is another excellent option for baking. Made from hard white wheat instead of the hard red wheat used to make regular whole wheat flour, white whole wheat flour is sweeter and lighter tasting than its red wheat counterpart. To substitute any of these whole wheat flours for refined white, use the following guidelines:

---

1 cup white flour =
1 cup whole wheat pastry flour
1 cup minus 1 tablespoon white whole wheat flour
1 cup minus 2 tablespoons regular
whole wheat flour

---

1 cup whole wheat pastry flour =
1 cup minus 1 tablespoon white whole wheat flour
1 cup minus 2 tablespoons regular
whole wheat flour

Sweeteners

Refined white sugar contains no nutrients. In fact, when eaten in excess, refined sugar can actually deplete body stores of essential nutrients like chromium and the B vitamins. Of course, a moderate amount of sugar is usually not a problem for people who eat an otherwise healthy diet. What is moderate? No more than

10 percent of your daily intake of calories should come from sugar. For an individual who needs 2,000 calories to maintain his or her weight, this amounts to an upper limit of 12.5 teaspoons (about ¼ cup) of sugar a day. Naturally, a diet that is lower in sugar is even better.

The baked goods and dessert recipes in this book contain 25 to 50 percent less sugar than traditional recipes do. Ingredients like fruit juices, fruit purées, and dried fruits; flavorings and spices like vanilla extract, nutmeg, and cinnamon; and mildly sweet oats and oat bran have often been used to reduce the need for sugar.

The recipes in this book call for moderate amounts of white sugar, brown sugar, and different liquid sweeteners. However, a large number of sweeteners are now available, and you should feel free to substitute one sweetener for another, using your own tastes, your desire for high-nutrient ingredients, and your pocketbook as a guide. (Some of the newer less-refined sweeteners are far more expensive than traditional sweeteners.) For best results, replace granular sweeteners with other granular sweeteners, and substitute liquid sweeteners for other liquid sweeteners. You can, of course, replace a liquid with granules, or vice versa, but adjustments in other recipe ingredients will have to be made. (For each cup of liquid sweetener substituted for a granulated sweetener, reduce the liquid by ¼ to ⅓ cup.) Also be aware that each sweetener has its own unique flavor and its own degree of sweetness, making some sweeteners better suited to particular recipes.

Following is a description of some of the sweeteners commonly available in grocery stores, health food stores, and gourmet shops. Those sweeteners that can't be found in local stores can usually be ordered by mail. (See the Resource List on pages 491–492.)

Apple Butter. Sweet and thick, apple butter is made by cooking down apples with apple juice and spices. Many brands also contain added sugar, but some are sweetened only with juice. Use apple butter as you would honey to sweeten products in which a little spice will enhance flavor. Spice cakes, bran muffins, and oatmeal cookies are all delicious when made with apple butter.

Brown Rice Syrup. Commonly available in health foods stores, brown rice syrup is made by converting the starch in brown rice into sugar. This syrup is mildly sweet—about 30 to 60 percent as sweet as sugar, depending on the brand—and has a delicate malt flavor. Perhaps most important, brown rice syrup retains most of the nutrients found in the rice from which it was made. This sweetener is a good substitute for honey or other liquid sweeteners whenever you want to tone down the sweetness of a recipe.

Brown Sugar. This granulated sweetener is simply refined white sugar that has been coated with a thin film of molasses. Light brown sugar is lighter in color than regular brown sugar, but not lower in calories, as the name might imply. Because this sweetener contains some molasses, brown sugar has more calcium, iron, and potassium than white sugar. But like most sugars, brown sugar is no nutritional powerhouse. The advantage to using this sweetener instead of white sugar is that it is more flavorful and so can be used in smaller quantities.

Date Sugar. Made from ground dried dates, date sugar provides copper, magnesium, iron, and B vitamins. With a distinct date flavor, date sugar is delicious in breads, cakes, and muffins. Because it does not dissolve as readily as white sugar does, it is best to mix date sugar with the recipe's liquid ingredients and let it sit for a few minutes before proceeding with the recipe. Date sugar is less dense than white sugar, and so is only about two-thirds as sweet. However, date sugar is more flavorful, and so can often be substituted for white sugar on a cup-for-cup basis.

Fruit Juice Concentrates. Frozen juice concentrates add sweetness and flavor to baked goods while enchancing nutritional value. Use the concentrates as you would honey or other liquid sweeteners, but beware—too much will be overpowering. Always keep cans of frozen orange and apple juice concentrate in the freezer just for cooking and baking. Pineapple and tropical fruit blends also make good sweeteners, and white grape juice is ideal when you want a more neutral flavor.

Fruit Source. Made from white grape juice and brown rice, this sweetener has a rather neutral flavor and is about as sweet as white sugar. Fruit Source is available in both granular and liquid forms. Use the liquid as you would honey, and the granules as you would sugar. The granules do not dissolve as readily as sugar does, so mix Fruit Source with the recipe's liquid ingredients and let it sit for a few minutes before proceeding with the recipe.

Fruit Spreads, Jams, and Preserves. Available in a variety of flavors, these products make delicious sweeteners. For best flavor and nutrition, choose a brand made from fruits and fruit juice concentrate, with little or no added sugar, and select a flavor that is compatible with the baked goods you're making. Use as you would any liquid sweetener.

Honey. Contrary to popular belief, honey is not significantly more nutritious than sugar, but it does add a nice flavor to baked goods. It also adds moistness, reducing the need for fat. The sweetest of the liquid sweeteners, honey is generally 20 to 30 percent sweeter than sugar. Be sure to consider this when making substitutions.

Maple Sugar. Made from dehydrated maple syrup, granulated maple sugar adds a distinct maple flavor to baked goods. Powdered maple sugar is also available, and can be used to replace powdered white sugar in glazes.

Maple Syrup. The boiled-down sap of sugar maple trees, maple syrup adds delicious flavor to all baked goods, and also provides some potassium and other nutrients. Use it as you would honey or molasses.

Molasses. Light, or Barbados, molasses is pure sugarcane juice boiled down into a thick syrup. Light molasses provides some calcium, potassium, and iron, and is delicious in spice cakes, muffins, breads, and cookies. Blackstrap molasses is a by-product of the sugar-refining process. Very rich in calcium, potassium, and iron, it has a slightly bitter, strong flavor, and is half as sweet as refined sugar. Because of its distinctive taste, more than a few tablespoons in a recipe is overwhelming.

Sucanat. Granules of evaporated sugarcane juice, Sucanat tastes similar to brown sugar. This sweetener provides small amounts of potassium, chromium, calcium, iron, and vitamins A and C. Use it as you would any other granulated sugar.

Sugarcane Syrup. The process used to make sugarcane syrup is similar to that of making light molasses. Consequently, the syrup has a molasses-like flavor and is nutritionally comparable to the other sweetener.

Throughout our discussion of sweeteners, we have mentioned that some sweeteners are higher in nutrients than others. Just how much variation is there among sweeteners? The table at the bottom of this page compares the amounts of selected nutrients found in one-quarter cup of different sweeteners. Pay special attention to how the sweeteners compare with white sugar, the most refined of all the sweeteners.

Other Ingredients

Aside from the ingredients already discussed, a few more items may prove useful as you venture into fat-free cooking. Some ingredients may already be familiar to you, while others may become new additions to your pantry.

Barley Nugget Cereal. Whenever you want to replace or reduce the nuts in a recipe, try using a crunchy, nutty cereal like Grape-Nuts. The flavorful nuggets make a nice addition to crumb toppings, cookies, muffins, and other baked goods.

Couscous. A staple in African and Middle Eastern diets, couscous is actually pasta that has been shaped into small grain-sized pieces. Most of the couscous available in supermarkets is made from refined flour, but whole wheat couscous is also available, and is definitely a better nutritional bargain. Cous-

cous cooks in less than five minutes, and is an excellent alternative to rice when used as a bed for stir-fries or in side dishes, salads, and casseroles.

Dried Fruits. A wide variety of dried fruits are available. Dried pineapple, apricots, prunes, dates, and peaches are available in most grocery stores, while health foods stores and gourmet shops often carry dried mangoes, papaya, cherries, blueberries, and cranberries. These fruits add interest to muffins, cookie, and other baked goods. If you cannot find the type of dried fruit called for in a recipe, feel free to substitute another type.

Fat-Free Cracker Crumbs. Use fat-free cracker crumbs as a crunchy coating for oven "fried" foods, or as a topping for casseroles.

Comparing Sweeteners

Sweetener (¼ cup)	Calories	Calcium (mg)	Iron (mg)	Potassium (mg)
Apple Butter	130	10	0.5	176
Brown Rice Syrup	256	3	0.1	140
Brown Sugar	205	47	1.2	189
Date Sugar	88	10	0.4	209
Fruit Juice Concentrate (apple)	116	14	0.6	315
Fruit Juice Concentrate (orange)	113	23	0.3	479
Fruit Preserves	216	8	0	12
Fruit Source (granules)	192	16	0.4	142
Fruit Source (syrup)	176	15	0.4	138
Honey	240	0	0.5	27
Maple Sugar	176	45	0.8	137
Maple Syrup	202	83	1.0	141
Molasses, Blackstrap	170	548	20.2	2,342
Molasses, Light	172	132	4.3	732
Sucanat	144	41	1.6	162
Sugarcane Syrup	210	48	2.9	340
White Sugar	192	1	0	2

To make this ingredient, simply crush any flavor of fat-free crackers, place in a blender or food processor, and process into crumbs. One ounce of crackers makes about one-fourth cup of crumbs.

Fat-Free Flour and Corn Tortillas. Flour tortillas have always been fairly low in fat, generally with less than 3 grams of fat each. Fat-free brands are now available, as well, and are an even better choice. The recipes in this book use fat-free flour tortillas as wrappers for appetizer finger sandwiches and burritos, and as pizza crusts. If you cannot find a fat-free product, feel free to use regular flour tortillas. Corn tortillas have always been fat-free. Use these handy wrappers to make enchiladas and a variety of other dishes.

Fat-Free Graham Crackers. Graham crackers have always been fairly low in fat, usually with less than 3 grams of fat each. Now that fat-free and low-fat brands are available, though, you have an even healthier option. The recipes in this book use fat-free graham crackers to make graham cracker pie crusts. If you cannot find fat-free grahams, feel free to substitute a regular or low-fat brand.

Fat-Free Granola. A wonderful substitute for nuts, fat-free granola adds nutty crunch and extra flavor to cookies, pancakes, muffins, and other baked goods. Low-fat granola is another good option. Look for brands with no more than 2 grams of fat per ounce.

Nonstick Cooking Spray. These handy sprays are available both unflavored and in butter and olive oil flavors. While they are pure fat, the amount that comes out of the can during a one-second spray is so small that it adds an insignificant amount of fat to a recipe. In this book, nonstick cooking sprays are used to promote the browning of foods and to prevent foods from sticking to pots and pans.

Olive Oil. While all oils should be limited in a low-fat eating plan, a small amount of olive oil is suggested in an occasional recipe to enhance flavor. When used in the recommended amounts, this ingredient will not blow your fat budget, so include it if you like, using extra-virgin olive oil for the most flavor.

What about "light" olive oil? In this case, light refers to flavor—which is mild and bland compared with that of extra-virgin oils. This means that you have to use more oil for the same amount of flavor, making this product a poor choice for low-fat cooking.

Sesame Oil. Like olive oil, sesame oil enhances the flavors of foods. Because it is so flavorful, a little bit goes a long way, making this oil a valuable ingredient in low-fat cooking.

Toasted Wheat Germ. This ingredient adds crunch and nutty flavor to baked goods. A super-nutritious food, with 80 percent less fat than nuts, wheat germ provides generous amounts of vitamin E and minerals.

Whole Wheat Bread Crumbs. Whole wheat bread crumbs can be used in stuffings, as a topping for casseroles, or as a filler for meat loaf. To make whole wheat bread crumbs, simply tear up slices of whole wheat bread, place them in a blender or food processor, and process into crumbs. One slice of bread makes about one-half cup of crumbs.

Gelatin Mixes. Available in a variety of flavors, in both sugar-free and sugar-sweetened versions, gelatin mixes have always been fat-free. These handy mixes can serve as the base for delightful pie fillings, puddings, mousses, and many other creations.

Nonfat Whipped Topping. With just 15 calories and less than half a gram of fat per 2-tablespoon serving, nonfat whipped toppings make it possible to create ultra-light and creamy frostings, fillings, mousses, and other sweet delights. Light whipped toppings, with 20 calories and 1 gram of fat per serving, are your next best bet. How do these products stack up to whipped cream? For each 2-tablespoon serving, you will save 36 calories and 5 grams of fat by replacing full-fat whipped cream with its nonfat counterpart, making your savings substantial. Look for brands like Cool Whip Free and Cool Whip Light. Many grocery stores now also carry their own brands of nonfat and light whipped toppings.

Nuts. It may surprise you to learn that the recipes in this book sometimes include nuts as an ingredient, or suggest them as an optional addition. True, nuts are high in fat. But when used in small amounts, these tasty morsels will not blow your fat budget, and will provide some of the fats, vitamins, and minerals that are essential for good health. Read more about using nuts in low-fat cooking on page 383.

Pie Fillings. Canned pie fillings make convenient fillings and toppings for parfaits, cheesecakes, pastries, and many other goodies. Most fruit-based pie fillings have always been fat-free. Light varieties are also available, with about a third less sugar and calories. Look for brands like Comstock Light, Lucky Leaf Lite, and Thank You Light.

Pudding Mixes. Fat-free pudding mixes are now available in a range of flavors, in both sugar-free and regular versions, and in cook-and-serve and instant varieties. While the directions on regular pudding mixes usually warn against preparing the product with skim milk, as this will result in a thin mixture, fat-free pudding mixes are meant especially for use with skim milk, and mix up into a thick, rich-tasting treat. These convenient mixes can form the base for fillings, frostings,

mousses, trifles, and many other sweet creations.

A Word About Salt

Salt, a combination of sodium and chloride, enhances the flavors of many foods. However, most health experts recommend a maximum of 2,400 milligrams of sodium per day, the equivalent of about one teaspoon of salt. For this reason, very little salt is added to the recipes in this book. A minimal use of salt-laden processed ingredients, as well as a wise use of herbs and spices, keeps the salt content under control without compromising taste.

ABOUT THE NUTRITIONAL ANALYSIS

The Food Processor II (ESHA Research) computer nutrition analysis system, along with the product information from manufacturers, was used to calculate the nutritional information for the recipes in this book. Nutrients are always listed per one piece, one muffin, one slice of bread, one cookie, one serving, etc.

Sometimes, recipes give you options regarding ingredients. For instance, you might be able to choose between nonfat cream cheese and reduced-fat cream cheese, nonfat mayonnaise and reduced-fat mayonnaise, 96-percent lean ground beef and ground turkey, or raisins and nuts. This will help you create dishes that suit your tastes. Just keep in mind that the nutritional analysis is based on the first ingredient listed.

In your quest for fat-free eating, you might be inclined to choose fat-free cheese over reduced-fat cheese, and to omit any optional nuts. Be aware, though, that if you are not used to nonfat cheeses, it might be wise to start by using reduced-fat products. Should you opt to omit the nuts? Not necessarily. Nuts are high in fat, but they also contain essential minerals and vitamin E. Some studies have even indicated that people who eat nuts as part of a healthy diet have less heart disease. If you like nuts, feel free to use them in your cooking and baking. In fat-free recipes like the ones in this book, you can afford to add a few nuts or to sometimes choose the higher-fat ingredient.

WHERE DOES THE FAT COME FROM IN FAT-FREE RECIPES?

You may notice that even though a recipe may contain no oil, butter, margarine, nuts, chocolate chips, or other fatty ingredient, it still contains a small amount of fat (less than one gram). This is because many natural ingredients contain some fat. Whole grains, for example, store a small amount of oil in their germ, the center portion of the grain. This oil is very beneficial because it is loaded with vitamin E, an antioxidant. The germ also provides an abundance of vitamins and minerals. Products made from refined grains and refined flours—ingredients that have been stripped of

the germ—do have slightly less fat than whole grain versions, but they also have far less nutrients.

Other ingredients, too, naturally contain small amounts of fat. For instance, fruits and vegetables, like grains, contain some oil. And, again, the oil also provides many important nutrients. Olives, nuts, and lean meats also contribute fat to some recipes. However, when used in small quantities, the amount of fat is significant. In fact, the majority of recipes in this book contain less than one gram of fat per serving.

This book is filled with recipes that will make any meal of the day special. The dishes are not only easy to make, satisfying, and delicious, but are also foods that you can feel good about serving to your family and friends. So get ready to create some new family favorites, and to experience the pleasures and rewards of cooking without fat.

2

Breakfasts for Champions

When it comes to high-fat, high-calorie foods, few meals can top a traditional breakfast. For decades, fatty eggs, cheese, sausage, and bacon were considered an essential part of morning fare. Of course, we now know that these foods are far from healthy. But for many of us, breakfast just isn't breakfast without a stack of golden French toast or a hearty Western omelette. What to do, what to do?

Fortunately, you need not discard your favorite breakfast fare in order to banish high-fat foods from the breakfast table. There is now a healthier fat-free or low-fat alternative to just about any breakfast food that comes to mind. Fat-free egg substitutes have been the biggest boon to breakfast lovers. With none of the fat or cholesterol of eggs, these substitutes can replace the eggs in all of your breakfast casseroles and omelettes. Fat-free cheeses and ultra-lean sausage, ham, and bacon are other breakfast favorites that can now take their place in a healthful lifestyle. In fact, many of the recipes in this chapter combine these new fat-free and low-fat ingredients to create delicious versions of previously taboo dishes.

Can pancakes, waffles, and French toast also be part of a low-fat breakfast menu? Happily, many of the traditional recipes for these treats have always been fairly low in fat. However, most recipes do contain unnecessary oil, egg yokes, and salt—unhealthy ingredients that can be trimmed away, leaving these treats just as delicious as always, but a great deal more healthful. Replace the usual refined white flour with whole grain ingredients, add some sweet yet wholesome toppings, and these dishes are more than just low in fat. They are high in many important nutrients.

When creating breakfast menus, you need not confine your choices to the selections in this chapter. Fresh juices, in-season fruits, and whole grain breads and muffins will add both diversity and balance to your menu. So heat up the griddle, and get ready for high-nutrient, taste-tempting breakfast foods that will not only get you out of bed, but will keep you going all morning long!

BANANA GRANOLA PANCAKES

Yield: *16 pancakes*

1½ cups whole wheat flour

1 tablespoon sugar

1 teaspoon baking soda

1¾ cups nonfat buttermilk

2 egg whites, lightly beaten

2 cups sliced bananas (about 2 medium)

½ cup nonfat or low-fat granola cereal

1. Combine the flour, sugar, and baking soda in a medium-sized bowl, and stir to mix well. Stir in the buttermilk and egg whites. Fold in the bananas and granola.

2. Coat a griddle or large skillet with nonstick cooking spray, and preheat over medium heat until a drop of water sizzles when it hits the heated surface. (If using an electric griddle, heat the griddle according to the manufacturer's directions.)

3. For each pancake, pour ¼ cup of batter onto the griddle, and spread into a 4-inch circle. Cook for 1 minute and 30 seconds, or until the tops are bubbly and the edges are dry. Turn and cook for an additional minute, or until the second side is golden brown. As the pancakes are done, transfer them to a serving plate and keep warm in a preheated oven.

4. Serve hot, topped with either honey or maple syrup.

NUTRITIONAL FACTS (PER PANCAKE)
Calories: 77 Cholesterol: 1 mg Fat: 0.5 g
Fiber: 1.9 g Protein: 3.3 g Sodium: 133 mg

Cottage Cheese Pancakes

1. Combine the whole wheat flour, orange rind, and baking powder in a medium-sized bowl, and stir to mix well. Add the milk, cottage cheese, and egg whites, and stir to mix well.

2. Coat a griddle or large skillet with nonstick cooking spray, and preheat over medium heat until a drop of water sizzles when it hits the heated surface. (If using an electric griddle, heat the griddle according to the manufacturer's directions.)

3. For each pancake, pour 3 tablespoons of batter onto the griddle, and spread into a 3-inch circle. Cook for 1 minute and 30 seconds, or until the tops are bubbly and the edges are dry. Turn and cook for an additional minute, or until the second side is golden brown. As the pancakes are done, transfer them to a serving plate and keep warm in a preheated oven.

4. Serve hot, topped with Berry Fresh Fruit Sauce (page 26) or Honey-Orange Syrup (page 27).

Yield: *16 pancakes*

1 cup whole wheat flour

1 teaspoon dried grated orange rind

1½ teaspoons baking powder

1 cup skim milk

1 cup dry curd or nonfat cottage cheese

4 egg whites, lightly beaten

NUTRITIONAL FACTS (PER PANCAKE)

Calories: 43 Cholesterol: 1 mg Fat: 0.2 g
Fiber: 1 g Protein: 4 g Sodium: 57 mg

Simple Syrup Alternatives

Deliciously sweet syrups add that crowning touch to pancakes, waffles, and French toast. While all syrups are fat-free, they are generally almost pure sugar, and add up to 60 calories for each tablespoon used. Instead of the usual refined, sugary syrups, try any of the following toppings over pancakes, waffles, and other breakfast treats. As low in calories as most reduced-calorie brands, these syrups are more natural, wholesome, and economical.

WARM APPLE SYRUP

Yield: *1¾ cups*

¾ cup plus 2 teaspoons apple juice, divided

½ cup molasses, honey, or maple syrup

1½ cups chopped peeled apple (about 2 medium)

2 teaspoons cornstarch

1. Combine ¾ cup of the apple juice and all of the molasses and apples in a 1-quart saucepan. Place over medium heat, and bring to a boil, stirring occasionally. Reduce the heat to low, cover, and simmer for 10 minutes, or until the apples are tender.

2. Combine the cornstarch and the remaining 2 teaspoons of apple juice in a small bowl. Add the mixture to the pan, and cook and stir for 1 minutes, or until the mixture is slightly thickened.

3. Serve warm over pancakes, French toast, or waffles. Store any leftovers in the refrigerator for up to a week.

NUTRITIONAL FACTS (PER 2-TABLESPOON SERVING)
Calories: 50 Cholesterol: 0 mg Fat: 0 g
Fiber: 0.4 g Protein: 0 g Sodium: 5 mg

BERRY FRESH FRUIT SAUCE

Yield: *2¼ cups*

¼ cup sugar

1 tablespoon cornstarch

¾ cup white grape juice

2 cups fresh or frozen raspberries, blueberries, blackberries, or sliced strawberries

1. Combine the sugar and cornstarch in a 1-quart saucepan. Slowly stir in the juice. Place over medium heat, and bring to a boil, stirring constantly.

2. Add the fruit to the juice mixture, and bring to a second boil. Reduce the heat to low, and cook, stirring occasionally, for about 5 minutes, or until the fruit begins to break down and the mixture is thickened and bubbly.

3. Serve warm over pancakes, French toast, or waffles. Store any leftovers in the refrigerator for up to a week.

NUTRITIONAL FACTS (PER ¼-CUP SERVING)
Calories: 51 Cholesterol: 0 mg Fat: 0.1 g
Fiber: 1.1 g Protein: 0.4 g Sodium: 1 mg

Honey-Orange Syrup

1. Combine the cornstarch and orange juice in a 1-quart saucepan, and stir until the cornstarch is dissolved. Stir in the honey.

2. Place the pan over medium heat, and cook and stir for about 3 minutes, or until the mixture is bubbly and slightly thickened.

3. Serve warm over pancakes, French toast, or waffles. Store any leftovers in the refrigerator for up to a week.

Yield: *1½ cups*

1 tablespoon cornstarch

1 cup orange juice

½ cup honey

NUTRITIONAL FACTS (PER 2-TABLESPOON SERVING)
Calories: 55 Cholesterol: 0 mg Fat: 0 g
Fiber: 0 g Protein: 0.2 g Sodium: 1 mg

Fruitful Breakfast Bars

Two of these bars plus a glass of milk make a quick and nutritious breakfast.

1. Combine the flour, wheat germ, oats, baking powder, and cinnamon, and stir to mix well. Add the Prune Butter, honey or molasses, and egg substitute, and stir to mix well. Fold in the raisins and apricots.

2. Coat an 8-inch square pan with nonstick cooking spray. Spread the mixture evenly in the pan, and bake at 350°F for about 25 minutes, or until lightly browned.

3. Cool to room temperature, cut into bars, and serve.

Yield: *10 servings*

¾ cup whole wheat flour

½ cup toasted wheat germ

¼ cup quick-cooking oats

½ teaspoon baking powder

½ teaspoon ground cinnamon

¼ cup Prune Butter (page 223)

¼ cup honey or molasses

3 tablespoons fat-free egg substitute

½ cup dark raisins

½ cup chopped dried apricots

NUTRITIONAL FACTS (PER SERVING)
Calcium: 19 mg Calories: 128 Cholesterol: 0 mg
Fat: 0.9 g Fiber: 3.1 g Iron: 1.6 mg
Potassium: 256 mg Protein: 4.1 g Sodium: 25 mg

Applesauce Pancakes

Yield: *12 pancakes*

1½ cups whole wheat flour

1 tablespoon baking powder

¾ cup unsweetened applesauce

1 cup nonfat or low-fat buttermilk

2 egg whites, lightly beaten

1. Combine the flour and baking powder in a medium-sized bowl, and stir to mix well. Stir in the applesauce, buttermilk, and egg whites.

2. Coat a griddle or large skillet with nonstick cooking spray, and preheat over medium heat until a drop of water sizzles when it hits the heated surface. (If using an electric griddle, heat the griddle according to the manufacturer's directions.)

3. For each pancake, pour ¼ cup of batter onto the griddle, and spread into a 4-inch circle. Cook for 1 minute and 30 seconds, or until the tops are bubbly and the edges are dry. Turn and cook for an additional minute, or until the second side is golden brown. As the pancakes are done, transfer them to a serving plate and keep warm in a preheated oven.

4. Serve hot, topped with Warm Apple Syrup (page 26) or the syrup of your choice.

NUTRITIONAL FACTS (PER PANCAKE)
Calories: 69 Cholesterol: 1 mg Fat: 0.4 g
Fiber: 2 g Protein: 3.3 g Sodium: 122 mg

Variation

To make Applesauce Buckwheat Cakes, substitute ½ cup of buckwheat flour for ½ cup of the whole wheat flour.

NUTRITIONAL FACTS (PER PANCAKE)
Calories: 69 Cholesterol: 1 mg Fat: 0.4 g
Fiber: 2 g Protein: 3.3 g Sodium: 122 mg

Light and Fluffy Oatcakes

1. Combine the oats and buttermilk in a medium-sized bowl. Set aside for 5 minutes.

2. Place the egg whites in the bowl of an electric mixer, and beat on high until stiff peaks form. Set aside.

3. Combine the flour, sugar, and baking powder in a large bowl, and stir to mix well. Add the oat mixture to the flour mixture, and stir to mix well. Gently fold in the egg whites.

4. Coat a griddle or large skillet with nonstick cooking spray, and preheat over medium heat until a drop of water sizzles when it hits the heated surface. (If using an electric griddle, heat the griddle according to the manufacturer's directions.)

5. For each pancake, pour ¼ cup of batter onto the griddle, and spread into a 4-inch circle. Cook for 1 minute and 30 seconds, or until the tops are bubbly and the edges are dry. Turn and cook for an additional minute, or until the second side is golden brown. As the pancakes are done, transfer them to a serving plate and keep warm in a preheated oven.

6. Serve hot, topped with Warm Apple Syrup (page 26), Berry Fresh Fruit Sauce (page 26), or Honey-Orange Syrup (page 27).

Yield: *12 pancakes*

¾ cup quick-cooking oats

1¾ cups nonfat or low-fat buttermilk

2 egg whites

1 cup whole wheat pastry flour

1 tablespoon sugar

2 teaspoons baking powder

NUTRITIONAL FACTS (PER PANCAKE)
Calories: 75 Cholesterol: 1 mg Fat: 0.8 g
Fiber: 1.8 g Protein: 3.9 g Sodium: 108 mg

Variation

To make Blueberry Oatcakes, fold ¾ cup of fresh or frozen blueberries into the batter.

NUTRITIONAL FACTS (PER PANCAKE)
Calories: 80 Cholesterol: 1 mg Fat: 0.8 g
Fiber: 2 g Protein: 4 g Sodium: 108 mg

Golden French Toast

Yield: *12 slices*

2 cups fat-free egg substitute

¼ cup skim milk

¼ teaspoon ground cinnamon

1 teaspoon vanilla extract

12 slices whole wheat bread

1. Combine the egg substitute, milk, cinnamon, and vanilla extract in a shallow bowl, and stir to mix well. Dip each slice of bread in the egg mixture, turning to coat both sides.

2. Coat a griddle or large skillet with nonstick cooking spray, and preheat over medium heat until a drop of water sizzles when it hits the heated surface. (If using an electric griddle, heat the griddle according to the manufacturer's directions.)

3. Lay the bread slices on the griddle, and cook for about 2 minutes on each side, or until golden brown. As the slices are done, transfer them to a serving plate and keep warm in a preheated oven.

4. Serve hot, either plain or topped with maple syrup, Berry Fresh Fruit Sauce (page 26), or Honey-Orange Syrup (page 27).

NUTRITIONAL FACTS (PER SLICE)

Calories: 82 Cholesterol: 0 mg Fat: 0.8 g

Fiber: 2 g Protein: 8.2 g Sodium: 194 mg

Variation

For a crunchy coating, sprinkle each side of the bread with 2 teaspoons of toasted wheat germ just before placing the slice on the griddle.

NUTRITIONAL FACTS (PER SLICE)

Calories: 118 Cholesterol: 0 mg Fat: 1.8 g

Fiber: 3.3 g Protein: 10.9 g Sodium: 194 mg

Crispy Cornmeal Waffles

Waffles are great for people with busy lifestyles, as they may be made in advance, placed in plastic zip-type bags, and frozen until needed. At breakfast time, heat the frozen waffles in the toaster, and serve.

1. Coat a waffle iron with nonstick cooking spray, and preheat according to the manufacturer's directions.

2. Combine the flour, cornmeal, sugar, baking powder, and baking soda in a large bowl, and stir to mix well. Set aside.

3. Place the egg whites in the bowl of an electric mixer, and beat on high until soft peaks form. Set aside.

4. Add the buttermilk to the flour mixture, and stir to mix well. Gently fold in the egg whites.

5. Spoon 1¼ cups of batter (or the amount stated by the manufacturer) onto the prepared waffle iron. Bake for 5 to 7 minutes, or until the iron has stopped steaming and the waffle is crisp and brown.

6. Serve hot, topped with Berry Fresh Fruit Sauce (page 26) or Honey-Orange Syrup (page 27).

***Yield:** 12 waffles*

1 cup whole wheat pastry flour

1 cup whole grain cornmeal

2 tablespoons sugar

2 teaspoons baking powder

¾ teaspoon baking soda

4 egg whites

1½ cups nonfat or low-fat buttermilk

NUTRITIONAL FACTS (PER WAFFLE)
Calories: 97 Cholesterol: 0 mg Fat: 0.7 g
Fiber: 2.0 g Protein: 4.3 g Sodium: 194 mg

Variation

For variety and added crunch, fold ¼ cup of toasted wheat germ into the batter.

NUTRITIONAL FACTS (PER WAFFLE)
Calories: 106 Cholesterol: 0 mg Fat: 1.0 g
Fiber: 2.3 g Protein: 5.1 g Sodium: 194 mg

Golden Pumpkin Waffles

Yield: *12 waffles*

1 cup whole wheat pastry flour

1 cup whole grain cornmeal or brown rice flour

2 tablespoons sugar

2 teaspoons baking powder

¾ teaspoon baking soda

2½ teaspoons pumpkin pie spice

4 egg whites

½ cup mashed cooked or canned pumpkin

1 cup skim milk

1. Coat a waffle iron with nonstick cooking spray, and preheat according to manufacturer's directions.

2. Combine the whole wheat flour, cornmeal or brown rice flour, sugar, baking powder, baking soda, and pumpkin pie spice in a large bowl, and stir to mix well. Set aside.

3. Place the egg whites in the bowl of an electric mixer, and beat on high until soft peaks form. Set aside.

4. Add the pumpkin and milk to the flour mixture, and stir to mix well. Gently fold in the egg whites.

5. Spoon 1¼ cups of batter (or the amount stated by the manufacturer) onto the prepared waffle iron. Bake for 6 to 8 minutes, or until the iron has stopped steaming and the waffle is crisp and brown.

6. Serve hot, topped with Warm Apple Syrup (page 26) or Honey-Orange Syrup (page 27).

NUTRITIONAL FACTS (PER WAFFLE)
Calories: 96 Cholesterol: 0 mg Fat: 0.6 g
Fiber: 2.2 g Protein: 4.1 g Sodium: 172 mg

FAT-FREE COOKING TIP

Getting the Fat Out of Your Waffle Recipes

To make your favorite waffles light, crisp, and fat-free:

❑ Replace the oil in the recipe with ¾ as much buttermilk, applesauce, or other liquid.

❑ Substitute 3 egg whites for every 2 whole eggs in the recipe, and whip the egg whites to soft peaks before folding them into the batter.

❑ For an extra-crisp texture, substitute brown rice flour or cornmeal for up to half of the wheat flour. These flours add a pleasing crunch to baked goods.

Southwestern Omelette

1. Coat an 8-inch skillet with nonstick cooking spray, and preheat over medium-low heat. Place the egg substitute in the skillet, and let the eggs cooks without stirring for about 2 minutes, or until set around the edges.

2. Use a spatula to lift the edges of the omelette, and allow the uncooked egg to flow below the cooked portion. Cook for another minute or 2, or until the eggs are almost set.

3. Arrange first the cheese, and then the ham, peppers, and onions over half of the omelette. Fold the other half over the filling, and cook for another minute or 2, or until the cheese is melted and the eggs are completely set.

4. Slide the omelette onto a plate, top with the tomatoes or picante sauce, and serve immediately.

Yield: *1 serving*

¾ cup fat-free egg substitute

3 tablespoons shredded nonfat Cheddar cheese, or 1 slice nonfat Cheddar cheese

2 tablespoons chopped ham (at least 97% lean)

1 tablespoon chopped green bell pepper

1 tablespoon chopped onion

2 tablespoons chopped tomato or picante sauce

NUTRITIONAL FACTS (PER SERVING)
Calories: 154 Cholesterol: 14 mg Fat: 0.7 g
Fiber: 0.5 g Protein: 29 g Sodium: 649 mg

Fruit Muesli

This supernutritious breakfast cereal is a snap to make.

1. Place all of the ingredients in a large bowl, and stir to mix well. Transfer to an airtight container, and store for up to 4 weeks.

2. To serve, place ⅓ cup of muesli in an individual serving bowl and add ½ cup of low-fat milk, nonfat vanilla or plain yogurt, or applesauce. Stir, and let sit for 3 to 5 minutes before serving.

Yield: *5 cups*

2 cups old-fashioned oats

¼ cup plus 2 tablespoons wheat bran

¾ cup barley nugget cereal

¼ cup toasted wheat germ

½ cup dark raisins or chopped dates

½ cup chopped dried apricots

½ cup chopped dried peaches

½ cup chopped pecans, hazelnuts, walnuts, or almonds (optional)

NUTRITIONAL FACTS (PER ⅓-CUP SERVING, CEREAL ONLY)
Calories: 108 Cholesterol: 0 mg Fat: 1 g
Fiber: 3.4 g Protein: 3.7 g Sodium: 40 mg

ZUCCHINI FRITTATA

Yield: *4 servings*

1½ medium zucchini, halved
   lengthwise and sliced ¼ inch
   thick

1 medium yellow onion, cut into
   thin wedges

½ medium green bell pepper, cut
   into thin strips

½ medium red bell pepper, cut
   into thin strips

1 teaspoon crushed fresh garlic

1 teaspoon dried Italian seasoning

¼ teaspoon ground black pepper

2 cups fat-free egg substitute

¾ cup shredded nonfat or
   reduced-fat mozzarella cheese

1 tablespoon plus 1½ teaspoons
   grated nonfat or reduced-fat
   Parmesan cheese

1. Coat a 10-inch ovenproof skillet with nonstick cooking spray. Place over medium-high heat, and add the zucchini, onions, bell peppers, garlic, Italian seasoning, and black pepper. Cook and stir for 3 minutes, or until the vegetables are crisp-tender.

2. Reduce the heat to low, and pour the egg substitute over the vegetables. Let the eggs cook without stirring for 10 to 12 minutes, or until almost set.

3. Remove the skillet from the heat, and place under a preheated broiler. Broil 6 inches from the heat for about 3 minutes, or until the eggs are set.

4. Sprinkle the cheeses over the frittata, and broil for an additional minute, or just until the cheese has melted. Cut the frittata into wedges, and serve immediately.

NUTRITIONAL FACTS (PER SERVING)
Calories: 119 Cholesterol: 6 mg Fat: 0.1 g
Fiber: 1.5 g Protein: 20.6 g Sodium: 370 mg

Potato-Crusted Sausage Quiche

1. Combine the egg substitute, cottage cheese, flour, pepper, and Tabasco sauce in a large bowl, and stir to mix well. Stir in the cheese, sausage, and scallions. Set aside.

2. Coat a 9-inch deep dish pan with nonstick cooking spray. Slice the unpeeled potatoes ¼ inch thick, and arrange the slices in a single layer over the bottom and sides of the pan to form a crust. Pour the egg mixture into the crust.

3. Bake uncovered at 375°F for 45 minutes, or until a sharp knife inserted in the center of the quiche comes out clean. Allow to cool at room temperature for 5 minutes before cutting into wedges and serving.

Yield: *5 servings*

1 cup fat-free egg substitute

1 cup dry curd or low-fat cottage cheese

1 tablespoon unbleached flour

⅛ teaspoon ground black pepper

½ teaspoon Tabasco pepper sauce

1 cup shredded nonfat or reduced-fat Cheddar cheese

4 ounces smoked turkey sausage (at least 97% lean), diced

2 scallions, finely chopped

2 medium potatoes, scrubbed

NUTRITIONAL FACTS (PER SERVING)
Calories: 190 Cholesterol: 16 mg Fat: 0.6 g
Fiber: 1.8 g Protein: 22 g Sodium: 489 mg

Ham and Cheese Breakfast Biscuits

1. Combine the flour, oat bran, and baking powder in a medium-sized bowl, and stir to mix well. Add the buttermilk, and stir to mix well. Fold in the cheese and ham.

2. Coat a 9-inch pan with nonstick cooking spray. Drop heaping tablespoons of the batter onto the pan, spacing the biscuits 1 inch apart.

3. Bake at 400°F for 20 minutes, or until lightly browned. Transfer to a serving platter, and serve hot.

Yield: *8 biscuits*

1 cup unbleached flour

½ cup oat bran

2 teaspoons baking powder

¾ cup nonfat buttermilk

½ cup shredded nonfat or reduced-fat Cheddar cheese

2 ounces ham (at least 97% lean), finely chopped

NUTRITIONAL FACTS (PER BISCUIT)
Calories: 98 Cholesterol: 5 mg Fat: 0.9 g
Fiber: 1.4 g Protein: 6.7 g Sodium: 231 mg

Eggchiladas

Yield: *4 servings*

8 corn tortillas (6-inch rounds)

1 cup shredded nonfat or
   reduced-fat Cheddar cheese

FILLING

1 cup diced cooked potato

¼ cup chopped green bell pepper

¼ cup chopped onion

½ teaspoon whole cumin seed

¼ teaspoon ground black pepper

2 cups fat-free egg substitute

SAUCE

1 can (8 ounces) unsalted tomato
   sauce

1 cup water, divided

1 tablespoon chili powder

1 tablespoon plus 1½ teaspoons
   unbleached flour

1. To make the filling, coat a large nonstick skillet with nonstick cooking spray, and preheat over medium-high heat. Add the potatoes, bell peppers, onions, cumin, and black pepper, and cook and stir for 2 to 3 minutes, or until the peppers and onions are crisp-tender.

2. Reduce the heat to medium-low, and add the egg substitute. Cook for 2 minutes without stirring. Then, stirring gently to scramble, cook for 2 additional minutes, or just until the eggs are cooked through. Remove the skillet from the heat, cover to keep warm, and set aside.

3. To make the sauce, place the tomato sauce, ¾ cup of the water, and the chili powder in an 8-inch skillet. (Note that this must be cooked in a skillet, rather than a saucepan, because you will later dip the tortillas in the sauce.) Place over medium heat, and bring to a boil.

4. Combine the flour and the remaining ¼ cup of water in a jar with a tight-fitting lid, and shake until smooth. Slowly add the flour mixture to the tomato sauce, stirring constantly, and cook until bubbly. Reduce the heat to low to keep the sauce warm.

5. Coat a 9-x-13-inch baking dish with nonstick cooking spray, and set aside. Using tongs, dip a tortilla in the warm sauce for 5 to 10 seconds, coating both sides, to soften. Lay the tortilla on a flat surface, and spoon ⅓ cup of the filling along the bottom. Roll the tortilla up to enclose the filling, and place seam side down in the prepared dish. Repeat with the remaining tortillas, leaving about ⅛ inch of space between the tortillas for easy serving.

6. Pour the remaining sauce over the filled tortillas, and sprinkle with the cheese. Bake at 375°F for 10 to 12 minutes, or until the dish is heated through and the cheese is melted. Serve immediately.

NUTRITIONAL FACTS (PER SERVING)
Calories: 265 Cholesterol: 5 mg Fat: 0.8 g
Fiber: 4.2 g Protein: 25 g Sodium: 235 mg

Hot Apple Kasha

1. Combine the millet and water in a 1½-quart saucepan, and bring to a boil over high heat. Reduce the heat to low, cover, and simmer for 15 minutes without stirring.

2. Combine the buckwheat and cinnamon in a small bowl, and add the mixture to the pot. Stir in the apple juice and chopped apple. Cover and cook, without stirring, for 10 minutes, or until the liquid has been absorbed and the grains are tender.

3. Remove the pot from the heat and let sit, covered, for 5 minutes. Serve hot, plain or with a topping of maple syrup and skim milk.

Yield: *4 servings*

½ cup uncooked millet

1¼ cups water

¼ cup uncooked roasted buckwheat kernels (kasha)

¼ teaspoon ground cinnamon

1 cup apple juice

1 medium apple, peeled and coarsely chopped

NUTRITIONAL FACTS (PER ¾-CUP SERVING)
Calories: 156 Cholesterol: 0 mg Fat: 0.9 g
Fiber: 3 g Protein: 3.2 g Sodium: 4 mg

Bulgur Wheat Breakfast

1. Combine all of the ingredients in a 1½-quart saucepan, and bring to a boil over high heat. Reduce the heat to low, cover, and simmer for 5 minutes without stirring.

2. Remove the pot from the heat and let sit, covered, for 15 to 20 minutes, or until the liquid has been absorbed and the grains are tender. Serve hot, plain or topped with honey and skim milk.

Yield: *5 servings*

1 cup uncooked bulgur wheat

3 tablespoons toasted wheat germ

⅓ cup chopped dried apricots

⅓ cup chopped prunes

2½ cups water

NUTRITIONAL FACTS (PER ¾-CUP SERVING)
Calories: 160 Cholesterol: 0 mg Fat: 0.9
Fiber: 7.4 g Protein: 5.3 g Sodium: 6 mg

Spinach and Mushroom Omelette

Yield: *1 serving*

¾ cup fat-free egg substitute

⅛ teaspoon ground black pepper

3 tablespoons shredded nonfat Cheddar cheese, or 1 slice nonfat Cheddar cheese

¼ cup (packed) chopped fresh spinach

2 tablespoons sliced fresh mushrooms

1 slice turkey bacon, cooked, drained, and crumbled (optional)

Ground paprika

By using fat-free egg substitute instead of whole eggs and nonfat cheese instead of a full-fat product, you will save 235 calories, 25 grams of fat, and 790 milligrams of cholesterol per omelette. Not a bad bargain, considering the great taste of this healthy breakfast dish!

1. Coat an 8-inch nonstick skillet with nonstick cooking spray, and preheat over medium-low heat. Place the egg substitute in the skillet, and sprinkle with the pepper. Let the eggs cook without stirring for about 2 minutes, or until set around the edges.

2. Use a spatula to lift the edges of the omelette, and allow the uncooked egg to flow below the cooked portion. Cook for another minute or 2, or until the eggs are almost set.

3. Arrange first the cheese, and then the spinach, the mushrooms, and, if desired, the bacon over half of the omelette. Fold the other half over the filling, and cook for another minute or 2, or until the cheese is melted and the eggs are completely set.

4. Slide the omelette onto a plate, sprinkle with the paprika, and serve immediately.

NUTRITIONAL FACTS (PER SERVING)
Calories: 125 Cholesterol: 4 mg Fat: 0.1 g
Fiber: 0.5 g Protein: 25 g Sodium: 431 mg

3

Bountiful Breads

Nothing warms the heart and tempts the taste buds like the smell of fresh-baked breads, rolls, muffins, and biscuits. Until very recently, though, most muffins, quick breads, and other baked goods were made with large amounts of butter, margarine, oil, and other high-fat ingredients—ingredients that must be kept to a minimum in a healthy diet. Fortunately, times have changed, and we now know that delicious baked goods can be made with little or no fat.

Most breads are simple to make, and when you bake your own, you can not only reduce or eliminate the fat, but also boost the nutritional value of your product by using a variety of whole grain flours and by reducing the amount of sugar used. In fact, the baked goods recipes in this book contain 25 to 50 percent less sugar than traditional recipes do. Naturally sweet and flavorful ingredients like fruit juices, fruit purées, and oats reduce the need for sugar while enhancing the taste and aroma of your home-baked treats.

Will your baked goods be dry if you leave out the oil and butter? Not if you replace the fat with fruit juices, fruit purées, nonfat buttermilk, and other healthful fat substitutes. The recipes in this chapter combine these natural substitutes with whole grain flours to produce an array of super-moist, tempting breads. From Jalapeño Cornbread to Apple Butter Bread to Very Blueberry Muffins, you'll find breads for every meal of the day. Just as important, you'll learn how to apply the secrets of fat-free baking to your own recipes so that you and your family can enjoy new, healthful versions of old family favorites.

Before mixing up the batter for your first fat-free muffin or loaf, you may want to turn to "About the Ingredients," on pages 6 to 21. That section will acquaint you with the whole grain flours you'll be using, and will guide you in substituting less-refined sweeteners for traditional sweeteners, if you wish to do so. Then take out your baking pans, preheat your oven, and get ready to create some of the healthiest, most flavorful breads you've ever tasted!

Broccoli Cheese Muffins

Yield: *16 muffins*

2 cups whole grain cornmeal

1 tablespoon sugar

1 tablespoon baking powder

½ teaspoon baking soda

1½ cups nonfat or low-fat buttermilk

3 egg whites, lightly beaten

1 package (10 ounces) frozen chopped broccoli, thawed and squeezed dry

1 cup shredded nonfat or reduced-fat Cheddar cheese

1. Combine the cornmeal, sugar, baking powder, and baking soda in a large bowl, and stir to mix well. Add the buttermilk and egg whites, and stir just until the dry ingredients are moistened. Fold in the broccoli and cheese.

2. Coat muffin cups with cooking spray, and fill ¾ full with the batter. Bake at 350°F for 16 to 18 minutes, or just until a wooden toothpick inserted in the center of a muffin comes out clean.

3. Remove the muffin tins from the oven, and allow them to sit for 5 minutes before removing the muffins. Serve warm.

NUTRITIONAL FACTS (PER MUFFIN)
Calories: 86 Cholesterol: 2 mg Fat: 0.8 g
Fiber: 1.7 g Protein: 5.4 g Sodium: 202 mg

Cranberry Apple Muffins

Yield: *12 muffins*

2 cups whole wheat pastry flour

¼ cup plus 2 tablespoons sugar

1 tablespoon baking powder

¼ teaspoon baking soda

½ teaspoon ground cinnamon

¾ cup plus 2 tablespoons apple juice

2 egg whites, lightly beaten

1 cup finely chopped apple (about 1½ medium)

⅓ cup coarsely chopped fresh or frozen cranberries

⅓ cup golden raisins

1. Combine the flour, sugar, baking powder, baking soda, and cinnamon in a large bowl, and stir to mix well. Add the apple juice, egg whites, and chopped apples, and stir just until the dry ingredients are moistened. Fold in the cranberries and raisins.

2. Coat muffin cups with cooking spray, and fill ¾ full with the batter. Bake at 350°F for 16 minutes, or just until a wooden toothpick inserted in the center of a muffin comes out clean.

3. Remove the muffin tins from the oven, and allow them to sit for 5 minutes before removing the muffins. Serve warm or at room temperature.

NUTRITIONAL FACTS (PER MUFFIN)
Calories: 124 Cholesterol: 0 mg Fat: 0.4 g
Fiber: 2.9 g Protein: 3.5 g Sodium: 128 mg

Getting the Fat Out of Your Muffin, Quick Bread, and Cake Recipes

As the recipes in this chapter illustrate, almost any moist ingredient can replace the fat in muffins, breads, and biscuits, as well as other baked goods. It is important to realize, though, that some recipes are better candidates for fat reduction than others. Quick breads and muffins are some of the most easily adapted recipes. Coffee cakes, carrot cakes, spice cakes, and those yeast breads that naturally have denser textures are also easily made fat-free. Any cakes and other baked goods that are meant to have a very light, tender texture are the most difficult to modify. However, you can easily eliminate one-half to three-fourths of the fat even in these recipes.

When you modify your recipes, try eliminating only half the fat at first. The next time you make the recipe, try replacing even more of the fat. Whenever you *completely* eliminate the fat from a recipe, it is best to substitute whole wheat flour for at least one-third of the white flour, or to substitute oat bran for one-fourth of the white flour. This will help maintain a pleasing texture.

As you begin working with fat substitutes, you will learn that each type of fat substitute has its own set of "rules"—guidelines that will allow you to successfully modify your particular recipe. For instance, it is usually necessary to lower the oven temperature, as fat-free products can become dry if baked in an overly hot oven. The remainder of this inset will look at the many available fat substitutes, and will guide you in using these substitutes to "defat" favorite muffin, quick bread, and cake recipes. For guidelines on modifying cookie and brownie recipes, see the inset on page 432.

Using Fat Substitutes in Muffins, Quick Breads, and Cakes

Fat Substitutes	In Which Items Do These Work Best?	How Should Your Recipes Be Modified When Using These Fat Substitutes?
Applesauce, mashed banana, puréed fruits, fruit juice, nonfat buttermilk, nonfat yogurt, and skim milk.	Use applesauce, nonfat buttermilk, nonfat yogurt, or skim milk to make biscuits, muffins, chocolate cakes, and other baked goods whose flavor you do not want to change. Use fruit juices and purées in carrot and spice cakes, breads, and muffins.	❑ Replace part or all of the butter, margarine, or other solid fat in muffins, breads, biscuits, scones, and cakes with half as much fat substitute. Replace part or all of the oil with three-fourths as much fat substitute. Mix up the batter, and add more substitute if the batter seems too dry. ❑ Replace each whole egg with one egg white. ❑ Reduce the oven temperature by 25°F. ❑ Check for doneness a few minutes before the end of the usual baking time.

Fat Substitutes	In Which Items Do These Work Best?	How Should Your Recipes Be Modified When Using These Fat Substitutes?
Honey, maple syrup, corn syrup, chocolate syrup, fruit jams and spreads, and fruit juice concentrates.	Use honey or fruit jam in muffins; maple syrup in spice cakes and muffins; fruit juice concentrates in muffins and breads; corn syrup in white cakes and other baked goods whose flavor you do not want to change; and chocolate syrup in chocolate cakes and other chocolate treats.	❑ Replace part or all of the butter, margarine, or other solid fat in muffins, breads, scones, and cakes with three-fourths as much fat substitute. Replace part or all of the oil with an equal amount of fat substitute. Mix up the batter, and add more substitute if the batter seems too dry. ❑ Replace each whole egg with one egg white. ❑ Reduce the sugar by the amount of fat substitute being added. ❑ Reduce the oven temperature by 25°F. ❑ Check for doneness a few minutes before the end of the usual baking time.
Prune Butter (page 223)	This substitute is delicious in chocolate cakes and in fruit- or spice-flavored muffins, breads, and cakes.	❑ Replace part or all of the butter, margarine, or other solid fat in muffins, breads, scones, and cakes with an equal amount of Prune Butter. ❑ Replace each whole egg with one egg white. ❑ Reduce the sugar by one-half to two-thirds the amount of Prune. ❑ Reduce the oven temperature by 25°F. ❑ Check for doneness a few minutes before the end of the usual baking time.
Prune Purée (page 223)	Because of Prune Purée's mild flavor, it works well in all recipes.	❑ Replace part or all of the butter, margarine, or other solid fat in muffins, breads, scones, and cakes with half as much Prune Purée. Replace part or all of the oil with three-fourths as much of the purée. Mix up the batter, and add more substitute if the batter seems too dry. ❑ Replace each whole egg with one egg white *or* two additional tablespoons of Prune Purée. ❑ Reduce the oven temperature by 25°F. ❑ Check for doneness a few minutes before the end of the usual baking time.

Fat Substitutes	In Which Items Do These Work Best?	How Should Your Recipes Be Modified When Using These Fat Substitutes?
Mashed cooked or canned pumpkin, butternut squash, and sweet potatoes.	Use these substitutes in biscuits, muffins, breads, and spice cakes. They work particularly well in citrus- and pineapple-flavored baked goods.	❑ Replace part or all of the butter, margarine, or other solid fat in muffins, breads, scones, biscuits, and cakes with three-fourths as much fat substitute. Replace part or all of the oil with an equal amount of fat substitute. Mix up the batter, and add more substitute if the batter seems too dry. ❑ Replace each whole egg with one egg white. ❑ Reduce the oven temperature by 25°F. ❑ Check for doneness a few minutes before the end of the usual baking time.

Honey Bran Muffins

1. Combine the bran and buttermilk in a medium-sized bowl. Stir to mix well, and set aside for 15 minutes.

2. Combine the flour and baking soda in a large bowl, and stir to mix well. Add the bran mixture, honey, and egg whites, and stir just until the dry ingredients are moistened. Fold in the apricots or prunes.

3. Coat muffin cups with cooking spray, and fill ¾ full with the batter. Bake at 350°F for 16 minutes, or just until a wooden toothpick inserted in the center of a muffin comes out clean.

4. Remove the muffin tins from the oven, and allow them to sit for 5 minutes before removing the muffins. Serve warm or at room temperature.

Yield: *12 muffins*

1 cup wheat bran

1¼ cups plus 2 tablespoons nonfat or low-fat buttermilk

1½ cups whole wheat pastry flour

1 teaspoon baking soda

¼ cup plus 2 tablespoons honey

2 egg whites, lightly beaten

½ cup chopped dried apricots or prunes

NUTRITIONAL FACTS (PER MUFFIN)
Calories: 120 Cholesterol: 0 mg Fat: 0.7 g
Fiber: 4.3 g Protein: 4.5 g Sodium: 145 mg

Banana Oat Bran Muffins

Yield: *12 muffins*

1½ cups whole wheat pastry flour

¾ cup oat bran

¼ cup light brown sugar

1 tablespoon baking powder

¼ teaspoon baking soda

¼ teaspoon ground nutmeg

1½ cups mashed very ripe banana (about 3 large)

¼ cup pineapple or orange juice

2 egg whites, lightly beaten

⅓ cup chopped dates or dried apricots

TOPPING

1 tablespoon finely chopped walnuts

1 tablespoon light brown sugar

1. Combine the topping ingredients in a small bowl. Stir to mix well, and set aside.

2. Combine the flour, oat bran, sugar, baking powder, baking soda, and nutmeg in a large bowl, and stir to mix well. Add the mashed bananas, juice, and egg whites, and stir just until the dry ingredients are moistened. Fold in the dates or apricots.

3. Coat muffin cups with cooking spray, and fill ¾ full with the batter. Sprinkle ½ teaspoon of the topping over each muffin, and bake at 350°F for 16 to 18 minutes, or just until a wooden toothpick inserted in the center of a muffin comes out clean.

4. Remove the muffin tins from the oven, and allow them to sit for 5 minutes before removing the muffins. Serve warm or at room temperature.

NUTRITIONAL FACTS (PER MUFFIN)
Calories: 131 Cholesterol: 0 mg Fat: 1 g
Fiber: 3.7 g Protein: 4.1 g Sodium: 128 mg

Fresh Pear Muffins

1. Combine the flour, oat bran, sugar, baking powder, cinnamon, and nutmeg in a large bowl, and stir to mix well. Add the nectar, egg whites, and chopped pear, and stir just until the dry ingredients are moistened. Fold in the raisins or walnuts.

2. Coat muffin cups with cooking spray, and fill ¾ full with the batter. Bake at 350°F for 15 to 17 minutes, or just until a wooden toothpick inserted in the center of a muffin comes out clean.

3. Remove the muffin tins from the oven, and allow them to sit for 5 minutes before removing the muffins. Serve warm or at room temperature.

Yield: *12 muffins*

1½ cups whole wheat pastry flour

¾ cup oat bran

⅓ cup sugar

1 tablespoon baking powder

¼ teaspoon ground cinnamon

¼ teaspoon ground nutmeg

1 cup pear nectar

2 egg whites, lightly beaten

¾ cup finely chopped pear (about 1 medium)

¼ cup dark raisins or chopped walnuts

NUTRITIONAL FACTS (PER MUFFIN)
Calories: 121 Cholesterol: 0 mg Fat: 0.7 g
Fiber: 3.3 g Protein: 3.8 g Sodium: 102 mg

Applesauce Maple Muffins

1. Combine the flour and baking powder, and stir to mix well. Add the applesauce, maple syrup, and egg whites, and stir just until the dry ingredients are moistened. Fold in the raisins or walnuts.

2. Coat muffin cups with nonstick cooking spray, and fill ¾ full with the batter. Bake at 350°F for 16 to 18 minutes, or just until a wooden toothpick inserted in the center of a muffin comes out clean.

3. Remove the muffin tin from the oven, and allow it to sit for 5 minutes before removing the muffins. Serve warm or at room temperature.

Yield: *12 muffins*

2 cups whole wheat pastry flour

1 tablespoon baking powder

1¼ cups unsweetened applesauce

½ cup maple syrup

2 egg whites

½ cup dark raisins or chopped walnuts

NUTRITIONAL FACTS (PER MUFFIN)
Calories: 130 Calcium: 26 mg Cholesterol: 0 mg
Fat: 0.4 g Fiber: 3.3 g Iron: 1 mg
Potassium: 188 mg Protein: 3.6 g Sodium: 94 mg

Very Blueberry Muffins

Yield: *12 muffins*

1¼ cups quick-cooking oats

¾ cup plain nonfat yogurt

½ cup orange juice

1¼ cups whole wheat pastry flour

⅓ cup sugar

1 tablespoon baking powder

¼ teaspoon baking soda

1 teaspoon dried grated orange
   rind, or 1 tablespoon fresh

2 egg whites, lightly beaten

1 cup fresh or frozen blueberries

TOPPING

1 tablespoon sugar

For variety, substitute coarsely chopped raspberries, blackberries, or sweet pitted cherries for the blueberries.

1. Combine the oats, yogurt, and orange juice in a medium-sized bowl. Stir to mix well, and set aside for 5 minutes.

2. Combine the flour, sugar, baking powder, baking soda, and orange rind in a large bowl, and stir to mix well. Add the oat mixture and egg whites, and stir just until the dry ingredients are moistened. Fold in the blueberries.

3. Coat muffin cups with cooking spray, and fill ¾ full with the batter. Sprinkle ¼ teaspoon of sugar over the top of each muffin, and bake at 350°F for 16 minutes, or just until a wooden toothpick inserted in the center of a muffin comes out clean.

4. Remove the muffin tins from the oven, and allow them to sit for 5 minutes before removing the muffins. Serve warm or at room temperature.

NUTRITIONAL FACTS (PER MUFFIN)
Calories: 123 Cholesterol: 0 mg Fat: 0.8 g
Fiber: 2.8 g Protein: 4.7 g Sodium: 140 mg

Tips for Super-Moist Fat-Free Baking

The most common complaint people have about fat-free baked goods is that they are too dry. The good news is that it is possible to produce deliciously moist fat-free muffins, quick breads, cakes, and other baked goods. Here are some important tips that you should keep in mind whenever you bake fat-free treats.

❑ *Avoid overbaking.* Fat-free treats bake more quickly than do those made with fat. Baked at too high a temperature or left in the oven too long, they will become dry. That's why the recipes in this book recommend lower-than-standard oven temperatures and shorter-than-standard baking times.

❑ *Use the toothpick test or another test of doneness.* The best way to check fat-free muffins, quick breads, and cakes for doneness is to do the toothpick test. Insert a wooden toothpick in the center of the product. When the toothpick comes out clean, the product should be removed from the oven. When using one of this book's cookie or brownie recipes, use the test of doneness provided in that recipe.

❑ *Keep your baked goods moist and fresh.* Fat-free baked goods made with the natural fat substitutes suggested in this book will have a high moisture content and no preservatives. It is a good idea to refrigerate any quick breads, muffins, and cakes not eaten within twenty-four hours. The recipes will let you know when a product must be refrigerated immediately after baking.

Orange Oatmeal Muffins

1. To make the topping, combine the topping ingredients until crumbly. Set aside.

2. Combine the oats and orange juice, and set aside for 20 minutes.

3. Combine the flour, sugar, baking powder, and baking soda, and stir to mix well. Add the orange juice mixture and the egg whites to the flour mixture, and stir just until the dry ingredients are moistened.

4. Coat muffin cups with nonstick cooking spray, and fill ¾ full with the batter. Sprinkle the topping over the batter. Bake at 350°F for 14 to 16 minutes, or just until a wooden toothpick inserted in the center of a muffin comes out clean.

5. Remove the muffin tin from the oven, and allow it to sit for 5 minutes before removing the muffins. Serve warm or at room temperature.

NUTRITIONAL FACTS (PER MUFFIN)
Calories: 131 Calcium: 17 mg Cholesterol: 0 mg
Fat: 0.7 g Fiber: 2.8 g Iron: 1 mg
Potassium: 150 mg Protein: 4.1 g Sodium: 106 mg

Yield: *12 muffins*

1 cup quick-cooking oats

1 cup plus 2 tablespoons orange juice

1½ cups whole wheat pastry flour or unbleached flour

½ cup sugar

1 teaspoon baking powder

1 teaspoon baking soda

2 egg whites

TOPPING

3 tablespoons quick-cooking oats

1 tablespoon frozen orange juice concentrate, thawed

1½ teaspoons sugar

Very Cranberry Muffins

1. Combine the oats and milk, and set aside for 15 minutes.

2. Combine the flour, baking powder, and sugar, and stir to mix well. Add the oat mixture and the remaining ingredients, and stir just until the dry ingredients are moistened.

3. Coat muffin cups with nonstick cooking spray, and fill ¾ full with the batter. Bake at 350°F for about 18 minutes, or just until a wooden toothpick inserted in the center of a muffin comes out clean.

4. Remove the muffin tin from the oven, and allow it to sit for 5 minutes before removing the muffins. Serve warm or at room temperature.

NUTRITIONAL FACTS (PER MUFFIN)
Calories: 137 Calcium: 44 mg Cholesterol: 0 mg
Fat: 0.7 g Fiber: 3.1 g Iron: 0.9 mg
Potassium: 125 mg Protein: 4.2 g Sodium: 107 mg

Yield: *12 muffins*

1 cup quick-cooking oats

¾ cup skim milk

1½ cups whole wheat pastry flour or unbleached flour

1 tablespoon baking powder

¼ cup sugar

1 cup whole berry cranberry sauce

2 egg whites

1 teaspoon vanilla extract

¼ cup chopped walnuts (optional)

Mandarin Blueberry Muffins

Yield: *12 muffins*

1¾ cups whole wheat pastry flour or unbleached flour

¾ cup oat bran

⅓ cup sugar

1 tablespoon baking powder

1 can (11 ounces) mandarin orange segments in light syrup, undrained

2 egg whites

1 teaspoon vanilla or almond extract

½ cup plus 2 tablespoons fresh or frozen blueberries

1. Combine the flour, oat bran, sugar, and baking powder, and stir to mix well. Crush the orange segments slightly and add the oranges and their syrup, the egg whites, and the vanilla extract to the flour mixture, and stir just until the dry ingredients are moistened. Fold in the blueberries.

2. Coat muffin cups with nonstick cooking spray, and fill ¾ full with the batter. Bake at 350°F for 15 to 18 minutes, or just until a wooden toothpick inserted in the center of a muffin comes out clean.

3. Remove the muffin tin from the oven, and allow it to sit for 5 minutes before removing the muffins. Serve warm or at room temperature.

NUTRITIONAL FACTS (PER MUFFIN)
Calories: 113 Calcium: 28 mg Cholesterol: 0 mg
Fat: 0.7 g Fiber: 3.9 g Iron: 1.1 mg
Potassium: 155 mg Protein: 4.2 g Sodium: 94 mg

Brown Sugar Banana Muffins

Yield: *12 muffins*

2 cups whole wheat pastry flour

⅓ cup brown sugar

1 tablespoon baking powder

1 cup mashed very ripe banana (about 2 large)

⅓ cup skim milk

1 teaspoon vanilla extract

2 egg whites

TOPPING

1 tablespoon brown sugar

1 tablespoon toasted wheat germ

1. To make the topping, stir together the brown sugar and wheat germ, and set aside.

2. Combine the flour, brown sugar, and baking powder, and stir to mix well. Add the banana, skim milk, vanilla extract, and egg whites, and stir just until the dry ingredients are moistened.

3. Coat muffin cups with nonstick cooking spray, and fill ¾ full with the batter. Sprinkle the topping over batter. Bake at 350°F for 14 to 16 minutes, or just until a wooden toothpick inserted in the center of a muffin comes out clean.

4. Remove the muffin tin from the oven, and allow it to sit for 5 minutes before removing the muffins. Serve warm or at room temperature.

NUTRITIONAL FACTS (PER MUFFIN)
Calories: 121 Calcium: 31 mg Cholesterol: 0 mg
Fat: 0.5 g Fiber: 3.1 g Iron: 1.1 mg
Potassium: 234 mg Protein: 3.7 g Sodium: 97 mg

Peachy Bran Muffins

1. Combine the flour, wheat bran, sugar, and baking powder, and stir to mix well. Set aside.

2. Drain the peaches, reserving the juice, and purée in a blender. Add enough juice to the puréed peaches to bring the volume up to 1½ cups. Add the peach purée and the egg whites to the flour mixture, and stir just until the dry ingredients are moistened. Fold in the dried peaches or pecans.

3. Coat muffin cups with nonstick cooking spray, and fill ¾ full with the batter. Bake at 350°F for 15 to 17 minutes, or just until a wooden toothpick inserted in the center of a muffin comes out clean.

4. Remove the muffin tin from the oven, and allow it to sit for 5 minutes before removing the muffins. Serve warm or at room temperature.

Yield: *12 muffins*

1½ cups whole wheat pastry flour or unbleached flour

⅔ cup wheat bran

½ cup sugar

1 tablespoon baking powder

1 can (1 pound) peaches packed in juice, undrained

2 egg whites

⅓ cup chopped dried peaches or chopped pecans

NUTRITIONAL FACTS (PER MUFFINS)
Calories: 121 Calcium: 26 mg Cholesterol: 0 mg
Fat: 0.5 g Fiber: 3.3 g Iron: 1.1 mg
Potassium: 183 mg Protein: 3.5 g Sodium: 94 mg

THREE-GRAIN Muffins

Yield: *12 muffins*

1½ cups wheat bran

¾ cup plus 2 tablespoons oat bran

½ cup whole grain cornmeal

⅓ cup brown sugar

1½ teaspoons baking soda

¾ cup apple or prune juice

1 cup nonfat buttermilk

3 tablespoons fat-free egg substitute

1 teaspoon vanilla extract

½ cup dark raisins or chopped dried apricots

1. Combine the wheat bran, oat bran, cornmeal, brown sugar, and baking soda, and stir to mix well. Add the remaining ingredients, and stir just until the dry ingredients are moistened. Cover, and refrigerate at least overnight. (This batter may be refrigerated for up to a week.)

2. Coat muffin cups with nonstick cooking spray, and fill ¾ full with the batter. Bake at 350°F for about 18 minutes, or until a wooden toothpick inserted in the center of a muffin comes out clean.

3. Remove the muffin tin from the oven, and allow it to sit for 5 minutes before removing the muffins. Serve warm or at room temperature.

NUTRITIONAL FACTS (PER MUFFIN)
Calories: 110 Calcium: 42 mg Cholesterol: 0 mg
Fat: 0.9 g Fiber: 4 g Iron: 1.7 mg
Potassium: 267 mg Protein: 4.1 g Sodium: 135 mg

APRICOT BRAN Muffins

Yield: *12 muffins*

1½ cups wheat bran

1¼ cups nonfat buttermilk

1 cup whole wheat pastry flour or unbleached flour

1 teaspoon baking soda

⅓ cup brown sugar

2 egg whites

1 cup chopped dried apricots

1. Combine the bran and buttermilk, and set aside for 15 minutes.

2. Combine the flour, baking soda, and brown sugar, and stir to mix well. Add the bran mixture and the egg whites, and stir just until the dry ingredients are moistened. Fold in the apricots.

3. Coat muffin cups with nonstick cooking spray, and fill ¾ full with the batter. Bake at 350°F for 16 to 18 minutes, or just until a wooden toothpick inserted in the center of a muffin comes out clean.

4. Remove the muffin tin from the oven, and allow it to sit for 5 minutes before removing the muffins. Serve warm or at room temperature.

NUTRITIONAL FACTS (PER MUFFIN)
Calories: 112 Calcium: 49 mg Cholesterol: 0 mg
Fat: 0.6 g Fiber: 4 g Iron: 1.9 mg
Potassium: 346 mg Protein: 4.4 g Sodium: 108 mg

Chocolate Crumb Muffins

1. To make the topping, combine the oats, cocoa, and brown sugar, and stir to mix well. Add the honey and stir until the mixture is moist and crumbly. Set aside.

2. Combine the flours, cocoa, brown sugar, and baking powder, and stir to mix well. Place the pears and their juice in a blender, and purée until smooth. Add 1½ cups of this mixture to the flour mixture. (Reserve the remaining purée for use in another recipe.) Add the egg whites and vanilla extract, and stir just until the dry ingredients are moistened.

3. Coat muffin cups with nonstick cooking spray, and fill ¾ full with the batter. Sprinkle a rounded teaspoonful of the topping over each muffin, and press very lightly into the batter. Bake at 350°F for 14 to 16 minutes, or just until a wooden toothpick inserted in the center of a muffin comes out clean.

4. Remove the muffin tin from the oven, and allow it to sit for 5 minutes before removing the muffins. Serve warm or at room temperature.

NUTRITIONAL FACTS (PER MUFFIN)
Calories: 147 Calcium: 39 mg Cholesterol: 0 mg
Fat: 1.4 g Fiber: 3.8 g Iron: 1.6 mg
Potassium: 174 mg Protein: 4 g Sodium: 119 mg

Yield: *12 muffins*

1 cup whole wheat pastry flour or unbleached flour

1 cup oat flour

¼ cup plus 2 tablespoons cocoa powder

½ cup light brown sugar

1 tablespoon baking powder

1 can (1 pound) pear halves packed in juice, undrained

2 egg whites

1 teaspoon vanilla extract

TOPPING

¼ cup plus 2 tablespoons quick-cooking oats

1 tablespoon cocoa powder

1 tablespoon brown sugar

1 tablespoon honey

Apple Date Muffins

Yield: *12 muffins*

2¼ cups whole wheat pastry flour

1½ teaspoons baking soda

⅓ cup brown sugar

¾ cup nonfat buttermilk

1½ cups finely chopped fresh apples (about 2 medium)

3 tablespoons fat-free egg substitute

1 teaspoon vanilla extract

½ cup chopped dates

1. Combine the flour, baking soda, and brown sugar, and stir to mix well. Add the buttermilk, apple, egg substitute, and vanilla extract, and stir just until the dry ingredients are moistened. Fold in the dates.

2. Coat muffin cups with nonstick cooking spray, and fill ¾ full with the batter. Bake at 350°F for 16 to 18 minutes, or just until a wooden toothpick inserted in the center of a muffin comes out clean.

3. Remove the muffin tin from the oven, and allow to sit for 5 minutes before removing the muffins. Serve warm or at room temperature.

NUTRITIONAL FACTS (PER MUFFIN)
Calcium: 36 mg Calories: 135 Cholesterol: 0 mg
Fat: 0.6 g Fiber: 3.7 g Iron: 1.3 mg
Potassium: 202 mg Protein: 4.1 g Sodium: 129 mg

Plum Delicious Bran Muffins

Yield: *12 muffins*

1½ cups whole wheat pastry flour or unbleached flour

½ cup wheat bran or oat bran

1 tablespoon baking powder

½ teaspoon baking soda

¾ cup apple butter

½ cup nonfat buttermilk or plain nonfat yogurt

2 egg whites

1 cup chopped skinned fresh plums (about 2 medium)

½ cup chopped prunes

1. Combine the flour, bran, baking powder, and baking soda, and stir to mix well. Add the apple butter, buttermilk or yogurt, and egg whites, and stir just until the dry ingredients are moistened. Fold in the plums and prunes.

2. Coat muffin cups with nonstick cooking spray, and fill ¾ full with the batter. Bake at 350°F for 16 to 18 muffins, or just until a wooden toothpick inserted in the center of a muffin comes out clean.

3. Remove the muffin tin from the oven, and allow it to sit for 5 minutes before removing the muffins. Serve warm or at room temperature.

NUTRITIONAL FACTS (PER MUFFIN)
Calories: 123 Calcium: 40 mg Cholesterol: 0 mg
Fat: 0.7 g Fiber: 3.3 g Iron: 1.1 mg
Potassium: 221 mg Protein: 3.7 g Sodium: 138 mg

Poppy Seed Muffins

1. Combine the flours, sugar, poppy seeds, and baking soda, and stir to mix well. Add the yogurt, egg whites, and vanilla or almond extract, and stir just until the dry ingredients are moistened. Fold in the almonds if desired.

2. Coat muffin cups with nonstick cooking spray, and fill ¾ full with the batter. Bake at 350°F for 14 to 16 minutes, or just until a wooden toothpick inserted in the center of a muffin comes out clean.

3. Remove the muffin tin from the oven, and allow it to sit for 5 minutes before removing the muffins. Serve warm or at room temperature.

Yield: 10 muffins

1 cup whole wheat pastry flour or unbleached flour

½ cup oat flour

⅓ cup sugar

3–4 teaspoons poppy seeds

1 teaspoon baking soda

¾ cup plain nonfat yogurt

2 egg whites

1 teaspoon vanilla or almond extract

¼ cup chopped almonds (optional)

NUTRITIONAL FACTS (PER MUFFIN)
Calories: 106 Calcium: 54 mg Cholesterol: 0 mg
Fat: 0.9 g Fiber: 2.2 g Iron: 0.8 mg
Potassium: 128 mg Protein: 4.4 g Sodium: 107 mg

Blueberry Bran Muffins

1. Combine the flour, bran, sugar, baking soda, and baking powder, and stir to mix well. Add the yogurt, egg whites, and vanilla extract, and stir just until the dry ingredients are moistened. Fold in the blueberries.

2. Coat muffin cups with nonstick cooking spray, and fill ¾ full with the batter. Bake at 350°F for 16 to 18 minutes, or just until a wooden toothpick inserted in the center of a muffin comes out clean.

3. Remove the muffin tin from the oven, and allow it to sit for 5 minutes before removing the muffins. Serve warm or at room temperature.

Yield: 12 muffins

1¼ cups whole wheat pastry flour or unbleached flour

¾ cup oat bran or wheat bran

⅓ cup sugar

1 teaspoon baking soda

2 teaspoons baking powder

1 cup vanilla or lemon nonfat yogurt

2 egg whites

1 teaspoon vanilla extract

¾ cup fresh or frozen blueberries

NUTRITIONAL FACTS (PER MUFFIN)
Calories: 106 Calcium: 47 mg Cholesterol: 0 mg
Fat: 0.9 g Fiber: 2.9 g Iron: 0.8 mg
Potassium: 138 mg Protein: 4.2 g Sodium: 145 mg

Cherry Walnut Muffins

Yield: *12 muffins*

1½ cups whole wheat pastry flour
   or unbleached flour

½ cup brown rice flour or whole
   grain cornmeal

½ cup sugar

2 teaspoons baking powder

1 teaspoon baking soda

1 cup plain nonfat yogurt

1½ teaspoons vanilla extract

2 egg whites

¾ cup coarsely chopped frozen
   pitted cherries

TOPPING

1 tablespoon sugar

1 tablespoon finely ground walnuts

1. To make the topping, combine the sugar and walnuts until crumbly. Set aside.

2. Combine the whole wheat flour, rice flour or cornmeal, sugar, baking powder, and baking soda, and stir to mix well. Add the yogurt, vanilla extract, and egg whites, and stir just until the dry ingredients are moistened. Fold in the cherries.

3. Coat muffin cups with nonstick cooking spray, and fill ¾ full with the batter. Sprinkle the topping over the batter. Bake at 350°F for 15 to 18 minutes, or just until a wooden toothpick inserted in the center of a muffin comes out clean.

4. Remove the muffin tin from the oven, and allow it to sit for 5 minutes before removing the muffins. Serve warm or at room temperature.

NUTRITIONAL FACTS (PER MUFFIN)
Calories: 137 Calcium: 56 mg Cholesterol: 0 mg
Fat: 0.8 g Fiber: 2.2 g Iron: 0.8 mg
Potassium: 164 mg Protein: 4.4 g Sodium: 148 mg

BANANA GRANOLA MUFFINS

1. Combine the flour and baking powder, and stir to mix well. Add the banana, skim milk, maple syrup or honey, and egg whites, and stir just until the dry ingredients are moistened. Stir in the 2 cups of granola.

2. Coat muffin cups with nonstick cooking spray, and fill ¾ full with the batter. Sprinkle the topping over the muffins, and press lightly into the batter. Bake at 350°F for 14 to 16 minutes, or just until a wooden toothpick inserted in the center of a muffin comes out clean.

3. Remove the muffin tin from the oven, and allow it to sit for 5 minutes before removing the muffins. Serve warm or at room temperature.

Yield: 12 muffins

1⅓ cups whole wheat pastry flour

1 tablespoon baking powder

¾ cup mashed very ripe banana (about 1½ large)

½ cup skim milk

¼ cup maple syrup or honey

2 egg whites

2 cups nonfat or low-fat granola cereal

TOPPING

¼ cup nonfat or low-fat granola cereal

NUTRITIONAL FACTS (PER MUFFIN)
Calories: 150 Calcium: 42 mg Cholesterol: 0 mg
Fat: 0.5 g Fiber: 3.5 g Iron: 1.5 mg
Potassium: 211 mg Protein: 5 g Sodium: 195 mg

CARROT SPICE MUFFINS

1. Combine the flour, baking powder, baking soda, cinnamon, and nutmeg, and stir to mix well. Add the maple syrup or honey, skim milk, egg whites, and carrot, and stir just until the dry ingredients are moistened. Fold in the raisins or pecans.

2. Coat muffin cups with nonstick cooking spray, and fill ¾ full with the batter. Bake at 350°F for 15 to 17 minutes, or just until a wooden toothpick inserted in the center of a muffin comes out clean.

3. Remove the muffin tin from the oven, and allow it to sit for 5 minutes before removing the muffins. Serve warm or at room temperature.

Yield: 12 muffins

2 cups whole wheat pastry flour

2 teaspoons baking powder

1 teaspoon baking soda

¾ teaspoon ground cinnamon

¾ teaspoon ground nutmeg

⅓ cup maple syrup or honey

⅓ cup skim milk

2 egg whites

2 cups grated carrots (about 4 medium)

⅓ cup golden raisins or chopped pecans

NUTRITIONAL FACTS (PER MUFFIN)
Calories: 119 Calcium: 46 mg Cholesterol: 0 mg
Fat: 0.8 g Fiber: 3.4 g Iron: 1.2 mg
Potassium: 206 mg Protein: 3.4 g Sodium: 145 mg

Pineapple Bran Muffins

Yield: *12 muffins*

1¼ cups skim milk

1½ cups wheat bran

½ cup date sugar or brown sugar

1½ cups whole wheat pastry flour or unbleached flour

1 tablespoon baking powder

1 can (8 ounces) crushed pineapple packed in juice, undrained

2 egg whites

⅓ cup chopped pecans (optional)

1. Combine the milk, wheat bran, and date or brown sugar, and set aside for 15 minutes.

2. Combine the flour and baking powder, and stir to mix well. Add the bran mixture, the pineapple with its juice, and the egg whites, and stir just until the dry ingredients are moistened. Fold in the pecans if desired.

3. Coat muffin cups with nonstick cooking spray, and fill ¾ full with the batter. Bake at 350°F for about 18 minutes, or just until a wooden toothpick inserted in the center of a muffin comes out clean.

4. Remove the muffin tin from the oven, and allow it to sit for 5 minutes before removing the muffins. Serve warm or at room temperature.

NUTRITIONAL FACTS (PER MUFFIN)
Calories: 106 Calcium: 60 mg Cholesterol: 0 mg
Fat: 0.6 g Fiber: 4.7 g Iron: 1.4 mg
Potassium: 224 mg Protein: 4.8 g Sodium: 105 mg

Orange Marmalade Muffins

Yield: *12 muffins*

1¼ cups whole wheat pastry flour or unbleached flour

1 cup oat bran or wheat bran

1 tablespoon baking powder

¾ cup plain nonfat yogurt

½ cup plus 1 tablespoon orange marmalade

2 egg whites

1 teaspoon vanilla extract

⅓ cup chopped pecans or ¾ cup fresh or frozen blueberries (optional)

1. Combine the flour, bran, and baking powder, and stir to mix well. Add the yogurt, marmalade, egg whites, and vanilla extract, and stir just until the dry ingredients are moistened. Fold in the pecans or blueberries if desired.

2. Coat muffin cups with nonstick cooking spray, and fill ¾ full with the batter. Bake at 350°F for about 15 minutes, or just until a wooden toothpick inserted in the center of a muffin comes out clean.

3. Remove the muffin tin from the oven, and allow it to sit for 5 minutes before removing the muffins. Serve warm or at room temperature.

NUTRITIONAL FACTS (PER MUFFIN)
Calories: 113 Calcium: 57 mg Cholesterol: 0 mg
Fat: 0.8 g Fiber: 3.1 g Iron: 1 mg
Potassium: 146 mg Protein: 4.5 g Sodium: 106 mg

Rise-and-Shine Muffins

1. Combine the cereal, milk, egg substitute, and vanilla extract, and set aside for 10 minutes.

2. Combine the flour, sugar, baking powder, and cinnamon, and stir to mix well. Add the cereal mixture, and stir just until the dry ingredients are moistened. Fold in the apricots or prunes and the sunflower seeds if desired.

3. Coat muffin cups with nonstick cooking spray, and fill ¾ full with the batter. Bake at 350°F for 16 to 18 minutes, or just until a wooden toothpick inserted in the center of a muffin comes out clean.

4. Remove the muffin tin from the oven, and allow it to sit for 5 minutes before removing the muffins. Serve warm or at room temperature.

Yield: *12 muffins*

2¼ cups bran flake-and-raisin cereal

1⅓ cups skim milk

3 tablespoons fat-free egg substitute

1 teaspoon vanilla extract

1½ cups whole wheat pastry flour or unbleached flour

½ cup sugar

1 tablespoon baking powder

¼ teaspoon ground cinnamon

½ cup chopped dried apricots or prunes

¼ cup hulled sunflower seeds (optional)

NUTRITIONAL FACTS (PER MUFFIN)
Calories: 135 Calcium: 62 mg Cholesterol: 0 mg
Fat: 0.4 g Fiber: 3.4 g Iron: 2.4 mg
Potassium: 234 mg Protein: 4.4 g Sodium: 180 mg

Jam'n'Apricot Muffins

1. Combine the flours and baking powder, and stir to mix well. Add the jam, buttermilk, egg whites, and vanilla extract, and stir just until the dry ingredients are moistened. Fold in the apricots.

2. Coat muffin cups with nonstick cooking spray, and fill ¾ full with the batter. Bake at 350°F for 15 to 17 minutes, or just until a wooden toothpick inserted in the center of a muffin comes out clean.

3. Remove the muffin tin from the oven, and allow it to sit for 5 minutes before removing the muffins. Serve warm or at room temperature.

Yield: *12 muffins*

1½ cups whole wheat pastry flour or unbleached flour

½ cup oat flour

1 tablespoon baking powder

½ cup apricot jam or preserves

⅔ cup nonfat buttermilk

2 egg whites

1 teaspoon vanilla extract

⅔ cup chopped dried apricots

NUTRITIONAL FACTS (PER MUFFIN)
Calories: 130 Calcium: 44 mg Cholesterol: 0 mg
Fat: 0.7 g Fiber: 3.1 g Iron: 1.3 mg
Potassium: 216 mg Protein: 4 g Sodium: 108 mg

German Chocolate Muffins

Yield: *14 muffins*

1½ cups whole wheat pastry flour
or unbleached flour

¾ cup oat flour

¼ cup cocoa powder

⅔ cup light brown sugar

1 tablespoon baking powder

1½ cups nonfat buttermilk

2 egg whites

1½ teaspoons vanilla extract

1 teaspoon coconut-flavored
extract

TOPPING

1 tablespoon shredded coconut

1 tablespoon light brown sugar

1. To make the topping, combine the coconut and brown sugar until crumbly. Set aside.

2. Combine the flours, cocoa, brown sugar, and baking powder, and stir to mix well. Add the buttermilk, egg whites, and extracts, and stir just until the dry ingredients are moistened.

3. Coat muffin cups with nonstick cooking spray, and fill ¾ full with the batter. Sprinkle the topping over the batter. Bake at 350°F for 14 to 16 minutes, or just until a wooden toothpick inserted in the center of a muffin comes out clean.

4. Remove the muffin tin from the oven, and allow it to sit for 5 minutes before removing the muffins. Serve warm or at room temperature.

NUTRITIONAL FACTS (PER MUFFIN)
Calories: 129 Calcium: 62 mg Cholesterol: 0 mg
Fat: 0.9 g Fiber: 2.8 g Iron: 1.3 mg
Potassium: 172 mg Protein: 4.4 g Sodium: 121 mg

Molasses Apple Muffins

1. Combine the flour, baking soda, baking powder, and cinnamon, and stir to mix well. Add the molasses, milk, egg whites, apples, and vanilla extract, and stir just until the dry ingredients are moistened. Fold in the raisins.

2. Coat muffin cups with nonstick cooking spray, and fill ¾ full with the batter. Bake at 350°F for 16 to 18 minutes, or just until a wooden toothpick inserted in the center of a muffin comes out clean.

3. Remove the muffin tin from the oven, and allow it to sit for 5 minutes before removing the muffins. Serve warm or at room temperature.

Yield: *12 muffins*

2 cups whole wheat pastry flour

1 teaspoon baking soda

1 teaspoon baking powder

½ teaspoon ground cinnamon

¼ cup plus 2 tablespoons molasses

¼ cup skim milk

2 egg whites

2 cups shredded Granny Smith apples (about 3 medium)

1 teaspoon vanilla extract

⅓ cup dark raisins

NUTRITIONAL FACTS (PER MUFFIN)
Calories: 121 Calcium: 35 mg Cholesterol: 0 mg
Fat: 0.5 g Fiber: 3.3 g Iron: 1.4 mg
Potassium: 250 mg Protein: 3.7 g Sodium: 116 mg

Sweet Corn Muffins

1. Combine the flour, cornmeal, baking powder, and baking soda, and stir to mix well. Add the buttermilk, molasses or sugarcane syrup and egg whites, and stir just until the dry ingredients are moistened. Fold in the dates.

2. Coat muffin cups with nonstick cooking spray, and fill ⅔ full with the batter. Bake at 350°F for about 15 minutes, or just until a wooden toothpick inserted in the center of a muffin comes out clean.

3. Remove the muffin tin from the oven, and allow it to sit for 5 minutes before removing the muffins. Serve warm or at room temperature.

Yield: *14 muffins*

1¼ cups whole wheat pastry flour or unbleached flour

1 cup whole grain cornmeal

1 tablespoon baking powder

½ teaspoon baking soda

1⅓ cups nonfat buttermilk

¼ cup plus 2 tablespoons molasses or sugarcane syrup

2 egg whites

½ cup chopped dates

NUTRITIONAL FACTS (PER MUFFIN)
Calories: 116 Calcium: 60 mg Cholesterol: 0 mg
Fat: 0.7 g Fiber: 2.8 g Iron: 1.2 mg
Potassium: 231 mg Protein: 3.6 g Sodium: 137 mg

Refrigerator Bran Muffins

Yield: *12 muffins*

1¼ cups whole wheat pastry flour or unbleached flour

1 teaspoon baking soda

1½ cups wheat bran

¾ cup nonfat buttermilk

½ cup orange or apple juice

¼ cup plus 2 tablespoons molasses or honey

2 egg whites

½ cup dark raisins or chopped dried fruit

¼ cup hulled sunflower seeds (optional)

1. Combine the flour and baking soda, and stir to mix well. Add the remaining ingredients, and stir just until the dry ingredients are moistened. Cover, and refrigerate overnight or up to 3 days.

2. When ready to bake, stir the batter well. Coat muffin cups with nonstick cooking spray, and fill ¾ full with the batter. Bake at 350°F for 16 to 18 minutes, or just until a wooden toothpick inserted in the center of a muffin comes out clean.

3. Remove the muffin tin from the oven, and allow it to sit for 5 minutes before removing the muffins. Serve warm or at room temperature.

NUTRITIONAL FACTS (PER MUFFIN)
Calories: 114 Calcium: 49 mg Cholesterol: 0 mg
Fat: 0.6 g Fiber: 3.9 g Iron: 1.9 mg
Potassium: 334 mg Protein: 4.3 g Sodium: 97 mg

Carrot Pineapple Muffins

Yield: *12 muffins*

2 cups whole wheat pastry flour

½ cup sugar

1 teaspoon baking soda

½ teaspoon ground cinnamon

1 can (8 ounces) crushed pineapple packed in juice, undrained

¼ cup Prune Purée (page 223)

2 egg whites

1 teaspoon vanilla extract

½ cup (packed) grated carrots (about 1 medium)

⅓ cup raisins or chopped pecans

1. Combine the flour, sugar, baking soda, and cinnamon, and stir to mix well. Add the pineapple, including the juice, and the Prune Purée, egg whites, and vanilla extract, and stir just until the dry ingredients are moistened. Fold in the carrots and the raisins or pecans.

2. Coat muffin cups with nonstick cooking spray, and fill ¾ full with the batter. Bake at 350°F for 15 to 17 minutes, or just until a wooden toothpick inserted in the center of a muffin comes out clean.

3. Remove the muffin tin from the oven, and allow it to sit for 5 minutes before removing the muffins. Serve warm or at room temperature.

NUTRITIONAL FACTS (PER MUFFIN)
Calories: 133 Calcium: 14 mg Cholesterol: 0 mg
Fat: 0.4 g Fiber: 3.2 g Iron: 1 mg
Potassium: 170 mg Protein: 3.6 g Sodium: 81 mg

Strawberry Streusel Muffins

1. To make the topping, stir the topping ingredients together until moist and crumbly. Set aside.

2. Combine the flours, sugar, and baking powder, and stir to mix well. Add the strawberries, orange juice, and egg whites, and stir just until the dry ingredients are moistened.

3. Coat muffin cups with nonstick cooking spray, and fill ¾ full with the batter. Sprinkle the topping over the batter. Bake at 350°F for about 15 minutes, or just until a wooden toothpick inserted in the center of a muffin comes out clean.

4. Remove the muffin tin from the oven, and allow it to sit for 5 minutes before removing the muffins. Serve warm or at room temperature.

NUTRITIONAL FACTS (PER MUFFIN)
Calories: 120 Calcium: 29 mg Cholesterol: 0 mg
Fat: 0.8 g Fiber: 3.3 g Iron: 1 mg
Potassium: 169 mg Protein: 4 g Sodium: 93 mg

Yield: *12 muffins*

1½ cups whole wheat pastry flour or unbleached flour

½ cup oat flour

⅓ cup sugar

1 tablespoon baking powder

1 cup puréed strawberries (about 2 cups fresh)

¼ cup plus 2 tablespoons orange juice

2 egg whites

TOPPING

½ cup quick-cooking oats

1 tablespoon whole wheat pastry flour or unbleached flour

2 tablespoons sugar

1 tablespoon frozen orange juice concentrate, thawed

Strawberry Oatmeal Muffins

Yield: *12 muffins*

1¼ cups quick-cooking oats

1¼ cups nonfat buttermilk

1¼ cups whole wheat pastry flour
   unbleached flour

⅓ cup sugar

1 tablespoon baking powder

¼ teaspoon baking soda

2 tablespoons plus 1½ teaspoons
   Prune Purée (page 223)

2 egg whites

1 teaspoon vanilla extract

1 cup chopped fresh or frozen
   strawberries

TOPPING

1 tablespoon sugar

1. Combine the oats and buttermilk, stir to mix well, and set aside for at least 5 minutes.

2. Combine the flour, sugar, baking powder, and baking soda, and stir to mix well. Add the oat-buttermilk mixture, Prune Purée, egg whites, and vanilla extract, and stir just until the dry ingredients are moistened. Fold in the strawberries.

3. Coat muffin cups with nonstick cooking spray, and fill ¾ full with the batter. Sprinkle ¼ teaspoon of sugar over the top of each muffin. Bake at 350°F for 15 to 17 minutes, or just until a wooden toothpick inserted in the center of a muffin comes out clean.

4. Remove the muffin tin from the oven, and allow it to sit for 5 minutes before removing the muffins. Serve warm or at room temperature.

NUTRITIONAL FACTS (PER MUFFIN)
Calcium: 55 mg Calories: 120 Cholesterol: 0 mg
Fat: 0.9 g Fiber: 2.9 g Iron: 0.9 mg
Potassium: 154 Protein: 4.6 g Sodium: 136 mg

Fantastic Fruit Muffins

1. Combine the oats and skim milk, stir to mix well, and set aside for at least 5 minutes.

2. Combine the flour, brown sugar, baking powder, and baking soda, and stir to mix well. Add the oat-milk mixture and the Prune Purée, egg whites, vanilla extract, and pears, and stir just until the dry ingredients are moistened. Fold in the cranberries and raisins.

3. Coat muffin cups with nonstick cooking spray, and fill ¾ full with the batter. Bake at 350°F for 15 to 17 minutes, or just until a wooden toothpick inserted in the center of a muffin comes out clean.

4. Remove the muffin tin from the oven, and allow it to sit for 5 minutes before removing the muffins. Serve warm or at room temperature.

Yield: *12 muffins*

¾ cup quick-cooking oats

¾ cup skim milk

1½ cups whole wheat pastry flour or unbleached flour

¼ cup plus 2 tablespoons brown sugar

1 tablespoon baking powder

¼ teaspoon baking soda

2 tablespoons plus 1½ teaspoons Prune Purée (page 223)

2 egg whites

1 teaspoon vanilla extract

1 cup finely chipped fresh pears (about 1½ medium)

⅓ cup coarsely chopped fresh or frozen cranberries

⅓ cup golden raisins

NUTRITIONAL FACTS (PER MUFFIN)
Calories: 130 Calcium: 52 mg Cholesterol: 0 mg
Fat: 0.7 g Fiber: 3.2 g Iron: 1.2 mg
Potassium: 195 mg Protein: 4.2 g Sodium: 120 mg

PEACH PERFECTION Muffins

Yield: *12 muffins*

1 cup whole wheat pastry flour or unbleached flour

1 cup oat bran

1 tablespoon baking powder

¼ cup plus 2 tablespoons honey

¼ cup plus 2 tablespoons plain nonfat yogurt

3 tablespoons Prune Purée (page 223)

2 egg whites

1 teaspoon vanilla extract

1 cup chopped fresh peaches (about 2 medium)

⅓ cup chopped dried dates or raisins

1. Combine the flour, oat bran, and baking powder, and stir to mix well. Add the honey, yogurt, Prune Purée, egg whites, and vanilla extract, and stir just until the dry ingredients are moistened. Fold in the peaches and the dates or raisins.

2. Coat muffin cups with nonstick cooking spray, and fill ¾ full with the batter. Bake at 350°F for 15 to 17 minutes, or just until a wooden toothpick inserted in the center of a muffin comes out clean.

3. Remove the muffin tin from the oven, and allow it to sit for 5 minutes before removing the muffins. Serve warm or at room temperature.

NUTRITIONAL FACTS (PER MUFFIN)
Calories: 115 Calcium: 40 mg Cholesterol: 0 mg
Fat: 0.8 g Fiber: 3.3 g Iron: 1 mg
Potassium: 184 mg Protein: 4 g Sodium: 98 mg

Pumpkin Praline Pecan Muffins

1. To make the topping, combine the pecans and brown sugar until crumbly. Set aside.

2. Combine the flour, oat bran, brown sugar, and baking powder, and stir to mix well. Add the remaining ingredients, and stir just until the dry ingredients are moistened.

3. Coat muffin cups with nonstick cooking spray, and fill ¾ full with the batter. Sprinkle the topping over the batter. Bake at 350°F for 15 to 18 minutes, or just until a wooden toothpick inserted in the center of a muffin comes out clean.

4. Remove the muffin tin from the oven, and allow it to sit for 5 minutes before removing the muffins. Serve warm or at room temperature.

Yield: *12 muffins*

1¾ cups whole wheat pastry flour or unbleached flour

½ cup oat bran

½ cup brown sugar

1 tablespoon baking powder

⅔ cup cooked mashed pumpkin

1 cup skim milk

2 egg whites

1 teaspoon vanilla extract

TOPPING

1 tablespoon finely chopped pecans

1 tablespoon brown sugar

NUTRITIONAL FACTS (PER MUFFIN)
Calories: 128 Calcium: 61 mg Cholesterol: 0 mg
Fat: 0.9 g Fiber: 3.2 g Iron: 1.5 mg
Potassium: 203 mg Protein: 4.5 g Sodium: 107 mg

Sweet Potato Corn Muffins

1. Combine the flour, cornmeal, and baking powder, and stir to mix well. Add the sweet potato, orange or apple juice, molasses, and egg whites, and stir just until the dry ingredients are moistened. Fold in the raisins or dates.

2. Coat muffin cups with nonstick cooking spray, and fill ¾ full with the batter. Bake at 350°F for 15 to 18 minutes, or just until a wooden toothpick inserted in the center of a muffin comes out clean.

3. Remove the muffin tin from the oven, and allow it to sit for 5 minutes before removing the muffins. Serve warm or at room temperature.

Yield: *12 muffins*

1¼ cups whole wheat pastry flour or unbleached flour

½ cup plus 2 tablespoons whole grain cornmeal

1 tablespoon baking powder

½ cup cooked mashed sweet potato

¾ cup orange or apple juice

¼ cup plus 2 tablespoons molasses

2 egg whites

⅓ cup dark raisins or chopped dates

NUTRITIONAL FACTS (PER MUFFIN)
Calories: 122 Calcium: 43 mg Cholesterol: 0 mg
Fat: 0.5 g Fiber: 2.8 g Iron: 1.4 mg
Potassium: 255 mg Protein: 3.3 g Sodium: 104 mg

Oatmeal, Fruit, and Nut Bread

Yield: *16 slices*

¾ cup quick-cooking oats

1¼ cups nonfat or low-fat buttermilk

1½ cups whole wheat pastry flour

½ cup light brown sugar

1 teaspoon baking powder

1 teaspoon baking soda

2 teaspoons vanilla extract

⅓ cup dried cherries, blueberries,
cranberries, or raisins

¼ cup chopped pecans

1. Combine the oats and buttermilk in a medium-sized bowl. Stir to mix well, and set aside.

2. Combine the flour, brown sugar, baking powder, and baking soda in a large bowl, and stir to mix well, pressing out any lumps. Add the buttermilk mixture and vanilla, and stir just until the dry ingredients are moistened. Fold in the fruits and nuts.

3. Coat an 8-x-4-inch loaf pan with cooking spray. Spread the batter in the pan, and bake at 325°F for 35 minutes, or just until a toothpick inserted in the center of the loaf comes out clean.

4. Remove the bread from the oven, and let sit for 10 minutes. Turn the loaf onto a wire rack, and cool before slicing.

NUTRITIONAL FACTS (PER SLICE)
Calories: 100 Cholesterol: 0 mg Fat: 1.9 g
Fiber: 2 g Protein: 3 g Sodium: 124 mg

Pumpkin Perfection Bread

Yield: *16 slices*

1⅔ cups whole wheat pastry flour

½ cup sugar

1 teaspoon baking powder

1 teaspoon baking soda

2 teaspoons pumpkin pie spice

1 cup mashed cooked or canned
pumpkin

¼ cup plus 2 tablespoons orange
juice

¼ cup Prune Purée (page 223)

¼ cup toasted wheat germ or
chopped pecans

1. Combine the flour, sugar, baking powder, baking soda, and pumpkin pie spice in a large bowl, and stir to mix well. Add the pumpkin, orange juice, and Prune Purée, and stir just until the dry ingredients are moistened. Fold in the wheat germ or pecans.

2. Coat an 8-x-4-inch loaf pan with nonstick cooking spray. Spread the batter evenly in the pan, and bake at 325°F for 40 to 45 minutes, or just until a wooden toothpick inserted in the center of the loaf comes out clean.

3. Remove the bread from the oven, and let sit for 10 minutes. Turn the loaf onto a wire rack, and cool before slicing.

NUTRITIONAL FACTS (PER SLICE)
Calories: 84 Cholesterol: 0 mg Fat: 0.5 g
Fiber: 2.3 g Protein: 2.5 g Sodium: 103 mg

Raisin Bran Bread

1. Combine the flour, wheat bran, and baking soda in a large bowl, and stir to mix well. Set aside.

2. Combine the milk, molasses, and lemon juice in a medium-sized bowl, and stir to mix well. Add the milk mixture to the flour mixture, and stir just until the dry ingredients are moistened. Fold in the raisins.

3. Coat an 8-x-4-inch loaf pan with nonstick cooking spray. Spread the batter evenly in the pan, and bake at 350°F for 35 minutes, or just until a wooden toothpick inserted in the center of the loaf comes out clean.

4. Remove the bread from the oven, and let sit for 10 minutes. Turn the loaf onto a wire rack, and cool before slicing.

Yield: *16 slices*

1⅔ cups whole wheat pastry flour

1¼ cups wheat bran

1 teaspoon baking soda

1⅓ cups skim milk

⅓ cup molasses

1 tablespoon lemon juice

⅓ cup dark raisins

NUTRITIONAL FACTS (PER SLICE)
Calories: 88 Cholesterol: 0 mg Fat: 0.5 g
Fiber: 3.6 g Protein: 3.2 g Sodium: 93 mg

Apple Butter Bread

1. Combine the flour, baking powder, baking soda, and nutmeg in a large bowl, and stir to mix well. Add the apple butter, apple juice, and vanilla extract, and stir just until the dry ingredients are moistened. Fold in the raisins or currants and, if desired, the walnuts.

2. Coat an 8-x-4-inch loaf pan with nonstick cooking spray. Spread the batter evenly in the pan, and bake at 350°F for 40 to 45 minutes, or just until a wooden toothpick inserted in the center of the loaf comes out clean.

3. Remove the bread from the oven, and let sit for 10 minutes. Turn the loaf onto a wire rack, and cool before slicing.

Yield: *16 slices*

2 cups whole wheat pastry flour

1 teaspoon baking powder

1 teaspoon baking soda

¼ teaspoon ground nutmeg

1 cup apple butter

½ cup plus 2 tablespoons apple juice

1 teaspoon vanilla extract

½ cup dark raisins or currants

¼ cup chopped walnuts (optional)

NUTRITIONAL FACTS (PER SLICE)
Calories: 103 Cholesterol: 0 mg Fat: 0.3 g
Fiber: 2.2 g Protein: 2.2 g Sodium: 103 mg

Pineapple-Poppy Seed Bread

Yield: *16 slices*

2 cups whole wheat pastry flour

⅓ cup sugar

1 teaspoon baking powder

1 teaspoon baking soda

1 can (8 ounces) crushed pineapple in juice, undrained

⅓ cup skim milk

1 teaspoon vanilla extract

½ teaspoon almond extract

2 tablespoons poppy seeds

1. Combine the flour, sugar, baking powder, and baking soda in a large bowl, and stir to mix well. Add the pineapple, including the juice, and the milk and extracts, and stir just until the dry ingredients are moistened. Fold in the poppy seeds.

2. Coat an 8-x-4-inch loaf pan with nonstick cooking spray. Spread the batter evenly in the pan, and bake at 350°F for 40 minutes, or just until a wooden toothpick inserted in the center of the loaf comes out clean.

3. Remove the bread from the oven, and let sit for 10 minutes. Turn the loaf onto a wire rack, and cool before slicing.

NUTRITIONAL FACTS (PER SLICE)
Calories: 83 Cholesterol: 0 mg Fat: 0.8 g
Fiber: 2.1 g Protein: 2.5 g Sodium: 105 mg

Carrot Raisin Bread

Yield: *16 slices*

2 cups whole wheat pastry flour

½ cup sugar

1 teaspoon baking powder

1 teaspoon baking soda

1 teaspoon ground cinnamon

1 cup apple or orange juice

1 cup finely grated carrots (about
2 medium)

⅓ cup dark or golden raisins

¼ cup toasted wheat germ

1. Combine the flour, sugar, baking powder, baking soda, and cinnamon in a large bowl, and stir to mix well. Add the juice and carrots, and stir just until the dry ingredients are moistened. Fold in the raisins and wheat germ.

2. Coat an 8-x-4-inch loaf pan with nonstick cooking spray. Spread the batter evenly in the pan, and bake at 350°F for 45 minutes, or just until a wooden toothpick inserted in the center of the loaf comes out clean.

3. Remove the bread from the oven, and let sit for 10 minutes. Turn the loaf onto a wire rack, and cool before slicing.

NUTRITIONAL FACTS (PER SLICE)
Calories: 102 Cholesterol: 0 mg Fat: 0.5 g
Fiber: 2.4 g Protein: 2.8 g Sodium: 105 mg

Jalapeño Cornbread

1. Combine the cornmeal, flour, sugar, baking powder, and baking soda in a large bowl, and stir to mix well. Add the buttermilk and egg whites, and stir just until the dry ingredients are moistened. Fold in the corn, cheese, and jalapeños.

2. Coat a 10-inch ovenproof skillet with nonstick cooking spray, and spread the batter evenly in the pan. Bake at 350°F for 25 to 30 minutes, or just until a wooden toothpick inserted in the center of the bread comes out clean.

3. Remove the bread from the oven, and let it sit for 5 minutes. Cut the bread into wedges, and serve hot.

Yield: 12 servings

1¼ cups whole grain cornmeal

¾ cup whole wheat pastry flour

1 tablespoon sugar

2 teaspoons baking powder

½ teaspoon baking soda

1½ cups nonfat or low-fat buttermilk

2 egg whites, lightly beaten

¾ cup fresh or frozen (thawed) whole kernel corn

½ cup shredded nonfat or reduced-fat Cheddar cheese

1–2 tablespoons finely chopped jalapeño peppers

NUTRITIONAL FACTS (PER SERVING)
Calories: 106 Cholesterol: 2 mg Fat: 0.8 g
Fiber: 2.1 g Protein: 5.5 g Sodium: 202 mg

Buttermilk Drop Biscuits

1. Combine the flour, oat bran, sugar, and baking powder in a large bowl, and stir to mix well. Add the buttermilk, and stir just until the dry ingredients are moistened. Add a little more buttermilk if needed to form a stiff batter.

2. Coat a baking sheet with nonstick cooking spray, and drop heaping tablespoonfuls of the batter onto the sheet. For crusty biscuits, space the spoonfuls 1 inch apart; for soft biscuits, space the spoonfuls so that they are barely touching.

3. Bake at 400°F for 18 minutes, or just until the tops are lightly browned. Transfer to a serving plate, and serve hot.

Yield: 12 biscuits

2 cups unbleached flour

½ cup oat bran

1 tablespoon sugar

1 tablespoon baking powder

1¼ cups plus 2 tablespoons nonfat or low-fat buttermilk

NUTRITIONAL FACTS (PER BISCUIT)
Calories: 101 Cholesterol: 0 mg Fat: 0.7 g
Fiber: 1.3 g Protein: 3.7 g Sodium: 121 mg

Pumpkin Drop Biscuits

Yield: *12 biscuits*

1 cup whole wheat pastry flour

1 cup unbleached flour

2 tablespoons sugar

4 teaspoons baking powder

½ cup cooked mashed pumpkin

1 cup nonfat buttermilk

1. Combine the flours, sugar, and baking powder, and stir to mix well. In a separate bowl, combine the pumpkin and buttermilk, and stir until blended. Add the pumpkin mixture to the flour mixture, and stir just until the dry ingredients are moistened.

2. Coat a baking sheet with nonstick cooking spray. Drop heaping tablespoonfuls of dough onto the sheet, placing the biscuits ½ inch apart for soft biscuits, or 1½ inches apart for crusty biscuits.

3. Bake at 375°F for about 18 minutes, or until lightly browned. Transfer to a serving plate, and serve hot.

NUTRITIONAL FACTS (PER BISCUIT)
Calories: 93 Calcium: 51 mg Cholesterol: 0 mg
Fat: 0.4 g Fiber: 1.7 g Iron: 1 mg
Potassium: 105 mg Protein: 3.2 g Sodium: 112 mg

Orange Poppy Seed Bread

Yield: *16 slices*

2 cups whole wheat pastry flour

½ cup sugar

1 teaspoon baking soda

1 tablespoon poppy seeds

1 cup orange juice

1 teaspoon vanilla extract

1. Combine the flour, sugar, baking soda, and poppy seeds, and stir to mix well. Add the orange juice and vanilla extract, and stir just until the dry ingredients are moistened.

2. Coat an 8-x-4-inch loaf pan with nonstick cooking spray. Spread the mixture evenly in the pan, and bake at 325°F for about 45 minutes, or just until a wooden toothpick inserted in the center of the loaf comes out clean.

3. Remove bread from oven, and let sit for 10 minutes. Invert loaf onto a wire rack, turn right side up, and cool before slicing and serving.

NUTRITIONAL FACTS (PER SLICE)
Calories: 84 Calcium: 14 mg Cholesterol: 0 mg
Fat: 0.5 g Fiber: 2 g Iron: 0.7 mg
Potassium: 91 mg Protein: 2.2 g Sodium: 52 mg

Butternut Oat Bran Biscuits

1. Combine the flour, oat bran, sugar, baking powder, and baking soda, and stir to mix well. In a separate bowl, combine the squash or pumpkin and the buttermilk, and stir until blended. Add the squash mixture to the flour mixture, and stir just until the dough leaves the sides of the bowl and rounds into a ball.

2. Turn the dough onto a floured surface, and pat into a ½-inch-thick sheet. Use a 2½-inch glass or biscuit cutter to cut out 12 biscuits, dipping the rim of the glass in flour to prevent sticking. Reroll the scraps as needed.

3. Coat a baking sheet with nonstick cooking spray. Arrange the biscuits on the baking sheet, placing them ½ inch apart for soft biscuits, or 1½ inches apart for crusty biscuits.

4. Bake at 375°F for 18 minutes, or until lightly browned. Transfer to a serving plate, and serve hot.

Yield: *12 biscuits*

1¾ cups plus 2 tablespoons unbleached flour

1 cup oat bran

1 tablespoon plus 1½ teaspoons sugar

1 tablespoon baking powder

¼ teaspoon baking soda

¼ cup plus 2 tablespoons cooked mashed butternut squash or pumpkin

1 cup plus 2 tablespoons nonfat buttermilk

NUTRITIONAL FACTS (PER BISCUIT)
Calories: 109 Calcium: 52 mg Cholesterol: 0 mg
Fat: 0.8 g Fiber: 2.1 g Iron: 1.4 mg
Potassium: 123 mg Protein: 4.2 g Sodium: 107 mg

WHOLE WHEAT APRICOT BREAD

Yield: *16 slices*

2 cups whole wheat pastry flour

⅓ cup sugar

1 teaspoon baking powder

1 teaspoon baking soda

1 can (1 pound) apricots in juice, undrained

1 teaspoon vanilla extract

⅓ cup finely chopped dried apricots

⅓ cup barley nugget cereal or chopped pecans

1. Combine the flour, sugar, baking powder, and baking soda in a large bowl, and stir to mix well. Set aside.

2. Drain the apricots, reserving the juice. Place the apricots in a blender, and process until smooth. Add enough of the reserved juice to bring the volume of the mixture up to 1½ cups.

3. Add the blended apricots and vanilla extract to the flour mixture, and stir just until the dry ingredients are moistened. Fold in the dried apricots and cereal.

4. Coat an 8-x-4-inch loaf pan with nonstick cooking spray. Spread the batter evenly in the pan, and bake at 325°F for 45 minutes, or just until a wooden toothpick inserted in the center of the loaf comes out clean.

5. Remove the bread from the oven, and let sit for 10 minutes. Turn the loaf onto a wire rack, and cool before slicing.

NUTRITIONAL FACTS (PER SLICE)
Calories: 94 Cholesterol: 0 mg Fat: 0.3 g
Fiber: 2.5 g Protein: 2.6 g Sodium: 119 mg

Pumpkin Spice Bread

1. Combine the flour, sugar, pumpkin pie spice, baking soda, and baking powder, and stir to mix well. Add the pumpkin and apple or orange juice, and stir just until the dry ingredients are moistened. Fold in the nuts if desired.

2. Coat an 8-x-4-inch loaf pan with nonstick cooking spray. Spread the mixture evenly in the pan, and bake at 350°F for 40 to 45 minutes, or just until a wooden toothpick inserted in the center of the loaf comes out clean.

3. Remove the bread from the oven, and let sit for 10 minutes. Invert the loaf onto a wire rack, turn right side up, and cool before slicing and serving.

Yield: *16 slices*

1¾ cups whole wheat pastry flour

½ cup sugar

1½ teaspoons pumpkin pie spice

1 teaspoon baking soda

1 teaspoon baking powder

1 cup cooked mashed pumpkin

½ cup apple or orange juice

¼ cup chopped pecans (optional)

NUTRITIONAL FACTS (PER SLICE)
Calories: 82 Calcium: 13 mg Cholesterol: 0 mg
Fat: 0.4 g Fiber: 2 g Iron: 0.8 mg
Potassium: 93 mg Protein: 1.5 g Sodium: 74 mg

Super-Moist Apple Bread

Yield: *16 slices*

2 cups whole wheat pastry flour

½ cup brown sugar

1 teaspoon baking soda

¾ cup apple juice

1 teaspoon vanilla extract

2 cups finely chopped apples

¼ cup chopped dark raisins or
   chopped walnuts (optional)

1. Combine the flour, brown sugar, and baking soda, and stir to mix well. Add the apple juice and vanilla extract, and stir just until the dry ingredients are moistened. Fold in the apples. Fold in the raisins or walnuts if desired.

2. Coat an 8-x-4-inch loaf pan with nonstick cooking spray. Spread the mixture evenly in the pan, and bake at 325°F for 50 to 55 minutes, or just until a wooden toothpick inserted in the center of the loaf comes out clean.

3. Remove the bread from the oven, and let sit for 10 minutes. Invert the loaf onto a wire rack, turn right side up, and cool before slicing and serving.

NUTRITIONAL FACTS (PER SLICE)
Calories: 89 Calcium: 13 mg Cholesterol: 0 mg
Fat: 0.3 g Fiber: 2.2 g Iron: 0.8 mg
Potassium: 114 mg Protein: 2 g Sodium: 54 mg

Applesauce Gingerbread

Yield: *16 servings*

1½ cups unbleached flour

1 cup whole wheat pastry flour

⅔ cup sugar

2½ teaspoons baking soda

1 teaspoon ground ginger

1 teaspoon ground cinnamon

1 teaspoon ground allspice

1½ cups unsweetened applesauce

1 cup molasses

3 egg whites

1. Combine the flours, sugar, baking soda, and spices, and stir to mix well. Add the remaining ingredients, and stir to mix well.

2. Coat a 9-x-13-inch pan with nonstick cooking spray. Spread the batter evenly in the pan, and bake at 325°F for 40 minutes, or just until a wooden toothpick inserted in the center of the cake comes out clean.

3. Cool the cake for at least 20 minutes. Cut into squares and serve warm or at room temperature with a light whipped topping if desired.

NUTRITIONAL FACTS (PER SERVING)
Calories: 157 Calcium: 38 mg Cholesterol: 0 mg
Fat: 0.3 g Fiber: 1.6 g Iron: 1.7 mg
Potassium: 255 mg Protein: 3.1 g Sodium: 146 mg

Fruitful Cranberry Bread

1. Combine the flour, oat bran, sugar, baking powder, and baking soda, and stir to mix well. Add the juice, banana, and vanilla extract, and stir just until the dry ingredients are moistened. Fold in the cranberries.

2. Coat an 8-x-4-inch loaf pan with nonstick cooking spray. Spread the mixture evenly in the pan, and bake at 350°F for about 45 minutes, or just until a wooden toothpick inserted in the center of the loaf comes out clean.

3. Remove the bread from the oven, and let sit for 10 minutes. Invert the loaf onto a wire rack, turn right side up, and cool before slicing and serving.

Yield: *16 slices*

1½ cups whole wheat pastry flour

½ cup oat bran

⅓ cup sugar

1 teaspoon baking powder

1 teaspoon baking soda

¾ cup orange or apple juice

½ cup mashed very ripe banana (about 1 large)

1 teaspoon vanilla extract

1 cup coarsely chopped fresh or frozen cranberries

NUTRITIONAL FACTS (PER SLICE)
Calories: 76 Calcium: 12 mg Cholesterol: 0 mg
Fat: 0.5 g Fiber: 2.5 g Iron: 0.7 mg
Potassium: 126 mg Protein: 2.2 g Sodium: 73 mg

Honey Banana Bread

1. Combine the flour, brown sugar, baking powder, baking soda, and nutmeg, and stir to mix well. Add the banana, honey, and milk, and stir just until the dry ingredients are moistened.

2. Coat an 8-x-4-inch loaf pan with nonstick cooking spray. Spread the mixture evenly in the pan, and bake at 325°F for 45 to 50 minutes, or just until a wooden toothpick inserted in the center of the loaf comes out clean.

3. Remove the bread from the oven, and let sit for 10 minutes. Invert the loaf onto a wire rack, turn right side up, and cool before slicing and serving.

Yield: *16 slices*

2 cups whole wheat pastry flour

¼ cup brown sugar

1½ teaspoons baking powder

¾ teaspoon baking soda

¼ teaspoon ground nutmeg

1 cup mashed very ripe banana (about 2 large)

⅓ cup honey

¼ cup skim milk

NUTRITIONAL FACTS (PER SLICE)
Calories: 99 Calcium: 21 mg Cholesterol: 0 mg
Fat: 0.4 g Fiber: 2.1 g Iron: 0.8 mg
Potassium: 140 mg Protein: 2.5 g Sodium: 73 mg

CARROT FRUIT BREAD

Yield: *16 slices*

1½ cups whole wheat pastry flour

1 teaspoon baking powder

1 teaspoon baking soda

½ cup brown sugar

¼ cup plus 1 tablespoon orange or pineapple juice

2 egg whites

1 teaspoon almond extract

1¼ cups grated carrots

⅓ cup chopped dates

⅓ cup chopped dried apricots

1. Combine the flour, baking powder, baking soda, and brown sugar, and stir to mix well. Add the juice, egg whites, and almond extract, and stir just until the dry ingredients are moistened. Fold in the remaining ingredients.

2. Coat an 8-x-4-inch loaf pan with nonstick cooking spray. Spread the mixture evenly in the pan, and bake at 350°F for about 45 minutes, or just until a wooden toothpick inserted in the center of the loaf comes out clean.

3. Remove the bread from the oven, and let sit for 10 minutes. Invert the loaf onto a wire rack, turn right side up, and cool before slicing and serving.

NUTRITIONAL FACTS (PER SLICE)
Calories: 89 Calcium: 22 mg Cholesterol: 0 mg
Fat: 0.4 g Fiber: 2.2 g Iron: 0.9 mg
Potassium: 173 mg Protein: 2.3 g Sodium: 105 mg

ANADAMA QUICK BREAD

Yield: *16 slices*

2⅓ cups whole wheat pastry flour

½ cup whole grain cornmeal

2 teaspoons baking powder

1 teaspoon baking soda

1½ cups plus 2 tablespoons non-fat buttermilk

⅓ cup molasses

2 egg whites, slightly beaten

1. Combine the flour, cornmeal, baking powder, and baking soda, and stir to mix well. Add the remaining ingredients, and stir just until the dry ingredients are moistened.

2. Coat an 8-x-4-inch loaf pan with nonstick cooking spray. Spread the mixture evenly in the pan, and bake at 350°F for about 45 minutes, or just until a wooden toothpick inserted in the center of the loaf comes out clean.

3. Remove the bread from the oven, and let sit for 10 minutes. Invert the loaf onto a wire rack, turn right side up, and cool before slicing and serving.

NUTRITIONAL FACTS (PER SLICE)
Calories: 100 Calcium: 53 mg Cholesterol: 0 mg
Fat: 0.6 g Fiber: 2.6 g Iron: 1.1 mg
Potassium: 186 mg Protein: 4 g Sodium: 128 mg

Two-Bran Breakfast Bread

1. Combine the wheat bran and orange juice, and set aside for at least 5 minutes.

2. Combine the flour, oat bran, sugar, baking powder, and baking soda, and stir to mix well.

3. Add the wheat bran mixture and the yogurt to the flour mixture, and stir just until the dry ingredients are moistened. Fold in the apricots and prunes.

4. Coat an 8-x-4-inch loaf pan with nonstick cooking spray. Spread the mixture evenly in the pan, and bake at 350°F for 35 to 40 minutes, or just until a wooden toothpick in the center of the loaf comes out clean.

5. Remove the bread from the oven, and let sit for 10 minutes. Invert the loaf onto a wire rack, turn right side up, and cool before slicing and serving.

Yield: *16 slices*

¼ cup wheat bran

⅓ cup orange juice

1⅔ cups whole wheat pastry flour

¼ cup oat bran

⅓ cup sugar

1 teaspoon baking powder

1 teaspoon baking soda

1 cup plain nonfat yogurt

⅓ cup chopped dried apricots

⅓ cup chopped prunes

NUTRITIONAL FACTS (PER SLICE)
Calories: 89 Calcium: 41 mg Cholesterol: 0 mg
Fat: 0.4 g Fiber: 2.7 g Iron: 0.9 mg
Potassium: 178 mg Protein: 3.1 g Sodium: 84 mg

BOSTON BANANA BROWN BREAD

Yield: *32 slices*

2 cups whole wheat pastry flour

1 cup whole grain cornmeal

1 teaspoon baking soda

¼ teaspoon ground nutmeg

1½ cups mashed very ripe banana (about 3 large)

1 cup nonfat buttermilk

½ cup molasses

¾ cup chopped dried dates

1. Combine the flour, cornmeal, baking soda, and nutmeg, and stir to mix well. Add the banana, buttermilk, and molasses, and stir just until the dry ingredients are moistened. Fold in the dates.

2. Coat 4 one-pound cans with nonstick cooking spray. Divide the batter among the cans, and bake at 300°F for about 40 minutes, or just until a wooden toothpick inserted in the center of a loaf comes out clean.

3. Remove the bread from the oven, and let sit for 10 minutes. Invert the loaves onto a wire rack, turn right side up, and cool before slicing and serving.

NUTRITIONAL FACTS (PER SLICE)

Calories: 74 Calcium: 22 mg Cholesterol: 0 mg
Fat: 0.4 g Fiber: 1.8 g Iron: 0.7 mg
Potassium: 168 mg Protein: 1.8 g Sodium: 36 mg

BANANA GINGERBREAD

Yield: *16 slices*

2 cups whole wheat pastry flour

¼ cup toasted wheat germ

1 teaspoon baking powder

1 teaspoon baking soda

1½ teaspoons ground ginger

1 teaspoon ground cinnamon

1½ cups mashed very ripe banana (about 3 large)

¼ cup molasses

1. Combine the flour, wheat germ, baking powder, baking soda, and spices, and stir to mix well. Add the remaining ingredients, and stir just until the dry ingredients are moistened.

2. Coat an 8-x-4-inch loaf pan with nonstick cooking spray. Spread the mixture evenly in the pan, and bake at 325°F for 40 to 45 minutes, or just until a wooden toothpick inserted in the center of the loaf comes out clean.

3. Remove the bread from the oven, and let sit for 10 minutes. Invert the loaf onto a wire rack, turn right side up, and cool before slicing and serving.

NUTRITIONAL FACTS (PER SLICE)

Calories: 89 Calcium: 19 mg Cholesterol: 0 mg
Fat: 0.6 g Fiber: 2.5 g Iron: 1 mg
Potassium: 209 mg Protein: 2.8 g Sodium: 74 mg

Whole Wheat Banana Bread

1. Combine the flour, baking soda, baking powder, and sugar, and stir to mix well. Add the banana, Prune Purée, and vanilla extract, and stir just until the dry ingredients are moistened. Fold in the walnuts if desired.

2. Coat an 8-x-4-inch loaf pan with nonstick cooking spray. Spread the mixture evenly in the pan, and bake at 350°F for about 50 minutes, or just until a wooden toothpick in the center of the loaf comes out clean.

3. Remove the bread from the oven, and let sit for 10 minutes. Invert the loaf onto a wire rack, turn right side up, and cool before slicing and serving.

Yield: 16 slices

2 cups whole wheat pastry flour

1 teaspoon baking soda

1 teaspoon baking powder

¼ cup plus 2 tablespoons sugar

1½ cups mashed very ripe banana (about 3 large)

¼ cup Prune Purée (page 223)

1 teaspoon vanilla extract

⅓ cup chopped walnuts (optional)

NUTRITIONAL FACTS (PER SLICE)
Calories: 92 Calcium: 15 mg Cholesterol: 0 mg
Fat: 0.3 g Fiber: 2.3 g Iron: 0.9 mg
Potassium: 169 mg Protein: 2.2 g Sodium: 74 mg

Cinnamon Raisin Bread

1. Combine the flour, brown sugar, baking soda, baking powder, and cinnamon, and stir to mix well. Add the buttermilk, Prune Purée, and vanilla extract, and stir just until the dry ingredients are moistened. Fold in the raisins.

2. Coat an 8-x-4-inch loaf pan with nonstick cooking spray. Spread the mixture evenly in the pan, and bake at 350°F for about 45 minutes, or just until a wooden toothpick inserted in the center of the loaf comes out clean.

3. Remove the bread from the oven, and let sit for 10 minutes. Invert the loaf onto a wire rack, turn right side up, and cool before slicing and serving.

Yield: 16 slices

2 cups whole wheat pastry flour

⅓ cup brown sugar

1 teaspoon baking soda

1 teaspoon baking powder

2 teaspoons ground cinnamon

1 cup nonfat buttermilk

¼ cup Prune Purée (page 223)

1 teaspoon vanilla extract

½ cup dark raisins

NUTRITIONAL FACTS (PER SLICE)
Calories: 93 Calcium: 36 mg Cholesterol: 0 mg
Fat: 0.5 g Fiber: 2.3 g Iron: 1 mg
Potassium: 146 mg Protein: 2.8 g Sodium: 90 mg

PRUNE and ORANGE BREAD

Yield: *16 slices*

2 cups whole wheat pastry flour

1 teaspoon baking soda

1 teaspoon baking powder

1 teaspoon dried grated orange rind, or 1 tablespoon fresh

¾ cup Prune Butter (page 223)

¾ cup orange juice

⅓ cup chopped pecans (optional)

1. Combine the flour, baking soda, baking powder, and orange peel, and stir to mix well. Add the Prune Butter and orange juice, and stir just until the dry ingredients are moistened. Fold in the pecans if desired.

2. Coat an 8-x-4-inch loaf pan with nonstick cooking spray. Spread the mixture evenly in the pan, and bake at 350°F for about 40 minutes, or just until a wooden toothpick inserted in the center of the loaf comes out clean.

3. Remove the bread from the oven, and let sit for 10 minutes. Invert the loaf onto a wire rack, turn right side up, and cool before slicing and serving.

NUTRITIONAL FACTS (PER SLICE)
Calories: 82 Calcium: 15 mg Cholesterol: 0 mg
Fat: 0.3 g Fiber: 3 g Iron: 0.9 mg
Potassium: 162 mg Protein: 2.4 g Sodium: 73 mg

CRANBERRY Pumpkin BREAD

Yield: *16 slices*

2 cups whole wheat pastry flour

⅓ cup light brown sugar

1 teaspoon baking soda

1 teaspoon baking powder

1 teaspoon pumpkin pie spice

1 cup whole berry cranberry sauce

¾ cup cooked mashed pumpkin

¼ cup apple or orange juice

1. Combine the flour, sugar, baking soda, baking powder, and pumpkin pie spice, and stir to mix well. Add the remaining ingredients, and stir just until the dry ingredients are moistened.

2. Coat an 8-x-4-inch loaf pan with nonstick cooking spray. Spread the mixture evenly in the pan, and bake at 350°F for about 50 minutes, or just until a wooden toothpick inserted in the center of the loaf comes out clean.

3. Remove the bread from the oven, and let sit for 10 minutes. Invert the loaf onto a wire rack, turn right side up, and cool before slicing and serving.

NUTRITIONAL FACTS (PER SLICE)
Calories: 100 Calcium: 18 mg Cholesterol: 0 mg
Fat: 0.3 g Fiber: 2.5 g Iron: 1 mg
Potassium: 110 mg Protein: 2.2 g Sodium: 78 mg

Pumpkin Gingerbread

1. Combine the flour, cornmeal, baking soda, ginger, and allspice, and stir to mix well. Add the pumpkin, apple or orange juice, and molasses, and stir just until the dry ingredients are moistened. Fold in the raisins if desired.

2. Coat 4 one-pound cans with nonstick cooking spray. Divide the batter among the cans, and bake at 300°F for 40 to 45 minutes, or just until a wooden toothpick inserted in the center of a loaf comes out clean.

3. Remove the bread from the oven, and let sit for 10 minutes. Invert the loaves onto a wire rack, turn right side up, and cool before slicing and serving.

Yield: *32 slices*

2 cups whole wheat pastry flour

1 cup whole grain cornmeal

1 teaspoon baking soda

2 teaspoons ground ginger

1 teaspoon ground allspice

1 cup cooked mashed pumpkin

1¼ cups apple or orange juice

¾ cup molasses

¾ cup dark raisins (optional)

NUTRITIONAL FACTS (PER SLICE)
Calories: 63 Calcium: 18 mg Cholesterol: 0 mg
Fat: 0.3 g Fiber: 1.5 g Iron: 0.9 mg
Potassium: 137 mg Protein: 1.4 g Sodium: 29 mg

Pumpkin Pineapple Bread

1. Combine the flour, oats, sugar, baking soda, baking powder, and pumpkin pie spice, and stir to mix well. Add the pineapple, including the juice, and the pumpkin, and stir just until the dry ingredients are moistened. Fold in the nuts if desired.

2. Coat an 8-x-4-inch loaf pan with nonstick cooking spray. Spread the batter evenly in the pan, and bake at 350°F for 45 to 50 minutes, or just until a wooden toothpick inserted in the center of the loaf comes out clean.

3. Remove the bread from the oven, and let sit for 10 minutes. Invert the loaf onto a wire rack, turn right side up, and cool before slicing and serving.

Yield: *16 slices*

1½ cups whole wheat pastry flour

¾ cup quick-cooking oats

½ cup sugar

1 teaspoon baking soda

1 teaspoon baking powder

1½ teaspoons pumpkin pie spice

1 can (8 ounces) crushed pineapple packed in juice, undrained

1 cup cooked mashed pumpkin

⅓ cup chopped pecans (optional)

NUTRITIONAL FACTS (PER SLICE)
Calories: 91 Calcium: 15 mg Cholesterol: 0 mg
Fat: 0.5 g Fiber: 2.3 g Iron: 0.9 mg
Potassium: 108 mg Protein: 2.4 g Sodium: 73 mg

Fresh Pear Bread

Yield: *16 slices*

2 cups whole wheat pastry flour

½ cup sugar

2 teaspoons baking powder

¾ teaspoon baking soda

¼ teaspoon ground nutmeg

¼ teaspoon ground cinnamon

¾ cup pear nectar

1 teaspoon vanilla extract

1⅓ cups finely chopped peeled
   pears (about 1½ medium)

¼ cup plus 2 tablespoons dried
   currants or dark raisins

¼ cup chopped walnuts (optional)

Make sure that the fresh pears you use for this recipe are perfectly ripe and sweet.

1. Place the flour, sugar, baking powder, baking soda, nutmeg, and cinnamon in a large bowl, and stir to mix well. Add the nectar, vanilla extract, and pears, and stir just until the dry ingredients are moistened. Fold in the currants or raisins and, if desired, the walnuts.

2. Coat an 8-x-4-inch loaf pan with nonstick cooking spray, and spread the mixture evenly in the pan. Bake at 325°F for about 45 minutes, or just until a wooden toothpick inserted in the center of the loaf comes out clean.

3. Remove the loaf from the oven, and let sit for 15 minutes. Invert the loaf onto a wire rack, turn right side up, and cool to room temperature. Wrap the loaf in plastic wrap or aluminum foil, and store for 8 hours or overnight before slicing and serving. (Overnight storage will develop the flavors and give the loaf a softer, moister crust.) Refrigerate any leftover not eaten within 24 hours.

NUTRITIONAL FACTS (PER SLICE)
Calories: 93 Carbohydrates: 22 g Cholesterol: 0 mg
Fat: 0.4 g Fiber: 2.5 g Protein: 2.2 g Sodium: 121 mg

You Save: Calories: 65 Fat: 6.8 g

Applesauce-Oatmeal Bread

1. Place the flour, oats, sugar, baking powder, baking soda, and cinnamon in a large bowl, and stir to mix well. Add the applesauce and vanilla extract, and stir just until the dry ingredients are moistened. Fold in the raisins or cranberries and, if desired, the nuts.

2. Coat an 8-x-4-inch loaf pan with nonstick cooking spray, and spread the mixture evenly in the pan. Bake at 325°F for about 45 minutes, or just until a wooden toothpick inserted in the center of the loaf comes out clean.

3. Remove the loaf from the oven, and let sit for 15 minutes. Invert the loaf onto a wire rack, turn right side up, and cool to room temperature. Wrap the loaf in plastic wrap or aluminum foil, and store for 8 hours or overnight before slicing and serving. (Overnight storage will develop the flavors and give the loaf a softer, moister crust.) Refrigerate any leftovers not eaten within 24 hours.

Yield: *16 slices*

1½ cups whole wheat pastry flour

¾ cup quick-cooking oats

½ cup sugar

2 teaspoons baking powder

¾ teaspoon baking soda

½ teaspoon ground cinnamon

1½ cups unsweetened applesauce

1½ teaspoons vanilla extract

¼ cup plus 2 tablespoons dark raisins or dried cranberries

⅓ cup chopped toasted walnuts or pecans (page 383) (optional)

NUTRITIONAL FACTS (PER SLICE)

Calories: 97 Carbohydrates: 22.3 g Cholesterol: 0 mg
Fat: 0.5 g Fiber: 2.2 g Protein: 2.3 g Sodium: 121 mg

You Save: Calories: 69 Fat: 6.8 g

Mocha Banana Bread

Yield: *16 slices*

2 teaspoons vanilla extract

½ teaspoon instant coffee granules

1¾ cups whole wheat pastry flour

¼ cup Dutch processed cocoa powder

½ cup plus 2 tablespoons sugar

2 teaspoons baking powder

¾ teaspoon baking soda

½ teaspoon ground cinnamon

2 cups mashed very ripe banana (about 4 large)

½ cup chopped toasted pecans, almonds, or macadamia nuts (page 383) (optional)

1. Place the vanilla extract and coffee granules in a small bowl, and stir to mix well. Set aside.

2. Place the flour, cocoa powder, sugar, baking powder, baking soda, and cinnamon in a large bowl, and stir to mix well. Add the banana and the vanilla extract mixture, and stir just until the dry ingredients are moistened. Fold in the nuts, if desired.

3. Coat an 8-x-4-inch loaf pan with nonstick cooking spray, and spread the mixture evenly in the pan. Bake at 325°F for about 55 minutes, or just until a wooden toothpick inserted in the center of the loaf comes out clean.

4. Remove the loaf from the oven, and let sit for 15 minutes. Invert the loaf onto a wire rack, turn right side up, and cool to room temperature. Wrap the loaf in plastic wrap or aluminum foil, and store for 8 hours or overnight before slicing and serving. (Overnight storage will develop the flavors and give the loaf a softer, moister crust.) Refrigerate any leftovers not eaten within 24 hours.

NUTRITIONAL FACTS (PER SLICE)
Calories: 104 Carbohydrates: 24.8 Cholesterol: 0 mg
Fat: 0.6 g Fiber: 2.6 g Protein: 2.4 g Sodium: 121 g

You Save: Calories: 68 Fat: 7.1 g

Golden Pumpkin Bread

1. Place the flour, baking powder, baking soda, and pumpkin pie spice in a large bowl, and stir to mix well. Set aside.

2. Place the pumpkin, orange juice, brown sugar, and vanilla extract in a medium-sized bowl, and stir to mix well and to dissolve the brown sugar. Add the pumpkin mixture to the flour mixture, and stir just until the dry ingredients are moistened. Fold in the wheat germ or pecans.

3. Coat an 8-x-4-inch loaf pan with nonstick cooking spray, and spread the mixture evenly in the pan. Bake at 325°F for about 55 minutes, or just until a wooden toothpick inserted in the center of the loaf comes out clean.

4. Remove the loaf from the oven, and let sit for 15 minutes. Invert the loaf onto a wire rack, turn right side up, and cool to room temperature. Wrap the loaf in plastic wrap or aluminum foil, and store for 8 hours or overnight before slicing and serving. (Overnight storage will develop the flavors and give the loaf a softer, moister crust.) Refrigerate any leftovers not eaten within 24 hours.

Yield: *16 slices*

2 cups whole wheat pastry flour

2 teaspoons baking powder

¾ teaspoon baking soda

2 teaspoons pumpkin pie spice

1¼ cups mashed cooked pumpkin or canned pumpkin

¾ cup orange juice

½ cup plus 2 tablespoons light brown sugar

1½ teaspoons vanilla extract

⅓ cup honey crunch wheat germ or chopped toasted pecans (page 383)

NUTRITIONAL FACTS (PER SLICE)
Calories: 93 Carbohydrates: 20.7 g Cholesterol: 0 mg
Fat: 0.5 g Fiber: 2.5 g Protein: 2.9 g Sodium: 124 mg

You Save: Calories: 79 Fat: 9.2 g

Pear-Cranberry Bread

Yield: *16 slices*

1 can (1 pound) pear halves in juice, undrained

⅓ cup oat bran

1¾ cups whole wheat pastry flour

½ cup sugar

2 teaspoons baking powder

¾ teaspoon baking soda

2 teaspoons vanilla extract

½ cup dried cranberries

⅓ cup honey crunch wheat germ or chopped walnuts

1. Drain the pears, reserving the juice. Place the drained pears in a blender or food processor, and process until smooth. Pour the pear purée into a 2-cup measuring cup, and add enough of the reserved juice to bring the volume to 1⅔ cups.

2. Place the oat bran in a medium-sized bowl, and add the pear purée. Stir with a wire whisk until well mixed, and set the mixture aside for at least 15 minutes to allow the oat bran to soften.

3. Place the flour, sugar, baking powder, and baking soda in a large bowl, and stir to mix well. Add the pear mixture and the vanilla extract to the flour mixture, and stir just until the dry ingredients are moistened. Fold in the cranberries and the wheat germ or walnuts.

4. Coat an 8-x-4-inch loaf pan with nonstick cooking spray, and spread the mixture evenly in the pan. Bake at 325°F for about 45 minutes, or just until a wooden toothpick inserted in the center of the loaf comes out clean.

5. Remove the loaf from the oven, and let sit for 15 minutes. Invert the loaf onto a wire rack, turn right side up, and cool to room temperature. Wrap the loaf in plastic wrap or aluminum foil, and store for 8 hours or overnight before slicing and serving. (Overnight storage will develop the flavors and give the loaf a softer, moister crust.) Refrigerate any leftovers not eaten within 24 hours.

NUTRITIONAL FACTS (PER SLICE)
Calories: 107 Carbohydrates: 25 g Cholesterol: 0 mg
Fat: 0.6 g Fiber: 2.6 g Protein: 2.7 g Sodium: 122 mg

You Save: Calories: 81 Fat: 9.5 g

Getting the Fat Out of Your Favorite Quick Bread Recipes

Many traditional quick bread recipes are loaded with fat. This is a shame, because these sweet treats can often be made with no fat at all. And as the recipes in this chapter show, just about any moist ingredient can replace the fat in quick breads. Applesauce and fruit purées perform especially well as fat substitutes in quick breads, but mashed cooked pumpkin and sweet potatoes, Prune Purée (page 223) and nonfat or low-fat buttermilk and yogurt can also act as fat substitutes. Use the following tricks of the trade to insure success when eliminating the fat from your favorite quick bread recipes.

❑ *Replace the desired amount of butter, margarine, or other solid shortening with half as much fat substitute.* For instance, if you are omitting ½ cup of butter from a recipe, replace it with ¼ cup of fruit purée, nonfat buttermilk, mashed cooked pumpkin, or other fat substitute. If the recipe calls for oil, substitute three-fourths as much fat substitute. Mix up the batter. If it seems too dry, add a little more fat substitute. For extra flavor and tenderness, try substituting fruit purée or nonfat buttermilk for the recipe's liquid, as well.

❑ *Eliminate only half the fat in a recipe at first.* The next time you make the recipe, try replacing even more fat. Continue reducing fat until you find the lowest amount that will give you the desired results. Realize that as you remove more and more fat from a recipe, the following tips—for using low-gluten flours and eliminating eggs, for instance—become even more important.

❑ *Use low-gluten flours.* Wheat flour contains proteins that, when mixed with liquid into a batter, form tough strands called gluten. Fat tenderizes baked goods by interfering with this process—which is why removing the fat from baked goods often makes them tough or rubbery. The good news is that you can leave out the fat and still have a tender texture if you use a low-gluten flour like whole wheat pastry flour in your fat-free quick breads. (Read more about whole wheat pastry flour on page 16.) Ingredients such as oats, bran, cornmeal, and cocoa powder also form little or no gluten, making them ideal ingredients for use in fat-free quick breads.

❑ *Minimize mixing.* Stirring batter excessively develops gluten and toughens the texture of baked goods. Stir only enough to mix well.

❑ *Avoid overbaking.* Reduced-fat baked goods tend to bake more quickly than do those made with fat, and if left in the oven too long, they can become dry. To prevent this, bake fat-free quick breads at 325°F to 350°F, and check the product for doneness a few minutes before the end of the usual baking time.

❑ *Eliminate the eggs.* You may have noticed that none of the fat-free quick breads in this book contains any eggs. Why? Fat adds tenderness to baked goods. Eggs, on the other hand, toughen the structure of baked goods as their proteins coagulate during baking and bind the batter together. For this reason, fat-free quick breads that contain too many eggs can have a tough texture. For maximum tenderness, substitute 2 tablespoons of your chosen fat substitute for each whole egg in your recipe.

❑ *Increase the leavening if necessary.* Fat lubricates batters and helps quick breads rise better. When fats are creamed with sugar, they also incorporate air into the batter, which further aids rising. For these reasons, when you eliminate the fat from your quick bread recipe, your bread might not rise as well. If this happens, try adding a little extra baking soda to your recipe, starting with ¼ teaspoon. (Alternatively, add a teaspoon of baking powder.) For each cup of acidic liquid—fruit purée or buttermilk, for instance—avoid using more than 1 teaspoon of baking soda, as more soda might cause the product to take on a bitter or soapy taste.

Fruit and Nut Bread

Yield: *32 slices*

3 cups whole wheat pastry flour

½ cup sugar

1 teaspoon baking soda

1¾ cups nonfat or low-fat buttermilk

¼ cup honey

2 teaspoons vanilla extract

½ cup dried cranberries or dried
pitted cherries

½ cup chopped dried apricots or
pineapples

½ cup dark raisins

½ cup golden raisins

⅔ cup chopped toasted pecans
(page 223)

1. Place the flour, sugar, and baking soda in a large bowl, and stir to mix well. Add the buttermilk, honey, and vanilla extract, and stir to mix well. Fold in the fruits and nuts.

2. Coat four 1-pound cans with nonstick cooking spray. Divide the batter among the cans, and bake at 300°F for about 45 minutes, or just until a wooden toothpick inserted in the center of a loaf comes out clean.

3. Remove the bread from the oven, and let sit for 15 minutes. Invert the loaves onto a wire rack, turn right side up, and cool to room temperature. Wrap the loaves in aluminum foil or plastic wrap, and let sit overnight before slicing and serving. (Overnight storage will develop the flavors and give the loaves a softer, moister crust.) Refrigerate any leftovers not eaten within 24 hours.

NUTRITIONAL FACTS (PER SLICE)
Calories: 104 Carbohydrates: 21 g Cholesterol: 0 mg
Fat: 2 g Fiber: 1.9 g Protein: 2.4 g Sodium: 55 mg

You Save: Calories: 59 Fat: 6.9 g

Baking Festive Round Loaves

Any quick bread recipe can be used to make festive round loaves by baking the batter in cans instead of loaf pans. These loaves can then be wrapped in colored plastic wrap, tied on top with a ribbon, and given as gifts during the holiday season or at any time of year.

Simply coat three or four 1-pound food cans with nonstick cooking spray, and divide the batter evenly among the cans, filling each half to two-thirds full. Bake at 300°F for about 45 minutes, or just until a wooden toothpick inserted in the center of a loaf comes out clean. Cool the bread in the cans for 10 to 15 minutes, remove the loaves from the cans, and cool completely before wrapping.

A word of caution is in order regarding the cans used to make these loaves. When choosing cans for baking, be sure to avoid those that have been lead-soldered. Lead is a toxic metal that can leach into foods during baking. Food cans produced in this country do not contain lead solder, as the United States canning industry eliminated this process in 1991. Some labels even state that the can is lead-free. Imported foods, however, may still be packaged in soldered cans.

To be safe, avoid baking bread in all cans with pronounced seams—a sign of possible lead soldering—and in all imported food cans. You will then be sure that your festive breads are as healthy as they are delicious.

Zucchini-Spice Bread

1. Place the flour, sugar, baking powder, baking soda, cinnamon, lemon rind, and nutmeg in a large bowl, and stir to mix well. Add the zucchini, milk, and vanilla extract, and stir just until the dry ingredients are moistened. Fold in the raisins or walnuts.

2. Coat an 8-x-4-inch loaf pan with nonstick cooking spray, and spread the mixture evenly in the pan. Bake at 325°F for 50 to 55 minutes, or just until a wooden toothpick inserted in the center of the loaf comes out clean.

3. Remove the loaf from the oven, and let sit for 15 minutes. Invert the loaf onto a wire rack, turn right side up, and cool to room temperature. Wrap the loaf in plastic wrap or aluminum foil, and store for 8 hours or overnight before slicing and serving. (Overnight storage will develop the flavors and give the loaf a softer, moister crust.) Refrigerate any leftovers not eaten within 24 hours.

Yield: *16 slices*

2 cups whole wheat pastry flour

⅔ cup sugar

2½ teaspoons baking powder

½ teaspoon baking soda

1 teaspoon ground cinnamon

1 teaspoon dried grated lemon rind, or 1 tablespoon fresh

½ teaspoon ground nutmeg

1¼ cups (packed) shredded unpeeled zucchini (about 1 medium-large)

¾ cup skim milk

1½ teaspoons vanilla extract

½ cup dark raisins or chopped walnuts, or ¼ cup each raisins and walnuts

---

NUTRITIONAL FACTS (PER SLICE)
Calories: 103 Carbohydrates: 23 g Cholesterol: 0 mg
Fat: 0.3 g Fiber: 2.2 g Protein: 2.8 g Sodium: 123 mg

You Save: Calories: 72 Fat: 9 g

CINNAMON-APPLE CHOP BREAD

Yield: *8 servings*

DOUGH

1¾ cups plus 2 tablespoons un-bleached flour

¼ cup plus 2 tablespoons quick-cooking oats

¼ cup sugar

2 teaspoons Rapid Rise yeast

¼ teaspoon salt

½ cup plus 2 tablespoons skim milk

1 teaspoon lemon juice

2 teaspoons skim milk

FILLING

1½ cups chopped peeled apples (about 2 medium)

¼ cup dark raisins

1 tablespoon sugar

½ teaspoon ground cinnamon

GLAZE

½ cup powdered sugar

2½ teaspoons skim milk

½ teaspoon vanilla extract

1. To make the dough, place ¾ cup of the flour and all of the oats, sugar, yeast, and salt in a large bowl, and stir to mix well. Set aside.

2. Place the milk in a small saucepan, and heat until very warm (125°F to 130°F). Add the milk to the flour mixture, and stir for 1 minutes. Stir in the lemon juice. Stir in enough of the remaining flour, 2 tablespoons at a time, to form a soft dough.

3. Sprinkle 2 tablespoons of the remaining flour over a clean dry surface, and turn the dough onto the surface. Knead the dough for 5 minutes, gradually adding just enough of the remaining flour to form a smooth, satiny ball.

4. Coat a large bowl with nonstick cooking spray, and place the dough in the bowl. Cover the bowl with a clean kitchen towel, and let rise in a warm place for about 40 minutes, or until doubled in size.

5. To make the filling, place the apples, raisins, sugar, and cinnamon in a small bowl, and toss to mix well. Set aside.

6. Place the dough on a large floured cutting board, and pat it into a 10-inch circle. Pile the apple mixture on top of the dough, and draw the dough up and around the apple mixture so that the edges of the dough meet in the middle, completely covering the apple filling. Flatten the dough into an 8-inch circle.

7. Using a large sharp knife, slice the mound 5 times in one direction, cutting through to the board. Then slice 5 times in the other direction to form pieces of dough that are about 1½ inches square. Use the knife to gently mix the dough and apple mixture by lifting the mixture from the bottom and piling it back on top.

8. Coat a baking sheet with nonstick cooking spray, and gently mound the dough onto the sheet. Using your hands, gently shape the dough into an 8-inch circle, making sure that most of the apple mixture is touching pieces of dough. (This will insure that the dough holds together as it bakes.)

9. Cover the dough with a clean kitchen towel, and let rise in a warm place for about 30 minutes, or until nearly doubled in size. Brush the top lightly with the 2 teaspoons of skim milk. Bake at 350°F for about 23 minutes, or until the bread is light golden brown and puffy. Remove the bread from the oven, and allow to cool for 3 to 5 minutes.

10. To make the glaze, place all of the glaze ingredients in a small bowl, and stir until smooth. Drizzle the glaze over the warm loaf. Immediately cut into wedges, or simply pull off chunks and serve warm.

NUTRITIONAL FACTS (PER SERVING)
Calories: 194 Carbohydrates: 44 g Cholesterol: 0 mg
Fat: 0.4 g Fiber: 1.4 g Protein: 4.1 g Sodium: 78 mg

You Save: Calories: 60 Fat: 8 g

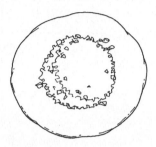

a. Pile the filling on the circle of dough.

b. Draw the dough up and around the filling.

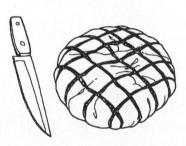

c. Slice the dough-wrapped mound 5 times in each direction.

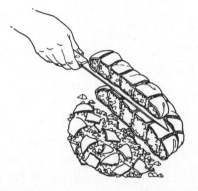

d. Use a knife to gently mix the dough and the filling.

Making Cinnamon-Apple Chop Bread.

Time-Saving Tip

To make the dough for Cinnamon-Apple Chop Bread in a bread machine, simply place all of the dough ingredients except for ¼ cup of the flour in the machine's bread pan. (Do not heat the milk.) Turn the machine to the "rise," "dough," "manual," or equivalent setting so that the machine will mix, knead, and let the dough rise once.

Check the dough about 5 minutes after the machine has started. If the dough seems too sticky, add more of the remaining flour, a tablespoon at a time. When the dough is ready, remove it from the bread machine and proceed to shape, fill, and bake it as directed in the recipe.

Prune-Filled Tea Bread

Yield: *16 slices*

DOUGH

2 cups unbleached flour

3 tablespoons sugar

2 teaspoons Rapid Rise yeast

½ teaspoon salt

¾ cup skim milk

1 egg white

¾ cup whole wheat pastry flour

2 teaspoons skim milk or beaten egg white

FILLING

1 cup chopped prunes

1 cup white grape juice

GLAZE

⅓ cup confectioners' sugar

1¼ teaspoons white grape juice

¼ teaspoon almond extract

For variety, substitute chopped dried apricots for the prunes.

1. To prepare the filling, combine the prunes and juice in a 1-quart saucepan, and bring to a boil over high heat. Reduce the heat to low, cover, and simmer for 15 to 20 minutes, or until the prunes have absorbed the liquid. Remove the pot from the heat and let the mixture cool to room temperature.

2. To make the dough, combine the unbleached flour with the sugar, yeast, and salt in a large bowl. Stir to mix well, and set aside.

3. Place the milk in a small saucepan, and heat until very warm (125°F to 130°F). Add the milk to the flour mixture, and stir for 1 minute. Stir in the egg white.

4. Add 2 tablespoons of the whole wheat flour to the dough, and stir to mix. Continue to add the flour in 2-tablespoon portions until a stiff dough is formed.

5. Sprinkle 2 tablespoons of the remaining whole wheat flour onto a flat surface, and turn the dough onto the surface. Knead the dough for 5 minutes, gradually adding enough of the remaining flour to form a smooth, satiny ball of dough.

6. Scrape the work surface, and lightly sprinkle it with flour. Return the dough to the surface, and, using a rolling pin, roll it into a 11-x-16-inch rectangle. Spread the cooled filling over the dough to within ½ inch of the edges, and roll the rectangle up jelly-roll style, beginning at the long end.

7. Coat a 12-inch round pizza pan or large baking sheet with nonstick cooking spray, and place the roll on the pan, bringing the ends together to form a ring. Using scissors, cut almost all of the way through the dough at 1-inch intervals. Twist each 1-inch segment to turn the cut side up. See illustration on page 93. Cover the pan with a clean kitchen towel, and let rise in a warm place for about 35 minutes or until doubled in size.

8. Lightly brush the top of the loaf with the skim milk or beaten egg white, and bake at 350°F for 16 to 18 minutes, or until lightly browned. Remove from the oven and let sit for 3 to 5 minutes.

9. To make the glaze, combine the glaze ingredients in a small bowl, stirring until smooth. Drizzle the glaze over the warm bread and serve immediately.

NUTRITIONAL FACTS (PER SLICE)
Calories: 135 Cholesterol: 0 mg Fat: 0.3 g
Fiber: 2.2 g Protein: 3.4 g Sodium: 78 mg

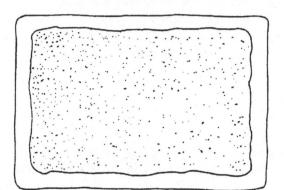

a. Spread the filling over the dough.

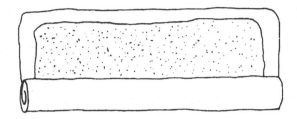

b. Roll the dough up jelly-roll style.

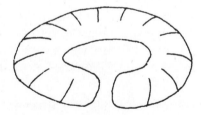

c. Bend the roll into a ring, and cut almost all the way through at 1-inch intervals.

d. Twist each 1-inch segment to turn the cut side up.

Time-Saving Tip

To make the dough for Prune-Filled Tea Bread in a bread machine, simply place all of the dough ingredients in the machine's bread pan. (Do not heat the liquids.) Turn the machine to the "rise," "dough," "manual," or an equivalent setting so that the machine will mix, knead, and let the dough rise once. Check the dough about 5 minutes after the machine has started. If the dough seems too sticky, add more flour, a tablespoon at a time. If it seems too stiff, add more liquid, a teaspoon at a time. When the dough is ready, remove it from the machine and proceed to shape and bake it as directed in the recipe.

Applesauce Sticky Buns

Yield: *12 buns*

DOUGH

1½ cups unbleached flour

2 tablespoons sugar

1½ teaspoons Rapid Rise yeast

¼ teaspoon salt

¾ cup plus 2 tablespoons
   unsweetened applesauce

1 egg white

¾ cup whole wheat pastry flour

FILLING

2 tablespoons maple syrup

¼ teaspoon ground cinnamon

¼ cup plus 2 tablespoons dark
   raisins

3 tablespoons chopped walnuts
   (optional)

GLAZE

⅓ cup maple syrup

1. To make the dough, combine the unbleached flour, sugar, yeast, and salt, and stir to mix well. Set aside.

2. Place the applesauce in a small saucepan, and heat until very warm (125°F to 130°F). Add the applesauce to the flour mixture and stir for 1 minute. Stir in the egg white.

3. Add 2 tablespoons of the whole wheat flour to the dough, and stir to mix. Continue to add the flour in 2-tablespoon portions until a stiff dough is formed.

4. Sprinkle 2 tablespoons of the remaining whole wheat flour onto a flat surface, and turn the dough onto the surface. Knead the dough for 5 minutes, gradually adding enough of the remaining flour to form a smooth, satiny ball of dough.

5. Scrape the work surface, and lightly sprinkle it with flour. Return the dough to the surface, and, using a rolling pin, roll into a 10-x-12-inch rectangle. Combine the 2 tablespoons maple syrup and the cinnamon, and spread the mixture over the dough to within ½ inch of the edges. Sprinkle the raisins and desired, the walnuts over the syrup, and roll the rectangle jelly-roll style, beginning at the long end.

6. Coat a 9-inch round pan with nonstick cooking spray, and pour the ⅓ cup of maple syrup over the bottom of the pan. Cut the rolled-up dough into 1-inch slices, and lay the slices in the pan, cut side up, spacing them ½ inch apart. Cover the pan with a clean kitchen towel, and let rise in a warm place for about 35 minutes, or until doubled in size.

7. Bake at 350°F for 20 minutes, or until lightly browned. Remove the pan from the oven, and run a knife around the edge of the pan to loosen the buns. Immediately invert the buns onto a serving plate, and serve warm.

NUTRITIONAL FACTS (PER BUN)
Calories: 143 Cholesterol: 0 mg Fat: 0.3 g
Fiber: 1.8 g Protein: 3.1 g Sodium: 52 mg

Time-Saving Tip

Like the dough for the Prune-Filled Tea Bread, the dough for Applesauce Sticky Buns may be mixed in a bread machine. Just follow the directions on page 93.

Cinnamon-Raisin Sticky Buns

1. To make the glaze, place the honey in a 1-quart saucepan. Stir the cornstarch into the juice, and add to the honey. Place the pot on medium heat, and cook, stirring constantly, until the mixture comes to a boil and thickens slightly. Remove the pot from the heat, and set aside.

2. To make the dough, combine 1 cup of the flour with all of the bran, sugar, yeast, and salt, and stir to mix well.

3. Place the milk in a small saucepan, and heat until very warm (125°F to 130°F). Add the milk to the flour mixture, and stir for 1 minute. Stir in the egg white.

4. Adding 2 tablespoons at a time, stir enough of the remaining flour into the flour mixture to form a stiff dough. Sprinkle 2 tablespoons of the flour over a flat surface, and turn the dough onto the surface. Knead the dough for 5 minutes, gradually adding enough of the remaining flour to form a smooth, satiny ball.

5. Using a rolling pin, roll the dough into a 10-x-12-inch rectangle. Remove 3 tablespoons of the glaze, place it in a small dish, and stir in the cinnamon. Spread the mixture over the dough, extending it to within ½ inch of the edges. Sprinkle the raisins and, if desired, the nuts over the syrup. Roll the rectangle up jelly-roll style, beginning with the long end. Set aside.

6. Coat a 9-inch round pan with nonstick cooking spray, and pour the remaining glaze over the bottom of the pan. Cut the dough roll into 1-inch slices, and lay the slices flat in the pan, spacing them ½ inch apart. Cover the pan with a clean kitchen towel, and let the buns rise in a warm place until double in size, about 35 minutes.

7. Bake at 350°F for 18 to 20 minutes, or until lightly browned. Remove the pan from the oven, and run a knife around the edges to loosen the buns. Immediately invert onto a serving platter, and serve warm.

Yield: *12 buns*

2 cups unbleached flour

½ cup oat bran

2 tablespoons sugar

1½ teaspoons Rapid Rise yeast

¼ teaspoon salt

¾ cup skim milk

1 egg white

½ teaspoon ground cinnamon

¼ cup plus 2 tablespoons dark raisins

¼ cup chopped pecans or walnuts (optional)

GLAZE

¼ cup plus 2 tablespoons honey

1½ teaspoons cornstarch

¼ cup plus 2 tablespoons orange or apple juice

NUTRITIONAL FACTS (PER SERVING)
Calories: 148 Calcium: 28 mg Cholesterol: 0 mg
Fat: 0.4 g Fiber: 1.2 g Iron: 1.2 mg
Potassium: 121 mg Protein: 3.5 g Sodium: 56 mg

A Dough for All Seasons

Warm, fragrant, and delicious, sweet yeast breads, cakes, and buns are always a special treat. And with just one recipe, you can make an infinite number of tantalizing baked goods. Use Whole Wheat Sweet Dough to prepare some of the yeast dessert breads presented in this chapter, or draw upon your imagination to create your own cinnamon rolls, coffee cakes, buns, and breads.

If the thought of making yeast dough from scratch scares you, fear not. This recipe is easily mixed by hand. Or, if you own a bread machine, follow the simple instructions provided at the end of the recipe to prepare this versatile dough with a minimum of fuss.

Whole Wheat Sweet Dough

Yield: *about 1 pound, or 16 servings*

¼ cup warm water (105°F–115°F)

2 teaspoons Rapid Rise yeast

⅓ cup sugar, divided

2 cups unbleached flour

¾ cup whole wheat pastry flour

½ teaspoon salt

½ cup plus 2 tablespoons nonfat or low-fat buttermilk, warmed to room temperature

1. Place the water, yeast, and 1 teaspoon of the sugar in a small bowl, and stir to dissolve the yeast. Set aside.

2. Place the remaining sugar, ¾ cup of the unbleached flour, and all of the whole wheat flour and salt in a large bowl, and stir to mix well.

3. Add the yeast mixture and the buttermilk to the flour mixture, and stir for 1 minute. Stir in enough of the remaining unbleached flour, 2 tablespoons at a time, to form a soft dough.

4. Sprinkle 2 tablespoons of the remaining unbleached flour over a dry surface, and turn the dough onto the surface. Knead the dough for 5 minutes, gradually adding just enough of the remaining flour to form a smooth, satiny ball.

5. Coat a large bowl with nonstick cooking spray, and place the dough in the bowl. Cover the bowl with a clean kitchen towel, and let rise in a warm place for about 1 hour, or until doubled in size. Then proceed to shape, fill, and bake the dough according to recipe directions.

NUTRITIONAL FACTS (PER SERVING)
Calories: 89 Carbohydrates: 19 g Cholesterol: 0 mg
Fat: 0.3 g Fiber: 1.1 g Protein: 2.5 g Sodium: 77 mg

You Save: Calories: 45 Fat: 5 g

Time-Saving Tip

To make Whole Wheat Sweet Dough in a bread machine, simply place all of the dough ingredients except for cup of the unbleached flour in the machine's bread pan. (Do not heat the water.) Turn the machine to the "rise," "dough," "manual," or equivalent setting so that the machine will mix, knead, and let the dough rise once.

Check the dough about 5 minutes after the machine has started. If the dough seems too sticky, add more of the remaining flour, a tablespoon at a time. When the dough is ready, remove it from the machine and proceed to shape, fill, and bake it as directed in the recipe of your choice.

Cinnamon-Raisin Ring

1. Place the dough on a lightly floured surface, and, using a rolling pin, roll it into an 11-x-16-inch rectangle. Place the margarine, sugar, and cinnamon in a small dish, stir to mix well, and spread the mixture over the dough to within ¼ inch of the edges. Sprinkle the raisins and, if desired, the nuts over the margarine mixture. Roll the rectangle up jelly-roll style, beginning at the long end.

2. Coat a 14-inch pizza pan or a large nonstick baking sheet with nonstick cooking spray, and place the roll on the pan, bringing the ends around to form a circle. Using scissors, cut almost all of the way through the dough at 1-inch intervals. Twist each 1-inch segment to turn the cut side up. (See the figure on page 93.) Cover with a clean kitchen towel, and let rise in a warm place for 35 to 45 minutes, or until doubled in size.

3. Lightly brush the top of the ring with the 2 teaspoons of skim milk, and bake at 350°F for about 15 minutes, or until lightly browned. Remove from the oven, and allow to cool for 3 minutes.

4. To make the glaze, place all of the glaze ingredients in a small bowl, and stir until smooth. Drizzle the glaze over the warm ring, and serve immediately.

NUTRITIONAL FACTS (PER SERVING)

Calories: 118 Carbohydrates: 27.5 g Cholesterol: 0 mg
Fat: 0.3 g Fiber: 1.1 g Protein: 2.6 g Sodium: 89 mg

You Save: Calories: 56 Fat: 7 g

Yield: *16 servings*

1 recipe Whole Wheat Sweet Dough (page 96)

2 teaspoons skim milk

FILLING

2 tablespoons tub-style nonfat margarine, or 3 tablespoons reduced-fat margarine or light butter, softened to room temperature

2 tablespoons sugar

¾ teaspoon ground cinnamon

½ cup dark raisins

⅓ cup chopped toasted pecans or walnuts (page 383) (optional)

GLAZE

½ cup powdered sugar

⅛ teaspoon ground cinnamon

2½ teaspoons skim milk

½ teaspoon vanilla extract

Cherry-Almond Ring

Yield: *16 servings*

1 recipe Whole Wheat Sweet Dough (page 96)

2 teaspoons skim milk

2 tablespoons sliced toasted almonds

FILLING

1 cup chopped pitted fresh or frozen (unthawed) cherries

¼ cup sugar

3 tablespoons white grape juice, divided

1 tablespoon cornstarch

GLAZE

½ cup powdered sugar

2½ teaspoons skim milk

¼ teaspoon vanilla extract

¼ teaspoon almond extract

1. To make the filling, place the cherries, sugar, and 2 tablespoons of the juice in a 1-quart pot, and bring to a boil over medium-high heat, stirring constantly. Reduce the heat to low, cover, and simmer for about 4 minutes, or until the cherries are soft.

2. Place the remaining tablespoon of juice and the cornstarch in a small bowl, and stir to dissolve the cornstarch. Add the cornstarch mixture to the cherries, and cook and stir for another minute or 2, or until the mixture is thick and bubbly. Remove the pot from the heat, and allow the mixture to cool to room temperature.

3. Place the dough on a lightly floured surface, and, using a rolling pin, roll it into an 11-x-16-inch rectangle. Spread the cherry filling frozen (unthawed) cherries over the dough to within ½ inch of the edges. Roll the rectangle up jelly roll-style, beginning at the long end.

4. Coat a 14-inch pizza pan or a large nonstick baking sheet with nonstick cooking spray, and place the roll on the pan, bringing the ends around to form a circle. Using scissors, cut almost all of the way through the dough at 1-inch intervals. Twist each 1-inch segment to turn the cut side up. (See the figure on page 93.) Cover with a clean kitchen towel, and let rise in a warm place for 35 to 45 minutes, or until doubled in size.

5. Lightly brush the top of the ring with the 2 teaspoons of skim milk, and bake at 350°F for about 15 minutes, or until lightly browned. Remove from the oven, and allow to cool for 3 minutes.

6. To make the glaze, place all of the glaze ingredients in a small bowl, and stir until smooth. Drizzle the glaze over the warm ring, sprinkle the almonds over the top, and serve immediately.

NUTRITIONAL FACTS (PER SERVING)
Calories: 125 Carbohydrates: 27 g Cholesterol: 0 mg
Fat: 0.6 g Fiber: 1.2 g Protein: 2.9 g Sodium: 78 mg

You Save: Calories: 60 Fat: 7.2 g

Apple Streusel Loaf

1. Place the dough on a lightly floured surface, and, using a rolling pin, roll it into a 10-x-14-inch rectangle. Coat a large baking sheet with nonstick cooking spray, and transfer the dough to the sheet.

2. Using a sharp knife, make 3¼-inch-long cuts at 1-inch intervals on both of the 14-inch sides. Spread the pie filling down the center third of the dough. Fold the strips diagonally over the filling, overlapping them to create a braided look. (See the figure on page 101.)

3. Cover the loaf with a clean kitchen towel, and let rise in a warm place for about 45 minutes, or until doubled in size.

4. To make the streusel topping, place the flour, brown sugar, and cinnamon in a small bowl, and stir to mix well. Add the nonfat margarine, and stir until the mixture is moist and crumbly. (If you are using reduced-fat margarine, use a pastry cutter or 2 knives to cut the margarine into the flour mixture until it is moist and crumbly.) If the mixture seems too dry, add more margarine, ¼ teaspoon at a time, until the proper consistency is reached. Stir in the wheat germ and the pecans or walnuts.

5. Lightly brush the top of the loaf with the skim milk. Sprinkle with the streusel topping.

6. Bake at 350°F for about 22 minutes, or until the loaf is lightly browned. Remove from the oven, and let sit for 3 minutes before adding the glaze.

7. To make the glaze, place all of the glaze ingredients in a small bowl, and stir until smooth. Drizzle the glaze over the loaf. Let the loaf sit for 5 minutes before slicing and serving warm.

Yield: *14 servings*

1 recipe Whole Wheat Sweet Dough (page 96)

1 can (20 ounces) light (reduced-sugar) apple pie filling

2 teaspoons skim milk

STREUSEL TOPPING

3 tablespoons whole wheat pastry flour

3 tablespoons light brown sugar

¼ teaspoon ground cinnamon

2 teaspoons chilled tub-style non-fat margarine, or 1 tablespoon chilled reduced-fat margarine, cut into pieces

2 tablespoons honey crunch wheat germ

2 tablespoons chopped toasted pecans or walnuts (page 383)

GLAZE

⅓ cup powdered sugar

1½ teaspoons skim milk

¼ teaspoon vanilla extract

⅛ teaspoon ground cinnamon

NUTRITIONAL FACTS (PER SERVING)
Calories: 162 Carbohydrates: 35 g Cholesterol: 0 mg
Fat: 1 g Fiber: 1.7 g Protein: 3.5 g Sodium: 111 mg

You Save: Calories: 62 Fat: 7.3 g

CHERRY-CHEESE LOAF

Yield: *14 slices*

1 recipe Whole Wheat Sweet Dough (page 96)

2 teaspoons skim milk

2 tablespoons chopped toasted almonds, pecans, walnuts, or hazelnuts (page 383)

FILLING

1 block (8 ounces) nonfat cream cheese, softened to room temperature

¼ cup sugar

2 tablespoons fat-free egg substitute, or 1 egg white

2 tablespoons unbleached flour

1 teaspoon vanilla extract

1 cup canned light (reduced-sugar) cherry pie filling

GLAZE

½ cup powdered sugar

2½ teaspoons skim milk

½ teaspoon vanilla extract

1. To make the filling, place the cream cheese and sugar in a medium-sized bowl, and beat with an electric mixer until smooth. Add the egg substitute or egg white, flour, and vanilla extract, and beat until smooth. Set aside.

2. Place the dough on a lightly floured surface, and, using a rolling pin, roll it into a 10-x-14-inch rectangle. Coat a large baking sheet with nonstick cooking spray, and transfer the dough to the sheet.

3. Using a sharp knife, make 3¼-inch-long cuts at 1-inch intervals on both of the 14-inch sides. Spread the cheese filling down the center third of the dough; then cover the cheese mixture with the cherry pie filling. Fold the strips diagonally over the filling, overlapping them to create a braided look.

4. Cover the loaf with a clean kitchen towel, and let rise in a warm place for about 45 minutes, or until doubled in size.

5. Lightly brush the top of the loaf with the skim milk. Bake at 350°F for about 22 minutes, or until the loaf is lightly browned. Remove the loaf from the oven, and set aside while you prepare the glaze.

6. To make the glaze, place all of the glaze ingredients in a small bowl, and stir until smooth. Drizzle the glaze over the loaf, and sprinkle with the nuts. Let sit for 10 minutes before slicing and serving warm.

NUTRITIONAL FACTS (PER SERVING)
Calories: 165 Carbohydrates: 34 g Cholesterol: 2 mg
Fat: 0.9 g Fiber: 1.3 g Protein: 6 g Sodium: 158 mg

You Save: Calories: 118 Fat: 13.1 g

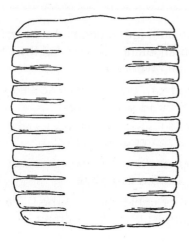

a. Make 3¼-inch-long cuts at 1-inch intervals on each side of the dough.

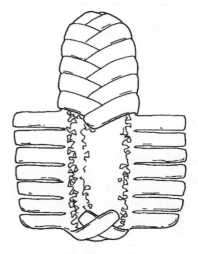

b. Fold the dough strips diagonally over the filling.

c. Continue folding the strips to create a "braided" loaf.

Making Cherry-Cheese Loaf.

REALLY RASPBERRY SCONES

Yield: *12 scones*

1½ cups unbleached flour

1 cup quick-cooking oats

2 tablespoons sugar

2 teaspoons baking powder

½ teaspoon baking soda

1 egg white

¾ cup plus 2 tablespoons lemon
   or vanilla nonfat yogurt

½ cup chopped fresh or frozen
   raspberries

Skim milk or 1 beaten egg white

1. Combine the flour, oats, sugar, baking powder, and stir to mix well. Stir in the egg white and just enough baking soda, and of the yogurt to form a stiff dough. Gently stir in the raspberries.

2. Form the dough into a ball, and turn onto a lightly floured surface. With floured hands, pat the dough into a 7-inch circle.

3. Coat a baking sheet with nonstick cooking spray. Place the dough on the sheet, and use a sharp floured knife to cut it into 12 wedges. Pull the wedges out slightly to leave a ½-inch space between. Brush the tops lightly with skim milk or beaten egg white.

4. Bake at 375°F for 20 minutes, or until lightly browned. Transfer to a serving plate, and serve hot with raspberry fruit spread.

NUTRITIONAL FACTS (PER SLICE)
Calories: 112 Calcium: 42 mg Cholesterol: 0 mg
Fat: 0.5 g Fiber: 1.5 g Iron: 1.1 mg
Potassium: 85 mg Protein: 3.8 g Sodium: 104 mg

Cherry Apple Scones

If you are unable to find dried cherries, substitute golden raisins or dried cranberries.

1. Combine the flours, sugar, baking powder, and baking soda, and stir to mix well. Stir in the egg white and just enough of the applesauce to form a stiff dough. Stir in the dried cherries.

2. Form the dough into a ball, and turn onto a lightly floured surface. With floured hands, pat the dough into a 7-inch circle.

3. Coat a baking sheet with nonstick cooking spray. Place the dough on the sheet, and use a sharp floured knife to cut it into 12 wedges. Pull the wedges out slightly to leave a ½-inch space between them. Brush the tops lightly with skim milk or beaten egg white.

4. Bake at 375°F for about 20 minutes, or until lightly browned. Transfer to a serving plate, and serve hot with cherry fruit spread or apple jelly.

Yield: *12 scones*

1½ cups unbleached flour

¾ cup whole wheat pastry flour

3 tablespoons sugar

2 teaspoons baking powder

½ teaspoon baking soda

1 egg white

¾ cup plus 2 tablespoons
    unsweetened applesauce

⅓ cup dried cherries

Skim milk or 1 beaten egg white

NUTRITIONAL FACTS (PER SCONE)

Calories: 118 Calcium: 18 mg Cholesterol: 0 mg
Fat: 0.3 g Fiber: 1.8 g Iron: 1.1 mg
Potassium: 99 mg Protein: 3.1 g Sodium: 95 mg

HONEY OAT SCONES

Yield: *12 scones*

1½ cups unbleached flour

1 cup quick-cooking oats

1 tablespoon baking powder

¼ cup honey

3 tablespoons fat-free egg
substitute

⅓ cup dark raisins

¼ cup plus 2 tablespoons nonfat
buttermilk

Skim milk

1. Combine the flour, oats, and baking powder, and stir to mix well. Stir in the honey, egg substitute, raisins, and buttermilk, adding just enough of the buttermilk to form a stiff dough.

2. Form the dough into a ball, and turn onto a lightly floured surface. With floured hands, pat the dough into a 7-inch circle.

3. Coat a baking sheet with nonstick cooking spray. Place the dough on the sheet, and use a sharp floured knife to cut it into 12 wedges. Pull the wedges out slightly to leave a ½-inch space between them. Brush the tops lightly with skim milk.

4. Bake at 375°F for about 20 minutes, or until lightly browned. Transfer to a serving plate, and serve hot.

NUTRITIONAL FACTS (PER SCONE)
Calories: 123 Calcium: 33 mg Cholesterol: 0 mg
Fat: 0.6 g Fiber: 1.4 g Iron: 1.2 mg
Potassium: 94 mg Protein: 3.4 g Sodium: 97 mg

Fruitful Scones

1. Combine the flours, baking soda, and baking powder, and stir to mix well. In a separate bowl, combine the Prune Butter, egg white, and yogurt, and stir to mix well. Add just enough of the prune mixture to the flour mixture to form a stiff dough. Stir in the raisins or cranberries and the nuts if desired.

2. Form the dough into a ball, and turn onto a lightly floured surface. With floured hands, pat the dough into a 7-inch circle.

3. Coat a baking sheet with nonstick cooking spray. Place the dough on the sheet, and use a sharp floured knife to cut it into 12 wedges. Pull the wedges out slightly to leave a ½-inch space between them. Brush the tops lightly with skim milk, and sprinkle with cinnamon sugar if desired.

4. Bake at 375°F for 18 to 20 minutes, or until golden brown. Transfer to a serving plate, and serve hot.

NUTRITIONAL FACTS (PER SCONE)
Calories: 103 Calcium: 38 mg Cholesterol: 0 mg
Fat: 0.3 g Fiber: 1.6 g Iron: 1.1 mg
Potassium: 114 mg Protein: 3.9 g Sodium: 81 mg

Yield: *12 scones*

1½ cups unbleached flour

¾ cup whole wheat pastry flour

¾ teaspoon baking soda

½ teaspoon baking powder

¼ cup plus 2 tablespoons Prune Butter (page 223)

1 egg white

¾ cup plain nonfat yogurt

¼ cup dark raisins or dried cranberries

¼ cup chopped walnuts or pecans (optional)

Skim milk

Cinnamon sugar (optional)

Sunday Morning Scones

Yield: *12 scones*

1 cup whole wheat pastry pastry flour

1 cup unbleached flour

½ teaspoon baking soda

2 teaspoons baking powder

¼ cup reduced-fat margarine or light butter

⅔ cup unsweetened applesauce

⅓ cup nonfat buttermilk

⅓ cup dark raisins (optional)

Skim milk

1. Combine the flours, baking soda, and baking powder, and stir to mix well. Use a pastry cutter to cut in the margarine or butter until the mixture resembles coarse meal. Stir in the applesauce and just enough of the buttermilk to form a stiff dough. Fold in the raisins if desired.

2. Form the dough into a ball, and turn onto a lightly floured surface. With floured hands, shape the dough into a 7-inch circle.

3. Coat a baking sheet with nonstick cooking spray. Place the dough on the sheet, and use a sharp floured knife to cut it into 12 wedges. Pull the wedges out slightly to leave a ½-inch space between them. Brush the tops lightly with skim milk

4. Bake at 400°F for 16 to 18 minutes, or until lightly browned. Transfer to a serving plate, and serve hot.

NUTRITIONAL FACTS (PER SCONE)
Calories: 97 Calcium: 24 mg Cholesterol: 0 mg
Fat: 2 g Fiber: 1.7 g Iron: 0.9 mg
Potassium: 74 mg Protein: 2.7 g Sodium: 142 mg

Fresh Pear Scones

1. Combine the flours and baking powder, and stir to mix well. Stir in the remaining ingredients, adding just enough of the milk to form a stiff dough.

2. Form the dough into a ball, and turn onto a lightly floured surface. With floured hands, pat the dough into a 7-inch circle.

3. Coat a baking sheet with nonstick cooking spray. Place the dough on that sheet, and use a sharp floured knife to cut it into 12 wedges. Pull the wedges out slightly to leave a ½-inch space between them. Brush the tops lightly with skim milk.

4. Bake at 375°F for about 20 minutes, or until lightly browned. Transfer to a serving plate, and serve hot.

Yield: *12 scones*

1 cup unbleached flour

¾ cup whole wheat pastry flour

1 tablespoon baking powder

3 tablespoons maple syrup

3 tablespoons fat-free egg substitute

¾ cup finely chopped fresh pears (about 1 medium)

⅓ cup currants or dark raisins

2–3 tablespoons skim milk

Skim milk

NUTRITIONAL FACTS (PER SCONE)

Calories: 97 Calcium: 33 mg Cholesterol: 0 mg
Fat: 0.3 g Fiber: 1.8 g Iron: 1.1 mg
Potassium: 107 mg Protein: 2.7 g Sodium: 90 mg

4

Hors d'Oeuvres with a Difference

Food and festivity are part of the American way. Let's face it—great food really does liven up a party. Who can resist those creamy dips, those saucy meatballs, or those savory canapés? Unfortunately, traditional party favorites top the list of foods high in fat, sugar, and salt—ingredients that must be limited in a healthy diet. Fatty dips, spreads, meats, cheeses, crackers, and chips are often featured fare on hors d'oeuvres tables. Have a sample of each, and you could easily consume a full day's worth of fat and calories in an hour or two!

Enter low- and no-fat cheeses, nonfat sour cream, light mayonnaise, ultra-lean ground meats, reduced-fat lunch meats, and a host of other products that can help take the fat out of celebrations and get-togethers. You will be delighted to learn how a few simple ingredient substitutions can make a big fat difference in traditional party favorites. For instance, a bowl of dip made with a cup of full-fat sour cream gets about 500 calories and 48 grams of fat from the sour cream alone. Prepare the same dip with nonfat sour cream, and you will eliminate 320 calories and all 48 grams of fat. Scoop up your dip with some low-fat whole grain crackers—or, better yet, with raw carrot and celery sticks—and you will have a wholesome snack that is every bit as tempting as its full-fat counterpart.

This chapter presents a wide range of hot and cold hors d'oeuvres, both plain and fancy. From Shrimp Bruschetta to Fiesta Roll-Ups to Zippy Artichoke Dip, you will find a wealth of festive, party-perfect foods. Add some trays of fresh vegetables, a selection of in-season fruit, and plenty of low-cal beverages, and your menu will be high on satisfaction, yet remarkably low in fat. Friends and family will appreciate this more than you know.

Shrimp Bruschetta

Yield: *48 appetizers*

6 ounces (about 1 cup) diced
    cooked shrimp

1 cup shredded nonfat or
    reduced-fat mozzarella cheese

¾ cup chopped plum tomatoes
    (about 2½ medium)

¾ cup chopped fresh spinach

¼ cup chopped scallions

1 teaspoon crushed fresh garlic

1 teaspoon dried oregano

1 long, thin loaf French bread
    (about 24 x 2 x 1 inches)

1. Combine the shrimp, cheese, tomatoes, spinach, scallions, garlic, and oregano in a medium-sized bowl, and stir to mix well. Set aside.

2. Slice the bread into 48 (½-inch) slices. Arrange the slices on a baking sheet, and bake at 300°F for 12 to 15 minutes, or until crisp and dry.

3. Spread each slice with 1 tablespoon of the shrimp mixture. Increase the oven temperature to 400°F, and return appetizers to the oven for 5 minutes, or just until the cheese is melted.

4. Arrange the appetizers on a serving platter, and serve hot.

NUTRITIONAL FACTS (PER APPETIZER)
Calories: 11 Cholesterol: 7 mg Fat: 0.1 g
Fiber: 0.2 g Protein: 2 g Sodium: 54 mg

Crab-Stuffed Mushrooms

1. Remove and discard the mushroom stems. Wash the mushroom caps and pat dry. Set aside.

2. Combine the bread crumbs, crab meat, cheese, bell peppers, scallions, thyme, and black pepper in a medium-sized bowl, and stir to mix well. Add the egg whites and mayonnaise or sour cream, and stir gently to blend.

3. Coat a shallow baking pan with nonstick cooking spray. Place a heaping teaspoonful of stuffing in each mushroom cap, and arrange the mushrooms in the prepared pan.

4. Bake at 400°F for 20 minutes, or until lightly browned on top. Transfer the mushrooms to a serving platter, garnish with the lemon wedges, and serve hot.

NUTRITIONAL FACTS (PER APPETIZER)
Calories: 19 Cholesterol: 4 mg Fat: 0.2 g
Fiber 0.2 g Protein: 1.9 g Sodium: 50 mg

Yield: *40 appetizers*

40 medium-large fresh mushrooms

2 cups soft bread crumbs

8 ounces (1½ cups) finely flaked cooked crab meat

⅓ cup grated nonfat or reduced-fat Parmesan cheese

⅓ cup finely chopped red bell pepper

⅓ cup finely chopped green bell pepper

¼ cup finely chopped scallions

½ teaspoon dried thyme

¼ teaspoon ground black pepper

2 egg whites, lightly beaten

¼ cup nonfat mayonnaise or nonfat sour cream

Lemon wedges (garnish)

Aloha Meatballs

Yield: *45 appetizers*

MEATBALLS

1 pound ground turkey breast or 95% lean ground beef

1 cup cooked brown rice

1 can (8 ounces) crushed pineapple in juice, drained

1 can (8 ounces) sliced water chestnuts, drained

½ cup chopped scallions

1 tablespoon reduced-sodium soy sauce

1 teaspoon ground ginger

SAUCE

¾ cup unsalted chicken broth

⅓ cup ketchup or chili sauce

3 tablespoons seasoned rice vinegar

2 tablespoons brown sugar

2 teaspoons cornstarch

½ teaspoon ground ginger

1. Combine the meatball ingredients in a medium-sized bowl, and mix thoroughly. Coat a baking sheet with nonstick cooking spray. Shape the meatball mixture into 45 (1-inch) balls, and place the meatballs on the baking sheet.

2. Bake at 350°F for about 25 minutes, or until thoroughly cooked. Transfer the meatballs to a chafing dish or Crock-Pot heated casserole to keep warm.

3. Combine the sauce ingredients in a small saucepan, and stir until the cornstarch is dissolved. Place over medium heat, and cook and stir until the mixture comes to a boil. Reduce the heat to low, and cook and stir for another minute, or until the mixture thickens slightly. Pour the sauce over the meatballs, toss gently to mix, and serve.

NUTRITIONAL FACTS (PER APPETIZER)
Calories: 24 Cholesterol: 6 mg Fat: 0.1 g
Fiber: 0.2 g Protein: 2.5 g Sodium: 49 mg

Time-Saving Tip

To avoid a last-minute rush, make the meatballs in advance. Just cook them as directed—without the sauce—and freeze them in freezer bags. The day before the party, thaw the meatballs in the refrigerator. The next day, simply make the sauce and heat it along with the meatballs.

Chicken Fingers with Honey Mustard Sauce

Yield: *20 appetizers*

3 cups corn flakes

½ teaspoon poultry seasoning

¼ teaspoon ground black pepper

3 tablespoons fat-free egg substitute

3 tablespoons skim milk

1 pound boneless skinless chicken breasts (about 4 breast halves)

Nonstick cooking spray

SAUCE

¼ cup plus 2 tablespoons nonfat or reduced-fat mayonnaise

3 tablespoons spicy mustard

3 tablespoons honey

2 tablespoons lemon juice

1. Place the corn flakes in a blender or food processor, and process into crumbs. (You should get about ¾ cup of crumbs. Adjust the amount if necessary.)

2. Combine the corn flake crumbs, poultry seasoning, and pepper in a shallow dish. Stir to mix well, and set aside.

3. Combine the egg substitute and milk in a shallow dish. Stir to mix well, and set aside.

4. Cut each chicken breast half into 5 long strips. Dip each strip first in the egg mixture, and then in the crumb mixture, turning to coat each side with crumbs.

5. Coat a large baking sheet with nonstick cooking spray, and arrange the strips in a single layer on the sheet. Spray the tops of the strips lightly with cooking spray, and bake at 400°F for 15 minutes, or until the strips are golden brown and no longer pink inside.

6. While the chicken is baking, combine the sauce ingredients in a small dish, and stir to mix well. Arrange the chicken strips on a serving platter, and serve hot, accompanied by the bowl of sauce.

NUTRITIONAL FACTS (PER APPETIZER, WITH 2 TEASPOONS OF SAUCE)
Calories: 51 Cholesterol: 13 mg Fat: 0.4 g
Fiber: 0.1 g Protein: 5.8 g Sodium: 111 mg

Stuffed Finger Sandwiches

Yield: *18 appetizers*

1 long, thin loaf French bread (about 24 x 2 x 1 inches)

½ cup plus 2 tablespoons nonfat cream cheese

½ teaspoon dried Italian seasoning

¾ teaspoon crushed fresh garlic

4 ounces thinly sliced cooked turkey breast

8–10 fresh tender spinach leaves

½ medium red bell pepper, cut in thin strips

½ cup chopped frozen (thawed) artichoke hearts, or ½ cup drained and chopped canned artichoke hearts

1. Using a serrated knife, slice the french bread lengthwise cutting off the top third of the loaf. Using your fingers, remove and discard enough of the soft inner bread to leave only a ½-inch-thick-shell.

2. Combine the cream cheese, Italian seasoning, and garlic in a small bowl, and stir to mix well. Spread half of this mixture evenly over the inside of the bottom shell. Roll up the turkey slices, and arrange them in an even layer over the cream cheese mixture. Lay the spinach leaves over the turkey, and top with a layer of pepper strips. Finish with a layer or artichokes.

3. Spread the remaining cream cheese mixture over the inside of the top shell. Place the top shell over the bottom shell to reform the loaf, and wrap the loaf tightly in aluminum foil or plastic wrap. Chill for several hours or overnight.

4. When ready to serve, unwrap the loaf, and use a serrated knife to cut the loaf diagonally into 1-inch slices. Secure each piece with a wooden toothpick, arrange on a platter, and serve.

NUTRITIONAL FACTS (PER APPETIZER)
Calories: 60 Cholesterol: 8 mg Fat: 0.2 g
Fiber: 0.7 g Protein: 5.5 g Sodium: 179 mg

Fiesta Roll-Ups

1. Combine the sour cream and picante sauce in a small bowl. Stir to mix, and set aside.

2. Spread each tortilla with 3 tablespoons of cream cheese, extending the cheese to the outer edges. Lay 2 ounces of sliced turkey or ham over the *bottom half only* of each tortilla, leaving a 1-inch margin on each outer edge. Place 1 ounce of Cheddar over the turkey, and spread with 1 tablespoon of the sour cream–picante mixture. Arrange 1 lettuce leaf over the cheese, and sprinkle with 1 tablespoon of olives. Arrange 3 tomato slices over the olive layer, and top with 2 tablespoons of scallions.

3. Starting at the bottom, roll each tortilla up tightly. Cut a 1¼-inch piece off each end, and discard. Slice the remainder of each tortilla into six 1¼-inch pieces. Arrange the rolls on a platter, and serve.

Yield: *48 appetizers*

¼ cup nonfat sour cream

¼ cup picante sauce

8 fat-free tortillas (10-inch rounds)

1½ cups nonfat or reduced-fat cream cheese

1 pound thinly sliced cooked turkey breast, or 1 pound thinly sliced ham (at least 97% lean)

8 ounces thinly sliced nonfat or reduced-fat Cheddar cheese

8 large fresh lettuce leaves

½ cup chopped black olives

24 very thin slices of tomato

½ cup sliced scallions

NUTRITIONAL FACTS (PER APPETIZER)
Calories: 48 Cholesterol: 9 mg Fat: 0.2 g
Fiber: 0.3 g Protein: 5.8 g Sodium: 136 mg

Time-Saving Tip

To avoid a last-minute rush, make Fiesta Roll-Ups the day before your party, cover the hors d'oeuvres with plastic wrap, and refrigerate. When guests arrive, simply remove the plastic wrap and serve.

Mexican Bean Dip

Yield: *2½ cups*

1 can (1 pound) pinto beans, rinsed and drained

¼ cup nonfat sour cream

2–3 teaspoons chili powder

½ teaspoon ground cumin

½ cup shredded nonfat or reduced-fat Cheddar cheese

¼ cup thinly sliced scallions

¼ cup sliced black olives

2 tablespoons finely chopped jalapeño peppers

1. Place the beans, sour cream, chili powder, and cumin in a food processor or blender, and process until smooth. Spread the mixture over the bottom of a 9-inch glass pie pan. Top with the cheese, followed by the scallions, olives, and jalapeños.

2. Serve at room temperature or hot. If using a microwave oven, heat at high power for 5 to 6 minutes, or until the edges are bubbly and the cheese is melted. If using a conventional oven, bake at 400°F for 20 minutes. Serve with fat-free tortilla chips.

NUTRITIONAL FACTS (PER TABLESPOON)
Calories: 14 Cholesterol: 0 mg Fat: 0.1 g
Fiber: 0.7 g Protein: 1.2 g Sodium: 44 mg

Blender Salsa

Yield: *2¼ cups*

1 can (1 pound) unsalted whole tomatoes, undrained

½ cup chopped onion

1–2 tablespoons chopped jalapeño peppers

1–2 tablespoons minced fresh cilantro

2 tablespoons red wine vinegar

1 teaspoon chili powder

½ teaspoon salt

This easy-to-make salsa has 75 percent less sodium than most bottled brands.

1. Place all of the ingredients in a food processor or blender, and blend for 5 to 10 seconds, or until well mixed but slightly chunky. Transfer the salsa to a serving dish, cover, and chill for several hours to blend the flavors.

2. Serve with fat-free tortilla chips.

NUTRITIONAL FACTS (PER TABLESPOON)
Calories: 4 Cholesterol: 0 mg Fat: 0 g
Fiber: 0.3 g Protein: 0.2 g Sodium: 35 mg

Zippy Artichoke Dip

1. Combine the sour cream, mayonnaise, mustard, garlic, and pepper in a medium-sized bowl, and stir to mix well. Stir in the artichokes. Transfer the dip to a serving dish, cover, and chill for several hours.

2. Serve with whole grain crackers and raw vegetables.

Yield: *2¼ cups*

1 cup nonfat sour cream

½ cup nonfat or reduced-fat mayonnaise

1 tablespoon grainy Dijon mustard

½ teaspoon crushed fresh garlic

¼ teaspoon coarsely ground black pepper

1 can (14 ounces) artichoke hearts, well drained and chopped

NUTRITIONAL FACTS (PER TABLESPOON)
Calories: 9 Cholesterol: 0 mg Fat: 0 g
Fiber: 0.4 g Protein: 0.7 g Sodium: 51 mg

Hot and Creamy Crab Dip

1. Cut the top from the bread loaf, and set aside. Hollow out the bread, leaving a 1-inch-thick shell. Set aside.

2. Coat a baking sheet with nonstick cooking spray. Cut the removed bread into cubes, and place on the baking sheet. Bake at 350°F for 10 minutes, or until lightly toasted. Set aside.

3. Place the cream cheese, milk, lemon juice, and Worcestershire sauce in a food processor, and process until smooth. Stir in the crab meat and onion. Evenly spread the mixture in the hollowed loaf, cover with the bread top, and wrap in aluminum foil.

4. Bake the filled loaf at 350°F for 1 hour and 15 minutes, or until the dip is hot and creamy. Place the loaf on a serving plate, remove and discard the top, and sprinkle the dip lightly with paprika. Serve hot with whole grain crackers and the toasted bread cubes.

Yield: *3¼ cups*

1 large round loaf sourdough bread

2 cups nonfat or reduced-fat cream cheese, softened

2 tablespoons skim milk

1 tablespoon lemon juice

1 tablespoon white wine Worcestershire sauce

1½ cups (about 8 ounces) flaked cooked crab meat

2 tablespoons finely chopped onion

Ground paprika

NUTRITIONAL FACTS (PER TABLESPOON)
Calories: 13 Cholesterol: 4 mg Fat: 0.1 g
Fiber: 0 g Protein: 2.2 g Sodium: 61 mg

Nut 'n' Honey Dip

Yield: *2¼ cups*

2 cups nonfat ricotta cheese

¼ cup honey

3–4 tablespoons smooth or
  chunky peanut butter

1. Place all of the ingredients in a food processor or blender, and process until well blended. Transfer the dip to a serving dish, cover, and chill for several hours.

2. Serve with sliced apples and pears, chunks of banana, whole fresh strawberries, and fresh pineapple spears.

NUTRITIONAL FACTS (PER TABLESPOON)
Calories: 23 Cholesterol: 1 mg Fat: 0.6 g
Fiber: 0 g Protein: 2 g Sodium: 29 mg

Commendable Crackers and Chips

One of the most healthful and satisfying complements to a tempting dip or spread is a bowl of low-fat whole grain crackers and chips. The list below includes just some of the lowest-fat brands now available in your grocery and health foods stores. When heartier accompaniments are desired, try thinly sliced rounds of whole grain bagels; fingers of firm whole wheat, rye, or pumpernickel bread; or wedges of toasted whole grain pita. These snacks are so delicious that you will find yourself serving them not just at party time, but whenever you're in the mood for a light and healthy snack.

Crackers
Finn Crisp
Hain Fat-Free
Harvest Crisps
Health Valley
Hol Grain
Kavli Norwegian Flatbread
Krispy Cakes
Melba Toast
Mini Rice Cakes

Crackers
Pepperidge Farm
  Wholesome Choice
Ry Vita
Rye Krisp
Stoned Wheat Thins
Triscuits (reduced fat)
Wasa Bread
Wheat Thins (reduced fat)

Chips
Baked Tostitos
Guiltless Gourmet Fat-Free
  Tortilla Chips
Louise's Fat-Free and
  Reduced-Fat Potato Chips
Louise's Reduced-Fat
  Tortilla Chips
Smart Temptations
  Tortilla Chips

Dilly Cucumber Dip

1. Place the cucumber in a food processor or blender, and process until finely chopped. Roll the cucumber in a clean kitchen towel, and squeeze out any excess moisture.

2. Combine the sour cream and mayonnaise in a medium-sized bowl, and fold in the cucumber and all of the remaining ingredients. Transfer the dip to a serving dish, cover, and chill for several hours.

3. Serve with raw vegetables, whole grain crackers, chunks of pumpernickel or sourdough bread, and smoked salmon.

Yield: 2¼ *cups*

1 medium cucumber, peeled, seeded, and cut into chunks

1½ cups nonfat sour cream

½ cup nonfat or reduced-fat mayonnaise

2 tablespoons finely chopped onion

1 tablespoon plus 1½ teaspoons finely chopped fresh dill

NUTRITIONAL FACTS (PER TABLESPOON)

Calories: 13 Cholesterol: 0 mg Fat: 0 g
Fiber: 0 g Protein: 0.4 g Sodium: 41 mg

Bacon and Cheddar Dip

1. Place the cream cheese, sour cream, and mayonnaise in a food processor, and process to mix well. Stir in the Cheddar cheese, bacon, and onion. Transfer the dip to a serving dish, cover, and chill for several hours.

2. Serve with whole grain crackers and raw vegetables.

Yield: 3 *cups*

1 cup nonfat cream cheese, softened

1 cup nonfat sour cream

½ cup nonfat or reduced-fat mayonnaise

1 cup shredded nonfat or reduced-fat Cheddar cheese

4 slices turkey bacon, cooked, drained, and crumbled

2 tablespoons plus 1½ teaspoons finely chopped onion

NUTRITIONAL FACTS (PER TABLESPOON)

Calories: 17 Cholesterol: 2 mg Fat: 0.2 g
Fiber: 0 g Protein: 1.8 g Sodium: 80 mg

5

Soups, Salads, and Vegetable Side Dishes

Mom was right when she told you to eat your vegetables. The most nutrient-rich of all foods, veggies are loaded with vitamins, minerals, and fiber—all powerful preventive medicines in the fight against cancer, heart disease, and many other disorders. As for fat and cholesterol, vegetables contain neither. And they're low in calories, too. A half cup of nonstarchy vegetables like asparagus, broccoli, cauliflower, green beans, or summer squash has a mere 25 calories. Even starchy vegetables like potatoes, corn, and peas have only about 80 calories per half cup. Compare this with the other foods on your plate—a three-ounce portion of roast chicken can have anywhere from 140 to 250 calories, for instance—and it's clear that veggies are a calorie counter's best friend.

Because of the many health benefits of vegetables, it is currently recommended that a healthy diet contain at least three to five servings of veggies a day. This isn't as much as it may seem, as a serving is only one half cup of cooked vegetables, or one cup of raw leafy vegetables. In other words, two good-sized portions of your favorite vegetables at dinner time will probably fulfill your minimum daily requirement.

Of course, when vegetables are fried in oil or swimming in butter or fat-laden sauces, nutritionally, they are not much better than a bowl of chips. But once you know the secrets of fat-free cooking, you will find that there are many ways to make vegetables and salads tasty and appealing without butter, margarine, fatty dressings, or other high-fat foods.

This chapter also presents a variety of delectable low-fat, low-salt soups. Whether you are looking for a golden broth floating with tender noodles and chunks of turkey or a thick and creamy chowder, there's a soup that will meet your needs deliciously. You'll even find tips for giving your favorite soup recipe a slimming makeover. So take out your kettle, and get ready to make soups a healthful part of your menus.

The recipes in this chapter use herbs, spices, and a variety of other ingredients to give vegetables flavor without fat—and without an unhealthy dose of sodium, too. Thanks to products like nonfat cheese and nonfat sour cream, you will find that even home-style vegetable casseroles and creamy Cheddar cheese toppings can be prepared with little or no fat. As an added bonus, these recipes often replace boiling with steaming, stir-frying, and other cooking techniques that minimize nutri-ent loss while keeping veggies bright in color and bursting with garden-fresh flavor. The result? Your vegetable dishes will be not just tasty, but also rich in the vitamins, minerals, and fiber that make them such an important part of your daily diet. Mom would be proud!

Pasta Fagioli Soup

1. Place the ground meat in a 4-quart pot, and brown over medium heat, stirring constantly to crumble, until the meat is no longer pink. Drain off any excess fat. (If the meat is 95-percent lean, there should be no fat.)

2. Add the onion, carrot, celery, tomatoes, seasonings, and beef broth to the pot, and bring to a boil over high heat. Reduce the heat to low, cover, and simmer for 15 minutes, or until the vegetables are tender.

3. Add the beans and pasta to the pot, cover, and simmer for 7 to 9 minutes, or just until the pasta is al dente. (Be careful not to overcook, as the pasta will continue to soften as long as it remains in the hot soup.)

4. Ladle the soup into individual serving bowls, and serve hot.

NUTRITIONAL FACTS (PER 1-CUP SERVING)
Calories: 154 Cholesterol: 25 mg Fat: 2.4 g
Fiber: 3.5 g Protein: 13 g Sodium: 295 mg

Yield: *12 servings*

1 pound 95% lean ground beef or ground turkey breast

1 large onion, chopped

1 large carrot, peeled, halved, and sliced

2 large stalks celery with leaves, thinly sliced

2 cans (1 pound each) unsalted tomatoes, crushed

1 teaspoon dried basil

1 teaspoon dried oregano

1 teaspoon crushed fresh garlic

¼ teaspoon ground black pepper

3 cups beef broth

1 can (1 pound) navy or garbanzo beans, rinsed and drained

6 ounces elbow macaroni or ziti pasta

Turkey Barley Soup

Yield: *8 servings*

6 cups unsalted chicken broth or water

¾ cup hulled barley

2 cups sliced fresh mushrooms

1 cup sliced carrots

1 cup sliced celery (include leaves)

1 cup chopped onion

2 teaspoons chicken bouillon granules

1 teaspoon dried thyme

¼ teaspoon ground black pepper

2 cups diced cooked turkey breast

1. Combine the broth or water and the barley in a 3-quart pot and bring to a boil over high heat. Reduce the heat to low, cover and simmer for 40 minutes, or until the barley is almost tender.

2. Add the mushrooms, carrots, celery, onion, bouillon granules, thyme, pepper, and turkey to the pot. Cover and simmer for 20 minutes, or until the barley and vegetables are tender.

3. Ladle the soup into individual serving bowls, and serve hot.

NUTRITIONAL FACTS (PER 1-CUP SERVING)
Calories: 135 Cholesterol: 30 mg Fat: 0.9 g
Fiber: 3.5 g Protein: 13 g Sodium: 285 mg

Golden Turkey Noodle Soup

1. Combine the broth or water, sweet potatoes, onion, bouillon granules, and pepper in a 3-quart pot, and bring to a boil over high heat. Reduce the heat to low, cover, and simmer for 15 minutes, or until the potatoes are tender.

2. Remove the pot from the heat. Using a slotted spoon, transfer the sweet potatoes to a blender. Add 1½ cups of the hot broth to the blender, and place the lid on the blender, leaving the top slightly ajar to allow steam to escape. Carefully blend the mixture at low speed until smooth.

3. Return the blended mixture to the pot, and place over high heat. Add the carrots and celery, and bring the mixture to a boil. Reduce the heat to low, cover, and simmer for 6 to 8 minutes, or until the vegetables are barely tender.

4. Add the noodles and turkey or chicken to the pot, cover, and simmer, stirring occasionally, for about 8 minutes, or just until the noodles are al dente. (Be careful not to overcook, as the pasta will continue to soften as long as it remains in the hot soup.)

5. Ladle the soup into individual serving bowls, and serve hot.

Yield: *8 servings*

6½ cups unsalted chicken broth or water

1½ cups diced peeled sweet potatoes (about 1½ medium)

1 medium onion, chopped

2 teaspoons chicken bouillon granules

⅛ teaspoon ground white pepper

1 medium carrot, peeled and diced

1 stalk celery with leaves, thinly sliced

4 ounces medium no-yolk noodles

2 cups diced cooked turkey breast or chicken breast

NUTRITIONAL FACTS (PER 1-CUP SERVING)
Calories: 151 Cholesterol: 30 mg Fat: 0.9 g
Fiber: 1.7 g Protein: 13 g Sodium: 287 mg

BARLEY AND CHEESE SOUP

Yield: *6 servings*

2 cups water

½ teaspoon chicken bouillon granules

½ cup plus 1 tablespoon quick-cooking barley

2 tablespoons finely chopped onion

3 cups skim milk, divided

2 tablespoons cornstarch

⅓ cup instant nonfat dry milk powder

⅛ teaspoon cayenne pepper or ground white pepper

1 cup shredded nonfat processed Cheddar cheese, or 1 cup shredded reduced-fat Cheddar cheese

3 tablespoons thinly sliced scallions (garnish)

1. Combine the water, bouillon granules, barley, and onion in a 2½-quart pot, and bring to a boil over high heat. Reduce the heat to low, cover, and simmer for 10 to 12 minutes, or until the barley is tender.

2. Combine ¼ cup of the milk and all of the cornstarch in a small bowl, and stir until the cornstarch dissolves. Set aside.

3. In a medium-sized bowl, combine the remaining 2¾ cups of milk with the milk powder and the cayenne or white pepper, and mix until smooth. Add the milk to the pot, increase the heat to medium, and cook, stirring constantly, just until the mixture begins to boil.

4. Stir the cornstarch mixture once, and add it to the pot. Cook and stir for 1 minute, or until the mixture thickens slightly.

5. Add the cheese to the pot, and stir until the cheese melts. Remove the pot from the heat, ladle the soup into individual serving bowls, and garnish each serving with a sprinkling of scallions. Serve hot.

NUTRITIONAL FACTS (PER 1-CUP SERVING)
Calories: 145 Cholesterol: 6 mg Fat: 0.5 g
Fiber: 1.6 g Protein: 13 g Sodium: 316 mg

Fresh Corn Chowder

1. Combine the water, potatoes, celery, onion, bouillon granules, savory, and pepper in a 3-quart pot, and bring to a boil over high heat. Reduce the heat to low, cover, and simmer for 15 minutes, or until the potatoes are almost tender.

2. Add the corn to the pot. Cover and simmer for 5 minutes, or until the potatoes and corn are tender.

3. Place the milk in a medium-sized bowl, and stir in the milk powder. Add the mixture to the pot, and cook, stirring constantly, for about 5 minutes, or until the mixture is heated through.

4. Remove 4 cups of soup—including both broth and vegetables—from the pot. Place 2 cups of the removed soup in a blender, and place the lid on the blender, leaving the top slightly ajar to allow steam to escape. Carefully blend the mixture at low speed until smooth. Return the blended mixture to the pot, and repeat this procedure with the remaining 2 cups of soup.

5. Simmer the soup for 5 additional minutes. Ladle the soup into individual serving bowls, and garnish each serving with a sprinkling of chives or scallions. Serve hot.

Yield: *9 servings*

1 cup water

4 cups diced peeled potatoes (about 1½ pounds)

½ cup thinly sliced celery

½ cup chopped onion

2½ teaspoons chicken bouillon granules

1½ teaspoons dried savory

¼ teaspoon ground white pepper

4 cups fresh or frozen (thawed) whole kernel corn (about 1½ pounds)

3 cups skim milk

¼ cup plus 2 tablespoons instant nonfat dry milk powder

3 tablespoons finely chopped fresh chives or scallions (garnish)

NUTRITIONAL FACTS (PER 1-CUP SERVING)
Calories: 164 Cholesterol: 2 mg Fat: 1.1 g
Fiber: 3.1 g Protein: 7.8 g Sodium: 360 mg

Getting the Fat Out of Your Soup Recipes

Almost everyone has a favorite soup recipe or two. Maybe it's a recipe for Grandma's Chicken Noodle Soup—the one she always made for you when you were sick. Or maybe it's a recipe for the Split Pea with Ham Soup that always appears on your mother's holiday table. More than likely, though, your favorite soup recipe is a little high in fat—especially if it's a cream soup or if it contains meat. If the recipe uses a commercial broth, it may also be high in salt. Fortunately, it's easy to reduce fat and salt in just about any soup recipe you can think of. Here are some tips.

Reducing Fat

❑ If your recipe contains beef, pork, or poultry, use the leanest cuts available, and trim off any visible fats. (See Chapter 1 for a discussion of lean meats and poultry.) If you have to brown the meat before adding it to the soup, be sure to drain off any fat before placing the meat in the soup pot.

❑ After preparing a meat stock or soup, refrigerate it for a few hours or overnight to allow the fat to rise to the top and harden. Lift off the hardened fat for a fat-free broth that has almost no calories.

❑ When there's no time to refrigerate your stock or broth, defat it quickly by placing it in a fat separator cup. This specially designed cup has a spout that pours stock from the bottom of the cup. The fat, which floats to the top, stays in the cup.

❑ If you don't have a fat separator cup, quickly defat your soup with ice cubes. Just place a few ice cubes in a pot of warm—not hot—soup, and let the cubes remain in the stock for a few seconds. Then remove the cubes, as well as the fat that clings to them.

❑ If you choose to use a canned broth, keep in mind that most broths are quite low in fat, and that any fat that is present will have floated to the top. When you open the can, simply spoon out and discard the fat. Now you have a fat-free broth!

❑ If your recipe contains milk, substitute 1-percent low-fat or skim milk for the whole milk. For a richer taste, add one to two tablespoons of instant nonfat dry milk powder to each cup of low-fat or skim milk.

❑ If your recipe contains cream, substitute evaporated skim milk—or one cup of skim or low-fat milk mixed with one-third cup of instant nonfat dry milk powder—for the high-fat cream.

❑ To add extra richness to low-fat cream soups, purée some of the broth and vegetables from the soup. Then return the mixture to the pot to thicken the soup.

❑ If your recipe contains sour cream, substitute a reduced-fat or nonfat brand for the full-fat product.

❑ If your recipe contains cheese, use a reduced-fat or nonfat brand. Most reduced-fat cheeses melt well, although they should be finely shredded for best results. When using nonfat cheeses, always choose a processed cheese, which is specifically designed to melt during cooking.

Reducing Salt

❑ If your recipe has a stock or bouillon base, either use a commercial salt-free or low-salt stock, or make your own stock.

❑ To make your soup more flavorful without using salt, reduce your stock or broth by simmering it uncovered until some of the liquid evaporates. This will intensify the flavors.

❑ To prevent your low-salt soup from tasting flat, add a little lemon juice or vinegar to the finished product. These ingredients give the impression of saltiness.

❑ When decreasing the amount of salt or salty bouillon in a recipe, increase the herbs and spices for added flavor.

❑ Add a pinch of white pepper to your pot of low-salt soup. The pungency of the spice will reduce the need for salt.

CREAMY MUSHROOM SOUP

1. Combine the mushrooms, onions, sherry, marjoram or thyme, salt, and pepper in a 2½-quart pot. Place over medium heat, and cook, stirring frequently, until the mushrooms are tender and most of the liquid has evaporated.

2. Add 2½ cups of the milk and all of the evaporated skim milk to the pot. Cook and stir until the mixture comes to a simmer.

3. Combine the remaining ½ cup of milk and the flour in a jar with a tight-fitting lid, and shake until smooth. Add the flour mixture to the soup, and cook and stir until thickened and bubbly.

4. Ladle the soup into individual serving bowls, and serve hot.

Yield: *5 servings*

4 cups sliced fresh mushrooms

½ cup chopped onion

2 tablespoons dry sherry

1 teaspoon dried marjoram or thyme

½ teaspoon salt

⅛ teaspoon ground white pepper

3 cups skim milk, divided

1 cup evaporated skim milk

⅓ cup toasted garbanzo flour* or unbleached flour

*An excellent thickener for soups, stews, and gravies, garbanzo flour is made by grinding toasted garbanzo beans. This wholesome flour adds a rich nutty flavor to dishes, and boosts nutritional value. Look for it in health foods stores and many grocery stores.

NUTRITIONAL FACTS (PER 1-CUP SERVING)
Calories: 140 Cholesterol: 0 mg Fat: 0.9 g
Fiber: 1.9 g Protein: 12 g Sodium: 330 mg

Summer Vegetable Soup

Yield: *7 servings*

1½ pounds ripe tomatoes (about 4 medium), diced

2 cups unsalted vegetable broth or water

4 cups chopped cabbage

1 cup fresh or frozen (thawed) whole kernel corn

1 cup fresh or frozen (thawed) cut green beans

1 medium onion, chopped

1 medium carrot, peeled, halved, and sliced

¾ teaspoon salt

¼ teaspoon ground black pepper

1 teaspoon dried thyme or marjoram

¼ teaspoon celery seed

2 tablespoons tomato paste

1. Combine the tomatoes and the broth or water in a 4-quart pot, and bring to a boil over high heat. Reduce the heat to low, cover, and simmer for 20 minutes, or until the tomatoes are soft.

2. Add the remaining ingredients to the pot, and simmer for 15 minutes, or until the vegetables are tender.

3. Ladle the soup into individual serving bowls, and serve hot.

NUTRITIONAL FACTS (PER 1-CUP SERVING)
Calories: 68 Cholesterol: 0 mg Fat: 0.8 g
Fiber: 3.7 g Protein: 2.9 g Sodium: 256 mg

TOMATO FLORENTINE SOUP

1. Coat a 3-quart pot with cooking spray or olive oil, and place over medium heat. Add the onions, and sauté for 3 minutes, or until the onions are soft.

2. Add the tomatoes, vegetable broth or water, tomato paste, salt, pepper, and Italian seasoning to the pot. Increase the heat to high, and bring to a boil. Add the pasta, cover, and cook over medium-low heat for 8 minutes, or until the pasta is almost al dente.

3. Add the spinach to the pot, and simmer for 1 to 2 minutes, or just until the pasta is al dente and the spinach is wilted. (Be careful not to overcook, as the pasta will continue to soften as long as it remains in the hot soup.)

4. Ladle the soup into individual bowls, topping each serving with a tablespoon of cheese, if desired. Serve hot.

NUTRITIONAL FACTS (PER 1-CUP SERVING)
Calories: 125 Cholesterol: 0 mg Fat: 0.7 g
Fiber: 3.4 g Protein: 4.5 g Sodium: 258 mg

Yield: *7 servings*

Olive oil cooking spray or 1 tablespoon olive oil

1 medium onion, chopped

1 can (1 pound) unsalted tomatoes, crushed

4 cups unsalted vegetable broth or water

2 tablespoons tomato paste

¾ teaspoon salt

¼ teaspoon ground black pepper

1 teaspoon dried Italian seasoning

4 ounces sea shell pasta

2 cups (packed) chopped fresh spinach

½ cup grated nonfat or reduced-fat Parmesan cheese (optional)

Golden Split Pea Soup

Yield: *8 servings*

1½ cups dried yellow split peas, cleaned (page 200)

1 medium yellow onion, chopped

2 medium sweet potatoes, peeled and diced

6 cups unsalted chicken broth or water

2 teaspoons chicken bouillon granules

2 teaspoons ground cumin

2 teaspoons ground coriander

½ teaspoon ground ginger

½ teaspoon ground turmeric

⅛ teaspoon ground white pepper

1. Combine all of the ingredients in a 3-quart pot, and bring to a boil over high heat. Reduce the heat to low, cover, and simmer, stirring occasionally, for 1 hour, or until the peas are soft and the liquid is thick.

2. Ladle the soup into individual serving bowls, and serve hot.

NUTRITIONAL FACTS (PER 1-CUP SERVING)
Calories: 177 Cholesterol: 0 mg Fat: 0.8 g
Fiber: 7 g Protein: 10 g Sodium: 255 mg

Spanish Bean Soup

1. Combine the beans and the chicken broth or water in a 4-quart pot, and bring to a boil over high heat. Reduce the heat to low, cover, and simmer, stirring occasionally, for 1½ to 2 hours, or until the beans are tender.

2. Add all of the remaining ingredients except for the parsley to the pot, cover, and simmer for about 30 minutes, or until the potatoes are tender.

3. Stir the parsley into the soup. Ladle the soup into individual serving bowls, and serve hot.

NUTRITIONAL FACTS (PER 1-CUP SERVING)
Calories: 172 Cholesterol: 9 mg Fat: 2.3 g
Fiber: 4.8 g Protein: 10 g Sodium: 327 mg

Yield: *9 servings*

1¼ cups dried garbanzo beans, cleaned and soaked (page 200)

8 cups unsalted chicken broth or water

1 large Spanish onion, chopped

1 teaspoon crushed fresh garlic

6 ounces ham (at least 97% lean), diced, or 6 ounces smoked turkey sausage (at least 97% lean), diced

1¼ teaspoons chicken bouillon granules

¼ teaspoon ground white pepper

¾ pound unpeeled potatoes (about 2 medium), diced

1 teaspoon dried saffron

3 tablespoons finely chopped fresh parsley

Antipasto Salad

Yield: *8 servings*

8 cups torn romaine lettuce

¾ cup shredded nonfat or reduced-fat mozzarella cheese

3 ounces thinly shaved turkey pastrami (at least 97% lean)

½ small red bell pepper, cut into thin rings

½ small green bell pepper, cut into thin rings

4 thin slices red onion, separated into rings

¾ cup canned garbanzo beans, rinsed and drained

8 cherry tomatoes, halved

8 Greek salad peppers

8 large pitted black olives (optional)

1. Arrange the lettuce over the bottom of a large serving platter and sprinkle with the cheese. Cut the pastrami into thin strips and arrange over the cheese. Spread the bell pepper and onion rings over the top.

2. Arrange the garbanzo beans, tomatoes, salad peppers, and olives, if desired, around the outer edges of the lettuce. Serve with a dish of bottled nonfat Italian dressing or Creamy Italian Dressing (page 140).

NUTRITIONAL FACTS (PER 1½-CUP SERVING)
Calories: 73 Cholesterol: 7 mg Fat: 0.9 g
Fiber: 2.1 g Protein: 8 g Sodium: 244 mg

Spicy Beet Salad

1. Place the beets, orange juice, salt, and spices in a 2-quart pot and bring to a boil over high heat. Reduce the heat to medium-low, cover, and simmer for 25 minutes, or until the beets are tender.

2. Remove the pot from the heat, and let the beets cool slightly. Add the vinegar and onions, and toss to mix well.

3. Transfer the mixture to a shallow dish, cover, and chill for 8 hours or overnight before serving.

NUTRITIONAL FACTS (PER ⅔-CUP SERVING)
Calories: 58 Cholesterol: 0 mg Fat: 0.2 g
Fiber: 1.8 g Protein: 1.8 g Sodium: 134 mg

Yield: *10 servings*

2 pounds beets (about 6 medium-large), peeled and sliced ¼-inch thick

1½ cups orange juice

¼ teaspoon salt

⅛ teaspoon ground white pepper

¼ teaspoon ground cinnamon

¼ teaspoon ground ginger

⅛ teaspoon ground cloves

¼ cup white vinegar

2 medium sweet onions, thinly sliced

California Carrot Salad

1. Place the carrots and raisins in a large bowl, and toss to mix well.

2. Combine the dressing ingredients in a small bowl, and stir to mix. Pour the dressing over the carrot mixture, and toss to mix well.

3. Cover the salad and chill for several hours or overnight before serving.

NUTRITIONAL FACTS (PER ⅔-CUP SERVING)
Calories: 105 Cholesterol: 0 mg Fat: 0.2 g
Fiber: 2.4 g Protein: 1.4 g Sodium: 101 mg

Yield: *10 servings*

6 cups grated carrots (about 12 medium)

1 cup golden raisins

DRESSING

⅓ cup frozen orange juice concentrate, thawed

⅓ cup nonfat or reduced-fat mayonnaise

⅓ cup nonfat sour cream

Broccoli and Basil Pasta Salad

Yield: *10 servings*

8 ounces rotini or penne pasta

2½ cups fresh broccoli florets

⅔ cup diagonally sliced carrots (about 1 large)

½ cup matchstick-sized pieces red bell pepper (about ½ medium)

DRESSING

½ cup nonfat or reduced-fat mayonnaise

⅓ cup nonfat sour cream

¼ cup orange juice

1 tablespoon mustard

1 tablespoon finely chopped fresh basil, or 1 teaspoon dried

¼ teaspoon ground white pepper

1. Cook the pasta until barely al dente according to package directions. Add the broccoli and carrots to the pot, and cook for another 30 to 60 seconds, or just until the broccoli turns bright green and is crisp-tender. Drain the pasta and vegetables, rinse with cold water, and drain again. Transfer the mixture to a large bowl, and toss in the red pepper.

2. In a small bowl, combine the dressing ingredients, and stir to mix. Pour the dressing over the pasta and vegetables, and toss gently to mix well.

3. Cover the salad and chill for at least 2 hours or overnight before serving.

NUTRITIONAL FACTS (PER ¾-CUP SERVING)
Calories: 115 Cholesterol: 0 mg Fat: 0.5 g
Fiber: 1.5 g Protein: 4 g Sodium: 140 mg

SEVEN-LAYER SLAW

1. Combine the lemon juice and sugar in a small bowl. Add the apples, and toss to mix. Set aside.

2. Combine the sour cream and mayonnaise in a small bowl, and stir to mix well. Set aside.

3. To assemble the salad, place the cabbage in a 2½-quart glass serving bowl. Arrange the apple mixture in a layer over the cabbage, followed by a layer of water chestnuts and a layer of peas. Spread the sour cream mixture over the peas, and sprinkle the cheese over the sour cream. If desired, top with a sprinkling of nuts.

4. Cover the salad and chill for several hours or overnight. To serve, dip a serving spoon down through all of the layers so that each serving includes some of each ingredient.

NUTRITIONAL FACTS (PER ⅔-CUP SERVING)

Calories: 81 Cholesterol: 2 mg Fat: 0.2 g
Fiber: 2 g Protein: 4.2 g Sodium: 264 mg

Yield: *12 servings*

2 teaspoons lemon juice

2 teaspoons sugar

1½ cups chopped peeled apples (about 1½ medium)

1 cup nonfat sour cream

1 cup reduced-fat or nonfat mayonnaise

6 cups shredded cabbage (about ½ medium head)

1 can (8 ounces) sliced water chestnuts, drained

1 cup (about 6 ounces) frozen green peas, thawed

¾ cup shredded nonfat or reduced-fat Cheddar cheese

¼ cup chopped pecans (optional)

Chinese Cucumber Salad

Yield: *8 servings*

3 cups peeled, sliced cucumbers
(about 3 medium)

1 medium onion, thinly sliced

DRESSING

¼ cup seasoned rice wine vinegar

1 tablespoon reduced-sodium soy
sauce

1 teaspoon sesame oil

⅛ teaspoon ground white pepper

1. Place the cucumbers and onions in a shallow dish, and toss to mix.

2. Combine the dressing ingredients in a small bowl, and stir to mix. Pour the dressing over the vegetables, and stir to mix well.

3. Cover the salad and chill for several hours or overnight before serving.

NUTRITIONAL FACTS (PER ½-CUP SERVING)
Calories: 29 Cholesterol: 0 mg Fat: 0.7 g
Fiber: 1.1 g Protein: 1.1 g Sodium: 174 mg

Crowning Touches

Scan the shelves of your local grocery store, and you'll find a dazzling array of reduced-fat and nonfat salad dressings. Unfortunately, many commercial brands contain far too much sodium—sometimes more than 200 milligrams per tablespoon. Make your own dressing, though, and the result will not only be low in sodium and fat, but also full of the fresh-made flavor that only homemade dressings have.

Do croutons have a place on a low-fat salad? Certainly, many commercial brands don't. But if you use the recipe on page 140, you will be able to enjoy crunchy garlicky croutons without paying a high-fat price.

SOUR CREAM-BLUE CHEESE DRESSING

1. Combine all of the ingredients except for ¼ cup of the blue cheese in a food processor or blender, and process for about 1 minute, or until the mixture is smooth. Stir in the remaining blue cheese.

2. Transfer the dressing to a covered container, and refrigerate for several hours before serving.

Yield: 1½ cups

½ cup nonfat sour cream

½ cup nonfat or reduced-fat mayonnaise

¼ cup white wine vinegar

2 cloves garlic

¼ teaspoon ground white pepper

½ cup crumbled blue cheese, divided

NUTRITIONAL FACTS (PER TABLESPOON)
Calories: 17 Cholesterol: 2 mg Fat: 0.6 g
Fiber: 0 g Protein: 0.7 g Sodium: 96 mg

HONEY MUSTARD DRESSING

1. Combine all of the ingredients in a small bowl, and stir to mix well.

2. Transfer the dressing to a covered container, and refrigerate for several hours before serving.

Yield: 1⅛ cups

½ cup nonfat or reduced-fat mayonnaise

¼ cup honey

¼ cup mustard

2 tablespoons lemon juice

NUTRITIONAL FACTS (PER TABLESPOON)
Calories: 21 Cholesterol: 0 mg Fat: 0.2 g
Fiber: 0.1 g Protein: 0.2 g Sodium: 119 mg

CREAMY ITALIAN DRESSING

Yield: *2⅛ cups*

¾ cup nonfat or reduced-fat mayonnaise

¾ cup skim milk

¼ cup red or white wine vinegar

3 cloves garlic

¼ teaspoon dried Italian seasoning

¼ teaspoon ground white pepper

½ cup grated nonfat or reduced-fat Parmesan cheese

1. Combine all of the ingredients in a food processor or blender and process for about 1 minute, or until the mixture is smooth.

2. Transfer the dressing to a covered container, and refrigerate for several hours before serving.

NUTRITIONAL FACTS (PER TABLESPOON)
Calories: 10 Cholesterol: 1 mg Fat: 0 g
Fiber: 0 g Protein: 0.7 g Sodium: 72 mg

GARLIC AND HERB CROUTONS

Yield: *4½ cups*

2 tablespoons chicken or vegetable broth

2 tablespoons grated nonfat or reduced-fat Parmesan cheese

2 teaspoons crushed fresh garlic

¾ teaspoon dried Italian seasoning

6 cups French bread cubes

1. Combine the broth, cheese, garlic, and Italian seasoning in a small dish, and stir to mix well. Rub the mixture over the inside of a large bowl. Place the bread cubes in the bowl, and toss gently to coat the cubes with the garlic mixture.

2. Coat a large baking sheet with nonstick cooking spray. Arrange the bread cubes in a single layer on the sheet, and bake at 350° for 16 to 18 minutes, or until the croutons are lightly browned and crisp.

3. Turn the oven off, and let the croutons cool in the oven with the door ajar for 30 minutes. Store in an airtight container until ready to use.

NUTRITIONAL FACTS (PER 3-TABLESPOON SERVING)
Calories: 21 Cholesterol: 0 mg Fat: 0.2 g
Fiber: 0.2 g Protein: 0.8 g Sodium: 51 mg

Fresh Tomato Dressing

1. Combine all of the ingredients in a food processor or blender, and process for about 1 minute, or until the mixture is smooth.

2. Transfer the dressing to a covered container, and refrigerate for several hours before serving.

Yield: *1½ cups*

1½ medium ripe tomatoes, chopped

¼ cup chopped onion

¼ cup plus 2 tablespoons red wine vinegar

2 tablespoons honey

1 tablespoon olive oil (optional)

1 tablespoon chopped fresh parsley, or 1 teaspoon dried

3 cloves garlic

2 teaspoons ground paprika

¾ teaspoon salt

¼ teaspoon ground black pepper

NUTRITIONAL FACTS (PER TABLESPOON)
Calories: 8 Cholesterol: 0 mg Fat: 0 g
Fiber: 0.1 g Protein: 0.1 g Sodium: 68 mg

South of the Border Salad

Yield: *6 servings*

1 can (1 pound) black beans, rinsed and drained

2 cups (about 12 ounces) frozen whole kernel corn, thawed

½ cup chopped green bell pepper

¼ cup chopped onion

DRESSING

½ cup picante sauce

1–2 tablespoons minced fresh cilantro

1 teaspoon crushed fresh garlic

½ teaspoon ground cumin

1 teaspoon sugar

1. Place the beans, corn, bell pepper, and onion in a large bowl, and toss to mix well.

2. Combine the dressing ingredients in a small bowl, and stir to mix. Pour the dressing over the bean mixture, and toss to mix well.

3. Cover the salad and chill for several hours or overnight before serving.

NUTRITIONAL FACTS (PER ⅔-CUP SERVING)
Calories: 123 Cholesterol: 0 mg Fat: 0.9 g
Fiber: 6.1 g Protein: 6.3 g Sodium: 222 mg

Dillicious Potato Salad

1. Cut the potatoes in ¾-inch pieces, and place in a microwave or stove-top steamer. Cover and cook at high power or on medium-high heat for 8 to 10 minutes, or until tender. Rinse with cool water and drain.

2. Place the potatoes in a large bowl. Add the peas, carrots, onions, and toss gently to mix.

3. Combine the dressing ingredients in a small bowl, and stir to mix well. Pour the dressing over the potato mixture, and toss gently to mix.

4. Cover the salad and chill for at least 2 hours or overnight before serving.

NUTRITIONAL FACTS (PER ¾-CUP SERVING)

Calories: 145 Cholesterol: 0 mg Fat: 0.2 g
Fiber: 3.4 g Protein: 3.7 g Sodium: 146 mg

Yield: *9 servings*

2 pounds unpeeled potatoes (about 6 medium)

1 cup (about 6 ounces) frozen green peas, thawed

⅓ cup finely chopped carrot

⅓ cup chopped onion

DRESSING

¼ cup plus 2 tablespoons nonfat sour cream

¼ cup plus 2 tablespoons nonfat or reduced-fat mayonnaise

1 tablespoon lemon juice

1 tablespoon Dijon mustard

¼ teaspoon ground white pepper

1 tablespoon finely chopped fresh dill, or 1 teaspoon dried

Italian Pasta Salad

Yield: *8 servings*

8 ounces rotini or penne pasta

1 medium tomato, chopped

¼ cup sliced scallions

¼ cup sliced black olives

⅓ cup bottled nonfat Italian dressing

¼ cup grated nonfat or reduced-fat Parmesan cheese

This is a basic salad that can be varied in many ways.

1. Cook the pasta al dente according to package directions. Drain, rinse with cold water, and drain again.

2. Place the pasta in a large bowl. Add the tomato, scallions, and olives, and toss to mix well. Add the Italian dressing and cheese, and toss to mix well.

3. Cover the salad and chill for at least 2 hours or overnight before serving.

NUTRITIONAL FACTS (PER ¾-CUP SERVING)

Calories: 130 Cholesterol: 2 mg Fat: 0.9 g

Fiber: 1.1 g Protein: 4.9 g Sodium: 226 mg

Variations

For variety, add any of the following:

- ½ cup chopped seeded cucumber and ½ cup chopped red bell pepper
- 1 cup lightly steamed broccoli florets
- ¾ pound cooked shrimp
- 1 cup chopped artichoke hearts
- ½ cup zucchini cut into matchstick-sized pieces and ½ cup grated carrot
- 1 cup cooked or canned kidney, garbanzo, or white beans

GREAT GARBANZO SALAD

1. To cook the couscous, place the water in a 1-quart pot, and bring to a boil over high heat. Stir in the couscous, cover, and remove the pot from the heat. Let sit for 5 minutes, or until the water is absorbed. Uncover the pot, and set aside to cool.

2. Place the couscous, garbanzo beans, tomato, cucumber, onion, and parsley in a large bowl, and toss to mix well.

3. Combine the dressing ingredients in a small bowl, and stir to mix. Pour the dressing over the couscous mixture, and toss to mix well.

4. Cover the salad and chill for at least 2 hours or overnight before serving.

NUTRITIONAL FACTS (PER ⅔-CUP SERVING)

Calories: 109 Cholesterol: 0 mg Fat: 0.9 g
Fiber: 2.5 g Protein: 4.7 g Sodium: 90 mg

Yield: *8 servings*

1⅓ cups water

⅔ cup uncooked couscous

1 can (15 ounces) garbanzo beans, rinsed and drained

1 medium tomato, diced

1 medium cucumber, peeled, seeded, and diced

⅓ cup chopped purple onion

2 tablespoons minced fresh parsley

DRESSING

¼ cup red or white wine vinegar

1 tablespoon olive oil (optional)

1 teaspoon dried oregano

⅛ teaspoon ground black pepper

Rainbow Fruit Salad

Yield: *5 servings*

1 cup sliced fresh strawberries

1 cup cubed cantaloupe

1 cup diced kiwi fruit

1 cup sliced bananas

1 cup fresh blueberries

DRESSING

2 tablespoons frozen orange juice
    concentrate, thawed

1 tablespoon honey

¾ teaspoon poppy seeds

1. Place the fruit in a large bowl, and toss to mix.

2. Combine the dressing ingredients in a small bowl, and stir to mix. Pour the dressing over the fruit, and toss to mix well.

3. Cover the salad and chill for 1 to 3 hours before serving.

NUTRITIONAL FACTS (PER 1-CUP SERVING)
Calories: 121 Cholesterol: 0 mg Fat: 0.8 g
Fiber: 4 g Protein: 1.7 g Sodium: 7 mg

ROSEMARY RICE SALAD

1. Place the rice, broccoli, carrots, celery, and raisins in a large bowl, and toss to mix well.

2. Combine the dressing ingredients in a small bowl, and stir to mix. Pour the dressing over the rice mixture, and toss to mix well.

3. Cover the salad and chill for at least 2 hours or overnight before serving.

NUTRITIONAL FACTS (PER ⅔-CUP SERVING)

Calories: 107 Cholesterol: 0 mg Fat: 0.7 g
Fiber: 2.1 g Protein: 2.5 g Sodium: 81 mg

Yield: *8 servings*

3 cups cooked brown rice

1 cup finely chopped fresh broccoli stems

½ cup grated carrots

⅓ cup finely chopped celery

¼ cup dark or golden raisins

DRESSING

¼ cup orange juice

2 tablespoons white wine vinegar

1 tablespoon olive oil (optional)

1 teaspoon crushed fresh garlic

1 tablespoon chopped fresh rosemary, or 1 teaspoon dried

½ teaspoon ground ginger

¼ teaspoon salt

Curried Rice and Bean Salad

Yield: *8 servings*

3 cups cooked brown rice

1 can (1 pound) red kidney beans, rinsed and drained

½ cup chopped green bell pepper

½ cup thinly sliced celery

⅓ cup thinly sliced scallions

¼ cup dark raisins

DRESSING

⅓ cup nonfat or reduced-fat mayonnaise

⅓ cup plain nonfat yogurt

1–2 teaspoons curry powder

⅛ teaspoon ground black pepper

1. Place the rice, beans, bell pepper, celery, scallions, and raisins in a large bowl, and toss to mix well.

2. Combine the dressing ingredients in a small bowl, and stir to mix. Pour the dressing over the rice mixture, and toss to mix well.

3. Cover the salad and chill for at least 2 hours or overnight before serving.

NUTRITIONAL FACTS (PER ¾-CUP SERVING)
Calories: 163 Cholesterol: 0 mg Fat: 0.9 g
Fiber: 4.9 g Protein: 6.2 g Sodium: 209 mg

Winter Fruit Salad

Yield: *8 servings*

3 cups diced unpeeled red delicious apples

1½ cups sliced celery

1 cup seedless green grapes, halved

½ cup dark raisins

DRESSING

¼ cup nonfat mayonnaise

¼ cup nonfat sour cream

1. Combine the apples, celery, grapes, and raisins in a large bowl, and toss to mix well.

2. Combine the dressing ingredients in a small bowl, and stir to mix. Pour the dressing over the apple mixture, and toss to mix well.

3. Cover the salad and chill for 1 to 3 hours before serving.

NUTRITIONAL FACTS (PER ¾-CUP SERVING)
Calories: 82 Cholesterol: 0 mg Fat: 0.3 g
Fiber: 1.6 g Protein: 0.9 g Sodium: 94 mg

Down-Home Lima Beans

1. Combine all of the ingredients in a 2½-quart pot, and bring to a boil over high heat. Reduce the heat to low, cover, and simmer, stirring occasionally, for 1 hour and 30 minutes, or until the beans are soft and the liquid is thick. Periodically check the pot during cooking, and add a little more broth or water if needed.

2. Remove the pot from the heat, and discard the bay leaf. Serve hot.

Yield: *9 servings*

2 cups dried large lima beans, cleaned and soaked (page 200)

5 cups unsalted chicken broth or water

1 medium onion, chopped

1½ teaspoons ham or chicken bouillon granules

1 bay leaf

2 teaspoons dried sage

¼ teaspoon ground black pepper

NUTRITIONAL FACTS (PER ⅔-CUP SERVING)
Calories: 140 Cholesterol: 0 mg Fat: 0.2 g
Fiber: 8 g Protein: 8.5 g Sodium: 175 mg

Country-Style Green Beans

1. Combine the green beans, water, bouillon granules or ham, mustard, and pepper in a 2½-quart pot, and bring to a boil over medium heat. Reduce the heat to low, and simmer uncovered, stirring occasionally, for 2 to 3 minutes, or until the beans turn bright green.

2. Cover the pot, and simmer, stirring occasionally, for 15 to 20 minutes, or until the beans are tender. Serve immediately.

Yield: *6 servings*

1½ pounds fresh green beans, cut into 1-inch pieces

½ cup water

1¼ teaspoons ham bouillon granules, or 3 ounces ham (at least 97% lean), diced

1 teaspoon dry mustard

⅛ teaspoon ground black pepper

NUTRITIONAL FACTS (PER ⅔-CUP SERVING)
Calories: 37 Cholesterol: 0 mg Fat: 0.2 g
Fiber: 3.9 g Protein: 2.2 g Sodium: 176 mg

Mom's Broccoli Casserole

Yield: *8 servings*

2 packages (10 ounces each) frozen chopped broccoli, thawed and squeezed dry

1½ cups cooked brown rice

1½ cups shredded nonfat or reduced-fat Cheddar cheese

2 tablespoons finely ground fat-free cracker crumbs

Nonstick cooking spray

SAUCE

1½ cups skim milk, divided

¼ cup instant nonfat dry milk powder

1 tablespoon plus 1½ teaspoons cornstarch

1 tablespoon water or unsalted chicken broth

½ cup finely chopped fresh mushrooms

½ cup finely chopped onion

¼ teaspoon dried thyme

¼ teaspoon ground black pepper

1. To make the sauce, combine ¼ cup of the milk and all of the milk powder and cornstarch in a small dish. Stir to mix well, and set aside.

2. Place the water or broth, mushrooms, onions, thyme, and pepper in a 2½-quart saucepan, and place the pan over medium heat. Cook and stir for about 2 minutes, or until the vegetables are tender and most of the liquid has evaporated.

3. Add the remaining 1¼ cups of milk to the pot, and continue to cook and stir just until the mixture starts to boil. Stir the cornstarch mixture once, and add it to the pot. Cook and stir for a minute or 2, or until the sauce is thickened and bubbly.

4. Remove the pot from the heat, and stir the broccoli, rice, and cheese into the sauce. Coat a 2-quart casserole dish with nonstick cooking spray, and spread the mixture evenly in the dish. Sprinkle the crumbs over the top of the mixture, and spray the crumbs lightly with nonstick cooking spray.

5. Bake at 350°F for 50 minutes to 1 hour, or until the top is golden brown and the edges are bubbly. Remove the dish from the oven, and let sit for 5 minutes before serving.

NUTRITIONAL FACTS (PER ¾-CUP SERVING)
Calories: 133 Cholesterol: 5 mg Fat: 0.5 g
Fiber: 3 g Protein: 12.7 g Sodium: 248 mg

FAT-FREE COOKING TIP

Sautéing Without Fat

When sautéing vegetables, replace part or all of the fat usually used with broth, sherry, white wine, or another liquid. For every tablespoon of butter you eliminate, you will save 100 calories and 11 grams of fat. Each time you eliminate a tablespoon of oil, you will save 120 calories and 14 grams of fat.

Cauliflower au Gratin

1. Combine the cauliflower and cheese sauce in a large bowl and toss to mix well. Coat a 1½-quart casserole dish with nonstick cooking spray, and spread the mixture evenly in the dish. Sprinkle the crumbs over the top of the mixture, and spray the crumbs lightly with nonstick cooking spray.

2. Bake at 350°F for 30 minutes, or until the top is browned and the edges are bubbly. Remove the dish from the oven, and let sit for 5 minutes before serving.

Yield: 5 servings

1 package (1 pound) frozen cauliflower florets, thawed and drained

1 recipe Cheddar Cheese Sauce (page 159)

2 tablespoons finely ground fat-free cracker crumbs (onion or herb flavor)

Nonstick cooking spray

NUTRITIONAL FACTS (PER ¾-CUP SERVING)
Calories: 80 Cholesterol: 4 mg Fat: 0.3 g
Fiber: 1.8 g Protein: 9 g Sodium: 221 mg

Carrot-Rice Casserole

1. Combine the carrots, rice, onions, herbs, and salt in a large bowl, and stir to mix well. Add the milk and egg substitute, and stir to mix. Coat a 2-quart casserole dish with nonstick cooking spray, and spread the mixture evenly in the dish. Sprinkle the cheese over the top.

2. Bake at 350°F for 50 minutes to 1 hour, or until a sharp knife inserted in the center of the dish comes out clean. Remove the dish from the oven, and let sit for 5 minutes before serving.

Yield: 8 servings

3 cups grated carrots (about 6 medium)

3 cups cooked brown rice

½ cup finely chopped onion

1 tablespoon minced fresh parsley, or 1 teaspoon dried

1 tablespoon minced fresh savory, or 1 teaspoon dried

¼ teaspoon salt

1½ cups evaporated skim milk

½ cup fat-free egg substitute

3 tablespoons grated nonfat or reduced-fat Parmesan cheese

NUTRITIONAL FACTS (PER ¾-CUP SERVING)
Calories: 154 Cholesterol: 3 mg Fat: 0.8 g
Fiber: 2.6 g Protein: 8.5 g Sodium: 184 mg

Cabbage and Potato Curry

Yield: *6 servings*

2 medium unpeeled potatoes, sliced ¼ inch thick

½ cup chicken or vegetable broth

½ medium head cabbage, halved and cut into 1-inch pieces

2–3 teaspoons curry powder

1. Combine the potatoes and broth in a large nonstick skillet. Place the skillet over medium-low heat, cover, and cook, stirring occasionally, for about 10 minutes, or until the potatoes are tender.

2. Add the cabbage and curry to the skillet, and stir to mix. Cover and cook, stirring occasionally, for 7 to 9 minutes, or until the cabbage is tender. Serve hot.

NUTRITIONAL FACTS (PER ¾-CUP SERVING)
Calories: 84 Cholesterol: 0 mg Fat: 0.3 g
Fiber: 2.9 g Protein: 2.8 g Sodium: 83 mg

Cooking Country Style

Southern-style vegetables are typically seasoned with bacon, lard, or ham hocks. Delicious? Absolutely! Healthy? As you might expect, these dishes are loaded with fat and salt. Fortunately, a variety of ingredients can be substituted for the usual Southern flavorings, resulting in mouthwatering dishes that are untraditionally low in fat. Here are some ideas:

❑ *Bouillon granules.* Ham bouillon granules can be added to a pot of beans or cabbage as a fat-free alternative to ham or bacon. Look for a brand like Goya, which is usually located in the ethnic foods section of grocery stores. Chicken- and vegetable-flavored bouillons are still another option. What about sodium? A teaspoon of the granules typically contains 1,000 milligrams of sodium—about half the amount in a teaspoon of salt. You can eliminate salt worries, though, by choosing a brand like Vogue Vege Base, a vegetable bouillon made mostly of powdered vegetables. Do keep in mind that most bouillons contain monosodium glutamate (MSG), and read labels carefully if you want to avoid this ingredient.

❑ *Lean ham.* Many hams—both turkey and pork—are very low in fat. Look for brands that are at least 97 percent lean. Then dice the ham and add small amounts to bean soups, greens, and other vegetables dishes.

❑ *Smoked turkey sausage.* Like lean ham, this product will add a smoky flavor to a variety of dishes. Look for brands like Healthy Choice, which is 97 percent lean, and use the sausage as you would lean ham.

❑ *Smoked turkey parts.* This is a great alternative to ham hocks. Add chunks of skinless smoked turkey to bean soups, green beans, and other vegetables.

❑ *Herbs and spices.* Because sage, fennel, and thyme are traditionally used to flavor sausage, these spices can be used instead of meat to add a country-style taste to bean soups and many vegetable dishes.

❑ *Vinegar.* A splash of vinegar or lemon juice tossed into vegetables just before serving adds zip, reducing the need for salty seasonings. Experiment with different types of vinegar, such as cider, white wine, red wine, rice wine, malt, and balsamic.

Confetti Corn Pudding

Puréed corn, rather than cream, adds richness to this cold dish.

Yield: *6 servings*

1. Place 1 cup of the corn and all of the onion, milk, egg substitute, flour, salt, and pepper in a blender or food processor. Process for 1 minute, or until the mixture is smooth. Add the parsley, and process for an additional 10 seconds.

2. Place the corn mixture in a large bowl, and add the remaining corn kernels and the peppers. Stir to mix well.

3. Coat a 1½-quart casserole dish with nonstick cooking spray and pour the corn mixture into the dish. Bake at 350°F for 1 hour or until a sharp knife inserted midway between the center of the dish and the rim comes out clean. Remove the dish from the oven and let sit for 5 minutes before serving.

1 pound frozen whole kernel corn, thawed, or 3⅓ cups fresh, divided

⅓ cup chopped onion

¾ cup plus 2 tablespoons skim milk

½ cup fat-free egg substitute

2 tablespoons unbleached flour

¼ teaspoon salt

⅛ teaspoon ground black pepper

1 tablespoon chopped fresh parsley, or 1 teaspoon dried

¼ cup finely chopped green bell pepper

¼ cup finely chopped red bell pepper

NUTRITIONAL FACTS (PER ⅔-CUP SERVING)
Calories: 98 Cholesterol: 0 mg Fat: 0.2 g
Fiber: 2.1 g Protein: 5.6 g Sodium: 141 mg

Skillet Squash and Onions

Yield: *6 servings*

1½ pounds zucchini or yellow squash (about 4–5 medium zucchini or 8–10 medium squash)

1 medium yellow onion, sliced ¼-inch thick

2 tablespoons water

2 teaspoons butter-flavored sprinkles

¼ teaspoon ground black pepper

1 tablespoon minced fresh dill, or 1 teaspoon dried

1. Cut each squash in half lengthwise; then cut each half in ¼-inch-thick slices. (There should be about 6 cups of squash. Adjust the amount if necessary.)

2. Place the squash and onions in a large nonstick skillet. Sprinkle the water, butter-flavored sprinkles, pepper, and dill on the top, and place the skillet over medium heat. Cover and cook, stirring occasionally, for 7 to 9 minutes, or just until the vegetables are tender. Serve hot.

NUTRITIONAL FACTS (PER ⅔-CUP SERVING)
Calories: 25 Cholesterol: 0 mg Fat: 0.2 g
Fiber: 1.6 g Protein: 1.5 g Sodium: 30 mg

Stuffed Eggplant Extraordinaire

1. Tear the bread into pieces, and place the pieces in a blender or food processor. Process into fine crumbs, and set aside.

2. Cut each eggplant in half lengthwise, and scoop out and reserve the flesh, leaving a ⅜-inch-thick shell. Trim a small piece off the bottom of each shell, if necessary, to allow each half to sit upright. Set aside.

3. Coat a large skillet with nonstick cooking spray. Finely chop the removed eggplant, and transfer to the skillet. Add the tomato, bell pepper, onion, celery, salt, and black pepper to the skillet, and place over medium heat. Cover and cook, stirring occasionally, for 5 minutes, or until the vegetables are almost tender.

4. Remove the skillet from the heat, and stir in the bread crumbs and parsley. Divide the eggplant mixture among the 4 hollowed-out eggplant shells.

5. Coat a shallow baking dish with nonstick cooking spray, and arrange the stuffed shells in the dish. Sprinkle 1½ teaspoons of cheese over the top of each stuffed shell, and bake at 350°F for 25 minutes, or until the filling is heated through and the top is golden brown.

Yield: *4 servings*

2 slices whole wheat bread

2 small eggplants (about 8 ounces each)

1 medium tomato, finely chopped

⅓ cup finely chopped green bell pepper

⅓ cup finely chopped onion

⅓ cup finely chopped celery

⅛ teaspoon salt

¼ teaspoon ground black pepper

2 tablespoons minced fresh parsley, or 2 teaspoons dried

2 tablespoons grated nonfat or reduced-fat Parmesan cheese

NUTRITIONAL FACTS (PER SERVING)

Calories: 75 Cholesterol: 1 mg Fat: 0.8 g
Fiber: 4.5 g Protein: 4.4 g Sodium: 163 mg

Swiss Onion Bake

Yield: *8 servings*

1½ pounds mild sweet onions (about 4 medium)

1 tablespoon minced fresh parsley, or 1 teaspoon dried

2 tablespoons dry sherry or unsalted chicken broth

1 cup evaporated skim milk

1 cup fat-free egg substitute

¼ teaspoon ground white pepper

1 cup shredded nonfat or reduced-fat Swiss cheese

4 slices uncooked turkey bacon, cut in half (optional)

1. Cut the onions into thin wedges. Coat a large skillet with nonstick cooking spray, and add the onions, parsley, and sherry or broth. Place over medium heat, and cook, stirring constantly, for about 5 minutes, or until the onions are tender. (Add a little more sherry or broth if the skillet becomes too dry.) Remove the skillet from the heat, and set aside for a few minutes to cool slightly.

2. Stir the milk into the onion mixture. Add the egg substitute, pepper, and cheese, and stir to mix.

3. Coat a 2-quart casserole dish with nonstick cooking spray, and spread the onion mixture evenly in the dish. Arrange the bacon slices over the top, if desired, and bake at 375°F for 45 minutes, or until a sharp knife inserted in the center of the dish comes out clean. Remove the dish from the oven, and let sit for 5 minutes before serving.

NUTRITIONAL FACTS (PER ⅔-CUP SERVING)
Calories: 93 Cholesterol: 4 mg Fat: 0.2 g
Fiber: 1.5 g Protein: 11 g Sodium: 189 mg

Stir-Fried Spinach

Yield: *4 servings*

1 pound fresh spinach

1 teaspoon crushed fresh garlic

⅛ teaspoon ground black pepper

2 teaspoons lemon juice

1. Thoroughly wash the spinach and remove all tough stems. Shake off any excess water, but do not dry completely. Set aside.

2. Coat a large skillet with nonstick cooking spray, and preheat over medium-high heat. Add the garlic, and stir-fry for 30 seconds. Add the spinach and pepper, and stir-fry for about 2 minutes, or just until the spinach is wilted and tender.

3. Remove the skillet from the heat, and toss in the lemon juice. Serve hot.

NUTRITIONAL FACTS (PER ½-CUP SERVING)
Calories: 25 Cholesterol: 0 mg Fat: 0.4 g
Fiber: 3.1 g Protein: 3.2 g Sodium: 89 mg

Golden Mashed Potatoes

1. Peel the rutabaga, and dice into ½-inch cubes. Place the rutabaga in 3-quart pot, add enough water to barely cover, and bring to a boil over high heat. Reduce the heat to low, cover, and simmer, stirring occasionally, for 20 minutes, or until the rutabaga is almost tender.

2. Peel the potatoes, and cut into 1-inch pieces. Add the potatoes to the cooking rutabaga, adding water if needed to barely cover the vegetables. Bring to a second boil. Reduce the heat to low, cover, and simmer for 20 minutes, or until the vegetables are very tender.

3. Remove the pot from the heat, and drain off and reserve the cooking liquid. Add the salt and pepper to the vegetables, and mash or beat until smooth. Stir in the sour cream or yogurt, adding a little of the reserved cooking liquid if the mixture is too stiff. Serve hot.

Yield: *8 servings*

1 medium rutabaga (about 1½ pounds)

1½ pounds baking potatoes (about 5–6 medium)

¼ teaspoon salt

⅛ teaspoon ground white pepper

⅓ cup nonfat sour cream or plain nonfat yogurt

NUTRITIONAL FACTS (PER ⅔-CUP SERVING)
Calories: 96 Cholesterol: 0 mg Fat: 0.2 g
Fiber: 3 g Protein: 2.5 g Sodium: 97 mg

Hearty Oven Fries

1. Combine the coating ingredients in a small dish, and stir to mix well. Set aside.

2. Scrub the potatoes, dry well, and cut into ½-inch-thick strips. Place the potatoes in a large bowl. Pour the egg white or egg substitute over the potatoes, and toss to coat evenly. Sprinkle the coating over the potatoes, and toss again to coat.

3. Coat a large baking sheet with nonstick cooking spray, and arrange the potatoes in a single layer on the sheet, making sure that the potato strips are not touching one another. Spray the tops lightly with cooking spray, and bake at 400°F for 25 to 30 minutes, or until nicely browned and tender. Serve hot.

Yield: *6 servings*

1½ pounds unpeeled baking potatoes (about 3 extra large)

1 egg white, lightly beaten, or 2 tablespoons fat-free egg substitute

Nonstick cooking spray

COATING

2 teaspoons ground paprika

1 teaspoon garlic powder

¼ teaspoon salt

¼ teaspoon ground black pepper

NUTRITIONAL FACTS (PER SERVING)
Calories: 129 Cholesterol: 0 mg Fat: 0.3 g
Fiber: 2.7 g Protein: 3.3 g Sodium: 98 mg

Stuffed Acorn Squash

Yield: *4 servings*

2 medium acorn squash (about 1 pound each)

1 cup cooked brown rice or bulgar wheat

1 medium tart apple, peeled and finely chopped

¼ cup thinly sliced celery

¼ cup finely chopped onion

¼ cup dark raisins

1 tablespoon butter-flavored sprinkles

¾ teaspoon dried thyme

1. Cut each squash in half crosswise, and scoop out and discard the seeds. Trim a small piece off the bottom of each squash half, if necessary, to allow the squash to sit upright.

2. Combine the remaining ingredients in a medium-sized bowl, and stir to mix well. Divide the mixture among the squash shells.

3. Coat a shallow baking dish with nonstick cooking spray, and arrange the stuffed shells in the dish. Cover the dish with aluminum foil, and bake at 350°F for 50 minutes to 1 hour, or until the squash are tender. Serve hot.

NUTRITIONAL FACTS (PER SERVING)

Calories: 208 Cholesterol: 0 mg Fat: 0.8 g
Fiber: 9.5 g Protein: 3.7 g Sodium: 77 mg

Cranapple Acorn Squash

Yield: *4 servings*

2 medium acorn squash (about 1 pound each)

2 cups finely chopped peeled apple (about 3 medium)

½ cup coarsely chopped fresh or frozen (do not thaw) cranberries

¼ cup golden raisins

3 tablespoons light brown sugar

2 tablespoons chopped pecans (optional)

¼ teaspoon ground nutmeg

1. Cut each squash in half crosswise, and scoop out and discard the seeds. Trim a small piece off the bottom of each squash half, if necessary, to allow the squash to sit upright.

2. Combine the apples, cranberries, raisins, brown sugar, and pecans, if desired, in a medium-sized bowl, and stir to mix well. Divide the mixture among the squash shells, and sprinkle a pinch of nutmeg over each stuffed shell.

3. Coat a shallow baking dish with nonstick cooking spray, and arrange the stuffed shells in the dish. Cover the dish with aluminum foil, and bake at 350°F for 50 minutes to 1 hour, or until the squash are tender. Serve hot.

NUTRITIONAL FACTS (PER SERVING)

Calories: 183 Cholesterol: 0 mg Fat: 0.4 g
Fiber: 8.8 g Protein: 2.3 g Sodium: 7 mg

Sauce It Up!

Vegetables blanketed with buttery or cheesy sauces are *not* what the doctor ordered. But take heart. Made properly, creamy rich-tasting sauces can still adorn your favorite veggies. Here are some ideas for fabulous fat-free toppings.

Cheddar Cheese Sauce

1. Combine the flour, ¼ cup of the milk, and the pepper in a small jar with a tight-fitting lid. Shake to mix well, and set aside.

2. Place the remaining ¾ cup of milk in a 1-quart saucepan. Place over medium heat, and cook, stirring constantly, until the mixture starts to boil. Stir in the flour mixture, and continue to cook and stir for a few seconds, or until the sauce is thickened and bubbly.

3. Reduce the heat to low, add the cheese, and continue to stir until the cheese melts. Serve hot over steamed broccoli, cauliflower, asparagus, potatoes, or other vegetables.

Yield: 1¼ cups

2 tablespoons unbleached flour

1 cup skim milk, divided

⅛ teaspoon ground white pepper

¾ cup shredded nonfat processed Cheddar cheese, or ¾ cup shredded reduced-fat Cheddar cheese

---

NUTRITIONAL FACTS (PER TABLESPOON)
Calories: 13 Cholesterol: 1 mg Fat: 0 g
Fiber: 0 g Protein: 1.9 g Sodium: 51 mg

Honey Mustard Sauce

1. Combine all of the ingredients in a 1-quart saucepan, and stir to mix well. Place over medium-low heat, and cook, stirring constantly, just until the sauce is heated through.

2. Serve hot over steamed broccoli, cauliflower, asparagus, or other vegetables.

Yield: 1¼ cups

½ cup nonfat or reduced-fat mayonnaise

¼ cup honey

¼ cup mustard

¼ cup lemon juice

NUTRITONAL FACTS (PER TABLESPOON)
Calories: 20 Cholesterol: 0 mg Fat: 0.1 g
Fiber: 0.1 g Protein: 0.2 g Sodium: 107 mg

CREAMY LEMON SAUCE

Yield: *1½ cups*

1 cup skim milk

¼ cup instant nonfat dry milk powder

1 tablespoon plus 1½ teaspoons cornstarch

½ teaspoon salt

⅛ teaspoon ground white pepper

1 pinch ground nutmeg

¼ cup fat-free egg substitute

3 tablespoons lemon juice

2 teaspoons freshly grated lemon rind

This sauce can beautifully replace hollandaise in any of your favorite recipes.

1. Place the milk, milk powder, cornstarch, salt, pepper, and nutmeg in a 1-quart saucepan, and stir until the cornstarch and milk powder are dissolved. Place over medium-low heat, and cook, stirring constantly, until the sauce is thickened and bubbly. Reduce the heat to low.

2. Place the egg substitute in a small bowl, and stir in ¼ cup of the hot milk mixture. Return the mixture to the pan, and continue to cook and stir for another minute, or until the mixture thickens slightly. Do not let the mixture boil.

3. Remove the pan from the heat, and slowly stir in the lemon juice and rind. Serve hot over steamed asparagus, broccoli, or cauliflower.

NUTRITIONAL FACTS (PER TABLESPOON)
Calories: 10 Cholesterol: 0 mg Fat: 0 g
Fiber: 0 g Protein: 0.9 g Sodium: 58 mg

Island Sweet Potatoes

Yield: *8 servings*

2 cans (1 pound each) sweet potatoes, drained

1 can (8 ounces) crushed pineapple in juice, undrained

1 large firm but ripe banana, sliced

⅓ cup golden raisins or chopped dates

¼ teaspoon ground nutmeg

1¾ cups miniature marshmallows

1. Cut the sweet potatoes into bite-sized pieces, and place in a large bowl. Add the pineapple, including the juice, and the banana slices, raisins or dates, and nutmeg. Toss gently to mix.

2. Coat a 2-quart casserole dish with nonstick cooking spray, and spread the mixture evenly in the dish. Arrange the marshmallows over the top, and bake at 350°F for 35 to 40 minutes, or until the edges are bubbly and the topping is golden brown. Serve hot.

NUTRITIONAL FACTS (PER ⅔-CUP SERVING)
Calories: 156 Cholesterol: 0 mg Fat: 0.3 g
Fiber: 2 g Protein: 2.3 g Sodium: 68 mg

Baked Butternut Pudding

1. Peel and seed the squash, and cut the remaining flesh into cubes. Place the squash the apple juice in a 4-quart pot, and bring to a boil over high meat. Reduce the heat to low, cover, and simmer, stirring occasionally, for 25 minutes, or until the squash is very tender.

2. Remove the pot from the heat, and drain off and discard the juice. Add the brown sugar, butter-flavored sprinkles, cinnamon, and nutmeg to the squash, and mash the mixture with a potato masher until smooth.

3. Place the egg substitute in a small bowl, and stir in ½ cup of the hot mashed squash. Return the mixture to the pot.

4. To make the topping, combine the topping ingredients in a small bowl, and stir to mix well. Set aside.

5. Coat a 2-quart casserole dish with nonstick cooking spray, and spread the squash mixture evenly in the dish. Sprinkle the topping over the squash, and bake at 350°F for 45 to 50 minutes, or until a sharp knife inserted in the center of the dish comes out clean. Remove the dish from the oven, and let sit for 5 minutes before serving.

Yield: *8 servings*

3 pounds butternut squash (about 2 medium)

2 cups apple juice

2 tablespoons light brown sugar

1 tablespoon plus 1 teaspoon butter-flavored sprinkles

½ teaspoon ground cinnamon

¼ teaspoon ground nutmeg

½ cup fat-free egg substitute

TOPPING

3 tablespoons light brown sugar

3 tablespoons toasted wheat germ or finely chopped pecans

NUTRITIONAL FACTS (PER ⅔-CUP SERVING)

Calories: 115 Cholesterol: 0 mg Fat: 0.6 g

Fiber: 4.5 g Protein: 3.8 g Sodium: 43 mg

6

Hearty Home-Style Entrées

Many people believe that a transition to low-fat cooking means waving good-bye to the hearty home-style dishes they love so much. The truth is that you don't have to give up pot roast with gravy, chicken and dumplings, shepherd's pie, or any of your other favorites just because you're cutting down on fat. Nor do you have to spend hours in specialty stores searching for exotic ingredients, or added time in the kitchen learning complicated cooking methods. By replacing high-fat ingredients with low-fat or no-fat foods, and by using a few simple cooking techniques, you can enjoy all of your favorite foods and many, new ones, as well. This chapter will show you how.

The entrées in this chapter begin with the freshest seafood or the leanest cuts of poultry, beef, or pork. Then, fat is kept to an absolute minimum by using nonstick skillets and non-stick cooking sprays, and by replacing full-fat dairy products with their healthful nonfat and reduced-fat counterparts. Of course, fresh vegetables, hearty grains, and savory seasonings play an important role in these dishes by adding their own great flavors and textures, and by boosting nutrition. The result? Satisfying home-style entrées, most of which have only 2 to 3 grams of fat per serving!

Delicious pasta entrées and crowd-pleasing meatless main dishes can also be found in this chapter. And, of course, many of your own family favorites can be easily "slimmed down" with the techniques and ingredients used within this chapter. Spicy jambalayas, "fried" chicken, juicy burgers, and more can all be part of a healthy diet once you learn the secrets of fat-free cooking!

Lemon-Herb Chicken with Vegetables

Yield: *4 servings*

4 boneless skinless chicken breast halves (4 ounces each)

¼ cup chicken broth

16 medium whole fresh mushrooms (about 8 ounces)

2 medium carrots, peeled, halved lengthwise, and cut into 2-inch pieces

2 medium zucchini, halved lengthwise and cut into ½-inch slices

MARINADE

2 tablespoons lemon juice

1 tablespoon brown sugar

1 teaspoon crushed fresh garlic

½ teaspoon coarsely ground black pepper

¼ teaspoon salt

1 teaspoon dried thyme, oregano, or rosemary

1. Rinse the chicken, and pat it dry with paper towels. Place the chicken in a shallow nonmetal container.

2. Combine the marinade ingredients in a small bowl, and pour over the chicken parts. Turn the chicken to coat, cover, and refrigerate for several hours or overnight

3. Coat a large skillet with nonstick cooking spray, and preheat over medium-high heat. Place the chicken in the skillet, reserving the marinade, and cook for about 2 minutes on each side, or until nicely browned.

4. Reduce the heat to low, and add the reserved marinade, broth, mushrooms, and carrots to the skillet. Cover and simmer for 10 minutes. Add the zucchini, and simmer for an additional 5 minutes, or until the chicken is no longer pink inside and the vegetables are tender.

5. Serve hot, accompanying each chicken breast with some of the vegetables and pan juices. Serve over brown rice if desired.

NUTRITIONAL FACTS (PER SERVING)
Calories: 192 Cholesterol: 72 mg Fat: 3.4 g
Fiber: 2.7 g Protein: 29 g Sodium: 263 mg

FAT-FREE COOKING TIP

Browning Without Fat

The traditional method of browning foods requires oil, butter, or margarine. Indeed, some recipes recommend several tablespoons of oil for browning! However, as the recipes in this chapter show, all that extra oil is simply not necessary. To brown meat, chicken, or vegetables with virtually no added fat, spray a thin film of nonstick cooking spray over the bottom of the skillet Then preheat the skillet over medium-high heat, and brown the food as usual. If the food starts to stick, add a few teaspoons of water or broth. If you use a nonstick skillet *and* nonstick cooking spray, it should not be necessary to add any liquid at all.

Baked Chicken with Garlic and Sun-Dried Tomatoes

As the garlic cloves cook, they become sweet and mild. For a real treat, spread the clones on hot French bread instead of butter.

Yield: *4 servings*

4 boneless skinless chicken breast halves (4 ounces each)

20 cloves garlic, peeled (about 2 heads)

1 medium onion, sliced ¼-inch-thick and separated into rings

½ cup chopped sun-dried tomatoes (not packed in oil)

¼ cup dry white wine

½ cup chicken broth

1 teaspoon dried oregano

¼ teaspoon ground black pepper

1. Rinse the chicken, and pat it dry with paper towels.

2. Coat a large ovenproof skillet with olive oil cooking spray, and pre-heat over medium-high heat Crush 2 of the garlic cloves, and place them in the skillet Place the chicken in the skillet, and arrange the remaining garlic cloves around the chicken.

3. Cook the chicken for about 2 minutes on each side, or until the chicken and garlic cloves are nicely browned. Remove the chicken from the skillet, and set aside. Remove the skillet from the heat

4. Lay the onions and tomatoes over the garlic cloves in the skillet. Arrange the chicken in a single layer over the tomatoes, onions, and garlic. Pour the wine and broth over the chicken, and sprinkle with the oregano and pepper.

5. Cover and bake at 350°F for 30 minutes, or until the chicken is tender and the juices run clear when the chicken is pierced.

6. Serve hot, accompanying each chicken breast with some of the vegetables and pan juices. Serve over brown rice or noodles if desired.

NUTRITIONAL FACTS (PER SERVING)
Calories: 209 Cholesterol: 72 mg Fat: 3.3 g
Fiber: 1.7 g Protein: 30 g Sodium: 305 mg

Poached Chicken
with Creamy Mushroom Sauce

Yield: *4 servings*

4 boneless skinless chicken breast
  halves (4 ounces each)

1 cup chicken broth

SAUCE

2 cups sliced fresh mushrooms

¾ cup nonfat sour cream

1 tablespoon unbleached flour

¼ teaspoon ground black pepper

1 tablespoon freshly grated lemon
  rind

1. Rinse the chicken, and arrange it in an unheated nonstick skillet. Add the broth, and bring to a boil over high heat. Reduce the heat to low, cover, and simmer for 20 to 25 minutes, or until the chicken is tender and no longer pink inside. Pour the broth into a measuring cup. Transfer the chicken to a serving platter, and cover to keep warm.

2. To make the sauce, place the mushrooms in the skillet along with 1 tablespoon of the reserved broth. Cook and stir over medium heat until the mushrooms are tender and all of the liquid has evaporated. Add ½ cup plus 2 tablespoons of the reserved broth, and bring to a boil. Reduce the heat to medium-low.

3. Combine the sour cream, flour, pepper, and lemon rind in a small bowl, and stir until smooth. Add the sour cream mixture to the mushroom mixture, and cook and stir for about 1 minute, or until the sauce is thickened and bubbly.

4. Pour the sauce over the chicken, and serve hot, accompanying the dish with brown rice or noodles if desired.

NUTRITIONAL FACTS (PER SERVING)
Calories: 207 Cholesterol: 72 mg Fat: 3.2 g
Fiber: 0.5 g Protein: 30 g Sodium: 231 mg

Chicken with Black Bean Salsa

1. Rinse the chicken, and pat it dry with paper towels. Spread each piece with some of the garlic, and sprinkle with the pepper.

2. Coat a large skillet with nonstick cooking spray, and preheat over medium-high heat. Arrange the chicken in the skillet, and cook for about 2 minutes on each side, or until nicely browned. Reduce the heat to low, and add the broth. Cover and simmer for 10 to 12 minutes, or until the chicken is tender and the juices run clear when the chicken is pierced. Transfer the chicken to a serving platter, and cover to keep warm.

3. Drain any liquid from the skillet, and add the undrained black beans and the salsa or picante sauce. Cook and stir over medium heat until heated through. Spoon the bean mixture over the chicken, sprinkle with the scallions, and serve hot, accompanying the dish with brown rice if desired.

Yield: *6 servings*

6 boneless skinless chicken breast halves (4 ounces each)

1 tablespoon crushed fresh garlic

¼ teaspoon ground black pepper

3 tablespoons chicken broth

1 can (15 ounces) black beans, undrained

½ cup salsa or picante sauce

3 tablespoons thinly sliced scallions

NUTRITIONAL FACTS (PER SERVING)
Calories: 212 Cholesterol: 72 mg Fat: 3.4 g
Fiber: 4.9 g Protein: 30 g Sodium: 436 mg

Crispy Cajun Chicken

Yield: *8 servings*

8 skinless chicken breast halves
   with bones (6 ounces each)

1¼ cups nonfat or low-fat buttermilk or yogurt

COATING

5 cups cornflakes

1 tablespoon ground paprika

2–3 teaspoons Cajun seasoning

Finely crushed cornflakes give this ultra-lean oven-fried chicken its crispy coating.

1. Rinse the chicken, and pat it dry with paper towels. Place the chicken in a shallow nonmetal dish, and pour the buttermilk or yogurt over the chicken. Turn the pieces to coat, cover, and refrigerate for several hours or overnight.

2. To make the coating, place the cornflakes in a blender or food processor, and process into crumbs. You should have about 1¼ cups of crumbs. (Adjust the amount if necessary.)

3. Combine the cornflake crumbs, paprika, and Cajun seasoning in a small plastic bag. Close the bag, and shake well to mix.

4. Remove 2 pieces of chicken from the buttermilk, place in the coating bag, and shake to coat evenly. Repeat with the remaining chicken.

5. Coat a large baking sheet with nonstick cooking spray, and arrange the chicken on the pan. Lightly spray each piece of chicken with non-stick cooking spray, and bake at 400°F for 50 minutes, or until the meat is tender and the juices run clear when the chicken is pierced. Serve hot.

NUTRITIONAL FACTS (PER SERVING)
Calories: 207 Cholesterol: 72 mg Fat: 3.2 g
Fiber: 0.4 g Protein: 28 g Sodium: 285 mg

Simply Delicious Chicken and Dumplings

1. Rinse the chicken, and place the chicken, water, bouillon granules, poultry seasoning, and pepper in a 4-quart pot. Bring the mixture to a boil over high heat Then reduce the heat to low, cover, and simmer for 25 to 30 minutes, or until the chicken is tender and the juices run clear when the chicken is pierced.

2. Remove the pot from the heat. Remove the chicken from the pot with a slotted spoon, reserving the liquid. Arrange the chicken on a plate to cool slightly.

3. Pour the cooking liquid into a fat separator cup, and pour the fat-free broth from the separator cup into a measuring cup. There should be 3 cups. (If necessary, add water to bring it up to measure.) Return the broth to the pot.

4. Remove the skin and bones from the chicken, and discard. Tear the remaining meat into bite-sized pieces, and return the chicken to the pot.

5. Add the carrots, celery, and onion to the pot. Place the pot over high heat, and bring to a boil. Reduce the heat to low, cover, and simmer for 5 minutes, or until the vegetables are almost tender. Add the peas to the pot

6. Combine the milk and flour in a jar with a tight-fitting lid, and shake until smooth. Pour the flour mixture into the pot, and cook, stirring constantly, for about 2 minutes, or until the broth is thickened and bubbly.

7. To make the dumplings, combine the flour, baking powder, and sugar in a medium-sized bowl, and stir to mix well. Stir in the buttermilk, and drop heaping teaspoonfuls of the batter onto the simmering stew. Cover and simmer over low heat for 10 to 12 minutes, or until the dumplings are fluffy and cooked through. Serve hot

Yield: *6 servings*

4 chicken breast halves with skin and bone (8 ounces each)

2½ cups water

1½ teaspoons chicken bouillon granules

½ teaspoon poultry seasoning

⅛ teaspoon ground white pepper

1 medium carrot, peeled, halved lengthwise, and sliced

1 stalk celery, thinly sliced (include leaves)

½ cup chopped onion

1 cup frozen green peas

½ cup skim milk

¼ cup plus 2 tablespoons unbleached flour

DUMPLINGS

1½ cups unbleached flour

2 teaspoons baking powder

1 teaspoon sugar

¾ cup nonfat or low-fat buttermilk

NUTRITIONAL FACTS (PER 1½-CUP SERVING)
Calories: 257 Cholesterol: 45 mg Fat: 1.8 g
Fiber: 2.9 g Protein: 24 g Sodium: 498 mg

Chicken Enchiladas

Yield: *6 servings*

1¼ pounds boneless skinless chicken breasts

2 cups water

1 teaspoon chicken bouillon granules

⅓ cup thinly sliced scallions

¼ cup minced fresh cilantro or parsley

1 teaspoon dried oregano

¼ teaspoon ground black pepper

12 corn tortillas (6-inch rounds)

1 cup shredded nonfat or reduced-fat Cheddar cheese

SAUCE

1 can (8 ounces) unsalted tomato sauce

1½ tablespoons chili powder

1½ teaspoons ground cumin

2 tablespoons unbleached flour

¼ cup water

TOPPINGS

¾ cup nonfat sour cream

¼ cup thinly sliced scallions

Softening the tortillas in tomato sauce instead of the usual oil or lard saves lots of fat and calories, as does using nonfat cheese and skinless chicken breasts.

1. Rinse the chicken, and place the chicken, water, and bouillon granules in a 2-quart pot Bring the mixture to a boil over high heat. Then reduce the heat to low, cover, and simmer for 20 minutes, or until the chicken is tender and the juices run clear when the chicken is pierced.

2. Remove the chicken from the pot with a slotted spoon reserving the liquid, and cool to room temperature. Tear the chicken into shreds, and transfer to a large bowl. Add the scallions, cilantro or parsley, oregano, and pepper, and stir to mix. Set aside.

3. To make the sauce, combine the tomato sauce, chili powder and cumin in a medium-sized skillet. Stir in 1½ cups of the reserved cooking liquid, and bring the mixture to a boil over medium heat.

4. Combine the flour and water in a jar with a tight-fitting lid, and shake until smooth. Stir the flour mixture into the simmering sauce, and continue to stir until the mixture is thickened and bubbly. Reduce the heat to low.

5. Coat a 9-x-13-inch baking pan with nonstick cooking spray. Dip a tortilla in the sauce for about 10 seconds—just long enough to soften the tortilla—coating each side with sauce. Lay the tortilla on a flat surface, and place ¼ cup of the chicken filling along one end. Roll the tortilla up jelly-roll style, and lay it in the pan, seam side down. Repeat with the remaining tortillas, leaving a ¼-inch space between the enchiladas to prevent them from sticking together.

6. Pour the remaining sauce over the enchiladas, and spread the cheese over the too. Bake uncovered at 450°F for 12 to 15 minutes, or until the cheese is melted and the dish is heated through. Top individual servings with 2 tablespoons of sour cream and 2 teaspoons of scallions, and serve hot.

NUTRITIONAL FACTS (PER 2-ENCHILADA SERVING)
Calories: 318 Cholesterol: 58 mg Fat: 2.8 g
Fiber: 3.7 g Protein: 32 g Sodium: 449 mg

Savory Turkey and Rice

1. Rinse the turkey, and pat it dry with paper towels. Coat a 9-inch square pan with nonstick cooking spray, and arrange the turkey in a single layer in the pan. Add 2 tablespoons of the broth or water, cover with aluminum foil, and bake at 350°F for 20 minutes. Remove the foil, and bake for 10 additional minutes, or until the meat is tender and the juices run clear when the turkey is pierced.

2. Remove the turkey from the pan, and cool to room temperature. Tear the meat into bite-sized pieces, and set aside.

3. Combine the rice, 4½ cups of the broth or water, and the bouillon granules in a 2½-quart pot. Bring the mixture to a boil over high heat, stir, and reduce the heat to low. Cover and simmer without stirring for 45 to 50 minutes, or until the liquid has been absorbed and the rice is tender. Remove the pot from the heat, and allow to sit, covered, for 5 minutes.

4. Combine the mushrooms, onion, garlic, poultry seasoning, pepper, and sherry in a large nonstick skillet. Sauté over medium heat until the mushrooms are tender and most of the liquid has evaporated. Add the peas, rice, turkey, and remaining ¼ cup of broth or water, and toss until heated through. Serve hot.

Yield: *6 servings*

1 pound turkey breast tenderloins

4¾ cups plus 2 tablespoons unsalted chicken broth or water, divided

2 cups uncooked brown rice

2 teaspoons chicken bouillon granules

1¼ cups sliced fresh mushrooms

1 medium yellow onion, chopped

1 teaspoon crushed fresh garlic

¾ teaspoon poultry seasoning

¼ teaspoon ground black pepper

2 tablespoons dry sherry

1 cup frozen green peas, thawed

NUTRITIONAL FACTS (PER 1½-CUP SERVING)
Calories: 341 Cholesterol: 49 mg Fat: 2.8 g
Fiber: 3.8 g Protein: 24 g Sodium: 403 mg

BREAST of TURKEY PROVENÇAL

Yield: *4 servings*

4 pieces (4 ounces each) turkey breast tenderloins or turkey cutlets

⅓ cup unbleached flour

¼ teaspoon salt

¼ teaspoon ground black pepper

½ cup dry white wine

2 teaspoons crushed fresh garlic

1 teaspoon dried rosemary

1 teaspoon dried oregano

1 bay leaf

½ cup chicken broth

1 medium tomato, cut into 8 wedges

¼ cup minced fresh parsley

1. Rinse the turkey, and pat it dry with paper towels. Place the turkey on a flat surface, and pound to ¼-inch thickness.

2. Combine the flour, salt, and pepper in a plastic bag. Close the bag, and shake well to mix. Place the turkey, 2 pieces at a time, in the coating bag, and shake well until evenly coated. Set aside.

3. Combine the wine, garlic, rosemary, and oregano in a small bowl. Set aside.

4. Coat a large nonstick skillet with olive oil cooking spray, and preheat over medium-high heat. Add the turkey, and cook for 2 to 3 minutes on each side, or until nicely browned.

5. Pour the wine mixture over the turkey, and add the bay leaf. Reduce the heat to medium-low, and cook until the wine is reduced by half, periodically scraping the bottom of the skillet. Add the chicken broth, and arrange the tomato wedges around the meat. Cover and simmer for 5 to 7 minutes, or until the turkey and tomatoes are tender.

6. Transfer the turkey, vegetables, and sauce to a serving platter, and sprinkle with the parsley. Serve over noodles or pasta if desired.

NUTRITIONAL FACTS (PER SERVING)
Calories: 177 Cholesterol: 73 mg Fat: 1.5 g
Fiber: 0.8 g Protein: 28 g Sodium: 283 mg

Turkey Jambalaya

For variety, make this savory dish with chicken instead of turkey.

Yield: *5 servings*

1. Rinse the turkey, and pat it dry with paper towels. Coat a large skillet with nonstick cooking spray, and preheat over medium-high heat. Add the turkey, and stir-fry for 2 to 3 minutes, or until browned.

2. Add the remaining ingredients to the skillet, and stir to mix well. Bring the mixture to a boil, reduce the heat to low, and cover. Simmer for about 50 minutes, or until the liquid has been absorbed and the rice is tender.

3. Remove the skillet from the heat, and allow to sit, covered, for 5 minutes. Serve hot.

¾ pound boneless skinless turkey breasts, cut into bite-sized pieces

1⅔ cups unsalted chicken broth

1½ cups uncooked brown rice

4 ounces smoked turkey sausage (at least 97% lean), diced

1 can (1 pound) unsalted tomatoes, crushed

½ cup thinly sliced celery (include leaves)

½ cup chopped green bell pepper

½ cup chopped onion

1 teaspoon crushed fresh garlic

1 bay leaf

1–2 teaspoons Cajun or Creole seasoning

NUTRITIONAL FACTS (PER 1½-CUP SERVING)

Calories: 340 Cholesterol: 56 mg Fat: 3.5 g
Fiber: 3.5 g Protein: 25 g Sodium: 386 mg

Mexican Skillet Dinner

Yield: *6 servings*

1 pound 95% lean ground beef

1 can (1 pound) Mexican-style
    tomatoes, crushed

2½ cups fresh or frozen (thawed)
    whole kernel corn

1 teaspoon crushed fresh garlic

8 ounces whole wheat macaroni

1⅓ cups unsalted beef broth or
    water

1 tablespoon chili powder

½ teaspoon dried oregano

¼ teaspoon ground black pepper

½ teaspoon salt (optional)

1. Place the meat in a large, deep skillet, and cook over medium heat, stirring to crumble, until the meat is no longer pink. Add all of the remaining ingredients, and stir to mix well.

2. Bring the mixture to a boil. Then reduce the heat to low, cover, and simmer, stirring occasionally, for 10 to 12 minutes, or until the pasta is tender and the liquid has been absorbed. If any liquid remains, remove the cover and simmer for several more minutes. Serve hot.

NUTRITIONAL FACTS (PER 1½-CUP SERVING)
Calories: 311 Cholesterol: 50 mg Fat: 4.3 g
Fiber: 6 g Protein: 24 g Sodium: 357 mg

Foil-Baked Flounder

Baking fish in a foil pouch allows the fish to steam in its own juices, sealing in flavor and nutrients. Vegetables, wine, and herbs—not fat or salt—provide added flavor and color.

1. Cut heavy-duty aluminum foil into four 8-x-12-inch pieces, and center a fish fillet on the lower half of each piece. Spread ½ teaspoon of garlic over each fillet, and top with ½ cup of snow peas, ½ cup of carrots, 1 tablespoon of scallions, 2 teaspoons of dill, ½ teaspoon of butter sprinkles, ⅛ teaspoon of pepper, and 1 tablespoon of wine.

2. Fold the upper half of the foil over the fish to meet the bottom half. Seal the edges together by making a tight ½-inch fold; then fold again to double-seal. Allow space for heat circulation and expansion. Use this technique to seal the remaining sides.

3. Arrange the pouches on a baking pan or directly on the oven rack, and bake at 450°F for about 15 minutes, or until the fish is opaque and the thickest part is easily flaked with a fork. Open each packet by cutting an "X" in the top of the foil, and serve hot.

Yield: *4 servings*

4 flounder, sole, snapper, or orange roughy fillets (6 ounces each)

2 teaspoons crushed fresh garlic

2 cups snow peas

2 cups thinly sliced carrots (about 2 medium)

¼ cup chopped scallions

2 tablespoons plus 2 teaspoons minced fresh dill

2 teaspoons butter-flavored sprinkles

½ teaspoon ground black pepper

¼ cup dry white wine

NUTRITIONAL FACTS (PER SERVING)
Calories: 223 Cholesterol: 82 mg Fat: 2.3 g
Fiber: 3.2 g Protein: 35 g Sodium: 176 mg

Spicy Shrimp Gumbo

Yield: *6 cups*

1 medium onion, chopped

1 medium green bell pepper, chopped

½ cup thinly sliced celery (include leaves)

2 teaspoons crushed fresh garlic

4 ounces smoked turkey sausage (at least 97% lean), diced

1 can (1 pound) unsalted tomato sauce

½ cup unsalted chicken broth

1 bay leaf

1 teaspoon Cajun or Creole seasoning (or more to taste)

1 cup frozen whole kernel corn

1 cup frozen cut okra

¾ pound cleaned raw shrimp

1. Combine the onion, bell pepper, celery, garlic, sausage, tomato sauce, broth, bay leaf, and Cajun or Creole seasoning in a 2½-quart pot, and bring to a boil over high heat. Reduce the heat to low, cover, and simmer for 20 minutes, or until the vegetables are tender.

2. Add the corn and okra to the sausage mixture. Increase the heat to high, and bring to a boil. Then reduce the heat to low, cover, and simmer for 5 minutes, or until the okra is barely tender.

3. Add the shrimp to the gumbo, cover, and simmer for 5 additional minutes, or until the shrimp turn pink. Serve hot, accompanying the dish with brown rice, if desired.

NUTRITIONAL FACTS (PER 1-CUP SERVING)
Calories: 134 Cholesterol: 91 mg Fat: 1.1 g
Fiber: 3.2 g Protein: 14.5 g Sodium: 357 mg

Pot Roast with Sour Cream Gravy

Top round roast—which is sometimes sold as London broil—is one of the leanest cuts available, and can be easily substituted for pot roasts and briskets in any of your favorite recipes.

1. Trim any visible fat from the meat. Rinse the meat, and pat it dry with paper towels. Spread the garlic over both sides of the meat, and sprinkle with the pepper.

2. Coat a large ovenproof skillet with nonstick cooking spray, and preheat over medium-high heat. Place the meat in the skillet, and brown for 2 to 3 minutes on each side. Remove the skillet from the heat, and spread the onions over the meat. Place the bay leaves in the skillet, and pour the broth into the bottom of the skillet. Cover tightly, and bake at 325°F for 1 hour and 45 minutes.

3. Remove the skillet from the oven, and carefully remove the cover. (Steam will escape.) Place the potatoes and carrots around the meat, cover, and return the skillet to the oven for 45 additional minutes, or until the meat and vegetables are tender. Transfer the meat and vegetables to a serving platter, and cover to keep warm.

4. To make the gravy, discard the bay leaves, and pour the meat drippings into a fat separator cup. Then pour the fat-free drippings into a 2-cup measure. (If the meat was well trimmed, there may not be any fat to remove.) If necessary, add water to the defatted drippings to bring the volume up to 1¼ cups.

5. Pour the drippings mixture into a 1-quart saucepan, add the bouillon granules, and bring to a boil over medium heat. Combine the flour and water in a jar with a tight-fitting lid, and shake until smooth. Slowly pour the flour mixture into the boiling gravy. Cook and stir with a wire whisk until the gravy is thickened and bubbly.

6. Reduce the heat to low, add the sour cream, and whisk just until heated through. Transfer the gravy to a warmed gravy boat or pitcher, and serve hot with the meat and vegetables.

Yield: *8 servings*

2½-pound top round roast or London broil

2 teaspoons crushed fresh garlic

¼ teaspoon coarsely ground black pepper

1 medium yellow onion, thinly sliced

2 bay leaves

¾ cup beef broth

1½ pounds potatoes (about 5 medium), scrubbed and quartered

1¼ pounds carrots (about 6 large), peeled and cut into 2-inch pieces

GRAVY

Meat drippings

1½ teaspoons beef bouillon granules

3 tablespoons unbleached flour

¼ cup water

½ cup nonfat sour cream

NUTRITIONAL FACTS (PER SERVING)
Calories: 300 Cholesterol: 59 mg Fat: 5.2 g
Fiber: 4.2 g Protein: 29 g Sodium: 335 mg

Italian-Style Pot Roast

Yield: *6 servings*

1¾-pound top round roast or London broil

2 teaspoons crushed fresh garlic

¼ teaspoon ground black pepper

1 cup chopped onion

1½ cups sliced fresh mushrooms

1 can (1 pound) unsalted tomatoes, crushed

1 can (6 ounces) unsalted tomato paste

¼ cup water

2 teaspoons dried Italian seasoning

1¾ teaspoons beef bouillon granules

1. Trim any visible fat from the meat Rinse the meat, and pat it dry with paper towels. Spread the garlic over both sides of the meat, and sprinkle with the pepper.

2. Coat a large ovenproof skillet with nonstick cooking spray, and preheat over medium-high heat. Place the meat in the skillet, and brown for 2 to 3 minutes on each side. Remove the skillet from the heat, and spread the onions and mushrooms over the meat. Combine the tomatoes, tomato paste, water, Italian seasoning, and bouillon granules in a large bowl, and pour over the meat and vegetables.

3. Cover tightly, and bake at 350°F for 2 hours, or until the meat is tender. Serve hot, accompanying the roast with spaghetti, linguini, or another pasta if desired.

NUTRITIONAL FACTS (PER SERVING)
Calories: 205 Cholesterol: 59 mg Fat: 5 g
Fiber: 3.3 g Protein: 27 g Sodium: 336 mg

Old-Fashioned Beef Stew

1. Trim any visible fat from the meat. Rinse the meat, and pat it dry with paper towels. Cut the meat into bite-sized pieces.

2. Coat a large deep skillet or Dutch oven with nonstick cooking spray, and preheat over medium-high heat. Add the meat, and brown for 2 to 3 minutes.

3. Stir the tomato sauce, water, pepper, herbs, bouillon granules, and Worcestershire sauce into the meat, and bring to a boil. Reduce the heat to low, cover, and simmer for 1 hour, or until the meat is tender.

4. Add the potatoes, carrots, onion, mushrooms, and celery to the meat. Cover and simmer for 30 minutes, or until the vegetables are tender. Add the peas, and simmer for 10 additional minutes. Serve hot.

NUTRITIONAL FACTS (PER 1-CUP SERVING)
Calories: 165 Cholesterol: 29 mg Fat: 2.6 g
Fiber: 3.4 g Protein: 16 g Sodium: 285 mg

Yield: *8 cups*

1 pound top round

1 can (1 pound) unsalted tomato sauce

2 cups water

¼ teaspoon ground black pepper

1 teaspoon dried thyme

1 teaspoon dried marjoram

2 bay leaves

1½ teaspoons beef bouillon granules

1 tablespoon Worcestershire sauce

2 medium potatoes, scrubbed and diced

2 medium carrots, peeled, halved, and sliced

1 medium yellow onion, diced

1 cup sliced fresh mushrooms

1 medium stalk celery, thinly sliced (include leaves)

1 cup frozen green peas, thawed

Mama Mia Meat Loaf

Yield: *8 servings*

LOAF

1½ pounds 95% lean ground beef

1 medium yellow onion, finely chopped

¼ cup finely chopped green bell pepper

1½ teaspoons crushed fresh garlic

2 tablespoons minced fresh parsley, or 2 teaspoons dried

¾ cup oat bran or quick-cooking oats

¼ cup unsalted tomato sauce

3 egg whites

1½ teaspoons dried Italian seasoning

¼ teaspoon ground black pepper

½ teaspoon salt (optional)

TOPPING

¾ cup unsalted tomato sauce

1 teaspoon sugar

½ teaspoon dried Italian seasoning

"Lean" meat loaf pans are great for low-fat cooking. These pans have an inner liner with holes in it that allows the fat to drain into the bottom of the pan instead of being reabsorbed into the meat.

1. Combine the loaf ingredients in a large bowl, and mix well. Coat a 9-x-5-inch meat loaf pan with nonstick cooking spray, and press the mixture into the pan to form a loaf.

2. Bake uncovered at 350°F for 35 minutes. Combine the topping ingredients in a small bowl, and pour the topping over the meat loaf. Bake for 30 additional minutes, or until the meat is no longer pink inside. Remove the loaf from the oven, and let sit for 10 minutes before slicing and serving.

NUTRITIONAL FACTS (PER SERVING)
Calories: 152 Cholesterol: 56 mg Fat: 4.8 g
Fiber: 2.1 g Protein: 22 g Sodium: 213 mg

Saucy Stuffed Peppers

1. Place the meat in a large skillet, and cook over medium heat, stirring to crumble, until the meat is no longer pink. Stir in the onion, chili powder, pepper, and salt, if desired, and continue to cook and stir for a few more minutes, or until the onion is tender. (Add a few tablespoons of water or broth if the skillet gets too dry.) Remove the skillet from the heat, and stir in first the rice, and then the cheese.

2. Cut the tops off the peppers, and remove the seeds and membranes. Divide the filling among the peppers, and replace the pepper tops.

3. To make the sauce, combine all of the sauce ingredients in a large bowl, and stir to mix. Place the peppers upright in an 8-x-12-inch casserole dish or Dutch oven, and pour the sauce around the peppers. Cover with aluminum foil and bake at 350°F for 1 hour, or until the peppers are tender. Serve hot.

Yield: *8 servings*

8 large green bell peppers

FILLING

1 pound 95% lean ground beef

1 medium onion, chopped

1 tablespoon chili powder

¼ teaspoon ground black pepper

½ teaspoon salt (optional)

4 cups cooked brown rice

1 cup shredded nonfat or
   reduced-fat Cheddar cheese

SAUCE

2 cans (1 pound each) unsalted
   tomato sauce

1 tablespoon chili powder

¼ teaspoon salt

NUTRITIONAL FACTS (PER SERVING)
Calories: 246 Cholesterol: 40 mg Fat: 3.9 g
Fiber: 4.8 g Protein: 21 g Sodium: 347 mg

Choosing the Leanest Ground Meat

No food adds more fat to the diet than ground beef. And the wide range of choices now available—lean, extra-lean, ground round, ground sirloin, and ground chuck, for instance—does not seem to make it any easier to find a lean product. Complicating your choice is the fact that many package labels do not state fat content.

How fatty is ground beef? At its worst, ground beef is almost *33 percent pure fat*. Are ground chuck, sirloin, or round any leaner? Not necessarily. The terms chuck, sirloin, and round merely describe the part of the animal the meat is from; they do not indicate the amount of fat it contains. (Extra fat is often added during grinding.)

The only way to be sure about fat content is to buy meat in packages that provide some nutrition information. The leanest ground beef commonly available—95-percent lean ground beef—has only 4.9 grams of fat per 3-ounce cooked serving, and contains 5 percent fat by weight. If you can't find ready-made 95-percent lean ground beef, select a lean piece of top round, and have the butcher trim off the visible fat and grind the remaining meat Ground beef made this way is about 95-percent lean. Or buy 93-percent ground beef, which is an acceptable—and widely available—choice.

Where does ground turkey fit in? Ground turkey may be substituted for ground beef in any recipe—as long as you like the taste of ground turkey, which is distinctly different from that of beef. Realize, though, that ground turkey is not necessarily leaner than ground beef. In fact, much of the ground turkey sold today is 85 percent lean, meaning that it contains 15 percent fat by weight. This product contains *twice* the fat of 93-percent lean ground beef. How can ground turkey be so fatty? Often, this product contains turkey skin and fat, as well as turkey meat. So read the labels, and look for the lowest fat content available. Ground turkey made from dark meat without added skin or fat contains about 8 percent fat by weight. Ground turkey made from skinless breast meat contains only 1 percent fat. What about ground chicken? Like ground turkey, it often contains added skin and fat, so, again, read the label before making your purchase.

The nutrition information for the ground beef recipes in this book has been calculated using 95-percent lean ground beef. When you use ground meat this lean, there is no fat to drain off. In fact, the meat may stick to the bottom of the pan during browning. When this happens, add a few tablespoons of water to the skillet

Using Meat Extenders and Substitutes

Whether you're making tacos, a casserole, or burgers, a number of excellent meat substitutes can replace part or all of the ground meat in your recipe. If your family is skeptical about these products, try replacing just half of the meat at first. You may find that after some time, you can create totally meatless versions of many of your favorite dishes using one of the following three alternatives.

Made from soy and other vegetable proteins, frozen meatless crumbles like Harvest Burger for Recipes and Morningstar Farms Burger Style Recipe Crumbles can be found in the freezer case of your grocery store. Thawed, these fat-free products can be added to chili and similar recipes. Use 2 cups of crumbles to replace 1 pound of ground meat. Or mix 1 cup of crumbles with ½ pound of cooked ground meat.

Another option is Tofu Crumbles—precooked mildly seasoned bits of tofu. Simply substitute 2 cups of crumbles for 1 pound of cooked ground meat. Or mix 1 cup of crumbles with ½ pound of cooked ground meat. Look for this low-fat product in the tofu section of your grocery store.

Made from defatted soy flour, textured vegetable protein (TVP) comes packaged as small nuggets that you rehydrate with water. TVP is sold in most health foods stores and some grocery stores. To replace 1 pound of ground meat, pour ⅞ cup of boiling water over 1 cup of TVP. Let the mixture sit for about 5 minutes, or until the liquid has been absorbed. To use

TVP as a meat extender, rehydrate ½ cup of the nuggets with 7 tablespoons of broth or water, and mix with ½ pound of cooked, crumbled ground meat. When used in chili and other spicy dishes, no one will suspect that this fat-free product is there.

To use any of these alternatives as extenders in burgers or meat loaf, mix 1 cup of thawed frozen meatless crumbles, Tofu Crumbles, or rehydrated TVP with ¾ to 1 pound of uncooked ground meat. Then shape and cook the mixture as desired.

Shepherd's Pie

1. To make the topping, peel the potatoes and cut them into 1-inch pieces. Place in a 2-quart pot, barely cover with water, and bring to a boil over high heat. Reduce the heat to medium, cover, and cook for 10 minutes, or until the potatoes are soft.

2. Drain all but 2 tablespoons of water from the potatoes, reserving the drained water. Add the sour cream or yogurt, salt, and pepper, and mash the potatoes with a potato masher until smooth. If the potatoes are too stiff, add a little of the reserved cooking liquid. Set aside.

3. Place the meat in a large, deep skillet, and cook over medium heat, stirring to crumble, until the meat is no longer pink. Stir in the tomato sauce, chili powder, oregano, and bouillon granules, if desired, and continue to cook and stir just until the mixture is heated through.

4. Coat a 2½-quart casserole dish with nonstick cooking spray, and spoon the beef mixture into the dish. Arrange the mixed vegetables in a layer over the beef mixture. Then spread the mashed potatoes over the vegetables.

5. Bake uncovered at 350°F for 25 minutes, or until the edges are bubbly. Top with the cheese, and bake for 5 additional minutes, or until the cheese is melted. Remove the dish from the oven, and let sit for 5 minutes before serving.

Yield: *6 servings*

1 pound 95% lean ground beef

1½ cups unsalted tomato sauce

2 teaspoons chili powder

½ teaspoon dried oregano

1 teaspoon beef bouillon granules (optional)

1 package (10 ounces) frozen mixed vegetables, thawed

TOPPING

1½ pounds baking potatoes (about 4 medium)

½ cup nonfat sour cream or plain nonfat yogurt

¼ teaspoon salt

⅛ teaspoon ground white pepper

1 cup shredded nonfat or reduced-fat Cheddar cheese

NUTRITIONAL FACTS (PER 1⅓-CUP SERVING)
Calories: 290 Cholesterol: 54 mg Fat: 4 g
Fiber: 5 g Protein: 27 g Sodium: 459 mg

Mushroom and Onion Burgers

Yield: *6 servings*

1 pound 95% lean ground beef

1½ cups chopped fresh mushrooms

½ cup chopped onion

1 cup soft whole wheat bread crumbs

2 tablespoons Worcestershire sauce

6 multigrain burger buns

TOPPINGS

6 slices tomato

6 thin slices onion

6 lettuce leaves

While these burgers cook, the chopped mushrooms and onions release their juices into the meat, keeping these ultra-lean burgers moist and flavorful.

1. Combine the ground beef, mushrooms, onions, bread crumbs, and Worcestershire sauce in a medium-sized bowl, and mix thoroughly. Gently shape the mixture into 6 (4-inch) patties.

2. Coat a large nonstick skillet with nonstick cooking spray, and preheat over medium heat. Place the patties in the skillet, and cook them for 4 to 5 minutes on each side, or until the meat is no longer pink inside. To cook the burgers on a barbecue grill, cook over medium heat for 7 to 9 minutes on each side, or until the meat is no longer pink inside.

3. Place each burger on a bun, and top with a slice of tomato, a slice of onion, and a lettuce leaf. Serve hot.

NUTRITIONAL FACTS (PER BURGER WITH BUN AND TOPPINGS)
Calories: 268 Cholesterol: 50 mg Fat: 5.1 g
Fiber: 4.8 g Protein: 27 g Sodium: 405 mg

SWEET AND SOUR PORK

1. To make the sauce, combine all of the sauce ingredients in a small dish. Set aside.

2. Trim the tenderloin of any visible fat and membranes. Rinse with cool water, and pat dry with paper towels. Cut the tenderloin into 1-inch cubes, and set aside.

3. Coat a large nonstick skillet with nonstick cooking spray, and preheat over medium-high heat. Add the garlic and pork, and stir-fry for 5 to 6 minutes, or until the pork is browned.

4. Drain the juice from the pineapple, reserving both the juice and the fruit. Add the juice to the pork mixture, and bring to a boil. Reduce the heat to low, cover, and simmer for 6 to 8 minutes, or until the pork is tender and cooked through.

5. Add the pineapple chunks, bell pepper, onion, and carrot to the pork mixture. Cover and simmer for 3 additional minutes, or until the vegetables are crisp-tender.

6. Stir the sauce to mix, and add it to the skillet. Cook, stirring constantly, until the sauce is thickened and bubbly. Serve hot, accompanying the dish with brown rice, if desired.

Yield: 5 servings

1-pound pork tenderloin

½ teaspoon crushed fresh garlic

1 can (20 ounces) pineapple chunks in juice, undrained

1 medium green bell pepper, cut into thin strips

1 medium yellow onion, cut into thin wedges

1 medium carrot, peeled and diagonally sliced

SAUCE

¼ cup chicken broth

¼ cup white wine vinegar or rice wine vinegar

2 tablespoons reduced-sodium soy sauce

2 tablespoons brown sugar

2 tablespoons cornstarch

½ teaspoon ground ginger

NUTRITIONAL FACTS (PER 1-CUP SERVING)
Calories: 226 Cholesterol: 54 mg Fat: 3.5 g
Fiber: 2 g Protein: 20 g Sodium: 292 mg

Spring Vegetable Quiche

Yield: *5 servings*

1½ cups cooked brown rice

1 egg white

1 cup chopped fresh asparagus
   or broccoli

½ cup fresh or frozen (thawed)
   whole kernel corn

⅓ cup finely chopped carrots

⅓ cup chopped fresh mushrooms

¼ cup finely chopped onion

2 tablespoons minced fresh
   parsley

1 cup shredded nonfat or
   reduced-fat mozzarella cheese

1 cup evaporated skim milk

1 cup fat-free egg substitute

2 tablespoons grated nonfat or
   reduced-fat Parmesan cheese

1. To make the crust, combine the brown rice and egg white in a medium-sized bowl, and stir to mix well. Coat a 9-inch deep dish pie pan with nonstick cooking spray, and use the back of a spoon to pat the mixture over the bottom and sides of the pan, forming an even crust.

2. Combine all of the remaining ingredients except for the Parmesan in a large bowl. Stir to mix well, and pour into the rice crust. Sprinkle the Parmesan over the top.

3. Bake at 375°F for about 50 minutes, or until the top is golden brown and a sharp knife inserted in the center of the quiche comes out clean. Remove the dish from the oven, and let sit for 5 minutes before slicing and serving.

NUTRITIONAL FACTS (PER SERVING)

Calories: 197 Cholesterol: 8 mg Fat: 0.9 g
Fiber: 2.5 g Protein: 20 g Sodium: 337 mg

Spinach and Barley Bake

For variety, substitute brown rice or bulgur wheat for the barley.

Yield: *4 servings*

1. Combine the barley and water in a 1½-quart pot, and bring to a boil over high heat. Reduce the heat to low, cover, and simmer for 45 to 50 minutes, or until the barley is tender and the liquid has been absorbed.

2. Combine the cooked barley and all of the remaining ingredients except for 2 tablespoons of the Parmesan in a large bowl, and stir to mix well. Coat a 1½-quart casserole dish with nonstick cooking spray, and spread the mixture evenly in the dish. Sprinkle the remaining Parmesan over the top.

3. Bake uncovered at 375°F for 50 to 60 minutes, or until golden brown and bubbly. Remove the dish from the oven, and let sit for 5 minutes before serving.

⅔ cup hulled barley

1⅔ cups water

1 package (10 ounces) frozen chopped spinach, thawed and squeezed dry

1 cup sliced fresh mushrooms

1 teaspoon crushed fresh garlic

1½ cups dry curd or nonfat cottage cheese

¼ cup plus 2 tablespoons grated nonfat or reduced-fat Parmesan cheese, divided

½ cup fat-free egg substitute

1 tablespoon unbleached flour

½ teaspoon dried thyme

⅛ teaspoon ground black pepper

NUTRITIONAL FACTS (PER 1¼-CUP SERVING)

Calories: 211 Cholesterol: 11 mg Fat: 0.8 g

Fiber: 5.9 g Protein: 20 g Sodium: 188 mg

Baked Macaroni and Cheese

Yield: *6 servings*

8 ounces elbow macaroni

2 cups skim milk, divided

2 tablespoons unbleached flour

¼ teaspoon ground white pepper

2 teaspoons dry mustard

2 cups shredded nonfat processed
   Cheddar cheese, or 2 cups
   shredded reduced-fat Cheddar
   cheese, divided

1. Cook the macaroni al dente according to package directions. Drain, rinse, and drain again. Set aside.

2. Place ½ cup of the milk and all of the flour, pepper, and mustard in a jar with a tight-fitting lid. Shake until smooth, and set aside.

3. Pour the remaining 1½ cups of milk into a 2-quart pot, and bring to a boil over medium heat, stirring constantly. Add the flour mixture, and cook, still stirring, for about 1 minute, or until thickened and bubbly. Reduce the heat to low, add 1½ cups of the cheese, and stir until the cheese melts.

4. Remove the pot from the heat, and stir in the macaroni. Coat a 2-quart casserole dish with nonstick cooking spray, and spread the macaroni mixture evenly in the dish. Sprinkle the remaining cheese over the top, and bake at 350°F for 30 to 35 minutes, or until bubbly around the edges. Remove the dish from the oven, and let sit for 5 minutes before serving.

NUTRITIONAL FACTS (PER 1-CUP SERVING)
Calories: 232 Cholesterol: 8 mg Fat: 0.7 g
Fiber: 1 g Protein: 20 g Sodium: 338 mg

FAT-FREE COOKING TIP

Cooking with Nonfat Cheeses

If you have been cooking with nonfat cheese for a while, you may have noticed that some brands do not melt as well as their full-fat counterparts. So how can you prepare a creamy nonfat cheese sauce, like the one in Baked Macaroni and Cheese? One option is to use a finely shredded brand of nonfat cheese. Finely shredded cheeses melt better than coarsely shredded products—although they still may not melt completely. Or use a processed nonfat cheese. Processed cheeses are specially made to melt, and will work in any sauce recipe. Processed cheeses tend to be higher in sodium than natural cheeses, though, so read labels and check the sodium counts before you make your purchase.

What about reduced-fat cheeses? Most brands melt very well and can be substituted for full-fat brands in any recipe, with very little difference in taste or texture. Only your waistline will know the difference.

FAT-FREE EGGS FOO YUNG

For variety, make a nonvegetarian version by adding 1 cup of chopped cooked shrimp or crab meat.

1. To make the sauce, combine the cornstarch and brown sugar in a 1-quart saucepan, and stir to mix well. Add the broth, the soy or hoison sauce, and the sesame oil. Place the pan over medium heat, and cook, stirring constantly, until thickened and bubbly. Cover to keep warm, and set aside.

2. Combine the egg substitute, sprouts, water chestnuts, scallions, and pepper in a large bowl, and stir to mix well.

3. Coat a griddle or large skillet with nonstick cooking spray, and preheat over medium heat. For each pancake, pour ½ cup of the egg mixture onto the griddle, spreading the bean sprouts out evenly to make a 4-inch cake. Cook for 3 minutes, or until the eggs are almost set. Flip the pancake over, and cook for 2 additional minutes, or until the eggs are completely set. As the pancakes are done, transfer them to a serving plate and keep warm in a preheated oven.

4. Serve hot, topping each serving with some of the sauce.

Yield: *4 servings*

1½ cups fat-free egg substitute

4 cups mung bean sprouts

1 can (8 ounces) water chestnuts, drained and chopped

2 scallions, thinly sliced

⅛ teaspoon ground black pepper

SAUCE

2 teaspoons cornstarch

1 teaspoon brown sugar

1 cup unsalted vegetable broth

2 tablespoons reduced-sodium soy sauce or hoison sauce

½ teaspoon sesame oil

NUTRITIONAL FACTS (PER 2-PANCAKE SERVING)
Calories: 88 Cholesterol: 0 mg Fat: 0.6 g
Fiber: 1.3 g Protein: 10 g Sodium: 411 mg

Eggplant Parmesan

Yield: *6 servings*

2 medium eggplants (about 1 pound each)

4 egg whites, beaten

½ cup dried Italian bread crumbs

¼ cup unbleached flour

½ cup grated nonfat or reduced-fat Parmesan cheese, divided

Olive oil cooking spray

1 cup shredded nonfat or reduced-fat mozzarella cheese

SAUCE

2 cans (1 pound each) unsalted tomatoes, crushed

1 can (6 ounces) tomato paste

1 medium onion, chopped

1½ teaspoons crushed fresh garlic

2 teaspoons dried Italian seasoning

¼ teaspoon ground black pepper

¼ teaspoon crushed red pepper

1. To make the sauce, combine all of the sauce ingredients in a 2-quart saucepan, and stir to mix well. Bring the mixture to a boil over high heat. Then reduce the heat to low, cover, and simmer for 20 minutes. Set aside to keep warm.

2. Trim the ends off the eggplants, but do not peel. Cut each eggplant crosswise into 9 slices, each approximately ½-inch thick.

3. Place the egg whites in a medium-sized shallow bowl. Combine the bread crumbs, flour, and ¼ cup of the Parmesan in another shallow bowl. Dip the eggplant slices first in the egg whites, and then in the crumb mixture.

4, Coat a large baking sheet with olive oil cooking spray, and arrange the eggplant slices in a single layer on the pan. Spray the tops of the slices very lightly with the cooking spray, and bake at 400°F for 15 to 20 minutes, or until the eggplant is golden brown and tender.

5. Coat a 9-x-13-inch baking pan with nonstick cooking spray. Transfer the eggplant slices to the dish, slightly overlapping the slices to allow them to fit in a single layer. Pour the sauce over the eggplant slices, and sprinkle with the mozzarella and the remaining Parmesan.

6. Bake at 400°F for 5 minutes, or until the cheese is melted. Serve hot with your choice of pasta.

NUTRITIONAL FACTS (PER SERVING)
Calories: 201 Cholesterol: 10 mg Fat: 1.1 g
Fiber: 6 g Protein: 15 g Sodium: 588 mg

Time-Saving Tip

To reduce preparation time, make Eggplant Parmesan with 4½ cups of bottled fat-free marinara sauce instead of using homemade sauce.

Fresh Tomato Pizza

1. To make the crust, combine I cup of the flour with the oat bran, yeast, sugar, and salt, and stir to mix well. Place the water in a saucepan, and heat until very warm (125°F to 130°F). Add the water to the flour mixture, and stir for 1 minute. Stir in enough of the remaining flour, 2 tablespoons at a time, to form a stiff dough.

2. Sprinkle 2 tablespoons of the remaining flour over a flat surface, and turn the dough onto the surface. Knead the dough for 5 minutes, gradually adding enough of the remaining flour to form a smooth, satiny ball. Coat a large bowl with nonstick cooking spray, and place the dough in the bowl. Cover the bowl with a clean kitchen towel, and let rise in a warm place for about 35 minutes, or until doubled in size.

3. When the dough has risen, punch it down, shape it into a ball, and turn it onto a lightly floured surface. Using a rolling pin, roll the dough into a 12-inch circle. Sprinkle the cornmeal over a 12-inch pizza pan, and place the dough in the pan.

4. Spread the garlic over the crust. Then arrange a single layer of tomato slices over the garlic, extending the tomatoes to within ½ inch of the edges. Sprinkle a layer of mozzarella over the tomatoes, and top with the pepper and onion rings. Finally, sprinkle with the oregano and Parmesan.

5. Bake at 450°F for 16 to 18 minutes, or until the cheese is browned and bubbly. Slice and serve immediately.

NUTRITIONAL FACTS (PER SLICE)
Calories: 153 Cholesterol: 4 mg Fat: 0.8 g
Fiber: 2.3 g Protein: 10 g Sodium: 189 mg

Time-Saving Tip

The dough for Fresh Tomato Pizza may be mixed in a bread machine. Just follow the directions on page 93.

Yield: 8 slices

CRUST

1¾ cups bread flour, divided

½ cup oat bran

1½ teaspoons Rapid Rise yeast

1 teaspoon sugar

¼ teaspoon salt

¾ cup water

1 teaspoon whole grain cornmeal

TOPPINGS

1 teaspoon crushed fresh garlic

3 large plum tomatoes, thinly sliced

1¼ cups shredded nonfat or reduced-fat mozzarella cheese

8 thin green bell pepper rings

3 thin onion slices, separated into rings

1½ teaspoons dried oregano or Italian seasoning

1 tablespoon nonfat or reduced-fat Parmesan cheese

Spinach and Cheese Calzones

Yield: *6 servings*

CRUST

2¼ cups bread flour, divided

⅔ cup oat bran

1½ teaspoons Rapid Rise yeast

1 teaspoon sugar

¼ teaspoon salt

¼ teaspoon celery seed

1 cup water

1 teaspoon whole grain cornmeal

FILLING

1¼ cups chopped fresh spinach

2 tablespoons finely chopped onion

1¼ cups nonfat ricotta cheese

¾ cup grated nonfat or reduced-fat mozzarella cheese

2 tablespoons grated Parmesan cheese

¾ teaspoon dried Italian seasoning

SAUCE (OPTIONAL)

2 cups bottled fat-free marinara sauce

1. To make the crust, in a large bowl, combine 1¼ cups of the flour with all of the oat bran, yeast, sugar, salt, and celery seed, and stir to mix well. Place the water in a saucepan, and heat until very warm (125°F to 130°F). Add the water to the flour mixture, and stir for 1 minute. Stir in enough of the remaining flour, 2 tablespoons at a time, to form a stiff dough.

2. Sprinkle 2 tablespoons of the remaining flour over a flat surface, and turn the dough onto the surface. Knead the dough for 5 minutes, gradually adding enough of the remaining flour to form a smooth, satiny ball. Coat a large bowl with nonstick cooking spray, and place the dough in the bowl. Cover the bowl with a clean kitchen towel, and let rise in a warm place for about 35 minutes, or until doubled in size.

3. When the dough has risen, punch it down, divide it into 6 portions, and shape each portion into a ball. Using a rolling pin, roll each ball into a 7-inch circle.

4. To make the filling, combine all of the filling ingredients in a medium-sized bowl, and stir to mix well. Spread ⅙ of the filling on the bottom half of each circle of dough, extending the filling to within ½ inch of the edges. Brush a little water around the outer edges of each circle, fold the top half over the bottom half, and firmly press the edges together to seal.

5. Sprinkle the cornmeal over a large baking sheet, and arrange the calzones on the sheet. Bake at 450°F for 15 to 17 minutes, or until golden brown. If desired, place the marinara sauce in a small saucepan, and cook over medium heat just until heated through. Serve the calzones hot, accompanying each serving with a small dish of the warm sauce.

NUTRITIONAL FACTS (PER CALZONE)
Calories: 264 Cholesterol: 13 mg Fat: 1 g
Fiber: 3.5 g Protein: 19.4 g Sodium: 336 mg

Time-Saving Tip

Like the Fresh Tomato Pizza dough, the dough for Spinach and Cheese Calzones may be mixed in a bread machine. Just follow the directions on page 93.

Zucchini-Rice Casserole

1. Coat a large skillet with nonstick cooking spray, and add the zucchini, mushrooms, onions, tomatoes, and garlic. Place the skillet over medium heat, and cook, stirring constantly, for several minutes, or until the vegetables are tender and most of the liquid has evaporated.

2. Remove the skillet from the heat, and set aside to cool slightly. Stir in first the rice, and then the egg substitute, yogurt, Swiss or mozzarella, and pepper.

3. Coat a 2-quart casserole dish with nonstick cooking spray, and spread the mixture evenly in the dish. Sprinkle the Parmesan over the top, and bake at 350°F for about 50 minutes, or until browned and bubbly. Remove the dish from the oven, and let sit for 5 minutes before serving.

NUTRITIONAL FACTS (PER 1¼-CUP SERVING)
Calories: 174 Cholesterol: 6 mg Fat: 1 g
Fiber: 3 g Protein: 13 g Sodium: 199 mg

Yield: *6 servings*

2 medium zucchini, scrubbed, halved lengthwise, and cut into ¼-inch slices

1½ cups sliced fresh mushrooms

½ cup chopped onion

2 medium plum tomatoes, chopped

1 teaspoon crushed fresh garlic

3 cups cooked brown rice

½ cup fat-free egg substitute

½ cup plain nonfat yogurt

1 cup shredded nonfat or reduced-fat Swiss or mozzarella cheese

¼ teaspoon ground black pepper

3 tablespoons grated nonfat or reduced-fat Parmesan cheese

Broccoli Quiche in Potato Crust

Yield: 5 servings

1 package (10 ounces) frozen chopped broccoli, thawed and squeezed dry

1 cup shredded nonfat or reduced-fat Cheddar or Swiss cheese

1 cup dry curd or nonfat cottage cheese

1 cup fat-free egg substitute

¼ cup finely chopped onion

1½ teaspoons Dijon mustard

1 tablespoon unbleached flour

⅛ teaspoon ground black pepper

2 medium potatoes, scrubbed

1. Combine all of the ingredients except for the potatoes in a large bowl, and stir to mix well. Set aside.

2. Coat a 9-inch deep dish pie pan with nonstick cooking spray. Slice the potatoes ¼-inch thick, and arrange the slices in a single layer over the bottom and sides of the pan to form a crust. Pour the broccoli mixture into the crust

3. Bake at 375°F for about 45 minutes, or until the top is golden brown and a sharp knife inserted in the center of the quiche comes out clean. Remove the dish from the oven, and let sit for 5 minutes before slicing and serving.

NUTRITIONAL FACTS (PER SERVING)

Calories: 175 Cholesterol: 6 mg Fat: 0.4 g
Fiber: 3.5 g Protein: 20 g Sodium: 289 mg

Chili Cheese Casserole

Yield: 6 servings

5 cups cooked brown rice

6 fresh or canned (drained) mild green chili or banana peppers, diced into ¾-inch pieces

1¼ cups shredded nonfat or reduced-fat Monterey jack or Cheddar cheese

1½ teaspoons ground cumin

¼ teaspoon salt (optional)

1. Combine all of the ingredients in a large bowl, and stir to mix well.

2. Coat a 2-quart casserole dish with nonstick cooking spray, and spread the mixture evenly in the dish. Cover with aluminum foil, and bake at 350°F for 50 to 60 minutes, or until the peppers are tender and the dish is heated through. Serve hot.

NUTRITIONAL FACTS (PER 1-CUP SERVING)

Calories: 223 Cholesterol: 5 mg Fat: 1.4 g
Fiber: 3.1 g Protein: 13 g Sodium: 208 mg

Two-Bean Chili

1. Combine the TVP and broth in a 3-quart pot, and bring to a boil over high heat Remove the pot from the heat, and let sit for 5 minutes, or until the liquid has been absorbed.

2. Add all of the remaining ingredients except for the cheese to the TVP mixture, and stir to mix well. Place over high heat, and bring to a boil. Reduce the heat to low, cover, and simmer for 25 to 30 minutes, or until the vegetables are tender.

3. Serve hot, topping each serving with some of the cheese if desired.

NUTRITIONAL FACTS (PER 1-CUP SERVING)
Calories: 156 Cholesterol: 0 mg Fat: 0.8 g
Fiber: 11 g Protein: 13 g Sodium: 302 mg

Yield: *8 cups*

1 cup texturized vegetable protein (TVP)

⅞ cup vegetable or beef broth

1 large onion, chopped

1 large green bell pepper, chopped

1 can (1 pound) unsalted tomatoes, crushed

1 can (1 pound) unsalted tomato sauce

1 can (1 pound) red kidney beans, drained

1 can (1 pound) pinto beans, drained

2–3 tablespoons chili powder

1 teaspoon dried oregano

½ teaspoon ground cumin

1 cup shredded nonfat or reduced-fat Cheddar cheese (optional)

BEAN BURRITOS SUPREME

Yield: *6 servings*

1¾ cups cooked pinto beans, or 1 can (1 pound) pinto beans, drained

2 teaspoons chili powder

¼ teaspoon ground cumin

½ cup finely chopped yellow onion

½ cup finely chopped tomato

6 fat-free flour tortillas (10-inch rounds)

½ cup nonfat sour cream

½ cup shredded nonfat or reduced-fat Cheddar cheese

¾ cup shredded lettuce

1. Place the beans in a medium-sized bowl, and mash with a fork until slightly chunky. Stir in the chili powder and cumin, and set aside.

2. Coat a large skillet with nonstick cooking spray, and add the onion and tomato. Place the pan over medium heat, cover, and cook, stirring occasionally, for about 5 minutes, or until the vegetables are soft.

3. Add the beans to the skillet mixture, and cook uncovered, stirring constantly, until the beans are heated through and the mixture has the consistency of thick refried beans. Remove the skillet from the heat, cover to keep warm, and set aside.

4. Preheat a large nonstick skillet over medium-high heat, and place a tortilla in the skillet. To warm the tortilla, cook for 15 seconds, turning after 8 seconds.

5. Lay the warm tortilla on a flat surface, and spoon ¼ cup of the warm bean mixture along the right side of the tortilla. Top the bean mixture with 1 tablespoon of the sour cream, 1 tablespoon of the cheese, and 2 tablespoons of the lettuce. Fold the bottom edge of the tortilla up about 1 inch. (This fold will prevent the filling from falling out) Then, beginning at the right edge, roll the tortilla up jelly-roll style.

6. Transfer the tortilla to a serving platter, cover with aluminum foil, and place in a 200°F oven to keep warm. Repeat with the remaining tortillas, and serve immediately.

NUTRITIONAL FACTS (PER BURRITO)
Calories: 223 Cholesterol: 2 mg Fat: 0.4 g
Fiber: 5.9 g Protein: 10.2 g Sodium: 437 mg

Making Bean Burritos Supreme.

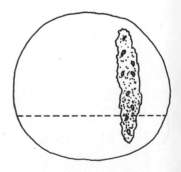

a. Arrange the filling along the right side of the tortilla.

Black Bean Pizzas

1. Place the beans in a medium-sized bowl, and mash with a fork until slightly chunky. Stir in the chili powder, and set aside.

2. Coat a large skillet with nonstick cooking spray, and add the tomato and cumin. Place over medium heat, cover, and cook, stirring occasionally, for about 5 minutes, or until the tomatoes are soft.

3. Add the beans to the skillet, and cook uncovered, stirring constantly, until the beans are heated through and the mixture has the consistency of thick refried beans. Remove the skillet from the heat, and set aside.

4. Coat a large baking sheet with nonstick cooking spray, and lay the tortillas on the sheet. Spread ¼ cup of the bean mixture over each tortilla, extending the mixture to within ½ inch of the edges. Top each tortilla with ¼ cup of the cheese, ⅙ of the onions, ⅙ of the olives, and 2 teaspoons of the jalapeños.

5. Bake uncovered at 400°F for 7 to 9 minutes, or until the pizzas are browned and crisp. Remove from the oven, top each pizza with 2 tablespoons each of the chopped tomato and shredded lettuce, and serve immediately.

Yield: *6 servings*

1¾ cups cooked black beans, or 1 can (1 pound) black beans, drained

1 tablespoon chili powder

¾ cup finely chopped tomato

¼ teaspoon whole cumin seed

6 fat-free flour tortillas (10-inch rounds)

1½ cups shredded nonfat or reduced-fat Cheddar cheese

6 thin onion slices, separated into rings

6 large black olives, thinly sliced

2 tablespoons finely chopped jalapeño peppers (optional)

¾ cup chopped tomato

¾ cup shredded lettuce

NUTRITIONAL FACTS (PER PIZZA)
Calories: 240 Cholesterol: 5 mg Fat: 1 g
Fiber: 6.2 g Protein: 15.8 g Sodium: 585 mg

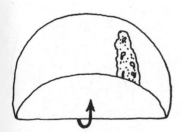

b. Fold the bottom edge of the tortilla up.

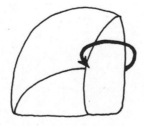

c. Fold the right side over the filling.

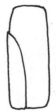

d. Continue folding to form a roll.

Lentil Chili

Yield: *8 cups*

¾ cup dried brown lentils, cleaned (page 200)

2 cups chicken, beef, or vegetable broth

1 can (1 pound) unsalted tomatoes, crushed

1 medium green bell pepper, chopped

1 medium yellow onion, chopped

1 teaspoon crushed fresh garlic

2 tablespoons chili powder

½ teaspoon ground cumin

¼ teaspoon ground allspice

1 can (1 pound) unsalted tomato sauce

2 cups fresh or frozen (thawed) whole kernel corn

1. Combine all of the ingredients except for the tomato sauce and corn in a 2½-quart pot, and bring to a boil over high heat. Reduce the heat to low, cover, and simmer, stirring occasionally, for 25 to 30 minutes, or until the lentils are tender.

2. Add the tomato sauce and corn to the lentil mixture. Stir to mix, cover, and simmer for 10 to 15 additional minutes. Serve hot.

NUTRITIONAL FACTS (PER 1-CUP SERVING)

Calories: 140 Cholesterol: 0 mg Fat: 0.8 g
Fiber: 5.6 g Protein: 9 g Sodium: 219 mg

Bean Burgers

1. Combine the lentils, broth, and pepper in a 1½-quart pot, and bring to a boil over high heat. Reduce the heat to low, cover, and simmer for 25 to 30 minutes, or until the lentils are soft. Remove the pot from the heat, drain off any excess water, and set aside to cool.

2. While the lentils are cooking, tear the bread into pieces. Place the bread in a food processor or blender, and process into fine crumbs. Transfer the crumbs to a small dish, and set aside.

3. Place the cooked lentils in a food processor (this mixture is too stiff for a blender), and process until the mixture is almost smooth. Add the carrot, mushrooms, scallions, and bread crumbs, and process to mix well. Add the cheese, and process just until mixed.

4. Shape scant ½-cup portions of the lentil mixture into 6 (3½-inch) patties. Coat a large nonstick skillet or griddle with nonstick cooking spray, and preheat over medium heat. Place the patties in the skillet, and cook for 7 to 9 minutes, turning every 3 minutes, until golden brown.

5. Place each pattie in a pita pocket or bun, and top with 1 leaf of lettuce, 1 slice of tomato, 2 tablespoons of sprouts, and 1 tablespoon of ranch dressing. Serve immediately.

NUTRITIONAL FACTS (PER BURGER)
Calories: 225 Cholesterol: 2 mg Fat: 1.6 g
Fiber: 7 g Protein: 17 g Sodium: 440 mg

Yield: *6 servings*

¾ cup dried brown lentils, cleaned (page 200)

1¾ cups unsalted vegetable or beef broth

¼ teaspoon ground black pepper

2 slices whole wheat bread

½ cup grated carrot

½ cup finely chopped fresh mushrooms

¼ cup finely chopped scallions

¾ cup shredded nonfat or reduced-fat Cheddar or mozzarella cheese

6 whole wheat pita pockets (6-inch rounds) or multigrain burger buns

6 lettuce leaves

6 slices tomato

¾ cup alfalfa sprouts

¼ cup plus 2 tablespoons bottled nonfat ranch dressing

Bean Basics

If you really want to get the fat out of your diet, think beans. A hearty and satisfying alternative to meat, beans are fat-free, and rich in protein, complex carbohydrates, B vitamins, iron, zinc, copper, and potassium. As for fiber, no other food surpasses beans. Just a half cup of cooked beans provides 4 to 8 grams of fiber—up to four times the amount found in most other plant foods. Beans have also been found to lower cholesterol. As an added bonus, beans stabilize blood sugar levels, making you feel full and satisfied long after the meal is over—a definite benefit if you're watching your weight

Some people avoid eating beans because of "bean bloat." What causes this problem? Complex sugars in beans, called oligosaccharides, sometimes form gas when broken down in the lower intestine. This side effect usually subsides when beans are made a regular part of the diet, and the body becomes more efficient at digesting them. The proper cleaning, soaking, and cooking of dried beans can also help prevent bean bloat. The following techniques will help you make beans a delicious and healthful part of your diet.

Cleaning

Because beans are a natural product, packages of dried beans sometimes contain shriveled or discolored beans, as well as small twigs and other items. Before cooking, sort through your beans and discard any discolored or blemished legumes. Rinse the beans well, cover them with water, and discard any that float to the top.

Soaking

There are two methods used to soak beans in preparation for cooking. If you have time—if you intend to cook your dish the next day, for instance—you may want to use the long method, as this technique is best for reducing the gas-producing oligosaccharides. If dinner is just a couple of hours away, though, the

quick method is your best bet. Keep in mind that not all beans must be soaked before cooking. Black-eyed peas, brown and red lentils, and split peas do not require soaking.

The Long Method

After cleaning the beans, place them in a large bowl or pot, and cover them with four times as much water. Soak the beans for at least four hours, and for as long as twelve hours. If soaking them for more than four, place the bowl or pot in the refrigerator. After soaking, discard the water and replace with fresh water before cooking.

The Quick Method

After cleaning the beans, place them in a large pot, and cover them with four times as much water. Bring the pot to a boil over high heat, and continue to boil for two minutes. Remove the pot from the heat, cover, and let stand for one hour. After soaking, discard the water and replace with fresh water before cooking.

Cooking

To cook beans for use in salads, casseroles, and other dishes that contain little or no liquid, clean and soak as described above, discard the soaking water, and replace with two cups of water for each cup of dried beans. When beans are to be cooked in soups or stews that include acidic ingredients—lemon juice, vinegar, or tomatoes, for instance—add these ingredients at the end of the cooking time. Acidic foods can toughen the beans' outer layer, slowing the rate at which the beans cook. You'll know that the beans are done when you can mash them easily with a fork. Keep in mind that old beans may take longer to cook. During long cooking times, periodically check the pot, and add more liquid if necessary.

The following table gives approximate cooking times for several different beans. Need a meal in a hurry? Lentils and split peas require no soaking and cook quickly. Lentils are the fastest cooking of all the legumes; they can be ready in less than thirty minutes. Split peas cook in less than an hour.

Cooking Times for Dried Beans and Legumes

Bean or Legume	Cooking Time
Black, garbanzo, great northern, kidney, navy, pinto, and white beans	1½–2 hours
Black-eyed peas*	1–1¼ hours
Lentils, brown*	25–30 minutes
Lentils, red*	15–20 minutes
Lima beans, baby	45 minutes–1¼ hours
Lima beans, large	1–1½ hours
Split peas*	45–50 minutes

*These beans do not require soaking.

Curried Lentils

1. Place all of the ingredients in a 2½-quart pot, and bring to a boil over high heat. Reduce the heat to low, cover, and simmer, stirring occasionally, for 25 to 30 minutes, or until the lentils are soft. (If you're using red lentils, cook the mixture for only 15 to 20 minutes.)

2. Serve hot, ladling each serving over brown rice or couscous, if desired.

NUTRITIONAL FACTS (PER 1-CUP SERVING)

Calories: 181 Cholesterol: 0 mg Fat: 0.7 g
Fiber: 7.2 g Protein: 12 g Sodium: 340 mg

Yield: *5 cups*

1 cup dried-brown or red lentils, cleaned (page 200)

3 cups unsalted chicken broth or water

1 large onion, chopped

2 medium carrots, peeled, halved, and sliced

2 stalks celery, thinly sliced (include leaves)

1 large apple, peeled and finely chopped

1 teaspoon crushed fresh garlic

1½ teaspoons chicken bouillon granules

2–3 teaspoons curry powder

SOUTHWESTERN Black Beans

Yield: *8 servings*

2½ cups black beans, cleaned and soaked (page 200)

7½ cups unsalted chicken broth or water

2 medium yellow onions, chopped

1 large green bell pepper, chopped

2 teaspoons crushed fresh garlic

2 teaspoons ham, chicken, or vegetable bouillon granules, or 6 ounces ham (at least 97% lean), diced

1 tablespoon chili powder

2 dried hot red chili pepper pods

1 teaspoon dried oregano

½ teaspoon ground cumin

¼ teaspoon ground black pepper

¼ cup distilled white vinegar

TOPPINGS

¾ cup shredded nonfat or reduced-fat Cheddar cheese

½ cup nonfat sour cream

¼ cup sliced scallions

1. Combine all of the ingredients except for the vinegar and toppings in a 4-quart pot, and bring to a boil over high heat. Reduce the heat to low, cover, and simmer, stirring occasionally, for 2 hours, or until the beans are soft and the liquid is thick. Periodically check the pot during cooking, and add a little more broth or water if needed.

2. Remove the pot from the heat, discard the pepper pods, and stir in the vinegar. Serve hot, topping each serving with 1½ tablespoons of cheese, 1 tablespoon of sour cream, and 1½ teaspoons of scallions. If desired, serve over brown rice.

NUTRITIONAL FACTS (PER 1-CUP SERVING)

Calories: 237 Cholesterol: 2 mg Fat: 0.8 g
Fiber: 16 g Protein: 16 g Sodium: 345 mg

Spicy Pinto Beans

1. Combine all of the ingredients except for the tomatoes and cilantro in a 3-quart pot, and bring to a boil over high heat. Reduce the heat to low, cover, and simmer, stirring occasionally, for 1 hour and 30 minutes, or until the beans are tender. Periodically check the pot during cooking, and add a little more broth or water if needed.

2. Add the tomatoes to the bean mixture, and cook for 30 additional minutes. Serve hot, topping the beans with cilantro or scallions. If desired, serve over brown rice.

NUTRITIONAL FACTS (PER 1-CUP SERVING)

Calories: 184 Cholesterol: 0 mg Fat: 0.9 g
Fiber: 15 g Protein: 11 g Sodium: 289 mg

Yield: *7 cups*

2 cups dried pinto beans, cleaned and soaked (page 200)

5½ cups unsalted chicken broth or water

1 medium onion, chopped

1 teaspoon crushed fresh garlic

1 tablespoon chopped jalapeño peppers

2 teaspoons ham, chicken, or vegetable bouillon granules

1½ teaspoons ground cumin

2 teaspoons chili powder

2 medium tomatoes, diced

⅓ cup chopped fresh cilantro or scallions

Jamaican Red Beans

Yield: *7 cups*

2 cups dried red kidney beans, cleaned and soaked (page 200)

6 cups unsalted chicken broth or water

2 medium onions, chopped

2 stalks celery, thinly sliced (include leaves)

2 teaspoons ham or chicken bouillon granules

2 teaspoons dried thyme

½ teaspoon ground allspice

¼ teaspoon ground black pepper

2 bay leaves

2–3 dried hot red chili pepper pods

2 tablespoons distilled white vinegar

1. Combine all of the ingredients except for the vinegar in a 3-quart pot, and bring to a boil over high heat. Reduce the heat to low, cover, and simmer, stirring occasionally, for 2 hours, or until the beans are soft and the liquid is thick. Add a little more liquid during cooking if needed.

2. Remove the pot from the heat, and discard the bay leaves and pepper pods. Stir in the vinegar, and serve hot, ladling the beans over brown rice if desired.

NUTRITIONAL FACTS (PER 1-CUP SERVING)
Calories: 193 Cholesterol: 0 mg Fat: 0.6 g
Fiber: 12 g Protein: 12 g Sodium: 247 mg

Fettuccine Almost Alfredo

1. Cook the pasta al dente according to package directions. Drain well, return the pasta to the pot, and cover to keep warm).

2. While the pasta is cooking, combine all of the sauce ingredients in a blender or food processor, and process until smooth. Pour the mixture into a 1-quart saucepan, place over low heat, and cook, stirring constantly, just until the mixture is heated through. Do not allow the sauce to boil.

3. Pour the sauce over the pasta, add the Parmesan, and toss gently to mix well. Serve immediately.

Yield: 5 servings

12 ounces fettuccine pasta

¾ cup grated nonfat or reduced-fat Parmesan cheese

SAUCE

1 cup nonfat ricotta cheese

¾ cup skim milk

1 tablespoon butter-flavored sprinkles

⅛ teaspoon ground white pepper

NUTRITIONAL FACTS (PER 1⅓-CUP SERVING)
Calories: 342 Cholesterol: 20 mg Fat: 1.1 g
Fiber: 1.6 g Protein: 22 g Sodium: 276 mg

Cajun Chicken Pasta

1. Cook the pasta al dente according to package directions. Drain well, return the pasta to the pot, and cover to keep warm.

2. While the pasta is cooking, coat a large nonstick skillet with non-stick cooking spray. Add the garlic and chicken, and stir-fry over medium-high heat for about 3 minutes, or until the chicken is browned.

3. Reduce the heat to low, and add all of the remaining ingredients except for the pasta to the skillet. Cover and simmer, stirring occasionally, for about 10 minutes, or until the vegetables are tender.

4. Add the pasta to the skillet mixture, and toss gently to mix. Remove the bay leaf and serve immediately.

Yield: 4 servings

8 ounces linguine or fettuccine pasta

2 teaspoons crushed fresh garlic

8 ounces boneless skinless chicken breasts, cut into thin strips

1 pound fresh tomatoes, chopped (about 3 medium)

½ cup chopped onion

½ cup sliced celery (include leaves)

½ cup chopped green bell pepper

¼ cup unsalted tomato paste

1 teaspoon Cajun seasoning (or more to taste)

1 bay leaf

NUTRITIONAL FACTS (PER 1½-CUP SERVING)
Calories: 324 Cholesterol: 33 mg Fat: 2.2 g
Fiber: 4 g Protein: 22 g Sodium: 342 mg

Sonoma Spaghetti

Yield: *4 servings*

½ cup chopped sun-dried tomatoes (not packed in oil)

½ cup water

8 ounces spaghetti or fettuccine pasta

1 cup nonfat or reduced-fat cream cheese

1 cup skim milk

¼ teaspoon ground white pepper

4 scallions, thinly sliced

2 tablespoons minced fresh basil

¼ cup grated nonfat or reduced-fat Parmesan cheese

1. Place the sun-dried tomatoes and water in a 1-quart saucepan, and bring to a boil over medium heat. Boil for 20 seconds, and remove the pot from the heat. Cover, and set aside for 20 minutes, or until the water has been absorbed

2. Cook the pasta al dente according to package directions. Drain well, return the pasta to the pot, and cover to keep warm.

3. While the pasta is cooking, combine the cream cheese, milk, and pepper in a blender or food processor, and process until smooth. Pour the mixture into a 1-quart saucepan, and place over low heat Cook and stir for about 2 minutes, or just until the sauce is heated through. Do not allow the sauce to boil. The sauce should be the consistency of heavy cream. Add a few tablespoons of skim milk, if necessary, to thin it to the desired consistency.

4. Drain any remaining liquid from the tomatoes, and add the tomatoes to the pasta. Add the sauce, scallions, and basil, and toss gently to mix. Serve immediately, topping each serving with a tablespoon of the Parmesan.

NUTRITIONAL FACTS (PER 1½-CUP SERVING)
Calories: 317 Cholesterol: 10 mg Fat: 1.2 g
Fiber: 2.4 g Protein: 20.4 g Sodium: 493 mg

COOKING TIP

Cooking with Fresh Pasta

A variety of fresh pastas is now available in the refrigerated section of most grocery stores, and in some specialty shops, as well. Like their dry counterparts, most fresh pastas contain no added fat. To substitute fresh pasta for dry pastas in any of the recipes in this book, replace the required amount of dry pasta with 1¼ times as much fresh. For example, if a recipe calls for 8 ounces of linguini, substitute 10 ounces of fresh linguini. Fresh pasta cooks much faster than dry, so be sure to check the label for the recommended cooking time. Then enjoy the incomparable tenderness and delicacy of fresh pasta in a delicious low-fat dish.

Linguini with Clam Sauce

1. Drain the clams, reserving ½ cup of the juice, and set aside.

2. Cook the pasta al dente according to package directions. Drain well, and return the pasta to the pot. If desired, add the olive oil and toss to mix. Cover the pot and set aside.

3. While the linguine is cooking, combine the onions, mushrooms, celery, garlic, basil, oregano, butter-flavored sprinkles, and pepper in a large skillet. Add the clams and the reserved juice, and bring to a boil over high heat. Reduce the heat to low, cover, and simmer, stirring occasionally, for 10 minutes, or until the vegetables are tender.

4. Add the cooked linguine and the parsley to the clam mixture, and toss gently until well mixed. Serve immediately, topping each serving with a rounded tablespoon of the Parmesan.

NUTRITIONAL FACTS (PER 1½-CUP SERVING)

Calories: 318 Cholesterol: 36 mg Fat: 1.9 g
Fiber: 2.4 g Protein: 22 g Sodium: 252 mg

Yield: *4 servings*

2 cans (6 ounces each) chopped clams, undrained

8 ounces linguine pasta

1 tablespoon olive oil (optional)

1 medium yellow onion, diced

1 cup sliced fresh mushrooms

½ cup thinly sliced celery (include leaves)

2 teaspoons crushed fresh garlic

¾ teaspoon dried basil

¾ teaspoon dried oregano

1 tablespoon butter-flavored sprinkles

⅛ teaspoon ground white pepper

¼ cup minced fresh parsley

⅓ cup grated nonfat or reduced-fat Parmesan cheese

Spaghetti with Shrimp and Sun-Dried Tomatoes

Yield: *4 servings*

8 ounces thin spaghetti

1 tablespoon olive oil (optional)

2 teaspoons crushed fresh garlic

1 pound cleaned raw shrimp

½ cup diced sun-dried tomatoes
(not packed in oil)

2 tablespoons dry white wine

½ cup chicken broth

1 teaspoon dried rosemary

¼ teaspoon ground black pepper

¼ cup minced fresh parsley

1. Cook the pasta al dente according to package directions. Drain well, and return the pasta to the pot. If desired, add the olive oil and toss to mix. Cover the pot and set aside.

2. While the pasta is cooking, coat a large skillet with nonstick cooking spray. Add the garlic, shrimp, tomatoes, wine, broth, rosemary, and pepper to the skillet, and stir to mix. Cover and cook over medium heat for 3 minutes, or until the shrimp turn pink and the tomatoes plump. Reduce the heat to low.

3. Add the pasta to the shrimp mixture. Tossing gently, cook for a minute or 2, or until the mixture is heated through. Toss in the parsley, and serve immediately.

NUTRITIONAL FACTS (PER 1½-CUP SERVING)

Calories: 318 Cholesterol: 166 mg Fat: 2.2 g
Fiber: 2.3 g Protein: 27 g Sodium: 434 mg

Pasta with Crab and Asparagus

1. Combine all of the sauce ingredients in a blender or food processor, and process until smooth. Set aside.

2. Cook the pasta until almost al dente according to package directions. Add the asparagus to the cooking water, and cook for another minute, or until the asparagus are crisp-tender. Drain the pasta and asparagus, and return the mixture to the pot.

3. Add the crab meat to the pasta mixture, and top with the sauce. Place the pot over low heat, and, tossing gently, cook until the sauce is heated through. If the sauce is too thick, add a little skim milk.

4. Serve immediately, topping each serving with a tablespoon of the Parmesan.

NUTRITIONAL FACTS (PER 1½-CUP SERVING)
Calories: 337 Cholesterol: 47 mg Fat: 1.6 g
Fiber: 2.7 g Protein: 29 g Sodium: 332 mg

Yield: *4 servings*

8 ounces penne or sea shell pasta

½ pound fresh asparagus spears, cut into 1-inch pieces

6 ounces (about 1 cup) flaked cooked crab meat

¼ cup grated nonfat or reduced-fat Parmesan

SAUCE

1 cup nonfat ricotta cheese

2 scallions, chopped

2 tablespoons dry sherry

2 tablespoons lemon juice

¼ teaspoon dried oregano

⅛ teaspoon ground white pepper

Getting the Fat Out of Your Pasta Recipes

It's a shame that most pasta recipes are so high in fat, as pasta is a natural for low-fat cooking. Happily, it's easy to do a healthy makeover of any pasta dish. Begin by leaving the oil—and the salt, too!—out of your cooking water. Pasta cooks up beautifully without this added fat. Then use the following table to replace high-fat foods like butter and sour cream with low- and no-fat ingredients.

Substitutions That Save Fat

Instead of:	Use:	You Save:	Special Considerations:
1 cup butter margarine.	1 cup Butter Buds liquid.	1,500 calories, 176 fat grams.	Butter Buds may be used in sauces, but not for sautéing.
	1 cup reduced-fat margarine or light butter.	800–1,200 calories, 88–112 fat grams.	Nonfat margarines generally do not melt well enough to be used in cooking.
1 cup cream.	⅔ cup nonfat ricotta cheese blended with ⅓ cup skim until smooth. (Add extra milk if the mixture is too thick.)	674 calories, 88 fat grams.	If using the ricotta mixture in a sauce that is to be heated, cook over low heat just until heated through. Some brands separate if boiled.
	1 cup evaporated skim milk.	622 calories, 88 fat grams.	Any of these substitutes may be used in cream sauces, casseroles, and other dishes.
	1 cup skim milk mixed with ⅓ cup instant nonfat dry milk powder.	622 calories, 88 fat grams.	
1 cup sour cream.	1 cup nonfat sour cream.	252 calories, 48 fat grams.	Some brands of sour cream separate when heated. Choose a brand like Land O Lakes, which is heat stable, if the sour cream will be used in a cooked sauce.
	1 cup plain nonfat yogurt.	355 calories, 48 fat grams.	All yogurts will separate if heated. To prevent this, stir 2 tablespoons of flour or 1 tablespoon of cornstarch into each cup of yogurt before adding it to the sauce.
1 cup whole-milk ricotta cheese.	1 cup nonfat ricotta cheese.	248 calories, 32 fat grams.	This ingredient makes an excellent substitute in lasagna and other dishes.
1 cup regular cream cheese.	1 cup nonfat cream cheese.	600 calories, 80 fat grams.	If using nonfat cream cheese in a sauce that is to be heated, cook over low heat just until heated through. Some brands separate if boiled.
1 cup whole-milk mozzarella cheese.	1 cup nonfat mozzarella cheese.	200 calories, 28 fat grams.	This ingredient makes an excellent substitute in lasagna and other dishes.

Bow Ties with Spicy Artichoke Sauce

1. Cook the pasta al dente according to package directions. Drain well, return the pasta to the pot, and cover to keep warm.

2. While the pasta is cooking, combine the tomatoes, onion, mushrooms, garlic, basil, oregano, cayenne, and black pepper in a large skillet. Place over medium-low heat, cover, and cook for 10 to 12 minutes, or until the tomatoes are soft.

3. Add the artichoke hearts, bell peppers, and lemon juice to the skillet mixture. Cover and cook for 2 additional minutes, or until the peppers are crisp-tender. Reduce the heat to low.

4. Add the pasta to the skillet mixture, and toss gently to mix. Add the Parmesan, toss gently, and serve immediately.

Yield: *5 servings*

8 ounces bow tie or rigatoni pasta

1 pound fresh tomatoes, diced (about 3 medium)

1 medium yellow onion, diced

1 cup sliced fresh mushrooms

1 tablespoon crushed fresh garlic

1 tablespoon dried basil

1 tablespoon dried oregano

¼ teaspoon cayenne pepper

¼ teaspoon ground black pepper

1 can (14 ounces) artichoke hearts, drained and quartered

½ red bell pepper, cut into thin strips

2 tablespoons lemon juice

½ cup plus 2 tablespoons grated nonfat or reduced-fat Parmesan cheese

---

NUTRITIONAL FACTS (PER 1½-CUP SERVING)
Calories: 235 Cholesterol: 6 mg Fat: 1.3 g
Fiber: 5.3 g Protein: 13 g Sodium: 148 mg

PASTA PRIMAVERA

Yield: *5 servings*

2½ teaspoons cornstarch

¼ teaspoon ground white pepper

1½ cups evaporated skim milk

8 ounces spaghetti or fettuccine pasta

2 teaspoons crushed fresh garlic

½ cup thinly sliced carrots

½ cup sliced fresh mushrooms

2 cups fresh broccoli florets

½ small red bell pepper, cut into thin strips

1 medium onion, cut into thin wedges

½ cup plus 2 tablespoons grated nonfat or reduced-fat Parmesan cheese

1. Combine the cornstarch, pepper, and milk in a jar with a tight-fitting lid, and shake until the cornstarch has dissolved. Set aside.

2. Cook the pasta al dente according to package directions. Drain well, return the pasta to the pot, and cover to keep warm.

3. Coat a large skillet with nonstick cooking spray. Place over medium-high heat, add the garlic, and stir-fry for 30 seconds. Add the vegetables along with 1 tablespoon of water. Cover and cook, stirring occasionally, for 3 to 5 minutes, or until the vegetables are crisp-tender. Add a little more water if the skillet becomes too dry.

4. Reduce the heat to medium, and add the pasta to the skillet mixture. Shake the milk mixture, and add it to the skillet. Toss gently over medium heat for about 2 minutes, or just until the sauce begins to boil and thicken slightly.

5. Remove the skillet from the heat, and add the Parmesan. Toss gently to mix, and serve immediately.

NUTRITIONAL FACTS (PER 1½-CUP SERVING)
Calories: 291 Cholesterol: 10 mg Fat: 1.1 g
Fiber: 3.2 g Protein: 17 g Sodium: 194 mg

Light and Lazy Lasagna

This lasagna is "lazy" because you don't cook the noodles before layering them in the pan. You can also prepare this entrée to the point of baking several hours—or even a day—in advance, and then refrigerate it until it's time to pop the dish into the oven.

1. To make the sauce, place the ground meat in a 4-quart pot. Cook over medium heat, stirring to crumble, until the meat is no longer pink. Drain off any fat. (If the meat is 95% lean, there will be no fat to drain.)

2. Add all of the remaining sauce ingredients to the browned meat, increase the heat to high, and bring to a boil. Reduce the heat to low, cover, and simmer for 25 minutes, or until the vegetables are tender. Set aside.

3. To make the filling, combine all of the filling ingredients in a large bowl, and stir to mix well. Set aside.

4. To assemble the lasagna, coat a 9-x-13-inch baking pan with nonstick cooking spray. Spoon 1 cup of the sauce over the bottom of the pan. Lay 4 of the uncooked noodles over the bottom of the pan, arranging 3 of the noodles lengthwise and 1 noodle crosswise. Allow a little space between the noodles for expansion. (You will have to break 1 inch off the crosswise noodle to make it fit in the pan.)

5. Top the noodles with half of the filling mixture, ¾ cup of the mozzarella, and 1½ cups of the sauce. Repeat the noodles, filling, mozzarella, and sauce layers. Finally, top with the remaining noodles, sauce, Parmesan, and mozzarella.

6. Cover the pan with aluminum foil, and bake at 350°F for 45 minutes. Remove the foil, and bake for 15 additional minutes, or until the edges are bubbly and the top is browned. Remove the dish from the oven, and let sit for 5 minutes before cutting and serving.

Yield: *10 servings*

12 lasagna noodles

2 cups shredded nonfat or reduced-fat mozzarella cheese

¼ cup grated nonfat or reduced-fat Parmesan cheese

FILLING

15 ounces nonfat ricotta cheese

1 cup dry curd or nonfat cottage cheese

¼ cup grated nonfat or reduced-fat Parmesan cheese

2 tablespoons finely chopped fresh parsley, or 2 teaspoons dried

SAUCE

8 ounces 95% lean ground beef or turkey Italian sausage

2 cans (1 pound each) unsalted tomato sauce

1 can (1 pound) unsalted tomatoes, crushed

2 tablespoons tomato paste

2 cups sliced fresh mushrooms

1 medium onion, chopped

1½ teaspoons crushed fresh garlic

2½ teaspoons dried Italian seasoning

NUTRITIONAL FACTS (PER SERVING)
Calories: 276 Cholesterol: 37 mg Fat: 2.0 g
Fiber: 3 g Protein: 28 g Sodium: 302 mg

Lasagna Roll-Ups

Yield: *4 servings*

8 lasagna noodles

1 cup shredded nonfat or reduced-fat mozzarella cheese

FILLING

15 ounces nonfat ricotta cheese

1 package (10 ounces) frozen chopped spinach, thawed and squeezed dry

½ cup grated carrot

2 tablespoons minced fresh parsley

SAUCE

1 can (1 pound) unsalted tomatoes, crushed

1 can (6 ounces) unsalted tomato paste

¼ cup unsalted vegetable broth or water

1 medium yellow onion, chopped

1 teaspoon dried Italian seasoning

1 teaspoon crushed fresh garlic

1. To make the sauce, combine all of the sauce ingredients in a 1½-quart pot, and bring to a boil over medium-high heat. Reduce the heat to low, cover, and simmer for 20 minutes.

2. To make the filling, combine all of the filling ingredients in a medium-sized bowl, and stir to mix well. Set aside.

3. Cook the noodles al dente according to package directions. Drain, rinse, and drain again.

4. Coat a 2½-quart casserole dish with nonstick cooking spray. To assemble the roll-ups, arrange the noodles on a flat surface, and spread ⅛ of the filling mixture along the length of each noodle. Roll each noodle up jelly-roll style, and place in the prepared dish, seam side down. Pour the sauce over the roll-ups.

5. Cover the dish with aluminum foil, and bake at 350°F for 30 minutes. Remove the foil, top with the mozzarella, and bake for 10 additional minutes, or until the cheese is melted. Serve hot.

NUTRITIONAL FACTS (PER SERVING)
Calories: 384 Cholesterol: 22 mg Fat: 1.4 g
Fiber: 6.0 g Protein: 35 g Sodium: 412 mg

Time-Saving Tip

In a hurry? Instead of preparing homemade sauce for your Lasagna Roll-Ups, use 3 cups of bottled fat-free marinara sauce.

Florentine Stuffed Shells

1. To make the sauce, combine all of the sauce ingredients in a 1½-quart pot, and bring to a boil over medium-high heat. Reduce the heat to low, cover, and simmer for 20 minutes.

2. To make the filling, combine all of the filling ingredients in a medium-sized bowl, and stir to mix well. Set aside.

3. Cook the pasta al dente according to package directions. Drain, rinse, and drain again. Set aside.

5. To assemble the dish, coat a 9-x-13-inch baking pan with nonstick cooking spray. Spoon 1 rounded tablespoon of the filling into each shell, and arrange the stuffed shells in a single layer in the pan. Pour the sauce over the shells.

5. Bake at 350°F for 25 to 30 minutes, or until heated through. Serve hot.

NUTRITIONAL FACTS (PER SERVING)
Calories: 257 Cholesterol: 9 mg Fat: 1.1 g
Fiber: 3.6 g Protein: 18 g Sodium: 361 mg

Time-Saving Tip

To speed preparation, make Florentine Stuffed Shells with 3 cups of bottled fat-free marinara sauce instead of the homemade sauce.

Yield: *8 servings*

24 jumbo pasta shells

FILLING

15 ounces nonfat ricotta cheese

½ cup shredded nonfat or reduced-fat mozzarella cheese

¼ cup grated nonfat or reduced-fat Parmesan cheese

1 package (10 ounces) frozen chopped spinach or broccoli, thawed and squeezed dry

¼ cup finely chopped onion

½ teaspoon dried Italian seasoning

SAUCE

1 can (1 pound) unsalted tomatoes, crushed

1 can (6 ounces) tomato paste

½ cup finely chopped onion

1 teaspoon crushed fresh garlic

¼ cup dry red wine, beef broth, or vegetable broth

2 tablespoons grated nonfat or reduced-fat Parmesan cheese

2 teaspoons dried Italian seasoning

¼ teaspoon ground black pepper

7

Creative Cakes

If you have ever tried to make a cake without fat, you understand the importance of this ingredient. Besides adding moistness and flavor, fat inhibits the development of gluten, a protein in flour that causes baked goods to become tough. Sugar does the same thing, which is why so many fat-free cakes contain additional sugar—as well as all the calories that go along with it.

Fortunately, there are better ways to reduce the fat in cakes and still maintain a pleasing texture. The secret? Include some healthful whole grain flours in your recipe. These are naturally lower in gluten than refined flours. With their mildly sweet flavor, oat flour and oat bran work especially well in no- and low-fat baked goods. Another excellent option is whole wheat pastry flour—a versatile product that will help you make the lightest, most tender cakes possible.

A variety of other products also help slash fat and add flavor in these recipes. Ingredients like applesauce and fruit purées, nonfat buttermilk, nonfat yogurt, and nonfat sour cream reduce the need for fat by adding moistness and richness to batters. Fat-free egg substitutes save more fat and cholesterol. And nonfat cream cheese, yogurt, and whipped toppings form the base of delightfully light and creamy fillings and frostings.

In a hurry? Busy cooks will be happy to know that cake mixes are easily prepared with no added fat. This chapter presents a variety of super-moist, meltingly tender made-from-mix treats with only a couple of grams of fat per serving.

So whether you are looking for a grand finale to an elegant meal or for a simple coffee cake for a casual get-together, you need look no further. With a little creativity, you and your family will be delighted to find that you can have your cake and eat it, too.

CARROT-PINEAPPLE CAKE

Yield: *16 servings*

2½ cups unbleached flour

1⅓ cups sugar

2 teaspoons baking soda

2 teaspoons ground cinnamon

2 cans (8 ounces each) crushed
    pineapple in juice, undrained

¼ cup skim milk

4 egg whites, lightly beaten, or
    ½ cup fat-free egg substitute

2 teaspoons vanilla extract

2 cups (packed) grated carrots
    (about 5 medium)

½ cup golden raisins

⅓ cup chopped pecans (optional)

CREAM CHEESE ICING

8 ounces nonfat or reduced-fat
    cream cheese

1 cup nonfat ricotta cheese

½ cup confectioners' sugar

1 teaspoon vanilla extract

1. Combine the flour, sugar, baking soda, and cinnamon in a medium-sized bowl, and stir to mix well. Stir in the pineapple, including the juice, and the milk, egg whites, and vanilla extract. Fold in the carrots, raisins, and, if desired, the pecans.

2. Coat a 9-x-13-inch pan with nonstick cooking spray. Spread the batter evenly in the pan, and bake at 325°F for 35 minutes, or just until a wooden toothpick inserted in the center of the cake comes out clean. Cool to room temperature.

3. To make the icing, combine all of the icing ingredients in a food processor, and process until smooth. Spread the icing over the cake, and serve immediately. Refrigerate any leftovers.

NUTRITIONAL FACTS (PER SERVING)
Calories: 215 Cholesterol: 3 mg Fat: 0.3 g
Fiber: 1.4 g Protein: 7.7 g Sodium: 268 mg

Minty Mocha-Fudge Cake

1. Combine the flours, sugar, cocoa, and baking soda in a large bowl, and stir to mix well. Set aside.

2. Combine the coffee, chocolate syrup, vinegar, and vanilla extract in a medium-sized bowl, and stir to mix well. Add the coffee mixture to the flour mixture, and stir with a wire whisk until well mixed.

3. Coat a 9-x-13-inch pan with nonstick cooking spray. Pour the batter into the pan, and bake at 350°F for 30 minutes, or just until a wooden toothpick inserted in the center of the cake comes out clean. Cool to room temperature.

4. To make the glaze, combine all of the glaze ingredients in a small bowl, and stir to mix well. If using a microwave oven, microwave the glaze, uncovered, at high power for 20 seconds, or until runny. If using a conventional stove top, combine the glaze ingredients in a small saucepan, and cook over medium heat, stirring constantly, for 20 seconds. Drizzle the glaze over the cake, and let the cake stand for at least 15 minutes, allowing the glaze to harden, before slicing and serving.

Yield: *16 servings*

2 cups unbleached flour

1 cup oat flour

1½ cups sugar

½ cup cocoa powder

2 teaspoons baking soda

2 cups coffee, cooled to room temperature

½ cup chocolate syrup

1 tablespoon distilled white vinegar

2 teaspoons vanilla extract

GLAZE

1 cup confectioners' sugar

1 tablespoon cocoa powder

4 drops peppermint extract

4–5 teaspoons skim milk

NUTRITIONAL FACTS (PER SERVING)
Calories: 207 Cholesterol: 0 mg Fat: 1 g
Fiber: 2.4 g Protein: 3.4 g Sodium: 168 mg

MACAROON SWIRL CAKE

Yield: *16 servings*

¼ cup plus 2 tablespoons reduced-fat margarine or light butter

1½ cups sugar

2 egg whites

1½ teaspoons vanilla extract

2 cups unbleached flour

¾ cup oat bran

1¼ teaspoons baking soda

1¼ cups plus 2 tablespoons nonfat or low-fat buttermilk

¼ cup sweetened flaked coconut

¾ teaspoon coconut extract

¼ cup plus 2 tablespoons cocoa powder

GLAZE

¼ cup plus 2 tablespoons confectioners' sugar

½ teaspoon coconut extract

1½ teaspoons skim milk

1 tablespoon sweetened flaked coconut

1. Place the margarine or butter and the sugar in the bowl of an electric mixer, and beat until smooth. Beat in the egg whites and vanilla extract until smooth, and set aside.

2. Combine the flour, oat bran, and baking soda in a medium-sized bowl, and stir to mix well. Add the flour mixture and the buttermilk to the margarine mixture, and beat just until well mixed.

3. Remove 1 cup of the batter, and place it in a small bowl. Stir in the flaked coconut and coconut extract, and set aside.

4. Add the cocoa to the large bowl of batter, and beat just until well mixed.

5. Coat a 12-cup bundt pan with nonstick cooking spray. Pour ¾ of the cocoa batter into the pan, spreading the batter evenly. Top with the coconut batter, followed by the remaining cocoa batter.

6. Bake at 350°F for 40 minutes, or just until a wooden toothpick inserted in the center of the cake comes out clean. Cool the cake in the pan for 20 minutes. Then invert onto a wire rack, and cool to room temperature.

7. To make the glaze, combine the confectioners' sugar, coconut extract, and milk in a small bowl, and stir until smooth. Transfer the cake to a serving platter, and drizzle the glaze over the cake. Sprinkle the coconut over the top of the glaze, and let sit for at least 15 minutes, allowing the glaze to harden, before slicing and serving.

NUTRITIONAL FACTS (PER SERVING)
Calories: 189 Cholesterol: 0 mg Fat: 3.3 g
Fiber: 1.9 g Protein: 4.1 g Sodium: 155 mg

Chocolate Cherry Tunnel Cake

1. Combine the flour, oat bran, sugar, cocoa, baking soda, and salt in a large bowl, and stir to mix well. Add the buttermilk, oil, egg whites, and vanilla extract, and stir to mix well.

2. Coat a 12-cup bundt pan with nonstick cooking spray, and spread the batter evenly in the pan. Spoon the cherry filling in a ring over the center of the batter. (As the cake bakes, the filling will sink into the batter.)

3. Bake at 350°F for about 40 minutes, or until the top springs back when lightly touched, and a wooden toothpick inserted near the sides of the cake comes out clean. Cool the cake in the pan for 40 minutes. Then invert onto a wire rack, and cool to room temperature.

4. To make the glaze, combine the confectioners' sugar, milk, and almond extract in a small bowl, and stir until smooth. Transfer the cake to a serving platter, and spoon the glaze over the cake. Let the cake sit for at least 15 minutes, allowing the glaze to harden, before slicing and serving.

NUTRITIONAL FACTS (PER SERVING)
Calories: 188 Cholesterol: 0 mg Fat: 3.3 g
Fiber: 2.1 g Protein: 4 g Sodium: 164 mg

Yield: *16 servings*

1¾ cups unbleached flour

¾ cup oat bran

1⅓ cups sugar

½ cup cocoa powder

1½ teaspoons baking soda

⅛ teaspoon salt

1¼ cups nonfat or low-fat buttermilk

3 tablespoons vegetable oil

2 egg whites, lightly beaten

1 teaspoon vanilla extract

FILLING

1¼ cups canned light (low-sugar) cherry pie filling

GLAZE

⅓ cup confectioners' sugar

1½ teaspoons skim milk

½ teaspoon almond extract

Pear Ginger Cake

Yield: *10 servings*

2 cans (1 pound each) pear halves in juice, undrained

⅓ cup brown sugar

10 walnut halves (optional)

1 cup unbleached flour

½ cup whole wheat pastry flour

¼ cup sugar

1 teaspoon baking powder

¾ teaspoon baking soda

¾ teaspoon ground ginger

½ teaspoon ground cinnamon

¼ teaspoon ground nutmeg

¼ cup plus 2 tablespoons molasses

¼ cup Prune Butter (page 223)

3 tablespoons fat-free egg substitute

For variety, substitute apricots or peaches for the pears.

1. Drain the pears, reserving the juice. Coat a 10-inch ovenproof skillet with nonstick cooking spray. Place 1½ tablespoons of the reserved pear juice in the bottom of the skillet, and distribute evenly. Sprinkle the brown sugar evenly over the pear juice. Arrange 10 pear halves over the brown sugar, with the cut side down and the widest part of the pears pointing toward the outer edge of the skillet. Fill the center with walnut halves, if desired. Set aside.

2. Combine the flours, sugar, baking powder, baking soda, and spices in a medium-sized bowl, and stir to mix well. Combine the molasses, Prune Butter, and ¾ cup of the reserved pear juice in a medium-sized bowl, and stir to mix well. Add the molasses mixture and egg substitute to the flour mixture, and stir to mix well.

3. Bake at 350°F for 30 minutes, or just until a wooden toothpick inserted in the center of the cake comes out clean. Cool the cake in the skillet for 15 minutes. Then invert onto a serving platter. Cool to room temperature before slicing and serving.

NUTRITIONAL FACTS (PER SERVING)

Calories: 177 Cholesterol: 0 mg Fat: 0.3 g
Fiber: 2.2 g Protein: 2.8 g Sodium: 147 mg

Making Prune Purée and Prune Butter

The dessert recipes in this book use a variety of substitutes, most of which are readily available in grocery stores. Two excellent fat substitutes, however, must be made at home. Prune Purée and Prune Butter will allow you to bake moist and flavorful cakes, cookies, and other treats with little or no fat, and will also add fiber and nutrients to your homemade goodies. Simply follow the recipes provided below, and keep these ingredients on hand for use in your fat-free baked goods.

PRUNE PURÉE

1. Place all of the ingredients in a blender or food processor, and process at high speed until the mixture is smooth.

2. Use immediately, or place in an airtight container and store in the refrigerator for up to 3 weeks.

Yield: *1½ cups*

3 ounces pitted prunes (about ½ cup)

1 cup water or fruit juice

2 teaspoons lecithin granules*

PRUNE BUTTER

1. Place both ingredients in a food processor, and process at high speed until the mixture forms a smooth paste. (Note that this mixture is too thick to be made in a blender.)

2. Use immediately, or place in an airtight container and store in the refrigerator for up to 3 weeks.

Yield: *1 cup*

8 ounces pitted prunes (about 1⅓ cups)

6 tablespoons water or fruit juice

* For information on lecithin, see the inset on page 233.

Apple Upside-Down Cake

Yield: *10 servings*

2 tablespoons frozen apple juice concentrate, thawed

¼ cup brown sugar

2 medium apples, peeled and sliced ¼ inch thick

1 cup unbleached flour

½ cup whole wheat pastry flour

¾ cup sugar

1 teaspoon baking soda

⅛ teaspoon ground nutmeg

1 cup apple juice

3 tablespoons fat-free egg substitute

1. Coat a 9-inch ovenproof skillet with nonstick cooking spray. Spread the apple juice concentrate over the bottom of the skillet, and sprinkle with the brown sugar. Arrange the apple slices in a circular pattern over the brown sugar. Set aside.

2. Combine the flours, sugar, baking soda, and nutmeg, and stir to mix well. Stir in the apple juice and egg substitute. Pour the batter over the apples, and bake at 350°F for 25 to 30 minutes, or just until a wooden toothpick inserted in the center of the cake comes out clean.

3. Cool at room temperature for 25 minutes; then invert onto a serving platter. Cut into wedges and serve warm or at room temperature.

NUTRITIONAL FACTS (PER SERVING)
Calories: 179 Calcium: 12 mg Cholesterol: 0 mg
Fat: 0.4 g Fiber: 1.6 g Iron: 1.2 mg
Potassium: 138 mg Protein: 2.7 g Sodium: 94 mg

Fresh Apple Cake

Yield: *16 servings*

1½ cups unbleached flour

1 cup whole wheat pastry flour

1½ cups sugar

1¼ teaspoons baking soda

1¼ teaspoons ground cinnamon

¾ cup apple juice

3 egg whites

2 teaspoons vanilla extract

3 cups thinly sliced fresh apples (about 3½ medium)

½ cup chopped walnuts (optional)

1. Combine the flours, sugar, baking soda, and cinnamon, and stir to mix well. Add the apple juice, egg whites, and vanilla extract, and stir to mix well. Fold in the apples and walnuts.

2. Coat a 9-x-13-inch pan with nonstick cooking spray. Spread the batter evenly in the pan, and bake at 325°F for 40 to 50 minutes, or just until a wooden toothpick inserted in the center of the cake comes out clean.

3. Cool the cake for at least 20 minutes. Cut into squares and serve warm or at room temperature with a light whipped topping if desired.

NUTRITIONAL FACTS (PER SERVING)
Calories: 163 Calcium: 7 mg Cholesterol: 0 mg
Fat: 0.3 g Fiber: 1 g Iron: 1 mg
Potassium: 69 mg Protein: 2.6 g Sodium: 78 mg

BROWN SUGAR AND SPICE CAKE

The spice in this cake is supplied by the apple butter.

Yield: *16 servings*

1. Combine the flours, brown sugar, baking powder, and baking soda, and stir to mix well. Stir in the buttermilk, apple butter, and egg whites.

2. Coat a 9-x-13-inch pan with nonstick cooking spray. Spread the batter evenly in the pan, and bake at 325°F for about 35 minutes, or just until a wooden toothpick inserted in the center of the cake comes out clean. Cool the cake to room temperature.

3. To make the icing, place the ricotta cheese in a food processor, and process until smooth. Add the confectioners' sugar and vanilla or maple extract, and process to mix well. Add the apple butter, and process just long enough to mix well.

4. Spread the icing over the cooled cake. Cut into squares and serve immediately or refrigerate.

1 cup whole wheat pastry flour

1⅔ cups unbleached flour

1 cup light brown sugar

1 teaspoon baking powder

1½ teaspoons baking soda

1⅓ cups nonfat buttermilk

¾ cup apple butter

2 egg whites

ICING

15 ounces nonfat ricotta cheese

¼ cup confectioners' sugar

1 teaspoon vanilla or maple extract

¼ cup apple butter

NUTRITIONAL FACTS (PER SERVING)

Calories: 197 Calcium: 188 mg Cholesterol: 0 mg
Fat: 0.6 g Fiber: 1.5 g Iron: 1.5 mg
Potassium: 176 mg Protein: 7.3 g Sodium: 164 mg

CINNAMON CARROT CAKE

Yield: *16 servings*

2½ cups unbleached flour

1¼ cups brown sugar

2 teaspoons baking soda

2 teaspoons ground cinnamon

¾ cup plus 2 tablespoons apple juice

4 egg whites

2 teaspoons vanilla extract

3 cups grated carrots (about 6 medium)

⅓ cup dark raisins or chopped walnuts

CREAM CHEESE ICING

8 ounces nonfat cream cheese

1 cup nonfat ricotta cheese

½ cup confectioners' sugar

1 teaspoon vanilla extract

1. Combine the flour, brown sugar, baking soda, and cinnamon, and stir to mix well. Add the juice, egg whites, and vanilla extract, and stir to mix well. Stir in the carrots and the raisins or walnuts.

2. Coat a 9-x-13-inch pan with nonstick cooking spray. Spread the batter evenly in the pan, and bake at 325°F for 30 to 35 minutes, or just until a wooden toothpick inserted in the center of the cake comes out clean. Cool to room temperature.

3. To make the icing, place the cream cheese and ricotta in a food processor, and process until smooth. Add the confectioners' sugar and vanilla extract, and process to mix well.

4. Spread the icing over the cooled cake. Cut into squares and serve immediately or refrigerate.

NUTRITIONAL FACTS (PER SERVING)
Calories: 205 Calcium: 205 mg Cholesterol: 0 mg
Fat: 0.3 g Fiber: 1.5 g Iron: 1.8 mg
Potassium: 216 mg Protein: 8 g Sodium: 247 mg

Peach Delight Cake

1. Combine the flours, sugar, baking soda, and nutmeg, and stir to mix well. Stir in the puréed peaches, vanilla extract, and egg substitute. Fold in the sliced peaches and the raisins or pecans.

2. Coat an 8-inch square pan with nonstick cooking spray. Spread the batter evenly in the pan, and bake at 350°F for about 35 minutes, or just until a wooden toothpick inserted in the center of the cake comes out clean.

3. Cool the cake for at least 20 minutes. Cut into squares and serve warm or at room temperature.

Yield: *8 servings*

¾ cup unbleached flour

½ cup whole wheat pastry flour

½ cup sugar

¾ teaspoon baking soda

⅛ teaspoon ground nutmeg

⅔ cup puréed fresh peaches

¾ teaspoon vanilla extract

3 tablespoons fat-free egg substitute

2 cups sliced fresh peaches (about 3 medium)

¼ cup dark raisins or chopped pecans

NUTRITIONAL FACTS (PER SERVING)
Calories: 161 Calcium: 12 mg Cholesterol: 0 mg
Fat: 0.3 g Fiber: 2.6 g Iron: 1.1 mg
Potassium: 212 mg Protein: 3.3 g Sodium: 86 mg

Busy Day Banana Cake

Yield: *8 servings*

1⅓ cups unbleached flour

½ cup sugar

1½ teaspoons baking powder

¼ teaspoon ground nutmeg

⅔ cup mashed very ripe banana
(about 1½ large)

⅓ cup maple syrup

3 tablespoons fat-free egg
substitute

ICING

1 cup nonfat ricotta cheese

2 tablespoons maple syrup

½ teaspoon vanilla extract

1. Combine the flour, sugar, baking powder, and nutmeg, and stir to mix well. Add the remaining ingredients, and stir to mix.

2. Coat an 8-inch square pan with nonstick cooking spray. Spread the batter evenly in the pan, and bake at 325°F for about 30 minutes, or just until a wooden toothpick inserted in the center of the cake comes out clean. Cool the cake to room temperature.

3. To make the icing, place the ricotta cheese, maple syrup, and vanilla extract in a food processor, and process until smooth. Spread the icing evenly over the cake, cut into squares, and serve immediately or refrigerate.

NUTRITIONAL FACTS (PER SERVING)
Calories: 215 Calcium: 186 mg Cholesterol: 0 mg
Fat: 0.3 g Fiber: 0.9 g Iron 1.3 mg
Potassium: 133 mg Protein: 6.8 g Sodium: 107 mg

Spiced Pear Cake

1. Combine the flours, sugar, baking soda, and spices, and stir to mix well. Stir in the pear nectar and egg substitute. Fold in the pear slices and raisins.

2. Coat an 8-inch square pan with nonstick cooking spray. Spread the batter evenly in the pan, and bake at 350°F for 25 to 30 minutes, or just until a wooden toothpick inserted in the center of the cake comes out clean.

3. Cool the cake for at least 20 minutes. Cut into squares and serve warm or at room temperature.

Yield: *8 servings*

¾ cup unbleached flour

½ cup whole wheat pastry flour

½ cup sugar

¾ teaspoon baking soda

¾ teaspoon ground cinnamon

⅛ teaspoon ground nutmeg

½ cup pear nectar

3 tablespoons fat-free egg substitute

2½ cups thinly sliced fresh pears (about 2½ medium)

¼ cup dark raisins

NUTRITIONAL FACTS (PER SERVING)
Calories: 169 Calcium: 15 mg Cholesterol: 0 mg
Fat: 0.4 g Fiber: 2.7 g Iron: 1.1 mg
Potassium: 245 mg Protein: 3.4 g Sodium: 85 mg

Putting Coconut in Perspective

Rich in saturated fat, coconut oil is usually avoided in heart-healthy diets. Does this mean that the meat of the coconut is also off limits? Not necessarily. While coconut does contain coconut oil (one cup of shredded sweetened coconut contains about 33 grams of fat, or about 6 teaspoons of oil), small amounts of coconut may be added to recipes, especially if the recipe contains little or no other fat.

For example, our recipe for Fresh Coconut Cake (see page 230) contains about 3⅓ ounces of fresh coconut in the whole cake. This means that each serving contains less than a half-teaspoon of coconut oil. Notice that the cake contains no other added fats such as butter, margarine, or oil. Coconut milk—which is extracted from the meat of the coconut, and therefore contains coconut oil—is not used. Instead, coconut water, the fat-free liquid found inside the coconut, helps to moisten the cake. The final result? One serving of Fresh Coconut Cake contains only 1.9 grams of fat. Not a high price to pay for the exotic sweetness of fresh coconut!

When reducing the fat in your own recipes, try to decrease the amount of coconut used instead of totally eliminating this flavorful ingredient. For example, instead of thickly covering the frosting with coconut, sprinkle the coconut sparingly over the top or just around the edge of the cake. This will enhance appearance and flavor without adding too much fat. A teaspoonful of coconut-flavored extract added to batter will reduce the amount of coconut needed.

Fresh Coconut Cake

Yield: *16 servings*

1¼ cups coconut water (use some skim milk if there is not enough coconut water)*

¾ cup diced fresh coconut

2¼ cups unbleached flour

1⅓ cups sugar

2 teaspoons baking powder

1 teaspoon baking soda

2 egg whites

1 teaspoon vanilla extract

1 teaspoon coconut-flavored extract

GLAZE

1 cup confectioners' sugar

4 teaspoons coconut water or skim milk

1 teaspoon coconut-flavored extract

2 tablespoons grated fresh coconut

* Coconut water is the fat-free liquid found inside the fresh coconut.

1. Place the coconut water and diced coconut in a food processor or blender, and process until the coconut is finely shredded. Set aside.

2. Combine the flour, sugar, baking powder, and baking soda, and stir to mix well. Add the coconut mixture, egg whites, vanilla extract, and coconut extract, and stir to mix well.

3. Coat a 9-x-13-inch pan with nonstick cooking spray. Spread the batter evenly in the pan, and bake at 325°F for 35 to 40 minutes, or just until a wooden toothpick inserted in the center of the cake comes out clean. Cool to room temperature.

4. To make the glaze, combine the glaze ingredients, stirring until smooth. Spread the glaze over the cooled cake, cut into squares, and serve.

NUTRITIONAL FACTS (PER SERVING)

Calories: 178 Calcium: 16 mg Cholesterol: 0 mg
Fat: 1.9 g Fiber: 1.1 g Iron: 1 mg
Potassium: 94 mg Protein: 2.7 g Sodium: 121 mg

PEAR Upside-Down Cake

1. Drain the pears, reserving the juice. Coat a 9-inch ovenproof skillet with nonstick cooking spray. Place 1½ tablespoons of the reserved pear juice in the bottom of the skillet and distribute evenly. Sprinkle the brown sugar evenly over the pear juice. Arrange 10 pear halves over the brown sugar with the cut side down and the widest part of the pears toward the outer edge of the skillet. Fill in the center with pecan halves if desired.

2. Combine the flours, sugar, baking powder, and baking soda, and stir to mix well. Stir in ¾ cup of the reserved pear juice and the honey or maple syrup, egg whites, and vanilla extract.

3. Pour the batter over the pears, spreading evenly. Bake at 350°F for 30 to 35 minutes, or just until a wooden toothpick inserted in the center of the cake comes out clean.

4. Let cool in the skillet for 15 minutes; then invert onto a serving platter. Cut into wedges and serve warm or at room temperature.

Yield: *10 servings*

2 cans (1 pound each) pear halves packed in juice, undrained

⅓ cup brown sugar

10 pecan halves (optional)

1 cup unbleached flour

⅔ cup whole wheat pastry flour

⅓ cup sugar

1 teaspoon baking powder

1 teaspoon baking soda

⅓ cup honey or maple syrup

2 egg whites

1 teaspoon vanilla extract

NUTRITIONAL FACTS (PER SERVING)
Calories: 196 Calcium: 23 mg Cholesterol: 0 mg
Fat: 0.3 g Fiber: 2.1 g Iron: 1.4 mg
Potassium: 132 mg Protein: 3.3 g Sodium: 132 mg

Blueberry Sunshine Cake

Yield: *16 servings*

2⅓ cups unbleached flour

⅔ cup oat bran

1¼ cups sugar

1 tablespoon plus 1½ teaspoons
lecithin granules*

1¼ teaspoons baking soda

2 teaspoons dried grated orange
rind, or 2 tablespoons fresh

1 cup orange juice

½ cup nonfat buttermilk

2 egg whites

¾ cup fresh or frozen blueberries

GLAZE

⅓ cup confectioners' sugar

2½ teaspoons frozen orange juice
concentrate, thawed

* For information on lecithin, see the
inset on page 233.

1. Combine the flour, oat bran, sugar, lecithin, baking soda, and orange rind, and stir to mix well. Add the orange juice, buttermilk, and egg whites, and stir to mix well. Fold in the blueberries.

2. Coat a 12-cup bundt pan with nonstick cooking spray. Spread the batter evenly in the pan, and bake at 350°F for 35 to 45 minutes, or just until a wooden toothpick inserted in the center of the cake comes out clean. Cool the cake in the pan for 20 minutes. Then invert onto a wire rack, and cool to room temperature.

3. To make the glaze, combine the confectioners' sugar with the juice concentrate. Transfer the cake to a serving platter, and drizzle the glaze over the cake. Let sit for at least 15 minutes before slicing and serving.

NUTRITIONAL FACTS (PER SERVING)
Calories: 167 Calcium: 26 mg Cholesterol: 0 mg
Fat: 0.9 g Fiber: 1.4 g Iron: 1.1 mg
Potassium: 104 mg Protein: 3.5 g Sodium: 83 mg

Lecithin—A Little Bit Goes a Long Way

Lecithin, a nutritious by-product of soybean-oil refining, is a perfect texture enhancer for fat-free baked goods. In fact, commercial bakers frequently use small amounts of lecithin in very low-fat and fat-free cakes, cookies, and other baked goods. Lecithin's unique chemical properties allow batters to rise better, and lend a softer texture to the finished product.

Lecithin is available in both liquid and granular forms. Both forms can be found in health foods stores, where lecithin is sold as a nutritional supplement. Lecithin liquid is very thick and sticky—so sticky that it's almost impossible to work with. Lecithin granules, however, are puffed-up bits of oil that are easily measured and added to batters. Because the granules are puffed, though, they cannot be substituted for the liquid on a measure-for-measure basis. The recipes in this book call for lecithin granules. For best results when using these granules, purchase a finely granulated brand, as coarse granules may not dissolve in the batter. If you find that your brand does not dissolve, simply process it in a blender with a little of the recipe's liquid ingredients before adding it to the batter. If you use the liquid form, use half as much. Regardless of the form you choose to use, keep your lecithin in the refrigerator to maintain freshness.

Lecithin granules do contain fat—6 grams per tablespoon. Unlike many fat-rich ingredients, though, lecithin is also rich in nutrients, especially vitamin E, iron, phosphorus, calcium, and choline, a nutrient that people on low-fat diets may not get enough of. Added in small amounts to a recipe, lecithin raises the fat content only slightly. For instance, most of the bundt cakes in this chapter contain 1½ tablespoons of lecithin. This adds 9 grams of fat to the whole recipe, or about 0.5 grams per serving. The improvement in texture is well worth the price.

Blueberry Lemon Tunnel Cake

Yield: *16 servings*

2¼ cups unbleached flour

¾ cup oat bran

1¼ cups sugar

1 tablespoon plus 1½ teaspoons
lecithin granules*

1½ teaspoons baking soda

1 teaspoon dried grated lemon
rind, or 1 tablespoon fresh

1½ cups nonfat buttermilk

2 egg whites

1½ teaspoons vanilla extract

FILLING

1¼ cups canned blueberry pie
filling

GLAZE

⅓ cup confectioners' sugar

1¾ teaspoons lemon juice

* For information on lecithin, see the
inset on page 233.

For variety, substitute lemon or cherry pie filling for the blueberry filling.

1. Combine the flour, oat bran, sugar, lecithin, baking soda, and lemon rind, and stir to mix well. Add the buttermilk, egg whites, and vanilla extract, and stir to mix well.

2. Coat a 12-cup bundt pan with nonstick cooking spray. Spread the batter evenly in the pan. Spoon the filling in a ring over the center of the batter. (The filling will sink into the batter as the cake bakes.)

3. Bake at 350°F for about 40 minutes, or until the top springs back when lightly touched, and a wooden toothpick inserted near the side comes out clean. Cool the cake in the pan for 40 minutes. Then invert onto a wire rack, and cool to room temperature.

4. To make the glaze, combine the confectioners' sugar with the lemon juice. Transfer the cake to a serving platter, and spoon the glaze over the cake. Let sit for at least 15 minutes before slicing and serving.

NUTRITIONAL FACTS (PER SERVING)
Calories: 179 Calcium: 40 mg Cholesterol: 0 mg
Fat: 1 g Fiber: 1.5 g Iron: 1.2 mg
Potassium: 103 mg Protein: 3.8 g Sodium: 114 mg

White Cake with Strawberries

1. Combine the topping ingredients. Cover and chill for several hours or overnight.

2. Combine the flour, sugar, baking powder, and baking soda, and stir to mix well. Stir in the buttermilk, egg white, and vanilla extract.

3. Coat a 9-inch round pan with nonstick cooking spray. Spread the batter evenly in the pan, and bake at 325°F for 15 to 20 minutes, or just until the center springs back when lightly touched and a wooden toothpick inserted in the center of the cake comes out clean.

4. Cool the cake to room temperature. Cut into wedges, top each serving with the strawberry mixture, and serve.

NUTRITIONAL FACTS (PER SERVING)
Calories: 152 Calcium: 43 mg Cholesterol: 0 mg
Fat: 0.6 g Fiber: 0.5 g Iron: 1.1 mg
Potassium: 179 mg Protein: 3.3 g Sodium: 121 mg

Yield: *8 servings*

1 cup plus 2 tablespoons unbleached flour

½ cup sugar

1 teaspoon baking powder

½ teaspoon baking soda

½ cup plus 2 tablespoons nonfat buttermilk

1 egg white

1 teaspoon vanilla extract

TOPPING

4 cups sliced fresh strawberries

2 tablespoons sugar

1 tablespoon amaretto liqueur

Banana Fudge Ripple Cake

Yield: *16 servings*

2 cups unbleached flour

¾ cup oat bran

1¼ cups sugar

1 tablespoon plus 1½ teaspoons lecithin granules*

1¼ teaspoon baking soda

1½ cups mashed very ripe banana (about 3 large)

½ cup nonfat buttermilk

2 egg whites

1½ teaspoon vanilla extract

⅓ cup chocolate syrup

1½ teaspoons confectioners' sugar

* For information on lecithin, see the inset on page 233.

1. Combine the flour, oat bran, sugar, lecithin, baking soda, and stir to mix well. Add the banana, buttermilk, egg whites, and vanilla extract, and stir to mix well. Remove ⅓ cup of the batter and mix with the chocolate syrup.

2. Coat a 12-cup bundt pan with nonstick cooking spray. Spread ⅓ of the plain batter evenly in the pan, top with half the chocolate mixture, add another ⅓ of the batter, top with the remaining chocolate mixture, and finish with the rest of the batter.

3. Bake at 350°F for about 40 minutes, or just until a wooden toothpick inserted in the center of the cake comes out clean. Cook the cake in the pan for 20 minutes. Then invert onto a wire rack, and cool to room temperature.

4. Transfer the cake to a serving platter. Sift the confectioners' sugar over the cooled cake, slice, and serve.

NUTRITIONAL FACTS (PER SERVING)
Calories: 170 Calcium: 25 mg Cholesterol: 0 mg
Fat: 1.1 g Fiber: 1.7 g Iron: 1.2 mg
Potassium: 161 mg Protein: 3.5 g Sodium: 87 mg

CHERRY ALMOND CAKE

For a change of pace, use blueberry, peach, or raspberry pie filling instead of the cherry filling.

Yield: *16 servings*

1. Combine the flour, sugar, lecithin, baking powder, and baking soda, and stir to mix well. Add the buttermilk, egg whites, vanilla extract, and almond extract, and stir to mix well.

2. Coat a 9-x-13-inch pan with nonstick cooking spray. Spread the batter evenly in the pan. Spoon the cherry filling back and forth over the cake in an "S" pattern. (The filling will sink into the batter as the cake bakes.)

3. Bake at 325°F for 45 to 50 minutes, or just until a wooden toothpick inserted in the center of the cake comes out clean. (Find a spot that is free of cherry filling.)

4. Cool the cake for at least 20 minutes. Cut into squares and serve warm or at room temperature.

2¼ cups unbleached flour

1¼ cups sugar

1 tablespoon lecithin granules*

2 teaspoons baking powder

1 teaspoon baking soda

1 cup plus 2 tablespoons nonfat buttermilk

2 egg whites

1 teaspoon vanilla extract

1 teaspoon almond extract

1 can (20 ounces) light (low-sugar) cherry pie filling

* For information on lecithin, see the inset on page 233.

NUTRITIONAL FACTS (PER SERVING)
Calories: 165 Calcium: 34 mg Cholesterol: 0 mg
Fat: 0.7 g Fiber: 1.4 g Iron: 1 mg
Potassium: 46 mg Protein: 2.4 g Sodium: 111 mg

Buttermilk Chocolate Cake

Yield: *16 servings*

1½ cups unbleached flour

½ cup oat flour

1½ cups sugar

½ cup plus 1 tablespoon cocoa
   powder

2 teaspoons baking soda

1½ cups nonfat buttermilk

¼ cup water

2 teaspoons vanilla extract

FROSTING

1 tablespoon cocoa powder

1 cup nonfat vanilla yogurt

1 cup light whipped topping

1. Combine the flours, sugar, cocoa, and baking soda, and stir to mix well. Stir in the buttermilk, water, and vanilla extract.

2. Coat a 9-x-13-inch pan with nonstick cooking spray. Spread the batter evenly in the pan, and bake at 350°F for 30 to 35 minutes, or until a wooden toothpick inserted in the center of the cake comes out clean. Cool the cake to room temperature.

3. To make the frosting, stir the cocoa into the yogurt. Then gently fold the yogurt into the whipped topping. Spread the frosting evenly over the cake, cut into squares, and serve immediately or refrigerate.

NUTRITIONAL FACTS (PER SERVING)
Calories: 156 Calcium: 56 mg Cholesterol: 0 mg
Fat: 1.3 g Fiber: 1.4 g Iron: 1.1 mg
Potassium: 70 mg Protein: 2.9 g Sodium: 136 mg

BANANA FUDGE CAKE

1. Combine the flours, cocoa, sugar, baking soda, and salt, if desired, and stir to mix well. Add the banana, buttermilk, egg whites, and vanilla extract, and stir to mix well.

2. Coat a 9-x-13-inch pan with nonstick cooking spray. Spread the batter evenly in the pan. Bake at 350°F for about 35 minutes, or just until a wooden toothpick inserted in the center of the cake comes out clean. Cool the cake to room temperature.

3. To make the glaze, combine the glaze ingredients in a small bowl. If using a microwave oven, microwave the glaze, uncovered, at high power for 35 seconds, or until runny. If using a conventional stove top, transfer the glaze to a small saucepan and place over medium heat for 30 seconds, stirring constantly. Drizzle the glaze over the cake, and let harden before cutting into squares and serving.

NUTRITIONAL FACTS (PER SERVING)
Calories: 197 Calcium: 25 mg Cholesterol: 0 mg
Fat: 0.9 g Fiber: 2.5 g Iron: 1.1 mg
Potassium: 165 mg Protein: 3.5 g Sodium: 146 mg

Yield: *16 servings*

1 cup whole wheat flour

1 cup unbleached flour

½ cup cocoa powder

1½ cups sugar

2 teaspoons baking soda

¼ teaspoon salt (optional)

1½ cups mashed very ripe banana (about 3 large)

½ cup nonfat buttermilk

2 egg whites

1½ teaspoons vanilla extract

GLAZE

1½ cups confectioners' sugar

1 tablespoon plus 1½ teaspoons cocoa powder

3 tablespoons skim milk

1 teaspoon vanilla extract

¼ cup plus 2 tablespoons chopped walnuts (optional)

Maple Spice Cake

Yield: *16 servings*

1⅓ cups unbleached flour

1⅓ cups whole wheat pastry flour

1 cup sugar

1 tablespoon baking powder

1 teaspoon ground cinnamon

½ teaspoon ground ginger

¼ teaspoon ground nutmeg

1⅓ cups skim milk

⅔ cup maple syrup

4 egg whites

FLUFFY MAPLE FROSTING

1 cup maple syrup

2 egg whites

1. Combine the flours, sugar, baking powder, and spices, and stir to mix well. Add the milk, maple syrup, and egg whites, and stir to mix well.

2. Coat a 9-x-13-inch pan with nonstick cooking spray. Spread the batter evenly in the pan, and bake at 350°F for 30 to 35 minutes, or just until a wooden toothpick inserted in the center of the cake comes out clean. Cool the cake to room temperature.

3. To make the frosting, place the maple syrup in a small saucepan. Bring the syrup to a boil over medium heat, and continue cooking without stirring until the temperature reaches 240°F on a candy thermometer inserted in the liquid. (If you don't have a candy thermometer, place a drop of syrup in a cup of cold water. When the syrup has reached the proper temperature, it will form a soft ball in the water and then flatten upon removal.) Just before the syrup reaches the desired temperature, beat the egg whites to soft peaks with an electric mixer. Slowly add the syrup to the egg whites while beating at high speed. Continue beating for about 5 minutes, or until the icing is glossy and firm enough to spread.

4. Spread the frosting over the cooled cake. Cut into squares and serve immediately, or refrigerate to prevent the frosting from separating.

NUTRITIONAL FACTS (PER SERVING)
Calories: 216 Calcium: 76 mg Cholesterol: 0 mg
Fat: 0.3 g Fiber: 1.5 g Iron: 1.2 mg
Potassium: 162 mg Protein: 4 g Sodium: 96 mg

GRANNY'S APPLE CAKE

1. Combine the flours, sugar, baking soda, and cinnamon, and stir to mix well. Add the maple syrup, egg whites, and vanilla extract, and stir to mix well. Fold in the remaining ingredients.

2. Coat a 9-x-13-inch pan with nonstick cooking spray. Spread batter evenly in pan, and bake at 350°F for 30 to 35 minutes, or just until a wooden toothpick inserted in center of cake comes out clean.

3. Cool the cake for at least 20 minutes. Cut into squares and serve warm or at room temperature.

NUTRITIONAL FACTS (PER SERVING)
Calcium: 14 mg Calories: 188 Cholesterol: 0 mg
Fat: 0.4 g Fiber: 2.3 g Iron: 1.2 mg
Potassium: 141 mg Protein: 3.4 g Sodium: 119 mg

Yield: *16 servings*

1¼ cups whole wheat pastry flour

1¼ cups unbleached flour

¾ cup sugar

2 teaspoons baking soda

2½ teaspoons ground cinnamon

¾ cup maple syrup

4 egg whites

2 teaspoons vanilla extract

4 cups chopped Granny Smith apples (about 5 medium)

½ cup dark raisins

½ cup chopped walnuts (optional)

BLACK FOREST CAKE

Yield: *10 servings*

1 cup unbleached flour

½ cup oat flour

¾ cup sugar

¼ cup cocoa powder

1 teaspoon baking soda

1 teaspoon vanilla extract

¼ cup chocolate syrup

1½ teaspoons white vinegar

1 cup water

FILLING

1 can (20 ounces) light (low-sugar) cherry pie filling

MERINGUE TOPPING

2 egg whites, brought to room temperature

⅛ teaspoon cream of tartar

5 tablespoons sugar

1 teaspoon vanilla or almond extract

This cake is made in a flan or tiara pan. The bottom of the pan has a raised center that makes an ideal place to put a filling after the cake has been baked, cooled, and inverted.

1. Combine the flours, sugar, cocoa, and baking soda, and stir to mix well. In a separate bowl, combine the vanilla extract, chocolate syrup, vinegar, and water. Add the chocolate mixture to the flour mixture, and stir to mix well.

2. Coat a 10-inch flan pan with nonstick cooking spray. Spread the batter evenly in the pan, and bake at 350°F for 15 to 20 minutes, or just until a wooden toothpick inserted in the center of the cake comes out clean.

3. Cool the cake to room temperature. Then invert onto a baking sheet. Fill the depression in the top of the cake with the cherry pie filling.

4. To make the meringue topping, whip the egg whites and cream of tartar with an electric mixer until soft peaks form. Still beating, slowly add the sugar and vanilla or almond extract. Continue to beat until stiff peaks form.

5. Pipe or spoon the meringue in a ring around the outer edge of the cherry filling. Place the cake in a 400°F oven for 3 to 5 minutes, or until the meringue is lightly browned.

6. Cool the cake to room temperature. Slice and serve immediately, or refrigerate to prevent the meringue from separating.

NUTRITIONAL FACTS (PER SERVING)
Calories: 219 Calcium: 9 mg Cholesterol: 0 mg
Fat: 0.9 g Fiber: 3.2 g Iron: 1.4 mg
Potassium: 73 mg Protein: 3.4 g Sodium: 116 mg

Blueberry Upside-Down Cake

1. Coat an 8-inch square pan with nonstick cooking spray. Evenly spread the juice concentrate on the bottom of the pan, and sprinkle with the brown sugar. Arrange the blueberries over the brown sugar.

2. Combine the flours, baking powder, and sugar, and stir to mix well. Add the remaining ingredients, and stir to mix well.

3. Pour the batter over the blueberries, spreading evenly. Bake at 350°F for 35 to 45 minutes, or just until a wooden toothpick inserted in the center of the cake comes out clean.

4. Cool the cake at room temperature for 10 minutes. Loosen the sides of the cake by running a sharp knife along the edges, and invert onto a serving platter. Serve warm or at room temperature, topping each piece with vanilla ice milk if desired.

Yield: *9 servings*

2 tablespoons frozen apple or orange juice concentrate, thawed

¼ cup brown sugar

1¼ cups fresh or frozen blueberries

1¼ cups unbleached flour

⅓ cup oat flour

1½ teaspoons baking powder

½ cup sugar

⅔ cup skim milk

⅓ cup honey

2 egg whites

1 teaspoon vanilla extract

NUTRITIONAL FACTS (PER SERVING)
Calories: 211 Calcium: 44 mg Cholesterol: 0 mg
Fat: 0.6 g Fiber: 1.4 g Iron: 1.3 mg
Potassium: 130 mg Protein: 4 g Sodium: 111 mg

Mocha Fudge Cake

Yield: *16 servings*

2 cups unbleached flour

1¼ cups sugar

½ cup cocoa powder

1 teaspoon baking powder

½ teaspoon baking soda

¼ teaspoon salt (optional)

¾ cup Prune Butter (page 223)

1½ cups plus 2 tablespoons
   coffee, at room temperature

2 teaspoons vanilla extract

½ cup chopped walnuts (optional)

3–4 tablespoons confectioners'
   sugar (optional)

1. Combine the flour, sugar, cocoa, baking powder, baking soda, and salt, if desired, and stir to mix well. In a separate bowl, combine the Prune Butter, coffee, and vanilla extract, and stir to mix well. Add the prune mixture to the flour mixture, and stir to mix well. Fold in the walnuts if desired.

2. Coat a 9-x-13-inch pan with nonstick cooking spray. Spread the batter evenly in the pan, and bake at 350°F for 30 to 35 minutes, or until the top springs back when lightly touched and a wooden toothpick inserted in the center of the cake comes out clean. Be careful not to overbake.

3. Cool the cake to room temperature. Sift the confectioners' sugar over the cake if desired, cut into squares, and serve.

NUTRITIONAL FACTS (PER SERVING)
Calories: 150 Calcium: 15 mg Cholesterol: 0 mg
Fat: 0 7 g Fiber: 2.2 g Iron 1.3 mg
Potassium: 114 mg Protein: 2.4 g Sodium: 66 mg

Sweet Potato Snack Cake

Yield: *8 servings*

1 cup whole wheat pastry flour

¾ cup light brown sugar

2 teaspoons baking powder

½ teaspoon ground cinnamon

⅛ teaspoon ground nutmeg

1½ cups cooked mashed sweet
   potato

2 egg whites

2 tablespoons skim milk

2 tablespoons confectioners'
   sugar (optional)

1. Combine the flour, brown sugar, baking powder, and spices, and stir to mix well. Add the remaining ingredients, and stir to mix well.

2. Coat an 8-inch square pan with nonstick cooking spray. Spread the batter evenly in the pan, and bake at 325°F for 40 to 45 minutes, or just until a wooden toothpick inserted in the center of the cake comes out clean.

3. Cool the cake to room temperature. Sift the confectioners' sugar over the cake if desired, cut into squares, and serve.

NUTRITIONAL FACTS (PER SERVING)
Calories: 183 Calcium: 57 mg Cholesterol: 0 mg
Fat: 0.4 g Fiber: 2.9 g Iron: 1.9 mg
Potassium: 252 mg Protein: 4 g Sodium: 141 mg

SUPER-MOIST PINEAPPLE CAKE

1. Combine the flour, sugar, and baking soda, and stir to mix well. Stir in the pumpkin, the crushed pineapple, including the juice, and the pineapple or orange juice and vanilla extract.

2. Coat a 9-x-13-inch pan with nonstick cooking spray. Spread the batter evenly in the pan, and bake at 350°F for 35 minutes, or just until a wooden toothpick inserted in the center of the cake comes out clean.

3. Cool the cake to room temperature. Sift the confectioners' sugar over the cake, cut into squares, and serve.

Yield: *16 servings*

2 cups unbleached flour

1½ cups sugar

1½ teaspoons baking soda

1 cup cooked mashed pumpkin

1 can (8 ounces) crushed pineapple packed in juice, undrained

½ cup pineapple or orange juice

1½ teaspoons vanilla extract

3–4 tablespoons confectioners' sugar

NUTRITIONAL FACTS (PER SERVING)
Calories: 154 Calcium: 10 mg Cholesterol: 0 mg
Fat: 0.2 g Fiber: 0.9 g Iron: 1 mg
Potassium: 53 mg Protein: 2.3 g Sodium: 85 mg

Raspberry Ripple Cake

Yield: *16 servings*

¾ cup fresh or frozen (thawed)
  raspberries

1 tablespoon sugar

¼ cup reduced-fat margarine or
  light butter

1¼ cups sugar

3 egg whites

1 teaspoon almond extract

2¼ cups unbleached flour

¾ cup oat bran

1¼ teaspoons baking soda

1¼ cups nonfat buttermilk

GLAZE

⅓ cup confectioners' sugar

¼ teaspoon almond extract

2 teaspoons nonfat buttermilk

For variety, substitute blueberries for the raspberries.

1. Place the raspberries and 1 tablespoon of sugar in a food processor or blender, and purée. Set aside.

2. Combine the margarine or butter and the sugar in the bowl of an electric mixer, and beat until smooth. Beat in the egg whites and almond extract until smooth. In a separate bowl, combine the flour, oat bran, and baking soda. Add the flour mixture and the buttermilk to the margarine mixture, and beat just until well mixed.

3. Remove ¾ cup of the batter, and mix with the raspberry purée. Set aside.

4. Coat a 12-cup bundt pan with nonstick cooking spray. Spread ⅔ of the plain batter evenly in the pan. Top with the raspberry batter, and follow with the remaining plain batter.

5. Bake at 350°F for 35 to 40 minutes, or just until a wooden toothpick inserted in the center of the cake comes out clean. Cool the cake in the pan for 10 minutes. Then invert onto a wire rack, and cool to room temperature.

6. To make the glaze, combine the glaze ingredients and stir until smooth. Transfer the cake to a serving platter, and drizzle the glaze over the cake. Let sit for at least 15 minutes before slicing and serving.

NUTRITIONAL FACTS (PER SERVING)
Calories: 169 Calcium: 29 mg Cholesterol: 0 mg
Fat: 2 g Fiber: 1.6 g Iron: 1.1 mg
Potassium: 83 mg Protein: 3.3 g Sodium: 117 mg

BANANA CRUNCH CAKE

1. To make the topping, combine the topping ingredients, and stir until moist and crumbly. Set aside.

2. Combine the flours, sugar, and baking powder, and stir to mix well. Add the banana, margarine or butter, egg whites, and vanilla extract, and stir just until mixed.

3. Coat a 9-inch round pan with nonstick cooking spray. Spread the batter evenly in the pan, and sprinkle the topping over the batter. Bake at 350°F for 30 minutes, or just until a wooden toothpick inserted in the center of the cake comes out clean. Cool the cake at room temperature for 10 minutes.

4. To make the glaze, combine the confectioners' sugar, milk, and cinnamon, and stir until smooth. Drizzle the glaze over the cake, cut into wedges, and serve warm or at room temperature.

NUTRITIONAL FACTS (PER SERVING)
Calories: 222 Calcium: 30 mg Cholesterol: 0 mg
Fat: 3.8 g Fiber: 2.2 g Iron: 1.5 mg
Potassium: 191 mg Protein: 4.6 g Sodium: 134 mg

Yield: *10 servings*

1 cup plus 2 tablespoons unbleached flour

½ cup whole wheat pastry flour

½ cup sugar

2 teaspoons baking powder

1 cup mashed very ripe banana (about 2 large)

¼ cup reduced-fat margarine or light butter, melted

2 egg whites

1 teaspoon vanilla extract

TOPPING

¾ cup quick-cooking oats

3 tablespoons brown sugar

2 tablespoons chopped walnuts

2 tablespoons maple syrup

GLAZE

¼ cup confectioners' sugar

1½ teaspoons skim milk

1 pinch ground cinnamon

Old-Fashioned Strawberry Shortcake

Yield: *10 servings*

1½ cups unbleached flour

½ cup oat bran

¼ cup sugar

1 tablespoon baking powder

4 tablespoons chilled reduced-fat margarine or light butter, cut into pieces

⅔ cup nonfat buttermilk

3 tablespoons fat-free egg substitute

FRUIT TOPPING

3 cups sliced fresh strawberries

⅓ cup sugar

CREAM TOPPING

½ cup nonfat vanilla yogurt

¾ cup light whipped topping

1. To make the fruit topping, combine the strawberries and sugar. Cover and refrigerate for several hours or overnight to allow the juices to develop.

2. To make the cream topping, gently fold the yogurt into the whipped topping. Chill until ready to serve.

3. Combine the flour, oat bran, sugar, and baking powder, and stir to mix well. Use a pastry cutter to cut in the margarine or butter until the mixture resembles coarse crumbs. In a separate bowl, combine the buttermilk and egg substitute. Add to the flour mixture, and stir just until moistened.

4. Coat a baking sheet with nonstick cooking spray. Drop heaping tablespoonfuls of the batter onto the sheet to make 10 biscuits. (Place ¾ inches apart for soft biscuits, or 2 inches apart for crusty biscuits.)

5. Bake at 400°F for 18 to 20 minutes, or until lightly browned." Remove from the oven, and let sit for at least 5 minutes. (The biscuits may be served warm or at room temperature.)

6. To assemble the shortcakes, slice each biscuit in half lengthwise. Place the bottom half of each biscuit on an individual serving plate, and top with 3 tablespoons of the strawberry topping. Add the top half of the biscuit and another 3 tablespoons of strawberries. Drop a heaping tablespoonful of the cream topping over the strawberries, and serve.

NUTRITIONAL FACTS (PER SERVING)
Calories: 198 Calcium: 79 mg Cholesterol: 0 mg
Fat: 3.8 g Fiber: 3.6 g Iron: 1.6 mg
Potassium: 255 mg Protein: 4.9 g Sodium: 186 mg

Glazed Pineapple Cake

1. Place the flours, sugar, milk powder, and baking soda in a large bowl, and stir to mix well. Add the pineapple with its juice and the egg substitute and vanilla extract, and stir just until well mixed.

2. Coat a 9-x-13-inch pan with nonstick cooking spray, and spread the mixture evenly in the pan. Bake at 325°F for about 40 minutes, or just until the top springs back when lightly touched and a wooden toothpick inserted in the center of the cake comes out clean. Allow the cake to cool for 20 minutes at room temperature.

3. While the cake is cooling, place all of the glaze ingredients in a small bowl, and stir to mix well. Spread the glaze in a thin layer over the top of the warm cake. Allow the cake to cool to room temperature before cutting into squares and serving.

Yield: *16 servings*

1 cup unbleached flour

1 cup oat flour or whole wheat pastry flour

1½ cups sugar

¼ cup instant nonfat dry milk powder

1 teaspoon baking soda

1 can (20 ounces) crushed pineapple in juice, undrained

¼ cup plus 2 tablespoons fat-free egg substitute

1½ teaspoons vanilla extract

GLAZE

1¼ cups powdered sugar

2 tablespoons skim milk or pineapple juice

¾ teaspoon almond extract

NUTRITIONAL FACTS (PER SERVING)
Calories: 190 Carbohydrates: 43 g Cholesterol: 0 mg
Fat: 0.6 g Fiber: 1.3 g Protein: 3 g Sodium: 96 mg

You Save: Calories: 163 Fat: 10.2 g

Citrus Carrot Cake

Yield: *18 serving:*

3 cups unbleached flour

1½ cups sugar

2 teaspoons baking soda

2 teaspoons baking powder

¼ teaspoon salt

2 teaspoons ground cinnamon

1⅓ cups orange juice

¾ cup fat-free egg substitute

2 teaspoons vanilla extract

4 cups (packed) grated carrots
(about 8 large)

½ cup golden or dark raisins

½ cup chopped toasted pecans or
walnuts (page 383) (optional)

1 recipe Fluffy Cream Cheese
Frosting (page 251)

1. Place the flour, sugar, baking soda, baking powder, salt, and cinnamon in a large bowl, and stir to mix well. Stir in the juice, egg substitute, and vanilla extract. Fold in the carrots, raisins, and, if desired, the nuts.

2. Coat a 9-x-13-inch pan with nonstick cooking spray, and spread the mixture evenly in the pan. Bake at 300°F for about 55 minutes, or just until the top springs back when lightly touched and a wooden toothpick inserted in the center of the cake comes out clean. Allow to cool to room temperature.

3. Spread the frosting over the cooled cake and refrigerate for at least 2 hours before cutting into squares and serving.

NUTRITIONAL FACTS (PER SERVING)
Calories: 211 Carbohydrates: 45 g Cholesterol: 1 mg
Fat: 0.5 g Fiber: 1.5 g Protein: 6.5 g Sodium: 327 mg

You Save: Calories: 220 Fat: 23.5 g

The Finishing Touch

Usually when you think of topping cakes, you think of frostings and icings. And certainly it is possible to make icings and frostings that are not only luscious enough to satisfy any sweet tooth, but also low in fat and calories. (See the inset on page 251.) But sometimes a simpler topping—rather than a conventional frosting—can lend the perfect finishing touch to your low-fat cake. Here are some ideas.

❑ Dust the top of your cake with a few tablespoons of powdered sugar instead of adding a gooey icing. Try sifting some powdered maple sugar over the tops of spice, banana, and applesauce cakes.

❑ Spread a thin layer of low-sugar fruit spread or jam over the top of your cake. Try raspberry spread on chocolate cake, pineapple spread on banana cake, and apricot or peach spread on spice cake.

❑ Spread your cake with yogurt cheese—a sweet, creamy spread made by draining the whey from yogurt (page 293). To cover a 9-x-13-inch cake, use 2 cups of yogurt cheese, which is made from about 4 cups of yogurt. Try vanilla, coffee, or raspberry yogurt cheese or chocolate cake; vanilla, pineapple, or banana yogurt cheese on banana cake; and lemon or vanilla yogurt cheese on lemon or carrot cake.

The Frosting on the Cake

Traditionally, recipes for cake frostings have often called for up to 3 cups of powdered sugar and a stick of butter. But is there an alternative that not only is lower in sugar and fat, but also satisfies everyone's expectations of a sweet and creamy topping? Of course there is! Instead of being laden with fat, the icings and frostings in this book are made from ingredients like nonfat cream cheese, nonfat whipped topping, and nonfat yogurt. Just as important, they contain just a fraction of the sugar found in traditional recipes. Enjoy the following three frostings on your own favorite cakes, as well as on the cakes in this chapter. (For more ideas on topping cakes, see the inset on page 263.)

FLUFFY CREAM CHEESE FROSTING

1. Place the cream cheese and vanilla extract in a large bowl, and beat with an electric mixer until smooth. Slowly add the sugar, a tablespoon at a time, beating constantly, until smooth and creamy.

2. Gently fold the whipped topping into the cream cheese mixture, and immediately spread the frosting over the cake.

Yield: about 3 cups, enough for a 9-x-13-inch cake or a 9-inch double layer cake

1½ blocks (8 ounces each) nonfat cream cheese, softened to room temperature

1½ teaspoons vanilla extract

¼ cup plus 2 tablespoons sugar

1½ cups nonfat or light whipped topping

NUTRITIONAL FACTS (PER 3-TABLESPOON SERVING)
Calories: 49 Carbohydrates: 8 g Cholesterol: 1 mg
Fat: 0.2 g Fiber: 0 g Protein: 3 g Sodium: 106 mg

You Save: Calories: 82 Fat: 11.3 g

YOGURT FLUFF FROSTING

1. Place the whipped topping in a medium-sized bowl. Gently fold in the yogurt, and immediately spread over the cake.

Yield: about 3 cups, enough for a 9-x-13-inch cake or a 9-inch double layer cake

2¼ cups nonfat or light whipped topping

¾ cup nonfat yogurt, any flavor

NUTRITIONAL FACTS (PER 3-TABLESPOON SERVING)
Calories: 29 Carbohydrates: 6 g Cholesterol: 0 mg
Fat: 0.3 g Fiber: 0 g Protein: 0.5 g Sodium: 14 mg

You Save: Calories: 53 Fat: 8 g

Pudding Perfection Frosting

Yield: *about 3 cups, enough for a 9-x-13-inch cake or a 9-inch double layer cake*

1 box (4-serving size) fat-free or regular instant pudding mix, any flavor

1 cup skim milk

2 cups nonfat or light whipped topping

1. Place the pudding mix and milk in a large bowl, and whisk with a wire whip for about 2 minutes, or until thick.

2. Gently fold the whipped topping into the pudding mixture, and immediately spread the frosting over the cake.

NUTRITIONAL FACTS (PER 3-TABLESPOON SERVING)

Calories: 43 Carbohydrates: 10 g Cholesterol: 0 mg
Fat: 0.3 g Fiber: 0 g Protein: 0.5 g Sodium: 104 mg

You Save: Calories: 40 Fat 5.4 g

Piña Colada Cake

1. Place the cake mix and pudding mix in a large bowl, and stir to mix well. Add the pineapple with its liquid and the sour cream, egg substitute, and water, and beat with an electric mixer for about 2 minutes, or until well mixed.

2. Coat a 9-x-13-inch pan with nonstick cooking spray, and spread the batter evenly in the pan. Bake at 350°F for about 35 minutes, or just until the top springs back when lightly touched and a wooden toothpick inserted in the center of the cake comes out clean. Be careful not to overbake.

3. Allow the cake to cool in the pan for 20 minutes. Using a small knife, poke holes in the cake at ½-inch intervals.

4. Place all of the syrup ingredients in a small bowl, and stir to mix well. Slowly pour the syrup over the cake, allowing it to be absorbed into the cake. Allow the cake to cool to room temperature.

5. To make the frosting, place the whipped topping in a medium-sized bowl, and gently fold in the yogurt. Spread the mixture over the cake, swirling the top with a knife. Sprinkle the coconut over the top, if desired. Cover and refrigerate for at least 3 hours before cutting into squares and serving.

NUTRITIONAL FACTS (PER SERVING)

Calories: 235 Carbohydrates: 46 g Cholesterol: 0 mg
Fat: 2.1 g Fiber: 0.5 g Protein: 4.8 g Sodium: 305 mg

You Save: Calories: 124 Fat: 18.5 g

Yield: *16 servings*

1 box (1 pound, 2.25 ounces) reduced-fat or regular yellow cake mix

1 package (4-serving size) fat-free or regular instant toasted coconut pudding mix*

1 can (8 ounces) crushed pineapple, undrained

1 cup nonfat sour cream

1 cup fat-free egg substitute

¼ cup water

SYRUP

½ cup fat-free sweetened condensed milk

¼ cup light rum

¾ teaspoon coconut-flavored extract

FROSTING

2 cups nonfat or light whipped topping

1 cup piña colada or coconut-flavored nonfat yogurt, regular or sugar-free

¼ cup shredded sweetened coconut (optional)

*If you cannot find toasted coconut pudding mix, substitute 1 package instant vanilla pudding mix plus ¾ teaspoon coconut-flavored extract and 2 tablespoons finely shredded toasted coconut.

LEMON CREAM CAKE

Yield: *16 servings*

1 box (1 pound, 2.25 ounces) reduced-fat or regular lemon or yellow cake mix

1 package (4-serving size) fat-free or regular instant lemon pudding mix

1 cup nonfat sour cream

1 cup fat-free egg substitute

½ cup water

3 tablespoons lemon juice

GLAZE

½ cup powdered sugar

1½ teaspoons lemon juice

1½ teaspoons nonfat sour cream

1. Place the cake mix and pudding mix in a large bowl, and stir to mix well. Add the sour cream, egg substitute, water, and lemon juice, and beat with an electric mixer for about 2 minutes, or until well mixed.

2. Coat a 12-cup bundt pan with nonstick cooking spray, and spread the batter evenly in the pan. Bake at 350°F for 40 to 45 minutes, or just until the top springs back when lightly touched and a wooden toothpick inserted in the center of the cake comes out clean. Be careful not to overbake.

3. Allow the cake to cool in the pan for 45 minutes. Then invert onto a serving platter and cool to room temperature.

4. To make the glaze, place the powdered sugar, lemon juice, and sour cream in a small bowl, and stir to mix well. If using a microwave oven, microwave on high power for 25 seconds, or until hot and runny. If using a stovetop, place the glaze in a small pot and cook over medium heat, stirring constantly, for about 25 seconds, or until hot and runny.

5. Drizzle the hot glaze over the cake. Allow the cake to sit for at least 15 minutes before slicing and serving.

NUTRITIONAL FACTS (PER SERVING)
Calories: 188 Carbohydrates: 39 g Cholesterol: 0 mg
Fat: 1.5 g Fiber: 0.4 g Protein: 3.1 g Sodium: 323 mg

You Save: Calories: 102 Fat: 12.5 g

Royal Raspberry Cake

For variety, substitute chocolate or lemon cake and pudding mix for the white cake mix and the white chocolate pudding mix. Use chocolate or lemon yogurt in the frosting.

1. Place the cake mix and pudding mix in a large bowl, and stir to mix well. Add the water, sour cream, and egg whites, and beat with an electric mixer for 2 minutes, or until well mixed.

2. Coat three 9-inch round cake pans with nonstick cooking spray, and divide the batter among the pans, spreading it evenly. Bake at 325°F for about 25 minutes, or just until the tops spring back when lightly touched. Allow the cakes to cool to room temperature in the pans. Be careful not to overbake.

3. To make the filling, transfer 1 tablespoon of the juice from the raspberries to a small bowl. Stir in the cornstarch, and set aside.

4. Place the berries and the remaining juice in a 1-quart pot, and place the pot over medium heat. Cook, stirring frequently, until the mixture comes to a boil and the berries begin to break down. Stir in the cornstarch mixture, and cook for another minute or 2, or until thickened and bubbly. Stir in the liqueur, remove from the heat, and allow to cool to room temperature.

5. To assemble the cake, place one layer, with the top side down, on a serving plate. Spread half of the raspberry filling over the cake layer. Place a second layer over the first, top side down, and spread with the remaining raspberry filling. Place the third layer on the cake, top side up.

6. Spread the frosting over the top and sides of the cake, swirling the frosting with a knife. Cover and refrigerate for at least 2 hours before serving.

Yield: *16 servings*

1 box (1 pound, 2.25 ounces) white cake mix

1 package (4-serving size) fat-free or regular instant white chocolate pudding mix

1¼ cups water

½ cup nonfat sour cream

3 egg whites

FILLING

1 package (10 ounces) frozen sweetened raspberries, thawed

1½ teaspoons cornstarch

2 tablespoons raspberry or amaretto liqueur

TOPPING

1 recipe Yogurt Fluff Frosting (page 251) made with vanilla or raspberry yogurt

---

NUTRITIONAL FACTS (PER SERVING)
Calories: 213 Carbohydrates: 43 g Cholesterol: 0 mg
Fat: 3 g Fiber: 1.2 g Protein: 2.3 g Sodium: 289 mg

You Save: Calories: 172 Fat: 17 g

SOUR CREAM FUDGE CAKE

Yield: *16 servings*

1½ cups unbleached flour

¾ cup oat flour

1½ cups sugar

¾ cup cocoa powder

2 teaspoons baking soda

¼ teaspoon salt

1 cup coffee, cooled to room
   temperature

1 cup unsweetened applesauce

½ cup nonfat sour cream

¼ cup fat-free egg substitute, or 2
   egg whites, lightly beaten

2 teaspoons vanilla extract

GLAZE

1¼ cups powdered sugar

¼ cup nonfat sour cream

2 tablespoons cocoa powder

1 teaspoon vanilla extract

1. Place the flours, sugar, cocoa, baking soda, and salt in a large bowl, and stir to mix well.

2. Place the coffee, applesauce, sour cream, egg substitute, and vanilla extract in a medium-sized bowl, and stir with a whisk to mix well. Add the coffee mixture to the flour mixture, and whisk to mix well.

3. Coat a 9-x-13-inch pan with nonstick cooking spray, and pour the batter into the pan. Bake at 325°F for about 35 minutes, or just until the top springs back when lightly touched and a wooden toothpick inserted in the center of the cake comes out clean. Be careful not to overbake. Remove the cake from the oven, and set aside.

4. To make the glaze, place all of the glaze ingredients in a small bowl, and stir until smooth. Add a little more sour cream if needed to make a thick frosting. Spread the glaze over the hot cake.

5. Allow the cake to cool to room temperature before cutting into squares and serving.

NUTRITIONAL FACTS (PER SERVING)
Calories: 194 Carbohydrates: 46 g Cholesterol: 0 mg
Fat: 1 g Fiber: 2.7 g Protein: 4 g Sodium: 200 mg

You Save: Calories: 98 Fat: 11.6 g

Slashing Fat in Half

Looking for a simple way to slash the fat in cakes and other baked goods? Try replacing the butter, margarine, or other solid shortening in cakes, muffins, quick breads, cookies, and other treats with half as much oil. For instance, if a recipe calls for ½ cup of butter, use ¼ cup of oil instead. Bake as usual, checking the product for doneness a few minutes before the end of the usual baking time. This technique makes it possible to produce moist and tender cakes, breads, and biscuits; crisp cookies; and tender pie crusts—all with about half the original fat.

Heavenly Lemon Cake

1. To make the filling, place the sugar and cornstarch in a 2-quart pot, and stir to mix well. Slowly add the milk while stirring constantly to dissolve the cornstarch and sugar.

2. Place the pot over medium heat, and bring the mixture to a boil, stirring constantly with a wire whisk. Continue to cook and stir for 1 minute, or until the mixture is thickened and bubbly.

3. Reduce the heat under the pot to low. Place the egg substitute in a small dish, and stir in ¼ cup of the hot milk mixture. Return the mixture to the pot while whisking constantly. Cook and stir for about 2 minutes, or until the mixture is thickened and bubbly.

4. Remove the pot from the heat, and whisk in the lemon rind. Slowly whisk in the lemon juice. Allow the mixture to sit for 20 minutes to cool slightly. Then stir, and pour into a medium-sized bowl. Cover the bowl and refrigerate for several hours, or until well chilled and thickened.

5. To assemble the cake, using a serrated knife, remove a ¾-inch-thick slice from the top of the cake, and set aside. Cut out the center of the cake, leaving a ¾-inch-thick shell on the bottom and sides. Place the hollowed out cake on a serving platter. Stir the lemon mixture; then spoon it into the hollow in the cake. Place the top back on the cake.

6. To make the frosting, place the whipped topping in a medium-sized bowl, and gently fold in the yogurt. Spread the frosting over the top and sides of the cake. Cover and refrigerate for at least 3 hours before slicing and serving.

Yield: *12 servings*

1 angel food cake (1 pound)

FILLING

⅔ cup sugar

¼ cup cornstarch

1¾ cups skim milk

¼ cup fat-free egg substitute

1 tablespoon freshly grated lemon rind, or 1 teaspoon dried

½ cup lemon juice

FROSTING

2 cups nonfat or light whipped topping

¾ cup nonfat or low-fat lemon yogurt

NUTRITIONAL FACTS (PER SERVING)
Calories: 184 Carbohydrates: 40 g Cholesterol: 0 mg
Fat: 0.8 g Fiber: 0.5 g Protein: 4.6 g Sodium: 293 mg

You Save: Calories: 100 Fat: 13.4 g

Tunnel of Fudge Cake

Yield: *20 servings*

2 cups unbleached flour

½ cup oat flour

½ cup Dutch processed cocoa powder

1½ cups sugar

1¼ teaspoons baking soda

¼ teaspoon salt

1 cup plus 2 tablespoons nonfat or low-fat buttermilk

¼ cup plus 2 tablespoons fat-free egg substitute

¼ cup walnut or canola oil

2 teaspoons vanilla extract

FUDGE FILLING

1¼ cups skim or 1% low-fat milk

1 box (4-serving size) fat-free instant chocolate or devil's food pudding mix

GLAZE

½ cup powdered sugar

1 tablespoon Dutch processed cocoa powder

½ teaspoon vanilla extract

1 tablespoon skim milk

1 tablespoon chopped walnuts (optional)

For variety, substitute white chocolate or vanilla. pudding mix for the chocolate or devil's food pudding mix.

1. To make the filling, place the milk and pudding mix in a small bowl, and stir with a wire whisk for a minute or 2, or until well mixed and thickened. Set the mixture aside for at least 5 minutes. (It will thicken a bit more during this time.)

2. Place the flours, cocoa, sugar, baking soda, and salt in a large bowl, and stir to mix well. Add the buttermilk, egg substitute, oil, and vanilla extract, and stir just enough to mix well.

3. Coat a 12-cup bundt plan with nonstick cooking spray, and spread the batter evenly in the pan. Spoon the filling in a ring over the center of the batter. (The filling will sink into the batter as the cake bakes.)

4. Bake at 350°F for about 45 minutes, or just until a wooden toothpick inserted on either side of the filling comes out clean. Cool the cake in the pan for 45 minutes. Then invert onto a serving platter and set aside while you prepare the glaze.

5. To make the glaze, place the powdered sugar and cocoa in a small bowl, and stir to mix well. Stir in the vanilla extract and just enough of the milk to make a thick but pourable glaze. Drizzle the glaze over the cake and, if desired, sprinkle with the walnuts.

6. Let the cake cool completely before slicing and serving. Refrigerate any leftovers.

NUTRITIONAL FACTS (PER SERVING)
Calories: 182 Carbohydrates: 36 g Cholesterol: 1 mg
Fat: 3.1 g Fiber: 1.3 g Protein: 3.6 g Sodium: 213 mg

You Save: Calories: 102 Fat: 11 g

Mocha-Zucchini Snack Cake

1. Place the flour, cocoa, sugar, baking powder, baking soda, salt, cinnamon, and coffee granules in a medium-sized bowl, and stir to mix well. Add the applesauce, zucchini, egg substitute or egg whites, and vanilla extract, and stir just until moistened. Fold in the raisins and, if desired, the nuts.

2. Coat an 8-inch square pan with nonstick cooking spray, and spread the mixture evenly in the pan. Bake at 325°F for 30 to 35 minutes, or just until the top springs back when lightly touched and a wooden toothpick inserted in the center of the cake comes out clean. Remove the cake from the oven, and set aside.

3. To make the glaze, place the milk and coffee granules in a small bowl, and stir to dissolve the coffee granules. Add the powdered sugar and cocoa, and stir until smooth. Spread the glaze over the hot cake.

4. Allow the cake to cool to room temperature before cutting into squares and serving.

NUTRITIONAL FACTS (PER SERVING)
Calories: 186 Carbohydrates: 41 g Cholesterol: 0 mg
Fat: 0.8 g Fiber: 2.6 g Protein: 3.6 g Sodium: 183 mg

You Save: Calories: 126 Fat 13.7 g

Yield: *8 servings*

¾ cup plus 3 tablespoons unbleached flour

¼ cup plus 2 tablespoons cocoa powder

¾ cup sugar

1 teaspoon baking powder

¼ teaspoon baking soda

¼ teaspoon salt

¾ teaspoon ground cinnamon

¾ teaspoon instant coffee granules

½ cup unsweetened applesauce

1 cup grated unpeeled zucchini (about 1 medium)

¼ cup fat-free egg substitute, or 2 egg whites, lightly beaten

1 teaspoon vanilla extract

¼ cup dark raisins

¼ cup chopped toasted pecans or walnuts (page 383) (optional)

GLAZE

1 tablespoon plus ½ teaspoon skim milk

¼ teaspoon instant coffee granules

½ cup powdered sugar

1 tablespoon cocoa powder

Applesauce-Spice Snack Cake

Yield: *8 servings*

¾ cup unbleached flour

½ cup whole wheat pastry flour

⅓ cup sugar

1 teaspoon baking soda

½ teaspoon ground cinnamon

½ teaspoon ground ginger

½ teaspoon ground allspice

¾ cup unsweetened applesauce

½ cup molasses or honey

3 tablespoons fat-free egg substitute

⅓ cup dark or golden raisins

¼ cup chopped walnuts (optional)

2 tablespoons powdered sugar (optional)

1. Place the flours, sugar, baking soda, and spices in a medium-sized bowl, and stir to mix well. Add the applesauce, molasses or honey, and egg substitute, and stir just until moistened. Fold in the raisins and, if desired, the walnuts.

2. Coat an 8-inch square pan with nonstick cooking spray, and spread the mixture evenly in the pan. Bake at 325°F for 30 to 35 minutes, or just until the top springs back when lightly touched and a wooden toothpick inserted in the center of the cake comes out clean. Be careful not to overbake.

3. Allow the cake to cool to room temperature. Then cover the pan with foil or plastic wrap, and set aside for at least 6 hours. (This will produce a softer, moister crust.) If desired, sift the powdered sugar over the top just before cutting into squares and serving.

NUTRITIONAL FACTS (PER SERVING)

Calories: 179 Carbohydrates: 4.3 g Cholesterol: 0 mg

Fat: 0.2 g Fiber: 1.6 g Protein: 3 g Sodium: 175 mg

You Save: Calories: 129 Fat: 14.9 g

Using Fat-Free Cream Cheese in Frostings and Fillings

If you've ever tried to defat a cream cheese frosting recipe by substituting fat-free cream cheese for the full-fat product, you probably ended up with a runny, watery mess. Why? Fat-free cream cheese has a higher water content than full-fat cream cheese. When more than a couple of tablespoons of sugar is added to the fat-free product, water is released from the cheese, resulting in a runny glaze.

The solution? Use a low-sugar frosting, like Fluffy Cream Cheese Frosting (page 251). Or beat a tablespoon or two of instant vanilla pudding mix into your fat-free frosting. This will thicken the mixture to the desired consistency. As another option, make the frosting with Neufchâtel—a reduced-fat cream cheese that has a relatively low water content.

Chocolate Cream Cake Roll

1. Line a 15¼-x-10¼-inch jelly roll pan with waxed paper by laying a 16-inch piece of waxed paper in the pan, and folding up the sides so that the paper covers the bottom and sides. Spray the waxed paper with nonstick cooking spray, and set aside.

2. Place the flour, sugar, cocoa, and baking soda in a medium-sized bowl, and stir to mix well. Add the applesauce, egg substitute, milk, and vanilla extract, and stir to mix well.

3. Spread the batter evenly in the waxed paper-lined pan, and bake at 350°F for 12 minutes, or just until the cake springs back when lightly touched in the center. Be careful not to overbake.

4. While the cake is baking, lay a clean kitchen towel out on a work surface. Remove the cake from the oven, and immediately invert it onto the towel. Peel off the waxed paper. Starting at the short end, loosely roll the cake and towel up together. (There should be 1½ inches of open space in the center to accommodate the filling.) Place the cake roll on a wire rack, and allow to cool to room temperature.

5. To make the filling, place the pudding mix and milk in a small bowl, and whip with a wire whisk for 2 minutes, or until well-mixed and thickened. Gently fold in the whipped topping, and set aside.

6. Gently unroll the cooled cake just enough to allow the filling to be spread over the top. Spread the filling to within ½ inch of each edge Roll the cake up, and transfer to a serving platter. Cover and chill for several hours or overnight.

7. Just before serving, trim ½ inch off each end of the chilled cake and discard. To make the glaze, place all of the glaze ingredients in a small bowl, and stir to mix well. If using a microwave oven, microwave on high power for about 30 seconds, or until hot and runny. If using a stove top, place the glaze in a small pot and cook over medium heat, stirring constantly, for about 30 seconds, or until hot and runny.

8. Drizzle the hot glaze over the cake. Allow the cake to sit for at least 15 minutes before slicing into ¾-inch-thick slices and serving.

Yield: *12 servings*

1⅓ cups unbleached flour

1 cup sugar

⅓ cup cocoa powder

1 teaspoon baking soda

¾ cup unsweetened applesauce

½ cup fat-free egg substitute

¼ cup skim milk

1 teaspoon vanilla extract

FILLING

1 package (4-serving size) fat-free instant chocolate, white chocolate, vanilla, or pistachio pudding mix

1 cup skim milk

1¼ cups nonfat or light whipped topping

GLAZE

¾ cup powdered sugar

1 tablespoon cocoa powder

1 tablespoon plus ½ teaspoon skim milk

½ teaspoon vanilla extract

NUTRITIONAL FACTS (PER SERVING)
Calories: 198 Carbohydrates: 46 g Cholesterol: 0 mg
Fat: 0.7 g Fiber: 1.3 g Protein: 3.5 g Sodium: 247 mg

You Save: Calories: 100 Fat: 11 g

Fudge Marble Cake

Yield: *18 servings*

⅔ cup oat bran

1 cup plus 2 tablespoons nonfat or low-fat buttermilk

2⅓ cups unbleached flour

1 teaspoon baking soda

1 stick (¼ pound) reduced-fat margarine or light butter, softened to room temperature

1½ cups sugar

¼ cup plus 2 tablespoons fat-free egg substitute

2½ teaspoons vanilla extract

FUDGE MARBLE

¼ cup Dutch processed cocoa powder

¼ cup chocolate syrup

GLAZE

½ cup powdered sugar

1 tablespoon Dutch processed cocoa powder

1 tablespoon skim milk

½ teaspoon vanilla extract

1. Place the oat bran and buttermilk in a small bowl, and whisk to mix well. Set aside for at least 10 minutes.

2. Place the flour and baking soda in a medium-sized bowl, and stir to mix well. Set aside.

3. Place the margarine or butter in a large bowl, and beat with an electric mixer until smooth. Beat in the sugar ½ cup at a time. Then beat in the egg substitute and vanilla extract.

4. Add the flour mixture and the oat bran mixture to the margarine mixture, and stir with a wooden spoon to mix well. Set aside.

5. To make the fudge marble, place 1 cup of the batter in a small bowl. Add the cocoa and chocolate syrup, and stir to mix well.

6. Coat a 12-cup bundt pan with nonstick cooking spray, and spoon three-fourths of the white batter into the pan. Top the white batter with all of the chocolate batter, and finish off with the remaining white batter.

7. Bake at 350°F for about 43 minutes, or just until a wooden toothpick inserted in the center of the cake comes out clean. Be careful not to overbake. Allow the cake to cool in the pan for 40 minutes. Then invert onto a serving platter, and let the cake cool to room temperature.

8. To make the glaze, place all of the glaze ingredients in a small bowl, and stir to mix well. Drizzle the glaze over the cooled cake. Allow the cake to sit for at least 15 minutes before slicing and serving.

NUTRITIONAL FACTS (PER SERVING)
Calories: 182 Carbohydrates: 38 g Cholesterol: 0 mg
Fat: 3 g Fiber: 1.4 g Protein: 3.5 g Sodium: 141 mg

You Save: Calories: 98 Fat: 10 g

Chocolate Flavor with a Fraction of the Fat

For rich chocolate flavor with a minimum of fat, substitute cocoa powder for high-fat baking chocolate. Simply use 3 tablespoons of cocoa powder plus I tablespoon of water or another liquid to replace each ounce of baking chocolate in cakes, brownies, puddings, and other goodies. You'll save 111 calories and 13.5 grams of fat for each ounce of baking chocolate that you replace!

For the deepest, darkest, richest cocoa flavor, use Dutch processed cocoa in your chocolate treats. Dutching, a process that neutralizes the natural acidity in cocoa, results in a darker, sweeter, more mellow-flavored cocoa. Look for a brand like Hershey's Dutch Processed European Style cocoa. Like regular cocoa, this product has only half a gram of fat per tablespoon—although some Dutch processed cocoa does contain more fat. Dutched cocoa can be substituted for regular cocoa in any recipe, and since it has a smoother, sweeter flavor, you may find that you can reduce the sugar in your recipe by up to 25 percent.

In the interest of keeping sugar to a minimum, you'll find that some of the recipes in this book call specifically for Dutch processed cocoa. In these recipes, the smoother, sweeter flavor of Dutch cocoa best complements the recipe. When a recipe simply calls for "cocoa powder," use either regular or Dutch processed cocoa, depending on your preference.

Here's another fat-cutting tip for chocolate lovers. Replace the butter, margarine, or other solid shortening in chocolate cookies, cakes, brownies, and other baked goods with Prune Butter (page 223). Dark, sweet, nutritious, and fat-free. Prune Butter adds moistness and enhances the flavor of chocolate. You will never miss the fat!

Cherry Tunnel Cake

Yield: *20 servings*

2⅓ cups unbleached flour

⅔ cup oat flour

1 teaspoon baking soda

1 teaspoon baking powder

½ teaspoon dried grated lemon rind, or 1½ teaspoons fresh

1 stick (¼ pound) reduced-fat margarine or light butter, softened to room temperature

1½ cups sugar

¼ cup plus 2 tablespoons fat-free egg substitute

2 teaspoons vanilla extract

1 cup nonfat or low-fat buttermilk

FILLING

1½ cups light (reduced-sugar) cherry pie filling

GLAZE

½ cup powdered sugar

⅛ teaspoon dried grated lemon rind, or ½ teaspoon fresh

½ teaspoon vanilla extract

2½ teaspoons skim milk

For variety, substitute blueberry or lemon pie filling for the cherry pie filling.

1. Place the flours, baking soda, baking powder, and lemon rind in a medium-sized bowl, and stir to mix well. Set aside.

2. Place the margarine or butter in a large bowl, and beat with an electric mixer until smooth. Beat in the sugar ½ cup at a time. Then beat in the egg substitute and vanilla extract.

3. Add the flour mixture and the buttermilk to the margarine mixture, and stir with a wooden spoon just enough to mix well.

4. Coat a 12-cup bundt pan with nonstick cooking spray, and spread the batter evenly in the pan. Spoon the filling in a ring over the center of the batter. (The filling will sink into the batter as the cake bakes.)

5. Bake at 350°F for about 45 minutes, or just until a wooden toothpick inserted on either side of the filling comes out clean. Cool the cake in the pan for 45 minutes. Then invert the cake onto a serving platter and set aside while you prepare the glaze.

6. To make the glaze, place the powdered sugar and lemon rind in a small bowl, and stir to mix well. Stir in the vanilla extract and just enough of the milk to make a thick but pourable glaze. Drizzle the glaze over the cake. Let the cake cool completely before slicing and serving.

NUTRITIONAL FACTS (PER SERVING)

Calories: 176   Carbohydrates: 34 g   Cholesterol: 0 mg
Fat: 2.6 g   Fiber: 0.9 g   Protein: 2.9 g   Sodium: 140 mg

You Save: Calories: 91   Fat: 9.4 g

Top: Very Cranberry Muffins (page 47)
Bottom Right: Three-Grain Muffins (page 50)
Bottom Left: Chocolate Crumb Muffins (page 51)

Top: Orange Poppy Seed Bread *(page 70)*
Bottom Left: Carrot Fruit Bread (page 76)
Bottom Right: Pumpkin Spice Bread (page 73)

Top: Cocoa Streusel Cake (page 275)
Bottom: Apple Butter Bundt Cake (page 285)

Top Left: Oatmeal Fudge Squares (page 439)
Top Right: West Indian Bread Pudding (page 392)
Bottom: Fat-Free Fudge Brownies (page 439)

Top: Banana Granola Muffins (page 55)
Bottom Left: Poppy Seed Muffins (page 53)
Bottom Right: German Chocolate Muffins (page 58)

Top: White Cake with Strawberries (page 235)
Bottom: Blueberry Sunshine Cake (page 232)

Top: Cherry Almond Cake (page 237)
Bottom: Banana Fudge Cake (page 239)

Top: Very Berry Cobbler (page 349)
Bottom: Blueberry Lemon Streusel Cake (page 273)

Top: Lemon Cheese Pie (page 334)
Bottom: Sweet Cherry Crisp (page 351)

Top Left: Chewy Coconut Brownies and Honey Oat Brownies (pages 453, 442)
Top Right: Fresh Pear Scones (page 107)
Bottom: Oatmeal Raisin Cookies (page 454)

Granny's Apple Cake (page 241)

Black Forest Cake (page 242)

Strawberry Swirl Cheesecake (page 294)

Top Left: Low-Fat Pound Cake (page 289)
Top Right: Almond Biscotti (page 465)
Bottom: Great Granola Cookies (page 468)

Top: Sweet Potato Corn Muffins (page 65)
Bottom: Cranberry Pumpkin Bread (page 80)

Raspberry Ripple Cake (page 246)

Top Left: Ham and Cheese Breakfast Biscuits (page 35)
Top Right: Golden French Toast (page 30)
Bottom: Crispy Cornmeal Waffles (page 31)

Top Left: Carrot Raisin Bread (page 68)
Top Right: Broccoli Cheese Muffins (page 40)
Bottom: Applesauce Sticky Buns (page 94)

Top: Fiesta Roll-Ups (page 115)
Center: Stuffed Finger Sandwiches (page 114)
Bottom: Shrimp Bruschetta (page 110)

Top Left: Zippy Artichoke Dip (page 117)
Top Right: Aloha Meatballs (page 112)
Bottom Left: Crab-Stuffed Mushrooms (page 111)
Bottom Right: Chicken Fingers with Sauce (page 113)

Top: Pasta Fagioli Soup (page 123)
Center: Spanish Bean Soup (page 133)
Bottom: Tomato Florentine Soup (page 131)

Top Right: Great Garbanzo Salad (page 145)
Center Left: Italian Pasta Salad (page 144)
Center Right: Broccoli and Basil Pasta Salad (page 136)
Bottom Left: Antipasto Salad (page 134)

Top: Stuffed Eggplant Extraordinaire (page 155)
Center: Mom's Broccoli Casserole (page 150)
Bottom: Cranapple Acorn Squash (page 158)

Top: Pasta with Crab and Asparagus (page 209)
Center: Bow Ties with Spicy Artichoke Sauce (page 211)
Bottom: Pasta Primavera (page 212)

Top: Lasagna Roll-Ups (page 214)
Bottom Left: Florentine Stuffed Shells (page 215)
Bottom Right: Light and Lazy Lasagna (page 213)

Top Left: Shepherd's Pie (page 183)
Top Right: Crispy Cajun Chicken (page 168)
Bottom: Lemon-Herb Chicken w/vegetables (page 164)

Top: Chicken Enchiladas (page 170)
Center: Old-Fashioned Beef Stew (page 179)
Bottom: Foil-Baked Flounder (page 175)

Top: Saucy Stuffed Peppers (page 181)
Center: Mama Mia Meat Loaf (page 180)
Bottom: Breast of Turkey Provençal (page 172)

Top: Eggplant Parmesan (page 190)
Center: Baked Macaroni and Cheese (page 188)
Bottom: Spring Vegetable Quiche (page 186)

Top: Bean Burritos Supreme (page 196)
Center: Two-Bean Chili (page 195)
Bottom: Fresh Tomato Pizza (page 191)

Top: Macaroon Swirl Cake (page 220)
Bottom Left: Chocolate Cherry Tunnel Cake (page 221)
Bottom Right: Blueberry Swirl Cheesecake (page 310)

Top: Razzleberry Trifle (page 391)
Bottom Left: Refreshing Fruit Pie (page 328)
Bottom Right: Pear Ginger Cake (page 222)

Top Left: Apple-Topped Cheesecake (page 296)
Center Right: No-Bake Cherry Cheesecake (page 307)
Bottom Left: Cappuccino Cheesecake (page 309)

Top Right: Royal Raspberry Cake (page 255)
Center Left: Sour Cream-Coconut Bundt Cake (page 283)
Bottom Right: Cranberry-Pear Coffee Cake (page 266)

Top Left: Peach Streusel Pie (page 340)
Top Right: Strawberry Angel Tarts (page 378)
Bottom: Apricot Custard Tart (page 377)

Top Right: Delightful Peach Trifle (page 408)
Center Left and Bottom Right: Tiramisu Treats (page 401)
Center Right and Bottom Left: Crème Caramel (page 410)

Top Left: Maple Oatmeal Cookies (page 477)
Bottom Left: Citrus Sugar Cookies (page 481)
Bottom Right: Cream Cheese Marble Brownies (page 489)

Top: Cool Chocolate-Raspberry Torte
(page 425)
Bottom Left: Strawberry Angel Parfaits
(page 423)
Bottom Right: Simple Apricot Sorbet
(page 421)

Top: Three-Fruit Cobbler (page 367)
Center Left: Cranberry-Pear Crumble
(page 365)
Center Right and Bottom: Ginger
Baked Peaches (page 383)

Center Left: Pear-Cranberry Bread (page 86)
Center Right: Fruit and Nut Bread (page 88)
Bottom: Golden Pumpkin Bread (page 85)

Getting the Fat Out of Your Favorite Cake Recipes

Everyone knows that cakes are loaded with sugar, but fat is often the bigger problem in these sweet treats. In fact, most traditional cakes get more calories from fat than they do from sugar. Consider a cake that contains one cup of oil and two cups of sugar. The oil provides almost 2,000 calories, while the sugar provides just under 1,600 calories. Fortunately, most cakes can be made with less fat, and some can be made with no fat at all, trimming a significant number of calories in the process.

Before you begin trimming the fat from your own recipes, realize that some cakes are better candidates for fat reduction than others. Naturally dense cakes—carrot cakes, fudgy chocolate cakes, and many coffee cakes, for instance—can be made with little or no fat. Packaged cake mixes can also be easily prepared with no added fats. Cakes that are meant to have a very light and tender texture, however, are more difficult to modify—although you can usually eliminate up to half of the fat from even these recipes.

Which fat substitutes perform best in cakes? Applesauce and other fruit purées (page 10), Prune Purée (page 223), and even mashed cooked pumpkin are all excellent fat substitutes in cakes. Nonfat or low-fat buttermilk and yogurt will also work well. Use the following tricks of the trade to insure success when eliminating the fat from your favorite cake recipes.

❑ *Replace the desired amount of butter, margarine, or other solid shortening with half as much fat substitute.* For instance, if you are omitting ½ cup of butter from a recipe, replace it with ¼ cup of fruit purée, Prune Purée, nonfat buttermilk, mashed cooked pumpkin, or other fat substitute. (If the recipe calls for oil, substitute three-fourths as much fat substitute.) Mix up the batter. If it seems too dry, add more fat substitute. For extra flavor and tenderness, try substituting fruit purée or nonfat buttermilk for the recipe's liquid, as well.

❑ *Eliminate only half the fat in a recipe at first.* The next time you make the recipe, try replacing even more fat. Continue reducing the fat until you find the lowest amount that will give you the desired results. Realize that as you remove more and more fat from a recipe, the following tips—for using low-gluten flours and reducing the amount of eggs, for instance—will become even more important.

❑ *Use low-gluten flours.* One of the main functions of fat in cakes is to prevent the development of gluten, a protein in wheat flour that causes a tough, coarse texture in baked goods. While fat substitutes like applesauce and fruit purées also help prevent gluten from forming, they do not perform this function nearly as well as fat does. However, if you use a low-gluten flour like whole wheat pastry flour or oat flour in your low- and no-fat cakes, you can achieve maximum tenderness with minimum fat. For best results, substitute whole wheat pastry flour or oat flour for a third to a half of the refined white flour in your recipe. Or substitute oat bran for a quarter of the flour in the recipe. (For the smoothest texture, soak the oat bran in the recipe's liquid for at least 10 minutes before adding it to the batter.) Read more about whole wheat pastry flour and other low-gluten options on pages 14 to 16.

❑ *Minimize mixing.* Stirring batter excessively develops gluten and toughens the texture of baked goods. Stir only enough to mix well.

❑ *Avoid overbaking.* Reduced-fat baked goods tend to bake more quickly than do those made with fat, and if left in the oven too long, they can become dry. To prevent this, reduce the oven temperature by 25°F, and check the product for doneness a few minutes before the end of the usual baking time

❑ *Reduce the amount of eggs.* You may have noticed that most of the fat-free cakes in this chapter contain a relatively small amount of eggs, and that some contain no eggs at all. Why? Fat adds tenderness to baked goods. Eggs, on the other hand, toughen the structure of baked goods as their proteins coagulate during baking and bind the batter together. For this reason, low- and no-fat cakes that contain too many eggs can have a tough texture. For maximum tenderness, substitute 1 egg white for each whole egg in your recipe. In some cases, you can alternatively substitute 2 tablespoons of your chosen fat substitute for each whole egg.

❑ *Increase the leavening, if necessary.* Fat lubricates batters and helps cakes rise better. When fats are creamed with sugar, they also incorporate air into the batter, which further aids rising. For these reasons, when you eliminate the fat from your cake recipe, your cake might not rise as well. If this happens, try adding a little extra baking soda to your recipe, starting with ¼ teaspoon. Avoid using more than 1 teaspoon of baking soda per cup of acidic liquid—such as fruit purée or buttermilk—as this may cause the product to take on a bitter, soapy taste. If a recipe contains little or no acidic liquids, try adding some extra baking powder for lightness, starting with ¾ to 1 teaspoon. For even greater lightness, whip the recipe's egg whites to soft peaks, and gently fold them into the prepared batter.

CRANBERRY-PEAR COFFEE CAKE

Yield: *8 servings*

¾ cup unbleached flour

½ cup whole wheat pastry flour

½ cup sugar

¾ teaspoon baking soda

½ cup plus 1 tablespoon orange juice

1½ cups finely chopped peeled pears (about 1½ medium)

1 teaspoon vanilla extract

⅓ cup dried cranberries

TOPPING

2 tablespoons light brown sugar

2 tablespoons honey crunch wheat germ or ground pecans, almonds, or walnuts

1. To make the topping, place the sugar and wheat germ or nuts in a small bowl, and stir to mix well. Set aside.

2. Place the flours, sugar, and baking soda in a medium-sized bowl, and stir to mix well. Add the orange juice, pears, and vanilla extract, and stir to mix well. (The batter will be thick.) Stir in the cranberries.

3. Coat an 8-inch square cake pan with nonstick cooking spray, and spread the batter evenly in the pan. Sprinkle the topping over the batter.

4. Bake at 325°F for about 30 minutes, or just until the top springs back when lightly touched and a wooden toothpick inserted in the center of the cake comes out clean. Be careful not to overbake.

5. Allow the cake to cool at room temperature for at least 30 minutes before cutting into squares and serving. Serve warm or at room temperature.

NUTRITIONAL FACTS (PER SERVING)

Calories: 174 Carbohydrates: 41 g Cholesterol: 0 mg
Fat: 0.6 g Fiber: 2.4 g Protein: 3.1 g Sodium: 120 mg

You Save: Calories: 117 Fat: 11.4 g

Caramel-Apple Coffee Cake

1. To make the topping, place the flour, sugar, and wheat germ or pecans in a small bowl, and stir to mix well. Add the juice concentrate, and stir until the mixture is moist and crumbly. Add a little more juice concentrate if needed. Set aside.

2. Place the flours, brown sugar, and cinnamon in a medium-sized bowl, and stir to mix well, using the back of a spoon to press out any lumps in the brown sugar. Add the baking soda, and stir to mix well.

3. Add the buttermilk, egg substitute, vanilla extract, and apples to the flour mixture, and stir to mix well. (The batter will be thick.)

4. Coat a 9-inch round cake pan with nonstick cooking spray, and spread the batter evenly in the pan. Sprinkle the topping over the batter.

5. Bake at 325°F for 35 to 40 minutes, or just until the top springs back when lightly touched and a wooden toothpick inserted in the center of the cake comes out clean. Be careful not to overbake.

6. Allow the cake to cool at room temperature for at least 30 minutes before cutting into wedges and serving. Serve warm or at room temperature.

NUTRITIONAL FACTS (PER SERVING)

Calories: 192 Carbohydrates: 43 g Cholesterol: 0 mg
Fat: 0.9 g Fiber: 2.6 g Protein: 4.7 g Sodium: 151 mg

You Save: Calories: 119 Fat: 12.5 g

Yield: *8 servings*

½ cup plus 2 tablespoons unbleached flour

½ cup whole wheat pastry flour

¾ cup light brown sugar

½ teaspoon ground cinnamon

¾ teaspoon baking soda

¼ cup plus 2 tablespoons nonfat or low-fat buttermilk

¼ cup fat-free egg substitute

1 teaspoon vanilla extract

2½ cups peeled Granny Smith or Rome apples diced into ⅓-inch pieces (about 3 medium)

TOPPING

¼ cup whole wheat pastry flour

¼ cup light brown sugar

⅓ cup honey crunch wheat germ or chopped toasted pecans (page 383)

1 tablespoon plus 1 teaspoon frozen apple juice concentrate, thawed

Black Forest Crumb Cake

Yield: *8 servings*

½ cup unbleached flour

¼ cup plus 2 tablespoons oat flour

¼ cup plus 2 tablespoons cocoa powder

¾ cup sugar

¾ teaspoon baking soda

⅛ teaspoon salt

1½ cups halved frozen pitted dark sweet cherries, thawed

½ cup plain nonfat yogurt

1 teaspoon vanilla extract

TOPPING

¼ cup honey crunch wheat germ, finely chopped walnuts, or finely chopped almonds

2 tablespoons whole wheat pastry flour

2 tablespoons cocoa powder

¼ cup light brown sugar

1 tablespoon plus 2 teaspoons chocolate syrup

1. To make the topping, place the wheat germ or nuts, flour, cocoa, and brown sugar in a small bowl, and stir to mix well. Add the chocolate syrup, and stir until the mixture looks like moist and crumbly cookie dough. Add a little more chocolate syrup if needed. Set aside.

2. Place the flours, cocoa, sugar, baking soda, and salt in a medium-sized bowl, and stir to mix well. Add the cherries (including the juice that accumulates during thawing), yogurt, and vanilla extract, and stir to mix well.

3. Coat a 9-inch round cake pan with nonstick cooking spray, and spread the batter evenly in the pan. Sprinkle the topping over the batter. If necessary, use your fingers to break the topping into smaller pieces.

4. Bake at 325°F for about 35 minutes, or just until the top springs back when lightly touched. Be careful not to overbake. Remove the cake from the oven, and allow it to cool to room temperature before cutting into wedges and serving.

NUTRITIONAL FACTS (PER SERVING)
Calories: 204 Carbohydrates: 46 g Cholesterol: 0 mg
Fat: 1.4 g Fiber: 3.7 g Protein: 4.6 g Sodium: 169 mg

You Save: Calories: 118 Fat: 14.3 g

Variation

To make Banana-Fudge Crumb Cake, substitute ¾ cup mashed very ripe banana (about 1½ large) for the cherries.

NUTRITIONAL FACTS (PER SERVING)
Calories: 201 Carbohydrates: 46 g Cholesterol: 0 mg
Fat: 1.4 g Fiber: 3.4 g Protein: 4.5 g Sodium: 170 mg

You Save: Calories: 121 Fat:14.3 g

ORANGE CRUMB CAKE

1. To make the topping, stir the topping ingredients together until moist and crumbly. Set aside.

2. Combine the flours, sugar, baking powder, and baking soda, and stir to mix well. Add the orange juice, pumpkin or butternut squash, egg substitute, and vanilla extract, and stir to mix well.

3. Coat an 8-inch round pan with nonstick cooking spray. Spread the batter evenly in the pan, and sprinkle the topping over the batter.

4. Bake at 350°F for 25 minutes, or just until a wooden toothpick inserted in the center of the cake comes out clean. Cover loosely with aluminum foil during the last 5 minutes of baking if the topping starts to brown too quickly. Cool at room temperature for 5 minutes.

5. To make the glaze, combine the glaze ingredients until smooth. Drizzle the glaze over the cake, cut into wedges, and serve warm.

NUTRITIONAL FACTS (PER SERVING)
Calories: 162 Calcium: 22 mg Cholesterol: 0 mg
Fat: 0.7 g Fiber: 2.1 g Iron: 1.5 mg
Potassium: 154 mg Protein: 4.1 g Sodium: 76 mg

Yield: *8 servings*

¾ cup unbleached flour

½ cup whole wheat pastry flour

½ cup sugar

1 teaspoon baking powder

¼ teaspoon baking soda

½ cup orange juice

¼ cup cooked mashed pumpkin or butternut squash

3 tablespoons fat-free egg substitute

1 teaspoon vanilla extract

CRUMB TOPPING

¼ cup plus 2 tablespoons quick-cooking oats

2 tablespoons toasted wheat germ or finely chopped pecans

1 tablespoon light brown sugar

1 tablespoon frozen orange juice concentrate, thawed

GLAZE

¼ cup confectioners' sugar

2 teaspoons frozen orange juice concentrate, thawed

Prune and Apple Coffee Cake

Yield: *8 servings*

1 cup unbleached flour

½ cup oat bran

¼ cup sugar

½ teaspoon baking powder

½ teaspoon baking soda

½ cup Prune Butter (page 223)

2 egg whites

½ cup plain nonfat yogurt

1 teaspoon vanilla extract

FILLING

¾ cup finely chopped fresh apples (about 1 medium)

2 tablespoons brown sugar

¼ teaspoon ground cinnamon

TOPPING

1 tablespoon brown sugar

2 teaspoons finely ground walnuts

1. To make the filling, combine the apple, brown sugar, and cinnamon, and stir to mix well. Set aside.

2. To make the topping, combine the brown sugar and walnuts until crumbly. Set aside.

3. Combine the flour, oat bran, sugar, baking powder, and baking soda, and stir to mix well. Add the remaining ingredients, and stir to mix well.

4. Coat an 8-inch round pan with nonstick cooking spray. Spread half of the batter evenly in the pan. Arrange the filling over the batter and spread the remaining batter over the filling. Sprinkle the topping over the batter.

5. Bake at 350°F for 30 to 35 minutes, or until the top springs back when lightly touched and a wooden toothpick inserted in the center of the cake comes out clean.

6. Cool the cake for at least 20 minutes. Cut into wedges and serve warm or at room temperature.

NUTRITIONAL FACTS (PER SERVING)
Calories: 170 Calcium: 51 mg Cholesterol: 0 mg
Fat: 0.9 g Fiber: 3 g Iron: 1.6 mg
Potassium: 237 mg Protein: 5 g Sodium: 99 mg

Pear Crumble Cake

1. To make the topping, stir the topping ingredients together until moist and crumbly. Set aside.

2. Combine the flours, sugar, baking powder, and nutmeg, and stir to mix well. Stir in the milk, Prune Purée, and egg white.

3. Coat a 9-inch round pan with nonstick cooking spray. Spread the batter evenly in the pan, and arrange the pear slices in a circular pattern over the batter. Sprinkle the topping over the pear slices.

4. Bake at 350°F for 30 to 35 minutes, or until a wooden toothpick inserted in the center of the cake comes out clean.

5. Cool the cake for at least 20 minutes. Cut into wedges and serve warm or at room temperature.

Yield: *8 servings*

⅔ cup unbleached pastry flour

⅔ cup whole wheat flour

½ cup sugar

1½ teaspoons baking powder

⅛ teaspoon ground nutmeg

⅔ cup skim milk

¼ cup Prune Purée (page 223)

1 egg white

1½ cups sliced peeled fresh pears (about 1½ medium)

TOPPING

¼ cup quick-cooking oats

2 tablespoons toasted wheat germ

2 tablespoons brown sugar

1 tablespoon maple syrup

NUTRITIONAL FACTS (PER SERVING)

Calories: 188 Calcium: 53 mg Cholesterol: 0 mg
Fat: 0.8 g Fiber: 3 g Iron: 1.4 mg
Potassium: 185 mg Protein: 4.6 g Sodium: 81 mg

Berry Peach Coffee Cake

Yield: *8 servings*

1 cup unbleached flour

½ cup whole wheat pastry flour

¼ cup plus 2 tablespoons sugar

2 teaspoons baking powder

¼ teaspoon ground cinnamon

¾ cup nonfat buttermilk

1 egg white

1 teaspoon vanilla extract

TOPPING

2 medium peaches, peeled and cut into ½-inch thick slices

½ cup fresh or frozen blueberries or raspberries

¼ cup toasted wheat germ

3 tablespoons brown sugar

1. Combine the flours, sugar, baking powder, and cinnamon, and stir to mix well. Stir in the buttermilk, egg white, and vanilla extract.

2. Coat a 9-inch round pan with nonstick cooking spray. Spread the batter evenly in the pan. Arrange the peach slices in a circular pattern over the batter, and spread the berries over the peaches. Comb the wheat germ and brown sugar, and sprinkle over the fruit.

3. Bake at 350°F for about 40 minutes, or until a wooden toothpick inserted in the center of the cake comes out clean.

4. Cool the cake for at least 20 minutes. Cut into wedges and serve warm or at room temperature.

NUTRITIONAL FACTS (PER SERVING)
Calories: 179 Calcium: 54 mg Cholesterol: 0 mg
Fat: 0.8 g Fiber: 2.5 g Iron: 1.6 mg
Potassium: 197 mg Protein: 5 g Sodium: 116 mg

Blueberry Lemon Streusel Cake

1. To make the topping, combine the oats, wheat germ, and nutmeg. Stir in the honey until the mixture is moist and crumbly. Set aside.

2. Combine the milk and lemon juice, and set aside for 2 minutes.

3. Combine the flours, sugar, baking powder, and lemon rind, and stir to mix well. Stir in the lemon juice mixture and the egg white. Fold in the blueberries.

4. Coat an 8-inch square pan with nonstick cooking spray. Spread the batter evenly in the pan, and sprinkle with the topping.

5. Bake at 350°F for 35 to 40 minutes, or until a wooden toothpick inserted in the center of the cake comes out clean.

6. Cool the cake for at least 20 minutes. Cut into squares and serve warm or at room temperature.

Yield: *9 servings*

⅔ cup skim milk

2 tablespoons lemon juice

1½ cups unbleached flour

½ cup oat flour

½ cup sugar

4 teaspoons baking powder

1 teaspoon dried grated lemon rind, or 1 tablespoon fresh

1 egg white

1½ cups fresh or frozen blueberries

TOPPING

¼ cup quick-cooking oats

1 tablespoon toasted wheat germ

⅛ teaspoon ground nutmeg

2 teaspoons honey

NUTRITIONAL FACTS (PER SERVING)

Calories: 184 Calcium: 58 mg Cholesterol: 0 mg
Fat: 0 9 g Fiber: 2.3 g Iron: 1.5 mg
Potassium: 124 mg Protein: 5 g Sodium: 164 mg

Cinnamon Nut Coffee Cake

Yield: *9 servings*

1 cup unbleached flour

½ cup whole wheat pastry flour

2 teaspoons baking powder

½ teaspoon baking soda

⅔ cup light brown sugar

½ cup unsweetened applesauce

½ cup nonfat buttermilk

3 tablespoons fat-free egg
    substitute

1 teaspoon vanilla extract

TOPPING

18 pecan halves

4½ teaspoons sugar

¾ teaspoon ground cinnamon

1. Combine the flours, baking powder, baking soda, and brown sugar, and stir to mix well. Add the applesauce, buttermilk, egg substitute, and vanilla extract, and stir to mix well.

2. Coat an 8-inch square pan with nonstick cooking spray. Spread the batter evenly in the pan. Arrange the pecan halves on top of the batter, pressing each nut slightly into the batter. Combine the sugar and cinnamon, and sprinkle over the top.

3. Bake at 350°F for about 25 minutes, or just until a wooden toothpick inserted in the center of the cake comes out clean.

4. Cool the cake for at least 20 minutes. Cut into squares and serve warm or at room temperature.

NUTRITIONAL FACTS (PER SERVING)
Calories: 172 Calcium: 51 mg Cholesterol: 0 mg
Fat: 1.9 g Fiber: 1.6 g Iron: 1.6 mg
Potassium: 147 mg Protein: 3.6 g Sodium: 148 mg

Cocoa Streusel Cake

1. To make the topping, combine the oats, flour, and brown sugar. Add the chocolate syrup, and stir until the mixture is moist and crumbly. Set aside.

2. Combine the flours, sugar, cocoa, and baking soda, and stir to mix well. Add the applesauce, milk, and vanilla extract, and stir to mix well.

3. Coat a 9-x-13-inch pan with nonstick cooking spray. Spread the batter evenly in the pan, and sprinkle with the topping. Bake at 325°F for about 50 minutes, or just until a wooden toothpick inserted in the center of the cake comes out clean.

4. Cool the cake to room temperature, cut into squares, and serve.

Yield: *16 servings*

1 cup unbleached flour

¾ cup whole wheat pastry flour

1¼ cups sugar

⅓ cup cocoa powder

2 teaspoons baking soda

1½ cups unsweetened applesauce

¾ cup skim milk

2 teaspoons vanilla extract

TOPPING

1½ cups quick-cooking oats

¼ cup unbleached flour

¼ cup brown sugar

¼ cup chocolate syrup

NUTRITIONAL FACTS (PER SERVING)
Calories: 188 Calcium: 29 mg Cholesterol: 0 mg
Fat: 1.1 g Fiber: 2.8 g Iron: 1.4 mg
Potassium: 129 mg Protein: 3.5 g Sodium: 133 mg

Pineapple Date Coffee Cake

Yield: *9 servings*

¾ cup whole wheat pastry flour

¾ cup unbleached flour

1½ teaspoons baking powder

½ teaspoon baking soda

1 can (8 ounces) crushed pineapple with juice, undrained

¼ cup mashed very ripe banana (about ½ large)

1 teaspoon vanilla or almond extract

⅔ cup finely chopped dates

TOPPING

1½ tablespoons brown sugar

1½ tablespoons shredded coconut

1. To make the topping, combine the sugar and coconut until crumbly. Set aside.

2. Combine the flours, baking powder, and baking soda, and stir to mix well. Stir in the pineapple (including the juice), banana, and vanilla or almond extract. Fold in the dates.

3. Coat an 8-inch square pan with nonstick cooking spray. Spread the batter evenly in the pan, and sprinkle with the topping. Bake at 325°F for 25 to 30 minutes, or just until a wooden toothpick inserted in the center of the cake comes out clean.

4. Cool the cake for at least 20 minutes. Cut into squares and serve warm or at room temperature.

NUTRITIONAL FACTS (PER SERVING)
Calories: 149 Calcium: 27 mg Cholesterol: 0 mg
Fat: 0.9 g Fiber: 3.2 g Iron: 1.3 mg
Potassium: 218 mg Protein: 3 g Sodium: 104 mg

Pear Streusel Coffee Cake

1. To make the topping, combine the brown sugar, flour, oats, and walnuts. Stir in the apple juice concentrate, and mix until moist and crumbly. Set aside.

2. Combine the flours, sugar, baking soda, and nutmeg, and stir to mix well. Stir in the apple juice and the chopped pear.

3. Coat an 8-inch round pan with nonstick cooking spray. Spread the batter evenly in the pan, and sprinkle with the topping. Bake at 350°F for about 25 minutes, or just until a wooden toothpick inserted in the center of the cake comes out clean.

4. Cool the cake for at least 20 minutes. Cut into wedges and serve warm or at room temperature.

NUTRITIONAL FACTS (PER SERVING)
Calories: 196 Calcium: 27 mg Cholesterol: 0 mg
Fat: 1.5 g Fiber: 3 g Iron: 1.9 mg
Potassium: 297 mg Protein: 4.2 g Sodium: 109 mg

Yield: *8 servings*

¾ cup unbleached flour

¾ cup whole wheat pastry flour

⅓ cup sugar

1 teaspoon baking soda

¼ teaspoon ground nutmeg

½ cup plus 1 tablespoon apple juice

1½ cups finely chopped fresh pears (about 2 medium)

TOPPING

3 tablespoons light brown sugar

2 tablespoons whole wheat pastry flour

2 tablespoons quick-cooking oats

2 tablespoons finely chopped walnuts

2½ teaspoons frozen apple juice concentrate, thawed

Apple Spice Coffee Cake

Yield: *8 servings*

½ cup whole wheat pastry flour

1 cup unbleached flour

½ cup brown sugar

1 teaspoon baking soda

¼ teaspoon ground cloves

½ teaspoon ground cinnamon

⅓ cup apple butter

⅔ cup nonfat buttermilk

1 egg white

¾ cup finely chopped fresh apples
   (about 1 medium)

TOPPING

1 tablespoon finely ground
   walnuts

1 tablespoon brown sugar

1. To make the topping, stir together the walnuts and brown sugar. Set aside.

2. Combine the flours, brown sugar, baking soda, and spices, and stir to mix well. Stir in the apple butter, buttermilk, and egg white. Fold in the chopped apple.

3. Coat an 8-inch round cake pan with nonstick cooking spray. Spread the batter evenly in the pan, and sprinkle with the topping. Bake at 325°F for 30 to 35 minutes, or just until a wooden toothpick inserted in the center of the cake comes out clean.

4. Cool the cake for at least 20 minutes. Cut into wedges and serve warm or at room temperature.

NUTRITIONAL FACTS (PER SERVING)
Calories: 185 Calcium: 45 mg Cholesterol: 0 mg
Fat: 0.9 g Fiber: 1.8 g Iron: 1.7 mg
Potassium: 187 mg Protein: 4.0 g Sodium: 136 mg

SOUR CREAM APPLE COFFEE CAKE

For variety, substitute sliced peaches or pears for the apples.

Yield: *8 servings*

1. To make the topping, combine the brown sugar and wheat germ or nuts in a small bowl, and stir to mix well. Set aside.

2. Combine the flours, sugar, baking soda, and cinnamon in a medium-sized bowl, and stir to mix well. Stir in the apple juice, sour cream, and egg white. Fold in the apples and raisins.

3. Coat a 9-inch round pan with nonstick cooking spray, and spread the batter evenly in the pan. Sprinkle the topping over the batter, and bake at 350°F for 30 to 33 minutes, or just until a wooden toothpick inserted in the center of the cake comes out clean.

4. Cool the cake to room temperature, cut into wedges, and serve.

1 cup unbleached flour

½ cup whole wheat pastry flour

½ cup sugar

1 teaspoon baking soda

½ teaspoon ground cinnamon

½ cup apple juice

¼ cup nonfat sour cream

1 egg white, lightly beaten

2½ cups thinly sliced peeled apples (about 3 medium)

¼ cup plus 2 tablespoons dark raisins

TOPPING

2 tablespoons light brown sugar

2 tablespoons toasted wheat germ or finely chopped walnuts

NUTRITIONAL FACTS (PER SERVING)
Calories: 163 Cholesterol: 0 mg Fat: 0.7 g
Fiber: 3.4 g Protein: 4 g Sodium: 199 mg

Golden Fruitcake

Yield: *20 slices*

1 cup plus 2 tablespoons whole wheat pastry flour

½ teaspoon baking powder

½ cup plus 2 tablespoons nonfat buttermilk

¼ cup cooked mashed pumpkin

2 tablespoons honey

2 egg whites

½ teaspoon vanilla extract

⅔ cup whole dried apricots

⅔ cup dried pineapple chunks

⅔ cup dried peach halves, cut in half

½ cup golden raisins

½ cup pecan halves (optional)

1. Combine the flour and baking powder, and stir to mix well. Add the buttermilk, pumpkin, honey, egg whites, and vanilla extract, and stir to mix well. Fold in the dried fruits and the nuts if desired.

2. Coat two 5¾-x-3-inch loaf pans with nonstick cooking spray. Divide the batter evenly between the pans, and bake at 325°F for about 45 minutes, or just until a wooden toothpick inserted in the center of a loaf comes out clean.

3. Remove the bread from the oven, and let sit for 10 minutes. Invert the loaves onto a wire rack, turn right side up, and cool to room temperature. Wrap in foil and let sit overnight before slicing and serving.

NUTRITIONAL FACTS (PER SLICE)
Calories: 78 Calcium: 21 mg Cholesterol: 0 mg
Fat: 0.3 g Fiber: 2.1 g Iron: 1 mg
Potassium: 243 mg Protein: 2.2 g Sodium: 24 mg

Fabulous Fruitcake

1. Combine the flour, brown sugar, and baking powder, and stir to mix well. Add the applesauce and egg whites, and stir to mix well. Fold in the fruits.

2. Coat two 5-x-3-inch loaf pans with nonstick cooking spray. Divide the mixture evenly between the pans and bake at 325°F for about 45 minutes, or just until a wooden toothpick inserted in the center of each loaf comes out clean.

3. Remove the bread from the oven, and let sit for 10 minutes. Invert the loaves onto a wire rack, turn right side up, and cool to room temperature. Wrap the bread in foil and let sit overnight before slicing and serving.

Yield: 20 slices

1 cup whole wheat pastry flour

¼ cup light brown sugar

½ teaspoon baking powder

¾ cup unsweetened applesauce

2 egg whites

⅔ cup whole dried apricots

⅔ cup dried pineapple chunks

⅔ cup whole pitted prunes

½ cup golden raisins

½ cup chopped dried dates or chopped walnuts

NUTRITIONAL FACTS (PER SERVING)
Calories: 101 Calcium: 18 mg Cholesterol: 0 mg
Fat: 0.2 g Fiber: 2.9 g Iron: 1.2 mg
Potassium: 306 mg Protein: 2 g Sodium: 17 mg

Cinnamon-Mocha Fudge Cake

Yield: *16 servings*

1 box (1 pound, 2.25 ounces) reduced-fat or regular devil's food or chocolate cake mix

1 package (4-serving size) fat-free or regular instant chocolate pudding mix

½ teaspoon ground cinnamon

1 cup fat-free egg substitute

¾ cup coffee, cooled to room temperature

½ cup unsweetened applesauce

GLAZE

½ cup powdered sugar

1 tablespoon cocoa powder

1 tablespoon coffee, cooled to room temperature

1. Place the cake mix, pudding mix, and cinnamon in a large bowl, and stir to mix well. Add the egg substitute, coffee, and applesauce, and beat with an electric mixer for about 2 minutes, or until well mixed.

2. Coat a 12-cup bundt pan with nonstick cooking spray, and spread the batter evenly in the pan. Bake at 350°F for about 40 minutes, or just until the top springs back when lightly touched and a wooden toothpick inserted in the center of the cake comes out clean. Be careful not to overbake.

3. Allow the cake to cool in the pan for 45 minutes. Then invert onto a serving platter, and cool to room temperature.

4. To make the glaze, place all of the glaze ingredients in a small bowl, and stir to mix well. If using a microwave oven, microwave on high power for 25 seconds, or until hot and runny. If using a stove top, place the glaze in a small pot and cook over medium heat, stirring constantly, for about 30 seconds, or until hot and runny.

5. Drizzle the hot glaze over the cake. Allow the cake sit for at least 15 minutes before slicing and serving.

NUTRITIONAL FACTS (PER SERVING)
Calories: 175 Carbohydrates: 36 g Cholesterol: 0 mg
Fat: 2.3 g Fiber: 1 g Protein: 3 g Sodium: 372 mg

You Save: Calories: 137 Fat: 14.5 g

SOUR CREAM-COCONUT BUNDT CAKE

1. Place the cake mix and pudding mix in a large bowl, and stir to mix well. Add the egg substitute, water, and sour cream, and beat with an electric mixer for about 2 minutes, or until well mixed.

2. Coat a 12-cup bundt pan with nonstick cooking spray, and spread the batter evenly in the pan. Bake at 350°F for 40 to 45 minutes, or just until the top springs back when lightly touched and a wooden toothpick inserted in the center of the cake comes out clean. Be careful not to overbake.

3. Allow the cake to cool in the pan for 45 minutes. Then invert onto a serving platter and cool to room temperature.

4. To make the glaze, place the powdered sugar, sour cream, and coconut extract in a small bowl, and stir to mix well. If using a microwave oven, microwave on high power for 30 seconds, or until hot and runny. If using a stovetop, place the glaze in a small pot and cook over medium heat, stirring constantly, for about 30 seconds, or until hot and runny.

5. Drizzle the hot glaze over the cake, and sprinkle the glaze with the coconut. Allow the cake to sit for at least 15 minutes before slicing and serving.

Yield: *16 servings*

1 box (1 pound, 2.25 ounces) reduced-fat or regular yellow, white, or chocolate cake mix

1 package (4-serving size) fat-free or regular instant toasted coconut pudding mix*

1 cup fat-free egg substitute

¾ cup water

¾ cup nonfat sour cream

GLAZE

½ cup powdered sugar

1 tablespoon plus 1 teaspoon nonfat sour cream

½ teaspoon coconut-flavored extract

2 tablespoons shredded sweetened coconut

---

* If you cannot find toasted coconut pudding mix, substitute 1 package instant vanilla pudding mix plus ¾ teaspoon coconut-flavored extract and 2 tablespoons finely shredded toasted coconut.

NUTRITIONAL FACTS (PER SERVING)

Calories: 188 Carbohydrates: 38.4 g Cholesterol: 0 mg
Fat: 2 g Fiber: 0.5 g Protein: 3 g Sodium: 281 mg

You Save: Calories: 106 Fat: 14 g

Variation

For a denser pound cake-like texture, reduce the water in the recipe to ½ cup, and bake for 35 to 40 minutes.

Pear and Walnut Bundt Cake

Yield: *16 servings*

1½ cups unbleached flour

1 cup whole wheat pastry flour

1 cup brown sugar

2 teaspoons baking soda

1 cup apple butter

½ cup plain nonfat yogurt

2 egg whites

1 teaspoon vanilla extract

1 cup finely chopped fresh pears
  (about 1 medium)

⅓ cup chopped walnuts (optional)

TOPPING

⅓ cup confectioners' sugar

1 tablespoon apple butter

1 tablespoon chopped walnuts

1. Combine the flours, brown sugar, and baking soda, and stir to mix well. Add the apple butter, yogurt, egg whites, and vanilla extract, and stir to mix well. Fold in the pears and walnuts.

2. Coat a 12-cup bundt pan with nonstick cooking spray. Spread the batter evenly in the pan, and bake at 325°F for 35 to 45 minutes, or just until a wooden toothpick inserted in the center of the cake comes out clean. Cool the cake in the pan for 20 minutes. Then invert onto a wire rack, and cool to room temperature.

3. To make the topping, combine the confectioners' sugar with the apple butter. Transfer the cake to a serving platter, and drizzle the topping over the cake. Sprinkle the walnuts over the glaze. Let sit for at least 15 minutes before slicing and serving.

NUTRITIONAL FACTS (PER SERVING)

Calories: 177 Calcium: 35 mg Cholesterol: 0 mg
Fat: 0.7 g Fiber: 1.8 g Iron: 1.5 mg
Potassium: 178 mg Protein: 3.3 g Sodium: 120 mg

Apple Butter Bundt Cake

1. Combine the flours and baking soda, and stir to mix well. Add the apple butter and egg whites, and stir to mix well. Stir in the apples and raisins.

2. Coat a 12-cup bundt pan with nonstick cooking spray. Spread the batter evenly in the pan, and bake at 350°F for 30 to 35 minutes, or just until a wooden toothpick inserted in the center of the cake comes out clean.

3. Cool the cake in the pan for 20 minutes. Then invert onto a wire rack, and cool to room temperature. Transfer to a serving plate, sift the confectioners' sugar over the top, slice, and serve.

NUTRITIONAL FACTS (PER SERVING)
Calories: 146 Calcium: 12 mg Cholesterol: 0 mg
Fat: 0.6 g Fiber: 2.3 g Iron: 1.1 mg
Potassium: 204 mg Protein: 2.9 g Sodium: 111 mg

Yield: *16 servings*

¾ cup whole wheat pastry flour

1½ cups unbleached flour

2 teaspoons baking soda

2 cups apple butter

2 egg whites

2 cups finely chopped peeled apples (about 3 medium)

½ cup dark raisins

1½ tablespoons confectioners' sugar

Cocoa Marble Bundt Cake

Yield: *16 servings*

2¼ cups unbleached flour

¾ cup oat bran

1⅓ cups sugar

1 tablespoon plus 1½ teaspoons lecithin granules*

1¼ teaspoons baking soda

1⅔ cups nonfat buttermilk

2 egg whites

1½ teaspoons vanilla extract

¼ cup chocolate syrup

¼ cup cocoa powder

GLAZE

⅓ cup confectioners' sugar

1 tablespoon cocoa powder

2 teaspoons skim milk

½ teaspoon vanilla extract

* For information on lecithin, see the inset on page 233.

1. Combine the flour, oat bran, sugar, lecithin, and baking soda, and stir to mix well. Add the buttermilk, egg whites, and vanilla extract and stir to mix well. Remove 1 cup of the batter and mix with the chocolate syrup and cocoa powder.

2. Coat a 12-cup bundt pan with nonstick cooking spray. Spread ¾ of the plain batter evenly in the pan, top with the chocolate mix and add the remaining batter.

3. Bake at 350°F for 35 to 45 minutes, or just until a wooden toothpick inserted in the center of the cake comes out clean. Cool the cake in the pan for 20 minutes. Then invert onto a wire rack, then cool to room temperature.

4. To make the glaze, combine the glaze ingredients, stirring until smooth. Transfer the cake to a serving platter, and drizzle the glaze over the cake. Let sit for at least 15 minutes before slicing and serving.

NUTRITIONAL FACTS (PER SERVING)
Calories: 174 Calcium: 35 mg Cholesterol: 0 mg
Fat: 1.3 g Fiber: 1.9 g Iron: 1.4 mg
Potassium: 106 mg Protein: 4.1 g Sodium: 112 mg

Butterscotch Bundt Cake

1. Combine the flour, oat bran, brown sugar, lecithin, and baking soda, and stir to mix well, pressing out any lumps with the back of a spoon. In a separate bowl, combine the buttermilk, squash or pumpkin, egg whites, honey, and vanilla extract. Add the buttermilk mixture to the flour mixture, and stir just enough to mix well.

2. Coat a 12-cup bundt pan with nonstick cooking spray. Spread the batter evenly in the pan, and bake at 350°F for about 40 minutes, or just until a wooden toothpick inserted in the center of the cake comes out clean.

3. Cool the cake in the pan for 20 minutes. Then invert onto a wire rack, and cool to room temperature. Transfer to a serving plate.

4. To make the glaze, combine the confectioners' sugar, brown sugar, and milk until smooth. Drizzle the glaze over the cake, and let sit for at least 15 minutes before slicing and serving.

NUTRITIONAL FACTS (PER SERVING)
Calories: 180 Calcium: 53 mg Cholesterol: 0 mg
Fat: 1.1 g Fiber: 1.4 g Iron: 1.8 mg
Potassium: 163 mg Protein: 3.7 g Sodium: 98 mg

Yield: *16 servings*

2⅓ cups unbleached flour

⅔ cup oat bran

1⅓ cups light brown sugar

1 tablespoon plus 1½ teaspoons lecithin granules*

1¼ teaspoons baking soda

1¼ cups nonfat buttermilk

½ cup cooked mashed butternut squash or pumpkin

2 egg whites

2 tablespoons honey

2 teaspoons vanilla extract

GLAZE

⅓ cup confectioners' sugar

2 teaspoons light brown sugar

2 teaspoons skim milk

* For information on lecithin, see the inset on page 233.

CITRUS POUND CAKE

Yield: *16 servings*

For variety, add 2 tablespoons of poppy seeds to the batter.

1 box (1 pound, 2.25 ounces) reduced-fat or regular lemon or yellow cake mix

1 box (4-serving size) fat-free or regular instant lemon pudding mix

1 can (11 ounces) mandarin oranges, undrained

¾ cup fat-free egg substitute

3 tablespoons powdered sugar (optional)

1. Place the cake mix and pudding mix in a large bowl, and stir to mix well. Add the mandarin oranges with their liquid and the egg substitute, and beat with an electric mixer for about 2 minutes, or until the ingredients are well mixed and the oranges are pulverized.

2. Coat a 12-cup bundt pan with nonstick cooking spray, and spread the batter evenly in the pan. Bake at 350°F for about 40 minutes, or just until the top springs back when lightly touched and a wooden toothpick inserted in the center of the cake comes out clean. Be careful not to overbake.

3. Allow the cake to cool in the pan for 45 minutes. Then invert onto a serving platter and cool to room temperature. If desired, sift the powdered sugar over the top just before slicing and serving.

NUTRITIONAL FACTS (PER SERVING)

Calories: 168 Carbohydrates: 36 g Cholesterol: 0 mg
Fat: 1.5 g Fiber: 0.4 g Protein: 2 g Sodium: 306 mg

You Save: Calories: 106 Fat: 13.2 g

Baking with Reduced-Fat Margarine and Light Butter

Contrary to popular belief, you *can* bake with reduced-fat margarine and light butter. These products make it possible to reduce fat by more than half and still enjoy light, tender, buttery-tasting cakes; crisp cookies; flaky pie crusts; and other goodies that are not easily made fat-free.

The secret to using these reduced-fat products successfully in your baked goods is to substitute three-fourths as much of the light product for the full-fat butter or margarine. This will compensate for the extra water that the reduced-fat products contain. For example, if a cake recipe calls for 1 cup of butter, substitute ¾ cup of light butter. And be sure to choose brands that contain 5 to 6 grams of fat and 50 calories per tablespoon. (Full-fat brands contain 11 grams of fat and 100 calories per tablespoon.) Brands with less fat than this do not generally work well in baking.

Be careful not to overbake your reduced-fat creations, as they can become dry. Bake cakes and quick breads at 325°F to 350°F, and biscuits and scones at 375°F to 400°F. Check the product for doneness a few minutes before the end of the usual baking time. Then enjoy! (For tips on using reduced-fat margarine and light butter in cookies, see the inset on pages 432 to 433.)

Low-Fat Pound Cake

1. Combine the margarine or butter and the sugar in the bowl of an electric mixer, and beat until smooth. Add the egg whites and vanilla extract, and beat until smooth. In a separate bowl, combine the flour, oat bran, and baking soda. Add the flour mixture and the yogurt to the margarine mixture, and beat just enough to mix well.

2. Coat an 8-x-4-inch loaf pan with nonstick cooking spray. Spread the mixture evenly in the pan, and bake at 350°F for 55 to 60 minutes, or just until a wooden toothpick inserted in the center of the loaf comes out clean.

3. Remove the cake from the oven, and let sit for 20 minutes. Invert the cake onto a wire rack, turn right side up, and cool to room temperature before slicing and serving.

Yield: *16 slices*

5 tablespoons reduced-fat margarine or light butter

1¼ cups sugar

3 egg whites

1½ teaspoons vanilla extract

1⅔ cups unbleached flour

½ cup oat bran

½ teaspoon baking soda

1 cup vanilla or lemon nonfat yogurt

NUTRITIONAL FACTS (PER SLICE)
Calories: 141 Calcium: 33 mg Cholesterol: 0 mg
Fat: 2.0 g Fiber: 0.9 g Iron: 0.8 mg
Potassium: 77 mg Protein: 3.3 g Sodium: 90 mg

LEMON-POPPY SEED POUND CAKE

Yield: *16 slices*

½ cup reduced-fat margarine or
   light butter

1½ cups sugar

3 egg whites

2⅓ cups unbleached flour

⅔ cup oat bran

1½ tablespoons poppy seeds

½ teaspoon baking soda

1 cup nonfat lemon yogurt

3 tablespoons lemon juice

1 tablespoon freshly grated lemon
   rind, or 1 teaspoon dried

GLAZE

⅓ cup confectioners' sugar

2 teaspoons lemon juice

1. Combine the margarine or butter and the sugar in the bowl of an electric mixer, and beat until smooth. Add the egg whites, and beat until smooth. In a separate bowl, combine the flour, oat bran, poppy seeds, and baking soda. Add the flour mixture and the yogurt, lemon juice, and lemon rind to the margarine mixture, and beat just until well mixed.

2. Coat a 12-cup bundt pan with nonstick cooking spray. Spread the batter evenly in the pan, and bake at 350°F for 40 minutes, or just until a wooden toothpick inserted in the center of the cake comes out clean. Cool the cake in the pan for 20 minutes. Then invert onto a wire rack, and cool to room temperature.

3. To make the glaze, combine the confectioners' sugar and lemon juice, and stir until smooth. Transfer the cake to a serving platter, and drizzle the glaze over the cake. Let sit for at least 15 minutes before slicing and serving.

NUTRITIONAL FACTS (PER SERVING)
Calories: 197 Calcium: 51 mg Cholesterol: 0 mg
Fat: 3.6 g Fiber: 1.3 g Iron: 1.2 mg
Potassium: 100 mg Protein: 4.3 g Sodium: 116 mg

Cool and Creamy Cheesecake

1. To make the crust, break the crackers into pieces, and place in the bowl of a food processor or blender. Process into fine crumbs. Measure the crumbs. There should be ¾ cup. (Adjust the amount if necessary.)

2. Return the crumbs to the food processor or blender, add the sugar, and process for a few seconds to mix. Add the egg substitute, and process until the mixture is moist and crumbly.

3. Coat a 9-inch springform pan with nonstick cooking spray, and use the back of a spoon to press the mixture over the bottom of the pan and ½-inch up the sides, forming an even crust. (Periodically dip the spoon in sugar, if necessary, to prevent sticking.) Bake at 350°F for 8 minutes, or until the edges feel firm and dry. Set aside to cool.

4. To make the filling, place the cream cheese, ricotta, egg substitute, sugar, flour, lemon rind, and vanilla extract in a food processor, and process until smooth. Spread the filling evenly over the crust, and bake at 325°F for 1 hour, or until the center is set. Turn the oven off, and allow the cake to cool in the oven with the door ajar for 30 minutes.

5. Remove the cake from the oven, and chill for at least 8 hours. Remove the collar of the pan just before slicing and serving. Top each serving with fresh fruit or canned cherry pie filling if desired.

NUTRITIONAL FACTS (PER SERVING)
Calories: 192 Cholesterol: 10 mg Fat: 0.3 g
Fiber: 0.4 g Protein: 14 g Sodium: 346 mg

Yield: *10 servings*

CRUST

4½ large (2½-x-5-inch) fat-free or reduced-fat graham crackers

1 tablespoon sugar

1 tablespoon fat-free egg substitute

FILLING

1 pound nonfat cream cheese, softened to room temperature

15 ounces nonfat ricotta cheese

½ cup fat-free egg substitute

¾ cup sugar

¾ cup plus 2 tablespoons unbleached flour

1 tablespoon freshly grated lemon rind, or 1 teaspoon dried

2 teaspoons vanilla extract

Vanilla Yogurt Cheesecake

Yield: *8 servings*

1½ large (2½-x-5-inch) reduced-
fat graham crackers

FILLING

1½ blocks (8 ounces each) nonfat
cream cheese, softened to
room temperature

1 teaspoon vanilla extract

½ cup sugar

2 tablespoons cornstarch

¼ cup plus 2 tablespoons fat-free
egg substitute

1½ cups vanilla yogurt cheese
(page 293)

TOPPING

1 cup plus 2 tablespoons canned
blueberry pie filling

For variety, substitute lemon yogurt cheese for the vanilla yogurt cheese.

1. Break the graham cracker into pieces, place in the bowl of a food processor, and process into fine crumbs. Measure the crumbs. There should be 3 tablespoons. (Adjust the amount if needed.)

2. Coat a 9-inch glass pie pan with nonstick cooking spray. Place the graham cracker crumbs in the pan, and tilt the pan to coat the bottom and sides with the crumbs. Set aside.

3. To make the filling, place the cream cheese and vanilla extract in a large bowl, and beat with an electric mixer until smooth. Add the sugar, and beat to mix well. Sprinkle the cornstarch over the cheese mixture, and beat to mix well. Add the egg substitute, and beat to mix well. Finally, add the yogurt cheese, and beat just until well mixed.

4. Spread the batter evenly in the pan, and bake at 300°F for 45 to 50 minutes, or until the center is firm to the touch. Turn the oven off, and allow the cake to cool in the oven with the door ajar for 1 hour. Remove the cake from the oven, cover, and chill for at least 6 hours, or until firm.

5. Spread the pie filling over the top of the cheesecake to within ½ inch of the edge. Chill for an additional 2 hours before slicing and serving.

NUTRITIONAL FACTS (PER SERVING)
Calories: 181 Carbohydrates: 33 g Cholesterol: 4 mg
Fat: 0.4 g Fiber: 0.7 g Protein: 11 g Sodium: 272 mg

You Save: Calories: 240 Fat: 30.9 g

Blueberry Cheesecake

1. Coat a 9-inch springform pan with nonstick cooking spray. Prepare the graham cracker crust as directed, but pat it over the bottom of the pan and ¾-inch up the side. Bake at 350°F for 8 to 9 minutes, or until the edges feel firm and dry. Set aside to cool.

2. Place the remaining ingredients, except for the blueberries, in a food processor or blender, and process until smooth. Fold in the blueberries.

3. Pour the filling into the crust. Bake at 350°F for about 50 minutes, or until the crust is lightly browned around the edges and the filling is set.

4. Turn the oven off, and let the cake cool in the oven with the door ajar for 1 hour. Refrigerate for at least 8 hours, cut into wedges, and serve.

Yield: *10 servings*

1 recipe Prune-the-Fat Pie Crust (page 321)

8 ounces nonfat cream cheese

15 ounces nonfat ricotta cheese

½ cup fat-free egg substitute

2 teaspoons vanilla extract

1 tablespoon fresh lemon juice

⅓ cup unbleached flour

¾ cup sugar

¾ cup fresh or frozen blueberries

NUTRITIONAL FACTS (PER SERVING)
Calories: 215 Calcium: 396 mg Cholesterol: 4 mg
Fat: 0.1 g Fiber: 0.9 g Iron: 1 mg
Potassium: 112 mg Protein: 13.5 g Sodium: 290 mg

Making and Using Yogurt Cheese

Yogurt cheese—a great substitute for cream cheese—is a wonderfully versatile food that can be used in dessert frostings and fillings, as a base for puddings and mousses, and, of course, in creamy cheesecakes.

To make yogurt cheese, start with any brand of fat-free or low-fat plain or flavored yogurt that does not contain gelatin, modified food starch, or vegetable gums like carrageenan and guar gum. These ingredients will prevent the yogurt from draining properly. Yogurts that contain pectin will drain nicely and can be used for making cheese.

Simply place the yogurt in a funnel lined with cheesecloth or a coffee filter, and allow it to drain into a jar in the refrigerator for at least 8 hours or overnight. Special funnels designed just for making yogurt cheese are also available in cooking shops. When the yogurt is reduced by half, it is ready to use. The whey that collects in the jar may be used in bread and muffin recipes, in place of the listed liquid.

When making baked cheesecakes, substitute yogurt cheese for cream cheese on a cup-for-cup basis, adding 1 to 1½ tablespoons of flour or 1½ to 2 teaspoons of cornstarch to the batter for each cup of yogurt cheese used. This will insure a firm-textured yet creamy cake. For best results, avoid using a blender or food processor for mixing, as this can cause the yogurt cheese to become thin. Instead, mix this ingredient into your batter with a spoon, wire whisk, or electric mixer.

Strawberry Swirl Cheesecake

Yield: *10 servings*

1 recipe Honey Graham Pie Crust (page 318)

⅔ cup low-sugar strawberry preserves

2 containers (15 ounces each) nonfat ricotta cheese

½ cup nonfat sour cream or plain nonfat yogurt

¾ cup fat-free egg substitute or 6 egg whites

⅔ cup sugar

¼ cup unbleached flour

2 teaspoons vanilla extract

1. Coat a 9-inch springform pan with nonstick cooking spray. Prepare the graham cracker crust as directed, but pat it over the bottom of the pan and ½ inch up the sides. Bake at 350°F for 8 minutes, or until the edges are firm and dry and lightly browned. Set aside to cool.

2. If using a microwave oven, place the jam in a microwave-safe bowl, and microwave uncovered at 50-percent power for 2 minutes or until runny. If using a conventional stove top, place the jam in a small saucepan over low heat and cook, stirring constantly, until runny. Set aside.

3. Place the ricotta, sour cream or yogurt, and egg substitute in the bowl of a food processor or in a blender, and process until smooth. Add the sugar, flour, and vanilla extract, and process until smooth.

4. Spread half of the cheese filling evenly over the graham cracker crust. Spoon half of the heated jam randomly over the filling. Top with the remaining filling. Then spoon the rest of the jam randomly over the top. Draw a knife through the batter to produce a marbled effect.

5. Bake at 350°F for 60 to 70 minutes, or until the center is set. Turn the oven off, and allow the cake to cool in the oven with the door ajar for 30 minutes.

6. Chill the cake for at least 8 hours. Remove the collar of the pan just before slicing and serving.

NUTRITIONAL FACTS (PER SERVING)

Calories: 239 Calcium: 479 mg Cholesterol: 0 mg
Fat: 1 g Fiber: 0.6 g Iron: 1 mg
Potassium: 72 mg Protein: 15 g Sodium: 243 mg

Lite and Luscious Lemon Cheesecake

1. To make the crust, break the graham crackers into pieces, place in the bowl of a food processor, and process into fine crumbs. Measure the crumbs. There should be ¾ cup. (Adjust the amount if needed.)

2. Return the crumbs to the food processor, add the sugar, and process for a few seconds to mix well. Add the margarine, and process for about 20 seconds, or until moist and crumbly. Add the wheat germ, and process for a few seconds to mix well.

3. Coat a 9-inch springform pan with nonstick cooking spray, and use the back of a spoon to press the crumb mixture against the bottom and sides of the pan, forming an even crust. (Periodically dip the spoon in sugar, if necessary, to prevent sticking.) Then use your fingers to finish pressing the crust firmly against the bottom and sides of the pan.

4. Bake at 350°F for about 8 minutes, or until the edges feel firm and dry. Set aside to cool to room temperature before filling.

5. To make the filling, place the cream cheese and vanilla extract in a large bowl, and beat with an electric mixer until smooth. Sprinkle the cornstarch over the cheese mixture, and beat until smooth. Add the sweetened condensed milk, and beat to mix well. Add the egg substitute, and beat to mix well. Finally, add the lemon juice and lemon rind, and beat to mix well.

6. Spread the cheesecake batter evenly over the crust, and bake at 325°F for about 50 minutes, or until the center is firm to the touch. (If you use a dark pan instead of a shiny one, reduce the oven temperature to 300°F.) Turn the oven off, and allow the cake to cool in the oven with the door ajar for I hour. Remove the cake from the oven, cover, and chill for at least 8 hours, or until firm.

7. Run a knife between the cheesecake and the collar of the pan, and remove the collar just before slicing and serving. Top individual servings with some of the fresh berries, and serve.

Yield: *10 servings*

CRUST

6 large (2½-x-5-inch) reduced-fat graham crackers

2 tablespoons sugar

1 tablespoon tub-style nonfat margarine, or 1 tablespoon plus 1½ teaspoons reduced-fat margarine

2 tablespoons honey crunch wheat germ

FILLING

2 blocks (8 ounces each) nonfat cream cheese, softened to room temperature

1½ teaspoons vanilla extract

3 tablespoons cornstarch

1 can (14 ounces) fat-free sweetened condensed milk

½ cup plus 2 tablespoons fat-free egg substitute

⅓ cup lemon juice

1½ teaspoons freshly grated lemon rind, or ½ teaspoon dried

TOPPING

2½ cups fresh raspberries or sliced fresh strawberries

NUTRITIONAL FACTS (PER SERVING)
Calories: 234 Carbohydrates: 43 g Cholesterol: 6 mg
Fat: 0.9 g Fiber: 1.5 g Protein: 13.1 g Sodium: 312 mg

You Save: Calories: 202 Fat: 25.6 g

Apple-Topped Cheesecake

Yield: *12 servings*

CRUST

6 large (2½-x-5-inch) reduced-fat graham crackers

2 tablespoons light brown sugar

1 tablespoon tub-style nonfat margarine, or 1 tablespoon plus 1½ teaspoons reduced-fat margarine

2 tablespoons honey crunch wheat germ or finely chopped toasted pecans (page 383)

FILLING

2½ cups nonfat cottage cheese

2 blocks (8 ounces each) nonfat cream cheese, softened to room temperature

2 teaspoons vanilla extract

¾ cup plus 2 tablespoons sugar

3 tablespoons cornstarch

¾ cup fat-free egg substitute

TOPPING

1 can (20 ounces) light (reduced-sugar) apple pie filling

1. To make the crust, break the graham crackers into pieces, place in the bowl of a food processor, and process into fine crumbs. Measure the crumbs. There should be ¾ cup. (Adjust the amount if needed.)

2. Return the crumbs to the food processor, add the brown sugar, and process for a few seconds to mix well. Add the margarine, and process for about 20 seconds, or until moist and crumbly. Add the wheat germ or pecans, and process for a few seconds to mix well.

3. Coat a 9-inch springform pan with nonstick cooking spray, and use the back of a spoon to press the crumb mixture against the bottom and sides of the pan, forming an even crust. (Periodically dip the spoon in sugar, if necessary, to prevent sticking.) Then use your fingers to finish pressing the crust firmly against the bottom and sides of the pan.

4. Bake at 350°F for about 8 minutes, or until the edges feel firm and dry. Set aside to cool to room temperature before filling.

5. To make the filling, place the cottage cheese in a large wire (fine mesh) strainer, and rinse with cool running water until all of the creaming mixture has been rinsed away. Using the bottom of a glass, push the curds against the bottom of the strainer to press out as much of the water as possible, leaving just the dry curds in the strainer.

6. Place the dry cottage cheese curds, cream cheese, vanilla extract, sugar, and cornstarch in the bowl of a food processor, and process until smooth. Add the egg substitute, and process to mix well.

7. Spread the batter over the crust, and bake at 325°F for 1 hour and 5 minutes, or until the center is firm to the touch. (If you use a dark pan instead of a shiny one, reduce the temperature to 300°F.) To minimize cracking, run a sharp, thin-bladed knife between the cheesecake and the collar of the pan. Turn the oven off, and allow the cake to cool in the oven with the door ajar for 1 hour. Remove the cake from the oven, cover, and chill for 6 hours, or until firm.

8. Spread the pie filling over the top of the cheesecake, extending the filling to the edge of the cake, and chill for at least 2 additional hours. Remove the collar of the pan just before serving.

NUTRITIONAL FACTS (PER SERVING)
Calories: 208 Carbohydrates: 37g Cholesterol: 6 mg
Fat: 0.9 g Fiber: 0.6 g Protein: 13 g Sodium: 308 mg

You Save: Calories: 238 Fat: 30.2 g

Busy Day Strawberry Cheesecake

1. Break the graham cracker into pieces, place in the bowl of a food processor, and process into fine crumbs. Measure the crumbs. There should be 3 tablespoons. (Adjust the amount if needed.)

2. Coat a 9-inch glass pie pan with nonstick cooking spray. Place the graham cracker crumbs in the pan, and tilt the pan to coat the bottom and sides with the crumbs. Set aside.

3. To make the filling, place the cream cheese, cottage cheese, and sugar in the bowl of a food processor, and process until smooth. Add the flour, egg substitute, and vanilla extract, and process until smooth.

4. Spread the batter evenly in the pan, and bake at 300°F for about 50 minutes, or until the center is firm to the touch. Turn the oven off, and allow the cake to cool in the oven with the door ajar for 1 hour. Remove the cake from the oven, cover, and chill for at least 6 hours, or until firm.

5. To make the topping, combine the strawberries and glaze in a medium-sized bowl, and toss to coat the berries with the glaze. Spread the glazed berries over the top of the cheesecake to within 1 inch of the edge. Cover and chill for at least 2 hours before slicing and serving.

Yield: *8 servings*

1½ large (2½-x-5-inch) reduced-fat graham crackers

FILLING

1½ blocks (8 ounces each) nonfat cream cheese, softened to room temperature

1½ cups nonfat cottage cheese

⅔ cup sugar

¼ cup unbleached flour

¼ cup plus 2 tablespoons fat-free egg substitute

1½ teaspoons vanilla extract

TOPPING

2 cups sliced fresh strawberries

½ cup ready-made strawberry pie glaze

NUTRITIONAL FACTS (PER SERVING)

Calories: 175 Carbohydrates: 33 g Cholesterol: 4 mg
Fat: 0.3 q Fiber: 0.8 g Protein: 10.2 g Sodium: 245 mg

You Save: Calories: 228 Fat: 31 g

No-Bake Pineapple Cheesecake

Yield: *8 servings*

1 prebaked Lite Graham Cracker
   Pie Crust (page 314) made
   with plain graham crackers

FILLING

½ cup unsweetened pineapple
   juice

1½ teaspoons unflavored gelatin

1½ blocks (8 ounces each) nonfat
   cream cheese, softened to
   room temperature

1 teaspoon vanilla extract

½ cup sugar

½ cup vanilla yogurt cheese
   (page 293)

¼ cup nonfat sour cream

TOPPING

1 can (8 ounces) crushed
   pineapple in juice, undrained

1 tablespoon cornstarch

1 tablespoon sugar

1 cup nonfat or light whipped
   topping

1. To make the filling, place the pineapple juice in a 1-quart pot. Sprinkle the gelatin over the juice and allow to sit for 2 minutes to soften.

2. Place the pot over low heat, and cook, stirring constantly, for a minute or 2, or until the gelatin is completely dissolved. Do not allow the juice to boil. Remove the pot from the heat and set aside for about 15 minutes, or until the juice cools to room temperature.

3. Place the cream cheese and vanilla extract in a large bowl, and beat with an electric mixer until smooth. Slowly add the sugar, a tablespoon at a time, beating constantly. Add the yogurt cheese and sour cream, and beat to mix well.

4. Slowly pour the pineapple juice-gelatin mixture into the cheese mixture, beating constantly with an electric mixer until smooth and creamy. Spread the cheese mixture evenly in the crust, cover, and chill for at least 3 hours, or until firm.

5. To make the topping, place the pineapple with its juice in a 1-quart pot. Add the cornstarch and sugar, and stir to dissolve the cornstarch. Place the pot over medium heat, and cook, stirring constantly, for several minutes, or until the mixture is thickened and bubbly. Remove the pot from the heat, and allow to cool to room temperature.

6. Gently fold the whipped topping into the cooled pineapple mixture. Spread the topping over the cheesecake, and chill for at least 1 additional hour before slicing and serving.

NUTRITIONAL FACTS (PER SERVING)
Calories: 237 Carbohydrates: 46 g Cholesterol: 3 mg
Fat: 1.4 g Fiber: 0.6 g Protein: 10.3g Sodium: 338 mg

You Save: Calories: 165 Fat: 19.9 g

Citrus Chiffon Cheesecake

1. To make the filling, place the lemon juice and water in a 1-quart pot. Place over medium heat, and cook for a minute or 2, or until the mixture comes to a boil.

2. Remove the pot from the heat, and sprinkle the gelatin over the juice mixture. Stir for about 1 minute, or until the gelatin is completely dissolved. Stir in the juice concentrate, and set aside for about 10 minutes, or until the mixture reaches room temperature.

3. Place the cream cheese and vanilla extract in a large bowl, and beat with an electric mixer until smooth. Slowly add the sugar, a tablespoon at a time, beating constantly. Add the yogurt cheese, and continue to beat to mix well.

4. Using clean beaters, beat the cooled gelatin mixture for about 3 minutes, or until light and fluffy. Add the whipped gelatin mixture to the cheese mixture, and beat to mix well.

5. Spread the cheese mixture evenly in the crust. Cover and chill for at least 3 hours, or until firm.

6. To make the topping, place the berries and marmalade in a 1-quart pot, and stir to mix well. Place the pot over medium heat, and cook, stirring occasionally, for about 5 minutes, or until hot and bubbly.

7. Place the orange juice in a small bowl, add the cornstarch, and stir to dissolve the cornstarch. Add the juice mixture to the berry mixture, and cook, stirring constantly, for a minute or 2, or until thickened and bubbly. Allow the topping to cool to room temperature.

8. Spread the topping over the top of the cheesecake to within 1 inch of the edge. Chill for 1 additional hour before slicing and serving.

NUTRITIONAL FACTS (PER SERVING)
Calories: 229 Carbohydrates: 45 g Cholesterol: 4 mg
Fat: 1.1 g Fiber: 1.1 g Protein: 20.1 g Sodium: 337 mg

You Save: Calories: 237 Fat: 27.3 g

Yield: *8 servings*

1 prebaked Lite Graham Cracker Pie Crust (page 314) made with plain graham crackers

FILLING

2 tablespoons lemon juice

2 tablespoons water

1½ teaspoons unflavored gelatin

¼ cup frozen orange juice concentrate, thawed

1½ blocks (8 ounces each) nonfat cream cheese, softened to room temperature

½ teaspoon vanilla extract

¼ cup plus 3 tablespoons sugar

¾ cup vanilla yogurt cheese (page 293)

TOPPING

1¼ cups fresh or frozen (unthawed) blueberries or raspberries

¼ cup orange marmalade

2 tablespoons orange juice

2½ teaspoons cornstarch

Classic Berry-Topped Cheesecake

Yield: 12 servings

CRUST

6 large (2½-x-5-inch) reduced-fat graham crackers

2 tablespoons sugar

1 tablespoon tub-style nonfat margarine, or 1 tablespoon plus 1½ teaspoons reduced-fat margarine

2 tablespoons honey crunch wheat germ

FILLING

2 blocks (8 ounces each) nonfat cream cheese, softened to room temperature

2 teaspoons vanilla extract

2 tablespoons plus 1 teaspoon cornstarch

1 teaspoon dried grated lemon rind, or 1 tablespoon fresh

1 can (14 ounces) fat-free sweetened condensed milk

½ cup plus 2 tablespoons fat-free egg substitute

1 cup vanilla yogurt cheese (page 293)

TOPPING

2 cups fresh strawberry halves or fresh whole raspberries

¼ cup plus 2 tablespoons seedless strawberry or raspberry jam

1. To make the crust, break the graham crackers into pieces, place in the bowl of a food processor, and process into fine crumbs. Measure the crumbs. There should be ¾ cup. (Adjust the amount if needed.)

2. Return the crumbs to the food processor, add the sugar, and process for a few seconds to mix well. Add the margarine, and process for about 20 seconds, or until moist and crumbly. Add the wheat germ, and process for a few seconds to mix well.

3. Coat a 9-inch springform pan with nonstick cooking spray, and use the back of a spoon to press the crumb mixture against the bottom and sides of the pan, forming an even crust. (Periodically dip the spoon in sugar, if necessary, to prevent sticking.) Then use your fingers to finish pressing the crust firmly against the bottom and sides of the pan.

4. Bake at 350°F for about 8 minutes, or until the edges feel firm and dry. Set aside to cool to room temperature before filling.

5. To make the filling, place the cream cheese and vanilla extract in a large bowl, and beat with an electric mixer until smooth. Sprinkle the cornstarch and lemon rind over the cheese mixture, and beat until smooth. Add the sweetened condensed milk, and beat until smooth. Add the egg substitute, and beat until smooth. Finally, add the yogurt cheese, and beat until smooth.

6. Spread the batter evenly over the crust, and bake at 325°F for about 1 hour, or until the center is firm to the touch. (If you use a dark pan instead of a shiny one, reduce the oven temperature to 300°F.) Turn the oven off, and allow the cake to cool in the oven with the door ajar for 1 hour. Remove the cake from the oven, cover, and chill for at least 6 hours, or until firm.

7. Arrange the berries in concentric circles over the top of the cheesecake. Place the jam in a small pot, and place over medium heat. Cook, stirring constantly, for about 1 minute, or until the jam is runny. Drizzle the jam over the berries, and chill for at least 2 additional hours. Remove the collar of the pan just before slicing and serving.

NUTRITIONAL FACTS (PER SERVING)
Calories: 226 Carbohydrates: 42 g Cholesterol: 6 mg
Fat: 0.7 g Fiber: 0.7 g Protein: 12.3 g Sodium: 314 mg

You Save: Calories: 227 Fat: 28 g

Tips for Making Perfect Fat-Free Cheesecakes

Cheesecake lovers rejoice! With the wide variety of slimmed-down creamy cheeses now available, it is finally possible to have your cheesecake and eat it, too. Here are a few basic tips that will insure the best possible success when making the ultra-light cheesecakes in this chapter, as well as when lightening up your own recipes.

❏ Unless otherwise directed, turn the oven off when the center of your fat-free cheesecake is set, or firm to the touch. If you stop baking your cheesecake before it reaches this point, it will most likely be soft and pudding-like in the center. Note that this test for doneness is different from that recommended in most traditional recipes, which direct you to stop baking the cake when it is still soft or "jiggly" in the center.

❏ Be aware that the kind of springform pan that you use to bake cheesecakes—shiny versus dark—can produce dramatic differences in baking times. The baking times and temperatures for the recipes in this chapter are based on using a shiny springform pan. If you use a dark pan, which absorbs heat more readily, reduce the oven temperature by 25°F. This will allow you to follow the baking times specified in the recipe.

❏ Keep in mind, too, that almost all cheesecakes—including high-fat and low-fat recipes—tend to crack on top as they cool. This is probably why most cheesecakes include toppings, as they cover up the cracks. You can minimize cracking by cooling the cheesecake in the oven with the door ajar. This prevents the rapid temperature changes that can exacerbate cracking. If you know that a particular cake is especially prone to cracking, run a sharp, thin-bladed knife between the cake and the collar of the pan as soon as it is done baking. This will minimize cracking as the cake cools and shrinks from the sides of the pan.

❏ See the inset on pages 306 to 307 for tips on substituting low- and no-fat cheeses for the full-fat cheese in your favorite cheesecake recipe.

Peach-Amaretto Cheesecake

Yield: *12 servings*

CRUST

6 large (2½-x-5-inch) reduced-fat graham crackers

2 tablespoons light brown sugar

1 tablespoon tub-style nonfat margarine, or 1 tablespoon plus 1½ teaspoons reduced-fat margarine

2 tablespoons honey crunch wheat germ or finely chopped toasted almonds (page 383)

FILLING

2 blocks (8 ounces each) nonfat cream cheese, softened to room temperature

2 teaspoons vanilla extract

2 tablespoons plus 2 teaspoons cornstarch

1 can (14 ounces) fat-free sweetened condensed milk

2 tablespoons amaretto liqueur

½ cup plus 2 tablespoons fat-free egg substitute

1 cup vanilla yogurt cheese (page 293)

TOPPING

3 cups diced peeled fresh peaches, divided (about 4 medium)

2 tablespoons light brown sugar

2 tablespoons amaretto liqueur

1. To make the crust, break the graham crackers into pieces, place in the bowl of a food processor, and process into fine crumbs. Measure the crumbs. There should be ¾ cup. (Adjust the amount if needed.)

2. Return the crumbs to the food processor and add the brown sugar. Process for a few seconds to mix well. Add the margarine, and process for about 20 seconds, or until moist and crumbly. Add the wheat germ or almonds, and process for a few seconds to mix well.

3. Coat a 9-inch springform pan with nonstick cooking spray, and use the back of a spoon to press the crumb mixture against the bottom and sides of the pan, forming an even crust. (Periodically dip the spoon in sugar, if necessary, to prevent sticking.) Then use your fingers to finish pressing the crust firmly against the bottom and sides of the pan.

4. Bake at 350°F for about 8 minutes, or until the edges feel firm and dry. Set aside to cool to room temperature before filling.

5. To make the filling, place the cream cheese and vanilla extract in a large bowl, and beat with an electric mixer until smooth. Sprinkle the cornstarch over the cheese, and beat to mix well. Add the sweetened condensed milk, and beat to mix well. Beat in first the liqueur and then the egg substitute. Finally, add the yogurt cheese, and beat to mix well.

6. Spread the batter over the crust, and bake at 325°F for 1 hour, or until the center is firm to the touch. (If you use a dark pan instead of a shiny one, reduce the temperature to 300°F.) Turn the oven off, and allow the cake to cool in the oven with the door ajar for 1 hour. Remove the cake from the oven, cover, and chill for 8 hours, or until firm.

7. To make the topping, place ¾ cup of the peaches and the brown sugar and liqueur in a blender or food processor, and process until smooth. Place the remaining peaches in a medium-sized bowl, add the puréed mixture, and mix well. Chill for at least 2 hours.

8. When ready to serve, run a sharp, thin-bladed knife between the cheesecake and the collar of the pan and remove the collar. Top each serving with a heaping tablespoon of the topping, and serve.

NUTRITIONAL FACTS (PER SERVING)
Calories: 235 Carbohydrates: 43 g Cholesterol: 6 mg
Fat: 0.7 g Fiber: 1 g Protein: 12.4 g Sodium: 276 mg

You Save: Calories: 227 Fat: 29.7 g

COCONUT-KEY LIME CHEESECAKE

1. To make the crust, break the graham crackers into pieces, place in a food processor, and process into fine crumbs. Measure the crumbs. There should be ¾ cup. (Adjust the amount if needed.)

2. Return the crumbs to the food processor, add the brown sugar, and process for a few seconds to mix well. Add the margarine and coconut extract, and process for about 20 seconds, or until moist and crumbly. Add the coconut, and process for a few seconds to mix well.

3. Coat a 9-inch springform pan with nonstick cooking spray, and use the back of a spoon to press the mixture against the bottom and sides of the pan, forming an even crust. (Periodically dip the spoon in sugar, if necessary, to prevent sticking.) Then use your fingers to finish pressing the crust firmly against the bottom and sides of the pan.

4. Bake at 350°F for about 8 minutes, or until the edges feel firm and dry. Set aside to cool to room temperature before filling.

5. To make the filling, place the cream cheese and vanilla in a large bowl, and beat with an electric mixer until smooth. Sprinkle the cornstarch over the cheese mixture, and beat until smooth. Add the condensed milk, and beat to mix well. Add the egg substitute, and beat to mix well. Finally, add the lime juice, and beat to mix well.

6. Spread the batter evenly over the crust, and bake at 325°F for about 50 minutes, or until the center is firm to the touch. (If you use a dark pan instead of a shiny one, reduce the oven temperature to 300°F.) Turn the oven off, and allow the cake to cool in the oven with the door ajar for I hour. Remove the cake from the oven, cover, and chill for at least 8 hours, or until firm.

7. To make the topping, place the strawberries and sugar in a medium-sized bowl, and stir to mix well. Cover and chill for at least 2 hours.

8. When ready to serve, run a sharp, thin-bladed knife between the cheesecake and the collar of the pan. Remove the collar, and cut the cheesecake into wedges. Top each serving with some of the strawberry topping, and serve.

Yield: *10 servings*

CRUST

6 large (2½-x-5-inch) reduced-fat graham crackers

2 tablespoons light brown sugar

1 tablespoon tub-style nonfat margarine, or 1 tablespoon plus 1½ teaspoons reduced-fat margarine

¼ teaspoon coconut-flavored extract

¼ cup shredded sweetened coconut

FILLING

2 blocks (8 ounces each) nonfat cream cheese, softened to room temperature

1½ teaspoons vanilla extract

3 tablespoons cornstarch

1 can (14 ounces) fat-free sweetened condensed milk

½ cup plus 2 tablespoons fat-free egg substitute

⅓ cup key lime juice

TOPPING

2 cups sliced fresh strawberries

2 tablespoons sugar

NUTRITIONAL FACTS (PER SERVING)
Calories: 241 Carbohydrates: 44 g Cholesterol: 6 mg
Fat: 1.5 g Fiber: 0.8 g Protein: 12.8 g Sodium: 361 mg

You Save: Calories: 220 Fat: 27 g

Chocolate Swirl Cheesecake

Yield: *12 servings*

CRUST

6 large (2½-x-5-inch) reduced-fat chocolate graham crackers

2 tablespoons sugar

1 tablespoon tub-style nonfat margarine, or 1 tablespoon plus 1½ teaspoons reduced-fat margarine

2 tablespoons honey crunch wheat germ or finely chopped toasted almonds (page 293)

FILLING

3 blocks (8 ounces each) nonfat cream cheese, softened to room temperature

2 teaspoons vanilla extract

1 cup nonfat ricotta cheese

3 tablespoons plus 1 teaspoon cornstarch

¾ cup plus 2 tablespoons sugar

½ cup fat-free egg substitute

CHOCOLATE SWIRL

2 tablespoons Dutch processed cocoa powder

¼ cup sugar

½ teaspoon vanilla extract

1. To make the crust, break the graham crackers into pieces, place in the bowl of a food processor, and process into fine crumbs. Measure the crumbs. There should be ¾ cup. (Adjust the amount if needed.)

2. Return the crumbs to the food processor, add the sugar, and process for a few seconds to mix well. Add the margarine, and process for about 20 seconds, or until moist and crumbly. Add the wheat germ or almonds, and process for a few seconds to mix well.

3. Coat a 9-inch springform pan with nonstick cooking spray, and use the back of a spoon to press the crumb mixture against the bottom and sides of the pan, forming an even crust. (Periodically dip the spoon in sugar, if necessary, to prevent sticking.) Then use your fingers to finish pressing the crust firmly against the bottom and sides of the pan.

4. Bake at 350°F for about 8 minutes, or until the edges feel firm and dry. Set aside to cool to room temperature before filling.

5. To make the filling, place the cream cheese and vanilla extract in a large bowl, and beat with an electric mixer until smooth. Add the ricotta, and beat for about 2 minutes, or until light, creamy, and smooth. Sprinkle the cornstarch over the cheese mixture, and beat until smooth. Add the sugar, and beat to mix well. Finally, add the egg substitute, and beat just enough to mix well.

6. To make the chocolate swirl, place 1½ cups of the cheese filling in a medium-sized bowl. Add the cocoa powder, sugar, and vanilla extract, and beat with an electric mixer to mix well.

7. Spread half of the plain cheesecake batter evenly over the crust. Spoon half of the cocoa batter randomly over the plain batter. Repeat the layers. Then draw a knife through the batter to produce a marbled effect.

8. Bake at 325°F for about 1 hour and 10 minutes, or until the center is firm to the touch. Note that sometimes cheesecakes made with ricotta will puff up during baking, making it difficult to tell if the center is firm. In this case, bake until the cake is just beginning to brown around the edges. (If you use a dark pan instead of a shiny one, reduce the oven temperature to 300°F.)

9. Run a sharp, thin-bladed knife between the cheesecake and the collar of the pan. (This will minimize cracking as the cake cools.) Turn the oven off, and allow the cake to cool in the oven with the door ajar for 1 hour. Remove the cake from the oven, cover, and chill for at least 8 hours, or until firm. Remove the collar of the pan just before slicing and serving.

NUTRITIONAL FACTS (PER SERVING)
Calories: 202 Carbohydrates: 35 g Cholesterol: 6 mg
Fat: 1 g Fiber: 0.5 g Protein: 13.9 g Sodium: 365 mg

You Save: Calories: 323 Fat: 31.5 g

Getting the Fat Out of Your Favorite Cheesecake Recipes

By far, most of the fat in cheesecake comes from the cream cheese that forms the base of its batter. Just one 8-ounce block of cream cheese contains 800 calories and 80 grams of fat—the equivalent of a stick of butter! Fortunately, a variety of creamy nonfat and low-fat cheeses can successfully replace the full-fat cream cheese in all your favorite cheesecake recipes, slashing calories and almost completely eliminating the fat. You'll note that many of the recipes in this chapter blend nonfat cream cheese with other low- or no-fat cheeses, as this results in a more traditional flavor and texture than you would get by using only nonfat cream cheese. The following table presents the healthful cheeses used in this chapter, looks at the fat and calorie savings offered by these great products, and gives you tips for using them successfully in your own recipes.

Using Nonfat and Low-Fat Cheeses in Cheesecakes

Cheese	Savings Per Cup When Substituted for Full-Fat Cream Cheese	Special Considerations
Neufchâtel (reduced-fat) cream cheese	230 calories 32 g fat	Substitute cup-for-cup for full-fat cream cheese. No adjustments are usually required.
Nonfat cottage cheese	640 calories 80 g fat	Substitute cup-for-cup for full-fat cream cheese. In baked cheesecakes, add 1 to 1½ tablespoons flour or 1½ to 2 teaspoons cornstarch per cup of nonfat cottage cheese to insure a firm texture. Some recipes instruct you to rinse the creaming mixture off the cottage cheese and press out any excess liquid, leaving just the dry curds. This also helps insure a firm texture.
Nonfat cream cheese	560 calories 80 g fat	Substitute cup-for-cup for full-fat cream cheese, and use the block-style cream cheese for best results. In baked cheesecakes, add 1 to 1½ tablespoons flour or 1½ to 2 teaspoons cornstarch per cup of nonfat cream cheese to insure a firm texture.
Nonfat ricotta cheese	560 calories 80 g fat	Substitute cup-for-cup for full-fat cream cheese. If any liquid has separated from the cheese, drain it off before using. In baked cheesecakes, add 1 to 1½ tablespoons flour or 1½ to 2 teaspoons cornstarch per cup of nonfat ricotta cheese to insure a firm texture.
Soft curd farmer cheese	400 calories 60 g fat	Substitute cup-for-cup for full-fat cream cheese. In baked cheesecakes, add 1 to 1½ tablespoons flour or 1½ to 2 teaspoons cornstarch per cup of farmer cheese to insure a firm texture.

Cheese	Savings Per Cup When Substituted for Full-Fat Cream Cheese	Special Considerations
Yogurt cheese (page 293)	630 calories 80 g fat	Substitute cup-for-cup for full-fat cream cheese. In baked cheesecakes, add 1 to 1½ tablespoons flour or 1½ to 2 teaspoons corn-starch per cup of yogurt cheese to insure a firm texture.

No-Bake Cherry Cheesecake

1. To make the filling, place the cream cheese or farmer cheese, sugar, and vanilla extract in the bowl of a food processor, and process until smooth. Set aside.

2. If using a microwave oven, place the lemon juice in a small microwave-safe bowl, and microwave at high power for about 30 seconds, or until the juice comes to a boil. If using a stove top, place the juice in a small pot, and place over medium heat for about 30 seconds, or until it comes to a boil. Remove the pot from the heat. Sprinkle the gelatin over the lemon juice and stir for about 1 minute, or until the gelatin is completely dissolved.

3. Add the gelatin mixture to the cheese mixture, and process until well mixed. Spread the cheese filling evenly over the crust, cover, and chill for at least 3 hours, or until set.

4. Spread the cherry pie filling over the top of the cheesecake, extending it all the way to the edges of the cake. Chill for at least 1 additional hour before slicing and serving.

NUTRITIONAL FACTS (PER SERVING)
Calories: 233 Carbohydrates: 46 g Cholesterol: 4 mg
Fat: 1 g Fiber: 1.2 g Protein: 9.9 g Sodium: 430 mg

You Save: Calories: 227 Fat: 26 g

Yield: 8 servings

1 prebaked Lite Graham Cracker Pie Crust (page 314) made with plain or chocolate graham crackers

FILLING

2 blocks (8 ounces each) nonfat cream cheese or soft curd farmer cheese, softened to room temperature

½ cup sugar

1 teaspoon vanilla extract

1 tablespoon plus 1 teaspoon lemon juice

1 teaspoon unflavored gelatin

TOPPING

1 can (20 ounces) light (reduced-sugar) cherry pie filling

No-Bake Mocha Mousse Cheesecake

Yield: *8 servings*

1 prebaked Lite Graham Cracker Pie Crust (page 314) made with chocolate graham crackers

FILLING

½ cup coffee, cooled to room temperature, divided

1 envelope (¼ ounce) unflavored gelatin

1 block (8 ounces) nonfat cream cheese, softened to room temperature

1 cup nonfat ricotta cheese

½ cup light brown sugar

2 tablespoons Dutch processed cocoa powder

2 tablespoons coffee liqueur

1½ teaspoons vanilla extract

1¼ cups nonfat or light whipped topping

1. To make the filling, place ¼ cup of the coffee in a blender. Sprinkle the gelatin over the top, and set aside for 2 minutes to allow the gelatin to soften.

2. Place the remaining ¼ cup of coffee in a small pot, and bring to a boil over medium-high heat. Pour the boiling hot coffee into the blender, cover with the lid, and blend at low speed for about 2 minutes, or until the gelatin is completely dissolved. Allow the mixture to sit for about 20 minutes, or until it has cooled to room temperature.

3. Add the cream cheese, ricotta, brown sugar, cocoa, liqueur, and vanilla extract to the blender, and blend until smooth. Transfer the mixture to a large bowl, cover, and chill for at least 4 hours, or until firm.

4. When the gelatin mixture has become firm, beat it with an electric mixer until it is the consistency of pudding. Gently fold in the whipped topping.

5. Spread the filling in the cooled crust, swirling the top with a knife. Cover and chill for at least 4 hours, or until set, before slicing and serving.

NUTRITIONAL FACTS (PER SERVING)
Calories: 205 Carbohydrates: 36 g Cholesterol: 4 mg
Fat: 1.5 g Fiber: 0.8 g Protein: 11.3 g Sodium: 263 mg

You Save: Calories: 259 Fat: 33.8 g

Cappuccino Cheesecake

1. To make the crust, break the graham crackers into pieces, place in the bowl of a food processor, and process into fine crumbs. Measure the crumbs. There should be ¾ cup. (Adjust the amount if needed.)

2. Return the crumbs to the food processor, and add the sugar. Process for a few seconds to mix well. Add the margarine, and process for about 20 seconds, or until moist and crumbly. Add the wheat germ or almonds, and process for a few seconds to mix well.

3. Coat a 9-inch springform pan with nonstick cooking spray, and use the back of a spoon to press the mixture against the bottom and sides of the pan, forming an even crust. (Periodically dip the spoon in sugar, if necessary, to prevent sticking.) Then use your fingers to finish pressing the crust firmly against the bottom and sides of the pan.

4. Bake at 350°F for about 8 minutes, or until the edges feel firm and dry. Set aside to cool to room temperature before filling.

5. To make the filling, place the cream cheese and vanilla extract in a large bowl, and beat with an electric mixer until smooth.

6. Place the liqueur and coffee granules in a small bowl, and stir to dissolve the coffee granules. Add the liqueur mixture to the cream cheese mixture, and beat to mix well.

7. Sprinkle the cornstarch over the cheese mixture, and beat to mix well. Sprinkle the cocoa and cinnamon over the cheese mixture, and beat to mix well. Add the sweetened condensed milk, and beat to mix well. Add the egg substitute, and beat to mix well. Finally, add the yogurt cheese, and beat to mix well.

8. Spread the cheesecake batter evenly over the crust, and bake at 325°F for about 1 hour, or until the center is firm to the touch. (If you use a dark pan instead of a shiny one, reduce the oven temperature to 300°F.) Turn the oven off, and allow the cake to cool in the oven with the door ajar for 1 hour. Remove the cake from the oven, cover, and chill for at least 8 hours, or until firm.

Yield: *12 servings*

CRUST

6 large (2½-x-5-inch) reduced-fat chocolate graham crackers

2 tablespoons sugar

1 tablespoon tub-style nonfat margarine, or 1 tablespoon plus 1½ teaspoons reduced-fat margarine

2 tablespoons honey crunch wheat germ or finely chopped almonds

FILLING

2 blocks (8 ounces each) nonfat cream cheese, softened to room temperature

2 teaspoons vanilla extract

2 tablespoons coffee liqueur

¾ teaspoon instant coffee granules

2 tablespoons plus 2 teaspoons cornstarch

1 tablespoon cocoa powder

¼ teaspoon ground cinnamon

1 can (14 ounces) fat-free sweetened condensed milk

½ cup plus 2 tablespoons fat-free egg substitute

1 cup vanilla yogurt cheese (page 293)

TOPPING

3 cups fresh raspberries or sliced fresh strawberries

¼ cup plus 2 tablespoons chocolate syrup

9. When ready to serve, run a sharp, thin-bladed knife between the cheesecake and the collar of the pan. Remove the collar, and cut the cheesecake into wedges. Top each serving with ¼ cup of the berries. Then drizzle 1½ teaspoons of the chocolate syrup over the top, and serve.

NUTRITIONAL FACTS (PER SERVING)
Calories: 241 Carbohydrates: 44 g Cholesterol: 6 mg
Fat: 1.3 g Fiber: 1.7 g Protein: 12.7 g Sodium: 281 mg

You Save: Calories: 229 Fat: 29 g

Blueberry Swirl Cheesecake

Yield: *12 servings*

CRUST

6 large (2½-x-5-inch) reduced-fat graham crackers

2 tablespoons sugar

1 tablespoon tub-style nonfat margarine, or 1 tablespoon plus 1½ teaspoons reduced-fat margarine

2 tablespoons honey crunch wheat germ

FILLING

2½ cups nonfat cottage cheese

2 blocks (8 ounces each) nonfat cream cheese, softened to room temperature

2½ teaspoons vanilla extract

1. To make the crust, break the graham crackers into pieces, place in the bowl of a food processor, and process into fine crumbs. Measure the crumbs. There should be ¾ cup. (Adjust the amount if needed.)

2. Return the crumbs to the food processor, add the sugar, and process for a few seconds to mix well. Add the margarine, and process for about 20 seconds, or until moist and crumbly. Add the wheat germ, and process for a few seconds to mix well.

3. Coat a 9-inch springform pan with nonstick cooking spray, and use the back of a spoon to press the mixture against the bottom and sides of the pan, forming an even crust. (Periodically dip the spoon in sugar, if necessary, to prevent sticking.) Then use your fingers to finish pressing the crust firmly against the bottom and sides of the pan.

4. Bake at 350°F for about 8 minutes, or until the edges feel firm and dry. Set aside to cool to room temperature before filling.

5. To make the filling, place the cottage cheese in a large wire (fine mesh) strainer, and rinse with cool running water until all of the creaming mixture has been rinsed away. Using the bottom of a glass, push the curds against the bottom of the strainer to press out as much of the water as possible, leaving just the dry curds in the strainer. Place the dry curds in a food processor, and process until smooth. Set aside.

6. Place the cream cheese and vanilla extract in a large bowl, and beat with an electric mixer until smooth. Add the puréed cottage cheese, and beat for about 2 minutes, or until light, creamy, and smooth. Sprinkle the flour and lemon rind over the mixture, and beat until smooth. Add the sugar, and beat to mix well. Finally, add the egg substitute, and beat just until well mixed.

7. Spread half of the cheesecake batter evenly over the crust. Then spoon the blueberry pie filling randomly over the batter. Top with the remaining batter, and draw a knife through the batter to produce a marbled effect.

8. Bake at 325°F for about 1 hour and 5 minutes, or until the center is firm to the touch. (If you use a dark pan instead of a shiny one, reduce the oven temperature to 300°F.) Run a sharp, thin-bladed knife between the cheesecake and the collar of the pan. (This will minimize cracking as the cake cools.) Turn the oven off, and allow the cake to cool in the oven with the door ajar for 1 hour.

9. Remove the cake from the oven, cover, and chill for at least 8 hours, or until firm before slicing and serving.

FILLING (CONT.)

¼ cup plus 2 tablespoons unbleached flour

½ teaspoon dried grated lemon rind, or 1½ teaspoons fresh

¾ cup plus 2 tablespoons sugar

¾ cup fat-free egg substitute

¾ cup canned blueberry pie filling

NUTRITIONAL FACTS (PER SERVING)

Calories: 193 Carbohydrates: 33 g Cholesterol: 6 mg
Fat: 0.5 g Fiber: 0.4 g Protein: 13.4 g Sodium: 303 mg

You Save: Calories: 259 Fat: 32.8 g

8

Pleasing Pies, Tarts, Cobblers, Crisps, and Pastries

Flaky and delicious, pies, tarts, and pastries are always a welcome treat. And whether made with a filling of juicy fruit or one of creamy custard, these goodies can easily be prepared with little or no added fat, and, in many cases, with less sugar than usual. In fact, if you compare the recipes in this chapter with those in traditional cookbooks, you will see that most have 90 percent less fat and 25 to 50 percent less sugar than traditional versions.

How do you trim the fat from pies, tarts, and pastries? The best place to start is with the crust, as most traditional crusts are loaded with butter, margarine, or other fats. Even worse, homemade pie crusts can be an ordeal to prepare from scratch. Not these. As you will see, low-fat crumb crusts prepared with graham crackers or other wholesome ingredients are a snap to make. Even a rolled

pie crust can be made with a minimum of fuss, and with less than half the fat of a traditional crust.

As for pie fillings, there are plenty of ways to reduce both fat and sugar. The custard, pudding, and cream pies in this chapter make use of a variety of nonfat dairy products, from nonfat yogurt to fat-free sweetened condensed milk. Many traditional fruit fillings are already low in fat, but most contain an overabundance of sugar. In contrast, the fruit pies in this chapter get much of their sweetness from fresh fruit, dried fruit, and juices. This natural sweetness is then enhanced by spices like cinnamon and nutmeg.

So take out your pie and tart pans, and get ready to enjoy a galaxy of homemade goodies. Lusciously sweet and meltingly tender, these are desserts that you will find yourself making time and time again.

PIE CRUSTS AND TART SHELLS

LITE GRAHAM CRACKER PIE CRUST

Yield: *One 9-inch pie crust*

8 large (2½-x-5-inch) reduced-fat plain or chocolate graham crackers

2 tablespoons sugar

1 tablespoon plus 1 teaspoon tub-style nonfat margarine, or 2 tablespoons reduced-fat margarine (do not melt)

1 tablespoon fat-free egg substitute

3 tablespoons honey crunch wheat germ

Fill this crust only with precooked or no-cook fillings, such as puddings.

1. Break the crackers into pieces, and place in the bowl of a food processor. Process into fine crumbs. Measure the crumbs. There should be 1 cup. (Adjust the amount if necessary.)

2. Return the crumbs to the food processor, add the sugar, and process for a few seconds to mix well. Add the margarine and egg substitute, and process for about 20 seconds, or until the mixture is moist (but not wet) and crumbly, and holds together when pinched. If the mixture seems too dry, mix in more margarine, ½ teaspoon at a time, until the proper consistency is reached. Add the wheat germ, and process for a few seconds to mix well.

3. Coat a 9-inch pie pan with nonstick cooking spray, and use the back of a spoon to press the mixture against the bottom and sides of the pan, forming an even crust. (Periodically dip the spoon in sugar, if necessary, to prevent sticking.) Then use your fingers to finish pressing the crust firmly against the bottom and sides of the pan.

4. Bake at 350°F for 9 minutes, or until the edges feel firm and dry. Cool to room temperature before filling.

NUTRITIONAL FACTS (PER ⅛ CRUST)
Calories: 79 Carbohydrates: 16 g Cholesterol: 0 mg Fat: 1 g
Fiber: 0.4 g Protein: 1. 8 g Sodium: 110 mg

You Save: Calories: 55 Fat: 8.8 g

Coconut Crunch Pie Crust

Like Lite Graham Cracker Pie Crust (page 314), this crust should be filled only with precooked or no-cook fillings.

1. Place the cereal in the bowl of a food processor, and process into fine crumbs. Measure the crumbs. There should be 1 cup. (Adjust the amount if necessary.)

2. Return the crumbs to the food processor, add the sugar, and process for a few seconds to mix well. Add the egg substitute, and process for about 20 seconds, or until the mixture is moist and crumbly. Add the coconut, and process for a few seconds, or just until well mixed.

3. Coat a 9-inch pie pan with nonstick cooking spray, and use the back of a spoon to press the mixture against the bottom and sides of the pan, forming an even crust. (Periodically dip the spoon in sugar, if necessary, to prevent sticking.)

4. Bake at 350°F for 10 minutes, or until the edges feel firm and dry. Cool to room temperature before filling.

Yield: *One 9-inch pie crust*

2 cups oat flake-and-almond breakfast cereal, such as Quaker Toasted Oatmeal or Oatmeal Crisp with Almonds

1 tablespoon sugar

1 tablespoon fat-free egg substitute

¼ cup shredded sweetened coconut

NUTRITIONAL FACTS (PER ⅛ CRUST)

Calories: 69 Carbohydrates: 12.7 g Cholesterol: 0 mg
Fat: 1.6 g Fiber: 0.9 g Protein: 1.5 g Sodium: 56 mg

You Save: Calories: 66 Fat: 8.8 g

Making Crumb Crusts in a Snap

If you find yourself making crumb crusts often, there is an easy way to speed the preparation of each individual crust Just whip up a large batch of graham cracker or cereal crumbs whenever you have the time, and store the crumbs in covered containers at room temperature for up to several months. You will then have a ready supply on hand to expedite the making of Lite Graham Cracker Pie Crust, Coconut Crunch Pie Crust, and many other recipes.

CRUNCHY NUTTY PIE CRUST

Yield: *One 9-inch pie crust*

1 cup barley nugget cereal

¼ cup honey crunch wheat germ or finely chopped pecans or almonds

2 tablespoons light brown sugar

3 tablespoons fat-free egg substitute

You can fill this crust with either precooked fillings or fillings that require baking.

1. Place the cereal, wheat germ or nuts, and brown sugar in a small bowl, and stir to mix well. Stir in the egg substitute.

2. Coat a 9-inch pie pan with nonstick cooking spray, and use the back of a spoon to pat the mixture against the bottom and sides of the pan, forming an even crust.

3. Bake at 350°F for about 12 minutes, or until the edges feel firm and dry. Cool the crust to room temperature and fill with a precooked filling, or fill and bake as directed in the recipe. (Note that this crust should be prebaked even when making pies that require additional baking, such as pumpkin and sweet potato pies. When further baking is required, cut 3-inch wide strips of aluminum foil, and fold them over the edges of the pie pan to prevent overbrowning.)

NUTRITIONAL FACTS (PER ⅛ CRUST)
Calories: 73 Carbohydrates: 15.6 g Cholesterol: 0 mg
Fat: 0.3 g Fiber: 1.5 g Protein: 2.9 g Sodium: 105 mg

You Save: Calories: 47 Fat: 7.7 g

Flaky Oat Pie Crust

This pie crust has less than half the fat of a traditional pie crust, with a tender flaky texture. Fill it with precooked fillings or with fillings that require baking.

1. Place the oats or oat bran, flour, baking powder, and salt in a medium-sized bowl, and stir to mix. Add the oil and just enough of the milk to form a stiff dough, stirring just until the mixture holds together and forms a ball.

2. Coat two 12-x-12-inch pieces of waxed paper with nonstick cooking spray. Lay the dough on 1 of the sheets of waxed paper, and pat it into a 7-inch circle. Place the other sheet of waxed paper over the circle of dough, and, using a rolling pin, roll the dough into an 11-inch circle.

3. Coat a 9-inch deep dish pie pan with nonstick cooking spray. Peel the top sheet of waxed paper from the pie crust, and invert the crust over the pie pan. Carefully peel the waxed paper from the crust, and press the crust into the pie pan. Pinch the edges of the crust or press with the tines of a fork to make a decorative edge. (As an alternative to steps 2 and 3, you can also pat the crust into the pan. Pinch off pieces of dough and press them in a thin layer against the sides of the pan. Then fill in the bottom with the remaining dough.)

4. For a prebaked crust, prick the crust with a fork at 1-inch intervals, and bake at 400°F for about 12 minutes, or until lightly browned. Allow the crust to cool to room temperature before filling. When a prebaked crust is not desired, simply fill and bake the crust as directed in the recipe.

Yield: *One 9-inch pie crust*

½ cup quick-cooking oats or oat bran

⅔ cup unbleached flour

½ teaspoon baking powder

⅛ teaspoon salt

2–3 tablespoons vegetable oil (try unrefined corn oil or walnut oil for extra flavor)

3 tablespoons plus 1 teaspoon skim milk

NUTRITIONAL FACTS (PER ⅛ CRUST)

Calories: 90 Carbohydrates: 11.5 g Cholesterol: 0 mg
Fat: 3.6 g Fiber: 1 g Protein: 2 g Sodium: 76 mg

You Save: Calories: 52 Fat: 6 g

HONEY GRAHAM PIE CRUST

Yield: *One 9-inch pie crust for 8 servings*

8 large (2½-x-5-inch) fat-free graham crackers

1½ tablespoons reduced-fat margarine or light butter, cut into pieces

1½ tablespoons honey

If you can't find fat-free graham crackers, use regular graham crackers, which are quite low in fat.

1. Break the crackers in pieces, and place in the bowl of a food processor or in a blender. Process into fine crumbs. Measure the crumbs. There should be 1¼ cups.

2. Return the crumbs to the food processor, and add the margarine or butter and the honey. Process until moist and crumbly.

3. Coat a 9-inch pie pan with nonstick cooking spray. Use the back of a spoon to press the crumbs against the sides and bottom of the pan, forming an even crust. Periodically dip the spoon in sugar to prevent sticking.

4. Bake the pie shell at 350°F for 10 minutes, or until the edges feel firm and dry. Cool the crust to room temperature, and fill as desired.

NUTRITIONAL FACTS (PER SERVING)

Calories: 93 Calcium: 8 mg Cholesterol: 0 mg
Fat: 1.1 g Fiber: 0.5 g Iron: 0.7 mg
Potassium: 75 mg Protein: 1.5 g Sodium: 152 mg

COCONUT OAT PIE CRUST

1. Combine the oats, flour, brown sugar, and coconut, and stir to mix well. Add the margarine or butter and the coconut extract, and stir until the mixture is moist and crumbly.

2. Coat a 9-inch pie pan with nonstick cooking spray. Use the back of a spoon to press the crumbs against the sides and bottom of the pan, forming an even crust. Periodically dip the spoon in sugar to prevent sticking.

3. Bake the pie shell at 350°F for 18 minutes, or until golden brown around the edges. Cool the crust to room temperature, and fill as desired.

Yield: One 9-inch pie crust for 8 servings

1 cup quick-cooking oats

¼ cup whole wheat pastry flour

2 tablespoons light brown sugar

2 tablespoons finely grated coconut

3 tablespoons melted reduced-fat margarine or light butter

½ teaspoon coconut-flavored extract

NUTRITIONAL FACTS (PER SERVING)

Calories: 91 Calcium: 11 mg Cholesterol: 0 mg
Fat: 3.5 g Fiber: 1.7 g Iron: 0.7 mg
Potassium: 71 mg Protein: 2.2 g Sodium: 53 mg

Plum Delicious Pie Crust

Yield: *One 9-inch pie crust for 8 servings*

8 large (2½-x-5-inch) fat-free graham crackers

¼ cup Prune Butter (page 223)

If you can't find a fat-free brand of graham crackers, just use regular graham crackers. All graham crackers are quite low in fat.

1. Break the crackers in pieces, and place in the bowl of a food processor or in a blender. Process into fine crumbs. Measure the crumbs. There should be 1¼ cups.

2. Return the crumbs to the food processor, and add the Prune Butter. Process until moist and crumbly.

3. Coat a 9-inch pie pan with nonstick cooking spray. Use the back of a spoon to press the crumbs against the sides and bottom of the pan, forming an even crust. Periodically dip the spoon in sugar to prevent sticking.

4. Bake the pie shell at 350°F for 10 minutes, or until the edges feel firm and dry. Cool the crust to room temperature, and fill as desired.

NUTRITIONAL FACTS (PER SERVING)
Calories: 89 Calcium: 11 mg Cholesterol: 0 mg
Fat: 0.2 g Fiber: 1.1 g Iron: 0.8 mg
Potassium: 125 mg Protein: 1.7 g Sodium: 126 mg

PRUNE-THE-FAT PIE CRUST

1. Break the crackers in pieces, and place in the bowl of a food processor or in a blender. Process into fine crumbs. Measure the crumbs.

2. Return the crumbs—approximately 1¼ cups—to the food processor, and add sugar and Prune Purée. Process until moist and crumbly.

3. Coat a 9-inch pie pan with nonstick cooking spray. Use back of spoon to press the crumbs against the sides and bottom of the pan, forming an even crust. Periodically dip the spoon in sugar to prevent sticking.

4. Bake the pie shell at 350°F for 10 minutes, or until the edges feel firm and dry. Cool the crust to room temperature, and fill as desired.

Yield: *One 9-inch pie crust for 8 servings*

8 large (2½-x-5-inch) fat-free graham crackers

2 tablespoons sugar

2 tablespoons Prune Purée (page 223)

NUTRITIONAL FACTS (PER SERVING)
Calories: 86 Calcium: 8 mg Cholesterol: 0 mg
Fat: 0.2 g Fiber: 1.8 g Iron: 0.7 mg
Potassium: 79 mg Protein: 1.5 g Sodium: 126 mg

Fruitful Graham Cracker Pie Crust

Yield: One 9-inch pie crust
for 8 servings

8 large (2½-x-5-inch) fat-free
graham crackers

3 tablespoons fruit spread or jam,
any flavor

If fat-free graham crackers aren't available, just use regular graham crackers, as they are quite low in fat. Use your imagination and choose the flavor fruit spread that would best complement your filling.

1. Break the crackers into pieces, and place in the bowl of a food processor or in a blender. Process into fine crumbs. Measure the crumbs. There should be 1¼ cups.

2. Return the crumbs to the food processor, and add the fruit spread. Process until moist and crumbly.

3. Coat a 9-inch pie pan with nonstick cooking spray. Use the back of a spoon to press the crumbs against the sides and bottom of the pan, forming an even crust. Periodically dip the spoon in sugar to prevent sticking.

4. Bake the pie shell at 350°F for 10 minutes, or until the edges feel firm and dry. Cool the crust to room temperature, and fill as desired.

NUTRITIONAL FACTS (PER SERVING)
Calories: 93 Calcium: 9 mg Cholesterol: 0 mg
Fat: 0.1 g Fiber: 0.5 g Iron: 0.7 mg
Potassium: 79 mg Protein: 1.6 g Sodium: 127 mg

CRUNCHY CEREAL PIE CRUST

This crust, like the one on page 322, may be tailor-made for different fillings by the use of different fruit spreads.

1. Place the cereal in the bowl of a food processor or in a blender. Process into fine crumbs. Measure the crumbs. There should be about 1¼ cups.

2. Return the crumbs to the food processor, and add the fruit spread. Process until moist and crumbly.

3. Coat a 9-inch pie pan with nonstick cooking spray. Use the back of a spoon to press the crumbs against the sides and bottom of the pan, forming an even crust. Periodically dip the spoon in sugar to prevent sticking.

4. Bake the pie shell at 350°F for 10 to 12 minutes, or until the edges feel firm and dry. Cool the crust to room temperature, and fill as desired.

Yield: *One 9-inch pie crust for 8 servings*

5 ounces (about 2½ cups) oat flakes, or oat flakes with almonds ready-to-eat cereal

3 tablespoons fruit spread or jam, any flavor

NUTRITIONAL FACTS (PER SERVING)
Calories: 86 Calcium: 9 mg Cholesterol: 0 mg
Fat: 0.2 mg Fiber: 0.6 g Iron: 1.6 mg
Potassium: 133 mg Protein: 3.3 g Sodium: 159 mg

Meringue Tart Shells

Yield: *8 shells*

3 egg whites, brought to room temperature

¼ teaspoon cream of tartar

Pinch salt

¾ cup sugar

¾ teaspoon vanilla extract

These light-as-air shells have always been fat-free, and make an elegant base for fresh fruits, puddings, and a variety of other fillings.

1. Place the egg whites, cream of tartar, and salt in a medium-sized bowl, and beat with an electric mixer until soft peaks form when the beaters are raised.

2. Gradually add the sugar, a tablespoon at a time, while beating continuously, until all of the sugar has been incorporated, the mixture is glossy, and stiff peaks form when the beaters are raised. (The total beating time will be about 7 minutes.) Beat in the vanilla extract.

3. Place a sheet of waxed paper over the bottom of a large baking sheet, and drop the meringue onto the sheet in 8 mounds, spaced about 4 inches apart. Using the back of a spoon, spread each mound into a 3½-inch circle, creating a center that is about ½ inch thick and building up the sides to about 1¼ inches in height.

4. Bake at 250°F for 1 hour, or until the shells are creamy white and firm to the touch. Turn the oven off, and allow the shells to cool in the oven for 1 hour with the door closed. Fill as desired. (Note that the shells may be prepared the day before you plan to use them, and stored in an airtight container until ready to fill.)

NUTRITIONAL FACTS (PER SHELL)
Calories: 79 Carbohydrates: 18.8 g Cholesterol: 0 mg
Fat: 0 g Fiber: 0 g Protein: 1.3 g Sodium: 34 mg

You Save: Calories: 0 Fat: 0 g

Variation

To make Almond Meringue Tart Shells, reduce the vanilla extract to ½ teaspoon, and add ½ teaspoon of almond extract along with the vanilla. Gently fold ¼ cup of finely ground toasted almonds into the finished meringue. Then shape and bake as directed in the recipe.

NUTRITIONAL FACTS (PER SHELL)
Calories: 102 Carbohydrates: 19.6 g Cholesterol: 0 mg
Fat: 2.1 g Fiber: 0 g Protein: 2.1 g Sodium: 34 mg

You Save: Calories: 48 Fat: 4.3 g

Making Foolproof Meringue

Light as air with a delightfully crisp texture, meringue can form the base for many a show-stopping dessert. As if that wasn't reason enough to enjoy this ethereal confection, meringue has always been fat-free. As versatile as it is delicious, meringue can either top a pie or form its crust. It can also be made into small tart shells, cookies, and many other treats.

Unless you know a few tricks of the trade, making meringue can be a frustrating experience. But once you learn the secrets of making foolproof meringue, you'll want to make it often. Here are some important tips for baking up the lightest, fluffiest meringue possible.

❑ When separating the egg whites, be sure not to let any of the yolk get mixed in. Egg yolks contain fat, which interferes with the ability of the whites to whip. If even a little yolk is mixed in with the whites, they will not whip properly. If you accidentally do get some yolk mixed in with the whites, simply scoop it out with a piece of egg shell.

❑ Allow the egg whites to come to room temperature before whipping.

❑ Make sure the mixing bowl and beaters are spotless. If there is any residue of fat or oil on either, the whites will not whip properly.

❑ Use a glass or metal bowl for best results when whipping egg whites. Egg whites whipped in plastic bowls may not reach their full volume.

❑ Beat the egg whites with cream of tartar and salt to soft peaks before you begin to add the sugar. Then add the sugar gradually, a tablespoon at a time, to achieve maximum lightness.

❑ For best results, make meringue on a clear, dry day. Meringue can pick up excess humidity from the air and become sticky.

Flaky Phyllo Tart Shells

Yield: *6 shells*

4 teaspoons sugar

¼ teaspoon dried grated lemon rind, or ¾ teaspoon fresh (optional)

4 sheets (each about 14 x 18 inches) phyllo pastry (about 3¼ ounces)

Butter-flavored cooking spray

Light and flaky, these shells make the perfect base for fillings of fresh fruit, pudding, or a scoop of your favorite ice cream.

1. Place the sugar and lemon rind in a small dish. Stir to mix well and set aside.

2. Spread the phyllo dough out on a clean dry surface. Cover the dough with plastic wrap to prevent it from drying out as you work. (Remove the sheets as you need them, being sure to re-cover the remaining dough.)

3. Remove 1 sheet of phyllo dough, and lay it on a clean dry surface. Spray the sheet lightly with the cooking spray, and sprinkle with 1 teaspoon of the sugar mixture. Top with another phyllo sheet, spray with the cooking spray, and sprinkle with another teaspoon of the sugar mixture. Repeat with the 2 remaining sheets.

4. Cut the stack of phyllo sheets lengthwise into two 18-inch-long strips. Then cut each strip crosswise to make 3 pieces, each measuring approximately 6 x 7 inches. You should now have 6 stacks of phyllo squares, each 4 layers thick.

5. Coat six jumbo muffin cups or six 6-ounce custard cups with non-stick cooking spray. Gently press 1 stack of phyllo squares into each cup, pleating as necessary to make it fit. Press the corners back slightly.

6. Bake at 350°F for about 8 minutes, or until golden brown. Remove the crusts from the oven and allow to cool for 5 minutes. Transfer the crusts to wire racks to cool completely. Then fill as desired. (Note that the shells may be prepared the day before you plan to use them, and stored in an airtight container until ready to fill.)

NUTRITIONAL FACTS (PER SERVING)
Calories: 56 Carbohydrates: 10.8 g Cholesterol: 0 mg
Fat: 0.9 g Fiber: 0 g Protein: 1.1 g Sodium: 74 mg

You Save: Calories: 68 Fat: 7.7 g

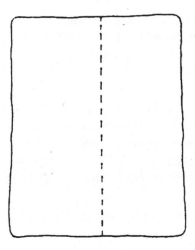

a. Cut the phyllo sheets into
2 long strips.

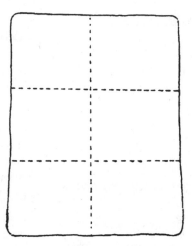

b. Cut each strip crosswise
to make 3 squares.

Making Flaky Phyllo Tart Shells.

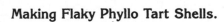

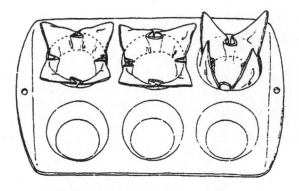

c. Press 1 stack of squares into
each muffin cup.

Refreshing Fruit Pie

Yield: *8 servings*

1 prepared Fruitful Graham Cracker Pie Crust made with seedless raspberry jam (page 322)

GLAZE

⅓ cup sugar

3 tablespoons plus 1½ teaspoons cornstarch

1½ cups white grape juice

¼ cup fresh raspberries, slightly crushed

FILLING

3 cups sliced peeled nectarines or peaches (about 3½ medium)

½ cup fresh blueberries

¼ cup fresh raspberries

1. To make the glaze, place the sugar and cornstarch in a 1-quart saucepan, and stir to mix well. Slowly add the juice, and stir to dissolve the cornstarch. Place the pan over medium heat, and bring to a boil, stirring constantly. Add the raspberries, and cook, still stirring, for another minute, or until the raspberries break up and the glaze turns red. Remove the pan from the heat, and set aside to cool for 15 minutes.

2. Stir the glaze, and spoon a thin layer over the bottom of the crust. Arrange half of the nectarines or peaches in a circular pattern over the crust. Top with the berries, and spoon half of the remaining glaze over the berries. Arrange the rest of the peaches over the glaze, and top with the remaining glaze.

3. Chili for several hours, or until the glaze is set. Cut into wedges and serve cold.

NUTRITIONAL FACTS (PER SERVING)
Calories: 195 Cholesterol: 0 mg Fat: 0.7 g
Fiber: 2 g Protein: 2.2 g Sodium: 118 mg

SWEET POTATO PIE

1. To make the crust, combine the cereal and sugar in a small bowl, and stir to mix well. Add the egg substitute, and stir to mix well.

2. Coat a 9-inch pie pan with nonstick cooking spray. Use the back of a spoon to press the crust mixture against the bottom and sides of the pan, forming an even crust. Bake at 350°F for 10 minutes, or until the edges feel firm and dry. Set aside to cool.

3. To make the filling, place all of the filling ingredients in a blender or food processor, and process for 1 minute, or until smooth. Pour the filling into the crust. Cut 3-inch wide strips of aluminum foil, and fold over the edges of the pie pan to shield the crust during baking.

4. Bake at 350°F for 50 minutes, or until a sharp knife inserted in the center of the pie comes out clean. Cool to room temperature before cutting into wedges and serving. Refrigerate any leftovers.

NUTRITIONAL FACTS (PER SERVING)
Calories: 175 Cholesterol: 1 mg Fat: 0.2 g
Fiber: 2.3 g Protein: 6.8 g Sodium: 175 mg

Yield: *8 servings*

CRUST

1 cup barley nugget cereal

2 tablespoons sugar

3 tablespoons fat-free egg substitute

FILLING

1 can (1 pound) sweet potatoes, drained

1 cup evaporated skim milk

½ cup fat-free egg substitute

½ cup light brown sugar

1½ teaspoons ground cinnamon

½ teaspoon ground nutmeg

1 teaspoon vanilla extract

LEMON MERINGUE PIE

Yield: *8 servings*

CRUST

8 large (2½-x-5-inch) fat-free or
   reduced-fat graham crackers

2 tablespoons sugar

2 tablespoons fat-free egg
   substitute

FILLING

¼ cup plus 3 tablespoons
   cornstarch

¾ cup sugar

1 cup water

¾ cup skim milk

½ cup fat-free egg substitute

¼ cup plus 2 tablespoons lemon
   juice

1 tablespoon freshly grated lemon
   find

MERINGUE TOPPING

3 egg whites, brought to room
   temperature

¼ teaspoon cream of tartar

⅛ teaspoon salt

¼ cup plus 1 tablespoon sugar

1 teaspoon vanilla extract

1. To make the crust, break the crackers into pieces, and place in the bowl of a food processor. Process into fine crumbs. Measure the crumbs. There should be about 1¼ cups. (Adjust the amount if necessary.) Return the crumbs to the food processor, add the sugar, and process for a few seconds to mix. Add the egg substitute, and process until the mixture is moist and crumbly.

2. Coat a 9-inch deep dish pie pan with nonstick cooking spray, and use the back of a spoon to press the mixture over the bottom and sides of the pan, forming an even crust. (Periodically dip the spoon in sugar, if necessary, to prevent sticking.) Bake at 350°F for 10 minutes, or until the edges feel firm and dry. Set aside to cool.

3. To make the filling, combine the cornstarch and sugar in a 2-quart saucepan. Slowly stir in the water and milk, and place over medium heat. Cook, stirring constantly with a wire whisk, until the mixture is thickened and bubbly. Reduce the heat to low.

4. Place the egg substitute in a small bowl. Remove ½ cup of the hot filling from the pot, and stir into the egg substitute. Return the mixture to the pot, and cook, stirring constantly, for 2 to 3 minutes, or until the mixture thickens slightly.

5. Remove the pot from the heat, and stir in the lemon juice and rind. Pour the filling into the pie crust, and set aside.

6. To make the meringue, place the egg whites in the bowl of an electric mixer, and beat until foamy. Beat in the cream of tartar and salt, and continue beating until soft peaks form when the beaters are removed. Slowly beat in the sugar, adding 1 tablespoon at a time. Add the vanilla extract, and beat until the mixture is glossy, and stiff peaks form when beaters are removed.

7. Spread the meringue over the warm filling, swirling it with a knife or spoon. Make sure the meringue touches all edges of the crust. Bake at 350°F for about 10 minutes, or just until the meringue is touched with brown.

8. Chill for at least 6 hours before cutting into wedges and serving. For easier serving, dip the knife in warm water before cutting each slice.

NUTRITIONAL FACTS (PER SERVING)
Calories: 234 Cholesterol: 0 mg Fat: 0.3 g
Fiber: 0.6 g Protein: 4.2 g Sodium: 199 mg

STRAWBERRY BANANA PIE

1. To make the glaze, combine the sugar and cornstarch in a medium-sized saucepan. Slowly stir in the juice. Place over medium heat and bring to a boil, stirring constantly. Reduce the heat to low, and cook and stir for another minute. Remove the saucepan from the heat, and set aside for 15 minutes.

2. Stir the glaze, and spoon a thin layer over the bottom of the pie crust. Arrange half of the strawberries and half of the bananas over the bottom of the crust. Spoon half of the remaining glaze over the fruit. Arrange the rest of the fruit over the glaze, and top with the remaining glaze.

3. Chill for several hours, or until the glaze is set. Cut into wedges and serve cold.

Yield: *8 servings*

1 prepared Fruitful Graham Cracker Pie Crust, made with strawberry fruit spread (page 322)

GLAZE

⅓ cup sugar

3 tablespoons cornstarch

1½ cups cran-strawberry juice, or another strawberry juice blend

FILLING

2 cups fresh strawberries, cut in half

2 cups sliced fresh bananas

NUTRITIONAL FACTS (PER SERVING)
Calories: 208 Calcium: 18 mg Cholesterol: 0 mg
Fat: 0.4 g Fiber: 2.2 g Iron: 1.1 mg
Potassium: 298 mg Protein: 2.2 g Sodium: 128 mg

PEACH PIZZAZ PIE

Yield: *8 servings*

1 prepared Crunchy Cereal Pie
  Crust, made with peach fruit
  spread (page 323)

GLAZE

⅓ cup sugar

3 tablespoons cornstarch

1½ cups peach nectar

FILLING

3 cups sliced fresh peaches
  (about 4 medium)

1 cup fresh blueberries or raspberries

1. To make the glaze, combine the sugar and cornstarch in a medium-sized saucepan. Slowly stir in the nectar. Place over medium heat and bring to a boil, stirring constantly. Reduce the heat to low, and cook for another minute. Remove the saucepan from the heat, and set aside for 15 minutes.

2. Stir the glaze, and spoon a thin layer over the bottom of the pie crust. Arrange half of the peaches in a circular pattern over the bottom of the crust. Top with the blueberries, and spoon half of the remaining glaze over the berries. Arrange the rest of the peaches over the glaze, and top with the remaining glaze.

3. Chill for several hours, or until the glaze is set. Cut into wedges and serve cold.

NUTRITIONAL FACTS (PER SERVING)

Calories: 193 Calcium: 16 mg Cholesterol: 0 mg
Fat: 0.3 g Fiber: 3.1 g Iron: 1.6 mg
Potassium: 232 mg Protein: 2.7 g Sodium: 111 mg

Fresh Nectarine Pie

This pie is equally good when made with strawberries, peaches, or other fruits.

1. To make the glaze, combine the sugar and cornstarch in a medium-sized saucepan. Slowly stir in the orange juice. Place over medium heat and cook, stirring constantly, until the glaze mixture is thickened and bubbly. Remove the saucepan from the heat, and set aside for 20 minutes.

2. Spoon a thin layer of the glaze over the bottom of the pie crust. Arrange half of the nectarine slices over the bottom of the crust. Spoon half of the remaining glaze over the nectarine slices. Arrange the rest of the nectarine slices over the glaze, and top with the remaining glaze.

3. Chill for several hours, or until the glaze is set. Cut into wedges and serve cold or at room temperature.

Yield: *8 servings*

1 prepared Plum Delicious Pie Crust (page 320)

GLAZE

⅓ cup sugar

3 tablespoons cornstarch

1½ cups orange juice

FILLING

4 cups sliced peeled fresh nectarines (about 4 medium)

NUTRITIONAL FACTS (PER SERVING)

Calories: 199 Calcium: 21 mg Cholesterol: 0 mg
Fat: 0.3 g Fiber: 2.4 g Iron: 1 mg
Potassium: 360 mg Protein: 2.7 g Sodium: 127 mg

Lemon Cheese Pie

Yield: *8 servings*

¾ cup sugar

½ cup cornstarch

1¾ cups nonfat buttermilk

1 tablespoon freshly grated lemon
   rind

½ cup fat-free egg substitute

⅓ cup fresh lemon juice

1 prepared Prune-the-Fat Pie
   Crust (page 321)

1. Combine the sugar and cornstarch in a medium-sized nonstick saucepan. Slowly stir in the buttermilk. Place over medium heat and cook, constantly stirring with a wire whisk, until the mixture is thickened and bubbly. Add the lemon rind to the buttermilk mixture, and continue to cook and stir for another minute or 2.

2. Reduce the heat to low, and blend about ½ cup of the hot mixture into the egg substitute. Then return the egg mixture to the pan. Cook and stir over low heat for 2 to 3 additional minutes. Do not allow the mixture to come to a boil.

3. Remove the mixture from the heat, and stir in the lemon juice, Pour the filling into the pie crust.

4. Chill for several hours, or until the filling is set. Cut into wedges and serve cold.

NUTRITIONAL FACTS (PER SERVING)
Calories: 220 Calcium: 76 mg Cholesterol: 0 mg
Fat: 0.2 g Fiber: 1.8 g Iron: 1 mg
Potassium: 184 mg Protein: 4.6 g Sodium: 203 mg

BANANA CREAM PIE

1. Combine the sugar, cornstarch, and nutmeg in a medium-sized saucepan. Slowly stir in the milk. Place over medium heat and cook, stirring constantly with a wire whisk, until the mixture comes to a boil. Reduce the heat to low, and cook and stir for another minute or 2.

2. Blend about ½ cup of the hot mixture into the egg substitute. Then return the egg mixture to the pan. Cook and stir over low heat for 2 to 3 minutes. Do not allow the mixture to come to a boil.

3. Remove the mixture from the heat, and stir in the vanilla extract. Let the mixture cool for 15 minutes, stirring every 5 minutes.

4. Spread a thin layer of the filling over the bottom of the pie crust. Top with half of the bananas and half of the remaining filling. Repeat the layers, ending with the filling. Sprinkle the top lightly with ground nutmeg if desired.

5. Chill for several hours, or until the filling is set. Cut into wedges and serve cold.

Yield: *8 servings*

½ cup sugar

3 tablespoons cornstarch

1 pinch ground nutmeg

2 cups skim milk

¼ cup plus 2 tablespoons fat-free egg substitute

1 teaspoon vanilla extract

1 prepared Prune-the-Fat Pie Crust (page 321)

3 large bananas, sliced ¼ inch thick

Ground nutmeg (optional)

NUTRITIONAL FACTS (PER SERVING)
Calories: 211 Calcium: 90 mg Cholesterol: 0 mg
Fat: 0.3 g Fiber: 1.3 g Iron: 1.1 mg
Potassium: 358 mg Protein: 5 g Sodium: 173 mg

Fabulous Fruit Pie

Yield: *8 servings*

1 prepared Coconut Oat Pie Crust
(page 319)

FILLING

1 cup sliced fresh strawberries

2 kiwi fruit, peeled and sliced ¼
inch thick

1 cup sliced bananas

5 strawberry slices

PINEAPPLE GLAZE

2½ tablespoons cornstarch

2 tablespoons sugar

¾ cup orange juice

1 can (8 ounces) crushed pineapple packed in juice, undrained

1. To make the glaze, combine the cornstarch and sugar in a medium-sized saucepan, and stir to mix well. Slowly stir in first the orange juice and then the crushed pineapple, including the juice. Place over medium-low heat and cook, stirring constantly, until the glaze mixture is thickened and bubbly. Remove the saucepan from the heat, and set aside for 15 minutes.

2. Spread half of the pineapple glaze evenly over the bottom of the pie crust. Arrange the strawberries in a circular pattern over the pineapple mixture. Arrange the kiwi slices over the strawberries. Arrange the banana slices over the kiwi. Top with the remaining glaze, and garnish with the strawberry slices.

3. Chill the pie for several hours, or until the glaze is set. Cut into wedges and serve cold.

NUTRITIONAL FACTS (PER SERVING)
Calories: 174 Calcium: 26 mg Cholesterol: 0 mg
Fat: 3.9 g Fiber: 3.5 g Iron: 1.1 mg
Potassium: 318 mg Protein: 3 g Sodium: 55 mg

CREAMY LEMON PIE

Yield: *8 servings*

1 prebaked Lite Graham Cracker Pie Crust (page 314) made with plain graham crackers

1. To make the filling, place the boiling water in a large bowl. Sprinkle the gelatin over the water, and whisk for 3 minutes, or until the gelatin is completely dissolved. Set the mixture aside for about 20 minutes, or until it has cooled to room temperature.

2. When the gelatin has cooled, whisk in the yogurt. Chill for 10 minutes. Stir the mixture; it should be the consistency of pudding. If necessary, chill for a few minutes longer.

3. When the gelatin mixture has reached the proper consistency, stir it well. Then gently fold in the whipped topping. Spoon the mixture into the prepared pie shell, swirling the top with a spoon, and chill for at least 3 hours, or until set, before cutting into wedges and serving.

FILLING

½ cup boiling water

1 package (4-serving size) regular or sugar-free lemon gelatin

1¾ cups regular or sugar-free nonfat or low-fat lemon yogurt

1½ cups nonfat or light whipped topping

NUTRITIONAL FACTS (PER SERVING)
Calories: 183 Carbohydrates: 38.8 g Cholesterol: 1 mg
Fat: 1.4 g Fiber: 0.4 g Protein: 4.5 g Sodium: 170 mg

You Save: Calories: 181 Fat: 24.3 g

KEY LIME CHEESE PIE

Yield: *8 servings*

1 prebaked Lite Graham Cracker Pie Crust (page 314) made with plain graham crackers or Coconut Crunch Pie Crust (page 315)

1. Place the condensed milk and cream cheese in a medium-sized bowl, and beat with an electric mixer until smooth. Add the lime juice, and beat until well mixed.

2. Pour the filling into the crust. Cover and chill for at least 8 hours, or until set, before cutting into wedges and serving.

FILLING

1 can (14 ounces) fat-free sweetened condensed milk

1 block (8 ounces) nonfat cream cheese, softened to room temperature

½ cup key lime juice

NUTRITIONAL FACTS (PER SERVING)
Calories: 247 Carbohydrates: 49 g Cholesterol: 4 mg
Fat: 1.1 g Fiber: 0.4 g Protein: 9.5 g Sodium: 300 mg

You Save: Calories: 142 Fat: 20.6 g

Razzleberry Pie

Yield: *8 servings*

1 prebaked Crunchy Nutty Pie
Crust (page 316) or Coconut
Crunch Pie Crust (page 315)

FILLING

3 cups fresh strawberry halves

2 cups fresh raspberries

GLAZE

¼ cup sugar

2 tablespoons cornstarch

1¼ cups water

1 package (4-serving size) regular or sugar-free raspberry
gelatin

TOPPING

1 cup nonfat or light whipped
topping (optional)

1. To make the glaze, place the sugar and cornstarch in a 1-quart pot, and stir to mix well. Add the water, and stir until the cornstarch is dissolved. Place the pot over medium heat, and cook, stirring constantly, for several minutes, or until the mixture comes to a boil and thickens slightly.

2. Remove the pot from the heat, and whisk in the gelatin. Continue to whisk for a minute or 2, or until the gelatin is completely dissolved. Set the glaze aside, stirring occasionally, for about 45 minutes, or until it has cooled to room temperature.

3. Place the glaze in the refrigerator. Stirring every few minutes, chill for about 10 minutes, or until the mixture has thickened slightly. It should be a little thicker than raw egg whites and a little thinner than pudding. Be careful not to chill the glaze too long, or it will congeal.

4. Place the berries in a large bowl, and toss to mix well. Pour the glaze over the berries, and toss gently to mix well. Spread the berry mixture evenly in the crust.

5. Cover and chill for at least 4 hours, or until set, before cutting into wedges and serving. Top each serving with 2 tablespoons of whipped topping, if desired.

NUTRITIONAL FACTS (PER SERVING)
Calories: 176 g Carbohydrates: 41 g Cholesterol: 0 mg
Fat: 0.6 g Fiber: 4.1 g Protein: 4.2 g Sodium: 145 mg

You Save: Calories: 148 Fat: 10.4 g

LITE AND LUSCIOUS KEY LIME PIE

1. To make the filling, place the egg substitute in a blender and sprinkle the gelatin over the egg substitute. Set aside for 2 minutes to allow the gelatin to soften.

2. Place ¼ cup of the lime juice in a small bowl. If using a microwave oven, microwave on high for about 1 minute, or until it comes to a boil. If using a stove top, place the juice in a small pot, and cook over medium heat for about 1 minute, or until it comes to a boil.

3. Add the boiling hot lime juice to the blender, place the lid on, and blend for about 1 minute, or until the ingredients are well mixed and the gelatin is completely dissolved. Add the remaining ¼ cup of lime juice, and blend for about 30 seconds, or until well mixed. Add the condensed milk, and blend for about 1 minute, or until well mixed. Immediately pour the filling into the crust.

4. Cover and chill for at least 6 hours, or until set, before cutting into wedges and serving. Top each serving with 2 tablespoons of whipped topping, if desired.

Yield: *8 servings*

1 prebaked Lite Graham Cracker Pie Crust (page 314) made with plain graham crackers, or Coconut Crunch Pie Crust (page 315)

FILLING

¼ cup fat-free egg substitute

1⅛ teaspoons unflavored gelatin

½ cup key lime juice, divided

1 can (14 ounces) fat-free sweetened condensed milk

TOPPING

1 cup nonfat or light whipped topping (optional)

NUTRITIONAL FACTS (PER SERVING)
Calories: 226 Carbohydrates: 47 g Cholesterol: 2 mg
Fat: 1 g Fiber: 0.4 g Protein: 6.4 g Sodium: 128 mg

You Save: Calories: 101 Fat: 14.9 g

Peach Streusel Pie

Yield: *8 servings*

1 unbaked Flaky Oat Pie Crust (page 317)

FILLING

6 cups peeled sliced peaches (about 6 medium-large)

¼ cup plus 2 tablespoons light brown sugar

1 tablespoon plus 2 teaspoons cornstarch

½ teaspoon ground cinnamon

¼ teaspoon ground nutmeg

TOPPING

¼ cup plus 2 tablespoons barley nugget cereal or chopped toasted pecans (page 383)

⅓ cup light brown sugar

¼ cup plus 1 tablespoon whole wheat pastry flour

½ teaspoon ground cinnamon

1 tablespoon plus 2 teaspoons frozen white grope juice concentrate, thawed

For variety, substitute sliced pears for the peaches.

1. To make the filling, place all of the filling ingredients In a large bowl, and toss to mix well.

2. Spread the mixture evenly in the pie shell. Cover the pie loosely with aluminum foil and bake at 400°F for 25 minutes, or until the fruit starts to soften and release its juices.

3. \While the pie is baking, make the topping by placing the cereal or pecans, brown sugar, flour, and cinnamon in a small bowl. Stir to mix well. Add the juice concentrate, and stir until the mixture is moist and crumbly. Add a little more juice concentrate if the mixture seems too dry.

4. Remove the pie from the oven, and sprinkle the topping over the pie. Reduce the temperature to 375°F, and bake uncovered for 25 to 30 additional minutes, or until the topping Is nicely browned and the filling is bubbly around the edges.

5. Allow the pie to cool at room temperature for at least 1 hour before cutting into wedges and serving. Serve warm or at room temperature, refrigerating any leftovers.

NUTRITIONAL FACTS (PER SERVING)
Calories: 243 Carbohydrates: 50 g Cholesterol: 0 mg
Fat: 3.9 g Fiber: 4.3 g Protein: 4.3 g Sodium: 136 mg

You Save: Calories: 193 Fat: 21.8 g

HARVEST PEAR PIE

For variety, substitute apples for the pears.

Yield: *8 servings*

1 unbaked Flaky Oat Pie Crust
(page 317)

1. Place the brown sugar, cornstarch, cinnamon, and nutmeg in a small bowl. Stir to mix well and set aside.

2. Place the pear slices in a large bowl. Add the sugar mixture, and toss to coat the pears with the mixture.

3. Arrange a layer of pear slices in a spiral pattern over the bottom of the prepared crust. Continue building layers in this manner until all of the slices are used.

4. Place the honey and juice concentrate in a small bowl, and stir to mix well. Drizzle the mixture over the top of the pie.

5. Spray a square of aluminum foil with nonstick cooking spray, and cover the pie loosely with the foil, placing it sprayed side down. Bake at 400°F for 15 minutes. Reduce the heat to 375°F, and bake for 40 additional minutes, or until the filling is bubbly around the edges. Remove the foil, and bake for 5 minutes more.

6. Allow the pie to cool to room temperature before cutting into wedges and serving.

FILLING

¼ cup light brown sugar

2 tablespoons plus 1 teaspoon cornstarch

½ teaspoon ground cinnamon

¼ teaspoon ground nutmeg

6 cups sliced peeled pears (about 6 medium-large)

¼ cup honey

1 tablespoon frozen orange juice concentrate, thawed

NUTRITIONAL FACTS (PER SERVING)
Calories: 223 Carbohydrates: 46 g Cholesterol: 0 mg
Fat: 3.9 g Fiber: 3.9 g Protein: 2.6 g Sodium: 79 mg

You Save: Calories: 82 Fat: 10.1 g

Sour Cream Apple Pie

Yield: *8 servings*

1 unbaked Flaky Oat Pie Crust
(page 317)

FILLING

1 cup nonfat sour cream

½ cup sugar

2 tablespoons unbleached flour

1 teaspoon vanilla extract

¼ cup fat-free egg substitute

4 cups sliced peeled apples
(about 6 medium)

¼ cup golden raisins (optional)

TOPPING

¼ cup barley nugget cereal or
chopped walnuts

3 tablespoons whole wheat pastry
flour

3 tablespoons light brown sugar

½ teaspoon ground cinnamon

1 tablespoon frozen apple juice
concentrate, thawed

1. To make the filling, place the sour cream, sugar, flour, vanilla extract, and egg substitute in a large bowl, and stir to mix well. Add the apples and, if desired, the raisins, and toss to mix well.

2. Spread the mixture evenly in the pie shell. Spray a square of aluminum foil with nonstick cooking spray, and cover the pie loosely with the foil, placing it sprayed side down. Bake at 400°F for 25 minutes, or until the filling begins to set around the edges.

3. While the pie is baking, make the topping by placing the cereal or walnuts, flour, brown sugar, and cinnamon in a small bowl, and stirring to mix well. Add the juice concentrate, and stir until the mixture is moist and crumbly.

4. Remove the pie from the oven, remove and discard the foil, and sprinkle the pie with the topping. Reduce the oven temperature to 375°F, and bake uncovered for 25 to 30 additional minutes, or until the topping is nicely browned and the filling just starts to bubble around the edges.

5. Allow the pie to cool for at least 1 hour before cutting into wedges and serving. Serve warm or at room temperature, refrigerating any leftovers.

NUTRITIONAL FACTS (PER SERVING)
Calories: 249 Carbohydrates: 48 g Cholesterol: 0 mg
Fat: 3.9 g Fiber: 2.7 g Protein: 5.7 g Sodium: 126 mg

You Save: Calories: 221 Fat: 22.6 g

Pie Apples That Please

Dozens of varieties of apples are available in grocery stores. Many of the crisp, sweet varieties that we love to eat out of hand, however, can become mushy when cooked. For best results when making pies, crisps, and tarts, use a firm-textured variety such as Crispin, Fuji, Golden Delicious, Granny Smith, Jonathan, Newton Pippin, Rome, or Winesap. The sweetest of these varieties—Crispin, Fuji, Golden Delicious, and Rome—will require the least amount of added sugar.

Pumpkin Cheese Pie

1. To make the filling, place ¼ cup of the orange juice in a blender. Sprinkle the gelatin over the top, and set aside for 2 minutes to soften the gelatin.

2. Place the remaining ¼ cup of juice in a small pot, and bring to a boll over medium heat. Add the boiling hot juice to the blender, place the lid on, and blend at low speed for about 2 minutes, or until the gelatin is completely dissolved. Allow the mixture to sit for about 20 minutes, or until it cools to room temperature.

3. Add the cream cheese, pumpkin, brown sugar, pumpkin pie spice, and vanilla extract to the blender, and blend until smooth. Pour the mixture into a large bowl, cover, and chill for at least 4 hours, or until firm.

4. When the gelatin mixture has become firm, beat it with an electric mixer until it is the consistency of pudding. Gently fold in the whipped topping.

5. Spread the mixture in the cooled crust, swirling the top with a knife. Cover and chill for at least 4 hours, or until set, before cutting into wedges and serving.

NUTRITIONAL FACTS (PER SERVING)
Calories: 179 Carbohydrates: 36 g Cholesterol: 2 mg
Fat: 1.3 g Fiber: 1.2 g Protein: 6.3 g Sodium: 233 mg

You Save: Calories: 161 Fat: 19.3 g

Yield: *8 servings*

1 prebaked Lite Graham Cracker Pie Crust (page 314) made with plain graham crackers

FILLING

½ cup orange juice, divided

1 envelope (¼ ounce) unflavored gelatin

1 block (8 ounces) nonfat cream cheese, softened to room temperature

1 cup mashed cooked or canned pumpkin

⅔ cup light brown sugar

1½ teaspoons pumpkin pie spice

1 teaspoon vanilla extract

1 cup nonfat or light whipped topping

Pear Phyllo Pie

Yield: *8 servings*

CRUST

2 tablespoons sugar

½ teaspoon ground cinnamon

¼ teaspoon ground nutmeg

6 sheets (about 14 x 18 inches)
  phyllo pastry (about 5 ounces)

Butter-flavored cooking spray

FILLING

⅓ cup sugar

2 tablespoons cornstarch

¼ teaspoon ground cinnamon

1¼ teaspoon ground nutmeg

6 cups sliced peeled pears (about
  6 medium)

¼ cup dark raisins or dried cranberries

For variety, substitute peaches for the pears.

1. To make the filling, place the sugar, cornstarch, cinnamon, and nutmeg in a small bowl. Stir to mix well, and set aside.

2. Place the pears in a large bowl. Sprinkle the sugar mixture over the pears, and toss to mix well. Toss in the raisins or cranberries, and set aside.

3. To make the crust, place the sugar, cinnamon, and nutmeg in a small dish, and stir to mix well. Set aside.

4. Spread the phyllo dough out on a clean dry surface. Cover the dough with plastic wrap to prevent it from drying out as you work. (Remove the sheets as you need them, being sure to re-cover the remaining dough.)

5. Remove 1 sheet of phyllo dough, and lay it on a clean dry surface. Spray the dough lightly with the cooking spray, and sprinkle with 1 teaspoon of the sugar mixture. Top with another phyllo sheet, spray with cooking spray, and sprinkle with 1 teaspoon of the sugar mixture.

6. Coat a 9-inch pie pan with nonstick cooking spray, and gently press the double-stacked phyllo sheets into the pan, allowing the ends to extend over the edges. Rotate the pie pan slightly, and repeat the procedure with 2 more sheets. Rotate the pan again, and repeat with the 2 remaining sheets.

7. Spread the filling evenly in the crust, and fold the phyllo in to cover the filling. Spray the top lightly with nonstick cooking spray, and sprinkle the remaining sugar mixture over the top. Using a sharp knife, score through the top crust to make 8 wedges. (This will prevent the top from flaking excessively when the pie is cut into serving pieces.)

8. Bake at 350°F for 45 minutes, or until the top is golden brown. Allow the pie to cool for 30 minutes to 1 hour before cutting into wedges and serving. Serve warm.

NUTRITIONAL FACTS (PER SERVING)

Calories: 183 Carbohydrates: 43 g Cholesterol: 0 mg
Fat: 1.4 g Fiber: 3.3 g Protein: 1.6 g Sodium: 69 mg

You Save: Calories: 103 Fat: 11.5 g

Making Pear Phyllo Pie.

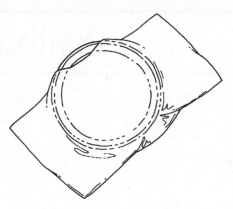

a. Press 1 set of phyllo sheets into the pan.

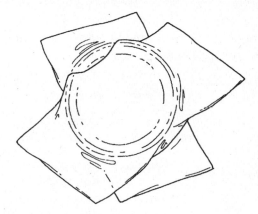

b. Rotate the pan, and press in another set of sheets.

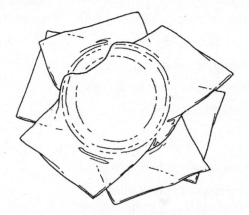

c. Rotate the pan, and press in the remaining sheets.

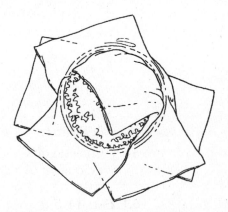

d. Fold the pastry over the filling.

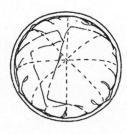

e. Score the pastry to make 8 wedges.

Praline Pumpkin Pie

Yield: *8 servings*

1 prebaked Crunchy Nutty Pie
   Crust (page 316) or unbaked
   Flaky Oat Pie Crust (page 317)

FILLING

1¾ cups mashed cooked or
   canned pumpkin (about one
   15-ounce can)

1 cup evaporated skimmed milk

½ cup fat-free egg substitute

¾ cup light brown sugar

2½ teaspoons pumpkin pie spice*

1½ teaspoons vanilla extract

TOPPING

3 tablespoons light brown sugar

3 tablespoons honey crunch
   wheat germ or finely chopped
   toasted pecans (page 383)

*If you don't have any pumpkin pie
spice on hand, you can use 1½ teaspoons ground cinnamon, ½ teaspoon
ground nutmeg, and ½ teaspoon
ground ginger.

1. To make the topping, place the brown sugar and the wheat germ or pecans in a small bowl, and stir to mix well. Set aside.

2. To make the filling, place all of the filling ingredients in a blender, and process until smooth.

3. Pour the filling into the crust, and bake at 400°F for 15 minutes. Sprinkle the topping over the top of the pie. Reduce the oven temperature to 350°F, and bake for about 45 additional minutes, or until a sharp knife inserted in the center of the pie comes out clean. (Note that if you use the Crunchy Nutty Pie Crust, you will need to shield the edges of the crust during baking with aluminum foil, as directed on page 316.)

4. Allow the pie to cool to room temperature before cutting into wedges and serving. Or refrigerate and serve chilled.

NUTRITIONAL FACTS (PER SERVING)
Calories: 197 Carbohydrates: 41 g Cholesterol: 1 mg
Fat: 0.8 g Fiber: 3.1 g Protein: 7.9 g Sodium: 176 mg

You Save: Calories: 138 Fat: 14.9 g

Old-Fashioned Peach Cobbler

1. To make the filling, place the orange juice, sugar, cornstarch, cinnamon, and nutmeg in a 2-quart pot, and stir to mix well. Place the pot over medium heat, and cook, stirring constantly, for 3 to 5 minutes, or until the mixture is thickened and bubbly.

2. Remove the pot from the heat, and stir the peach slices into the glaze, tossing gently to coat. Coat a 2-quart casserole dish with non-stick cooking spray, and spread the peach mixture evenly in the dish.

3. To make the batter, place the flour, oat bran, sugar, baking powder, and baking soda in a medium-sized bowl, and stir to mix well. Stir in the buttermilk.

4. Spread the batter evenly over the fruit, and bake at 350°F for 35 to 40 minutes, or until the topping is golden brown and the filling Is bubbly around the edges. (Loosely cover the dish with aluminum foil during the last 10 minutes of baking if the top starts to brown too quickly.) Remove the dish from the oven, and let stand for at least 10 minutes. Serve warm or at room temperature.

NUTRITIONAL FACTS (PER ¾-CUP SERVING)
Calories: 172 Cholesterol: 0 mg Fat: 0.6 g
Fiber: 2.7 g Protein: 3.3 g Sodium: 172 mg

Yield: *8 servings*

FRUIT FILLING

½ cup orange juice

¼ cup sugar

2 tablespoons cornstarch

¼ teaspoon ground cinnamon

⅛ teaspoon ground nutmeg

4½ cups sliced peeled peaches (about 5 medium), or 4½ cups frozen (thawed) sliced peaches

BATTER

¾ cup unbleached flour

¾ cup oat bran

⅓ cup sugar

1½ teaspoons baking powder

½ teaspoon baking soda

¾ cup nonfat low-fat buttermilk

Pear-Raisin Crisp

Yield: *6 servings*

FRUIT FILLING

5 cups sliced peeled pears (about 5 medium)

⅓ cup dark raisins

TOPPING

¼ cup barley nugget cereal or chopped walnuts

¼ cup light brown sugar

3 tablespoons whole wheat flour

⅛ teaspoon ground cinnamon

⅛ teaspoon ground nutmeg

1 tablespoon frozen apple juice concentrate, thawed

1. To make the filling, combine the pear slices and raisins in a large bowl, and toss to mix well. Coat a 9-inch deep dish pie pan with non-stick cooking spray, and spread the fruit evenly in the pan. Set aside.

2. To make the topping, combine the cereal or walnuts, brown sugar, flour, cinnamon, and nutmeg in a medium-sized bowl, and stir to mix well. Add the juice concentrate, and stir until the mixture is moist and crumbly.

3. Sprinkle the topping over the fruit, and bake uncovered at 350°F for 50 minutes, or until the topping is browned and the filling is bubbly around the edges. Remove the dish from the oven, and let stand for at least 5 minutes. Serve warm or at room temperature.

NUTRITIONAL FACTS (PER ¾-CUP SERVING)

Calories: 165 Cholesterol: 0 mg Fat: 0.6 g
Fiber: 4.5 g Protein: 1.9 g Sodium: 36 mg

Very Berry Cobbler

1. To make the fruit filling, place the sugar and cornstarch in a medium-sized saucepan, and stir to mix well. Stir in the orange juice fruit. Cook over medium heat, stirring constantly, for about 5 minutes, or until the mixture is thick and bubbly.

2. Coat a 2-quart casserole dish with nonstick cooking spray. Pour fruit filling into the dish, and set aside.

3. To make the topping, combine the flour, oat bran, sugar, baking powder, and baking soda, and stir to mix well. Stir in the butter. Pour the batter over the fruit.

4. Bake at 350°F for about 30 minutes, or until golden brown. Serve warm with vanilla ice milk if desired.

NUTRITIONAL FACTS (PER SERVING)
Calories: 186 Calcium: 55 mg Cholesterol: 0 mg
Fat: 0.5 g Fiber: 2.4 g Iron: 1.1 mg
Potassium: 272 mg Protein: 3.6 g Sodium: 138 mg

Yield: *8 servings*

FRUIT FILLING

3 tablespoons sugar

2 tablespoons cornstarch

¼ cup plus 2 tablespoons orange juice

5 cups fresh or frozen cherries, blueberries or blackberries (or any combination)

TOPPING

⅔ cup unbleached flour

⅓ cup oat bran

⅓ cup sugar

1½ teaspoons baking powder

½ teaspoon baking soda

¾ cup nonfat buttermilk

Raspberry Peach Cobbler

Yield: *8 servings*

FRUIT FILLING

5 cups sliced fresh peaches (about 6 medium)

1¼ cups fresh or frozen raspberries

½ cup light brown sugar

4½ teaspoons cornstarch

TOPPING

¾ cup oat bran

¾ cup unbleached flour

¼ cup sugar

2 teaspoons baking powder

¾ cup nonfat buttermilk

1. To make the fruit filling, combine the fruit, brown sugar, and cornstarch, and toss to mix well.

2. Coat a 2-quart casserole dish with nonstick cooking spray. Pour the fruit filling into the dish, and set aside.

3. To make the topping, combine the oat bran, flour, sugar, and baking powder, and stir to mix well. Stir in the buttermilk. Drop heaping tablespoonfuls of the batter onto the fruit to make 8 biscuits.

4. Bake at 375°F for 35 to 40 minutes, or until the fruit is bubbly and the biscuits are golden brown. If the top starts to brown too quickly, cover the dish loosely with aluminum foil during the last 10 minutes of baking. Serve warm.

NUTRITIONAL FACTS (PER SERVING)
Calories: 209 Calcium: 69 mg Cholesterol: 0 mg
Fat: 0.9 g Fiber: 4.8 g Iron: 1.7 mg
Potassium: 384 mg Protein: 4.4 g Sodium: 111 mg

Sweet Cherry Crisp

1. To make the fruit filling, combine the cherries with the cornstarch and the sugar, and toss to mix well.

2. Coat a 2-quart casserole dish with nonstick cooking spray. Pour the fruit filling into the dish, and set aside.

3. To make the topping, combine the topping ingredients and mix until moist and crumbly. Sprinkle the topping over the fruit.

4. Bake at 375°F for 30 to 35 minutes, or until the filling is bubbly and the topping is golden brown. Serve warm.

NUTRITIONAL FACTS (PER SERVING)
Calories: 165 Calcium: 31 mg Cholesterol: 0 mg
Fat: 0.8 g Fiber: 2.8 g Iron: 1.3 mg
Potassium: 348 mg Protein: 3.2 g Sodium: 4 mg

Yield: *8 servings*

FRUIT FILLING

6 cups pitted sweet cherries or 2 packages (12 ounces each) frozen cherries, thawed

4½ teaspoons cornstarch

2 tablespoons sugar

TOPPING

½ cup plus 2 tablespoons quick-cooking oats

¼ cup light brown sugar

¼ cup toasted wheat germ

4½ teaspoons frozen orange or apple juice concentrate, thawed

Peach Raisin Crisp

Yield: *6 servings*

FRUIT FILLING

4 cups fresh or frozen (thawed) sliced peaches (about 5 medium)

¼ cup plus 2 tablespoons dark raisins

TOPPING

¾ cup quick-cooking oats

3 tablespoons whole wheat pastry flour or unbleached flour

¼ cup brown sugar

½ teaspoon ground cinnamon

3 tablespoons reduced-fat margarine or light butter, cut into pieces

1. To make the fruit filling, toss the peach slices with the raisins. Coat a 9-inch deep dish pie pan with nonstick cooking spray, and spread the fruit evenly in the pan.

2. To make topping, combine oats, flour, brown sugar, and cinnamon, and stir to mix well. Use a pastry cutter to cut margarine or butter into the oat mixture until crumbly. Sprinkle topping over the fruit.

3. Bake at 375°F for 30 to 35 minutes, or until the topping is golden brown. Serve warm with nonfat vanilla yogurt if desired.

NUTRITIONAL FACTS (PER SERVING)
Calories: 190 Calcium: 26 mg Cholesterol: 0 mg
Fat: 3.6 g Fiber: 3.9 g Iron: 1.2 mg
Potassium: 384 mg Protein: 3.3 g Sodium: 73 mg

Mini Cherry Cobblers

1. To make the filling, combine the filling ingredients and toss to mix well. Coat six 6-ounce custard cups with nonstick cooking spray, and divide the mixture evenly among the cups. Set aside.

2. To make the crust, combine the flours and sugar, and stir to mix well. Use a pastry cutter to cut in the margarine or butter until the mixture resembles coarse crumbs. Add the milk, and stir just until moistened.

3. Divide the dough into 6 pieces, and shape each piece into a ball. One at a time, place each ball on a lightly floured surface, and roll into a 4-inch circle. Place each crust over a filled custard cup, and pinch the dough to form a decorative edging. Brush the tops lightly with egg white, and sprinkle with sugar if desired. Using a sharp knife, cut 4 slits in the center of each crust to allow the steam to escape.

4. Place the cups on a baking sheet, and bake at 375°F for 30 minutes, or until the filling is bubbly and the crust is golden brown. Serve warm.

NUTRITIONAL FACTS (PER SERVING)
Calories: 202 Calcium: 27 mg Cholesterol: 0 mg
Fat: 3.9 g Fiber: 2.6 g Iron: 1.2 mg
Potassium: 282 mg Protein: 3.7 g Sodium: 77 mg

Yield: *6 servings*

FILLING

4 cups pitted fresh or frozen (thawed) sweet cherries

3 tablespoons sugar

1 tablespoon frozen apple juice concentrate, thawed

4 teaspoons cornstarch

CRUST

½ cup unbleached flour

⅓ cup whole wheat pastry flour

1 tablespoon sugar

3 tablespoons chilled reduced-fat margarine or light butter, cut into pieces

2 tablespoons plus 1 teaspoon skim milk

1 egg white, beaten

Sugar (optional)

Apple Blackberry Cobbler

Yield: *8 servings*

FRUIT FILLING

6 cups sliced peeled fresh apples (about 7 medium)

1½ cups fresh or frozen (thawed) blackberries

⅓ cup light brown sugar

1½ tablespoons cornstarch

1 tablespoon frozen apple juice concentrate, thawed

CRUST

½ cup oat bran

½ cup unbleached flour

½ teaspoon baking powder

3 tablespoons chilled reduced-fat margarine or light butter, cut into pieces

2–3 tablespoons cold water

GLAZE

2 teaspoons beaten egg white

2 teaspoons water

1 tablespoon sugar

1. To make the fruit filling, combine all of the filling ingredients, and toss to mix well. Coat a 10-inch pie pan with nonstick cooking spray, and spread the fruit evenly in the pan.

2. To make the crust, combine the oat bran, flour, and baking powder, and stir to mix well. Use a pastry cutter to cut the margarine or butter into the flour mixture until the mixture resembles coarse crumbs. Stir in just enough of the water to make a stiff dough that leaves the sides of the bowl and forms a ball.

3. Turn the dough onto a generously floured surface, and roll into an 11-inch circle. Use a knife or pizza wheel to cut the circle into ½-inch strips. Lay half of the crust strips over the filling, spacing the strips ½ inch apart. Lay the remaining strips over the filling in the opposite direction to form a lattice top. Trim the edges to make the dough conform to the shape of the pan.

4. Combine the egg white and water, and brush over the crust. Sprinkle the sugar over the egg white mixture. Bake at 375°F for 45 minutes, or until the filling is bubbly and the crust is lightly browned. Cool for at least 15 minutes, and serve warm or at room temperature.

NUTRITIONAL FACTS (PER SERVING)

Calories: 164 Calcium: 29 mg Cholesterol: 0 mg
Fat: 2.9 g Fiber: 4.4 g Iron: 1.2 mg
Potassium: 214 mg Protein: 2.2 g Sodium: 75 mg

Cherry-Vanilla Cobbler

1. To make the filling, place the cherries in a large bowl. Set aside.

2. Place the sugar and cornstarch in a small bowl, and stir to mix well. Sprinkle the mixture over the fruit. (If the fruit is tart, you may need to add another couple of tablespoons of sugar.) Toss to mix well. Add the juice, and toss to mix well.

3. Coat a 2-quart casserole dish with nonstick cooking spray, and spread the mixture evenly in the dish. Cover the dish with aluminum foil, and bake at 375°F for 30 to 40 minutes, or until hot and bubbly.

4. To make the biscuit topping, place the flour, oat bran, sugar, and baking powder in a medium-sized bowl, and stir to mix well. Add just enough of the yogurt to make a moderately thick batter, stirring just until the dry ingredients are moistened. Drop heaping tablespoonfuls of the batter onto the hot fruit filling to make 8 biscuits.

5. Bake uncovered at 375°F for 18 to 20 minutes, or until the biscuits are lightly browned. Remove the dish from the oven, and allow to cool at room temperature for at least 10 minutes before serving warm.

Yield: *8 servings*

5 cups fresh or frozen (partially thawed) pitted sweet cherries

⅓ cup sugar

1 tablespoon plus

1 teaspoon cornstarch

¼ cup white grape juice

BISCUIT TOPPING

¾ cup unbleached flour

⅓ cup oat bran

¼ cup sugar

1½ teaspoons baking powder

¾ cup plus 1 tablespoon nonfat or low-fat vanilla yogurt

NUTRITIONAL FACTS (PER SERVING)

Calories: 198 Carbohydrates: 46 g Cholesterol: 1 mg
Fat: 0.9 g Fiber: 3.3 g Protein: 3.8 g Sodium: 108 mg

You Save: Calories: 108 Fat: 13.3 g

Peach-Almond Crisp

Yield: *8 servings*

5 cups sliced peeled peaches
(about 7 medium)

¼ cup golden raisins or chopped
dates

⅓ cup sugar

2 teaspoons cornstarch

TOPPING

2 cups oat flake-and-almond
cereal*

2 tablespoons whole wheat pastry
flour

⅓ cup light brown sugar

¼ teaspoon ground cinnamon

⅛ teaspoon ground nutmeg

1 tablespoon plus 1 teaspoon
chilled tub-style nonfat margarine, or 2 tablespoons
chilled reduced-fat margarine,
cut into pieces

¼ cup honey crunch wheat germ
or sliced toasted almonds
(page 383)

*Quaker Toasted Oatmeal and General
Mills Oatmeal-Almond Crisp are good
choices.

1. To make the filling, place the peaches and the raisins or dates in a large bowl, and toss to mix well. Set aside.

2. Place the sugar and cornstarch In a small bowl, and stir to mix well. Sprinkle the mixture over the fruit, and toss to mix well. Coat a 9-inch deep dish pie pan with nonstick cooking spray, and spread the fruit mixture evenly in the pan. Set aside.

3. To make the topping, place the cereal in a blender or food processor, and process into crumbs. Measure the crumbs. There should be ¾ cup. (Adjust the amount if needed.)

4. Place the crumbs, flour, brown sugar, cinnamon, and nutmeg in a small bowl, and stir to mix well. Add the nonfat margarine, and stir until the mixture is moist and crumbly. (If you are using reduced-fat margarine, use a pastry cutter or 2 knives to cut the margarine into the oat mixture until it is moist and crumbly.) If the mixture seems too dry, add more margarine, ½ teaspoon at a time, until the proper consistency is reached. Stir in the wheat germ or almonds, and sprinkle the topping over the filling.

5. Bake uncovered at 375°F for 35 to 40 minutes, or until the filling is bubbly and the topping is golden brown. Cover loosely with aluminum foil during the last few minutes of baking if the topping starts to brown too quickly. Allow to cool at room temperature for at least 15 minutes, and serve warm or at room temperature.

NUTRITIONAL FACTS (PER SERVING)

Calories: 178 Carbohydrates: 42 g Cholesterol: 0 mg
Fat: 1 g Fiber: 3.1 g Protein: 3 g Sodium: 57 mg

You Save: Calories: 128 Fat: 13.2 g

Trimming the Fat from Crumb Toppings

Deliciously crisp and crunchy, the crumb toppings that adorn fruit crisps and crumbles are typically loaded with fat and calories. The reason? Often a full stick of butter or margarine is used to hold the crumbs together. But you can easily reduce or even eliminate the fat in these toppings by moistening the mixture with fruit juice concentrate; a liquid sweetener like maple syrup, honey, or fruit spread; reduced-fat margarine or light butter; or even nonfat margarine. The secret to using these low- and no-fat substitutes is to add only the amount needed to moisten the crumb topping mixture. If you use too much, the moisture in these fat substitutes will make your topping doughy instead of crisp or crumbly.

When mixing up no- and low-fat crumb toppings, start with only a tablespoon or two of your chosen fat substitute. Mix up the topping; if it seems too dry, add more fat substitute, a quarter to a half teaspoon at a time, until the mixture is moist and crumbly. If you are using a liquid sweetener as your fat substitute, reduce the sugar in the recipe accordingly to prevent the topping from being overly sweet. Sprinkle the topping over the fruit filling, and bake as usual. If the top starts to brown too quickly, cover it loosely with aluminum foil during the last few minutes of baking.

To save even more fat in crumb toppings, replace part or all of the nuts with honey crunch wheat germ or a barley nugget cereal like Grape-Nuts. Or toast the nuts using the directions on page 383, and reduce the amount by half. You will still get a nutty taste and a crunchy texture, but with a lot less fat and calories.

Strawberry-Apple Cobbler

Yield: *9 servings*

4 cups sliced peeled apples
(about 5½ medium)

2 cups sliced strawberries

½ cup sugar

1 tablespoon cornstarch

¼ cup apple juice

BISCUIT TOPPING

1 cup unbleached flour

⅓ cup quick-cooking oats

⅓ cup plus 1½ teaspoons sugar,
divided

1½ teaspoons baking powder

½ cup plus 3 tablespoons nonfat
or low-fat buttermilk

Pinch ground cinnamon

1. To make the filling, place the apples and strawberries in a large bowl, and toss to mix well. Set aside.

2. Place the sugar and cornstarch in a small bowl, and stir to mix well. Sprinkle the mixture over the fruit, and toss to mix well. Add the juice, and toss to mix well.

3. Coat a 2½-quart casserole dish with nonstick cooking spray, and spread the fruit mixture evenly in the dish. Cover the dish with aluminum foil, and bake at 375°F for 30 to 40 minutes, or until hot and bubbly.

4. To make the biscuit topping, place the flour, oats, ⅓ cup of the sugar, and the baking powder in a medium-sized bowl, and stir to mix well. Add just enough of the buttermilk to make a moderately thick batter, stirring just until the dry ingredients are moistened. Drop heaping tablespoonfuls of the batter onto the hot fruit filling to make 9 biscuits. Combine the remaining 1½ teaspoons of sugar and the cinnamon in a small bowl, stir to mix, and sprinkle over the biscuits.

5. Bake uncovered at 375°F for 18 to 20 minutes, or until the biscuits are lightly browned. Allow to cool at room temperature for at least 10 minutes before serving warm.

NUTRITIONAL FACTS (PER SERVING)
Calories: 206 Carbohydrates: 49 g Cholesterol: 0 mg
Fat: 0.7 g Fiber: 2.3 g Protein: 3 g Sodium: 112 mg

You Save: Calories: 118 Fat: 12.5 g

Trimming the Fat from Cobbler Toppings

Biscuit toppings add that down-home touch to cobblers. Unfortunately, they can also add a lot of fat. The good news is that it's a simple matter to reduce or even eliminate the fat in your biscuit toppings. Try replacing part or all of the butter, margarine, or other solid shortening in biscuit toppings with half as much nonfat or low-fat buttermilk or yogurt. (Replace oil with three-fourths as much buttermilk or yogurt.) Mix the batter just until the dry ingredients are moistened, being careful not to overmix. If the mixture seems too dry, add a bit more buttermilk or yogurt. For an extra-moist and tender texture, substitute oat bran or quick-cooking oats for a fourth of the flour in the recipe. Drop the biscuits onto your cobbler, bake as usual, and enjoy!

Another way to slash fat in your cobbler toppings is to substitute reduced-fat margarine or light butter for full-fat shortenings. See the inset on page 288 for tips on using these products.

Mixed Fruit Crisp

1. To make the filling, place the apples, pears, plums, and raisins or dried cranberries in a large bowl, and toss to mix well. Set aside.

2. Place the sugar and cornstarch in a small bowl, and stir to mix well. Sprinkle the mixture over the fruit, and toss to mix well. Coat a 9-inch deep dish pie pan with nonstick cooking spray, and spread the fruit mixture evenly in the pan. Set aside.

3. To make the topping, break the graham crackers into pieces, place in the bowl of a food processor, and process into crumbs. Measure the crumbs. There should be ¾ cup. (Adjust the amount if needed.)

4. Place the crumbs, brown sugar, cinnamon, and ginger in a small bowl, and stir to mix well. Add the nonfat margarine, and stir until the mixture is moist and crumbly. (If you are using reduced-fat margarine, use a pastry cutter or 2 knives to cut the margarine into the crumb mixture until it is moist and crumbly.) If the mixture seems too dry, add more margarine, ½ teaspoon at a time, until the proper consistency is reached. Stir in the wheat germ or walnuts. Sprinkle the topping over the filling.

5. Bake uncovered at 375°F for 35 to 40 minutes, or until the filling is bubbly and the topping is golden brown. Cover loosely with aluminum foil during the last few minutes of baking if the topping starts to brown too quickly. Allow to cool at room temperature for at least 15 minutes, and serve warm or at room temperature.

NUTRITIONAL FACTS (PER SERVING)
Calories: 177 Carbohydrates: 42 g Cholesterol: 0 mg
Fat: 1.3 g Fiber: 2.4 g Protein: 2 g Sodium: 81 mg

You Save: Calories: 154 Fat: 10.5 g

Yield: *8 servings*

2 medium apples, peeled and sliced

2 medium pears, peeled and cut into ¾-inch chunks

2 medium unpeeled red plums, cut into ¾-inch slices

¼ cup dark raisins or dried cranberries

⅓ cup sugar

1½ teaspoons cornstarch

TOPPING

4½ large (2½-x-5-inch) low-fat graham crackers

¼ cup light brown sugar

¼ teaspoon ground cinnamon

¼ teaspoon ground ginger

1 tablespoon plus 1½ teaspoons chilled tub-style nonfat margarine, or 2 tablespoons plus 1 teaspoon chilled reduced-fat margarine, cut into pieces

¼ cup honey crunch wheat germ or chopped walnuts

Spiced Peach Cobbler

Yield: *8 servings*

1 tablespoon plus 1½ teaspoons cornstarch

½ cup plus 2 tablespoons peach nectar or white grape juice, divided

¼ cup plus 2 tablespoons sugar

¼ teaspoon ground cinnamon

¼ teaspoon ground allspice

¼ teaspoon ground nutmeg

4½ cups sliced peeled peaches (about 6 medium)

BISCUIT TOPPING

¾ cup plus 2 tablespoons unbleached flour

¼ cup oat bran

¼ cup plus 1½ teaspoons sugar, divided

1¾ teaspoons baking powder

½ cup plus 3 tablespoons nonfat or low-fat vanilla yogurt

For variety, substitute pears for the peaches.

1. To make the filling, place the cornstarch and 2 tablespoons of the nectar or juice in a small bowl, and stir to dissolve the cornstarch. Set aside.

2. Place the sugar and spices in a 3-quart pot, and stir to mix well Add the remaining ½ cup of nectar or juice, and stir to mix well. Add the peaches, and bring to a boil over medium-high heat, stirring frequently. Reduce the heat to medium-low, cover, and simmer, stirring occasionally, for about 5 minutes, or just until the peaches are tender.

3. Stir the cornstarch mixture, and slowly pour it into the boiling peach mixture, stirring constantly. Cook and stir for another minute, or until the mixture has thickened. Remove the pot from the heat, cover, and set aside.

4. To make the biscuit topping, place the flour, oat bran, ¼ cup of the sugar, and the baking powder in a medium-sized bowl, and stir to mix well. Add just enough of the yogurt to make a moderately thick batter, stirring just until the dry ingredients are moistened.

5. Coat a 2-quart baking dish with nonstick cooking spray, and spread the hot peach mixture evenly in the dish. Drop heaping tablespoonfuls of the batter onto the fruit filling to make 8 biscuits. Sprinkle the remaining 1½ teaspoons of sugar over the biscuit topping,

6. Bake uncovered at 375°F for about 20 minutes, or until the biscuits are lightly browned. Allow to cool at room temperature for at least 10 minutes before serving warm.

NUTRITIONAL FACTS (PER SERVING)
Calories: 187 Carbohydrates: 45 g Cholesterol: 1 mg
Fat: 0.5 g Fiber: 2.5 g Protein: 3.6 g Sodium: 122 mg

You Save: Calories: 119 Fat: 13.7 g

Hawaiian Pineapple Crisp

1. To make the filling, place the pineapple in a large bowl. Set aside.

2. Place the sugar, cornstarch, and nutmeg in a small bowl, and stir to mix well. Sprinkle the mixture over the fruit. (If the fruit is tart, you may need to add another couple of tablespoons of sugar.) Toss to mix well. Coat a 9-inch deep dish pie pan with nonstick cooking spray, and spread the fruit mixture evenly in the pan. Set aside.

3. To make the topping, place the oats, flour, and brown sugar in a small bowl, and stir to mix well. Add the nonfat margarine, and stir until the mixture is moist and crumbly. (If you are using reduced-fat margarine, use a pastry cutter or 2 knives to cut the margarine into the oat mixture until it is moist and crumbly.) If the mixture seems too dry, add more margarine, ½ teaspoon at a time, until the proper consistency is reached. Stir in the coconut and the wheat germ or nuts. Sprinkle the topping over the filling.

4. Bake uncovered at 375°F for 35 to 40 minutes, or until the filling is bubbly and the topping is golden brown. Cover loosely with aluminum foil during the last few minutes of baking if the topping starts to brown too quickly. Allow to cool at room temperature for at least 15 minutes, and serve warm or at room temperature.

NUTRITIONAL FACTS (PER SERVING)
Calories: 149 Carbohydrates: 31 g Cholesterol: 0 mg
Fat: 2.4 g Fiber: 2.2 g Protein: 2.3 g Sodium: 30 mg

You Save: Calories: 157 Fat: 12.8 g

Yield: *8 servings*

4 cups bite-sized pieces of fresh pineapple (about 1 medium)

¼ cup sugar

2 teaspoons cornstarch

⅛ teaspoon ground nutmeg

TOPPING

½ cup quick-cooking oats

¼ cup whole wheat pastry flour

⅓ cup light brown sugar

1 tablespoon plus 1½ teaspoons chilled tub-style nonfat margarine, or 2 tablespoons plus 1 teaspoon chilled reduced-fat margarine, cut into pieces

⅓ cup shredded sweetened coconut

3 tablespoons honey crunch wheat germ or chopped toasted macadamia nuts or almonds (page 383)

Cherry-Apple Crisp

Yield: *8 servings*

3½ cups sliced peeled apples (about 4½ medium)

1½ cups fresh or frozen (unthawed) pitted sweet cherries

⅓ cup sugar

2 teaspoons cornstarch

TOPPING

4½ large (2½-x-5-inch) low-fat graham crackers

¼ cup light brown sugar

¼ teaspoon ground cinnamon

1 tablespoon plus 1½ teaspoons chilled tub-style nonfat margarine, or 2 tablespoons plus 1 teaspoon chilled reduced-fat margarine, cut into pieces

¼ cup honey crunch wheat germ or chopped toasted pecans (page 383)

1. To make the filling, place the apples and cherries in a large bowl, and toss to mix well. Set aside.

2. Place the sugar and cornstarch in a small bowl, and stir to mix well. Sprinkle the mixture over the fruit, and toss to mix well. Coat a 9-inch deep dish pie pan with nonstick cooking spray, and spread the fruit mixture evenly in the pan. Set aside.

3. To make the topping, break the graham crackers into pieces, place in the bowl of a food processor, and process into crumbs. Measure the crumbs. There should be ¾ cup. (Adjust the amount if needed.)

4. Place the crumbs, brown sugar, and cinnamon in a small bowl, and stir to mix well. Add the nonfat margarine, and stir until the mixture is moist and crumbly. (If you are using reduced-fat margarine, use a pastry cutter or 2 knives to cut the margarine into the mixture until it is moist and crumbly.) If the mixture seems too dry, add more margarine, ½ teaspoon at a time, until the proper consistency is reached. Stir in the wheat germ or pecans. Sprinkle the topping over the filling.

5. Bake uncovered at 375°F for 35 to 40 minutes, or until the filling is bubbly and the topping is golden brown. Cover loosely with aluminum foil during the last few minutes of baking if the topping starts to brown too quickly. Allow to cool at room temperature for at least 15 minutes, and serve warm or at room temperature.

NUTRITIONAL FACTS (PER SERVING)
Calories: 157 Carbohydrates: 36 g Cholesterol: 0 mg
Fat: 1 g Fiber: 2 g Protein: 1.9 g Sodium: 91 mg

You Save: Calories: 149 Fat: 13.2 g

Plum Delicious Crisp

1. To make the filling, place the plums in a large bowl. Set aside.

2. Place the brown sugar and cornstarch in a small bowl, and stir to mix well. Sprinkle the mixture over the fruit, and toss to mix well. (If the fruit is tart, you may need to add another couple of tablespoons of sugar.) Coat a 9-inch deep dish pie pan with nonstick cooking spray, and spread the fruit mixture evenly in the pan. Set aside.

3. To make the topping, place the oats, flour, brown sugar, and cinnamon in a small bowl, and stir to mix well. Add the maple syrup, and stir until the mixture is moist and crumbly. (If the mixture seems too dry, add more maple syrup, ¼ teaspoon at a time, until the proper consistency is reached.) Stir in the wheat germ or walnuts. Sprinkle the topping over the filling.

4. Bake uncovered at 375°F for 35 to 40 minutes, or until the filling is bubbly and the topping is golden brown. Cover loosely with aluminum foil during the last few minutes of baking if the topping starts to brown too quickly. Allow to cool at room temperature for at least 15 minutes, and serve warm or at room temperature.

Yield: *8 servings*

5 cups ¾-inch-thick slices unpeeled red or purple plums (about 10 medium)

⅓ cup light brown sugar

1 tablespoon cornstarch

TOPPING

½ cup quick-cooking oats

¼ cup whole wheat pastry flour

⅓ cup light brown sugar

½ teaspoon ground cinnamon

2 tablespoons maple syrup

¼ cup honey crunch wheat germ or chopped walnuts

NUTRITIONAL FACTS (PER SERVING)
Calories: 164 Carbohydrates: 37 g Cholesterol: 0 mg
Fat: 1.3 g Fiber: 3.2 g Protein: 2.9 g Sodium: 6 mg

You Save: Calories: 142 Fat: 12.9 g

Apple-Raisin Crisp

Yield: *8 servings*

4¾ cups sliced peeled apples
   (about 6½ medium)

⅓ cup dark raisins

⅓ cup light brown sugar

1½ teaspoons cornstarch

2 tablespoons water

TOPPING

¼ cup plus 2 tablespoons quick-
   cooking oats

¼ cup plus 2 tablespoons whole
   wheat pastry flour

⅓ cup light brown sugar

½ teaspoon ground cinnamon

2 tablespoons frozen (thawed)
   apple juice concentrate or
   maple syrup

⅓ cup honey crunch wheat germ,
   chopped toasted pecans (page
   383), or chopped walnuts

For variety, substitute dates, dried pitted cherries, dried cranberries, or chopped dried apricots for the raisins.

1. To make the filling, place the apples and raisins in a large bowl, and toss to mix well. Set aside.

2. Place the brown sugar and cornstarch in a small bowl, and stir to mix well. Sprinkle the mixture over the fruit, and toss to mix well. (If the fruit is tart, you may need to add another couple of tablespoons of sugar.) Add the water, and toss to mix well. Coat a 9-inch deep dish pie pan with nonstick cooking spray, and spread the fruit mixture evenly in the pan. Set aside.

3. To make the topping, place the oats, flour, brown sugar, and cinnamon in a small bowl, and stir to mix well. Add the juice concentrate or maple syrup, and stir until the mixture is moist and crumbly. (If the mixture seems too dry, add more juice concentrate or maple syrup, ¼ teaspoon at a time, until the proper consistency is reached.) Stir in the wheat germ or nuts. Sprinkle the topping over the filling.

4. Bake uncovered at 375°F for 35 to 40 minutes, or until the filling is bubbly and the topping is golden brown. Cover loosely with aluminum foil during the last few minutes of baking if the topping starts to brown too quickly. Allow to cool at room temperature for at least 15 minutes, and serve warm or at room temperature.

NUTRITIONAL FACTS (PER SERVING)
Calories: 160 Carbohydrates: 37 g Cholesterol: 0 mg
Fat: 1 g Fiber: 2.8 g Protein: 2.7 g Sodium: 7 mg

You Save: Calories: 146 Fat: 13.2 g

CRANBERRY-PEAR CRUMBLE

1. To make the filling, place the pears and cranberries in a large bowl, and toss to mix well. Set aside.

2. Place the brown sugar and cornstarch in a small bowl, and stir to mix well. Sprinkle the mixture over the fruit, and toss to mix. (If the fruit is tart, you may need to add another couple of tablespoons of sugar.) Coat a 9-inch deep dish pie pan with nonstick cooking spray, and spread the fruit mixture evenly in the pan. Set aside.

3. To make the topping, place the oats, flour, brown sugar, and cinnamon in a small bowl, and stir to mix well. Add the juice concentrate, and stir until the mixture is moist and crumbly. (If the mixture seems too dry, add more juice concentrate, ¼ teaspoon at a time, until the proper consistency is reached.) Stir in the wheat germ or pecans. Sprinkle the topping over the filling.

4. Bake uncovered at 375°F for 35 to 40 minutes, or until the filling is bubbly and the topping is golden brown. Cover loosely with aluminum foil during the last few minutes of baking if the topping starts to brown too quickly. Allow to cool at room temperature for at least 15 minutes before serving warm.

Yield: *8 servings*

4½ cups diced peeled pears (about 5 medium)

½ cup coarsely chopped fresh or frozen (unthawed) cranberries

⅓ cup light brown sugar

2 teaspoons cornstarch

TOPPING

¼ cup plus 2 tablespoons quick-cooking oats

¼ cup plus 2 tablespoons whole wheat pastry flour

⅓ cup light brown sugar

½ teaspoon ground cinnamon

2 tablespoons frozen orange juice concentrate, thawed

⅓ cup honey crunch wheat germ or chopped toasted pecans (page 383)

NUTRITIONAL FACTS (PER SERVING)
Calories: 163 Carbohydrates: 38 g Cholesterol: 0 mg
Fat: 1.1 g Fiber: 3.8 g Protein: 2.9 g Sodium: 5 mg

You Save: Calories: 143 Fat: 13.1 g

Cocoa Fruit Crisp

Yield: *6 servings*

4½ cups sliced peeled pears (about 4½ medium)

¼ cup plus 2 tablespoons dried pitted cherries

⅓ cup sugar

2 teaspoons cornstarch

TOPPING

⅓ cup quick-cooking oats

¼ cup whole wheat pastry flour

2 tablespoons plus 1½ teaspoons Dutch processed cocoa powder

¼ cup plus 2 tablespoons light brown sugar

2 tablespoons chilled tub-style nonfat margarine, or 3 tablespoons chilled reduced-fat margarine, cut into pieces

⅓ cup honey crunch wheat germ or chopped walnuts

1. To make the filling, place the pears and dried cherries in a large bowl, and toss to mix well. Set aside.

2. Place the sugar and cornstarch in a small bowl, and stir to mix well. Sprinkle the mixture over the fruit, and toss to mix well. (If the fruit is tart, you may need to add another couple of tablespoons of sugar.) Coat a 9-inch deep dish pie pan with nonstick cooking spray, and spread the fruit mixture evenly in the pan. Set aside.

3. To make the topping, place the oats, flour, cocoa, and brown sugar in a small bowl, and stir to mix well. Add the nonfat margarine, and stir until the mixture is moist and crumbly. (If you are using reduced-fat margarine, use a pastry cutter or 2 knives to cut the margarine into the oat mixture until it is moist and crumbly.) If the mixture seems too dry, add more margarine, ½ teaspoon at a time, until the proper consistency is reached. Stir in the wheat germ or walnuts. Sprinkle the topping over the filling.

4. Bake uncovered at 375°F for 35 to 40 minutes, or until the filling is bubbly and the topping is golden brown. Cover loosely with aluminum foil during the last few minutes of baking if the topping starts to brown too quickly. Remove the dish from the oven, and allow to cool at room temperature for at least 15 minutes. Serve warm or at room temperature.

NUTRITIONAL FACTS (PER SERVING)
Calories: 181 Carbohydrates: 42 g Cholesterol: 0 mg
Fat: 1.4 g Fiber: 4 g Protein: 2.7 g Sodium: 26 mg

You Save: Calories: 140 Fat: 13.5 g

Three-Fruit Cobbler

1. To make the filling, drain the apricots, peaches, and oranges, reserving ¾ cup of the mixed juice. Cut the apricot halves in half. If the peach slices are large, cut them in half, also. Combine the fruits in a medium-sized bowl, and set aside.

2. Place the sugar, cornstarch, and cinnamon in a 2½-quart pot, and stir to mix well. Add half of the reserved juice, and stir until the cornstarch is dissolved. Stir in the remaining juice.

3. Place the pot over medium heat, and cook, stirring constantly, for several minutes, or until thickened and bubbly. Add the fruit to the pot, and cook and stir for about 30 seconds to coat it with the juice mixture.

4. Coat a 10-inch pie pan with nonstick cooking spray, and spread the fruit mixture evenly in the pan. Set aside.

5. To make the crust, place the flour, oat bran, sugar, and baking powder in a medium-sized bowl, and stir to mix well. Using a pastry cutter or 2 knives, cut in the margarine or butter until the mixture resembles coarse crumbs. Add just enough of the buttermilk to make a stiff dough, stirring just until the dough holds together and forms a ball.

6. Turn the dough onto a floured surface, and pat into a 7-inch circle. Then, using a rolling pin, roll the dough into an 11-inch circle. Use a knife or pizza wheel to cut the circle into ½-inch strips.

7. Arrange half of the strips over the filling, spacing them ½-inch apart. Arrange the remaining strips over the filling in the opposite direction to form a lattice top. Trim the edges to make the dough conform to the shape of the pan.

8. To glaze the crust, combine the egg substitute and water in a small dish, and brush over the crust. Sprinkle the sugar over the crust.

9. Bake at 375°F for 25 to 30 minutes, or until the filling is bubbly and the crust is lightly browned. Allow to cool at room temperature for at least 10 minutes before serving warm.

Yield: *8 servings*

1 can (1 pound) apricot halves in juice, undrained

1 can (1 pound) sliced peaches in juice, undrained

1 can (10 ounces) mandarin orange segments in juice, undrained

⅓ cup sugar

1 tablespoon plus 1½ teaspoons cornstarch

¼ teaspoon ground cinnamon

CRUST

¾ cup unbleached flour

½ cup oat bran

1 tablespoon sugar

¾ teaspoon baking powder

3 tablespoons chilled reduced-fat margarine or light butter

3 tablespoons nonfat or low-fat buttermilk

GLAZE

2 teaspoons fat-free egg substitute

2 teaspoons water

1 tablespoon sugar

NUTRITIONAL FACTS (PER SERVING)
Calories: 183 Carbohydrates: 39 g Cholesterol: 0 mg
Fat: 2.4 g Fiber: 2.4 g Protein: 3 g Sodium: 88 mg

You Save: Calories: 120 Fat: 10.8 g

California Crumble

Yield: *6 servings*

1 can (1 pound) sliced peaches in juice, drained

1 can (1 pound) apricot halves in juice, drained

3 tablespoons light brown sugar

¼ cup plus 1 tablespoon dark raisins, chopped dates dried pitted cherries, or chopped pitted prunes

TOPPING

¼ cup plus 2 tablespoons quick-cooking oats

¼ cup plus 2 tablespoons whole wheat pastry flour

⅓ cup light brown sugar

½ teaspoon ground cinnamon

2 tablespoons chilled tub-style nonfat margarine, or 3 table-spoons chilled reduced-fat margarine, cut into pieces

⅓ cup honey crunch wheat germ or chopped toasted almonds or walnuts (page 383)

1. To make the filling, cut the peaches and apricots into bite-sized pieces, and place them in a large bowl. Add the brown sugar, and toss to mix well. Add the raisins, dates, cherries, or prunes, and toss to mix well.

2. Coat a 9-inch deep dish pie pan with nonstick cooking spray, and spread the fruit mixture evenly in the pan. Set aside.

3. To make the topping, place the oats, flour, brown sugar, and cinnamon in a small bowl, and stir to mix well. Add the nonfat margarine, and stir until the mixture is moist and crumbly. (If you are using reduced-fat margarine, use a pastry cutter or 2 knives to cut the margarine into the oat mixture until it is moist and crumbly.) If the mixture seems too dry, add more margarine, ½ teaspoon at a time, until the proper consistency is reached. Stir in the wheat germ or nuts. Sprinkle the topping over the filling.

4. Bake uncovered at 375°F for 30 to 35 minutes, or until the filling Is bubbly and the topping is golden brown. Cover loosely with aluminum foil during the last few minutes of baking if the topping starts to brown too quickly. Allow to cool at room temperature for at least 15 minutes, and serve warm or at room temperature.

NUTRITIONAL FACTS (PER SERVING)
Calories: 186 Carbohydrates: 40 g Cholesterol: 0 mg
Fat: 1.3 g Fiber: 3.4 g Protein: 4.2 g Sodium: 38 mg

You Save: Calories: 143 Fat: 13.4 g

Very Blueberry Crisp

1. To make the filling, place the blueberries in a large bowl. Set aside.

2. Place the sugar, cornstarch, and lemon rind in a small bowl, and stir to mix well. Sprinkle the mixture over the fruit, and toss to mix well.

3. Coat a 9-inch deep dish pie pan with nonstick cooking spray, and spread the fruit mixture evenly in the pan. Cover the dish with aluminum foil, and bake at 375°F for about 20 minutes, or until the berries start to soften and release their juices.

4. While the berries are cooking, place the oats, flour, brown sugar, and cinnamon in a small bowl, and stir to mix well. Add the nonfat margarine, and stir until the mixture is moist and crumbly. (If you are using reduced-fat margarine, use a pastry cutter or 2 knives to cut the margarine into the oat mixture until it is moist and crumbly.) If the mixture seems too dry, add more margarine, ½ teaspoon at a time, until the proper consistency is reached. Stir in the wheat germ or nuts.

5. Sprinkle the filling over the hot berries, and bake uncovered for about 25 additional minutes, or until the filling is bubbly and the topping is golden brown. Cover loosely with aluminum foil during the last few minutes of baking if the topping starts to brown too quickly. Allow to cool at room temperature for at least 15 minutes, and serve warm or at room temperature.

Yield: *6 servings*

4 cups fresh or frozen (partially thawed) blueberries

⅓ cup sugar

2½ teaspoons cornstarch

¾ teaspoon dried grated lemon rind, or 2¼ teaspoons fresh

TOPPING

¼ cup plus 2 tablespoons quick-cooking oats

¼ cup plus 2 tablespoons whole wheat pastry flour

⅓ cup light brown sugar

½ teaspoon ground cinnamon

2 tablespoons chilled tub-style nonfat margarine, or 3 tablespoons chilled reduced-fat margarine, cut into pieces

⅓ cup honey crunch wheat germ or chopped toasted pecans or walnuts (page 383)

NUTRITIONAL FACTS (PER SERVING)

Calories: 206 Carbohydrates: 47 g Cholesterol: 0 mg
Fat: 1.5 g Fiber: 4.3 g Protein: 3.9 g Sodium: 40 mg

You Save: Calories: 143 Fat: 13.2 g

Cinnamon-Apple Cobbler

Yield: *9 servings*

2½ teaspoons cornstarch

¾ cup water or apple juice, divided

¼ cup plus 3 tablespoons light brown sugar

¾ teaspoon ground cinnamon

6 cups sliced peeled apples (about 8 medium)

¼ cup dark raisins

BISCUIT TOPPING

1 cup unbleached flour

⅓ cup quick-cooking oats

⅓ cup plus 1½ teaspoons sugar, divided

1½ teaspoons baking powder

½ cup plus 3 tablespoons nonfat or low-fat buttermilk

Pinch ground cinnamon

1. To make the filling, place the cornstarch and 2 tablespoons of the water or juice in a small bowl, and stir to dissolve the cornstarch. Set aside.

2. Place the brown sugar and cinnamon in a 3-quart pot, and stir to mix well. Add the remaining water or juice, and stir to mix well. Add the apples and raisins, and bring to a boil over medium-high heat. Reduce the heat to medium-low, cover, and cook, stirring occasionally, for about 5 minutes, or just until the apples are tender.

3. Stir the cornstarch mixture, and slowly pour it into the boiling apple mixture, stirring constantly. Cook and stir for another minute, or until the mixture has thickened. Remove the pot from the heat, cover, and set aside.

4. To make the biscuit topping, place the flour, oats, ⅓ cup of the sugar, and the baking powder in a medium-sized bowl, and stir to mix well. Add just enough of the buttermilk to make a moderately thick batter, stirring just until the dry ingredients are moistened.

5. Coat a 2½-quart baking dish with nonstick cooking spray, and spread the hot apple mixture evenly in the dish. Drop heaping tablespoonfuls of the batter onto the fruit filling to make 9 biscuits. Combine the remaining 1½ teaspoons of sugar and the cinnamon in a small bowl, stir to mix well, and sprinkle over the biscuit topping.

6. Bake uncovered at 375°F for about 20 minutes, or until the biscuits are lightly browned. Remove the dish from the oven, and allow to cool at room temperature for at least 10 minutes before serving warm.

NUTRITIONAL FACTS (PER SERVING)
Calories: 178 Carbohydrates: 42 g Cholesterol: 0 mg
Fat: 0.6 g Fiber: 2.1 g Protein: 2.7 g Sodium: 104 mg

You Save: Calories: 128 Fat: 12.6 g

Apricot-Ginger Crisp

For variety, substitute canned peaches or pears for the apricots.

Yield: *6 servings*

1. Cut the apricots into bite-sized pieces. Coat a 9-inch deep dish pie pan with nonstick cooking spray, and spread the apricots evenly in the pan. Set aside.

2. To make the topping, break the gingersnaps into pieces, place them in the bowl of a food processor, and process into crumbs. Measure the crumbs. There should be ¾ cup plus 2 tablespoons. (Adjust the amount if needed.)

3. Place the crumbs and brown sugar in a small bowl, and stir to mix well. Add the nonfat margarine, and stir until the mixture is moist and crumbly. (If you are using reduced-fat margarine, use a pastry cutter or 2 knives to cut the margarine into the mixture until it is moist and crumbly.) If the mixture seems too dry, add more margarine ½ teaspoon at a time, until the proper consistency is reached. Stir in the wheat germ or pecans. Sprinkle the topping over the filling.

4. Bake uncovered at 375°F for about 25 minutes, or until the filling is bubbly and the topping is golden brown. Cover loosely with aluminum foil during the last few minutes of baking if the topping starts to brown too quickly. Allow to cool at room temperature for at least 15 minutes, and serve warm or at room temperature.

2 cans (1 pound each) apricots in juice or light syrup, drained

TOPPING

14 low-fat gingersnaps

¼ cup plus 1 tablespoon light brown sugar

1 tablespoon plus ½ teaspoon chilled tub-style nonfat margarine, or 2 tablespoons chilled reduced-fat margarine, cut into pieces

⅓ cup honey crunch wheat germ or chopped toasted pecans (page 383)

NUTRITIONAL FACTS (PER SERVING)
Calories: 175 Carbohydrates: 36 g Cholesterol: 0 mg
Fat: 2.4 g Fiber: 2.3 g Protein: 3.3 g Sodium: 125 mg

You Save: Calories: 131 Fat: 12.8 g

Summer Fruit Crisp

Yield: *8 servings*

4 cups sliced peeled peaches or nectarines (about 6 medium)

1 cup fresh or frozen (unthawed) blueberries, raspberries, or pitted sweet cherries

⅓ cup sugar

1 tablespoon cornstarch

TOPPING

¼ cup plus 2 tablespoons quick-cooking oats

¼ cup plus 2 tablespoons whole wheat pastry flour

¼ cup plus 2 tablespoons light brown sugar

½ teaspoon ground cinnamon

2 tablespoons chilled tub-style nonfat margarine, or 3 table-spoons chilled reduced-fat margarine, cut into pieces

⅓ cup honey crunch wheat germ or chopped toasted pecans (page 383)

1. To make the filling, place the peaches or nectarines and the blueberries, raspberries, or cherries in a large bowl, and toss to mix well. Set aside.

2. Place the sugar and cornstarch in a small bowl, and stir to mix well. Sprinkle the mixture over the fruit, and toss to mix well. (If the fruit is tart, you may need to add another couple of tablespoons of sugar.) Coat a 9-inch deep dish pie pan with nonstick cooking spray, and spread the fruit mixture evenly in the pan. Set aside.

3. To make the topping, place the oats, flour, brown sugar, and cinnamon in a small bowl, and stir to mix well. Add the nonfat margarine, and stir until the mixture is moist and crumbly. (If you are using reduced-fat margarine, use a pastry cutter or 2 knives to cut the margarine into the oat mixture until it is moist and crumbly.) If the mixture seems too dry, add more margarine, ½ teaspoon at a time, until the proper consistency is reached. Stir in the wheat germ or pecans. Sprinkle the topping over the filling.

4. Bake uncovered at 375°F for 35 to 40 minutes, or until the filling is bubbly and the topping is golden brown. Cover loosely with aluminum foil during the last few minutes of baking if the topping starts to brown too quickly. Allow to cool at room temperature for at least 15 minutes, and serve warm or at room temperature.

NUTRITIONAL FACTS (PER SERVING)
Calories: 163 Carbohydrates: 37 g Cholesterol: 0 mg
Fat: 1 g Fiber: 3.4 g Protein: 3.2 g Sodium: 27 mg

You Save: Calories: 143 Fat: 13.2 g

Mini Blackberry Cobblers

For variety, substitute blueberries, raspberries, or diced peeled peaches for the blackberries.

1. To make the filling, place the blackberries in a large bowl. Set aside.

2. Place the sugar, cornstarch, and lemon or orange rind in a small bowl, and stir to mix well. Sprinkle the mixture over the fruit, and toss to mix well. (If the fruit is tart, you may need to add another couple of tablespoons of sugar.) Coat six 6-ounce custard cups with nonstick cooking spray, and divide the mixture evenly among the cups. Set aside.

3. To make the crust, place the flour, oats, sugar, baking powder, and salt in a medium-sized bowl, and stir to mix well. Using a pastry cutter or 2 knives, cut in the margarine or butter until the mixture resembles coarse crumbs. Add just enough of the milk to make a stiff dough, stirring just until the dough holds together and forms a ball.

4. Shape the dough into 6 balls. Using a rolling pin and working on a lightly floured surface, roll each ball into a 4-inch circle, and lay 1 crust over the fruit filling in each cup. Pinch the edges of each circle to make a decorative edge.

5. To glaze the crusts, brush each lightly with the egg substitute or egg white, and sprinkle with ¼ teaspoon of sugar. Using a sharp knife, cut 4 slits in the center of each crust to allow steam to escape during baking.

6. Place the cups on a baking sheet, and bake at 375°F for 30 minutes, or until the filling is bubbly and the crusts are lightly browned. Remove the cobblers from the oven, and allow to cool at room temperature for at least 10 minutes before serving warm.

Yield: *6 servings*

4 cups fresh or frozen (partially thawed) blackberries

¼ cup plus 2 tablespoons sugar

1 tablespoon cornstarch

¾ teaspoon dried grated lemon or orange rind, or 2¼ teaspoons fresh

CRUST

¾ cup unbleached flour

⅓ cup quick-cooking oats

1 tablespoon plus 1½ teaspoons sugar

½ teaspoon baking powder

⅛ teaspoon salt

2 tablespoons plus 1½ teaspoons chilled reduced-fat margarine or light butter

3 tablespoons evaporated skimmed milk

GLAZE

2 tablespoons fat-free egg substitute or 1 egg white, beaten

1½ teaspoons sugar

NUTRITIONAL FACTS (PER SERVING)
Calories: 215 Carbohydrates: 44 g Cholesterol: 0 mg
Fat: 3 g Fiber: 4.9 g Protein: 3.2 g Sodium: 86 mg

You Save: Calories: 94 Fat: 10.2 g

Biscuit-Topped Blueberry Cobbler

Yield: *8 servings*

5 cups fresh or frozen (partially thawed) blueberries

¼ cup plus 2 tablespoons sugar

1 tablespoon plus ½ teaspoon cornstarch

1 tablespoon plus 1 teaspoon frozen orange juice concentrate, thawed

BISCUIT TOPPING

¾ cup plus 2 tablespoons unbleached flour

¼ cup oat bran

⅓ cup plus 1½ teaspoons sugar, divided

1¾ teaspoons baking powder

½ cup plus 2 tablespoons nonfat or low-fat buttermilk

Pinch ground cinnamon

For variety, substitute blackberries or pitted sweet cherries for the blueberries.

1. To make the filling, place the blueberries in a large bowl. Set aside.

2. Place the sugar and cornstarch in a small bowl, and stir to mix well. Sprinkle the mixture over the fruit, and toss to mix well. (If the fruit is tart, you may need to add another couple of tablespoons of sugar.) Add the juice concentrate, and toss to mix well.

3. Coat a 2-quart casserole dish with nonstick cooking spray, and spread the fruit mixture evenly in the dish. Cover the dish with aluminum foil, and bake at 375°F for 30 to 40 minutes, or until hot and bubbly.

4. To make the biscuit topping, place the flour, oat bran, ⅓ cup of the sugar, and the baking powder in a medium-sized bowl, and stir to mix well. Add just enough of the buttermilk to make a moderately thick batter, stirring just until the dry ingredients are moistened.

5. Drop heaping tablespoonfuls of the batter onto the hot fruit filling to make 8 biscuits. Combine the remaining 1½ teaspoons of sugar and the cinnamon in a small bowl, and stir to mix well. Sprinkle the mixture over the biscuit topping.

6. Bake uncovered at 375°F for 18 to 20 minutes, or until the biscuits are lightly browned. Allow to cool at room temperature for at least 10 minutes before serving warm.

NUTRITIONAL FACTS (PER SERVING)
Calories: 190 Carbohydrates: 46 g Cholesterol: 0 mg
Fat: 0.7 g Fiber: 3.2 g Protein: 3.1 g Sodium: 120 mg

You Save: Calories: 128 Fat: 12.2 g

Raspberry Apple Turnovers

1. To make the filling, combine the cornstarch and 1 tablespoon of the apple juice, and set aside. Combine the remaining apple juice, apples, raisins, and sugar in a small saucepan. Cover, and cook over medium-low heat for 5 to 7 minutes, stirring occasionally, until the apples are tender. Stir in the raspberries, and cook uncovered for another minute or 2, until the raspberries are soft and begin to break up. Stir in the cornstarch mixture, and cook for another minute or 2, stirring constantly, until the mixture is thickened and bubbly. Remove from the heat and set aside to cool.

2. To make the pastry, combine the flour, oat bran, sugar, and baking powder, and stir to mix well. Use a pastry cutter to cut in the margarine or butter until the mixture resembles coarse crumbs. Stir in just enough of the buttermilk to make a stiff dough that leaves the sides of the bowl and forms a ball.

3. Turn the dough onto a generously floured surface, and divide into 2 pieces. Use a rolling pin to roll each piece into an 8-x-12-inch rectangle. Use a knife or pizza wheel to cut each rectangle into six 4-inch squares.

4. Place a slightly rounded tablespoon of filling in the center of each square. Bring one corner over the filling and match up with the opposite corner to form a triangle. Seal the turnovers by crimping the edges with the tines of a fork. Dip the fork in sugar to prevent sticking if necessary

5. Coat a baking sheet with nonstick cooking spray. Lift the turnovers with a spatula and transfer to the baking sheet. Combine the egg white and water, and brush over the tops of the pastries. Sprinkle ¼ teaspoon of sugar over each turnover.

6. Bake at 375°F for 20 minutes, or until the edges are lightly browned. Transfer to a serving platter, and serve warm.

Yield: *12 turnovers*

FILLING

1 tablespoon cornstarch

3 tablespoons apple juice

1¼ cups finely chopped fresh apples (about 2 medium)

¼ cup golden raisins

2 tablespoons sugar

½ cup fresh or frozen raspberries

PASTRY

1¼ cups unbleached flour

1 cup oat bran

2 tablespoons sugar

½ teaspoon baking powder

4 tablespoons chilled reduced-fat margarine or light butter, cut into pieces

½ cup plus 2 tablespoons nonfat buttermilk

GLAZE

1 tablespoon beaten egg white

1 tablespoon water

1 tablespoon sugar

NUTRITIONAL FACTS (PER TURNOVER)
Calcium: 28 mg Calories: 132 Cholesterol: 0 mg
Fat: 2.7 g Fiber: 2.5 g Iron: 1.2 mg
Potassium: 130 mg Protein: 3.3 g Sodium: 74 mg

HAMANTASCHEN

Yield: *40 pastries*

FILLING

1 cup finely chopped dried apricots, prunes, or other dried
   fruit

1 cup water

2 tablespoons honey

PASTRY

5 tablespoons reduced-fat margarine or light butter

¼ cup plus 2 tablespoons sugar

3 egg whites

1¼ cups whole wheat pastry flour

1¼ cups unbleached flour

1½ teaspoons baking powder

GLAZE

2 tablespoons beaten egg white

1 teaspoon water

Sugar (optional)

These fruit-filled treats are traditionally served on the Jewish holiday Purim.

1. To make the glaze, combine the egg white and water, mixing well. Set aside.

2. To make the filling, combine the apricots, water, and honey in a small saucepan, and bring to a boil over high heat. Reduce the heat to low, cover, and simmer for about 20 minutes, stirring occasionally, until the liquid is absorbed. Remove from the heat and cool to room temperature.

3. Combine the margarine or butter and the sugar in the bowl of an electric mixer, and beat until smooth. Add the egg whites, and beat until smooth. In a separate bowl, combine the flours and baking powder, and stir to mix well. Add the flour mixture to the margarine mixture, and beat until the dough leaves the sides of the bowl and forms a ball.

4. Place ¼ of the dough on a floured surface, leaving the remaining dough covered to prevent it from drying out. Roll the dough out to ¹⁄₁₆-inch thickness, and use a 3-inch glass or cookie cutter to cut rounds out of the dough. (If the dough is too sticky to handle, place it in the freezer for a few minutes.)

5. Brush a small amount of glaze around the outer edges of each circle. Place 1 teaspoon of filling in the center of each round, and fold up 3 sides of each circle about ½ inch to form a tricorn—a 3-sided hat. Note that the filling should not be totally covered by the pastry. Pinch the corners together so that the edges remain up.

6. Coat a baking sheet with nonstick cooking spray, and transfer the pastries to the sheet. Brush some glaze over each pastry, and lightly sprinkle with sugar if desired. Bake at 325°F for about 20 minutes, or until golden brown. Transfer to wire racks, and cool completely before serving.

NUTRITIONAL FACTS (PER PASTRY)
Calories: 53 Calcium: 6 mg Cholesterol: 0 mg
Fat: 0.8 g Fiber: 0.8 g Iron: 0.5 mg
Potassium: 69 mg Protein: 1.4 g Sodium: 35 mg

Apricot Custard Tart

1. To make the filling, pour the milk into a medium-sized bowl. Add the pudding mix, and beat with a wire whisk or electric mixer for 2 minutes, or until the mixture starts to thicken. Immediately pour the pudding into the cooled shell. Chill for at least 10 minutes, or until the pudding starts to set.

2. Drain the apricot halves well, reserving the juice and 1 of the halves. Arrange the remaining apricot halves, cut side down, on top of the pudding.

3. Place ½ cup of the reserved apricot juice, the reserved apricot half, the sugar, and the cornstarch in a blender, and blend until smooth. Pour the mixture into a small saucepan, place over medium heat, and cook, stirring constantly, until the mixture is thickened and bubbly. Allow to cool for 5 minutes. Then stir the mixture and drizzle it over the tart, covering the apricots.

4. Cover and chill for several hours, or until set, before cutting into wedges and serving.

NUTRITIONAL FACTS (PER SERVING)
Calories: 180 Carbohydrates: 40 g Cholesterol: 1 mg
Fat: 1.1 g Fiber: 0.9 g Protein: 3.9 g Sodium: 308 mg

You Save: Calories: 106 Fat: 10 g

Yield: *8 servings*

1 prebaked Life Graham Cracker Pie Crust (page 314) made with plain graham crackers, and pressed over the bottom and 1 inch up the sides of a 9-inch tart or springform pan

FILLING

1¾ cups skim or 1% low-fat milk

1 package (4-serving size) instant fat-free vanilla pudding mix

TOPPING

1 can (1 pound) apricot halves in juice, undrained

2 tablespoons sugar

1 tablespoon cornstarch

STRAWBERRY ANGEL TARTS

Yield: *8 torts*

8 Meringue Tart Shells, plain or almond (page 324)

2 cups nonfat or light whipped topping

3 cups sliced fresh strawberries

½ cup seedless strawberry jam

1. Place one tart shell on each of 8 serving plates. Fill the center of each tart shell with ¼ cup of the whipped topping; then place ¼ cup plus 2 tablespoons of the strawberries over the whipped topping, allowing a few of the berry slices to tumble down the sides.

2. Place the jam in a small pot. Cook over medium heat, stirring constantly, for about 1 minute, or until runny. Drizzle 1 tablespoon of the jam over the fruit, and serve immediately.

NUTRITIONAL FACTS (PER TART)
Calories: 176 Carbohydrates: 42 g Cholesterol: 0 mg
Fat: 0.8 g Fiber: 1.2 g Protein: 1.8 g Sodium: 52 mg

You Save: Calories: 81 Fat: 10 g

Variation

To make Raspberry Angel Tarts, substitute fresh raspberries for the strawberries, and chocolate syrup for the strawberry jam. (Do not heat the chocolate syrup; just drizzle it over the berries straight from the bottle.)

NUTRITIONAL FACTS (PER TART)
Calories: 172 Carbohydrates: 41 g Cholesterol: 0 mg
Fat: 1 g Fiber: 2.2 g Protein: 2.1 g Sodium: 62 mg

You Save: Calories: 81 Fat: 10 g

Lemon-Raspberry Tarts

1. To make the custard, place the sugar, cornstarch, and milk powder in a 1½-quart pot, and stir to mix well. Slowly add the milk, stirring constantly with a wire whisk to mix well. Place the pot over medium heat, and cook, stirring constantly, for about 5 minutes, or until the mixture is thickened and bubbly.

2. Reduce the heat to medium-low. Place the egg substitute in a small bowl. Remove ¼ cup of the hot milk mixture from the pot, and stir it into the egg substitute. Slowly whisk the egg mixture back into the pudding.

3. Add the lemon rind to the custard mixture, and cook and stir for a couple of minutes, or until the mixture thickens slightly and begins to boil. Remove the pot from the heat, and whisk in the lemon juice. Transfer the custard to a covered container, and chill for at least 4 hours, or until well-chilled and set.

4. When ready to assemble the tarts, place one tart shell on each of 6 serving plates. Stir the custard with a wire whisk until smooth. Then fill the center of each tart shell with ⅓ cup of the custard. Place ⅓ cup of the berries over the pudding.

5. Place the jam in a small pot. Cook over medium heat, stirring constantly, for about 1 minute, or until runny. Drizzle 2 teaspoons of the jam over the berries on each tart, and serve immediately.

Yield: *6 tarts*

6 Flaky Phyllo Tart Shells (page 326)

2 cups fresh raspberries

¼ cup seedless raspberry jam

LEMON CUSTARD

½ cup plus 2 tablespoons sugar

¼ cup cornstarch

3 tablespoons instant nonfat dry milk powder

1½ cups skim or 1% low-fat milk

¼ cup fat-free egg substitute

1½ teaspoons freshly grated lemon rind, or ½ teaspoon dried

¼ cup plus 3 tablespoons lemon juice

NUTRITIONAL FACTS (PER TART)
Calories: 248 Carbohydrates: 54 g Cholesterol: 1 mg
Fat: 1.3 g Fiber: 2.1 g Protein: 5.4 g Sodium: 136 mg

You Save: Calories: 153 Fat: 16.8 g

Mini Cherry Strudels

Yield: *24 pastries*

CRUSTS

12 sheets (about 14 x 18 inches) phyllo pastry (about 10 ounces)

Butter-flavored cooking spray

2 tablespoons powdered sugar (optional)

FILLING

¼ cup plus 2 tablespoons sugar

2 tablespoons plus 1½ teaspoons cornstarch

2 tablespoons white grape juice or orange juice

1 bag (1 pound) frozen pitted cherries, unthawed

GLAZE

1 tablespoon plus 1 teaspoon fat-free egg substitute

1 tablespoon plus 1 teaspoon sugar

1. To make the filling, place the sugar and cornstarch in a 1½-quart pot, and stir to mix well. Stir in first the juice, and then the cherries. Place the pot over medium heat, and cook, stirring constantly, for about 5 minutes, or until the cherries are thawed and the mixture is thickened and bubbly. Remove the pot from the heat, and set aside to cool to room temperature.

2. To make the glaze, place the egg substitute and sugar in a small bowl. Stir to mix well, and set aside.

3. Spread the phyllo dough out on a clean, dry surface, with the short end facing you. Cut the phyllo lengthwise down the center to make 2 stacks, each measuring about 18 x 7 inches. Lay one stack on top of the other to make one 18-x-7-inch stack of 24 phyllo sheets. Cover the dough with plastic wrap to prevent it from drying out as you work. (Remove strips as you need them, being sure to recover the remaining dough.)

4. Remove 1 strip of the phyllo dough, and lay it flat on a clean dry surface. Spray the strip lightly with cooking spray. Fold the bottom up to form a double layer of phyllo measuring approximately 9 x 7 inches.

5. Spread 1 level tablespoon of filling over the bottom of the phyllo sheet, leaving a 2-inch margin on each side. Fold the left and right edges inward to enclose the filling. Then roll the pastry up from the bottom, jelly-roll style. Repeat steps 4 and 5 with the remaining filling and phyllo sheets to make 24 strudels. (At this point, the strudels may be frozen for future use. See the Time-Saving Tip on page 382.)

6. Coat a large baking sheet with nonstick cooking spray, and arrange the strudels on the sheets. Brush the top of each strudel with some of the glaze.

7. Bake at 375°F for 12 to 15 minutes, or until golden brown. Allow to cool for at least 15 minutes before serving warm. Sift the powdered sugar over the strudels just before serving, if desired.

NUTRITIONAL FACTS (PER PASTRY)
Calories: 65 Carbohydrates: 13 g Cholesterol: 0 mg
Fat: 0.9 g Fiber: 0.5 g Protein: 1.1 g Sodium: 59 mg

You Save: Calories: 31 Fat: 4.6 g

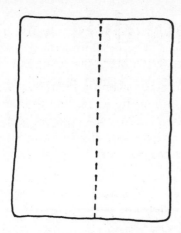

a. Cut the phyllo sheets into 2 long strips.

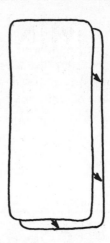

b. Lay 1 stack of strips on top of the other.

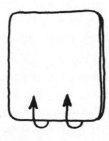

c. Fold the bottom of each strip up to double the strip.

d. Spread the filling over the bottom of each strip. Fold the left and right edges inward.

Making Mini Cherry Strudels.

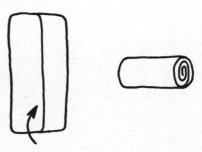

e. Roll the pastry up jelly-roll style.

Time-Saving Tip

To save time on the day you bake Mini Cherry Strudels (page 380) or Apricot-Apple Turnovers (page 384), prepare the pastries ahead of time to the point of baking, and arrange them in single layers in airtight containers, separating the layers with sheets of waxed paper. Then place the pastries in the freezer until needed. When ready to bake, arrange the frozen pastries on a coated sheet and allow them to sit at room temperature for 45 minutes before baking.

GREEK CUSTARD TARTS

Yield: *6 tarts*

6 Flaky Phyllo Tart Shells
   (page 326)

CUSTARD

2¼ cups skim or 1% low-fat milk

⅓ cup quick-cooking Cream of
   Wheat cereal or farina

⅓ cup sugar

½ cup fat-free egg substitute

3 tablespoons finely chopped
   dried apricots

½ teaspoon vanilla extract

⅛ teaspoon ground nutmeg

SYRUP

3 tablespoons orange juice

¾ teaspoon cornstarch

3 tablespoons honey

1. To make the filling, place the milk in a 2-quart pot. Place the pot over medium heat, and cook, stirring constantly, until the milk begins to boil. Whisk in the cereal and the sugar, reduce the heat to medium-low, and cook, still stirring, for 3 to 4 additional minutes, or until the mixture thickens slightly.

2. Place the egg substitute in a small bowl. Remove ½ cup of the hot milk mixture from the pot, and stir it into the egg substitute. Slowly whisk the egg mixture back into the pot. Cook and stir for a couple of minutes, or until the mixture thickens slightly and begins to boil.

3. Remove the pot from the heat, and stir in the apricots, vanilla extract, and nutmeg. Allow the custard to cool at room temperature for 15 minutes.

4. To make the syrup, place the orange juice and cornstarch in a small pot, and stir to dissolve the cornstarch. Add the honey, and stir to mix well. Place over medium heat, and cook, stirring constantly, until the mixture thickens slightly and begins to boil. Remove the pot from the heat, and set aside.

5. To assemble the tarts, stir the custard, and place ½ cup of the warm mixture in each crust. Drizzle 1 tablespoon of the hot syrup over the custard and the edges of the pastry, and serve immediately.

NUTRITIONAL FACTS (PER TART)
Calories: 223 Carbohydrates: 46 g Cholesterol: 2 mg
Fat: 1.2 g Fiber: 1.5 g Protein: 7.4 g Sodium: 156 mg

You Save: Calories: 179 Fat: 16.8 g

GINGER BAKED PEACHES

This dessert is equally delicious when made with pears.

Yield: *6 servings*

1. To make the filling, place the wheat germ, brown sugar, flour, ginger, and cinnamon in a small bowl, and stir to mix well. Add the juice concentrate, and stir just until the mixture is moist and crumbly. (If the mixture seems too dry, add more juice concentrate, ¼ teaspoon at a time, until the proper consistency is reached.) Stir in the pecans if desired. Set aside.

2. Peel the peaches. Then cut each in half lengthwise, and remove the pit. Cut a thin slice off the bottom of each peach half so that it will sit upright. Place a rounded tablespoon of the filling in the cavity of each peach half, mounding it up.

3. Pour the orange juice into the bottom of a 9-inch square pan, and arrange the peaches in the pan. Bake uncovered at 375°F for 25 to 30 minutes, or until the peaches are tender and the filling is golden brown. Cover the peaches loosely with aluminum foil during the last few minutes of baking if the filling starts to brown too quickly. Serve warm, accompanying each serving with a scoop of low-fat vanilla ice cream, if desired.

3 large fresh peaches (about 8 ounces each)

⅓ cup orange juice

3 cups nonfat or low-fat vanilla ice cream (optional)

FILLING

¼ cup plus 1 tablespoon honey crunch wheat germ

¼ cup plus 1 tablespoon light brown sugar

¼ cup whole wheat pastry flour

¼ teaspoon ground ginger

¼ teaspoon ground cinnamon

1 tablespoon plus 1 teaspoon frozen orange juice concentrate, thawed

2 tablespoons chopped toasted pecans (below) (optional)

NUTRITIONAL FACTS (PER SERVING)

Calories: 116 Carbohydrates: 27 g Cholesterol: 0 mg
Fat: 0.7 g Fiber: 2.7 g Protein: 2.8 g Sodium: 3 mg

You Save: Calories: 91 Fat: 12.4 g

Getting the Most Out of Nuts

Nuts add crunch, great taste, and essential nutrients to all kinds of baked goods. Unfortunately, nuts also add fat. But you can greatly reduce the fat—without sacrificing flavor—by toasting nuts before adding them to your recipe. Toasting intensifies the flavor of nuts so much that you can often cut the amount used in half.

Simply arrange the nuts in a single layer on a baking sheet, and bake at 350°F for about 10 minutes, or until lightly browned with a toasted, nutty smell. Be sure to check the nuts often, as once they begin to turn color, they can quickly burn. (For sliced almonds or chopped nuts, bake for only 6 to 8 minutes.) To save time, toast a large batch and store leftovers in an airtight container in the refrigerator for several weeks, or keep them in the freezer for several months.

Apricot-Apple Turnovers

Yield: *20 pastries*

CRUSTS

10 sheets (about 14 x 18 inches)
   phyllo pastry (about 8 ounces)

Butter-flavored cooking spray

2 tablespoons powdered sugar
   (optional)

FILLING

3 cups chopped peeled apples
   (about 4 medium)

½ cup apricot preserves

2 tablespoons water, divided

1 tablespoon cornstarch

GLAZE

1 tablespoon plus 1 teaspoon fat-
   free egg substitute

1 tablespoon plus 1 teaspoon
   sugar

1. To make the filling, place the apples, apricot preserves, and 1 tablespoon of the water in a 2-quart pot. Stir to mix well, cover, and cook over medium-low heat, stirring occasionally, for about 5 minutes, or until the apples are tender.

2. Place the cornstarch and remaining tablespoon of water in a small bowl, and stir to dissolve the cornstarch. Add the cornstarch mixture to the simmering apple mixture, and cook, stirring constantly, for about 1 minute, or until the mixture is thick and bubbly. Remove the pot from the heat, and set aside to cool to room temperature.

3. To make the glaze, place the egg substitute and sugar in a small bowl. Stir to mix well, and set aside.

4. Spread the phyllo dough out on a clean, dry surface, with the short end facing you. Cut the phyllo lengthwise into 4 long strips, each measuring about 3½ x 18 inches. Cover the dough with plastic wrap to prevent it from drying out as you work. (Remove strips as you need them, being sure to re-cover the remaining dough.)

5. Remove 2 strips of phyllo dough and stack 1 on top of the other. Spray the top strip lightly with the cooking spray. Spread 1 level tablespoon of the filling over the bottom right-hand corner of the double phyllo strip. Fold the filled corner up and over to the left, so that the corner meets the left side of the strip. Continue folding in this manner until you form a triangle of dough. Repeat with the remaining filling and dough to make 20 pastries. (At this point, the turnovers may be frozen for future use. See the Time-Saving Tip on page 382.)

6. Coat a large baking sheet with nonstick cooking spray, and arrange the pastries seam side down on the sheet. Brush the top of each pastry with some of the glaze.

7. Bake at 375°F for 12 to 15 minutes, or until golden brown. Allow to cool for at least 15 minutes before serving warm. Sift the powdered sugar over the strudels just before serving, if desired.

NUTRITIONAL FACTS (PER PASTRY)
Calories: 59 Carbohydrates: 12.3 g Cholesterol: 0 mg
Fat: 0.8 g Fiber: 0.4 g Protein: 0.8 g Sodium: 50 mg

You Save: Calories: 36 Fat: 4.8 g

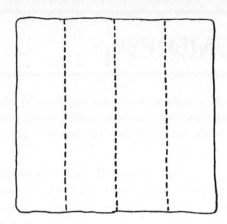

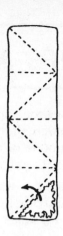

a. Cut the phyllo sheets into 4 strips.   **b. Fold the filled corner up and over.**   **c. Continue folding to form a triangle**

Making Apricot-Apple Turnovers.

Blueberries and Dumplings

Yield: *6 servings*

¼ cup plus 2 tablespoons sugar

1 tablespoon plus 1½ teaspoons cornstarch

¼ cup orange or white grape juice

½ cup water

4 cups fresh or frozen (unthawed) blueberries, pitted sweet cherries, or blackberries

DUMPLINGS

¾ cup unbleached flour

¼ cup sugar

1 teaspoon baking powder

2 tablespoons chilled reduced-fat margarine or light butter, cut into pieces

2 tablespoons fat-free egg substitute

2 tablespoons nonfat or low-fat buttermilk or plain nonfat yogurt

1. Place the sugar and cornstarch in a large nonstick skillet, and stir to mix well. (If the fruit is tart, you may need to add another couple of tablespoons of sugar.) Add the juice, and stir to dissolve the cornstarch. Stir in first the water, and then the fruit.

2. Place the skillet over medium heat, and cook, stirring constantly, for about 5 minutes, or until the mixture is thickened and bubbly. Remove the skillet from the heat while you prepare the dumplings.

3. To make the dumplings, place the flour, sugar, and baking powder in a small bowl, and stir to mix well. Using a pastry cutter or 2 knives, cut in the margarine or butter until the mixture is the consistency of coarse meal. Add the egg substitute and just enough of the buttermilk or yogurt to form a thick batter, stirring just until the dry ingredients are moistened.

4. Return the fruit mixture to the heat, and bring to a boil over medium-high heat. Then reduce the heat to medium-low. Drop heaping teaspoonfuls of the batter onto the simmering fruit to make 12 dumplings. Cover the skillet, and simmer without stirring for about 10 minutes, or until the dumplings are firm to the touch. (Adjust the heat if necessary to maintain a gentle simmer.) Remove the skillet from the heat, and allow to sit uncovered for 5 minutes before serving warm.

NUTRITIONAL FACTS (PER SERVING)
Calories: 222 Carbohydrates: 48 g Cholesterol: 0 mg
Fat: 2.2 g Fiber: 2.9 g Protein: 2.9 g Sodium: 126 mg

You Save: Calories: 101 Fat: 10.8 g

Variation

To make Peaches and Dumplings, substitute diced peeled fresh or frozen peaches for the blueberries. Add ¼ teaspoon each cinnamon and nutmeg along with the cornstarch, and increase the water to ¾ cup.

9

Creamy Puddings, Mousses, Trifles, and Frozen Desserts

Rich, creamy, and inviting, puddings are among the most popular of comfort foods. Puddings are versatile, too. Hearty noodle puddings and baked custards make healthful snacks, or can provide a sweet conclusion to a home-style family dinner. Elegant mousses and trifles fill the bill when you want a dessert for that special-occasion dinner.

Unfortunately, most puddings and mousses are loaded with an unhealthy amount of fat. In traditional recipes, whole milk, cream, and egg yolks top the list of ingredients. Consider, for instance, a traditionally prepared dish of chocolate mousse. Believe it or not, just one moderate serving can contain up to 25 grams of fat!

The good news is that puddings are among the easiest of desserts to prepare with little or no fat. But can you skim the fat without sacrificing flavor? Absolutely! Fat-saving products like evaporated skimmed milk, nonfat sour cream, and nonfat whipped toppings add creamy richness with no fat, and with a lot less calories than their traditional counterparts. More fat and calories are saved by using fat-free egg substitutes instead of whole eggs to thicken puddings and custards.

Cool and refreshing, frozen desserts are everyone's favorite treat on a sizzling summer day. But don't limit these icy confections to the summer months. Elegant and surprisingly simple to make, frozen desserts are perfect for year-round entertaining. And since they must be prepared in advance, these toothsome temptations are a real boon to the busy cook.

Besides being ultra-low in fat, many of the desserts found in the following pages contain only moderate amounts of sugar. Fruits and juices, as well as sweet flavorings like cinnamon, add natural sweetness to many of these recipes, reducing the need for added sugar.

This chapter offers a pleasing assortment of deceptively rich-tasting desserts, ranging from down-home Sour Cream and Apple Bread Pudding to elegant Chocolate-Hazelnut Mousse. But the proof is in the pudding. So whip up a creamy dish of comfort, and enjoy a treat that is so sweetly satisfying, even you will find it hard to believe that it's also guilt-free!

Whole Wheat Bread Pudding

Yield: *6 servings*

5 slices stale whole wheat bread

⅓ cup dark raisins

½ cup sugar

½ teaspoon ground cinnamon

2 cups skim milk

¼ cup plus 2 tablespoons fat-free
    egg substitute

1½ teaspoons vanilla extract

1. Cut the bread into ½-inch cubes, and measure the cubes. There should be 5 cups. (Adjust the amount if necessary.)

2. Place the bread cubes in a medium-sized bowl. Add the raisins, and toss to mix. Set aside.

3. Place the sugar and cinnamon in a medium-sized bowl, and stir to mix well. Add the milk, egg substitute, and vanilla extract, and stir to mix well.

4. Pour the milk mixture over the bread cube mixture, and stir gently to mix. Let the mixture sit at room temperature for 10 minutes.

5. Coat a 1½-quart casserole dish with nonstick cooking spray, and pour the bread mixture into the dish. Bake at 350°F for 1 hour, or until a sharp knife inserted in the center of the pudding comes out clean. Let sit for at least 20 minutes before serving. Serve warm or at room temperature, and refrigerate any leftovers.

NUTRITIONAL FACTS (PER ¾-CUP SERVING)
Calories: 178 Cholesterol: 1 mg Fat: 0.9 g
Fiber: 2.8 g Protein: 8 g Sodium: 172 mg

Spiced Cornmeal Pudding

1. Combine the cornmeal, sugar, cinnamon, and ginger in a 2½-quart pot, and stir to mix well. Slowly stir in the milk and the evaporated milk.

2. Place the pot over medium heat, and cook, stirring constantly, for 10 to 12 minutes, or until the mixture comes to a boil. Reduce the heat to low, and continue to cook and stir for 2 minutes, or until slightly thickened. Slowly stir in the molasses.

3. Place the egg substitute in a small bowl. Remove 1 cup of the hot cornmeal mixture from the pot, and stir it into the egg substitute. Slowly stir the egg mixture into the pudding. Cook and stir for 2 minutes, or until slightly thickened. Remove the pot from the heat, and stir in the vanilla extract and raisins.

4. Coat a 1½-quart round casserole dish with nonstick cooking spray. Pour the pudding mixture into the dish, and place the dish in a pan filled with 1 inch of hot water.

5. Bake uncovered at 350°F for 1 hour and 20 minutes, or until set. When done, a sharp knife inserted midway between the center of the pudding and the rim of the dish should come out clean. Remove the pudding from the oven, and let sit for 30 minutes. Serve warm, or refrigerate for several hours and serve chilled.

Yield: 8 servings

¼ cup plus 3 tablespoons whole grain cornmeal

2 tablespoons sugar

½ teaspoon ground cinnamon

½ teaspoon ground ginger

2½ cups skim milk

1 cup evaporated skim milk

⅓ cup molasses

1 cup fat-free egg substitute

1½ teaspoons vanilla extract

⅓ cup dark raisins

NUTRITIONAL FACTS (PER ⅔-CUP SERVING)
Calories: 157 Cholesterol: 2 mg Fat: 0.4 g
Fiber: 0.7 g Protein: 8.7 g Sodium: 136 mg

FAT-FREE COOKING TIP

Creamy Richness without the Cream

To make creamy custards, puddings, and other desserts without the cream, simply replace this high-fat ingredient with an equal amount of evaporated skim milk. Or substitute 1 cup of skim milk plus ⅓ cup of instant nonfat dry milk powder for each cup of cream. Either way, you will save 620 calories and 88 grams of fat for each cup of cream you replace.

CREAMY PINEAPPLE CUSTARD

Yield: *7 servings*

3 cups skim milk

½ cup instant nonfat dry milk powder

1 cup fat-free egg substitute

½ cup sugar

1 teaspoon vanilla extract

1 can (8 ounces) crushed pineapple in juice, undrained

¼ teaspoon ground nutmeg

1. Place the milk, milk powder, egg substitute, sugar, and vanilla extract in a blender, and blend for 30 seconds to mix well. Stir in the pineapple, including the juice.

2. Coat a 1½-quart baking dish with nonstick cooking spray. Pour the custard mixture into the dish, and sprinkle the top with nutmeg. Place the dish in a pan filled with 1 inch of hot water.

3. Bake uncovered at 350°F for 1 hour and 15 minutes, or until set. When done, a sharp knife inserted midway between the center of the custard and the rim of the dish should come out clean.

4. Remove the dish from the oven, and let cool at room temperature for 1 hour. Cover the dish, and chill for several hours or overnight before serving.

NUTRITIONAL FACTS (PER ¾-CUP SERVING)
Calories: 146 Cholesterol: 3 mg Fat: 0.2 g
Fiber: 0.2 g Protein: 9 g Sodium: 138 mg

Razzleberry Trifle

1. Combine the strawberries, raspberries, and sugar in a medium-sized bowl, and stir to mix well. Set the mixture aside for 20 minutes to let the juices develop.

2. Prepare the pudding with the skim milk according to package directions. Set aside. (If you're using regular pudding, let it chill for 1 to 2 hours before proceeding with the recipe.)

3. Spread one side of each cake slice with a thin layer of the jam. Arrange half of the slices over the bottom of a 3-quart trifle bowl or other decorative glass bowl. Top first with half of the fruit, and then with half of the pudding. Repeat the layers.

4. To make the topping, place the whipped topping in a small bowl, and fold the yogurt into the topping. Swirl the mixture over the top of the trifle, cover, and chili for at least 2 hours before serving.

Yield: 10 servings

2½ cups sliced fresh strawberries

1 cup fresh or frozen (thawed) raspberries

2 tablespoons sugar

1 package regular or instant vanilla pudding mix (6-serving size)

3 cups skim milk

10 slices (½-inch each) fat-free loaf cake

¼ cup low-sugar raspberry jam

TOPPING

¾ cup light whipped topping

¾ cup nonfat vanilla yogurt

NUTRITIONAL FACTS (PER 1-CUP SERVING)

Calories: 191 Cholesterol: 1 mg Fat: 1 g
Fiber: 1.5 g Protein: 5.4 g Sodium: 221 mg

West Indian Bread Pudding

Yield: 9 servings

5 cups French bread cubes (about 6 ounces)

⅓ cup golden raisins

1 cup mashed very ripe banana (about 2 large)

¼ cup plus 2 tablespoons honey

1¼ cups skim milk

1 cup fat-free egg substitute

¼ teaspoon ground nutmeg

1 teaspoon vanilla extract

1. Combine the bread cubes and raisins. In a separate bowl, combine the remaining ingredients, and pour over the bread cubes. Stir gently to mix, and let the mixture sit for 10 minutes.

2. Coat a 1½-quart casserole dish with nonstick cooking spray. Spread the bread mixture evenly in the dish, and bake at 350°F for 50 to 60 minutes, or until a sharp knife inserted in the center comes out clean.

3. Let stand for 10 minutes. Serve warm, and refrigerate any leftovers.

NUTRITIONAL FACTS (PER SERVING)
Calories: 182 Calcium: 72 mg Cholesterol: 0 mg
Fat: 0.8 g Fiber: 1.2 g Iron: 1.5 mg
Potassium: 275 mg Protein: 6.3 g Sodium: 185 mg

Sour Cream and Apple Bread Pudding

For variety, substitute diced peaches for the apples.

1. Place the bread cubes in a large bowl and set aside.

2. Place the milk, sour cream, egg substitute, sugar, and vanilla extract in a large bowl, and whisk until smooth. Pour the milk mixture over the bread cubes, and set aside for 10 minutes.

3. Stir the apples and raisins into the bread mixture. Coat a 2-quart casserole dish with nonstick cooking spray, and pour the mixture into the dish.

4. To make the topping, place the sugar and cinnamon in a small bowl, and stir to mix well. Sprinkle the topping over the pudding.

5. Bake at 350°F for about 1 hour, or until a sharp knife inserted in the center of the dish comes out clean. Allow to cool at room temperature for 45 minutes before serving. Serve warm or at room temperature, refrigerating any leftovers.

NUTRITIONAL FACTS (PER ¾-CUP SERVING)
Calories: 161 Carbohydrates: 32 g Cholesterol: 1 mg
Fat: 0.9 g Fiber: 1.8 g Protein: 6.7 g Sodium: 180 mg

You Save: Calories: 69 Fat: 10 g

Yield: *8 servings*

5 cups ½-inch cubes firm multi-grain or French bread (about 6 ounces)

1¾ cups skim or 1% low-fat milk

½ cup nonfat sour cream

½ cup plus 2 tablespoons fat-free egg substitute

¼ cup plus 2 tablespoons sugar

1½ teaspoons vanilla extract

¾ cup diced peeled apples (about 1 medium)

¼ cup golden or dark raisins

TOPPING

1 tablespoon plus 1½ teaspoons sugar

⅛ teaspoon ground cinnamon

Rum-Raisin Bread Pudding

Yield: *6 servings*

¼ cup dark raisins

2 tablespoons light rum

4 cups ½-inch cubes firm multi-grain or oatmeal bread (about 5 ounces)

1 can (12 ounces) evaporated skimmed milk

½ cup skim or 1% low-fat milk

¼ cup plus 2 tablespoons fat-free egg substitute

¼ cup plus 2 tablespoons light brown sugar

1 teaspoon vanilla extract

1 tablespoon sugar

1. Place the raisins and rum in a small bowl, and stir to mix well. Set aside for at least 15 minutes.

2. Place the bread cubes in a large bowl and set aside.

3. Place the evaporated milk, skim milk, egg substitute, brown sugar, and vanilla extract in a large bowl, and whisk until smooth. Pour the milk mixture over the bread cubes, and set aside for 10 minutes.

4. Stir the raisin mixture into the bread mixture. Coat a 1½-quart casserole dish with nonstick cooking spray, and pour the mixture into the dish. Sprinkle the sugar over the pudding.

5. Bake at 350°F for about 1 hour, or until a sharp knife inserted in the center of the dish comes out clean. Allow to cool at room temperature for 45 minutes before serving. Serve warm or at room temperature, refrigerating any leftovers.

NUTRITIONAL FACTS (PER ¾-CUP SERVING)
Calories: 184 Carbohydrates: 33 g Cholesterol: 2 mg
Fat: 0.4 g Fiber: 1.1 g Protein: 8.4 g Sodium: 227 mg

You Save: Calories: 65 Fat: 10.6 g

CREAMY TAPIOCA PUDDING

1. Place the milk, milk powder, tapioca, and sugar in a 2-quart pot, and stir to mix well. Place the pot over medium heat, and cook, stirring frequently, until the mixture comes to a boil. Reduce the heat to low, and simmer, stirring frequently, for 5 minutes, or until the tapioca begins to swell and becomes translucent.

2. Place the egg substitute in a small bowl, and stir in ½ cup of the hot tapioca mixture. Slowly stir the mixture back into the pot. Cook and stir over low heat for another couple of minutes, or until the mixture begins to boil and thickens slightly.

3. Remove the pot from the heat, and stir in the vanilla extract. Allow the pudding to cool at room temperature for 15 minutes.

4. Divide the pudding among five 8-ounce serving dishes, cover, and chill for several hours, or until thick and creamy. (The mixture will thicken as it cools.) Serve chilled.

Yield: *5 servings*

3 cups skim or 1% low-fat milk

⅓ cup instant nonfat dry milk powder

¼ cup plus 2 tablespoons small pearl tapioca

¼ cup plus 2 tablespoons sugar

⅓ cup fat-free egg substitute

1 teaspoon vanilla extract

NUTRITIONAL FACTS (PER ⅔-CUP SERVING)
Calories: 176 Carbohydrates: 44 g Cholesterol: 3 mg
Fat: 0.3 g Fiber: 0.1 g Protein: 11.3 g Sodium: 175 mg

You Save: Calories: 55 Fat: 7.5 g

Variation

To make Tapioca Pudding Parfaits, prepare the pudding as directed through Step 3. Then pour the warm pudding into a medium-sized bowl, cover, and chill for several hours or until thick and creamy. To assemble the parfaits, place 2 tablespoons of light cherry, blueberry, chopped apple, or chopped peach pie filling in the bottom of each of six 8-ounce parfait or wine glasses. Top the pie filling with ¼ cup of the pudding; then repeat the layers. Cover each parfait with plastic wrap, and chill for at least 2 hours before serving.

NUTRITIONAL FACTS (PER ¾-CUP SERVING)
Calories: 199 Carbohydrates: 42 g Cholesterol: 3 mg
Fat: 0.7 g Fiber: 0.5 g Protein: 8 g Sodium: 123 mg

Your Save: Calories: 67 Fat: 6 g

Pineapple Tapicoa Pudding

Yield: *5 servings*

2½ cups skim or 1% low-fat milk

⅓ cup instant nonfat dry milk powder

¼ cup plus 2 tablespoons small pearl tapioca

¼ cup plus 2 tablespoons sugar

½ cup plus 2 tablespoons fat-free egg substitute

1 can (8 ounces) crushed pineapple in juice, undrained

1 teaspoon vanilla extract

1. Place the milk, milk powder, tapioca, and sugar in a 2-quart pot, and stir to mix well. Place the pot over medium heat, and cook, stirring frequently, until the mixture comes to a boil. Reduce the heat to low, and simmer, stirring frequently, for 5 minutes, or until the tapioca begins to swell and becomes translucent.

2. Place the egg substitute in a small bowl, and stir in ½ cup plus 2 tablespoons of the hot tapioca mixture. Slowly stir the mixture back into the pot. Cook and stir over low heat for another couple of minutes, or until the mixture begins to boil and thickens slightly.

3. Remove the pot from the heat, and stir in the pineapple with its juice and the vanilla extract. Allow the pudding to cool at room temperature for 15 minutes.

4. Divide the pudding among five 8-ounce serving dishes, cover, and chill for several hours, or until thick and creamy. (The mixture will thicken as it cools.) Serve chilled.

NUTRITIONAL FACTS (PER ¾-CUP SERVING)
Calories: 197 Carbohydrates: 41 g Cholesterol: 3 mg
Fat: 0.3 g Fiber: 0.4 g Protein: 9 g Sodium: 138 mg

You Save: Calories: 63 Fat: 6.9 g

Variation

To make Ambrosia Tapioca Pudding, prepare the pudding as directed through Step 3. Then pour the warm pudding into a medium-sized bowl, cover, and chill for several hours or until thick and creamy. Add 1 can (10 ounces) well-drained mandarin oranges, 1 cup miniature marshmallows, and ¼ cup shredded sweetened coconut, and stir to mix well. Cover and chill for at least 2 hours. Divide the pudding among seven 8-ounce dessert dishes, and serve immediately.

NUTRITIONAL FACTS (PER ¾-CUP SERVING)
Calories: 192 Carbohydrates: 39 g Cholesterol: 2 mg
Fat: 1.4 g Fiber: 0.6 g Protein: 6.8 g Sodium: 112 mg

You Save: Calories: 51 Fat: 6.6 g

Cherry Chiffon Pudding

1. Place the pie filling, pineapple, and yogurt or yogurt cheese in a large bowl, and stir to mix well. Fold in the marshmallows and, if desired, the pecans. Gently fold in the whipped topping.

2. Divide the pudding among four 8-ounce wine glasses or dessert dishes. Cover the puddings, and chill for at least 2 hours before serving.

NUTRITIONAL FACTS (PER ¾-CUP SERVING)
Calories: 192 Carbohydrates: 43 g Cholesterol: 1 mg
Fat: 0.9 g Fiber: 0.8 g Protein: 3.1 g Sodium: 52 mg

You Save: Calories: 149 Fat: 15.3 g

Yield: *4 servings*

1 cup canned light (reduced-sugar) cherry pie filling

1 can (8 ounces) crushed pineapple in juice, well drained

¾ cup regular or sugar-free nonfat or low-fat vanilla yogurt, or ¾ cup yogurt cheese made from nonfat or low-fat vanilla yogurt (page 293)*

½ cup miniature marshmallows

¼ cup chopped toasted pecans (page 383) (optional)

1 cup nonfat or light whipped topping

*Using yogurt cheese instead of yogurt will result in a thicker, creamier pudding.

STRAWBERRIES 'N' CREAM

Yield: *6 servings*

1 package (10 ounces) frozen sweetened sliced strawberries, undrained

½ cup boiling water

1 package (4-serving size) regular or sugar-free strawberry gelatin

½ cup nonfat sour cream

2 cups nonfat or light whipped topping

For variety, substitute raspberry gelatin and frozen raspberries for the strawberry gelatin and frozen strawberries.

1. Drain the strawberries, reserving the juice. Set both the strawberries and the juice aside.

2. Pour the boiling water into a blender, and sprinkle the gelatin over the top. Cover with the lid, and carefully blend at low speed for about 30 seconds, or until the gelatin is completely dissolved. Allow the mixture to sit in the blender for about 20 minutes, or until it reaches room temperature.

3. When the gelatin mixture has cooled to room temperature, add the sour cream and the reserved juice from the strawberries, and blend for about 30 seconds, or until well mixed. Pour the mixture into a large bowl, and chill for 15 minutes. Stir the mixture; it should be the consistency of pudding. If it is too thin, return it to the refrigerator for a few minutes.

4. When the gelatin mixture has reached the proper consistency, stir it with a wire whisk until smooth. Gently fold in first the strawberries, and then the whipped topping.

5. Divide the mixture among six 8-ounce wine glasses, cover, and chill for at least 3 hours, or until set, before serving.

NUTRITIONAL FACTS (PER ¾-CUP SERVING)
Calories: 159 Carbohydrates: 36 g Cholesterol: 0 mg
Fat: 0.9 g Fiber: 0.9 g Protein: 2.5 g Sodium: 67 mg

You Save: Calories: 117 Fat: 17.9 g

PEACH BAVARIAN

For variety, substitute canned apricots and apricot gelatin for the canned peaches and peach gelatin.

1. Drain the peaches, reserving the juice. Dice the peaches and set aside.

2. Place ¾ cup of the reserved juice in a small pot. (If there is not enough juice, add water to bring the volume to ¾ cup.) Bring the mixture to a boil over high heat.

3. Pour the boiling juice into a large bowl. Sprinkle the gelatin over the top, and stir for about 3 minutes, or until the gelatin is completely dissolved. Set the mixture aside for about 20 minutes, or until it reaches room temperature.

4. When the gelatin mixture has cooled to room temperature, whisk in the yogurt. Chill for 15 minutes. Stir the mixture; it should be the consistency of pudding. If it is too thin, return it to the refrigerator for a few minutes.

5. When the gelatin mixture has reached the proper consistency, stir it with a wire whisk until smooth. Gently fold in first the diced peaches, and then the whipped topping.

6. Divide the mixture among six 8-ounce wine glasses, cover, and chill for at least 3 hours, or until set, before serving.

Yield: *6 servings*

1 can (1 pound) sliced peaches in juice, undrained

1 package (4-serving size) peach gelatin mix

1 cup regular or sugar-free non-fat peach yogurt

2 cups nonfat or light whipped topping

NUTRITIONAL FACTS (PER ¾-CUP SERVING)
Calories: 161 Carbohydrates: 36.7 g Cholesterol: 0 mg
Fat: 0.9 g Fiber: 1.3 g Protein: 3.3 g Sodium: 77 mg

You Save: Calories: 160 Fat: 21.8 g

Banana Pudding Parfaits

Yield: *4 servings*

2 cups skim or 1% low-fat milk

1 package (4-serving size) fat-free cook-and-serve or instant vanilla pudding mix, regular or sugar-free

1¼ cups sliced bananas (about 1¼ large)

16 reduced-fat vanilla wafers

½ cup nonfat or light whipped topping (optional)

For variety, substitute chocolate pudding and chocolate wafers for the vanilla pudding and vanilla wafers.

1. Use the skim milk to prepare the pudding according to package directions. Cover the mixture and chill for at least 2 hours for cook-and-serve pudding or 30 minutes for instant pudding, or until chilled and thickened.

2. To assemble the parfaits, spoon 1 tablespoon of pudding into the bottom of each of four 8-ounce wine or parfait glasses. Top the pudding with 2½ tablespoons of sliced bananas, 2 crumbled vanilla wafers, and a scant ¼ cup of pudding. Repeat the banana, wafer, and pudding layers.

3. Serve immediately, topping each serving with a rounded tablespoon of whipped topping, if desired. Or cover each glass with plastic wrap and chill for up to 2 hours before serving.

NUTRITIONAL FACTS (PER 1-CUP SERVING)
Calories: 237 Carbohydrates: 51 g Cholesterol: 2 mg
Fat: 2.1 g Fiber: 1.1 g Protein: 5.6 g Sodium: 229 mg

You Save: Calories: 46 Fat: 6 g

Tiramisu Treats

Creamy pudding replaces high-fat mascarpone cheese in this slimmed-down recipe.

1. To make the berry mixture, place the berries and sugar in a small bowl, and mash with a fork. Set aside.

2. To make the liqueur mixture, place the liqueur and cocoa in a small bowl, and stir to mix. Set aside.

3. To make the pudding mixture, use the skim or low-fat milk to prepare the pudding according to package directions. Cover and chill for at least 2 hours for cook-and-serve pudding or for at least 30 minutes for instant pudding, or until chilled and thickened.

4. To assemble the desserts, place 1 tablespoon of the berry mixture in the bottom of each of four 8-ounce parfait or wine glasses Crumble one ladyfinger over the berries in each glass. Drizzle 1½ teaspoons of liqueur over each ladyfinger, and top with ¼ cup of the pudding. Repeat the berry, ladyfinger, liqueur, and pudding layers.

5. Cover each glass with plastic wrap, and chill for at least 3 hours. If desired, top each serving with a rounded tablespoon of whipped topping and a sprinkling of cocoa powder just before serving.

NUTRITIONAL FACTS (PER ⅞-CUP SERVING)
Calories: 260 Carbohydrates: 51 g Cholesterol: 27 mg
Fat: 1.2 g Fiber: 1.1 g Protein: 5.8 g Sodium: 265 mg

You Save: Calories: 253 Fat: 34.3 g

Yield: *4 servings*

8 unsplit ladyfingers

BERRY MIXTURE

1 cup fresh or frozen (thawed) sliced strawberries or raspberries

1 tablespoon sugar

LIQUEUR MIXTURE

¼ cup coffee liqueur

1½ teaspoons cocoa powder

PUDDING MIXTURE

2 cups skim or 1% low-fat milk

1 package (4-serving size) fat-free cook-and-serve or instant vanilla pudding mix, regular or sugar-free

TOPPINGS (OPTIONAL)

½ cup nonfat or light whipped topping

½ teaspoon cocoa powder

Black Forest Pudding

Yield: *9 servings*

2 cups skim or 1% low-fat milk

1 package (4-serving size) fat-free cook-and-serve or instant chocolate pudding mix, regular or sugar-free

8 slices (½-inch each) fat-free chocolate loaf cake

2 tablespoons amaretto or hazelnut liqueur

1 can (20 ounces) light (reduced-sugar) cherry pie filling

TOPPING

1½ cups nonfat or light whipped topping

¾ cup regular or sugar-free nonfat or low-fat vanilla yogurt

3 tablespoons sliced toasted almonds (page 383) (optional)

1. Use the skim milk to prepare the pudding according to package directions. Cover the mixture and chill for at least 2 hours for cook-and-serve pudding or for at least 30 minutes for instant pudding, or until chilled and thickened.

2. Arrange 4 of the cake slices in a single layer over the bottom of a 2-quart glass bowl, and drizzle 1 tablespoon of liqueur over the cake slices. Spread half of the pudding over the cake, and follow with a layer of half the pie filling. Repeat the cake, liqueur, pudding, and pie filling layers.

3. To make the topping, place the whipped topping in a medium-sized bowl, and gently fold in the yogurt. Spread the mixture over the top of the pie filling.

4. Cover the dish, and chill for at least 3 hours. If desired, sprinkle the almonds over the top just before serving.

NUTRITIONAL FACTS (PER ¾-CUP SERVING)
Calories: 222 Carbohydrates: 48 g Cholesterol: 1 mg
Fat: 1 g Fiber: 0.8 g Protein: 4.8 g Sodium: 224 mg

You Save: Calories: 277 Fat: 23.1 g

Apple Cheesecake Parfaits

For variety, substitute light cherry pie filling for the light apple pie filling.

1. Place the cream cheese and sugar in a medium-sized bowl, and beat with an electric mixer until smooth. Add the milk, and beat until smooth. Add the yogurt cheese, and beat just until well mixed.

2. To assemble the parfaits, spoon 2½ tablespoons of the pie filling into the bottom of each of each of four 8-ounce wine or parfait glasses. Top with 2½ tablespoons of the cheese mixture. Repeat the pie filling and cheese layers.

3. Cover each glass with plastic wrap, and chill for at least 3 hours. Top each parfait with a tablespoon of the graham cracker or cookie crumbs just before serving.

Yield: *4 servings*

¾ cup nonfat cream cheese softened to room temperature

2 tablespoons sugar

2 tablespoons skim or 1% low-fat milk

¾ cup yogurt cheese made from vanilla yogurt (page 293)

1¼ cups canned light (reduced-sugar) apple pie filling

¼ cup crushed reduced-fat graham crackers, low-fat vanilla wafers, or low-fat gingersnaps

NUTRITIONAL FACTS (PER ⅔-CUP SERVING)

Calories: 191 Carbohydrates: 34 g Cholesterol: 4 mg
Fat: 0.8 g Fiber: 0.6 g Protein: 11.9 g Sodium: 227 mg

You Save: Calories: 227 Fat: 25.2 g

Apple-Raisin Risotto

Yield: *6 servings*

½ cup plus 2 tablespoons uncooked arborio rice*

3 cups skim or 1% low-fat milk

1 cup chopped peeled Granny Smith or Rome apple (about 1 large)

¼ cup dark raisins

¼ cup plus 2 tablespoons evaporated skimmed milk

¼ cup plus 2 tablespoons fat-free egg substitute

¼ cup plus 2 tablespoons sugar

¼ teaspoon ground cinnamon

1 teaspoon vanilla extract

*Arborio rice, a short grain rice that is best for making risotto, is available in most supermarkets and specialty stores.

1. Place the rice and milk in a heavy 2½-quart pot, and place over medium heat. Cook, stirring frequently, until the milk comes to a boil. Reduce the heat to low, cover, and simmer, stirring occasionally, for 15 minutes.

2. Add the apple to the rice mixture. Cover and simmer, stirring occasionally, for 10 additional minutes, or until the most of the milk has been absorbed and the rice is tender.

3. Add the raisins to the rice mixture. Cover and simmer for about 2 minutes, or until the raisins begin to soften.

4. Place the evaporated milk, egg substitute, sugar, cinnamon, and vanilla extract in a small bowl, and stir to mix well. Slowly stir the evaporated milk mixture into the rice mixture. Cook, stirring constantly, for 3 to 5 minutes, or until the mixture is thick and creamy.

5. Remove the pot from the heat, and allow to cool at room temperature for 10 minutes. Stir the pudding, and divide among six 8-ounce dessert dishes. Serve warm, refrigerating any leftovers.

NUTRITIONAL FACTS (PER ¾-CUP SERVING)

Calories: 187 Carbohydrates: 39 g Cholesterol: 2 mg
Fat: 0.4 g Fiber: 0.7 g Protein: 8 g Sodium: 107 mg

You Save: Calories: 95 Fat: 13.9 g

Chocolate-Hazelnut Mousse

For variety, substitute amaretto or coffee liqueur for the hazelnut liqueur.

1. Place ¼ cup plus 2 tablespoons of the milk in a blender, and sprinkle the gelatin over the top. Set aside for 2 minutes to allow the gelatin to soften.

2. Place the remaining ½ cup of milk in a small pot, and cook over medium heat, stirring frequently, until the milk comes to a boil.

3. Add the boiling hot milk to the blender, place the lid on, and blend at low speed for about 2 minutes, or until the gelatin is completely dissolved. Set the mixture aside for about 20 minutes, or until it cools to room temperature.

4. Add the ricotta, brown sugar, cocoa, liqueur, and vanilla extract to the blender, and blend until smooth. Pour the mixture into a large bowl, cover, and chill for at least 6 hours, or until the mixture is completely set and very firm. (You can complete this step the day before you prepare the mousse and let it chill overnight, if you wish.)

5. When the gelatin mixture has set, beat it with an electric mixer until it is the consistency of pudding. Gently fold in the whipped topping.

6. Divide the mixture among four 8-ounce wine glasses or dessert dishes. Cover each glass with plastic wrap, and chill for at least 3 hours. Top each serving with a rounded tablespoon of whipped topping, a splash of liqueur, and a sprinkling of nuts just before serving, if desired.

Yield: *4 servings*

¾ cup plus 2 tablespoons skim or 1% low-fat milk, divided

1 envelope (¼ ounce) unflavored gelatin

1 cup nonfat ricotta cheese

¼ cup plus 2 tablespoons light brown sugar

2 tablespoons Dutch processed cocoa powder

2 tablespoons Frangelico (hazelnut) liqueur

1 teaspoon vanilla extract

1 cup nonfat or light whipped topping

TOPPINGS (OPTIONAL)

¼ cup plus 2 tablespoons nonfat or light whipped topping

2 teaspoons Frangelico (hazelnut) liqueur

1 tablespoon plus 1 teaspoon chopped toasted hazelnuts (page 383)

NUTRITIONAL FACTS (PER ¾-CUP SERVING)
Calories: 199 Carbohydrates: 32 g Cholesterol: 5 mg
Fat: 0.9 g Fiber: 0.8 g Protein: 13.7 g Sodium: 108 mg

You Save: Calories: 221 Fat: 26.5 g

Trimming the Fat from Your Favorite Pudding Recipes

It's a shame that most pudding recipes are so high in fat because, when properly prepared, pudding makes a great low-fat snack or dessert. Happily, it's easy to do a slimming makeover of virtually any pudding recipe. Just use the following table to replace the high-fat ingredients in your own treasured pudding recipes with low-fat and no-fat ingredients. You'll find that any pudding—from hearty bread puddings and light-as-air mousses to custard-filled trifles—can be made ultra-light without sacrificing the creamy richness you love.

Fat-Saving Substitutions in Puddings

Instead of	Use	You Save	Special Considerations
1 cup whole milk	1 cup skim milk	65 calories 8 g fat	For extra richness, add 2 table-spoons of instant nonfat dry milk powder to each cup of skim or low-fat milk.
	1 cup 1% low-fat milk	50 calories 6 g fat	
1 cup cream	1 cup evaporated skimmed milk	622 calories 88 g fat	This ingredient may be used in cooked puddings and custards.
	1 cup skim milk mixed with ⅓ cup instant nonfat dry milk powder	622 calories 88 g fat	This ingredient may be used in cooked puddings and custards.
	⅔ cup nonfat ricotta cheese blended with ⅓ cup skim milk until smooth	674 calories 88 g fat	This ingredient may be used only in uncooked puddings and mousses.
1 cup regular cream cheese	1 cup nonfat cream cheese	600 calories 80 g fat	For best results, use a firm block-style nonfat cream cheese.
	1 cup reduced-fat (Neufchâtel) cream cheese	240 calories 26 g fat	
1 cup sour cream	1 cup nonfat sour cream	252 calories 48 g fat	Some brands of sour cream will separate when heated. Choose a brand like Land O Lakes or Breakstone's, both of which are heat-stable, if the sour cream will be used in a cooked pudding.
1 cup sour cream	1 cup nonfat yogurt	355 calories 48 g fat	All yogurts will separate if heated. To prevent this, stir 2 tablespoons of flour or 1 table-spoon of cornstarch into each cup of yogurt before adding it to a pudding that will be cooked.

Instead of	Use	You Save	Special Considerations
1 cup whipped cream	1 cup light whipped topping	250 calories 36 g fat	
	1 cup fat-free whipped topping	290 calories 42 g fat	
1 cup butter or margarine	1/2 cup Butter Buds liquid	1,500 calories 176 g fat	
	¾ cup reduced-fat margarine or light butter	800–1,200 calories 88–112 g fat	
1 large egg	3 tablespoons fat-free egg substitute	60 calories 5 g fat	
1 egg yolk	1 tablespoon fat-free egg substitute	40 calories 5 g fat	
1 ounce baking chocolate	3 tablespoons cocoa powder plus 1 tablespoon water or another liquid	111 calories 13.5 g fat	

Delightful Peach Trifle

Yield: *9 servings*

PUDDING MIXTURE

2 cups skim or 1% low-fat milk

1 package (4-serving size) fat-free cook-and-serve or instant vanilla pudding mix, regular or sugar-free

PEACH MIXTURE

2 cups diced peeled fresh peaches

1 tablespoon sugar

2 tablespoons amaretto liqueur

CAKE MIXTURE

8 slices (½-inch each) fat-free vanilla loaf cake or fat-free pound cake

2 tablespoons plus 2 teaspoons raspberry jam

TOPPING

1½ cups nonfat or light whipped topping

¾ cup regular or sugar-free non-fat or low-fat vanilla yogurt

3 tablespoons sliced toasted almonds (page 383) (optional)

1. Use the skim milk to prepare the pudding according to package directions. Cover the mixture and chill for at least 2 hours for cook-and-serve pudding or for at least 30 minutes for instant pudding, or until chilled and thickened.

2. To make the peach mixture, place the peaches, sugar, and liqueur in a medium-sized bowl, and stir to mix well. Set aside for 15 minutes to allow the juices to develop.

3. To make the cake mixture, arrange the cake slices on a flat surface, and spread each slice with 1 teaspoon of the jam.

4. To assemble the trifle, arrange half of the cake slices, jam side up, in a single layer over the bottom of a 2-quart glass bowl. Spread half of the peach mixture over the cake slices, and cover the peaches with half of the pudding. Repeat the cake, peach, and pudding layers.

5. To make the topping, place the whipped topping in a medium-sized bowl, and gently fold in the yogurt. Spread the mixture over the top of the pudding.

6. Cover and chill for at least 3 hours. If desired, sprinkle the almonds over the top just before serving.

NUTRITIONAL FACTS (PER ¾-CUP SERVING)
Calories: 205 Carbohydrates: 45 g Cholesterol: 2 mg
Fat: 0.8 g Fiber: 1 g Protein: 4.3 g Sodium: 206 mg

You Save: Calories: 123 Fat: 16.4 g

Baked Brown Rice Pudding

1. Place the rice, water, 1 cup of the milk, and the orange rind in a 2½-quart pot, and bring to a boil over medium-high heat. Reduce the heat to low, cover, and simmer for 45 minutes, or until the rice is tender and most of the liquid has been absorbed.

2. Place the remaining 1½ cups of milk and all of the egg substitute, sugar, milk powder, and vanilla extract in a medium-sized bowl. Stir to mix well.

3. Add the milk mixture and the raisins or dried cherries to the rice, and cook over medium heat, stirring constantly, for about 5 minutes, or until the mixture thickens slightly.

4. Coat a 1½-quart casserole dish with nonstick cooking spray. Pour the pudding into the dish, and sprinkle with the nutmeg. Set the casserole dish in a large roasting pan, and add hot tap water to the pan until it reaches halfway up the sides of the dish.

5. Bake uncovered at 325°F for 50 minutes, or until a sharp knife inserted midway between the center of the dish and the rim comes out clean.

6. Allow the pudding to cool at room temperature for at least 1 hour. Serve warm, or refrigerate for several hours and serve chilled. Refrigerate any leftovers.

Yield: *6 servings*

⅔ cup uncooked brown rice

1 cup water

2½ cups skim or 1% low-fat milk, divided

½ teaspoon dried grated orange rind, or 1½ teaspoons fresh

½ cup plus 2 tablespoons fat-free egg substitute

¼ cup plus 2 tablespoons sugar

¼ cup instant nonfat dry milk powder

1½ teaspoons vanilla extract

¼ cup golden or dark raisins or dried cherries

Ground nutmeg (garnish)

NUTRITIONAL FACTS (PER ¾-CUP SERVING)
Calories: 204 Carbohydrates: 41 g Cholesterol: 2 mg
Fat: 0.8 g Fiber: 1.1 g Protein: 8.9 g Sodium: 114 mg

You Save: Calories: 178 Fat: 21.9 g

CRÈME CARAMEL

Yield: *4 servings*

⅔ cup sugar, divided

¼ cup plus 2 tablespoons fat-free egg substitute

1½ teaspoons vanilla extract

1 can (12 ounces) evaporated skimmed milk

1. To make the caramel sauce, place ⅓ cup of the sugar in a heavy 1-quart saucepan. Cook over medium-high heat without stirring for about 1 minute, shaking the saucepan occasionally, until the sugar begins to liquefy around the edges. Reduce the heat to medium, and cook, stirring constantly, for another minute or 2, or until the sugar has completely liquefied and has turned a golden caramel color. Be careful not to cook the sugar too long, as it will continue to cook and darken after you remove it from the heat.

2. Immediately pour about 1 tablespoon of the caramel mixture into the bottom of each of four 6-ounce custard cups. (Be aware that the caramel mixture will be very hot!) Swirl each cup to coat the bottom and about ½-inch up the sides with the caramel mixture. Set the cups aside for 10 minutes to allow the caramel mixture to harden.

3. To make the custard, place the egg substitute, the remaining ⅓ cup of sugar, and the vanilla extract in a small bowl, and stir to dissolve the sugar. Set aside.

4. Place the evaporated milk in a 1-quart pot, and cook over medium heat, stirring frequently, just until the milk begins to boil. Remove the pot from the heat, and slowly whisk in the egg substitute mixture. Pour the custard into the caramel-lined cups.

5. Place the custards in a 9-x-9-inch baking pan, and add hot tap water to the pan until it reaches halfway up the sides of the custard cups. Bake at 325°F for about 50 minutes, or until a sharp knife inserted slightly off center in the custards comes out clean.

6. Remove the custards from the pan, and allow to cool to room temperature. Cover with plastic wrap, and chill for at least 24 hours before serving. (During this time, the hardened caramel sauce will become liquid.)

7. To serve, carefully run a sharp knife around the edge of the custards, taking care not to cut into the pudding itself. Invert the cups onto individual serving plates, allowing the sauce to flow over and around the custards. Serve immediately.

NUTRITIONAL FACTS (PER SERVING)
Calories: 205 Carbohydrates: 43 g Cholesterol: 3 mg
Fat: 0.2 g Fiber: 0 g Protein: 8.7 g Sodium: 135 mg

You Save: Calories: 152 Fat: 19.8 g

Polenta Pudding

1. Place the cornmeal in a 2½-quart pot, and slowly stir in the milk and the evaporated milk. Cook over medium heat, stirring constantly, for 10 to 12 minutes, or until the mixture comes to a boil. Reduce the heat to low, and continue cooking for 2 additional minutes, or until slightly thickened. Slowly stir in the honey.

2. Place the egg substitute in a small bowl, and stir in 1 cup of the hot cornmeal mixture. Slowly stir the egg mixture into the pudding, and continue cooking and stirring for 2 minutes, or until slightly thickened. Remove the pot from the heat, and stir in the vanilla extract and the raisins or apricots.

3. Coat a 2-quart round casserole dish with nonstick cooking spray. Pour the pudding mixture into the dish, and sprinkle with the nutmeg. Place the dish in a pan filled with 1 inch of hot water.

4. Bake uncovered at 350°F for 1 hour, or until set. When done, a sharp knife inserted midway between the center of the pudding and the rim of the dish will come out clean.

5. Allow the pudding to cool at room temperature for at least 30 minutes. Serve warm, or refrigerate for several hours and serve chilled. Refrigerate any leftovers.

Yield: *8 servings*

¼ cup plus 2 tablespoons whole grain cornmeal

2½ cups skim or 1% low-fat milk

1 cup evaporated skimmed milk

¼ cup plus 2 tablespoons honey

1 cup fat-free egg substitute

2 teaspoons vanilla extract

⅓ cup golden raisins or chopped dried apricots

Ground nutmeg (garnish)

NUTRITIONAL FACTS (PER ⅔-CUP SERVING)

Calories: 156 Carbohydrates: 30 g Cholesterol: 2 mg
Fat: 0.5 g Fiber: 0.8 g Protein: 9 g Sodium: 150 mg

You Save: Calories: 89 Fat: 10.1 g

Spiced Pumpkin Flan

Yield: *6 servings*

½ cup sugar

1 can (12 ounces) evaporated skimmed milk

½ cup mashed cooked or canned pumpkin

½ cup plus 1 tablespoon fat-free egg substitute

¼ cup orange juice

½ cup light brown sugar

2 teaspoons vanilla extract

1 teaspoon pumpkin pie spice

1. To make the caramel sauce, place the ½ cup of sugar in a heavy 1-quart saucepan. Cook over medium-high heat without stirring for about 1 minute, shaking the saucepan occasionally, until the sugar begins to liquefy around the edges. Reduce the heat to medium, and cook, stirring constantly, for another minute or 2, or until the sugar has completely liquefied and has turned a golden caramel color. Be careful not to cook the sugar too long, as it will continue to cook and darken after you remove it from the heat.

2. Immediately pour about 1 tablespoon of the caramel mixture into the bottom of each of four 6-ounce custard cups. (Be aware that the caramel mixture will be very hot!) Swirl each cup to coat the bottom and about ½ inch up the sides with the caramel mixture. Set the cups aside for 10 minutes to allow the caramel mixture to harden.

3. To make the custard, place all of the remaining ingredients in a blender, and process until smooth. Pour the custard mixture into the caramel-lined cups.

4. Place the custards in a 9-x-13-inch baking pan, and add hot tap water to the pan until it reaches halfway up the sides of the custard cups. Bake at 350°F for about 45 minutes, or until a sharp knife inserted slightly off center in the custards comes out clean.

5. Remove the custards from the pan, and allow to cool to room temperature. Cover with plastic wrap, and chill for at least 24 hours before serving. (During this time, the hardened caramel sauce will become liquid.)

6. To serve, carefully run a sharp knife around the edge of the custards, taking care not to cut into the pudding itself. Invert the cups onto individual serving plates, allowing the sauce to flow over and around custards. Serve immediately.

NUTRITIONAL FACTS (PER SERVING)
Calories: 177 Carbohydrates: 38 g Cholesterol: 2 mg
Fat: 0.2 g Fiber: 0.6 g Protein: 6.8 g Sodium: 109 mg

You Save: Calories: 61 Fat: 9.7 g

Peach Noodle Pudding

For variety, substitute diced apples for the peaches.

Yield: *8 servings*

1. Cook the noodles according to package directions until tender. Drain well, and return the noodles to the pot.

2. While the noodles are cooking, place the cream cheese and sugar in a medium-sized bowl, and stir until smooth. Add the cottage cheese, sour cream, egg substitute, and vanilla extract, and stir to mix well.

3. Pour the cheese mixture over the drained noodles, and toss to mix well. Add the peaches and raisins, and toss to mix well.

4. Coat an 8-x-8-inch (2-quart) casserole dish with nonstick cooking spray, and spread the noodle mixture evenly in the dish. Set aside.

5. To make the topping, place the sugar and cinnamon in a small bowl, and stir to mix well. Sprinkle the sugar mixture over the top of the noodle mixture. Then spray the top lightly with the cooking spray.

6. Bake at 350°F for about 1 hour, or until a sharp knife inserted in the pudding about 1 inch off center comes out clean. Allow the pudding to sit at room temperature for 1 hour before cutting into squares and serving. Serve warm or at room temperature, refrigerating any leftovers.

4 ounces wide or extra-broad no-yolk egg noodles (about 3 cups)

1 block (8 ounces) nonfat cream cheese, softened to room temperature

½ cup sugar

1 cup nonfat cottage cheese

¾ cup nonfat sour cream

¾ cup fat-free egg substitute

2½ teaspoons vanilla extract

1½ cups diced peeled fresh or frozen (thawed) peaches (about 2 medium)

¼ cup plus 2 tablespoons dark or golden raisins

TOPPING

2 tablespoons sugar

½ teaspoon ground cinnamon

Butter-flavored cooking spray

NUTRITIONAL FACTS (PER ¾-CUP SERVING)
Calories: 203 Carbohydrates: 37 g Cholesterol: 4 mg
Fat: 0.3 g Fiber: 1.4 g Protein: 12.7 g Sodium: 237 mg

You Save: Calories: 105 Fat: 16.1 g

Creamy Clafouti

Yield: *6 servings*

2 cups peeled fresh peaches or
  apricots cut into ¾-inch chunks,
  or 2 cups fresh pitted dark
  sweet cherries (or any combination)

½ cup plus 2 tablespoons fat-free
  egg substitute

¼ cup plus 2 tablespoons sugar

2 teaspoons vanilla extract

2 tablespoons cornstarch

¼ cup instant nonfat dry milk
  powder

1¼ cups skim or 1% low-fat milk

1 tablespoon powdered sugar

This baked fruit and custard dessert is a slimmed-down version of a French classic. When fresh fruit is not available, substitute 2 cups of frozen peaches or cherries (thawed and drained), or a 1-pound can of peaches or apricots (drained and chopped).

1. Coat a 9-inch deep dish pie pan with nonstick cooking spray, and spread the fruit over the bottom of the pan. Alternatively, coat six 6-ounce custard cups with cooking spray, and divide the fruit among the cups. Set aside.

2. Place the egg substitute, sugar, and vanilla extract in a medium-sized bowl, and stir to mix well. Set aside.

3. Place the cornstarch and milk powder in a 2-quart pot. Add ¼ cup of the milk, and stir to dissolve the cornstarch and milk powder. Slowly stir in the remaining milk. Place the pot over medium heat and cook, stirring constantly, for about 5 minutes, or until the mixture is thickened and bubbly.

4. Remove the pot from the heat. Stir the egg substitute mixture, and add it to the hot milk mixture in a thin stream while whisking constantly. Pour the egg-milk mixture over the fruit, and bake at 375°F for about 25 minutes, or until the clafouti is puffed around the edges and just beginning to brown. If you are baking the custard in individual custard cups, arrange them on a baking sheet before placing in the oven, and bake for only about 23 minutes.

5. Allow the clafouti to sit at room temperature for at least 15 minutes. (It will fall a bit.) Sift the powdered sugar over the top, and serve warm, refrigerating any leftovers.

NUTRITIONAL FACTS (PER ⅔-CUP SERVING)
Calories: 128 Carbohydrates: 26.8 g Cholesterol: 1 mg
Fat: 0.2 g Fiber: 1 g Protein: 5.6 g Sodium: 84 mg

You Save: Calories: 81 Fat: 8.3 g

Tangy Peach Sherbet

For variety, substitute fresh sliced strawberries or nectarines for the peaches.

1. Place the peaches and sugar in a 2-quart pot, stir to mix well, and place over medium heat. Cover and cook, stirring occasionally, for about 5 minutes, or until the peaches are soft and the liquid is syrupy.

2. Place the peach mixture in a blender, and sprinkle the gelatin and nutmeg over the top. Leaving the lid slightly ajar to allow steam to escape, carefully process at low speed for about 1 minute, or until the mixture is smooth and the gelatin is completely dissolved. Return the mixture to the pot, and allow to cool to room temperature.

3. When mixture has cooled, whisk in the buttermilk and vanilla extract.

4. Pour the mixture into a 1½-quart ice cream maker, and proceed as directed by the manufacturer. (If you don't own an ice cream maker, see the inset on page 419 for directions on making the sherbet in your freezer.) Scoop into individual dessert dishes, and serve immediately.

Yield: *6 servings*

4 cups diced peeled peaches (about 5½ medium)

½ cup plus 2 tablespoons sugar

1¼ teaspoons unflavored gelatin

⅛ teaspoon ground nutmeg

1¼ cups nonfat or low-fat buttermilk

1¼ teaspoons vanilla extract

NUTRITIONAL FACTS (PER ⅞-CUP SERVING)

Calories: 150 Carbohydrates: 36 g Cholesterol: 2 mg
Fat: 0.5 g Fiber: 2 g Protein: 2.5 g Sodium: 54 mg

You Save: Calories: 80 Fat: 3 g

Fresh Mango Sorbet

Yield: *6 servings*

1½ cups pineapple juice

½ cup sugar

¾ teaspoon unflavored gelatin

3 cups diced peeled fresh mangoes (about 2 large)

1. Place the juice and sugar in a small pot, and bring to a boil over high heat. Reduce the heat to low, cover, and simmer for 3 minutes, stirring occasionally.

2. Remove the pot from the heat, and sprinkle the gelatin over the juice mixture. Whisk for about 2 minutes, or until the gelatin is completely dissolved. Set aside for about 30 minutes to cool to room temperature.

3. Place the mangoes and the cooled juice mixture in a blender, and process until smooth.

4. Pour the mixture into a 1½-quart ice cream maker, and proceed as directed by the manufacturer. (If you don't own an ice cream maker, see the inset on page 419 for directions on making the sorbet in your freezer.) Scoop into individual dessert dishes, and serve immediately.

NUTRITIONAL FACTS (PER ¾-CUP SERVING)

Calories: 150 Carbohydrates: 38 g Cholesterol: 0 mg
Fat: 0.2 g Fiber: 2.4 g Protein: 0.7 g Sodium: 2 mg

You Save: Calories: 66 Fat: 0 g

Strawberry-Cheesecake Sherbet

For variety, substitute fresh peaches for the strawberries.

Yield: *5 servings*

1. Place the strawberries and sugar in a 2½-quart pot, stir to mix well, and place over medium heat. Cover the pot, and cook, stirring occasionally, for about 5 minutes, or until the strawberries are soft and the liquid is syrupy. Remove the pot from the heat, and allow to cool to room temperature.

2. Place the cooled strawberry mixture in a blender or food processor. Add the cream cheese and vanilla extract, and process until smooth.

3. Pour the mixture into a 1½-quart ice cream maker, and proceed as directed by the manufacturer. (If you don't own an ice cream maker, see the inset on page 419 for directions on making the sherbet in your freezer.) Scoop into individual dessert dishes, and serve immediately.

5 cups sliced fresh strawberries

½ cup plus 2 tablespoons sugar

1 block (8 ounces) nonfat cream cheese

1½ teaspoons vanilla extract

NUTRITIONAL FACTS (PER ⅞-CUP SERVING)
Calories: 187 Carbohydrates: 39 g Cholesterol: 3 mg
Fat: 0.6 g Fiber: 2.5 g Protein: 8 g Sodium: 221 mg

You Save: Calories: 112 Fat: 16 g

VERY STRAWBERRY ICE CREAM

Yield: *8 servings*

6 cups sliced fresh strawberries

1 can (12 ounces) fat-free sweetened condensed milk

1 cup nonfat sour cream

2 teaspoons vanilla extract

For variety, substitute other fruits, such as peaches, nectarines, pineapples, bananas, or apricots, for the strawberries.

1. Place all of the ingredients in a food processor, and process until smooth.

2. Pour the mixture into a 2-quart ice cream maker, and proceed as directed by the manufacturer. (If you don't own an ice cream maker, see the inset on page 419 for directions on making the dessert in your freezer.) Scoop into individual dessert dishes, and serve immediately.

NUTRITIONAL FACTS (PER ⅞-CUP SERVING)

Calories: 182 Carbohydrates: 39 g Cholesterol: 2 mg
Fat: 0.4 g Fiber: 1.6 g Protein: 5.6 g Sodium: 67 mg

You Save: Calories: 45 Fat: 10.1 g

TROPICAL BREEZE FREEZE

Yield: *5 servings*

3 cans (8 ounces each) crushed pineapple in juice, undrained

1 cup nonfat vanilla or coconut yogurt

½ cup fat-free sweetened condensed milk

¾ teaspoon vanilla extract

1. Place the pineapple with its juice and the yogurt, condensed milk, and vanilla extract in a blender or food processor, and process until smooth.

2. Pour the mixture into a 1½-quart ice cream maker, and proceed as directed by the manufacturer. (If you don't own an ice cream maker, see the inset on page 419 for directions on making the sherbet in your freezer.) Scoop into individual dessert dishes, and serve immediately.

NUTRITIONAL FACTS (PER ⅞-CUP SERVING)

Calories: 179 Carbohydrates: 40 g Cholesterol: 3 mg
Fat: 0.2 g Fiber: 0.8 g Protein: 5.1 g Sodium: 60 mg

You Save: Calories: 118 Fat: 15.8 g

Fruitful Frozen Yogurt

1. Place all of the ingredients in a food processor, and process until smooth.

2. Pour the mixture into a 2-quart ice cream maker, and proceed as directed by the manufacturer. (If you don't own an ice cream maker, see the inset below for directions on making the dessert in your freezer.) Scoop into individual dessert dishes, and serve immediately.

Yield: *9 servings*

3½ cups coarsely chopped fresh fruit (try strawberries, peaches, apricots, pineapples, bananas, or blueberries)

3 cups plain nonfat yogurt

1 can (14 ounces) fat-free sweetened condensed milk

2 teaspoons vanilla extract

NUTRITIONAL FACTS (PER ⅞-CUP SERVING)

Calories: 188 Carbohydrates: 37.4 g Cholesterol: 4 mg
Fat: 0.5 g Fiber: 0.9 g Protein: 9 g Sodium: 109 mg

You Save: Calories: 33 Fat: 6.2 g

Making Ice Cream, Sherbet, Sorbet, and Frozen Yogurt in Your Freezer

An ice cream maker will produce the smoothest, creamiest fat-free ice creams, sherbets, and sorbets imaginable. Inexpensive machines that do not require any ice, salt, or electricity are now widely available. The simplest machines have an inner canister that you store in the freezer until you are ready to make your frozen confection. You then pour your mixture into the canister, place the canister in the machine, and turn the handle every few minutes. Machines like these, as well as fancier models, are convenient to have on hand if you plan on making your own frozen desserts on a regular basis. However, if you don't have an ice cream maker, you can still enjoy frozen treats by using the following steps to prepare them in your freezer.

1. Prepare the ice cream, sorbet, or sherbet mixture as directed in the recipe, but instead of transferring the mixture to an ice cream maker, pour it into an 8-inch square pan. Cover the pan with aluminum foil, and place in the freezer for several hours, or until the outer 2-inch edge of the mixture is frozen. If you prefer, you can prepare the mixture a few days ahead of time. Then remove it from the freezer, and allow it to sit at room temperature for about 20 minutes, or until thawed enough to break into chunks, before proceeding with Step 2.

2. Break the mixture into chunks, and place in the bowl of a food processor or electric mixer. Process for several minutes, or until light, creamy, and smooth. (Note that, depending on the capacity of your food processor, you may have to process the mixture in 2 batches.)

3. Return the mixture to the pan, cover, and return to the freezer. Freeze for at least 2 hours, or until firm.

4. About 20 minutes before serving, remove the dessert from the freezer and allow it to soften slightly at room temperature. Scoop into individual dessert dishes, and serve immediately.

PRESTO PEACH ICE CREAM

Yield: *4 servings*

½ cup nonfat sour cream

⅓ cup sugar

1 teaspoon vanilla extract

1 bag (1 pound) frozen sliced
   peaches, unthawed

1. Place the sour cream, sugar, and vanilla extract in a small bowl, and stir to mix well. Set aside.

2. Dice the frozen peaches into ¾-inch chunks. Place the peaches in the bowl of a food processor, and process for a couple of minutes, or until finely ground.

3. Add the sour cream mixture to the food processor, and process for a couple of minutes, or until the mixture is light, creamy, and smooth. Serve immediately. Freeze leftovers in a covered container, and let sit at room temperature for about 10 minutes, or until slightly softened, before serving.

NUTRITIONAL FACTS (PER ¾-CUP SERVING)
Calories: 143 Carbohydrates: 34 g Cholesterol: 0 mg
Fat: 0.1 g Fiber: 2 g Protein: 2.6 g Sodium: 22 mg

You Save: Calories: 82 Fat: 11.9 g

Simple Apricot Sorbet

1. Place the apricots with their juice and the juice concentrate in a blender, and process until smooth.

2. Pour the mixture into an 8-x-4-inch loaf pan. Cover the pan with aluminum foil, and place in the freezer for about 3 hours and 30 minutes, or until the outer 1-inch edge of the mixture is frozen.

3. Place the partially frozen mixture in the bowl of a food processor or electric mixer, breaking up the frozen outer edges. Process for about 2 minutes, or until light, creamy, and smooth.

4. Return the mixture to the pan, cover, and return the pan to the freezer. Freeze for at least 2 hours, or until firm.

5. About 10 minutes before serving, remove the dessert from the freezer and allow it to soften slightly at room temperature. Scoop into individual dessert dishes, and serve immediately.

Yield: *4 servings*

1 can (1 pound) apricot halves in juice, undrained

¼ cup plus 1 tablespoon frozen white grape juice concentrate, unthawed

---

NUTRITIONAL FACTS (PER ⅔-CUP SERVING)
Calories: 107 Carbohydrates: 27 g Cholesterol: 0 mg
Fat: 0 g Fiber: 1.3 g Protein: 0.7 g Sodium: 4 mg

You Save: Calories: 93 Fat: 0 g

Very Cranberry Granita

Yield: 5 servings

3 cups cranberry juice cocktail, divided

¼ cup plus 1 tablespoon sugar

3 tablespoons frozen (thawed or unthawed) or liquid cranberry juice cocktail concentrate

1. Place 1 cup of the juice and all of the sugar in a 1-quart pot, and stir to mix. Bring the mixture to a boil over medium-high heat. Reduce the heat to low, cover, and simmer, stirring occasionally, for a minute or 2, or until the sugar is completely dissolved and the liquid is slightly syrupy. Remove the pot from the heat, and allow the mixture to cool to room temperature.

2. Pour the cooled sugar mixture into an 8-inch square pan, and add the remaining juice and the juice concentrate. Stir to mix well.

3. Place the pan in the freezer for about 25 minutes, or until ice crystals begin to form around the sides of the pan. Using a spoon, stir the frozen crystals from around the edges and bottom of the pan back into the liquid portion. Repeat the scraping process every 20 minutes for about 2 hours, or until the mixture is icy and granular.

4. Spoon the granita into four 8-ounce wine glasses, and serve immediately.

NUTRITIONAL FACTS (PER ¾-CUP SERVING)
Calories: 153 Carbohydrates: 39 g Cholesterol: 0 mg
Fat: 0.1 g Fiber: 0.2 g Protein: 0 g Sodium: 4 mg

You Save: Calories: 45 Fat: 0 g

Strawberry Angel Parfaits

1. Place 1 tablespoon of the strawberries in the bottom of each of five 10-ounce balloon wine glasses.

2. Crumble a half-slice of cake over the berries in each glass. Top the cake with ⅓ cup of ice cream, and then spoon 2 tablespoons of strawberries over the ice cream.

3. Repeat the cake, ice cream, and strawberry layers, and serve immediately.

Yield: *5 servings*

10 ounces frozen sliced sweetened strawberries, thawed

5 slices (½-inch each) angel food cake

3⅓ cups nonfat or low-fat vanilla ice cream

NUTRITIONAL FACTS (PER SERVING)
Calories: 248 Carbohydrates: 56.4 g Cholesterol: 2 mg
Fat: 0.3 g Fiber: 1.5 g Protein: 7.3 g Sodium: 21.4 mg

You Save: Calories: 117 Fat: 16 g

Tiramisu Sundaes

1. Place the liqueur and 2½ teaspoons of the cocoa in a small bowl and stir to dissolve the cocoa powder. Set aside.

2. Crumble 1 ladyfinger into the bottom of each of four 10-ounce balloon wine glasses. Drizzle 2 teaspoons of the liqueur mixture over the lady finger. Then top with ⅓ cup of the ice cream. Repeat the ladyfinger, liqueur, and ice cream layers.

3. Drizzle ½ teaspoon of the liqueur mixture over the top of each sundae. Then top each sundae with a rounded tablespoon of whipped topping and a sprinkling of cocoa. Serve immediately.

Yield: *4 servings*

¼ cup plus 2 tablespoons coffee liqueur

1 tablespoon Dutch processed cocoa powder, divided

8 ladyfingers

2⅔ cups nonfat or low-fat vanilla, cappuccino, or cheesecake ice cream

¼ cup plus 2 tablespoons nonfat or light whipped topping

NUTRITIONAL FACTS (PER SERVING)
Calories: 268 Carbohydrates: 49 g Cholesterol: 27 mg
Fat: 1.2 g Fiber: 0.6 g Protein: 5.4 g Sodium: 181 mg

You Save: Calories: 160 Fat: 21.3 g

Light Ice Cream Sandwiches

Yield: *8 servings*

8 large (2½-x-5-inch) reduced-fat
chocolate graham crackers

2 cups nonfat or low-fat ice
cream, any flavor, slightly
softened

For variety, try making these sandwiches with different ice cream flavors, such as vanilla, cherry vanilla, chocolate, raspberry ripple, cappuccino, and praline swirl.

1. Break each graham cracker in half so that you have 16 squares, each measuring 2½ x 2½ inches.

2. Spread ¼ cup of the ice cream over 1 square, top with another square, and gently press the crackers together. Smooth the edges of the ice cream with a knife. Wrap the sandwich in plastic wrap, and place in the freezer. Repeat with the remaining ingredients to make 8 sandwiches.

3. Freeze the sandwiches for at least 1 hour before serving.

NUTRITIONAL FACTS (PER SERVING)
Calories: 105 Carbohydrates: 20.5 g Cholesterol: 1 mg
Fat: 1.5 g Fiber: 0.2 g Protein: 2.5 g Sodium: 117 mg

You Save: Calories: 40 Fat: 6.6 g

Cool Chocolate-Raspberry Torte

For variety, substitute low-fat cappuccino, cookies and cream, mint chocolate chip, or peanut butter ice cream for the raspberry ice cream or sherbet

1. To make the crust, break the crackers into pieces, and place in the bowl of a food processor. Process into fine crumbs. Measure the crumbs. There should be 1 cup. Adjust the amount if necessary.

2. Return the crumbs to the food processor, add the sugar, and process for a few seconds to mix well. Add the margarine, and process for about 20 seconds, or until the mixture is moist (but not wet) and crumbly, and holds together when pinched. If the mixture seems too dry, mix in more margarine, ½ teaspoon at a time, until the proper consistency is reached. Add the wheat germ or nuts, and process to mix well.

3. Coat a 9-inch springform pan with nonstick cooking spray, and use the back of a spoon to press the mixture against the bottom and sides of the pan, forming an even crust. (Periodically dip the spoon in sugar, if necessary, to prevent sticking.) Then use your fingers to finish pressing the crust firmly against the bottom and sides of the pan.

4. Bake at 350°F for 10 minutes, or until the edges feel firm and dry. Set aside to cool to room temperature before filling.

5. Allow the chocolate ice cream to sit at room temperature for about 10 minutes, or until slightly softened. Spread the ice cream evenly in the crust. Cover the pan, and freeze for at least 1 hour. Then top with the raspberry ice cream or sherbet in the same manner. Freeze for at least 2 hours.

6. To make the optional fudge topping, place the sugar, cocoa, and cornstarch in a 1-quart pot, and stir to mix well. Slowly stir in the milk, and cook over medium heat, stirring constantly, for about 5 minutes, or until the mixture is thickened and bubbly.

7. Remove the pot from the heat, and stir in the vanilla extract. Transfer the topping to a covered container and refrigerate for at least 2 hours, or until well chilled.

Yield: *12 servings*

CRUST

8 large (2½-x-5-inch) reduced-fat chocolate graham crackers

2 tablespoons sugar

1 tablespoon plus 1½ teaspoons tub-style nonfat margarine, or 2 tablespoons plus ½ teaspoon reduced-fat margarine or light butter, cut into pieces

3 tablespoons honey crunch wheat germ or finely chopped toasted walnuts or almond (page 383)

FILLING

4 cups nonfat or low-fat chocolate ice cream

4 cups nonfat or low-fat raspberry ripple ice cream or raspberry sherbet

FUDGE TOPPING (OPTIONAL)

½ cup sugar

¼ cup Dutch processed cocoa powder

1 tablespoon plus 1½ teaspoons cornstarch

¾ cup skim milk

1 teaspoon vanilla extract

8. Stir the chilled topping, and spread it over the top of the torte. Return the torte to the freezer, and freeze for at least 2 additional hours.

9. When ready to serve, remove the torte from the freezer, and allow to sit at room temperature for 5 minutes. Run a sharp knife between the edge of the torte and the rim of the pan, and remove the collar. Slice and serve immediately.

NUTRITIONAL FACTS (PER SERVING)
Calories: 175 Carbohydrates: 35 g Cholesterol: 3 mg
Fat: 1.4 g Fiber: 0.8 g Protein: 5.5 g Sodium: 154 mg

You Save: Calories: 192 Fat: 19.3 g

Time-Saving Tip

Instead of making the fudge sauce from scratch, substitute 1 cup of ready-made fat-free hot fudge topping.

Cool Peach Melba

1. Place the orange juice in the bottom of a microwave or conventional steamer, and arrange the peach halves in the steamer. Cover and cook at high power or over high heat for about 4 minutes, or until the peaches are tender but not mushy. Transfer the peaches and juice to a covered container, and chill for several hours or overnight.

2. Just before serving, make the sauce by placing the cornstarch and sugar in a 1-quart pot. Remove ½ cup of juice from the container of peaches, and add it to the sugar mixture, stirring until the cornstarch is dissolved.

3. Place the saucepan over medium heat, and cook, stirring constantly, for about 2 minutes, or until the mixture becomes thickened and bubbly. Add the raspberries, and bring to a second boil. Cook and stir just until the berries begin to break up. Remove the pot from the heat, and set aside.

4. To assemble the desserts, place a ½-cup scoop of ice cream in each of 6 dessert bowls. Top each scoop with a well-drained peach half, placing the hollow side down. Top with 3 tablespoons of the warm sauce, and serve immediately.

Yield: 6 servings

¾ cup orange juice

3 medium peaches, peeled, halved, and pitted

3 cups nonfat or low-fat vanilla ice cream

SAUCE

1 tablespoon plus 1 teaspoon cornstarch

3 tablespoons sugar

1¼ cups fresh or frozen (unthawed) raspberries

NUTRITIONAL FACTS (PER SERVING)
Calories: 161 Carbohydrates: 37 g Cholesterol: 2 mg
Fat: 0.5 g Fiber: 1.9 g Protein: 3.7 g Sodium: 55 mg

You Save: Calories: 96 Fat: 12 g

Mocha Meringue Tarts

Yield: 8 servings

8 Meringue Tart Shells (page 324)

1 quart nonfat or low-fat mocha or cappuccino ice cream

2 cups fresh raspberries

½ cup chocolate syrup

1. Place each tart on an individual serving dish, and place a ½-cup scoop of ice cream in the center of each tart.

2. Scatter ¼ cup of berries over and around the ice cream in each tart, and drizzle 1 tablespoon of the chocolate syrup over the top. Serve immediately.

NUTRITIONAL FACTS (PER SERVING)
Calories: 224 Carbohydrates: 51 g Cholesterol: 2 mg
Fat: 0.5 g Fiber: 1.6 g Protein: 4.9 g Sodium: 107 mg

You Save: Calories: 89 Fat: 12 g

Ice Cream with Cherry-Amaretto Sauce

Yield: 4 servings

2 tablespoons sugar

2¼ teaspoons cornstarch

¼ cup plus 2 tablespoons orange juice

1 bag (12 ounces) frozen sweet pitted cherries, unthawed (about 2¼ cups)

2 tablespoons amaretto liqueur

3 cups nonfat or low-fat vanilla, chocolate, or fudge ripple ice cream

1. Place the sugar and cornstarch in a 1-quart pot, and stir to mix well. Slowly add the orange juice while stirring to dissolve the cornstarch. Add the frozen cherries.

2. Place the pot over medium heat and cook, stirring constantly, for about 5 minutes, or until the mixture is thickened and bubbly. Add the amaretto, and stir for 30 additional seconds. Remove from the heat.

3. Place ¾ cup of ice cream in each of 4 serving bowls, and top each serving with ⅓ cup of the warm cherry sauce. Serve immediately.

NUTRITIONAL FACTS (PER SERVING)
Calories: 256 Carbohydrates: 54 g Cholesterol: 3 mg
Fat: 0.4 g Fiber: 1.9 g Protein: 5.3 g Sodium: 83 mg

You Save: Calories: 157 Fat: 17.7 g

Frozen Mocha Pie

For variety, substitute raspberry ripple or chocolate ice cream for the cappuccino ice cream.

1. To make the syrup, place the chocolate syrup and liqueur in a small bowl, and stir to mix well. Set aside.

2. To make the topping, place the whipped topping in a medium-sized bowl, and gently fold in 1 tablespoon of the chocolate syrup mixture. Set aside.

3. To assemble the pie, first split each of the ladyfingers in half lengthwise. (Most ladyfingers come presplit.) Line the bottom and sides of a 9-inch deep dish pie pan with about two-thirds of the ladyfinger halves, arranging them split side up. Drizzle half of the chocolate syrup mixture over the ladyfingers that line the bottom of the pan.

4. Spread the ice cream over the ladyfingers. Then top with the remaining ladyfingers, this time arranging them split side-down.

5. Drizzle the remaining chocolate syrup mixture over the ladyfingers; layer. Then spread the whipped topping mixture over the syrup, swirling the topping.

6. Cover the pie loosely with aluminum foil, and freeze for several hours or overnight. When ready to serve, sprinkle the cocoa over the top of the pie. Cut the pie into wedges, place the wedges on individual serving plates, and allow to sit at room temperature for 5 minutes before serving.

Yield: *8 servings*

¼ cup chocolate syrup

2 tablespoons coffee or amaretto liqueur

2 cups nonfat or light whipped topping

4 ounces ladyfingers (about 16 whole cookies)

4 cups nonfat or low-fat cappuccino ice cream, slightly softened

1 teaspoon cocoa powder

NUTRITIONAL FACTS (PER SERVING)
Calories: 202 Carbohydrates: 42 g Cholesterol: 27 mg
Fat: 1.4 g Fiber: 0.4 g Protein: 4.4 g Sodium: 176 mg

You Save: Calories: 93 Fat: 12.6 g

Chocolate Ice Cream Cake

Yield: *16 servings*

5 cups nonfat or low-fat vanilla or chocolate ice cream

CAKE

1 box (1 pound, 2.25 ounces) reduced-fat or regular chocolate cake mix

1 cup water or coffee, cooled to room temperature

¾ cup plain nonfat yogurt

½ cup fat-free egg substitute

FROSTING

2 tablespoons Dutch processed cocoa powder

2 tablespoons chocolate syrup

3 cups nonfat or light whipped topping

For variety, try making this cake with different ice cream flavors, such as cherry vanilla, raspberry ripple, cappuccino, banana, chocolate mint, pistachio, and others.

1. To make the cake, place the cake mix in a large bowl. Add the water or coffee, yogurt, and egg substitute, and beat with an electric mixer for about 2 minutes, or until well mixed.

2. Coat three 9-inch round cake pans with nonstick cooking spray, and divide the batter evenly among the pans. Bake at 350°F for about 23 minutes, or just until the tops spring back when lightly touched and a wooden toothpick inserted in the center of the cakes comes out clean. Be careful not to overbake. Allow the cakes to cool to room temperature.

3. When ready to assemble the cake, place the ice cream in a large bowl, and set aside for about 10 minutes, or until soft enough to spread.

4. Place one cake layer on a serving platter, with the bottom facing up. Spread half of the ice cream over the cake layer. Place another cake layer over the ice cream, bottom side up, and spread with the remaining ice cream. Top with the remaining cake layer, top side up. Cover with aluminum foil, and place in the freezer for at least 1 hour.

5. To make the frosting, place the cocoa powder and chocolate syrup in a medium-sized bowl and stir to mix well. Add ½ cup of the whipped topping, and gently fold the mixture together. Fold in the remaining whipped topping.

6. Spread the frosting over the top and sides of the cake. Cover loosely with foil or a cake lid, and return to the freezer for at least 4 hours, or until firm. Remove the cake from the freezer and allow to sit at room temperature for about 10 minutes before slicing and serving.

NUTRITIONAL FACTS (PER SERVING)
Calories: 223 Carbohydrates: 45 g Cholesterol: 2 mg
Fat: 2.8 g Fiber: 0.9 g Protein: 5 g Sodium: 328 mg

You Save: Calories: 140 Fat: 19.4 g

10

Colossal Cookies and Brownies

Cookies are the perfect treat when you want a bite of something sweet. A crisp, crunchy biscotti is just the right accompaniment to a steaming cup of cappuccino. And a soft oatmeal cookie makes a satisfyingly chewy mid-morning snack.

Unfortunately, cookies also tend to contain higher proportions of fat, sugar, and refined flour than other sweet treats do. In response to consumer demand, manufacturers have flooded the market with low- and no-fat cookies. But while lower in fat, these treats often contain extra sugar to help maintain a pleasing texture. As a result, the calorie count remains high—and the nutrient count, low.

The good news is that when made properly, cookies can provide great taste and nutrition without an overabundance of fat, sugar, and calories. Unlike most cookie recipes, the recipes in this chapter feature wholesome ingredients like whole wheat flour and whole grain cereals. Just as important, these recipes keep fat to a minimum. The secret? Prune

Purée, an easy-to-prepare fat substitute, is often used to replace the fat. Slightly sweet and mild in flavor, Prune Purée is one of the very best fat substitutes for cookies. Reduced-fat margarine and light butter also slash fat, while helping maintain the texture that you love.

Although it is impossible to make a good cookie without some sugar, the following recipes avoid adding the abundance of extra sugar found in many fat-free cookies. Instead, ingredients like whole grain flours and nonfat dry milk powder help provide texture, while dried fruits and flavorings like vanilla enhance sweetness.

So get out your cookie sheets and mixing bowl, and get ready to make some temptingly sweet, guilt-free treats. From Mocha Oatmeal Cookies to Cinnamon-Raisin Biscotti to Moist and Chewy Fudge Brownies, this chapter presents a variety of delightful cookies that will satisfy even the most discriminating of cookie monsters.

Getting the Fat Out of Your Cookie and Brownie Recipes

As the recipes in this chapter show, a variety of ingredients can be used to replace the fat in cookies and brownies. You can use these same ingredients to get the fat out of your own favorite recipes.

The remainder of this inset will look at the available fat substitutes, and will guide you in using these substitutes to "defat" your cookie and brownie recipes. (For guidelines on modifying cake recipes, see page 265.) At first, try replacing only half the fat in your recipe. Then try reducing the fat even more. Eventually, your family favorite will be as healthful as it is delicious.

Using Fat Substitutes in Cookies and Brownies

Fat Substitutes	In Which Items Do These Work Best?	How Should Your Recipes Be Modified When Using These Fat Substitutes?
Applesauce, mashed banana, puréed fruits, non-fat buttermilk, and nonfat yogurt.	Use applesauce, buttermilk, or yogurt when you want to change the taste as little as possible. Use mashed bananas, puréed raspberries, and other fruits for a change of pace.	❑ Replace part or all of the butter, margarine, or other solid fat in brownies with half as much fat substitute. Replace part or all of the oil with three-fourths as much fat substitute. Mix up the batter, and add more substitute if the batter seems too dry. ❑ Using the same guidelines, replace up to half the fat in cookie recipes. ❑ Replace each whole egg in brownie and cookie recipes with three tablespoons of fat-free egg substitute, if desired. ❑ Bake reduced-fat brownies at 325°F, and check for doneness a few minutes before the end of the usual baking time. Remove the brownies from the oven as soon as the edges are firm and the center is almost set. ❑ Bake reduced-fat cookies at 275°F to 300°F, and bake for 15 to 20 minutes, or until lightly browned.
Honey, maple syrup, molasses, corn syrup, Fruit Source liquid, chocolate syrup, fruit jams and spreads, and fruit juice concentrates.	Use honey or fruit jam in oatmeal cookies; chocolate syrup in brownies; and maple syrup or molasses in spice cookies. (Use corn syrup and Fruit Source liquid when you want to change the taste as little as possible. Use fruit juice concentrates in oatmeal and spice cookies.	❑ Replace part or all of the butter, margarine, or other solid fat in cookies and brownies with three-fourths as much fat substitute. Replace part or all of the oil with an equal amount of fat substitute. Mix up the batter, and add more substitute if the batter seems too dry. Note that totally fat-free cookies will be chewy in texture. If you want crisp cookies, replace no more than half the fat. ❑ Replace each whole egg in cookie recipes with two tablespoons of water. Replace each whole egg in brownie recipes with three tablespoons of fat-free egg substitute, if desired. ❑ Reduce the sugar in cookie and brownie recipes by the amount of substitute being added. ❑ Bake reduced-fat brownies at 325°F and check for doneness a few minutes before the end of the usual baking time. Remove the brownies from the oven as soon as the edges are firm and the center is almost set. ❑ Bake reduced-fat cookies at 275°F to 300°F. Bake for 15 to 20 minutes, or until lightly browned.

Fat Substitutes	In Which Items Do These Work Best?	How Should Your Recipes Be Modified When Using These Fat Substitutes?
Prune Butter (page 223)	This substitute is delicious in brownies and in spice, oatmeal, and chocolate cookies.	❑ Replace part or all of the butter, margarine, or other solid fat in brownies and cookies with an equal amount of fat substitute. ❑ Replace each whole egg in brownie and cookie recipes with three tablespoons of fat-free egg substitute, if desired. ❑ Reduce the sugar in cookie and brownie recipes by one-half to two-thirds the amount of fat substitute being used. ❑ Bake reduced-fat brownies at 325°F, and check for doneness a few minutes before the end of the usual baking time. Remove the brownies from the oven as soon as the edges are firm and the center is almost set. ❑ Bake reduced-fat cookies at 350°F, and check for doneness a few minutes before the end of the usual baking time.
Prune Purée (page 223)	Because of Prune Purée's wild flavor, it works well in all recipes.	❑ Replace part or all of the butter, margarine, or other solid fat in cookies and brownies with half as much Prune Purée. Replace part or all of the oil with three-fourths as much of the purée. ❑ Replace each whole egg in brownie recipes with three tablespoons of egg substitute, if desired. Replace each whole egg in cookie recipes with one egg white or two additional tablespoons of Prune Purée. ❑ Bake reduced-fat brownies at 325°F, and check for doneness a few minutes before the end of the usual baking time. Remove the brownies from the oven as soon as the edges are firm and the center is almost set. ❑ Bake reduced-fat cookies at 350°F, and check for doneness a few minutes before the end of the usual baking time.
Mashed cooked or canned pumpkin, butternut squash, and sweet potatoes	Use any of these substitutes in oatmeal, spice, and chocolate cookie recipes, and in brownies.	❑ Replace part or all of the butter, margarine. or other solid fat in brownies with one-half to three-fourths as much fat substitute. ❑ Replace part or all of the oil with one-half to three-fourths as much fat substitute. Mix up the batter, and add more substitute if the batter seems too dry. ❑ Replace part or all of the butter, margarine, or other solid fat in cookies with one-half to three-fourths as much fat substitute. Replace half of the oil with three-fourths as much fat substitute. Mix up the batter, and add more substitute if the batter seems too dry. ❑ Replace each whole egg in cookie and brownie recipes with three tablespoons of fat-free egg substitute, if desired. ❑ Bake reduced-fat brownies at 325°F, and check for doneness a few minutes before the end of the usual baking time. Remove the brownies from the oven as soon as the edges are firm and the center is almost set. ❑ Bake reduced-fat cookies at 275°F to 300°F, and check for doneness a few minutes before the end of the usual baking time.

Fat Substitutes	In Which Items Do These Work Best?	How Should Your Recipes Be Modified When Using These Fat Substitutes?
Reduced-fat margarine and light butter	These work well in any recipe.	❑ Be sure to choose a brand of butter or margarine that contains 5 to 6 grams of fat and 50 calories per tablespoon. Brands with less fat than this do not generally work well in baking. ❑ Avoid using reduced-fat margarine and light butter in cookie recipes that already contain liquid ingredients such as applesauce, pumpkin, or milk. Since these cookies already contain some water, a reduced-fat product will likely produce a cakey or rubbery texture. ❑ Replace all of the full-fat margarine, butter, or other solid fat with three-fourths as much reduced-fat margarine or light butter. ❑ Bake reduced-fat cookies at 300°F to 325°F until golden brown. This will generally take about 12 to 15 minutes, depending on the size of the cookie. ❑ Bake reduced-fat brownies at 325°F until the edges are firm and the center is almost set. Be careful not to overbake.

A few more general tips will help insure the best possible results when trimming the fat from your favorite cookie and brownie recipes.

❑ If your recipe is made with 100 percent white flour, substitute whole wheat pastry flour for at least half of the flour in the recipe. Or substitute oat flour, quick-cooking oats, or oat bran for at least a third of the flour. Since these products are lower in gluten than white flour, they will help maintain a pleasing texture.

❑ Try adding a few tablespoons of instant nonfat dry milk powder to the recipe. This will improve the texture, promote browning, and boost nutritional value.

❑ If you find that your low- and no-fat drop cookies do not spread enough during baking, try flattening them slightly with your fingertips or the tip of a spoon before putting them in the oven. Or add a little extra baking soda—about ¼ teaspoon—to the recipe.

❑ Realize that you may have to experiment a bit to perfect your recipe. For instance, if your cookies spread too much during baking, you may need to reduce the amount of liquid or slightly increase the amount of flour.

Orange Oatmeal Cookies

1. Combine the flour, oats, sugar, and baking soda in a large bowl, and stir to mix well. Add the corn syrup, Prune Butter, and orange juice, and stir to mix well. Fold in the raisins or cranberries and the pecans.

2. Coat a baking sheet with nonstick cooking spray. Drop rounded teaspoonfuls of dough onto the sheet, placing them 1½ inches apart. Slightly flatten each cookie with the tip of a spoon.

3. Bake at 275°F for 18 to 20 minutes, or until golden brown. Cool the cookies on the pan for 1 minute. Then transfer the cookies to wire racks, and cool completely. Serve immediately, or transfer to an air-tight container and arrange in single layers separated by sheets of waxed paper.

Yield: *42 cookies*

1 cup plus 2 tablespoons whole wheat pastry flour

1 cup plus 2 tablespoons quick-cooking oats

⅔ cup sugar

1 teaspoon baking soda

3 tablespoons light corn syrup

2 tablespoons Prune Butter (page 223)

¼ cup plus 2 tablespoons orange juice

½ cup dark raisins or dried cranberries

¼ cup toasted pecans (see page 383)

NUTRITIONAL FACTS (PER COOKIE)
Calories: 48 Cholesterol: 0 mg Fat: 0.6 g
Fiber: 0.8 g Protein: 0.9 g Sodium: 32 mg

Really Raisin Cookies

Yield: *42 cookies*

1 cup plus 2 tablespoons whole wheat pastry flour

¾ cup sugar

1 teaspoon baking soda

¼ cup plus 2 tablespoons Prune Purée (page 223)

1 tablespoon honey

1 teaspoon vanilla extract

2 cups bran flake cereal

⅓ cup dark raisins

⅓ cup golden raisins

¼ cup toasted wheat germ or chopped walnuts

1. Combine the flour, sugar, and baking soda in a large bowl, and stir to mix well. Add the Prune Purée, honey, and vanilla extract, and stir to mix well. Fold in first the cereal, and then the raisins and the wheat germ or walnuts.

2. Coat a baking sheet with nonstick cooking spray. Drop rounded teaspoonfuls of dough onto the sheet, placing them 1½ inches apart. Slightly flatten each cookie with the tip of a spoon. (Note that the dough will be slightly crumbly, so that you may have to press it together lightly to make it hold its shape.)

3. Bake at 350°F for 8 to 9 minutes, or until lightly browned. Cool the cookies on the pan for 1 minute. Then transfer the cookies to wire racks, and cool completely. Serve immediately, or transfer to an airtight container and arrange in single layers separated by sheets of waxed paper.

NUTRITIONAL FACTS (PER COOKIE)
Calories: 44 Cholesterol: 0 mg Fat: 0.2 g
Fiber: 1 g Protein: 1 g Sodium: 44 mg

Milk Chocolate Chippers

1. Combine the flour, milk powder, sugars, and baking soda in a large bowl, and stir to mix well. Add the Prune Purée and vanilla extract, and stir to mix well. (The mixture will seem dry at first, but will form a stiff dough as you keep stirring.) Fold in the chocolate chips, the raisins, and, if desired, the walnuts.

2. Coat a baking sheet with nonstick cooking spray. Drop rounded teaspoonfuls of dough onto the sheet, placing them 1½ inches apart. Slightly flatten each cookie with the tip of a spoon.

3. Bake at 350°F for 9 minutes, or until lightly browned. Cool the cookies on the pan for 1 minute. Then transfer the cookies to wire racks, and cool completely. Serve immediately, or transfer to an airtight container and arrange in single layers separated by sheets of waxed paper.

Yield: *42 cookies*

1⅓ cups whole wheat pastry flour

¼ cup instant nonfat dry milk powder

½ cup sugar

¼ cup plus 2 tablespoons brown sugar

¾ teaspoon baking soda

¼ cup plus 2 tablespoons Prune Purée (page 223)

1 teaspoon vanilla extract

½ cup milk chocolate or semi-sweet chocolate chips

⅓ cup dark raisins

¼ cup chopped walnuts (optional)

NUTRITIONAL FACTS (PER COOKIE)
Calories: 43 Cholesterol: 0 mg Fat: 0.7 g
Fiber: 0.7 g Protein: 0.7 g Sodium: 26 mg

Moist and Chewy Brownies

1. Combine the flour, oat bran, cocoa, sugar, milk powder, and baking soda in a large bowl, and stir to mix well. Stir in the chocolate syrup, egg whites, and vanilla extract. Fold in the nuts if desired.

2. Coat an 8-inch square pan with nonstick cooking spray. Spread the batter evenly in the pan, and bake at 325°F for 23 minutes, or just until the edges are firm and the center is almost set.

3. Cool to room temperature, cut into squares, and serve.

Yield: *16 brownies*

¼ cup plus 1 tablespoon unbleached flour

¼ cup oat bran

⅓ cup cocoa powder

¾ cup sugar

¼ cup instant nonfat dry milk powder

1 pinch baking soda

¼ cup chocolate syrup

3 egg whites

1 teaspoon vanilla extract

⅓ cup chopped walnuts (optional)

NUTRITIONAL FACTS (PER SERVING)
Calories: 71 Cholesterol: 0 mg Fat: 0.4 g
Fiber: 1 g Protein: 2 g Sodium: 28 mg

Double Fudge Delights

Yield: *36 cookies*

1¼ cups whole wheat pastry flour

½ cup oat bran

½ cup plus 2 tablespoons sugar

¼ cup cocoa powder

¾ teaspoon baking soda

¼ cup plus 2 tablespoons Prune Butter (page 223)

¼ cup plus 2 tablespoons chocolate syrup

1 egg white

1 teaspoon vanilla extract

36 pecan halves (optional)

1. Combine the flour, oat bran, sugar, cocoa, and baking soda in a large bowl, and stir to mix well. Add the Prune Butter, chocolate syrup, egg white, and vanilla extract, and stir to mix well. (The mixture will seem dry at first, but will form a stiff dough as you keep stirring.)

2. Coat a baking sheet with nonstick cooking spray. Roll the dough into 1-inch balls, and place 1½ inches apart on the sheet. (If the dough is too sticky to handle, place it in the freezer for a few minutes.) Using the bottom of a glass dipped in sugar, flatten the cookies to ¼-inch thickness. As an alternative, press a pecan half in the center of each cookie to flatten the dough.

3. Bake at 325°F for 10 minutes, or until lightly browned. Cool the cookies on the pan for one minute. Then transfer the cookies to wire racks, and cool completely. Serve immediately, or transfer to an airtight container and arrange in single layers separated by sheets of waxed paper.

NUTRITIONAL FACTS (PER COOKIE)
Calories: 44 Cholesterol: 0 mg Fat: 0.2 g
Fiber: 1.2 g Protein: 1 g Sodium: 30 mg

Oatmeal Fudqe Squares

1. Combine the oats and applesauce or banana, and let sit for 5 minutes. Add the remaining ingredients, and stir to mix well.

2. Coat an 8-inch square pan with nonstick cooking spray. Spread the batter evenly in the pan, and bake at 325°F for about 22 minutes, or just until the edges are firm and the center is almost set.

3. Cool to room temperature, cut into squares, and serve.

Yield: *16 servings*

½ cup plus 2 tablespoons quick-cooking oats

¼ cup unsweetened applesauce or mashed banana

½ cup sugar

⅓ cup cocoa powder

2 tablespoons unbleached flour

¼ teaspoon salt (optional)

¼ cup honey

2 egg whites

1 teaspoon vanilla extract

¼ cup chopped walnuts (optional)

NUTRITIONAL FACTS (PER SERVING)
Calories: 64 Calcium: 5 mg Cholesterol: 0 mg
Fat: 0.5 g Fiber: 1 g Iron: 0.4 mg
Potassium: 35 mg Protein: 1.4 g Sodium: 20 mg

Fat-Free Fudqe Brownies

1. Combine the flour, cocoa, sugar, and salt, if desired, and stir to mix well. Stir in the applesauce, egg whites, and vanilla extract. Fold in the nuts if desired.

2. Coat an 8-inch square pan with nonstick cooking spray. Spread the batter evenly in the pan, and bake at 325°F for 23 to 25 minutes, or just until the edges are firm and the center is almost set.

3. Cool to room temperature, cut into squares, and serve.

Yield: *16 servings*

¾ cup unbleached flour

¼ cup plus 2 tablespoons cocoa powder

1 cup sugar

¼ teaspoon salt (optional)

⅓ cup unsweetened applesauce

3 egg whites

1 teaspoon vanilla extract

¼ cup chopped walnuts (optional)

NUTRITIONAL FACTS (PER SERVING)
Calories: 80 Calcium: 4 mg Cholesterol: 0 mg
Fat: 0.4 g Fiber: 0.8 g Iron: 0.5 mg
Potassium: 32 mg Protein: 1.6 g Sodium: 25 mg

Cocoa Banana Brownies

Yield: *16 servings*

1 cup oat bran

⅓ cup cocoa powder

1 cup sugar

¾ cup mashed very ripe banana
   (about 1½ large)

3 egg whites

1 teaspoon vanilla extract

¼ cup chopped walnuts (optional)

1. Combine the oat bran, cocoa, and sugar, and stir to mix well. Stir in the remaining ingredients.

2. Coat an 8-inch square pan with nonstick cooking spray. Spread the batter evenly in the pan, and bake at 325°F for 25 to 30 minutes, or just until the edges are firm and the center is almost set.

3. Cool to room temperature, cut into squares, and serve.

NUTRITIONAL FACTS (PER SERVING)
Calories: 80 Calcium: 7 mg Cholesterol: 0 mg
Fat: 0.8 g Fiber: 1.7 g Iron: 0.5 mg
Potassium: 96 mg Protein: 2.1 g Sodium: 23 mg

Applesauce Oatmeal Cookies

Yield: *50 cookies*

3 cups quick-cooking oats

1 cup whole wheat pastry flour

1 teaspoon baking soda

¼ teaspoon ground nutmeg

1 cup unsweetened applesauce

1 cup sugar

1 teaspoon vanilla extract

⅔ cup dark raisins

1. Combine the oats, flour, baking soda, and nutmeg, and stir to mix well. Add the applesauce, sugar, and vanilla extract, and stir to mix well. Stir in the raisins.

2. Coat cookie sheets with nonstick cooking spray. Roll the dough into 1-inch balls, and place the balls 1½ inches apart on the cookie sheets. (If the dough is too sticky to handle, place it in the freezer for a few minutes.) Using the bottom of a glass dipped in sugar, flatten the cookies to ¼-inch thickness.

3. Bake at 275°F for about 22 minutes, or until lightly browned. Transfer the cookies to wire racks, and cool completely. Serve immediately, or transfer to an airtight container and arrange in single layers separated by sheets of waxed paper.

NUTRITIONAL FACTS (PER COOKIE)
Calories: 49 Calcium: 5 mg Cholesterol: 0 mg
Fat: 0.3 g Fiber: 1 g Iron: 0.4 mg
Potassium: 48 mg Protein: 1.2 g Sodium: 17 mg

PEPPERMINT BROWNIES

1. Combine the oats, yogurt, and water, and set aside for 5 minutes.

2. Combine the flour, sugar, and cocoa, and stir to mix well. Add the oat mixture, egg whites, and vanilla extract to the flour mixture, and stir to mix well.

3. Coat an 8-inch square pan with nonstick cooking spray. Spread the batter evenly in the pan, and bake at 325°F for about 22 minutes, or just until the edges are firm and the center is almost set. Cool to room temperature.

4. To make the icing, combine the icing ingredients in a small bowl, and stir until smooth. If using a microwave oven, microwave the icing, uncovered, at high power for 20 seconds. If using a conventional stove top, transfer the icing to a small saucepan and place over medium heat for 20 seconds, stirring constantly. Drizzle the icing over the brownies, and let the glaze set for at least 10 minutes before cutting into squares and serving.

NUTRITIONAL FACTS (PER SERVING)
Calories: 85 Calcium: 11 mg Cholesterol: 0 mg
Fat: 0.5 g Fiber: 0.9 g Iron: 0.5 mg
Potassium: 42 mg Protein: 1.9 g Sodium: 28 mg

Yield: *16 servings*

⅓ cup quick-cooking oats

¼ cup plain nonfat yogurt

2 tablespoons water

½ cup unbleached flour

¾ cup plus 2 tablespoons sugar

¼ cup plus 2 tablespoons cocoa powder

3 egg whites

1½ teaspoons vanilla extract

ICING

½ cup confectioners' sugar

2 drops peppermint extract

1 drop green or red food coloring

2 teaspoons skim milk

HONEY GRANOLA BARS

Yield: *12 servings*

1¼ cups quick-cooking oats

¼ cup whole wheat pastry flour or unbleached flour

¼ cup toasted wheat germ

¼ teaspoon ground cinnamon

¼ cup plus 2 tablespoons honey

⅓ cup dark raisins or chopped dried apricots

1. Combine the oats, flour, wheat germ, and cinnamon, and stir to mix well. Add the honey, and stir until the mixture is moist and crumbly. Fold in the raisins or apricots.

2. Coat an 8-inch square pan with nonstick cooking spray. Pat the mixture into the pan, and bake at 300°F for 18 to 20 minutes, or until lightly browned.

3. Cool to room temperature, cut into bars, and serve.

NUTRITIONAL FACTS (PER SERVING)
Calories: 95 Calcium: 9 mg Cholesterol: 0 mg
Fat: 0.7 g Fiber: 1.8 g Iron: 0.8 mg
Potassium: 95 mg Protein: 2.4 g Sodium: 2 mg

HONEY OAT BROWNIES

Yield: *16 servings*

¾ cup quick-cooking oats

¼ cup unbleached flour

¼ cup plus 2 tablespoons cocoa powder

½ cup sugar

⅛ teaspoon baking powder

⅛ teaspoon salt (optional)

¼ cup plus 2 tablespoons honey

¼ cup water

1 teaspoon vanilla extract

¼ cup chopped walnuts (optional)

1. Combine the oats, flour, cocoa, sugar, baking powder, and salt, if desired, and stir to mix well. Stir in the remaining ingredients.

2. Coat an 8-inch square pan with nonstick cooking spray. Spread the batter evenly in the pan, and bake at 325°F for about 20 minutes, or until the edges are firm and the center is almost set.

3. Cool to room temperature, cut into squares, and serve.

NUTRITIONAL FACTS (PER SERVING)
Calories: 75 Calcium: 6 mg Cholesterol: 0 mg
Fat: 0.6 g Fiber: 1.1 g Iron: 0.5 mg
Potassium: 33 mg Protein: 1.2 g Sodium: 18 mg

BROWN RICE BISCOTTI

Yield: 24 biscotti

1. Combine the flours, sugar, and baking powder, and stir to mix well. Add the remaining ingredients, and stir just until the dough holds together.

2. Turn the dough onto a lightly floured surface, and shape into two 9-x-2-inch logs. Coat a baking sheet with nonstick cooking spray, and place the logs on the sheet. Bake at 350°F for 18 to 20 minutes, or until lightly browned.

3. Cool the logs at room temperature for 10 minutes. Then use a serrated knife to slice the logs diagonally into ½-inch-thick slices.

4. Place the slices on a baking sheet in a single layer, and bake at 325°F for 18 to 20 minutes, or until lightly browned, turning after 10 minutes.

5. Transfer the biscotti to wire racks, and cool completely. Serve immediately or store in an airtight container.

1 cup unbleached flour

½ cup whole wheat pastry flour

½ cup brown rice flour

¼ cup sugar

2 teaspoons baking powder

¼ cup honey or brown rice syrup

3 egg whites

1 teaspoon vanilla extract

⅓ cup finely chopped dried apricots

2 tablespoons finely ground pecans

NUTRITIONAL FACTS (PER BISCOTTI)

Calories: 60 Calcium: 8 mg Cholesterol: 0 mg
Fat: 0.5 g Fiber: 0.7 g Iron: 0.5 mg
Potassium: 52 mg Protein: 1.5 g Sodium: 35 mg

Chocolate Oatmeal Jumbles

Yield: *42 cookies*

1 cup whole wheat pastry flour or unbleached flour

1 cup quick-cooking oats

¼ cup sugar

2 tablespoons cocoa powder

1 teaspoon baking soda

½ cup plus 2 tablespoons chocolate syrup

2 tablespoons plus 2 teaspoons water

1 teaspoon vanilla extract

¼ cup dark raisins

¼ cup chopped walnuts

¼ cup chocolate chips

1. Combine the flour, oats, sugar, cocoa, and baking soda, and stir to mix well. Add the chocolate syrup, water, and vanilla extract, and stir to mix well. Stir in the remaining ingredients.

2. Coat a baking sheet with nonstick cooking spray. Drop rounded teaspoonfuls of dough onto the baking sheet, placing them 1½ inches apart. Slightly flatten each cookie with the tip of a spoon.

3. Bake at 275°F for 18 to 20 minutes, or until lightly browned. Cool the cookies on the pan for 1 minute. Then transfer the cookies to wire racks, and cool completely. Serve immediately, or transfer to an airtight container and arrange in single layers separated by sheets of waxed paper.

NUTRITIONAL FACTS (PER COOKIE)
Calories: 46 Calcium: 4 mg Cholesterol: 0 mg
Fat: 0.9 g Fiber: 0.9 g Iron: 0.4 mg
Potassium: 46 mg Protein: 1.1 g Sodium: 27 mg

Molasses Oatmeal Treats

1. Combine the flour, oats, sugar, and baking soda, and stir to mix well. Add the molasses, water, and vanilla extract, and stir to mix well. Stir in the remaining ingredients.

2. Coat a baking sheet with nonstick cooking spray. Drop rounded teaspoonfuls of dough onto the baking sheet, placing them 1½ inches apart. Slightly flatten each cookie with the tip of a spoon.

3. Bake at 275°F for 18 to 20 minutes, or until lightly browned. Cool the cookies on the pan for 1 minute. Then transfer the cookies to wire racks, and cool completely. Serve immediately, or transfer to an airtight container and arrange in single layers separated by sheets of waxed paper.

Yield: 42 cookies

1 cup whole wheat pastry flour or unbleached flour

1 cup quick-cooking oats

¼ cup sugar

1 teaspoon baking soda

½ cup plus 2 tablespoons molasses

2 tablespoons plus 2 teaspoons water

1 teaspoon vanilla extract

¼ cup toasted wheat germ

1 cup bran flake-and-raisin cereal

⅔ cup chopped dried apricots or other dried fruit

NUTRITIONAL FACTS (PER COOKIE)
Calories: 43 Calcium: 12 mg Cholesterol: 0 mg
Fat: 0.3 g Fiber: 1 g Iron: 0.8 mg
Potassium: 105 mg Protein: 1 g Sodium: 27 mg

Whole Wheat Ginger Snaps

Yield: *24 cookies*

1⅓ cups whole wheat pastry flour

¼ cup sugar

¾ teaspoon baking soda

½ teaspoon ground ginger

¼ cup molasses

3 tablespoons frozen orange juice concentrate, thawed

1. Combine the flour, sugar, baking soda, and ginger, and stir to mix well. Stir in the molasses and orange juice concentrate.

2. Coat a baking sheet with nonstick cooking spray. Roll the dough into 1-inch balls, and place 1½ inches apart on the baking sheet. (If the dough is too sticky to handle, place it in the freezer for a few minutes.) Using the bottom of a glass dipped in sugar, flatten the cookies to ¼-inch thickness.

3. Bake at 300°F for about 12 minutes, or until lightly browned. Cool the cookies on the pan for 1 minute. Then transfer the cookies to wire racks, and cool completely. Serve immediately, or transfer to an airtight container and arrange in single layers separated by sheets of waxed paper.

NUTRITIONAL FACTS (PER COOKIE)
Calories: 41 Calcium: 8 mg Cholesterol: 0 mg
Fat: 0.1 g Fiber: 0.8 g Iron: 0.4 mg
Potassium: 72 mg Protein: 0.9 g Sodium: 26 mg

BANANA MUESLI COOKIES

1. Combine the flour, oats, and baking soda, and stir to mix well. Add the banana and maple syrup, and stir to mix well. Stir in the cereal.

2. Coat a baking sheet with nonstick cooking spray. Roll the dough into 1-inch balls, and place 1½ inches apart on the baking sheet. (If the dough is too sticky to handle, place it in the freezer for a few minutes.) Using the bottom of a glass dipped in sugar, flatten the cookies to ¼-inch thickness. As an alternative, press a pecan half in the center of each cookie to flatten the dough.

3. Bake at 275°F for about 18 minutes, or until lightly browned. Cool the cookies on the pan for 1 minute. Then transfer the cookies to wire racks, and cool completely. Serve immediately, or transfer to an airtight container and arrange in single layers separated by sheets of waxed paper.

Yield: *30 cookies*

1 cup whole wheat pastry flour or unbleached flour

1 cup quick-cooking oats

¾ teaspoon baking soda

⅔ cup mashed very ripe banana (about 1½ large)

¼ cup plus 2 tablespoons maple syrup

1 cup ready-to-eat muesli cereal

30 pecan halves (optional)

NUTRITIONAL FACTS (PER COOKIE)
Calories: 46 Calcium: 9 mg Cholesterol: 0 mg
Fat: 0.4 g Fiber: 1 g Iron: 0.3 mg
Potassium: 60 mg Protein: 1.2 g Sodium: 28 mg

Jam 'n' Oatmeal Cookies

Yield: *60 cookies*

1½ cups whole wheat pastry flour
   or unbleached flour

2 cups quick-cooking oats

¾ cup light brown sugar

1¼ teaspoons baking soda

½ teaspoon ground cinnamon

¾ cup jam or fruit spread (try
   apricot, peach, pineapple,
   raspberry, or strawberry)

¼ cup water

1 teaspoon vanilla extract

¾ cup dark raisins, chopped
   dried fruit, or chopped nuts

1. Combine the flour, oats, brown sugar, baking soda, and cinnamon, and stir to mix well. Add the jam or fruit spread, water, and vanilla extract, and stir to mix well. Stir in the fruit or nuts.

2. Coat a baking sheet with nonstick cooking spray. Drop rounded teaspoonfuls of dough onto the baking sheet, placing them 1½ inches apart. Slightly flatten each cookie with the tip of a spoon.

3. Bake at 275°F for about 18 minutes, or until lightly browned. Cool the cookies on the pan for 1 minute. Then transfer the cookies to wire racks, and cool completely. Serve immediately, or transfer to an airtight container and arrange in single layers separated by sheets of waxed paper.

NUTRITIONAL FACTS (PER COOKIE)
Calories: 48 Calcium: 7 mg Cholesterol: 0 mg
Fat: 0.2 g Fiber: 0.8 g Iron: 0.4 mg
Potassium: 55 mg Protein: 0.9 g Sodium: 15 mg

Apricot Tea Cookies

1. Combine the flour, oat bran, sugar, and baking soda, and stir to mix well. Add the jam and water, and stir to mix well. Stir in the dried apricots.

2. Coat a baking sheet with nonstick cooking spray. Roll the dough into 1-inch balls, and place 1½ inches apart on the baking sheet. (If the dough is too sticky to handle, place it in the freezer for a few minutes.) Using the bottom of a glass dipped in sugar, flatten the cookies to ¼-inch thickness. As an alternative, press a pecan half or almond in the center of each cookie to flatten the dough.

3. Bake at 300°F for 15 to 18 minutes, or until lightly browned. Cool the cookies on the pan for 1 minute. Then transfer the cookies to wire racks, and cool completely. Serve immediately, or transfer to an airtight container and arrange in single layers separated by sheets of waxed paper.

Yield: *35 cookies*

1¼ cups unbleached flour

1 cup oat bran

¼ cup plus 2 tablespoons sugar

¾ teaspoon baking soda

¼ cup plus 2 tablespoons apricot jam

¼ cup water

½ cup chopped dried apricots

36 pecan halves or whole almonds (optional)

NUTRITIONAL FACTS (PER COOKIE)

Calories: 45 Calcium: 4 mg Cholesterol: 0 mg
Fat: 0.2 g Fiber: 0.7 g Iron: 0.5 mg
Potassium: 43 mg Protein: 1 g Sodium: 19 mg

Very Best Fudge Brownies

Yield: *36 servings*

4 squares (1 ounce each)
    unsweetened baking chocolate

1½ cups sugar

½ cup plus 1 tablespoon fat-free
    egg substitute

¾ cup Prune Butter (page 223)

2 teaspoons vanilla extract

1 cup unbleached flour

¼ teaspoon salt (optional)

¾ cup chopped walnuts (optional)

1. If using a microwave oven to melt the chocolate, place the chocolate in a mixing bowl and microwave uncovered at high power for 3 to 4 minutes, or until almost melted. Remove the bowl from the oven and stir the chocolate until completely melted. If melting the chocolate on the stove top, place the chocolate in a small saucepan and cook over low heat, stirring constantly, until melted.

2. Add the sugar, egg substitute, Prune Butter, and vanilla extract to the chocolate, and stir to mix well. Stir in the flour and, if desired, the salt and nuts.

3. Coat a 9-x-13-inch pan with nonstick cooking spray. Spread the batter evenly in the pan, and bake at 325°F for 35 to 40 minutes, or until the edges are firm and the center is almost set.

4. Cool to room temperature, cut into squares, and serve.

NUTRITIONAL FACTS (PER SERVING)
Calories: 74 Calcium: 6 mg Cholesterol: 0 mg
Fat: 1.7 g Fiber: 1.1 g Iron: 0.6 mg
Potassium: 72 mg Protein: 1.3 g Sodium: 21 mg

Very Best Cake Brownies

1. If using a microwave oven to melt the chocolate, place the chocolate in a mixing bowl and microwave uncovered at high power for 3 to 4 minutes, or until almost melted. Remove the bowl from the oven and stir the chocolate until completely melted. If melting the chocolate on the stove top, place the chocolate in a small saucepan and cook over low heat, stirring constantly, until melted.

2. Add the sugar, egg substitute, milk, Prune Butter, and vanilla extract to the chocolate, and stir to mix well. Stir in the flour and, if desired, the salt and nuts.

3. Coat a 9-x-13-inch pan with nonstick cooking spray. Spread the batter evenly in the pan, and bake at 325°F for 35 to 40 minutes, or until the center springs back when lightly touched.

4. Cool to room temperature, cut into squares, and serve.

Yield: *36 servings*

4 squares (1 ounce each) unsweetened baking chocolate

1½ cups sugar

½ cup plus 1 tablespoon fat-free egg substitute

½ cup skim milk

¾ cup Prune Butter (page 223)

2 teaspoons vanilla extract

1½ cups unbleached flour

¼ teaspoon salt (optional)

¾ cup chopped walnuts (optional)

NUTRITIONAL FACTS (PER SERVING)
Calories: 90 Calcium: 6 mg Cholesterol: 0 mg
Fat: 1.7 g Fiber: 1.3 g Iron: 0.8 mg
Potassium: 87 mg Protein: 1.7 g Sodium: 32 mg

Fudgy Cocoa Brownies

Yield: *16 servings*

½ cup Prune Butter (page 223)

¾ cup sugar

3 egg whites

¼ cup plus 2 tablespoons cocoa
   powder

¼ cup plus 2 tablespoons
   unbleached flour

¼ cup oat bran

⅛ teaspoon salt (optional)

1 teaspoon vanilla extract

⅓ cup chopped nuts (optional)

1. Combine the Prune Butter, sugar, and egg whites, and stir to mix well. Add the remaining ingredients and stir well.

2. Coat an 8-inch square pan with nonstick cooking spray. Spread the batter evenly in the pan, and bake at 325°F for 23 to 25 minutes, or until the edges are firm and the center is almost set.

3. Cool to room temperature, cut into squares, and serve.

NUTRITIONAL FACTS (PER SERVING)
Calories: 76 Calcium: 10 mg Cholesterol: 0 mg
Fat: 0.5 g Fiber: 1.6 g Iron: 0.8 mg
Potassium: 82 mg Protein: 1.5 g Sodium: 23 mg

Milk Chocolate Brownies

Yield: *16 servings*

½ cup Prune Butter (page 223)

¾ cup sugar

3 egg whites

2 teaspoons vanilla extract

½ cup unbleached flour

¼ cup plus 2 tablespoons cocoa
   powder

3 tablespoons nonfat dry milk

⅛ teaspoon salt (optional)

⅓ cup chopped nuts (optional)

1. Combine the Prune Butter, sugar, egg whites, and vanilla extract, and stir to mix well. Stir in the remaining ingredients.

2. Coat an 8-inch square pan with nonstick cooking spray. Spread the batter evenly in the pan, and bake at 325°F for 25 to 30 minutes, or just until the edges are firm and the center is almost set.

3. Cool to room temperature, cut into squares, and serve.

NUTRITIONAL FACTS (PER SERVING)
Calories: 78 Calcium: 17 mg Cholesterol: 0 mg
Fat: 0.5 g Fiber: 1.4 g Iron: 0.6 mg
Potassium: 85 mg Protein: 1.9 g Sodium: 29 mg

Chewy Coconut Brownies

1. Combine the oats, flour, cocoa, sugar, and salt, if desired, and stir to mix well. Stir in the Prune Purée, egg whites, and extracts. Fold in the coconut.

2. Coat an 8-inch square pan with nonstick cooking spray. Spread the batter evenly in the pan, and bake at 325°F for about 22 minutes, or until the edges are firm and the center is almost set.

3. Cool to room temperature, cut into squares, and serve.

NUTRITIONAL FACTS (PER SERVING)
Calories: 79 Calcium: 5 mg Cholesterol: 0 mg
Fat: 0.8 g Fiber: 1 g Iron: 0.5 mg
Potassium: 45 mg Protein: 1.5 g Sodium: 24 mg

Yield: *16 servings*

¼ cup plus 2 tablespoons quick-cooking oats

¼ cup plus 2 tablespoons unbleached flour

¼ cup plus 2 tablespoons cocoa powder

1 cup sugar

⅛ teaspoon salt (optional)

¼ cup Prune Purée (page 223)

2 egg whites

1 teaspoon vanilla extract

1 teaspoon coconut-flavored extract

2 tablespoons shredded coconut

Oatmeal Raisin Cookies

Yield: *40 cookies*

1 cup whole wheat pastry flour or unbleached flour

1½ cups quick-cooking oats

½ cup sugar

1 teaspoon baking soda

¼ cup Prune Purée (page 223)

¼ cup plus 2 tablespoons honey or molasses

1 teaspoon vanilla extract

½ cup dark raisins

½ cup chopped walnuts (optional)

1. Combine the flour, oats, sugar, and baking soda, and stir to mix well. Add the Prune Purée, honey or molasses, and vanilla extract, and stir to mix well. (If the dough seems crumbly, keep stirring until it holds together.) Stir in the raisins and nuts if desired.

2. Coat a baking sheet with nonstick cooking spray. Drop rounded teaspoonfuls of dough onto the sheet, placing them 1½ inches apart. Slightly flatten each cookie with the tip of a spoon.

3. Bake at 350°F for about 9 minutes, or until golden brown. Cool the cookies on the pan for 1 minute. Then transfer the cookies to wire racks, and cool completely. Serve immediately, or transfer to an airtight container and arrange in single layers separated by sheets of waxed paper.

NUTRITIONAL FACTS (PER COOKIE)
Calories: 48 Calcium: 5 mg Cholesterol: 0 mg
Fat: 0.3 g Fiber: 0.8 g Iron: 0.3 mg
Potassium: 43 mg Protein: 0.7 g Sodium: 21 mg

Raisin and Bran Jumbles

1. Combine the flour, sugar, and baking soda, and stir to mix well. Add the Prune Purée, maple syrup, and vanilla extract, and stir to mix well. Stir in the cereal, apricots, and prunes.

2. Coat a baking sheet with nonstick cooking spray. Drop rounded teaspoonfuls of dough onto the sheet, placing them 1½ inches apart. Slightly flatten each cookie with the tip of a spoon.

3. Bake at 350°F for about 9 minutes, or until golden brown. Cool the cookies on the pan for 1 minute. Then transfer the cookies to wire racks, and cool completely. Serve immediately, or transfer to an airtight container and arrange in single layers separated by sheets of waxed paper.

NUTRITIONAL FACTS (PER COOKIE)

Calories: 42 Calcium: 5 mg Cholesterol: 0 mg
Fat: 0.1 g Fiber: 0.9 g Iron: 0.6 mg
Potassium: 58 mg Protein: 0.8 g Sodium: 36 mg

Yield: *42 cookies*

1 cup plus 2 tablespoons whole wheat pastry flour or unbleached flour

¾ cup sugar

1 teaspoon baking soda

¼ cup Prune Purée (page 223)

3 tablespoons maple syrup

1 teaspoon vanilla extract

2 cups bran flake-and-raisin cereal

⅓ cup chopped dried apricots

⅓ cup chopped prunes

CRANBERRY SPICE COOKIES

Yield: *42 cookies*

1 cup whole wheat pastry flour

¾ cup plus 2 tablespoons unbleached flour

⅔ cup sugar

1 teaspoon baking soda

½ teaspoon ground cinnamon

⅛ teaspoon ground nutmeg

¼ cup plus 2 tablespoons Prune Purée (page 223)

¼ cup honey

1 teaspoon vanilla extract

½ cup dried cranberries or golden raisins

1 cup oat flakes or other ready-to-eat cereal flakes

1. Combine the flours, sugar, baking soda, and spices, and stir to mix well. Add the Prune Purée, honey, and vanilla extract, and stir to mix well. Stir in the cranberries or raisins and the cereal flakes.

2. Coat a baking sheet with nonstick cooking spray. Drop rounded teaspoonfuls of dough onto the sheet, placing them 1½ inches apart. Slightly flatten each cookie with the tip of a spoon.

3. Bake at 350°F for about 9 minutes, or until golden brown. Cool the cookies on the pan for 1 minute. Then transfer the cookies to wire racks, and cool completely. Serve immediately, or transfer to an airtight container and arrange in single layers separated by sheets of waxed paper.

NUTRITIONAL FACTS (PER COOKIE)
Calories: 47 Calcium: 3 mg Cholesterol: 0 mg
Fat: 0.1 g Fiber: 0.6 g Iron: 0.5 mg
Potassium: 37 mg Protein: 0.8 g Sodium: 25 mg

Colossal Chocolate Chippers

1. Combine the flours, sugar, and baking soda, and stir to mix well. Add the Prune Purée, honey, and vanilla extract, and stir to mix well. (If the dough seems crumbly, keep stirring until it holds together.) Stir in the chocolate chips and nuts if desired.

2. Coat a baking sheet with nonstick cooking spray. Drop slightly rounded teaspoonfuls of dough onto the sheet, placing them 1½ inches apart. Slightly flatten each cookie with the tip of a spoon.

3. Bake at 350°F for about 9 minutes, or until golden brown. Cool the cookies on the pan for 1 minute. Then transfer the cookies to wire racks, and cool completely. Serve immediately, or transfer to an airtight container and arrange in single layers separated by sheets of waxed paper.

Yield: *30 cookies*

¾ cup whole wheat pastry flour

½ cup unbleached flour

⅔ cup sugar

¾ teaspoon baking soda

¼ cup Prune Purée (page 223)

2 tablespoons honey

1 teaspoon vanilla extract

⅓ cup chocolate chips

⅓ cup chopped walnuts (optional)

NUTRITIONAL FACTS (PER COOKIE)
Calories: 49 Calcium: 2 mg Cholesterol: 0 mg
Fat: 0.7 g Fiber: 0.5 g Iron: 0.3 mg
Potassium: 25 mg Protein: 0.7 g Sodium: 21 mg

Mint Chocolate Drops

Yield: *30 cookies*

1 cup plus 1 tablespoon whole wheat pastry flour or unbleached flour

2 tablespoons cocoa powder

½ cup sugar

¾ teaspoon baking soda

¼ cup Prune Purée (page 223)

3 tablespoons chocolate syrup

1 teaspoon vanilla extract

⅓ cup mint chocolate chips

1. Combine the flour, cocoa, sugar, and baking soda, and stir to mix well. Add the Prune Purée, chocolate syrup, and vanilla extract, and stir to mix well. (If the dough seems crumbly, keep stirring until it holds together.) Stir in the chocolate chips.

2. Coat a baking sheet with nonstick cooking spray. Drop rounded teaspoonfuls of dough onto the sheet, placing them 1½ inches apart. Slightly flatten each cookie with the tip of a spoon.

3. Bake at 350°F for about 10 minutes, or until golden brown. Cool the cookies on the pan for 1 minute. Then transfer the cookies to wire racks, and cool completely. Serve immediately, or transfer to an airtight container and arrange in single layers separated by sheets of waxed paper.

NUTRITIONAL FACTS (PER COOKIE)
Calories: 43 Calcium: 3 mg Cholesterol: 0 mg
Fat: 0.8 g Fiber: 0.8 g Iron: 0.3 mg
Potassium: 34 mg Protein: 0.8 g Sodium: 25 mg

Carrot Raisin Cookies

Yield: *32 cookies*

1. Combine the flour, oats, baking soda, and cinnamon, and stir to mix well. Add the Prune Butter, honey, and carrots, and stir to mix well. Stir in the raisins.

2. Coat a baking sheet with nonstick cooking spray. Roll the dough into 1-inch balls, and place 1½ inches apart on the sheet. (If the dough is too sticky to handle, place it in the freezer for a few minutes.) Using the bottom of a glass dipped in sugar, flatten the cookies to ¼-inch thickness. As an alternative, press a pecan half in the center of each cookie to flatten the dough.

3. Bake at 275°F for about 18 minutes, or until golden brown. Cool the cookies on the pan for 1 minute. Then transfer the cookies to wire racks, and cool completely. Serve immediately, or transfer to an airtight container and arrange in single layers separated by sheets of waxed paper.

1¼ cups whole wheat pastry flour or unbleached flour

1 cup quick-cooking oats

1 teaspoon baking soda

½ teaspoon ground cinnamon

¼ cup Prune Butter (page 223)

¼ cup plus 2 tablespoons honey

¾ cup finely grated carrots

⅓ cup golden raisins

32 pecan halves (optional)

NUTRITIONAL FACTS (PER COOKIE)

Calories: 48 Calcium: 6 mg Cholesterol: 0 mg
Fat: 0.3 g Fiber: 1.2 g Iron: 0.4 mg
Potassium: 64 mg Protein: 1.2 g Sodium: 27 mg

Georgia Fudge Bars

Yield: *16 servings*

⅓ cup unbleached flour

⅓ cup oat bran

⅓ cup cocoa powder

1 cup sugar

⅛ teaspoon salt (optional)

½ cup cooked mashed sweet potato

3 egg whites

1 teaspoon vanilla extract

⅓ cup chopped pecans (optional)

1. Combine the flour, oat bran, cocoa, sugar, and salt, if desired, and stir to mix well. Add the sweet potato, egg whites, and vanilla extract, and stir to mix well. Fold in the nuts if desired.

2. Coat an 8-inch square pan with nonstick cooking spray. Spread the mixture evenly in the pan, and bake at 325°F for about 25 minutes, or until the edges are firm and the center is almost set. Cool to room temperature, cut into squares, and serve.

3. Cool to room temperature, cut into squares, and serve.

NUTRITIONAL FACTS (PER SERVING)

Calories: 78 Calcium: 6 mg Cholesterol: 0 mg
Fat: 0.5 g Fiber: 1.1 g Iron: 0.5 mg
Potassium: 51 mg Protein: 1.7 g Sodium: 29 mg

Light and Luscious Brownies

Yield: *16 servings*

6 tablespoons reduced-fat margarine or light butter

1 cup sugar

3 egg whites

1 teaspoon vanilla extract

¾ cup unbleached flour

⅓ cup cocoa powder

⅓ cup chopped nuts (optional)

1. Place the margarine or butter in a medium-sized saucepan, and melt over low heat. Remove the pan from the heat, and stir in first the sugar, and then the egg whites and vanilla extract. Stir in the flour and cocoa powder. Fold in the nuts if desired.

2. Coat an 8-inch square pan with nonstick cooking spray. Spread the batter evenly in the pan, and bake at 325°F for about 25 minutes, or until the edges are firm and the center is almost set. Cool to room temperature, cut into squares, and serve.

NUTRITIONAL FACTS (PER SERVING)

Calories: 95 Calcium: 4 mg Cholesterol: 0 mg
Fat: 2.4 g Fiber: 0.7 g Iron: 0.5 mg
Potassium: 29 mg Protein: 1.6 g Sodium: 74 mg

Pumpkin Spice Bars

1. Combine the flours, sugar, baking soda, and spices, and stir to mix well. Add the pumpkin, molasses, water, and egg whites, and stir to mix well. Fold in the raisins and nuts.

2. Coat a 9-x-13-inch pan with nonstick cooking spray. Spread the mixture evenly in the pan, and bake at 350°F for 30 to 35 minutes, or until a wooden toothpick inserted in the center comes out clean.

3. Cool to room temperature, cut into squares, and serve.

NUTRITIONAL FACTS (PER SERVING)
Calories: 76 Calcium: 17 mg Cholesterol: 0 mg
Fat: 0.7 g Fiber: 0.9 g Iron: 0.9 mg
Potassium: 118 mg Protein: 1.6 g Sodium: 43 mg

Yield: *32 servings*

1½ cups unbleached flour

1 cup whole wheat pastry flour

½ cup sugar

1½ teaspoons baking soda

1 teaspoon ground cinnamon

1 teaspoon ground cloves

¼ teaspoon ground nutmeg

½ cup cooked mashed pumpkin

⅔ cup molasses

1 cup water

2 egg whites

½ cup golden raisins

¼ cup chopped walnuts

GREAT PUMPKIN COOKIES

Yield: *38 cookies*

1 cup whole wheat pastry flour or unbleached flour

1 cup oat bran

¾ cup light brown sugar

¾ teaspoon baking soda

½ cup cooked mashed pumpkin

¼ cup maple syrup

COATING

2 tablespoons finely ground pecans

2 tablespoons sugar

1. To make the coating, combine the ground pecans and 2 tablespoons of sugar in a small bowl, and stir to mix well. Set aside.

2. Combine the flour, oat bran, brown sugar, and baking soda, and stir to mix well. Stir in the pumpkin and maple syrup.

3. Coat a baking sheet with nonstick cooking spray. Roll the dough into 1-inch balls. (If the dough is too sticky to handle, place it in the freezer for a few minutes.) Roll each ball in the pecan mixture until coated, and place the balls 1½ inches apart on the baking sheet. Use the bottom of a glass to flatten each cookie to ¼-inch thickness.

4. Bake at 300°F for 15 minutes, or until lightly browned. Cool the cookies on the pan for 1 minute. Then transfer the cookies to wire racks, and cool completely. Serve immediately, or transfer to an air-tight container and arrange in single layers separated by sheets of waxed paper.

NUTRITIONAL FACTS (PER COOKIE)
Calories: 45 Calcium: 9 mg Cholesterol: 0 mg
Fat: 0.5 g Fiber: 0.9 g Iron: 0.5 mg
Potassium: 54 mg Protein: 0.9 g Sodium: 18 mg

CARROT RAISIN BARS

1. Combine the margarine or butter and brown sugar in the bowl of a food processor or electric mixer, and process until smooth. Add the egg white and vanilla extract, and process until smooth.

2. In a separate bowl, combine the flour, oats, wheat germ, cinnamon, and baking powder. Add the flour mixture to the margarine mixture, and process to mix well. Fold in the carrots and raisins.

3. Coat an 8-inch square pan with nonstick cooking spray. Pat the mixture evenly in the pan, and bake at 350°F for 25 to 30 minutes, or until a wooden toothpick inserted in the center comes out clean. Cool to room temperature, cut into squares, and serve.

Yield: *16 servings*

3 tablespoons reduced-fat margarine or light butter

¾ cup brown sugar

1 egg white

1 teaspoon vanilla extract

¾ cup whole wheat pastry flour or unbleached flour

¾ cup quick-cooking oats

¼ cup toasted wheat germ

1 teaspoon ground cinnamon

1 teaspoon baking powder

1¼ cups grated carrots (about 2½ medium)

½ cup golden raisins

NUTRITIONAL FACTS (PER SERVING)

Calories: 108 Calcium: 22 mg Cholesterol: 0 mg
Fat: 1.6 g Fiber: 1.9 g Iron: 1 mg
Potassium: 159 mg Protein: 2.4 g Sodium: 57 mg

Pineapple Almond Bars

Yield: *16 servings*

¾ cup unbleached flour

¾ cup quick-cooking oats

¼ cup plus 2 tablespoons light brown sugar

½ teaspoon baking soda

5 tablespoons reduced-fat margarine or light butter, cut into pieces

1 teaspoon almond extract

2 tablespoons sliced almonds

½ cup pineapple preserves

For variety, make these delicious bars with raspberry or apricot preserves.

1. Place the flour, oats, brown sugar, and baking soda in the bowl of a food processor, and process for a few seconds to mix well. Add the margarine or butter and the almond extract, and process until crumbly.

2. Remove ½ cup of the crumbs, and mix with the almonds. Set aside.

3. Coat an 8-inch square pan with nonstick cooking spray. Pat the plain crumb mixture into an even layer on the bottom of the pan. Spread the preserves in a layer over the crust, extending the filling to within ¼ inch of each edge. Sprinkle the crumb-almond mixture over the preserves.

4. Bake at 350°F for 30 minutes, or until browned and crisp. Cool to room temperature, cut into squares, and serve.

NUTRITIONAL FACTS (PER SERVING)
Calories: 100 Calcium: 11 mg Cholesterol: 0 mg
Fat: 2.3 g Fiber: 0.7 g Iron: 0.8 mg
Potassium: 51 mg Protein: 1.5 g Sodium: 73 mg

Almond Biscotti

1. Combine the flours, sugar, and baking powder, and stir to mix well. Use a pastry cutter to cut in the margarine or butter until the mixture resembles coarse meal. Stir in the egg whites and the vanilla and almond extracts. Fold in the almonds.

2. Turn the dough onto a lightly floured surface, and shape into two 9-x-2-inch logs. Coat a baking sheet with nonstick cooking spray, and place the logs on the sheet, leaving 4 inches of space between the logs to allow for spreading. Bake at 350°F for about 25 minutes, or until lightly browned.

3. Cool the logs at room temperature for 10 minutes. Then use a serrated knife to slice the logs diagonally into ½-inch-thick slices.

4. Place the slices on an ungreased baking sheet in a single layer, cut side down. Bake at 350°F for 18 to 20 minutes, or until dry and crisp, turning the slices over after 10 minutes.

5. Transfer the biscotti to wire racks, and cool completely. Serve immediately or store in an airtight container.

Yield: *24 biscotti*

1 cup unbleached flour

1 cup whole wheat pastry flour

⅔ cup sugar

2 teaspoons baking powder

4 tablespoons reduced-fat margarine or light butter

3 egg whites

1 teaspoon vanilla extract

1 teaspoon almond extract

¼ cup finely chopped almonds

NUTRITIONAL FACTS (PER BISCOTTI)
Calories: 76 Calcium: 12 mg Cholesterol: 0 mg
Fat: 1.8 g Fiber: 1 g Iron: 0.5 mg
Potassium: 43 mg Protein: 1.9 g Sodium: 57 mg

Whole Wheat Chocolate Chippers

Yield: *40 cookies*

6 tablespoons reduced-fat margarine or light butter

¾ cup light brown sugar

3 tablespoons fat-free egg substitute

1 teaspoon vanilla extract

1¼ cups whole wheat pastry flour or unbleached flour

½ teaspoon baking soda

½ cup chocolate chips

⅓ cup Grape-Nuts cereal or chopped walnuts

1. Combine the margarine or butter, brown sugar, egg substitute, and vanilla extract in the bowl of a food processor or electric mixer, and process until smooth. In a separate bowl, combine the flour and baking soda. Add the flour mixture to the margarine mixture, and process to mix well. Stir in the remaining ingredients.

2. Coat a baking sheet with nonstick cooking spray. Drop rounded teaspoonfuls of dough onto the baking sheet, placing them 1-½ inches apart.

3. Bake at 300°F for about 16 minutes, or until golden brown. Cool the cookies on the pan for 1 minute. Then transfer the cookies to wire racks, and cool completely. Serve immediately, or transfer to an airtight container.

NUTRITIONAL FACTS (PER COOKIE)

Calories: 50 Calcium: 6 mg Cholesterol: 0 mg
Fat: 1.6 g Fiber: 0.5 g Iron: 0.4 mg
Potassium: 42 mg Protein: 0.8 g Sodium: 41 mg

BUTTERSCOTCH CRISPS

1. Combine the margarine or butter, sugar, egg substitute, molasses, and vanilla extract in the bowl of a food processor or electric mixer, and process until smooth. In a separate bowl, combine the flour and baking soda. Add the flour mixture to the margarine mixture, and process to mix well. Stir in the remaining ingredients.

2. Coat a baking sheet with nonstick cooking spray. Drop rounded teaspoonfuls of dough onto the baking sheet, placing them 1½ inches apart.

3. Bake at 300°F for about 16 minutes, or until golden brown. Cool the cookies on the pan for 1 minute. Then transfer the cookies to wire racks, and cool completely. Serve immediately, or transfer to an airtight container.

Yield: *40 cookies*

6 tablespoons reduced-fat margarine or light butter

½ cup plus 2 tablespoons sugar

3 tablespoons fat-free egg substitute

1 tablespoon molasses

1 teaspoon vanilla extract

1¼ cups whole wheat pastry flour or unbleached flour

½ teaspoon baking soda

½ cup butterscotch chips

⅔ cup Grape-Nuts cereal

NUTRITIONAL FACTS (PER COOKIE)
Calories: 52 Calcium: 5 mg Cholesterol: 0 mg
Fat: 1.6 g Fiber: 0.7 g Iron: 0.4 mg
Potasium: 44 mg Protein: 1 g Sodium: 48 mg

Great Granola Cookies

Yield: *36 cookies*

6 tablespoons reduced-fat margarine or light butter

¾ cup light brown sugar

3 tablespoons fat-free egg substitute

1 teaspoon vanilla extract

½ cup plus 2 tablespoons whole wheat pastry flour

½ cup unbleached flour

½ teaspoon baking soda

1 cup nonfat or low-fat granola cereal

½ cup chopped dried apricots

¼ cup hulled sunflower seeds or chopped nuts (optional)

1. Combine the margarine, brown sugar, egg substitute, and vanilla extract in the bowl of a food processor or electric mixer, and process to mix well. In a mixing bowl, combine the flours and baking soda. Add the flour mixture to the margarine mixture, and process to mix well. Stir in the remaining ingredients.

2. Coat a baking sheet with nonstick cooking spray. Drop slightly rounded teaspoonfuls of dough onto the baking sheet, placing them 1½ inches apart. Flatten each cookie slightly with the tip of a spoon.

3. Bake at 300°F for about 15 minutes, or until golden brown. Cool the cookies on the pan for 1 minute. Then transfer the cookies to wire racks, and cool completely. Serve immediately, or transfer to an airtight container.

NUTRITIONAL FACTS (PER COOKIE)

Calories: 51 Calcium: 6 mg Cholesterol: 0 mg
Fat: 1 g Fiber: 0.7 g Iron: 0.5 mg
Potassium: 60 mg Protein: 0.8 g Sodium: 40 mg

Ultimate Oatmeal Cookies

1. Combine the margarine or butter, brown sugar, egg substitute, and vanilla extract in the bowl of a food processor or electric mixer, and process until smooth. In a separate bowl, combine the flour, oats, and baking soda. Add the flour mixture to the margarine mixture, and process to mix well. Stir in the remaining ingredients.

2. Coat a baking sheet with nonstick cooking spray. Drop rounded teaspoonfuls of dough onto the baking sheet, placing them 1½ inches apart. Flatten each cookie slightly with the tip of a spoon.

3. Bake at 300°F for 15 to 18 minutes, or until lightly browned and crisp. Cool the cookies on the pan for 1 minute. Then transfer the cookies to wire racks, and cool completely. Serve immediately, or transfer to an airtight container.

Yield: 42 cookies

6 tablespoons reduced-fat margarine or light butter

¾ cup light brown sugar

3 tablespoons fat-free egg substitute

1 teaspoon vanilla extract

1 cup whole wheat pastry flour or unbleached flour

1 cup quick-cooking oats

½ teaspoon baking soda

½ cup dark raisins, chopped dried apricots, or other chopped dried fruit

¼ cup chopped walnuts, pecans, or almonds (optional)

NUTRITIONAL FACTS (PER COOKIE)
Calories: 45 Calcium: 6 mg Cholesterol: 0 mg
Fat: 0.9 g Fiber: 0.7 g Iron: 0.3 mg
Potassium: 41 mg Protein: 0.9 g Sodium: 31 mg

Thumbprint Cookies

Yield: *36 cookies*

4 tablespoons reduced-fat margarine or light butter

½ cup plus 2 tablespoons sugar

3 tablespoons frozen orange juice concentrate, thawed

1 teaspoon vanilla or almond extract

1 cup plus 2 tablespoons unbleached flour

¾ cup oat bran

¾ teaspoon baking soda

⅓ cup finely ground nuts (optional)

3 tablespoons fruit spread or jam, any flavor

1. Combine the margarine or butter and the sugar in the bowl of a food processor or electric mixer, and process until smooth. Add the juice concentrate and vanilla or almond extract, and process until smooth. In a separate bowl, combine the flour, oat bran, and baking soda. Add the flour mixture to the margarine mixture, and process until the dough leaves the sides of the bowl and forms a ball.

2. Coat a baking sheet with nonstick cooking spray. Roll the dough into 1-inch balls. (If the dough is too sticky to handle, place it in the freezer for a few minutes.) Roll the balls in the nuts if desired, and place them on the sheet, spacing them 1½ inches apart. Using the back of a ¼-teaspoon measuring spoon, make a depression in the center of each ball. (Dip the spoon in sugar, if necessary, to prevent sticking.) Fill each depression with ¼ teaspoon of jam.

3. Bake at 300°F for 18 to 20 minutes. To check for doneness, lift a cookie from the sheet with a spatula, The bottom should be golden brown. Cool the cookies on the pan for 1 minute. Then transfer the cookies to wire racks, and cool completely. Serve immediately, or transfer to an airtight container.

NUTRITIONAL FACTS (PER COOKIE)
Calories: 44 Calcium: 3 mg Cholesterol: 0 mg
Fat: 0.8 g Fiber: 0.5 g Iron: 0.3 mg
Potassium: 27 mg Protein: 0.8 g Sodium: 33 mg

Chocolate Raspberry Treats

1. Combine the margarine or butter and the brown sugar in the bowl of a food processor or electric mixer, and process until smooth. Add the chocolate syrup, water, and vanilla extract, and process until smooth. In a separate bowl, combine the flour, oats, cocoa, and baking soda. Add the flour mixture to the margarine mixture, and process until the dough leaves the sides of the bowl and forms a ball.

2. Coat a baking sheet with nonstick cooking spray. Roll the dough into 1-inch balls, and place the balls on the sheet, spacing them 1½ inches apart. (If the dough is too sticky to handle, place it in the freezer for a few minutes.) Using the back of a ¼-teaspoon measuring spoon, make a depression in the center of each ball. (Dip the spoon in sugar, if necessary, to prevent sticking.) Fill each depression with ¼ teaspoon of jam.

3. Bake at 300°F for 18 to 20 minutes. To check for doneness, lift a cookie from the sheet with a spatula. The bottom should be nicely browned. Cool the cookies on the pan for 1 minute. Then transfer the cookies to wire racks, and cool completely. Serve immediately, or transfer to an airtight container.

Yield: *42 cookies*

4 tablespoons reduced-fat margarine or light butter

¾ cup light brown sugar

¼ cup chocolate syrup

1 tablespoon plus 1 teaspoon water

1 teaspoon vanilla extract

1½ cups whole wheat pastry flour or unbleached flour

1 cup quick-cooking oats

2 tablespoons cocoa powder

¾ teaspoon baking soda

3 tablespoons plus 1½ teaspoons raspberry fruit spread or jam

NUTRITIONAL FACTS (PER COOKIE)
Calories: 50 Calcium: 7 mg Cholesterol: 0 mg
Fat: 0.8 g Fiber: 0.9 g Iron: 0.5 mg
Potassium: 45 mg Protein: 1 g Sodium: 33 mg

Maple-Date Drops

Yield: *40 cookies*

1 cup plus 2 tablespoons whole wheat pastry flour

¾ cup sugar

1 teaspoon baking soda

½ teaspoon ground cinnamon

¼ cup maple syrup

¼ cup water

1 teaspoon vanilla extract

2 cups bran flake and raisin cereal

½ cup chopped dates or dark raisins

¼ cup plus 2 tablespoons chopped toasted pecans or walnuts (page 383)

1. Place the flour, sugar, baking soda, and cinnamon in a large bowl, and stir to mix well. Add the maple syrup, water, and vanilla extract, and stir to mix well. Finally, add the cereal, dates or raisins, and nuts, and stir to mix well.

2. Coat a baking sheet with nonstick cooking spray. Drop rounded teaspoonfuls of dough onto the sheet, placing them 1½ inches apart. Slightly flatten each cookie with the tip of a spoon. (Note that the dough will be slightly crumbly, so that you may have to press it together slightly to make it hold its shape.)

3. Bake at 275°F for about 18 minutes, or until lightly browned. Cool the cookies on the pan for 2 minutes. Then transfer the cookies to wire racks, and cool completely. Serve immediately, or transfer to an airtight container and arrange in single layers separated by sheets of waxed paper.

NUTRITIONAL FACTS (PER COOKIE)
Calories: 53 Carbohydrates: 11.5 g Cholesterol: 0 mg
Fat: 0.9 g Fiber: 1 g Protein: 0.9 g Sodium: 50 mg

You Save: Calories: 21 Fat: 2.1 g

Apricot-Almond Drops

For variety, substitute dried cranberries or cherries for the apricots, and toasted pecans for the almonds.

1. Place the flour, sugar, and baking soda in a large bowl, and stir to mix well. Add the Prune Purée, maple syrup, water, and vanilla extract, and stir to mix well. The mixture will seem dry at first, but will become moist and hold together as you keep stirring. (Add a little more water, ½ teaspoon at a time, only if needed.) Finally, add the cereal, apricots, and almonds, and stir to mix well.

2. Coat a baking sheet with nonstick cooking spray. Drop rounded teaspoonfuls of dough onto the sheet, placing them 1½ inches apart. Slightly flatten each cookie with the tip of a spoon. (Note that the dough will be slightly crumbly, so that you may have to press it together slightly to make it hold its shape.)

3. Bake at 350°F for about 9 minutes, or until lightly browned. Cool the cookies on the pan for 2 minutes. Then transfer the cookies to wire racks, and cool completely. Serve immediately, or transfer to an airtight container and arrange in single layers separated by sheets of waxed paper.

Yield: *40 cookies*

1 cup plus 2 tablespoons whole wheat pastry flour

¾ cup sugar

1 teaspoon baking soda

3 tablespoons Prune Purée (page 223)

3 tablespoons maple syrup

1 tablespoon water

1 teaspoon vanilla extract

1⅞ cups oat bran flakes* or wheat bran flakes

⅔ cup chopped dried apricots

¼ cup plus 2 tablespoons chopped toasted almonds (page 223)

*Kellogg's Common Sense Oat Bran flakes are a good choice.

NUTRITIONAL FACTS (PER COOKIE)
Calories: 48 Carbohydrates: 10.5 g Cholesterol: 0 mg
Fat: 0.6 g Fiber: 1 g Protein: 1 g Sodium: 49 mg

You Save: Calories: 27 Fat: 2.4 g

Fat-Free Marshmallow Treats

Yield: *18 bars*

1 tablespoon nonfat margarine, or 1 tablespoon plus 1½ teaspoons reduced-fat margarine

6 cups miniature marshmallows

6 cups crisp rice cereal, regular or cocoa-flavored

1. Coat a 4-quart pot with butter-flavored nonstick cooking spray. Add the margarine and marshmallows, cover, and cook over low heat without stirring for 3 minutes. Then remove the lid and continue to cook, stirring constantly, for 2 to 3 additional minutes, or until the mixture is melted and smooth.

2. Remove the pot from the heat, and stir in the cereal. Coat a 9-x-13-inch pan with nonstick cooking spray, and use the back of a wooden spoon to pat the mixture firmly into the pan. (Coat the spoon with cooking spray to help prevent sticking.)

3. Allow the mixture to cool to room temperature before cutting into squares. Serve immediately, or store in an airtight container in single layers separated by sheets of waxed paper.

NUTRITIONAL FACTS (PER BAR)

Calories: 86 Carbohydrates: 20.7 g Cholesterol: 0 mg
Fat: 0.1 g Fiber: 0.1 g Protein: 0.8 g Sodium: 81 mg

You Save: Calories: 30 Fat: 3.4 g

Variation

To make Peanut Butter Marshmallow Treats, add ¼ cup plus 2 tablespoons reduced-fat or regular peanut butter to the pot along with the margarine and marshmallows.

NUTRITIONAL FACTS (PER BAR)

Calories: 116 Carbohydrates: 23 g Cholesterol: 0 mg
Fat: 1.9 g Fiber: 0.5 g Protein: 2.2 g Sodium: 106 mg

You Save: Calories: 31 Fat: 4.3 g

Mocha Oatmeal Cookies

1. Place the flour, oats, cocoa, and brown sugar in a large bowl, and stir to mix well. Using the back of a wooden spoon, press out any lumps in the brown sugar. Add the baking soda and cinnamon, and stir to mix well. Set aside.

2. Place the Prune Purée, coffee granules, and vanilla extract in a small bowl, and stir to dissolve the coffee granules. Add the Prune Purée mixture to the oat mixture, and stir to mix well. The mixture will seem dry at first, but will become moist and hold together as you keep stirring. (Add a little more Prune Purée, ½ teaspoon at a time, only if needed.)

3. Add the chocolate chips, fruit, and nuts to the dough, and stir to mix well. Coat a baking sheet with nonstick cooking spray. Drop rounded teaspoonfuls of dough onto the sheet, placing them 1½ inches apart. Slightly flatten each cookie with the tip of a spoon.

4. Bake at 350°F for about 9 minutes, or until lightly browned. Cool the cookies on the pan for 2 minutes. Then transfer the cookies to wire racks, and cool completely. Serve immediately, or transfer to an airtight container and arrange in single layers separated by sheets of waxed paper.

Yield: *42 cookies*

¾ cup plus 1 tablespoon whole wheat pastry flour

1 cup quick-cooking oats

3 tablespoons Dutch processed cocoa powder

¾ cup plus 2 tablespoons light or dark brown sugar

¾ teaspoon baking soda

¼ teaspoon ground cinnamon

¼ cup plus 3 tablespoons Prune Purée (page 223)

½ teaspoon instant coffee granules

1 teaspoon vanilla extract

⅓ cup semi-sweet chocolate chips

⅓ cup dark raisins, chopped dried apricots, or dried cherries

⅓ cup chopped toasted almonds, pecans, or walnuts (page 383)

NUTRITIONAL FACTS (PER COOKIE)
Calories: 45 Carbohydrates: 8.6 g Cholesterol: 0 mg
Fat: 1.2 g Fiber: 0.9 g Protein: 1 g Sodium: 24 mg

You Save: Calories: 24 Fat: 2.8 g

Chocolate Jumbles

Yield: *42 cookies*

1 cup whole wheat pastry flour

2 tablespoons Dutch processed cocoa powder

¾ cup sugar

1 teaspoon baking soda

3 tablespoons Prune Purée (page 223)

3 tablespoons chocolate syrup

1 tablespoon water

1 teaspoon vanilla extract

2 cups oat bran flakes* or wheat bran flakes

⅔ cup semi-sweet, milk chocolate, or white chocolate chips

⅓ cup chopped toasted almonds, pecans, hazelnuts, or macadamia nuts (page 383)

*Kellogg's Common Sense Oat Bran flakes are a good choice.

1. Place the flour, cocoa powder, sugar, and baking soda in a large bowl, and stir to mix well. Add the Prune Purée, chocolate syrup, water, and vanilla extract, and stir to mix well. The mixture will seem dry at first, but will become moist and hold together as you keep stirring. (Add a little more Prune Purée, ½ teaspoon at a time, only if needed.) Finally, add the cereal, chocolate chips, and nuts, and stir to mix well.

2. Coat a baking sheet with nonstick cooking spray. Drop rounded teaspoonfuls of dough onto the sheet, placing them 1½ inches apart. Slightly flatten each cookie with the tip of a spoon. (Note that the dough will be slightly crumbly, so that you may have to press it together slightly to make it hold its shape.)

3. Bake at 350°F for about 9 minutes, or until lightly browned. Cool the cookies on the pan for 2 minutes. Then transfer the cookies to wire racks, and cool completely. Serve immediately, or transfer to an air-tight container and arrange in single layers separated by sheets of waxed paper.

NUTRITIONAL FACTS (PER COOKIE)
Calories: 52 Carbohydrates: 10.1 g Cholesterol: 0 mg
Fat: 1.5 g Fiber: 1 g Protein: 1 g Sodium: 49 mg

You Save: Calories: 19 Fat: 2.5 g

Variation

To make Peanutty Chocolate Jumbles, substitute peanut butter chips for the chocolate chips, and use chopped roasted unsalted peanuts for the nuts.

NUTRITIONAL FACTS (PER COOKIE)
Calories: 52 Carbohydrates: 10.1 g Cholesterol: 0 mg
Fat: 1.5 g Fiber: 1 g Protein: 1 g Sodium: 49 mg

You Save: Calories: 19 Fat: 2.5 g

Maple Oatmeal Cookies

1. Place the flour, oats, sugar, baking soda, cinnamon, and nutmeg in a large bowl, and stir to mix well. Add the maple syrup, water, and vanilla extract, and stir to mix well. Finally, add the raisins and walnuts, and stir to mix well.

2. Coat a baking sheet with nonstick cooking spray. Drop rounded teaspoonfuls of dough onto the sheet, placing them 1½ inches apart. Slightly flatten each cookie with a tip of a spoon.

3. Bake at 275°F for about 18 minutes, or until lightly browned. Cool the cookies on the pan for 2 minutes. Then transfer the cookies to wire racks, and cool completely. Serve immediately, or transfer to an airtight container and arrange in single layers separated by sheets of waxed paper.

Yield: 36 cookies

1 cup whole wheat pastry flour

1 cup quick-cooking oats

⅔ cup sugar

¾ teaspoon baking soda

½ teaspoon ground cinnamon

½ teaspoon ground nutmeg

¼ cup maple syrup

¼ cup water

1 teaspoon vanilla extract

½ cup dark raisins

⅓ cup chopped walnuts

NUTRITIONAL FACTS (PER COOKIE)

Calories: 52 Carbohydrates: 10.8 g Cholesterol: 0 mg
Fat: 0.9 g Fiber: 0.8 g Protein: 1.1 g Sodium: 27 mg

You Save: Calories: 22 Fat: 2.1 g

Chewy Chocolate Chip Cookies

Yield: *42 cookies*

1⅓ cups whole wheat pastry flour

¼ cup instant nonfat dry milk powder

½ cup plus 2 tablespoons sugar

¼ cup dark brown sugar

¾ teaspoon baking soda

¼ cup plus 2 tablespoons Prune Purée (page 223)

1 teaspoon vanilla extract

⅔ cup semi-sweet chocolate chips

⅓ cup chopped toasted walnuts or pecans (page 383)

1. Place the flour, milk powder, and sugars in a large bowl, and stir to mix well. Using the back of a wooden spoon, press out any lumps in the brown sugar.

2. Add the baking soda to the flour mixture, and stir to mix well. Add the Prune Purée and vanilla extract, and stir to mix well. The mixture will seem dry at first, but will become moist and hold together as you keep stirring. (Add a little water, ½ teaspoon at a time, only if needed.) Finally, add the chocolate chips and nuts, and stir to mix well.

3. Coat a baking sheet with nonstick cooking spray. Drop rounded teaspoonfuls of dough onto the sheet, placing them 1½ inches apart. Slightly flatten each cookie with a tip of a spoon.

4. Bake at 350°F for about 9 minutes, or until lightly browned. Cool the cookies on the pan for 2 minutes. Then transfer the cookies to wire racks, and cool completely. Serve immediately, or transfer to an air-tight container and arrange in single layers separated by sheets of waxed paper.

NUTRITIONAL FACTS (PER COOKIE)

Calories: 49 Carbohydrates: 9.2 g Cholesterol: 0 mg
Fat: 1.4 g Fiber: 0.8 g Protein: 1 g Sodium: 26 mg

You Save: Calories: 20 Fat: 2.6 g

Chewy Chocolate-Chocolate Chip Cookies

1. Place the flour, cocoa, milk powder, and sugars in a large bowl, and stir to mix well. Using the back of a wooden spoon, press out any lumps in the brown sugar.

2. Add the baking soda to the flour mixture, and stir to mix well. Add the Prune Purée and vanilla extract, and stir to mix well. The mixture will seem dry at first, but will become moist and hold together as you keep stirring. (Add a little water, ½ teaspoon at a time, only if needed.) Finally, add the chocolate chips and nuts, and stir to mix well.

3. Coat a baking sheet with nonstick cooking spray. Drop rounded teaspoonfuls of dough onto the sheet, placing them 1½ inches apart. Slightly flatten each cookie with the tip of a spoon.

4. Bake at 350°F for about 9 minutes, or until lightly browned. Cool the cookies on the pan for 2 minutes. Then transfer the cookies to wire racks, and cool completely. Serve immediately, or transfer to an airtight container and arrange in single layers separated by sheets of waxed paper.

Yield: *42 cookies*

1 cup plus 2 tablespoons whole wheat pastry flour

3 tablespoons plus 1 teaspoon Dutch processed cocoa powder

¼ cup instant nonfat dry milk powder

½ cup plus 2 tablespoons sugar

¼ cup dark brown sugar

¾ teaspoon baking soda

¼ cup plus 2 tablespoons Prune Purée (page 223)

1 teaspoon vanilla extract

⅔ cup semi-sweet, milk chocolate, or white chocolate chips

⅓ cup chopped toasted almonds, macadamia nuts, hazelnuts, or pecans (page 383)

NUTRITIONAL FACTS (PER COOKIE)
Calories: 48 Carbohydrates: 9 g Cholesterol: 0 mg
Fat: 1.5 g Fiber: 0.8 g Protein: 1 g Sodium: 26 mg

You Save: Calories: 21 Fat: 2.5 g

Orange Oatmeal Cookies

Yield: *42 cookies*

1 cup whole wheat pastry flour

1 cup quick-cooking oats

¾ cup plus 2 tablespoons light brown sugar

¾ teaspoon baking soda

½ teaspoon dried grated orange rind, or 1½ teaspoons fresh

¼ cup plus 2 tablespoons Prune Purée (page 223)

1 tablespoon frozen orange juice concentrate, thawed

1 teaspoon vanilla extract

⅔ cup dark raisins or dried cranberries

⅓ cup chopped toasted pecans or walnuts (page 383)

1. Place the flour, oats, and brown sugar in a large bowl, and stir to mix well. Using the back of a wooden spoon, press out any lumps in the brown sugar.

2. Add the baking soda and orange rind to the flour mixture, and stir to mix well. Add the Prune Purée, juice concentrate, and vanilla extract, and stir to mix well. The mixture will seem dry at first, but will become moist and hold together as you keep stirring. (Add a little more Prune Purée, ½ teaspoon at a time, only if needed.) Finally, add the raisins or dried cranberries and the nuts, and stir to mix well.

3. Coat a baking sheet with nonstick cooking spray. Drop rounded teaspoonfuls of dough onto the sheet, placing them 1½ inches apart. Slightly flatten each cookie with the tip of a spoon.

4. Bake at 350°F for about 9 minutes, or until lightly browned. Cool the cookies on the pan for 2 minutes. Then transfer the cookies to wire racks, and cool completely. Serve immediately, or transfer to an airtight container and arrange in single layers separated by sheets of waxed paper.

NUTRITIONAL FACTS (PER COOKIE)
Calories: 44 Carbohydrates: 9 g Cholesterol: 0 mg
Fat: 0.8 g Fiber: 0.8 g Protein: 0.9 g Sodium: 24 mg

You Save: Calories: 24 Fat: 1.9 g

Keeping Fat-Free Cookies Soft and Moist

Fat-free cookies have the best texture within a few hours of coming out of the oven. Then, as they stand, they tend to take on a chewier and sometimes tough texture. If this happens, simply place some ¼-inch-thick unpeeled apple wedges in with the cookies. Place one wedge with each layer of cookies, making sure the apple wedge is not touching any of the cookies. (The layers should be separated by sheets of waxed paper.) Cover and let stand for several hours or overnight. The moisture from the apples will seep into the cookies and help soften them.

As an alternative, tear slices of bread into 1½- to 2-inch pieces, and place with the cookies. The bread will become stale as its moisture is released and absorbed by the cookies. When the cookies reach the desired degree of softness, remove the apple wedges or bread pieces to prevent further softening.

Citrus Sugar Cookies

1. Place the margarine or butter, sugar, juice concentrate, and vanilla extract in a large bowl, and beat with an electric mixer until smooth. Set aside.

2. Place the flour, oat bran, milk powder, baking soda, and lemon rind in a medium-sized bowl, and stir to mix well. Add the flour mixture to the margarine mixture, and beat to mix well. (Add 1 to 2 teaspoons of additional orange juice concentrate if the mixture seems too dry.)

3. Place the sugar coating in a small shallow dish, and set aside.

4. Coat a baking sheet with nonstick cooking spray. Using your hands, shape the dough into 1-inch balls. (If the dough is too sticky to handle, place it in the freezer for a few minutes.) Roll the balls in the sugar coating; then arrange on the baking sheet, spacing them 1½ inches apart. Using the bottom of a glass, flatten each ball to ¼-inch thickness.

5. Bake at 300°F for about 14 minutes. To check for doneness, lift a cookie from the sheet with a spatula. The bottom should be lightly browned. Cool the cookies on the pan for 2 minutes. Then transfer the cookies to wire racks, and cool completely. Serve immediately, or transfer to an airtight container.

Yield: *36 cookies*

¼ cup plus 1 tablespoon reduced-fat margarine or light butter, softened to room temperature

½ cup plus 2 tablespoons sugar

3 tablespoons frozen orange juice concentrate, thawed

1 teaspoon vanilla extract

1 cup plus 2 tablespoons unbleached flour

¾ cup oat bran

¼ cup instant nonfat dry milk powder

¾ teaspoon baking soda

1 teaspoon dried grated lemon rind, or 1 tablespoon fresh

COATING

1 tablespoon plus 1½ teaspoons sugar

NUTRITIONAL FACTS (PER COOKIE)
Calories: 45 Carbohydrates: 8.8 g Cholesterol: 0 mg
Fat: 0.9 g Fiber: 0.4 g Protein: 0.9 g Sodium: 39 mg

You Save: Calories: 31 Fat: 2.8 g

Molasses Spice Cookies

Yield: 40 cookies

¼ cup plus 2 tablespoons reduced-fat margarine or light butter, softened to room temperature

⅔ cup light brown sugar

¼ cup molasses

1 tablespoon unsweetened applesauce

1 teaspoon vanilla extract

2 cups whole wheat pastry flour

2 tablespoons instant nonfat dry milk powder

¾ teaspoon baking soda

1¼ teaspoons ground ginger

1¼ teaspoons ground cinnamon

COATING

2 tablespoons sugar

1. Place the margarine, brown sugar, molasses, applesauce, and vanilla extract in a large bowl, and beat with an electric mixer until smooth. Set aside.

2. Place the flour, milk powder, baking soda, ginger, and cinnamon in a medium-sized bowl, and stir to mix well. Add the flour mixture to the margarine mixture, and beat to mix well. (Add a couple of teaspoons of additional applesauce if the mixture seems too dry.)

3. Place the sugar coating in a small shallow dish, and set aside.

4. Coat a baking sheet with nonstick cooking spray. Using your hands, shape the dough into 1-inch balls. (If the dough is too sticky to handle, place it in the freezer for a few minutes.) Roll the balls in the sugar coating; then arrange on the baking sheet, spacing them 1½ inches apart. Using the bottom of a glass, flatten each ball to ¼-inch thickness.

5. Bake at 300°F for about 14 minutes. To check for doneness, lift a cookie from the sheet with a spatula. The bottom should be lightly browned. Cool the cookies on the pan for 2 minutes. Then transfer the cookies to wire racks, and cool completely. Serve immediately, or transfer to an airtight container.

NUTRITIONAL FACTS (PER COOKIE)
Calories: 47 Carbohydrates: 8.9 g Cholesterol: 0 mg
Fat: 0.9 g Fiber: 0.8 g Protein: 0.9 g Sodium: 38 mg

You Save: Calories: 21 Fat: 2.4 g

Maple Snickerdoodles

1. Place the margarine, sugar, maple syrup, lemon juice, and vanilla extract in a large bowl, and beat with an electric mixer until smooth. Set aside.

2. Place the flour, oat bran, milk powder, and baking soda in a medium-sized bowl, and stir to mix well. Add the flour mixture to margarine mixture, and beat to mix well.

3. To make the coating, place the sugar and cinnamon in a small shallow dish, and stir to mix well. Set aside.

4. Coat a baking sheet with nonstick cooking spray. Using your hands, shape the dough into 1-inch balls. (If the dough is too sticky to handle, place it in the freezer for a few minutes.) Roll the balls in the sugar coating; then arrange on the baking sheet, spacing them 1½ inches apart. Using the bottom of a glass, flatten each ball to ¼-inch thickness.

5. Bake at 300°F for about 14 minutes. To check for doneness, lift a cookie from the sheet with a spatula. The bottom should be lightly browned. Cool the cookies on the pan for 2 minutes. Then transfer the cookies to wire racks, and cool completely. Serve immediately, or transfer to an airtight container.

Yield: *40 cookies*

¼ cup plus 2 tablespoons reduced-fat margarine or light butter, softened to room temperature

¾ cup sugar

3 tablespoons maple syrup

1 tablespoon lemon juice

1½ teaspoons vanilla extract

1¼ cups unbleached flour

¾ cup plus 2 tablespoons oat bran

¼ cup instant nonfat dry milk powder

¾ teaspoon baking soda

COATING

1 tablespoon plus 1½ teaspoons sugar

1½ teaspoons ground cinnamon

NUTRITIONAL FACTS (PER COOKIE)
Calories: 48 Carbohydrates: 9.4 g Cholesterol: 0 mg
Fat: 0.9 g Fiber: 0.4 g Protein: 0.9 g Sodium: 37 mg

You Save: Calories: 26 Fat: 2.8 g

Cinnamon-Raisin Biscotti

Yield: *28 biscotti*

1 cup whole wheat pastry flour

1 cup unbleached flour

¾ cup plus 2 tablespoons light brown sugar

1 teaspoon ground cinnamon

2½ teaspoons baking powder

¼ cup (⅛ pound) chilled reduced-fat margarine or light butter, cut into pieces

½ cup dark raisins

⅓ cup honey crunch wheat germ or chopped toasted walnuts (page 383)

¼ cup plus 1 tablespoon fat-free egg substitute

1½ teaspoons vanilla extract

1. Place the flours, brown sugar, and cinnamon in a large bowl, and stir to mix well. Using the back of a wooden spoon, press out any lumps in the brown sugar. Add the baking powder, and stir to mix well.

2. Using a pastry cutter or 2 knives, cut the margarine or butter into the flour mixture until it resembles coarse meal. Stir in the raisins and the wheat germ or walnuts.

3. Add the egg substitute and vanilla extract to the dough, and stir just until the dry ingredients are moistened and the dough holds together. Add a little more egg substitute if the mixture seems too dry.

4. Spray your hands with nonstick cooking spray, and divide the dough into 2 pieces. Shape each piece into a 9-x-2½-inch log. Coat a large baking sheet with nonstick cooking spray, and place the logs on the sheet, spacing them 4 inches apart to allow for spreading. Bake at 325°F for 25 to 30 minutes, or until lightly browned and firm to the touch.

5. Using a spatula, carefully transfer the logs to a wire rack, and allow to cool at room temperature for 10 minutes. Then place the logs on a cutting board, and use a serrated knife to slice them diagonally into ½-inch-thick slices.

6. Arrange the slices in a single layer on an ungreased baking sheet, cut side down. Bake for 6 minutes at 325°F. Turn the slices and bake for 6 additional minutes, or until dry and crisp.

7. Transfer the biscotti to wire racks, and cool completely. Serve immediately, or transfer to an airtight container.

NUTRITIONAL FACTS (PER BISCOTTI)
Calories: 69 Carbohydrates: 13.7 g Cholesterol: 0 mg
Fat: 0.9 g Fiber: 0.7 g Protein: 1.7 g Sodium: 61 mg

You Save: Calories: 46 Fat: 3.6 g

Triple Chocolate Biscotti

1. Place the flour, cocoa, sugar, baking powder, and baking soda in a large bowl, and stir to mix well. Set aside.

2. Place the egg substitute, chocolate syrup, and vanilla extract in a small bowl, and stir to mix well. Add the egg mixture, chocolate chips, and, if desired, the nuts to the flour mixture, and stir just until the dry ingredients are moistened and the dough holds together. Add a little more egg substitute if the mixture seems too dry.

3. Spray your hands with nonstick cooking spray, and divide the dough into 2 pieces. Shape each piece into a 9-x-2½-inch log. Coat a large baking sheet with nonstick cooking spray, and place the logs on the sheet, spacing them 4 inches apart to allow for spreading. Bake at 325°F for 25 to 30 minutes, or until lightly browned and firm to the touch.

4. Using a spatula, carefully transfer the logs to a wire rack, and allow to cool at room temperature for 10 minutes. Then place the logs on a cutting board, and use a serrated knife to slice them diagonally into ½-inch-thick slices.

5. Arrange the slices in a single layer on an ungreased baking sheet, cut side down. Bake for 6 minutes at 325°F. Turn the slices and bake for 6 additional minutes, or until dry and crisp.

6. Transfer the biscotti to wire racks, and cool completely. Serve immediately, or transfer to an airtight container.

Yield: *28 biscotti*

1⅔ cups whole wheat pastry flour

⅓ cup Dutch processed cocoa powder

¾ cup sugar

2 teaspoons baking powder

¼ teaspoon baking soda

¼ cup plus 1 tablespoon fat-free egg substitute

1¼ cup chocolate syrup

2 teaspoons vanilla extract

½ cup semi-sweet, milk chocolate, or white chocolate chips

½ cup chopped toasted pecans, hazelnuts, walnuts, or almonds (page 383) (optional)

NUTRITIONAL FACTS (PER BISCOTTI)
Calories: 74 Carbohydrates: 15.8 g Cholesterol: 0 mg
Fat: 1.5 g Fiber: 1.4 g Protein: 2 g Sodium: 54 mg

You Save: Calories: 41 Fat: 3.5 g

Mocha Meringues

Yield: *24 cookies*

1 teaspoon vanilla extract

½ teaspoon instant coffee granules

2 large egg whites, wormed to room temperature

¼ teaspoon cream of tartar

⅛ teaspoon salt

¼ cup plus 2 tablespoons sugar

1 tablespoon cocoa powder (use regular, not Dutch processed)

½ cup semi-sweet or white chocolate chips

⅓ cup chopped toasted pecans or hazelnuts (page 383) (optional)

1. Place the vanilla extract and coffee granules in a small bowl, and stir to mix well. Set aside.

2. Place the egg whites in the bowl of an electric mixer, and beat on high speed until foamy. Add the cream of tartar and salt, and continue beating until soft peaks form. Still beating, slowly add the sugar, 1 tablespoon at a time. Beat the mixture just until stiff peaks form when the beaters are raised. Then beat in first the cocoa, and then the vanilla-coffee mixture.

3. Remove the beaters from the meringue mixture. Fold in the chocolate chips and, if desired, the nuts.

4. Line a large baking sheet with aluminum foil. (Do not grease the sheet or coat it with cooking spray.) Drop heaping teaspoonfuls of the mixture onto the baking sheet, spacing them 1 inch apart.

5. Bake at 250°F for 45 minutes, or until firm to the touch. Turn the oven off , and allow the meringues to cool in the oven for 2 hours with the door closed. Remove the pans from the oven, and peel the meringues from the foil. Serve immediately, or transfer to an airtight container.

NUTRITIONAL FACTS (PER COOKIE)

Calories: 30 Carbohydrates: 5.4 g Cholesterol: 0 mg
Fat: 1 g Fiber: 0.2 g Protein: 0.4 g Sodium: 16 mg

You Save: Calories: 20 Fat: 2.2 g

Toasted Coconut Meringues

Yield: *24 cookies*

1. Spread the coconut in a thin layer on a small baking sheet, and bake at 350°F, stirring occasionally, for about 5 minutes, or until the coconut turns light golden brown. Remove from the oven and set aside to cool to room temperature.

2. Place the egg whites in the bowl of an electric mixer, and beat on high speed until foamy. Add the cream of tartar and salt, and continue beating until soft peaks form. Still beating, slowly add the sugar, 1 tablespoon at a time. Beat the mixture just until stiff peaks form when the beaters are raised. Beat in the extracts.

3. Remove the beaters from the meringue mixture, and fold in the coconut.

4. Line a large baking sheet with aluminum foil. (Do not grease the sheet or coat it with cooking spray.) Drop heaping teaspoonfuls of the mixture onto the baking sheet, spacing them 1 inch apart.

5. Bake at 250°F for 45 minutes, or until firm to the touch. Turn the oven off, and allow the meringues to cool in the oven for 2 hours with the door closed. Remove the pans from the oven, and peel the meringues from the foil. Serve immediately, or transfer to an airtight container.

½ cup plus 2 tablespoons shredded sweetened coconut

2 large egg whites, warmed to room temperature

⅛ teaspoon cream of tartar

⅛ teaspoon salt

¼ cup plus 2 tablespoons sugar

½ teaspoon coconut-flavored extract

½ teaspoon vanilla extract

NUTRITIONAL FACTS (PER COOKIE)
Calories: 25 Carbohydrates: 4.3 g Cholesterol: 0 mg
Fat: 0.7 g Fiber: 0.1 g Protein: 0.4 g Sodium: 22 mg

You Save: Calories: 20 Fat: 2.2 g

Moist and Chewy Fudge Brownies

Yield: *16 brownies*

⅔ cup oat flour

¼ cup Dutch processed cocoa powder

¾ cup sugar

2 tablespoons instant nonfat dry milk powder

1 pinch baking soda

¼ cup plus 2 tablespoons fat-free egg substitute

¼ cup chocolate syrup

1 tablespoon water or strong black coffee, cooled to room temperature

1 teaspoon vanilla extract

⅓ cup chopped toasted walnuts, pecans, hazelnuts, macadamia nuts, or almonds (page 383) (optional)

1. Place the flour, cocoa, sugar, milk powder, and baking soda in a medium-sized bowl, and stir to mix well. Add the egg substitute, chocolate syrup, water or coffee, and vanilla extract, and stir to mix well. Set the batter aside for 15 minutes.

2. If desired, stir the nuts into the batter. Coat the bottom only of an 8-x-8-inch pan with nonstick cooking spray, and spread the mixture evenly in the pan. Bake at 325°F for about 23 minutes, or just until the edges are firm and the center is almost set. Be careful not to overbake.

3. Allow the brownies to cool to room temperature before cutting into squares and serving. For easier cutting, rinse the knife off periodically.

NUTRITIONAL FACTS (PER BROWNIE)
Calories: 72 Carbohydrates: 16.4 g Cholesterol: 0 mg
Fat: 0.5 g Fiber: 1 g Protein: 1.9 g Sodium: 22 mg

You Save: Calories: 65 Fat: 7.8 g

CREAM CHEESE MARBLE BROWNIES

1. Prepare the brownie mix as directed on the package. Coat the bottom only of a 9-x-13-inch pan with nonstick cooking spray, and spread the mixture evenly in the pan. Set aside.

2. Place the cream cheese and sugar in a medium-sized bowl, and beat with an electric mixer until smooth. Add the flour, and beat to mix well. Add the egg substitute and vanilla extract, and beat to mix well.

3. Pour the cheese mixture over the brownie batter in an "S" pattern. Then draw a knife through the batter to create a marbled effect.

4. Bake at 325°F for 30 to 33 minutes, or just until the edges are firm and the center is almost set. Be careful not to overbake.

5. Allow the brownies to cool to room temperature before cutting into squares and serving. For easier cutting, rinse the knife off periodically.

Yield: *24 brownies*

1 package (about 1 pound, 5 ounces) low-fat fudge brownie mix, such as Betty Crocker Sweet Rewards*

1 block (8 ounces) nonfat cream cheese, softened to room temperature

⅓ cup sugar

1 tablespoon unbleached flour

3 tablespoons fat-free egg substitute

1 teaspoon vanilla extract

*Alternatively, use a regular brownie mix, replacing the fat with a fat substitute, as directed on pages 432 through 434.

NUTRITIONAL FACTS (PER BROWNIE)

Calories: 119 Carbohydrates: 23 g Cholesterol: 0 mg
Fat: 1.5 g Fiber: 0.7 g Protein: 3.1 g Sodium: 132 mg

You Save: Calories: 64 Fat: 10.2 g

Resource List

Most of the ingredients used in the recipes in this book are readily available in any supermarket, or can be found in your local health foods store or gourmet shop. But if you are unable to locate what you're looking for, the following list should guide you to a manufacturer who can either sell the desired product to you directly or inform you of the nearest retail outlet.

Whole Grains and Flours

Arrowhead Mills, Inc.
Box 2059
Hereford, TX 79045
(800) 749-0730

Whole wheat pastry flour, oat flour, and other flours and whole grains.

The Baker's Catalogue and King Arthur Flour
PO Box 876
Norwich, VT 05055
(800) 827-6836

White whole wheat flour, whole wheat pastry flour, unbleached pastry flour and other flours, whole grains, and baking products.

Mountain Ark Trading Company
PO Box 3170
Fayetteville, AR 72702
(800) 643-8909

Whole grains and flours, unrefined sweeteners, dried fruits, fruit spreads, and a wide variety of other natural foods.

Sweeteners

Advanced Ingredients
331 Capitola Avenue
Suite F
Capitola, CA 95010
(909) 464-9891

Fruit Source granulated and liquid sweetners.

Fruit Source
1803 Mission Street, Suite 401
Santa Cruz, CA 95060
(408) 457-1136

Fruit Source granulated and liquid sweeteners.

Lundberg Family Farms
PO Box 369
Richvale, CA 95974-0369
(916) 882-4551

Brown rice syrup.

NutraCane, Inc.
5 Meadowbrook Parkway
Milford, NH 03055
(603) 672-2801

Sucanat granulated sweetener.

Sucanat North America Corporation/
Wholesome Foods
525 Fenters Boulevard
Daytona Beach, FL 32114
(904) 258-4708

Sucanat granulated sweetener.

Vermont Country Maple, Inc.
PO Box 53
Jericho Center, VT 05465
(800) 528-7021

Maple sugar, maple syrup, and other maple products.

Westbrae Natural Foods
1065 East Walnut
Carson, CA 90746
(310) 886-8200

Brown rice syrup.

Dutch Processed Cocoa Powder

The Baker's Catalogue
PO Box 876
Norwich, VT 05055-0876
(800) 827-6836

Hershey's Chocolate World
(800) 544-1347

Meat Substitutes

Harvest Direct, Inc.
PO Box 4514
Decatur, IL 62525-4514
(800) 835-2867

Harvest Burger mixes, and texturized vegetable protein (TVP).

Nondairy Cheeses

Sharon's Finest
PO Box 5020
Santa Rosa, CA 95402
(800) 656-9669

Almondrella Cheese, Tofurella Cheese, and Veganrella Cheese.

Metric Conversion Tables

Common Liquid Conversions

Measurement	=	Milliliters
¼ teaspoon	=	1.25 milliliters
½ teaspoon	=	2.50 milliliters
¾ teaspoon	=	3.75 milliliters
1 teaspoon	=	5.00 milliliters
1¼ teaspoons	=	6.25 milliliters
1½ teaspoons	=	7.50 milliliters
1¾ teaspoons	=	8.75 milliliters
2 teaspoons	=	10.0 milliliters
1 tablespoon	=	15.0 milliliters
2 tablespoons	=	30.0 milliliters

Measurement	=	Liters
¼ cup	=	0.06 liters
½ cup	=	0.12 liters
¾ cup	=	0.18 liters
1 cup	=	0.24 liters
1¼ cups	=	0.30 liters
1½ cups	=	0.36 liters
2 cups	=	0.48 liters
2½ cups	=	0.60 liters
3 cups	=	0.72 liters
3½ cups	=	0.84 liters
4 cups	=	0.96 liters
4½ cups	=	1.08 liters
5 cups	=	1.20 liters
5½ cups	=	1.32 liters

Converting Fahrenheit to Celsius

Fahrenheit	=	Celsius
200–205	=	95
220–225	=	105
245–250	=	120
275	=	135
300–305	=	150
325–330	=	165
345–350	=	175
370–375	=	190
400–405	=	205
425–430	=	220
445–450	=	230
470–475	=	245
500	=	260

Conversion Formulas

LIQUID		
When You Know	**Multiply By**	**To Determine**
teaspoons	5.0	milliliters
tablespoons	15.0	milliliters
fluid ounces	30.0	milliliters
cups	0.24	liters
pints	0.47	liters
quarts	0.95	liters

WEIGHT		
When You Know	**Multiply By**	**To Determine**
ounces	28.0	grams
pounds	0.45	kilograms

Index